WOODWORKING FOR INDUSTRY

Technology and Practice
(REVISED)

JOHN L. FEIRER

Head, Industrial Education Department,
Western Michigan University,
Kalamazoo, Michigan

B

CHAS. A. BENNETT CO., INC.
809 W. Detweiller Dr.   Peoria, Ill. 61614

turn to page 93

Library of Cong. Cat. No. 63-14887
PRINTED IN THE UNITED STATES OF AMERICA

ISBN 87002-053-6

77 78 79 RRD 10 9 8 7 6 5 4

CAPTION FOR FRONTISPIECE (other side of this page):

Dramatic and modern, the wing-like sections of the Forest Products Pavilion
in Oregon demonstrate the freedom of design that is possible with wood.

Table of Contents

LIST OF COLOR ILLUSTRATIONS

ACKNOWLEDGMENT LIST

Adjustable Clamp Company
Albion Malleable Iron Company
American Corporation
American Forest Products
   Industries
American Hardboard
   Association
American Plywood Association
American-Saint Gobain
   Corporation
Andersen Corporation
Armstrong Machine Company
Asphast Roofing Industry
   Bureau
Atlas Press Company
Baker Furniture Company
G. M. Basford Company
Behr-Manning Company
Bell Machine Company
The Black Brothers Company
Boice Crane Company
Bonditron
Borg-Warner Corporation
The Brandt Cabinet Works,
   Incorporated
Brunswick Corporation
Buck Brothers Company
Buss Machine Works,
   Incorporated
Samuel Cabot, Incorporated
California Redwood Association
Cleveland Twist Drill Company
Curtis Companies, Incorporated
Dansk Designs, Incorporated
The DeVilbiss Company
Drexel Furniture Company
Dunbar Furniture Corporation
   of Indiana
E. I. du Pont de Nemours and
   Company, Incorporated
Ekstrom, Carlson and Company
Filon Plastics Corporation
Fine Hardwoods Association
Ford Motor Company
Forest City Tool Company
Forest Products Laboratory
Formica Corporation
W. P. Fuller and Company
Gamble Brothers
General Electric Company
Georgia-Pacific Corporation
Greenlee Bros. and Company
Hardwood Dimension
   Manufacturers Association

Hardwood Plywood Institute
Heritage Furniture Company
Heywood-Wakefield Company
Huther Brothers, Incorporated
Independent Nail and
   Packing Company
Industrial Forestry Association
International Harverster
   Corporation
International Paper Company
   — Flakeboard Products
Janet Rosenblum
Jens Risdon Design,
   Incorporated
Kewaunee Manufacturing
   Company
Lockheed Corporation
Lufkin Rule Company
Mahogany Association,
   Incorporated
B. L. Marble Furniture,
   Incorporated
Masonite Corporation
Mattison Woodworking
   Machinery
Mereen-Johnson Machine
   Company
Millers Falls Company
Minnesota Mining and
   Manufacturing Company
Minnesota and Ontario Paper
   Company
Minnesota Woodworkers
   Supply Company
Misener Manufacturing
   Company, Incorporated
National Lock Company
National Lumber
   Manufacturers Association
National Safety Council
National Woodwork
   Manufacturers Association
Nicholson File Company
Northfield Foundry and
   Machine Company
Oliver Machinery Company
Owens-Corning Fiberglas
   Corporation
Pacific Plywood Company
Panelyte Division,
   St. Regis Paper Company
Frank Paxton Lumber Company

Philippine Mahogany
   Association, Incorporated
Pittsburgh Plate Glass Company
Pope and Talbot, Incorporated
Porter-Cable Machine Company
H. K. Porter Company,
   Incorporated
Portland Cement Company
Powermatic Machine Company
Production Publishing
   Company
Red Devil Tools
Republic Steel Corporation
Richmond Homes, Incorporated
Rockwell Manufacturing
   Company
Royale Manufacturing
   Company
Saranac Machine Company
Sherwin-Williams Company
Simpson Redwood Company
Solem Machine Company
Southern Pine Association
Standard Oil of California
Stanley Tools
John Stuart Incorporated
Thonet Industries, Incorporated
Timber Engineering Company
20th Century Homes
U. S. Government
   Printing Office
United States Gypsum
   Company
United States Plywood
   Corporation
Unit Structures, Incorporated
Virginia Machine Tool
   Company
West Coast Lumbermen's
   Association
Western Pine Association
West Virginia Pulp and
   Paper Company
Weyerhaeuser Company
Whitney Publications,
   Incorporated
Wilkenson Manufacturing
   Company
Wisconsin Knife Works
Yale and Towne
   Manufacturing Company
Yates-American Machine
   Company

The author wishes to express his thanks to William Purdy and Eugene Terlisner.
Cover: Mereen-Johnson Machine Company

TO THE TEACHER

The importance of woodwork in our American economy is increasing. However, the idea of *woodworking for industry* is not adequately presented in many schools. Although courses in woodworking have been taught for seventy years in schools, they have been limited to a large extent to hand and machine woodworking. Today there are more students enrolled in woodworking courses than at any other time in history; but there is a need for improvement of these courses to bring them up to date and in line with present practices in industry.

While wood is a very old material that has been used as long as man has been on this earth, only in recent years has it developed into a material with thousands of uses. This is particularly true of the many man-made wood products now utilized in furniture and building construction.

WOODWORKING FOR INDUSTRY is designed primarily to fill the need for a modern, advanced woodworking course in senior high schools. However, because of its comprehensiveness, this book may also prove useful in vocational and technical schools, and at the college level. The textbook presents current information on materials, tools, and processes. Technological developments in products, tools, and building techniques are given great emphasis. This book acquaints students with the sources, uses, and limitations of wood products. It describes the way in which man has applied modern technology to this basic, natural material to mold it to his many needs.

Most important, this book truly represents the broad field of woodworking. It gives equal emphasis to the important areas of building construction and cabinetmaking. It represents the work of all major occupational groups. This book gives the student a basic knowledge of woodworking that will be useful to him regardless of the occupational choice he makes in later life. It will stimulate him to think about choosing an occupation directly or indirectly related to the field of woodworking, in which he will find rewarding opportunities and a chance to make a worthwhile contribution to our economy. Today, the chance of a student's securing employment in a woodworking craft is better than ever before. However, a great majority of these opportunities lie in the areas of carpentry and building construction which have not been given adequate attention in most woodworking classes.

The subject matter of this textbook was selected after careful and extensive research. The author made detailed studies of governmentally and commercially published materials related to woodworking. He also examined advanced courses of study for schools in several cities and states. WOODWORKING FOR INDUSTRY is based on the results of this research. The important things have been emphasized and described in clear, interesting fashion. The author has been guided to a large extent by research done by the Forest Products Laboratory of Madison, Wisconsin. All of the units relating to wood materials have been checked for technical accuracy by this organization.

The units have been organized around the basic areas of instruction. The book is designed in such a way that any or all of the units may be selected for instructional purposes. The author has attempted to use the essential and desirable technical vocabulary and to explain the new terms as they are used. A *glossary* of important terms is included.

The reading level of this book is appropriate for the age level of the students for which it is designed. The content is presented in a manner that should appeal to advanced high school and technical school students. *Illustrations form a large portion of the instructional content.* There are drawings and photographs representing actual working conditions.

Many units in this textbook will be useful in connection with manipulative activities; others provide necessary depth by giving students a clear understanding of the importance of woodworking in our economic life.

Great pains have been taken to make sure that the material included in the book is *technically accurate*. The author visited furniture manufacturing concerns, home-building organizations, and on-the-job craftsmen to check on techniques and practices. While not every method of completing each process can be described, because of space limitations and the differences of opinion among craftsmen on many points, the ones described are accurate and technically correct.

WOOD IS . . .

Wood is one of the most unusual and valuable raw materials of industry. It is beautiful, relatively inexpensive, and available in a wide choice of weights, strengths, colors, and textures. Its machining characteristics are excellent. Wood can be bent, sliced, planed, sawed, and sanded. With glue, nails, or screws, it can be fastened to another piece of wood or to other material such as plastic, paper, or metal. It can be finished naturally or painted to match other materials. In our industrial society, wood is a most vital and useful product.

Wood has been on this earth longer than man; however, its value to society is still increasing. This is because man is continuing to learn more about

wood. To build intelligently with any material, you must understand the material itself. Continuing programs of research are making new information on wood available to the forest products industry.

For example, the Forest Products Laboratory at Madison, Wisconsin, regularly conducts many kinds of research and experiments to improve the usefulness of wood and man-made wood products. Many large concerns also devote substantial funds for similar research. Without this scientific work, much of what we know about wood never would have been discovered, and the great value of this material would have been largely wasted.

Some of man's earliest buildings were made of wood. The progress that has been made since those early, crude structures is shown in this handsome building, in which wood has an important structural and decorative part. Much of this progress is the result of knowing how to make the best use of wood — knowledge that has been gained through research.

Section A

APPROACH TO WOODWORKING

Wood is a material with a thousand uses. This research worker is searching for more possible uses for this wonderful natural resource. Many of you will find your future in an occupation directly or indirectly related to wood. Can you name several other professions in which a knowledge of wood is important?

Unit 1: INTRODUCTION

A century ago anyone who wanted to make something, regardless of what it was, thought of wood as the building material. Almost everything that was used by man was made of wood. Early Americans used wood, not only for their utensils, furniture, and homes, but also for their vehicles, bridges, and even much of their machinery. Wood was then, as it is now, a most versatile and universally used construction material. Today, however, so many things are made of metal, plastics, clay, and rubber that some people may have begun to think that wood and wood products are not so important to our American way of life as they once were. The jet plane, the missile, the satellite, all are made of non-wooden materials. Does this mean that woodworking is becoming obsolete? Certainly not. Almost everything that is made today, whether a missile, car model, or commercial building of steel or concrete, is first made of wood as a model. *Fig. 1–1.* Also, wood remains the favorite building material for homes, furniture, boats, musical instruments, sports equipment, and thousands of other items. *Fig. 1–2.*

Far from becoming obsolete, wood and wood products are growing more and more indispensable. Not only do we see them in the old, familiar things, but through research there are also many new combinations. For example, there are manufactured

1-1. A wood mock-up or model is made of every product, including this seat for a jet airplane.

13

1-2a.   A sailboat.

wood materials such as plywood,* hardboard,* and particle board.* There are thousands of other uses for wood that we no longer recognize as wood—plastics, cloth, chemicals, flavoring extracts, and paper. In the United States only 50 per cent less wood per person is used today than in 1860 when almost *everything* was made of wood. The amount of wood used for constructing homes and industrial buildings is increasing at a tremendous rate.

As Frank Lloyd Wright, late dean of American architects, has said, "Wood is a friend of mine; the best

---

*If you do not understand these terms, look them up in the *glossary* which begins on page 646. By making a practice of looking up new or forgotten terms, you will more clearly understand what you read, and soon you will become familiar with many important phrases and ideas used in woodworking industries.

friend on earth of a man is the tree. When we use the tree respectfully and economically, we have one of the greatest resources of the earth."

The technique of gluing pieces of lumber together (called laminating) has brought many new uses for wood as an engineering material in both light and heavy construction. Glued, laminated structures are indispensable in ship building, in framing for churches, barns, and other large buildings, in constructing bridges and towers, and in many other commercial uses. *Fig. 1-3.*

Per capita consumption of lumber in the United States is three and a half times the average of world consumption. Metal manufacturers employ more semi-skilled production workers, but your chances for a *skilled trade job* are far better in woodworking than in metalworking. This seems certain to remain true for many, many years.

WHAT WILL THIS COURSE TEACH ME?

This course will deal with aspects of woodworking that are important for industry. It includes the tools, materials, processes, and the "why" as well as the "how" of machine woodworking, cabinetmaking, carpentry, patternmaking, and boatbuilding. *Fig. 1-4.*

While painting and wood finishing are not strictly in the woodworking area, they are included because the development of most wood products involves some kind of finish. In wood technology, you will not only learn about the skills necessary to work woods, but you will also study the materials and major developments that have taken place in the industry. These developments include: (1) the use of new and better machinery and tools, (2) the use of carbide-tipped tools for greater efficiency, (3) the use of adhesives and glues including many of the new waterproof adhesives, (4) the use of manufactured wood products including plywood, hardboard, and particle board, and (5) the use of new techniques in building construction, particularly in the use of component building parts. *Fig. 1–5.*

WHY TAKE A COURSE IN WOODWORKING?

There is a good deal more to woodworking for industry than making a few small furniture items.

You can develop vocational skills that will help you in deciding on your life work and in training for it.

1-3. Laminated beams are used in commercial construction.

Woodworking offers many opportunities at every level of work. For example, your chances for a job in one of the skilled occupations today are

1-2b. A violin of select spruce and matched maple. The scroll has been hand carved. This instrument was built by a ninth grade student in woodwork.

1-4. Furniture making is one important area of woodworking.

1-5. Assembling component house parts — joists of box beam construction.

better in woodworking than in any other field; the largest single skilled trade in this country is that of carpentry. If you are interested in business, there are many opportunities in wholesale and retail lumber and furniture concerns. If you plan to enter one of the professions, you might consider such occupations as forester, industrial education teacher, or architect. If you are interested in one of the skilled trades such as carpentry, patternmaking, or cabinetmaking, then you should know what a vocationally competent worker is. He is one who works with accuracy and precision. *Fig. 1–6.* He appreciates and promotes good design and craftsmanship, and possesses skills and abilities in such fundamental processes as reading, writing, and

arithmetic. He gets along with other people, knows how to work, takes pride in his job well done, has marketable skills, and appreciates the value of his work in society.

If you are planning a career in some area of woodworking, you need to know something about the occupation and about yourself. Let's first take a look at several major occupational groups in woodworking. All woodworking occupations can be grouped into six areas; namely, aesthetic, commercial, mechanical, natural, scientific, and social. There are opportunities for a future in all of these areas in woodworking:

Aesthetic—furniture   designer   or wood carver.
Commercial—retail   lumber   yard

1–6.   This skilled woodworker is making an accurate wood model of a new design for a vertical milling machine.

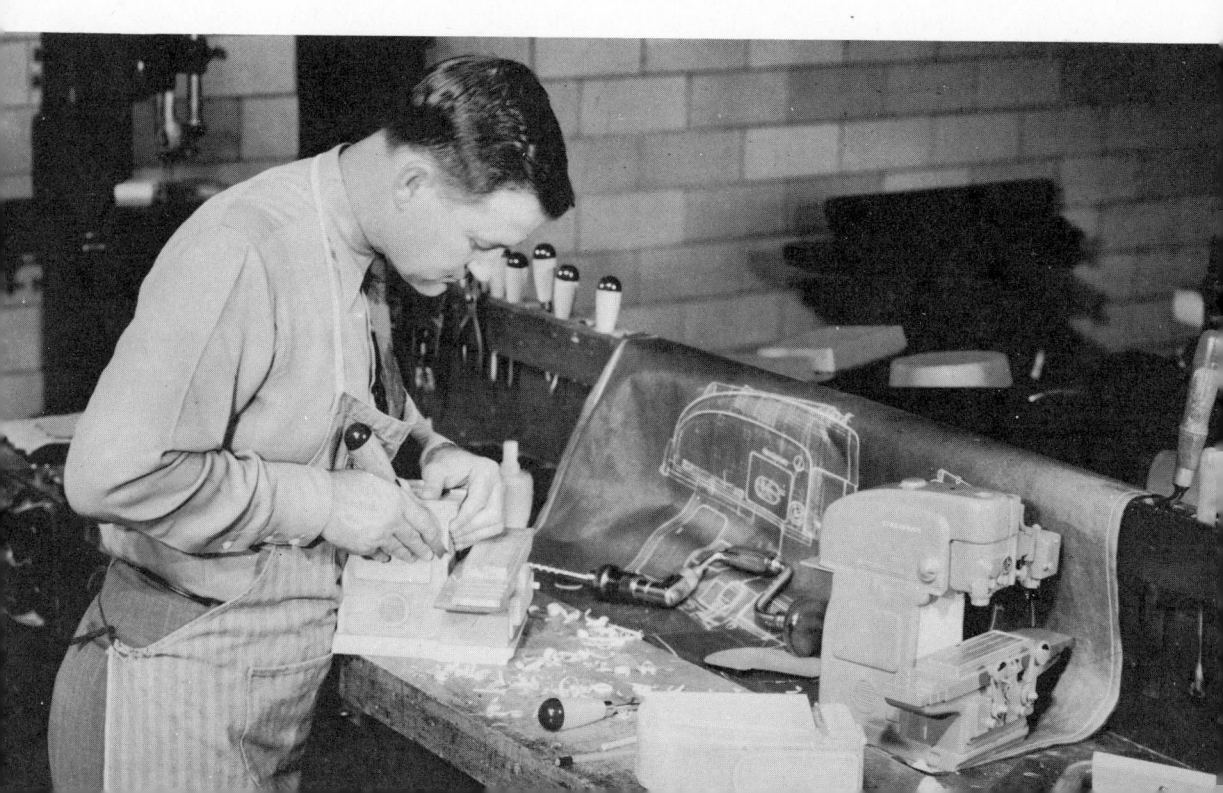

man, lumber wholesaler, furniture salesman, or realtor.

Mechanical—carpenter, patternmaker, boatbuilder, or cabinetmaker.

Natural—forester, or forest farmer.

Scientific—wood chemist, paper chemist, or forest products researcher.

Social—industrial education teacher.

You should also know some things about yourself. Some questions you should ask are:

What is my vocational interest?
What are my aptitudes and abilities, or what do I do well?
What kind of personality do I have?
What is my family and personal background?

As you study and work in the woodshop you should make an honest attempt to learn more about yourself and about the existing occupational opportunities.

You can develop abilities that

1-7. This "do-it-yourselfer" is building his own garage and enjoying it.

will make you an intelligent "do-it-yourselfer" in and around your home. Even if you don't enter a woodworking occupation you will some day buy or rent a home or apartment. You will also furnish it. A good many things in and around the home are made of wood. With your woodshop experiences you can do home maintenance, build on to your home, garage, or cottage, and build or repair furniture. *Fig. 1–7.* Woodworking is the most popular area of "do-it-yourself" activities.

You can learn a hobby or a good leisure-time activity. Many "do-it-yourself" tasks are done of necessity, not desire. However, you might enjoy just making things of wood, not necessarily because of economic necessity, but for pure enjoyment. Your hobby might be anything from model boatbuilding or wood carving to picture frame making and wood turning. *Fig. 1–8.*

You will learn about technological development in wood: modern methods of house construction, new techniques in making furniture, and unusual uses for wood.

You will know more about wood products—how to select and buy them. You will use this knowledge countless times, when making the simplest purchases as well as when you choose your furniture and your home itself, perhaps the most important purchases you will ever make. *Fig. 1–9.* Industry also finds many unusual uses for wood such as storage tanks for chemical materials, wood pipe for carrying sea water, wood structures for mining operations. These are only a very few. The

18

modern car, refrigerator, and many other "metal" products contain wood in the form of hardboard and plastics.

You will develop safety habits and practices in the use of tools and machines.

THE TEAM APPROACH IN WOODWORKING

In almost every job you might choose you will be a member of a team. This is particularly true of many of the jobs in woodworking. Let's look for a moment at the construction industry. The people who build homes, commercial buildings, bridges, and other structures must work as a team to get these things

1-9.   You will learn to judge what is good construction in the furniture you buy.

1-8.   It's fun to work with woods and that is why it is the most popular creative hobby in America.

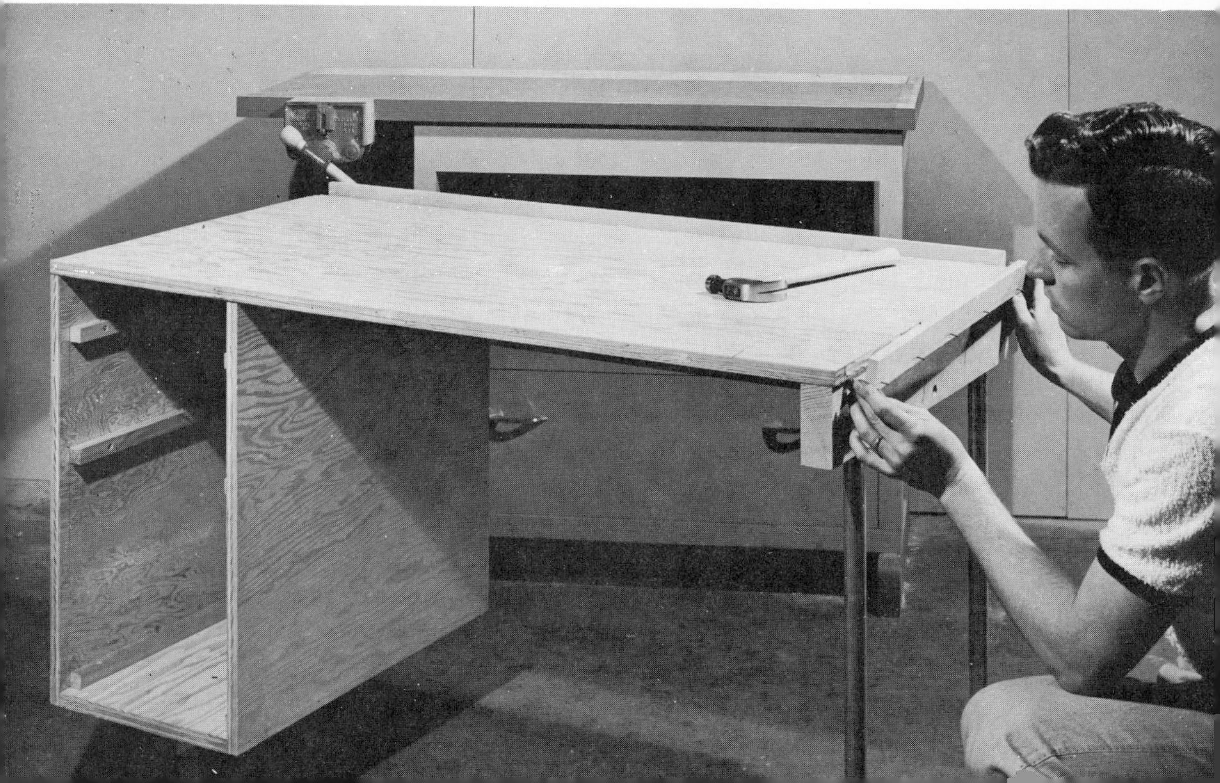

1–10. Building a home is a job for a *team* of men. Craftsmen in many areas of the building trades must co-operate.

done. *Fig. 1–10.* In a construction industry the team is composed of the architect and the client, the business people who supply the material, the contractor, and skilled workers. For example, if a home is to be built, the client and architect work together to determine the kind of home that will satisfy the needs and wishes of the client. The architect then designs the home to meet these requirements. When this has been completed and the design has been approved, drawings and prints are made. Specifications are written. These are then sent out for *bids.* A contractor will bid on the job, based on his knowledge of the cost of materials and labor. This means that he names a price at which he feels he can do the job and make a reasonable profit. If his bid is accepted, then he begins to assemble his own team for the actual building of the house. This team includes such skilled tradesmen (some of whom will be sub-contractors) as the cement worker, bricklayer, carpenter, plumber, electrician, tile setter, roofer, and painter. The contractor must also work with the people who sell building supplies and lumber. It is the *team approach* that gets things done.

Another illustration of the team

approach is found in the furniture industry. This is one of many manufacturing areas in which the principal material used is wood. The manufacturer selects and hires the team. In addition to all of the necessary office personnel, he needs skilled people to help in many ways. The furniture designer, for example, will create the design for all of the new furniture pieces; the designer and draftsman along with the shop foreman and skilled cabinetmaker will make a model of each new item to be produced. Drawings and models are studied and the jigs, fixtures, and tools built so that the furniture can be produced. Then, using automatic machinery and semi-skilled workers, the parts of the product are manufactured. These are assembled and the necessary hand work for finishing and upholstery completed.

SOME PEOPLE WHO WORK WITH WOODS

Each area of woodwork offers many different careers and jobs, from semi-skilled work in the furniture industry to professional occupations.

Professional Occupations.

Architect. Fig. 1–11.

DUTIES: Confers with clients about cost and style; makes preliminary plans and working drawings (including engineering drawings); prepares specifications; prepares list of building contractors; inspects and supervises projects as they are built.

NUMBER: About 24,000 registered and about 5,000 more who are without license.

EDUCATION AND TRAINING: A license usually requires a mini-

1–11. The architect is checking the prints with the carpenter as the building progresses. This is only one of his many responsibilities.

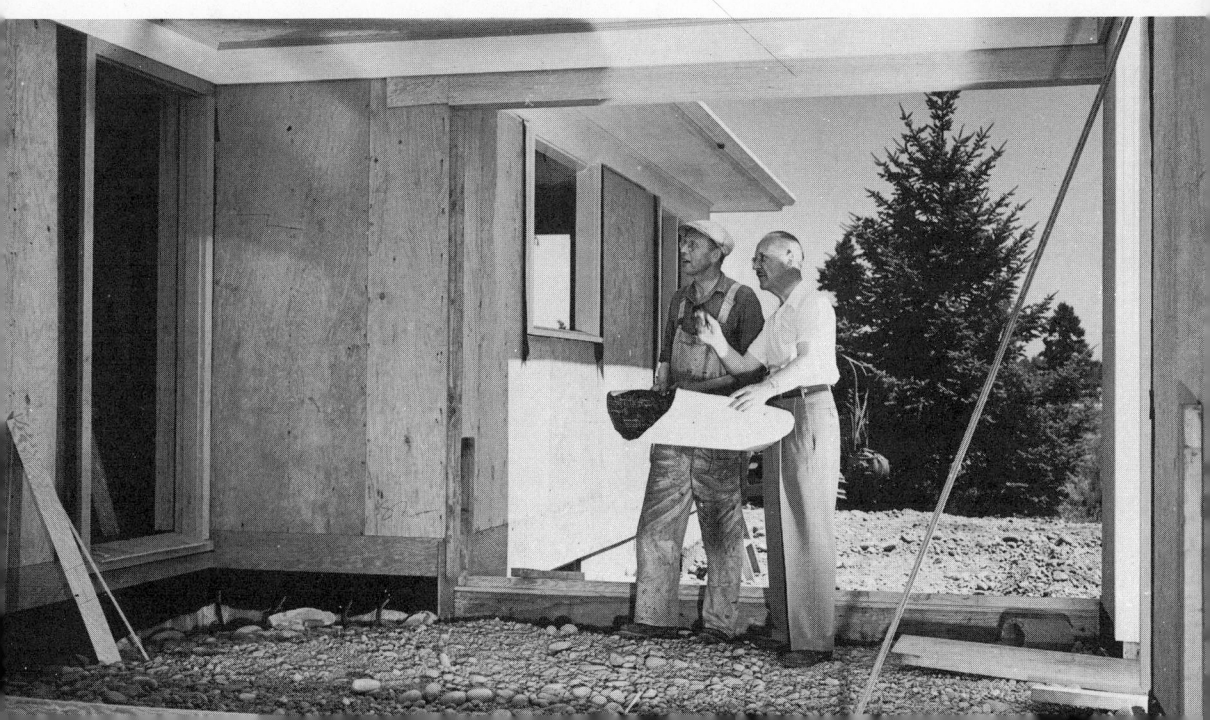

mum of a college or a university degree in architecture plus three years of practical experience in an architect's office.

FUTURE: A great future because of the building boom.

Industrial Education Teacher. Fig. 1–12.

DUTIES: Teaches junior or senior high school woodshop or general shop classes. Teaches carpentry, patternmaking, cabinetmaking or boatbuilding in a vocational or technical school. Must be able to organize instructional materials, teach, and maintain the shop. Works in all kinds of schools including junior high, senior high, vocational or technical, in cities and towns of every size.

NUMBER: About 50 per cent of the 50,000 industrial education teachers teach woodworking full or part time.

EDUCATION AND TRAINING: A four-year college degree with a specialization in technical and professional courses in industrial education.

FUTURE: Tremendous demand for industrial education teachers because about 50 per cent of the graduates enter industry each year.

Furniture Designer. Fig. 1–13.

DUTIES: Develops, designs, and creates models of possible new furniture pieces; makes finished drawings and diagrams.

NUMBER: Small numbers are em-

1–12. Would you be interested in teaching? If you like people and like to work with tools and materials, this may be the job for you.

ployed by independent designing firms and furniture factories.

EDUCATION AND TRAINING: Formal training in art, design, and construction in trade or technical schools, or colleges.

FUTURE: There is a limited outlook because of the small number employed.

Interior Designer. Fig. 1–14.

DUTIES: Plans and supervises the furnishing of private homes, offices, and other structures. Selects type of decor, schemes and furnishings; arranges the furniture, draperies, wall and floor coverings, lighting fixtures, lamps, and decorative accessories. Designs and has built special pieces of furniture.

NUMBER: Total is somewhat over 10,000.

1–13. The furniture designer not only must be creative, he must be able to do drafting.

EDUCATION AND TRAINING: Best preparation is a three-year course in art or a four-year degree from

1–14. Interior designers must be able to visualize the way a room will look, even in earliest planning stages. Notice that in this building the interior and exterior blend remarkably well.

Forester. Fig 1–15.

DUTIES: Protects, manages, and evaluates valuable forest land. Safeguards forests from fires, destructive insects, and diseases. Promotes and facilitates forestation; estimates the amount of lumber on forested land, and appraises the value of such land.

NUMBER: About 17,000.

EDUCATION AND TRAINING: Four years of college leading to a bachelor's degree.

FUTURE: Excellent.

1–15. Most foresters work out-of-doors a good deal of the time.

Skilled Trades and Technical Occupations.

Carpenters. Fig. 1–16.

DUTIES: Rough carpenters make the framework including sub-flooring, sheathing, partitions, floor joists, studding, and rafters. Finish carpenters install wood

a college with a major in interior decorating.

FUTURE: The outlook is excellent because of the many homes and offices built each year.

1–16. The all-around carpenter must be able to do both *rough* and *finish* work required to build a house.

paneling, cabinets, built-ins, window sashes, door frames, and hardware. Carpenters work in the construction industry, and in alteration and modernization. They also do maintenance work in factories, hotels, and other large buildings. Some carpenters also do roofing, glazing, and painting.

NUMBER: 1,200,000.

EDUCATION AND TRAINING: Training in a vocational or technical school or a four-year apprenticeship program for carpenters.

FUTURE: Excellent.

Cabinetmakers. Fig. 1–17.

DUTIES: Uses both hand and machine tools; cuts and shapes parts; assembles parts into furniture pieces.

NUMBER: About 100,000. Most carpenters, however, do some cabinetmaking. Others work in custom and production furniture plants, in retail furniture stores, and in shops that produce office and store fixtures.

EDUCATION AND TRAINING: Vocational or technical school program or a three- or four-year apprenticeship.

FUTURE: Limited number of opportunities because of mass production in the furniture industry.

Patternmaker. Fig. 1–18.

DUTIES: Studies blueprints and plans the pattern. Considers the way the object will be cast and the kind of metal used. Selects the proper wood, makes the layout, designs the parts, and fabri-

1–17. This skilled cabinetmaker is making a new leg for this chair. Notice the array of tools which he must know how to use.

cates them with hand and power tools.

NUMBER: There are about 7,500

1–18. This wood patternmaker is making engineering changes on the wood pattern for a tractor oil pan.

wood patternmakers—roughly as many as all other kinds of patternmakers combined.

EDUCATION AND TRAINING: Good trade school and/or five-year apprenticeship.

FUTURE: Slow increase in the number needed.

Painters and Finishers. Fig. 1–19.

DUTIES: Erects scaffolds; mixes paints and finishes; handles brushes and other painting tools; uses spray guns and rollers; must know the characteristics of common types of paints and finishes. Applies finishes.

NUMBER: About 400,000.

EDUCATION AND TRAINING: A good trade or technical school or four-year formal apprenticeship.

FUTURE: Excellent.

1-19. The painter must know his colors and he must understand materials, particularly wood and how it will take paint.

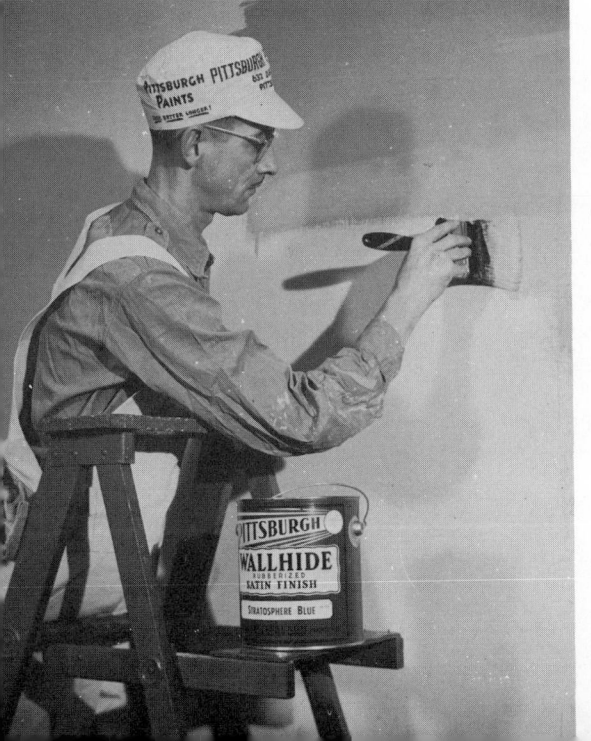

Business Occupations. There are about 4,000 lumber wholesalers who employ approximately 50,000 people. Some 30,000 retail lumber dealers employ about 250,000 people. *Fig. 1–20.* About 60 per cent of all the retail lumber dealers are located in towns of 5,000 population or less.

VALUES OF WOOD AS A BUILDING MATERIAL

• *A renewable abundance of supply.* We can and are *growing more timber,* while we are merely using up our coal, iron ore, and petroleum.

• *A wide variety of types.* Many species of softwoods are available for structural and framing lumber, plywood sheathing, roofing and subflooring, hardwood for flooring, paneling, cabinetwork and furniture, sports equipment, and musical instruments.

• *A durable material.* Wood has been tested and proved by centuries of hard, practical use. Examples: Beams discovered in an ancient Oriental tomb were found to be perfectly sound after 2,700 years; many homes of wood which were built more than 200 years ago are as sound today as when they were new. Wood has been found to be the best material for tanks for storing many kinds of chemicals.

• *A strong material.* Weight for weight, wood is stronger in compression and tension than many materials.

• *An attractive material.* The beauty, warmth, and richness of wood for furniture, panels, floors, and interiors cannot be equalled by any comparable material. *Fig. 1-21.*

1-20. A lumber dealer needs a thorough knowledge not only of the materials he sells but also of related products. This lumber yard dealer is conferring with a paint salesman. What he learns about new finishes will enable him to advise his own customers when they purchase unfinished lumber.

• *An easily worked material.* Wood can be cut, shaped, jointed, and finished with simple hand tools, portable tools, or machinery. It is the ideal do-it-yourself material for the man or boy who enjoys making improvements and repairs, furniture, models, toys, and sculpture.

• *A versatile material.* Wood can be made into products such as plywood, hardboard, particle board, and insulation board.

1-21. How many different uses of wood can you find in this interior?

Unit 2: SAFETY

Safety is the most important aspect of your woodshop experience. Your own safety, of course, comes first. No tool, machine, or product is as important as you are. However, real safety means safeguarding against damage to machines, tools, and materials, as well as preventing personal injury. All of these matters need close attention. Now is the time to develop good safety habits which will be valuable to you all your life—in school, on your job, and at home.

The furniture and building industries are vitally concerned with safety. Millions of dollars are spent each year in developing safety programs. Because efficient production and safety go hand in hand, present-day industry needs and wants *safe as well as efficient workers*. A permanent injury, such as the loss of a finger or an eye, can seriously impair your usefulness and have a lasting effect on your life.

WAYS TO BE SAFETY-SMART

Some people consider guards, goggles, and other safety devices beneath the dignity of the "real he-man." These people have not yet learned that *it is smart to be safe*. The following general safety rules apply to all of your work. Specific safety practices are also listed later with the discussion of individual machines.

Clothing and Personal Dress. Wear a short-sleeved shirt or roll up your sleeves. *Fig. 2–1*. Tuck in or remove your tie. For some kinds of work it is important to wear an apron or shopcoat. Rings, loose neckties, and

2–1. Dress appropriately for the work to be done.

28

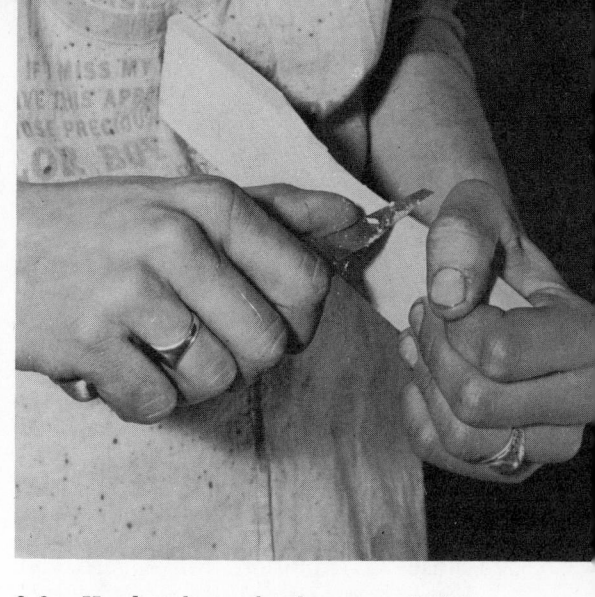

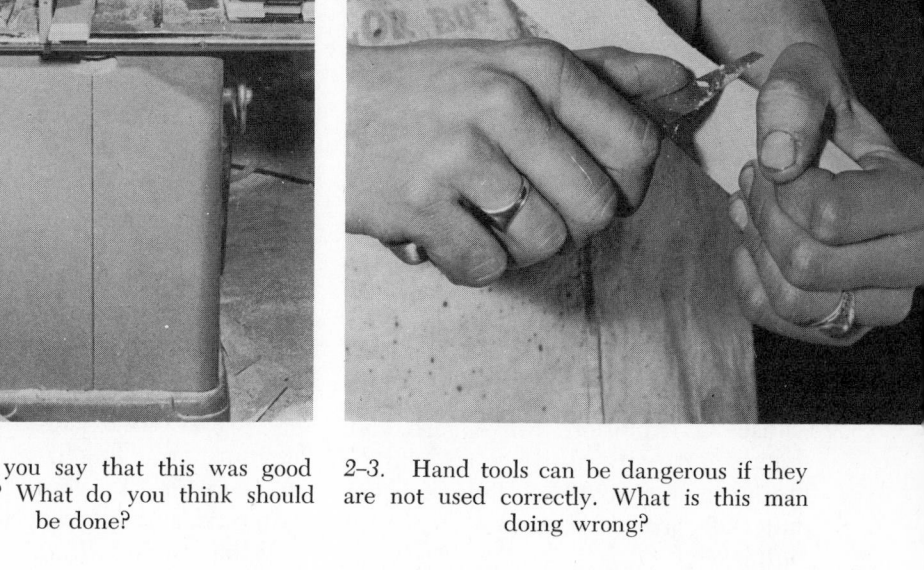

2-2. Would you say that this was good housekeeping? What do you think should be done?

2-3. Hand tools can be dangerous if they are not used correctly. What is this man doing wrong?

long, loose sleeves have caused many an accident.

Housekeeping. Remove all hazards around the machine. Place scrap wood in the scrap box. Pile materials neatly so that they will not fall when taken from the stock rack. Do not block the aisle, stairway, or area near equipment. *Fig. 2-2.* Good housekeeping means cleanliness and order. Keep the machines clean. A clean shop is usually a safe shop.

Hand Tools. Dull tools are dangerous. Always keep them sharp. Do not leave hand tools on the machine beds. Keep sharp tools out of your pockets. Always use the right tool for the job—it gets the job done faster and more safely. There is a right and wrong way to use every hand tool. Learn to use each one correctly. *Fig. 2-3.* Hand tool injuries are often caused by defective tools, using the wrong tools, or using them in an unsafe manner.

Portable Electric Tools. Remember that 110 volts can kill you or give a serious burn or shock. This is especially true when a tool is used around dampness or moisture. *Fig. 2-4.* Check the tool before using it for a broken plug, bad connector, broken switch, or poor insulation on the cord. Be sure that a portable tool is grounded. Keep the cord away from hot, rough, or oily places. Do not use electrical tools in the presence of inflammable gas or vapors; a spark can

2-4. Be sure you use portable power tools in a dry place.

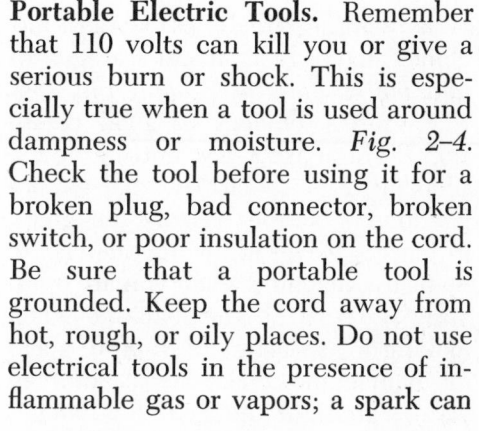

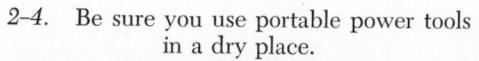

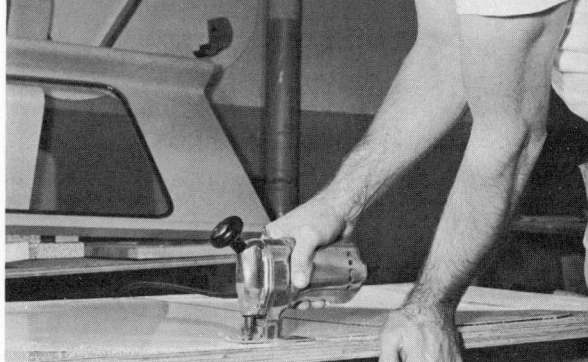

2–5a. Using the guards on the machines is safe practice.

cause an explosion. Make sure your hands and feet are dry when using a portable electrical tool. Pull the plug, not the cord, to remove it from the outlet.

Woodworking Machines. Modern machines have mechanical safeguards and *you should use them. Fig. 2–5.* Keep safety devices in good condition. (There are a few cutting operations on the circular saw that cannot be done with the basket-type guard in place.) Never allow anyone else to be near a machine when you are operating it. Turn off the machine when making all adjustments. Before starting a machine, check to see that all clamps are tight and that all wrenches and other tools are removed. Operate

2–5b. A good example of using a guard.

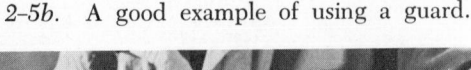

a machine *only after you have received thorough instructions.*

Special Protective Devices. Wear goggles for grinding and other operations in which there is danger from flying particles. *Fig. 2–6.* Wear heavy shoes when handling heavy materials. Wear the right kind of respirator for spraying.

Lifting Materials. Lift with your legs to avoid back and stomach injuries. Set loads down carefully to avoid pinching your fingers or toes. Always get help in handling bulky or long materials. Pile all materials in such a way that they will not slip or fall. Be careful in carrying anything, especially long pieces of stock, to keep from striking other students.

Using Ladders. Be sure that the ladder has a secure footing. Keep it at

2-6. This computer technician wears his safety glasses and hard hat at all times on the job. In woodworking and other industries this is a good practice for anyone whose work may take him near dangerous machinery.

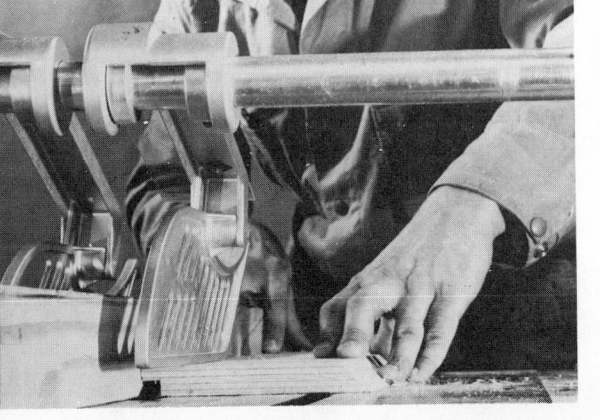

the correct angle, about 75 degrees. Face the ladder and use both hands when going up or down. Never try to overreach when on a ladder. Never use a ladder with weak or damaged rails or steps. Open a step ladder and set the brace before using it.

Horseplay. Practical jokes and horseplay around machines and tools are very dangerous. Conduct yourself like a good workman. Do not scuffle, push, or wrestle. *Fig. 2–7.*

Accidents and First Aid. Most shop accidents can be avoided. If one does occur, however, report it immediately and get proper first aid or medical attention. Do not laugh off a small injury. Even the slightest scratch can cause an infection and result in a permanent injury. Never try to remove foreign bodies from your eye by yourself. Get help from some competent person.

Fire. Keep oily rags in covered metal containers. Be sure that the proper fire extinguisher is available. Keep fire doors closed. Learn to use fire-extinguishing equipment.

Remember, safety is everybody's business. Always be careful. Play safe, and enjoy your woodshop.

2-7.   Can you find twenty unsafe practices? If not, you do not know your safety regulations.

NATIONAL SAFETY COUNCIL

Unit 3: DESIGN

There are many kinds of design in woodwork. A well-designed furniture piece is one that adheres to a certain style, has beautiful wood and finish, fine construction, and attractive cabinet hardware. *Fig. 3–1.* A well-designed boat not only looks sleek, but it also rides well in the water, handles easily, and is low in maintenance costs. A well-designed house is one that is structurally sound, suits the needs of the family, and has an attractive, well-defined appearance. *Fig. 3–2.* Several aspects of designing are often combined in one job. For instance, in building a house, there is *landscape design* for the surroundings, *room design* for a kitchen, and *structural design* for the roof rafters.

In all of these examples, there are

3–1. A well-designed piece of furniture. Its beauty is in the simplicity of line and shape and in the quality of the wood.

3-2. A well-planned home shows all the elements of good design—interesting lines, shape and form, and striking tone and texture.

three keys to good design. The product must *function* as well as possible. It must have an *attractive appearance*. It must be *structurally sound*. In other words, good design includes function, appearance, and sound construction.

One of the best ways to learn about good design is to watch for it at all times. You will find examples of good design everywhere—in better stores, in the work of good builders, and in a study of the designs shown in the best commercial and trade magazines. Design is all-important in wood products. It is useless to spend time and money constructing something that fails to meet the three keys to good design.

SOME ELEMENTS OF DESIGN

The design of any wood object involves *line, shape, mass, color,* and *tones and texture*.

Line. The four principal lines are straight, curved, S-shaped, and circular. These can be combined to form objects of almost any shape. Much contemporary furniture is largely composed of straight lines. *Fig. 3-3.*

3-3a. *Lines* not only define and give shape to the object but also help the eye see the total form.

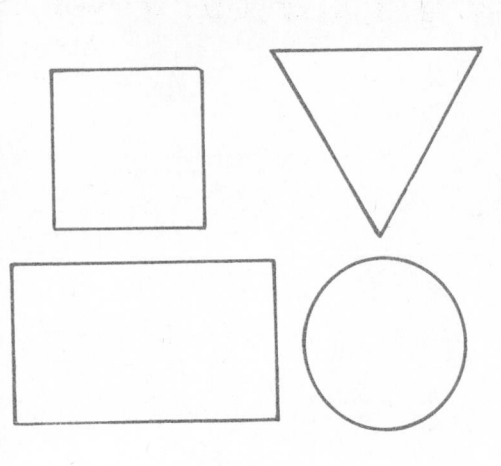

3–4a. *Shapes.*

3–3b. These chairs demonstrate a practical use of intersecting lines which the eye sees as a total form.

Early American furniture has many curved lines.

Shape. Lines make up shape. The four basic shapes are square, round, rectangular, and triangular. *Fig. 3–4a.* If you look at a house design,

3–4b. Notice that the architect has used all the basic shapes in this attractive entrance.

Color. Nature has given each species of wood a color all its own. Some of these are so beautiful that we give them a *natural finish* to preserve their warm, rich colors. *Fig. 3–6.* We can also add color by painting, staining, and finishing. The colors in home dec-

3–6.   Here you see a simple explanation of the color system. Six primary and six secondary colors or hues are indicated. Pairs of adjacent colors on this wheel are known as "harmonious" hues. Colors opposite to each other are complementaries. The ability of a surface to reflect a pure color is called hue. The architect and designer think of color as a design element that is just as important as line or form. They use the natural wood colors or add color with stains and paints.

3–5.   A solid is a three-dimensional object that occupies space. The architect and designer think in terms of form rather than solidity. The form may be open as in these tables or closed as in a house, boat, or wood pattern.

for example, you can see all of these shapes: a rectangle in a door opening, a square in a window, a circle in a door knob, and a triangle in the roof line. Look at the house in *Fig. 3–4b* and see how many of these shapes you can find.

Mass. Mass or form is a 3-dimensional shape or combination of shapes, having substance. Pieces of lumber come in many shapes, such as cubes, rods, and rectangles. When you put two or more of them together to make an object, the resulting product has mass. For example, it may have the mass or form of a house, a chair, or a simple wood pattern. Mass usually refers to an object of considerable size. *Fig. 3–5.*

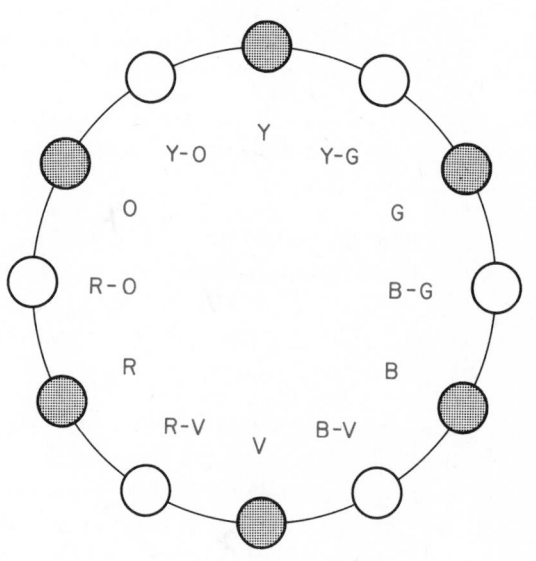

Y	YELLOW	V	VIOLET
Y-G	YELLOW-GREEN	R-V	RED-VIOLET
G	GREEN	R	RED
B-G	BLUE-GREEN	R-O	RED-ORANGE
B	BLUE	O	ORANGE
B-V	BLUE-VIOLET	Y-O	YELLOW-ORANGE

3-7. All except black surfaces reflect light, thus producing *tone*. White surfaces reflect all the light while black reflects none. Colors fall somewhere in between white and black. *Texture*, when speaking of color, means the pattern of contrasts in light reflections. This picture shows an excellent example of light reflection and surface texture. Everyone can appreciate the beauty in this interesting use of natural and man-made wood products.

oration are added for beauty. Color also can be applied for very practical reasons such as the colors used in wood patterns to identify various parts.

Tones and texture. Tones are the light-colored areas and darks or shadows in a material. *Fig. 3–7.* You can see examples of this in the heartwood and sapwood of a tree. Texture in wood refers to contrasts in the grain surface. In a living material such as wood, each species has its own texture. There are also many man-made textures such as those you see on special plywood surfaces.

PRINCIPLES OF DESIGN

Several people, asked to judge a single wood product, will not always agree. Some prefer modern or contemporary furniture and homes, while others prefer traditional. However, regardless of personal preference, there are certain rules or principles that must be observed if we are to design a product that has merit. The important principles are proportion, balance, harmony, rhythm, and emphasis.

Proportion. Proportion is the relationship of the parts of a product to each other. In general, a rectangular shape is considered to have better proportion than a square. It is difficult for the eye to see the exact relationship between height and width in a rectangle; this difficulty creates interest. Many consider the "golden mean" rectangle to have the most nearly perfect proportions, about 5 to 8. *Fig. 3–8.* In furniture, picture frames, and even houses there are many examples of this proportion. This rectangle can be divided vertically into two equal parts. If it is divided horizontally into three or four unequal parts, the largest is usually placed at the bottom. In dividing the rectangle into three parts vertically, the center part is often made the largest or smallest and the other two of equal size and shape. Proportion is extremely important when planning any wood product. For example, a home is not attractive if it is too "boxy" in appearance.

Balance. Balance is that quality which makes an object appear to be stable or at rest. Most things in nature are in balance, for instance, the arms and legs of the human body. Anything not in balance appears to be unstable, as if it may tip over at any moment. There are two kinds of balance: formal and informal. In *formal balance* a vertical line through the center of an object would divide it symmetrically, or equally on both sides. In *informal balance*, objects or the parts of an object appear to be equal because of their relative size

and position. Study houses and pieces of furniture to see if you can tell if they represent formal or informal balance. *Fig. 3–9.*

Harmony. Harmony is the way the various parts of an object blend together. The use of too many materials, textures, or colors prevents harmony. In house construction, unattractive homes are often those made of too many materials and textures—brick, wood, cement, glass—and too many

3–8.   The designer keeps in mind the proportions of the "golden rectangle" when designing tables, cabinets, and other furniture. Which rectangles in this picture have approximately the 5:8 proportion? Why do you think the designers sometimes choose other ratios?

3-9. Balance and symmetry spring from nature's law of equilibrium. We look for balance in all visible objects. Most of us can recognize this balance. Here is a good example of both formal and informal balance. The cabinet itself is in perfect formal balance: When it is divided in the middle, both sides are exactly the same. The accessories on the top of the cabinet show informal symmetry in which there is balance between the lamp and small globe on one side and the decorative candles on the other.

3-10. Rhythm in design is marked by the occurrence of certain features or elements at regular intervals. This effect causes eye movements. Here you see the use of rhythm in architectural design. What examples of rhythm can you find in other pictures in this chapter?

colors. Harmony is found not only in color and texture, but in space relationships, shapes, and other important elements.

Rhythm. Rhythm is the repetition of shape, color, or line which gives distinct character to an object. *Fig. 3-10.*

Emphasis. Emphasis is the center of interest or the point of greatest importance—a beautiful entrance door or an excellent piece of cabinet hardware, for example.

3–11.   Three beautiful coffee tables in popular styles. *a.* Modern, or contemporary, in walnut with an oil finish.

EXAMPLES OF DESIGN

Furniture Styles. Good design in furniture usually follows some well-established style. The three most popular styles in American furniture are *modern* or *contemporary*, *traditional*, and *early American* or *colonial*. *Fig. 3–11.* There are many adaptations of these styles, for example, contemporary furniture influenced by Scandinavian or Oriental fashions.

3–11b.   Traditional in mahogany with walnut burl accents.

3–11c. Colonial of cherry veneer and pecan.

3–12. This chest and mirror show the Oriental influence found in much of contemporary design.

Fig. 3–12. Traditional design is actually a combination of the best of the 18th Century designers. Early American or colonial has a distinctly homey, American flavor typified by the use of many turned parts.

Home Designs. There are many kinds of design in the home. Among these are:

• *Landscape design.* This includes such factors as view from the house, location and grading of the site, and the plantings.

• *Room design.* This includes kitchen cabinets, location of built-in units, architectural space relationships within each room, location of doors and windows, traffic pattern, relationship of each room to the rest of the house, and efficiency of use.

40

3–13. Mass-produced, prefabricated homes are available in a variety of styles.
a. Contemporary.

• *House design.* The design of homes tends to center around certain regional styles such as Cape Cod, colonial, contemporary, and western modern. *Fig. 3–13.* Each is designed for a certain climate and way of living. Good design of any home should provide good solutions to these questions: (a) Does the floor plan meet the needs and interests of the family? (b) Is the home economical to build? (c) Are the right materials used?

3–13b. Modified Cape Cod.

3–13c. Modified Colonial.

(d) Is it solidly constructed? (e) Is it easy to maintain and clean? (f) Is it attractive?

3–14. A cathedral type box beam used in home construction. This home is being built with components rather than pieces.

Structural Design. In addition to the appearance of any wood product there are two other highly important considerations: how well the product is made, and whether it will serve the purpose for which it is intended.

In modern house construction, developments in design include trussed roofs, box beams, stressed skin panels, and component units for assembling a house. *Fig. 3–14.* These advances in structural design are not only improvements in the soundness of construction, but also save money by using less material and requiring less labor time.

Structural design today involves new kinds of man-made wood materials, and new methods of joining parts together, depending on the strength needed. For example, home construction requires considering such information as snow loads, wind velocity, heating and air conditioning requirements.

42

Unit 4: READING PRINTS, ESTIMATING, AND PLANNING

The ability to read and understand drawings, prints, and plans is basic to all woodworking. Sketches, drawings, and prints are the written language that tells you what must be built, and the materials needed. *Fig. 4–1*. By means of lines, symbols, and dimensions, the ideas of the designer or architect are conveyed to you. To be a good worker you must be able to interpret the sketch, drawing, or print correctly so you can visualize the size and shape of the product to be built. *Fig. 4–2*. This is true whether the product is *a wood pattern, a piece of furniture, a boat, or a house. Fig. 4–3*. It would be impossible to convey this information in any other way.

A sketch or drawing of something to be built is the original idea put on paper. A print is an exact copy of a drawing. In the building industry most prints are called blueprints; the paper has a blue background with white lines. Blueprints are commonly used in house construction and other building trades because they do not fade when exposed to sunlight. In other areas a black-and-white print is more common. Most of you have had

a course in drawing or drafting so you should know how to *make* and *read* mechanical drawings. If not, you must review a good book on drawing at this point.

KINDS OF WOODWORKING DRAWINGS

The techniques used in preparing woodworking drawings and prints depend largely on the product involved. Drawings used in the pattern-making trade are not of the same kind as those used in the building trade. Here are some of the ways in which woodworking drawings differ from metalworking drawings:

4–1a. Attractive, well-designed homes such as this one are the result of careful planning. Plans must be drawn with great accuracy, and the builders must read them correctly.

43

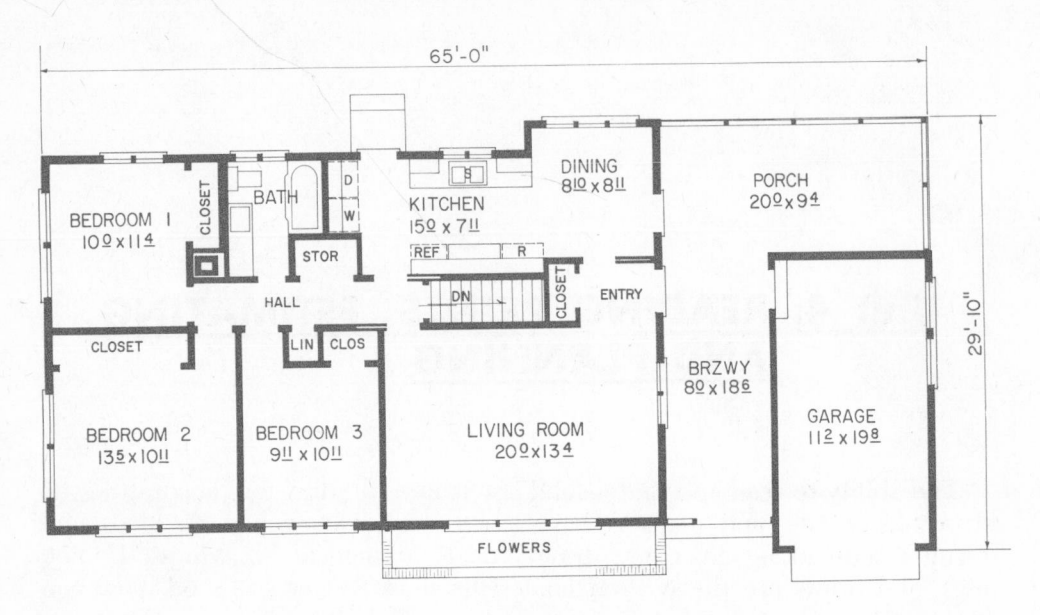

65'-0"

29'-10"

BEDROOM 1
10⁰ x 11⁴

CLOSET

BATH

D
W

STOR

HALL

KITCHEN
15⁰ x 7¹¹

REF

R

DN

CLOSET

ENTRY

DINING
8¹⁰ x 8¹¹

PORCH
20⁰ x 9⁴

CLOSET

LIN CLOS

BEDROOM 2
13⁵ x 10¹¹

BEDROOM 3
9¹¹ x 10¹¹

LIVING ROOM
20⁰ x 13⁴

BRZWY
8⁰ x 18⁶

GARAGE
11² x 19⁸

FLOWERS

4–1b. This floor plan is just one of many drawings you would have to understand if you were to build the house in *Fig. 4–1a.*

• A woodworking drawing is often a combination of several types of drawings. Part of it might be a *working view* drawing while another part might show a *perspective* or *cabinet view. Fig. 4–4.*

4–2a. To build this modern desk you need a working drawing, a bill of materials, and a plan of procedure.

• In a *multiview (orthographic projection)* drawing, the views are not always in their proper position as they are in machine drawing.

• In a woodworking drawing many details are not included. For example, the kind of joint or fastener is not always indicated.

• Many woodworking drawings have inch marks on all dimensions. *Fig. 4–5.* In popular books and magazines furniture drawings frequently are made in the form of isometric or cabinet drawings. For even greater clarity, *exploded isometrics* or *perspectives* are often used.

Drawings in Cabinetmaking and Furniture Manufacture. There are four types of drawings used in cabinetmaking and furniture manufacture: the *multiview working* drawing, the *cabinet* drawing, the *perspective* drawing, and the *isometric* drawing.

44

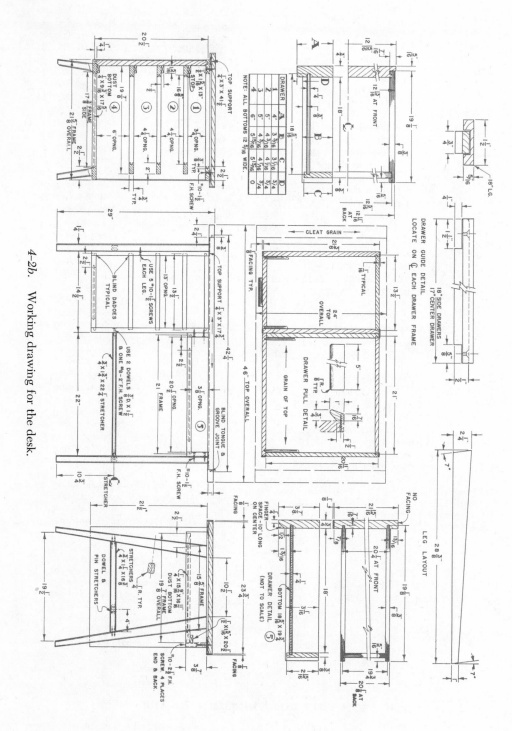

45

4-2b. Working drawing for the desk.

4-2c. BILL OF MATERIALS FOR KNEE HOLE DESK

Important: All dimensions listed below are FINISHED size.

No. of Pieces	Part Name	Thickness	Width	Length	Material
4	Top and Bottom Frame — Front and Back	3/4"	2 1/2"	13 1/2"	Solid White Oak
4	Top and Bottom Frame — Sides	3/4"	2 1/2"	17 3/8"	Hardwood
6	Drawer Frame — Front and Back	3/4"	2"	13 1/2"	Hardwood
6	Drawer Frame — Sides	3/4"	2"	16 5/8"	Hardwood
2	Center Drawer Frame — Front and Back	3/4"	2 1/2"	21"	Hardwood
2	Center Drawer Frame — Sides	3/4"	2 1/2"	15 5/8"	Hardwood
2	End Drawer — Case Sides	3/4"	21 3/8"	21 1/2"	Comb Grain White Oak Plywood S1S
1	Back Panel	3/4"	13 1/2"	20 1/2"	Comb Grain White Oak Plywood S1S
1	Center Drawer — Case Back	3/4"	3 3/8"	21"	Comb Grain White Oak Plywood S1S
2	Center Drawer — Case Side	3/4"	3 3/8"	20 1/8"	Comb Grain White Oak Plywood S1S
1	Drawer Front	3/4"	4"	12 15/16"	Comb Grain White Oak Plywood S1S
2	Drawer Fronts	3/4"	5"	12 15/16"	Comb Grain White Oak Plywood S1S
1	Drawer Front	3/4"	6"	12 15/16"	Comb Grain White Oak Plywood S1S
1	Drawer Front	3/4"	3 3/8"	21 15/16"	Comb Grain White Oak Plywood S1S
2	Drawer Sides	3/8"	3 3/16"	19 1/8"	Solid Oak
1	Drawer Back	3/8"	3 1/16"	12 5/16"	Solid Oak
4	Drawer Sides	3/8"	4 3/16"	19 1/8"	Solid Oak
2	Drawer Backs	3/8"	4 1/16"	12 5/16"	Solid Oak
2	Drawer Sides	3/8"	5 3/16"	19 1/8"	Solid Oak
1	Drawer Back	3/8"	5 3/16"	12 5/16"	Solid Oak
2	Drawer Sides	3/8"	3 1/16"	19 3/8"	Solid Oak
1	Drawer Back	3/8"	2 15/16"	19 3/8"	Solid Oak
4	Drawer Bottoms	1/4"	12 5/16"	18 5/16"	Birch Plywood S1S
1	Drawer Bottom	1/4"	18 5/8"	19 3/4"	Birch Plywood S1S
1	Dust Bottom	1/4"	9 3/8"	17 5/16"	Birch Plywood S1S
1	Dust Bottom	1/4"	15 5/16"	16 11/16"	Birch Plywood S1S
4	Legs	1 1/2"	2 1/4"	28 3/8"	Solid White Oak
2	Stretchers	3/4"	1 1/4"	16 3/8"	Solid White Oak
1	Stretcher	3/4"	1 3/4"	22 1/4"	Solid White Oak
4	Drawer Pulls	3/8"	1"	5"	Solid White Oak
2	Top Cleats	1"	2 1/4"	24"	Solid White Oak
4	Facing Strips	1/8"	3/4"	21 1/2"	Solid White Oak
3	Facing Strips	1/8"	3/4"	3 7/8"	Solid White Oak
2	Facing Strips	1/8"	1"	41 1/2"	Solid White Oak
4	Drawer Stops	1/2"	1 5/16"	13"	Hardwood
1	Drawer Stop	1/2"	1 5/16"	20 1/2"	Hardwood
4	Drawer Guides	1/2"	3/4"	18"	Hardwood
1	Drawer Guide	1/2"	3/4"	17"	Hardwood
5	Drawer Guides	5/16"	1 1/2"	18"	Hardwood
1	Top	3/4"	23 3/4"	42 1/4"	Comb Grain White Oak Plywood S1S
1	Top Supports	1/4"	3"	41 1/2"	Plywood
2	Top Supports	1/4"	3"	17 3/4"	Plywood
8	No. 10 x 2 1/2" F. H. Wood Screws				
10	No. 6 x 1" F. H. Wood Screws				
18	No. 10 x 1 1/2" F. H. Wood Screws				
4	No. 10 x 1 1/4" F. H. Wood Screws				
1	No. 8 x 2" F. H. Wood Screws				

4-2d. PLAN OF PROCEDURE FOR THE KNEE HOLE DESK

1. On circular saw, cut to size all frame members and pieces for both drawer cases.

2. Set up dado head for $\frac{1}{4}$" wide cut. Groove all front and back frame members for tongue and groove joints. Groove bottom and center drawer frame members for dust bottoms. Cut tongues on side members of all frames.

3. Glue up all frames.

4. Change dado head to make $\frac{3}{8}$" wide cut. Stop-dado sides of case for top and bottom frames. Also cut dadoes for center drawer frame. Cut grooves for back panels. Rabbet four sides of back end panel, and two ends of back knee hole panel. Rabbet sides of top, bottom and center drawer frames.

5. Change dado head for $\frac{3}{4}$" wide cut and dado sides of case for drawer frames.

6. Drill and countersink screw shank holes in top frame, and in outside case panels, for attaching top and legs. Drill inside case panel for two dowels and one screw for securing end of knee hole stretcher.

7. Drill and counterbore side and back panel of center drawer case for top mounting screws.

8. Glue up end drawer case. Glue and screw center drawer case to end case.

9. Cut legs and stretchers to size on circular saw.

10. Taper legs with taper jig on circular saw. Cut angles on ends of end stretchers.

11. Round leg and stretcher corners on shaper or drill press shaper attachment.

12. Locate and drill all dowel holes. Cut dowels to length.

13. Assemble legs and end stretchers. Attach leg assemblies and knee hole stretcher to case assembly.

14. Check drawer dimensions and cut all pieces to size on circular saw. (Note: Drawers are made narrower in back than in front for smoother operation).

15. Set dado head for $\frac{1}{4}$" wide cut and cut tongue and rabbet on ends of narrow drawer fronts. Dado both ends of narrow drawer sides, back ends of center drawer sides and ends of center drawer front.

Groove all drawer members to receive bottoms. Cut tongue on end of center drawer sides. Drill and countersink screw holes in drawer pulls. Notch drawer backs for drawer guides.

16. Chamfer back bottom edge of center drawer front for finger grip.

17. Assemble all drawers with glue and wire brads.

18. Make drawer pulls and screw into place.

19. Make drawer guides and stops and install.

20. Cut top to size and cut tenons on each end. Trim tenon for blind joint.

21. Cut end cleats to size. Either cut stop groove or cut groove all the way through and inlay end grain for a blind joint.

22. Glue top cleats in place.

23. Cut and glue top supports in place.

24. Cut all edge facing strips to size and glue in place.

25. Attach top with flat-head wood screws.

26. Finish sand entire project.

27. Apply blond oak finish.

4–3a. This interestingly designed cottage is constructed of many man-made materials such as plywood.

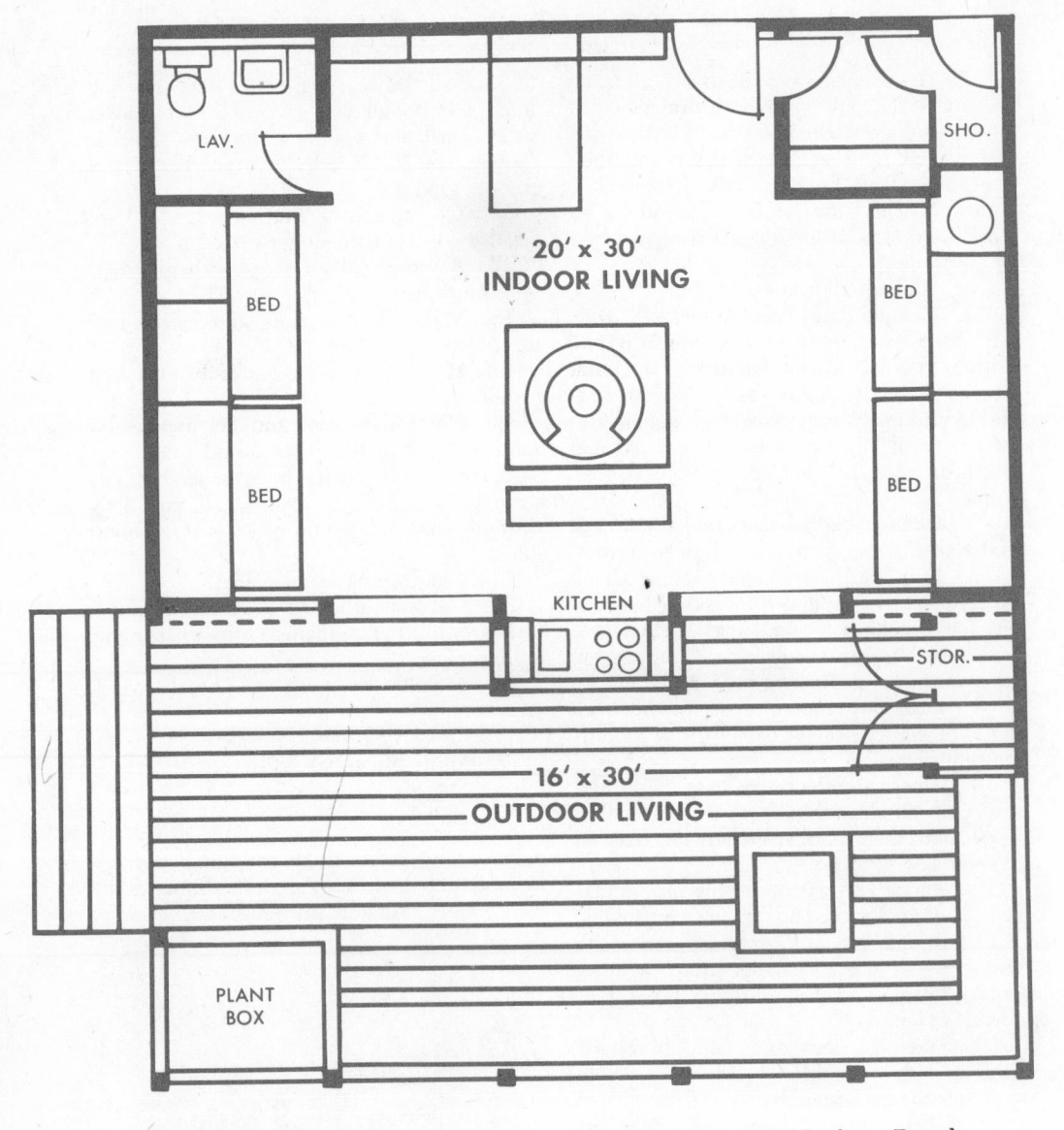

LAV.

SHO.

BED

20' x 30'
INDOOR LIVING

BED

BED

BED

KITCHEN

STOR.

16' x 30'
OUTDOOR LIVING

PLANT
BOX

4–3b. Floor plan for the cottage. Complete plans are available from Douglas
Fir Plywood Association.

The designer makes a full-size, multiview drawing of new items, showing important details of design and construction. This full-size drawing is used in the experimental shop to make a working model. After the mistakes are corrected and changes made in the working model, drawings (to some smaller scale) are made of each part of the furniture piece. These drawings become a part of the process route order (procedure sheet) that is used in actual production. See Unit 41.

ARCHITECTURAL DRAWINGS

The views of a house are shown in *general* and *detail* drawings. General drawings include the plans and elevations, while detail drawings are the sectionals or sections explained on page 68. They are small drawings of certain parts of the house, made to some scale to show proportions. All information as to size must be shown by dimensions written in figures. The selection of the scale is determined by the size of the house as it is related to the size of the paper. Scales commonly used are:

General drawings use a scale of $\frac{1}{4}'' = 1'-0''$. Less frequently a scale of $\frac{1}{8}'' = 1'-0''$ is used. Detail drawings are prepared to scales of $\frac{3}{8}'' = 1'-0''$, $\frac{1}{2}'' = 1'-0''$, $\frac{3}{4}'' = 1'-0''$ or $1\frac{1}{2}'' = 1'-0''$.

The scale used by the draftsman is determined by the size needed to be clear and easy to read. A complete set of working drawings such as is shown in *Fig. 4–6* consists of the following:

Presentation Drawing or Pictorial Rendering. These are perspective drawings of a house showing how it will look when completed, as lifelike as photographs.

Plans. A plan view is a top view. The several types include:

Site or Plot Plan. This plan shows the outline of the lot and the location of the building on it. On more complete site plans, the contours,

boundaries, existing roads, utilities and other physical details such as trees are shown.

Foundation or Basement Plan. This plan is the top view of the footings or foundation walls showing the exact size and location of foundations. It may also include the major utilities such as the location of the furnace, floor drains, and other items that appear in the basement.

Building or Floor Plan. This is a cross-section view of the house, showing the outside shape of the building, the arrangement, size, and shape of rooms, the types of materials, the thickness of walls and partitions, and the type, size, and location of doors and windows. Since the plan is drawn to a very small scale, symbols are used to indicate fixtures and materials. Other information, such as the

(CONT'D ON PAGE 68)

4–4a. A practical cabinet for storing hunting and fishing equipment. Plans for building it are on the next page.

49

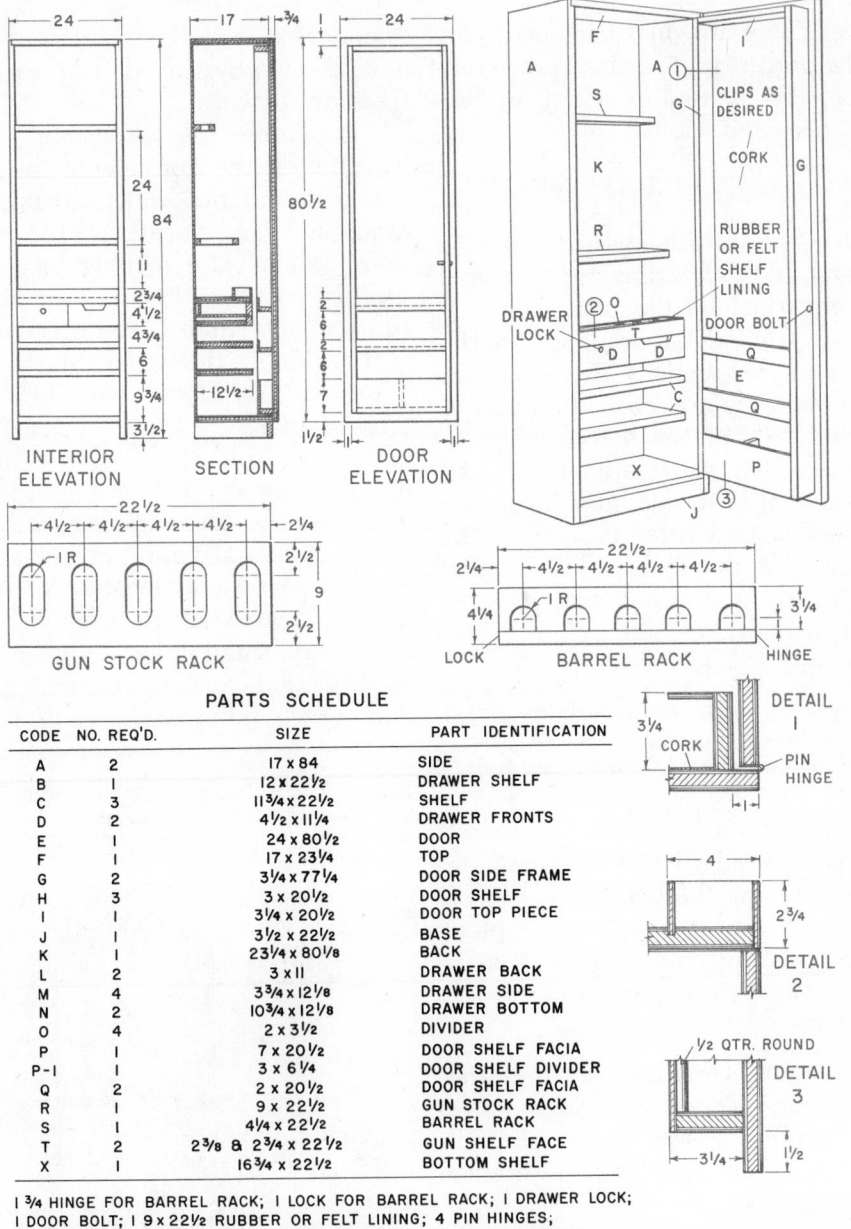

INTERIOR ELEVATION

SECTION

DOOR ELEVATION

CLIPS AS DESIRED

CORK

RUBBER OR FELT SHELF LINING

DRAWER LOCK

DOOR BOLT

GUN STOCK RACK

LOCK **BARREL RACK** HINGE

DETAIL 1

CORK

PIN HINGE

DETAIL 2

½ QTR. ROUND

DETAIL 3

PARTS SCHEDULE

CODE	NO. REQ'D.	SIZE	PART IDENTIFICATION
A	2	17 x 84	SIDE
B	1	12 x 22½	DRAWER SHELF
C	3	11¾ x 22½	SHELF
D	2	4½ x 11¼	DRAWER FRONTS
E	1	24 x 80½	DOOR
F	1	17 x 23¼	TOP
G	2	3¼ x 77¼	DOOR SIDE FRAME
H	3	3 x 20½	DOOR SHELF
I	1	3¼ x 20½	DOOR TOP PIECE
J	1	3½ x 22½	BASE
K	1	23¼ x 80⅛	BACK
L	2	3 x 11	DRAWER BACK
M	4	3¾ x 12⅛	DRAWER SIDE
N	2	10¾ x 12⅛	DRAWER BOTTOM
O	4	2 x 3½	DIVIDER
P	1	7 x 20½	DOOR SHELF FACIA
P-1	1	3 x 6¼	DOOR SHELF DIVIDER
Q	2	2 x 20½	DOOR SHELF FACIA
R	1	9 x 22½	GUN STOCK RACK
S	1	4¼ x 22½	BARREL RACK
T	2	2⅜ & 2¾ x 22½	GUN SHELF FACE
X	1	16¾ x 22½	BOTTOM SHELF

1 ¾ HINGE FOR BARREL RACK; 1 LOCK FOR BARREL RACK; 1 DRAWER LOCK;
1 DOOR BOLT; 1 9 x 22½ RUBBER OR FELT LINING; 4 PIN HINGES;
¼ x 20½ x 56 CORK BACKING; 1½ LIN. FT. ½" QTR. RD. NAILING STRIP.

MISCELLANEOUS — 4D & 6D FINISHING NAILS & GLUE; CLIPS AS REQ'D.

4–4b. Drawings for the cabinet pictured on page 49. Note that several types of drawings are combined here.

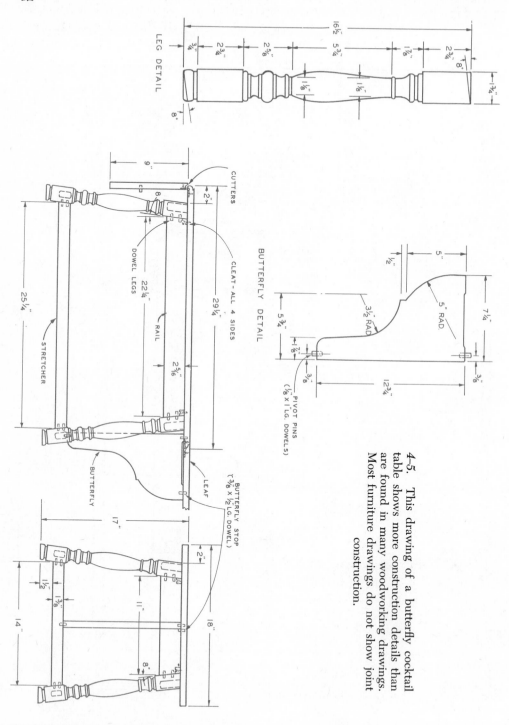

LEG DETAIL

BUTTERFLY DETAIL

CUTTERS

CLEAT - ALL 4 SIDES

DOWEL LEGS

RAIL

STRETCHER

BUTTERFLY

LEAF

BUTTERFLY STOP
(⅜ x ½ LG. DOWEL)

PIVOT PINS
(⅛ x 1 LG. DOWELS)

4–5. This drawing of a butterfly cocktail table shows more construction details than are found in many woodworking drawings. Most furniture drawings do not show joint construction.

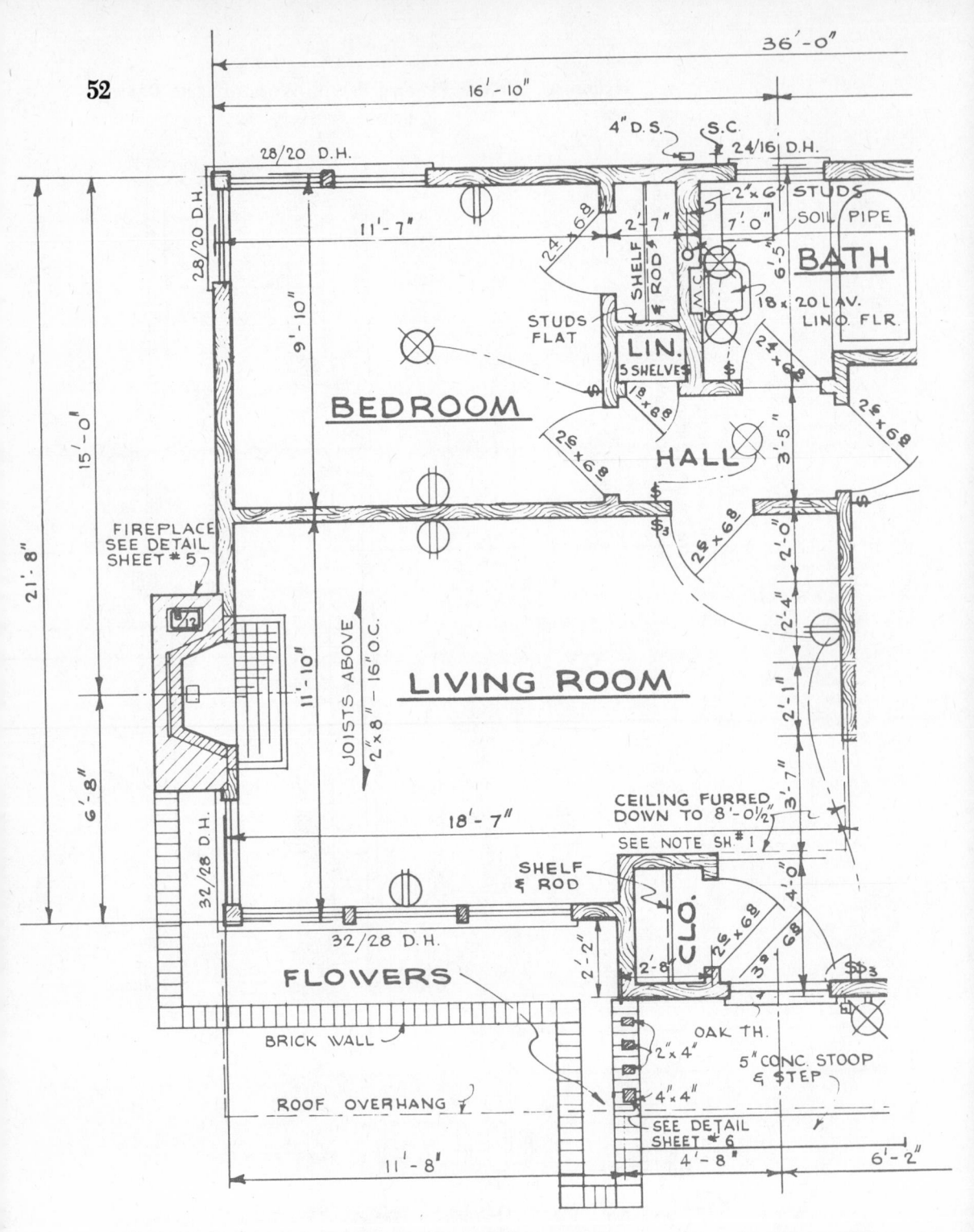

4-6a. On the following 16 pages is a complete set of working drawings for building a small, two-bedroom home. Note that the scales marked on the drawings no longer apply. Samples of the materials list and specifications for this same home are shown on pages 76–77.

FLOOR

SCALE:

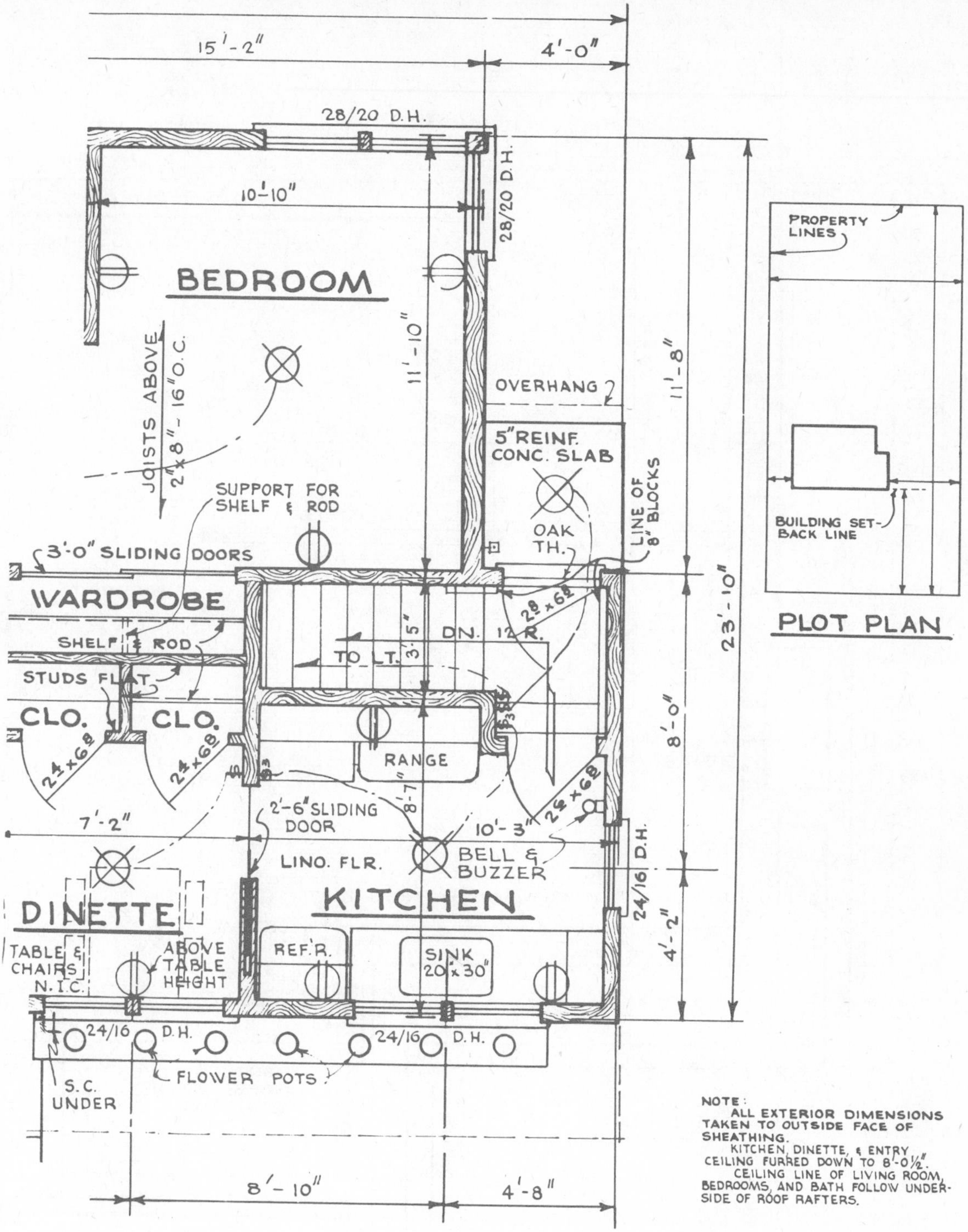

PLAN

¼" = 1'-0"

28/20 D.H.

15'-2"   4'-0"

10'-10"

BEDROOM

28/20 D.H.

11'-10"

JOISTS ABOVE 2"x 8"- 16" O.C.

OVERHANG

5" REINF. CONC. SLAB

11'-8"

SUPPORT FOR SHELF & ROD

OAK TH.

LINE OF 8" BLOCKS

3'-0" SLIDING DOORS

WARDROBE

23'-10"

SHELF & ROD

2"x 6"

STUDS FLAT

DN. 12 R.

3'-5"

TO LT.

CLO.   CLO.

RANGE

2"x 6"

2"x 6"

24x68   24x68

8'-0"

7'-2"

2'-6" SLIDING DOOR

10'-3"

BELL & BUZZER

24/16 D.H.

DINETTE

LINO. FLR.

KITCHEN

ABOVE TABLE HEIGHT

4'-2"

TABLE & CHAIRS N.I.C.

REF'R.

SINK 20"x 30"

24/16 D.H.   24/16 D.H.

S.C. UNDER

FLOWER POTS

8'-10"   4'-8"

PLOT PLAN

PROPERTY LINES

BUILDING SET-BACK LINE

NOTE :
ALL EXTERIOR DIMENSIONS TAKEN TO OUTSIDE FACE OF SHEATHING.
KITCHEN, DINETTE, & ENTRY CEILING FURRED DOWN TO 8'-0½".
CEILING LINE OF LIVING ROOM, BEDROOMS, AND BATH FOLLOW UNDERSIDE OF ROOF RAFTERS.

53

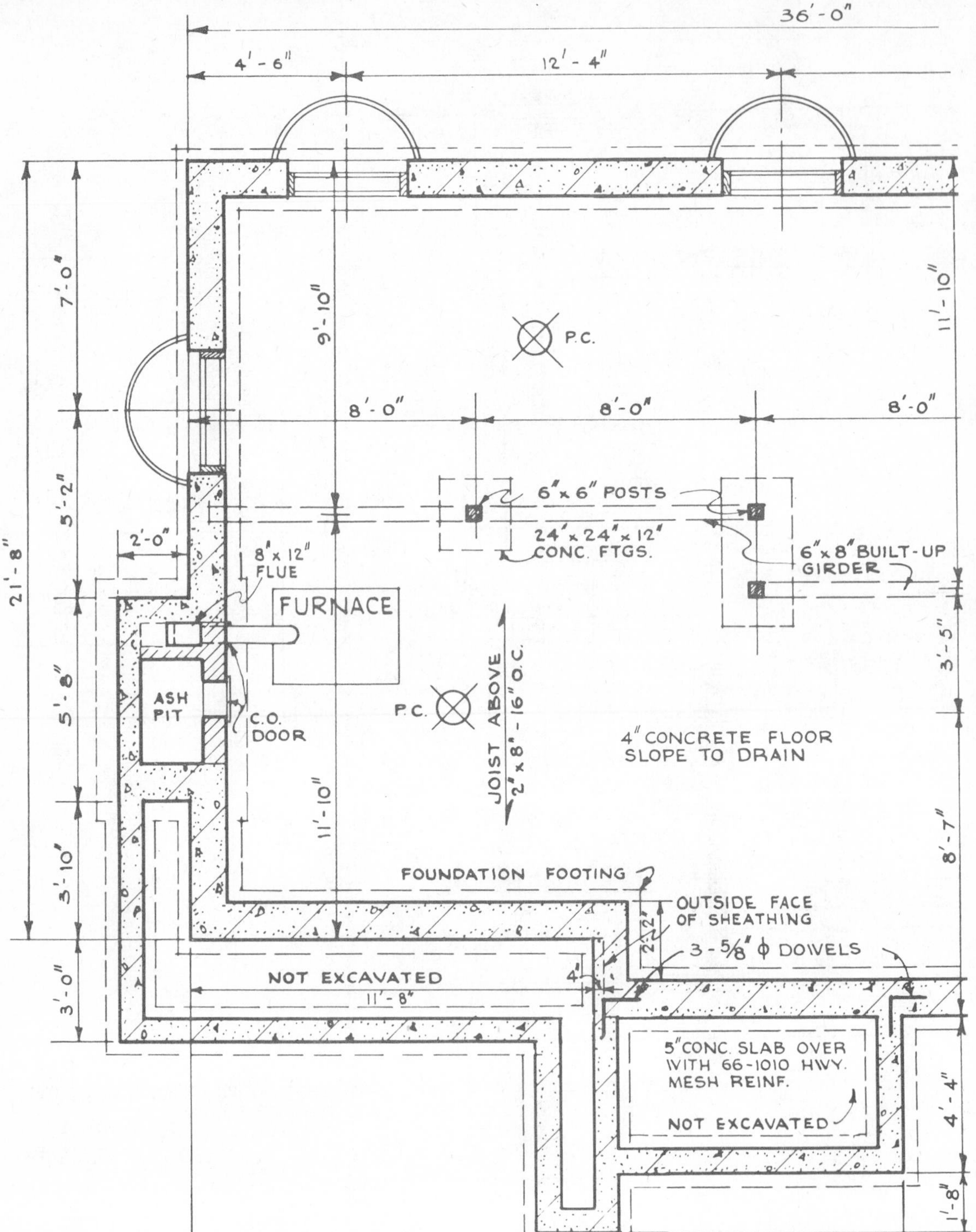
36'-0"
4'-6"
12'-4"
7'-0"
9'-10"
P.C.
11'-10"
8'-0"
8'-0"
8'-0"
5'-2"
6"x 6" POSTS
24"x 24"x 12"
CONC. FTGS.
6"x 8" BUILT-UP
GIRDER
2'-0"
8"x 12"
FLUE
21'-8"
FURNACE
3'-5"
5'-8"
ASH
PIT
C.O.
DOOR
P.C.
JOIST ABOVE
2"x 8" - 16" O.C.
4" CONCRETE FLOOR
SLOPE TO DRAIN
11'-10"
8'-7"
3'-10"
FOUNDATION FOOTING
OUTSIDE FACE
OF SHEATHING
2 1/2"
3 - 5/8" ϕ DOWELS
3'-0"
NOT EXCAVATED
4"
11'-8"
5" CONC. SLAB OVER
WITH 66-1010 HWY.
MESH REINF.
NOT EXCAVATED
4'-4"
1'-8"
10'-2"
2'-4"
7'-6"

BASEMENT

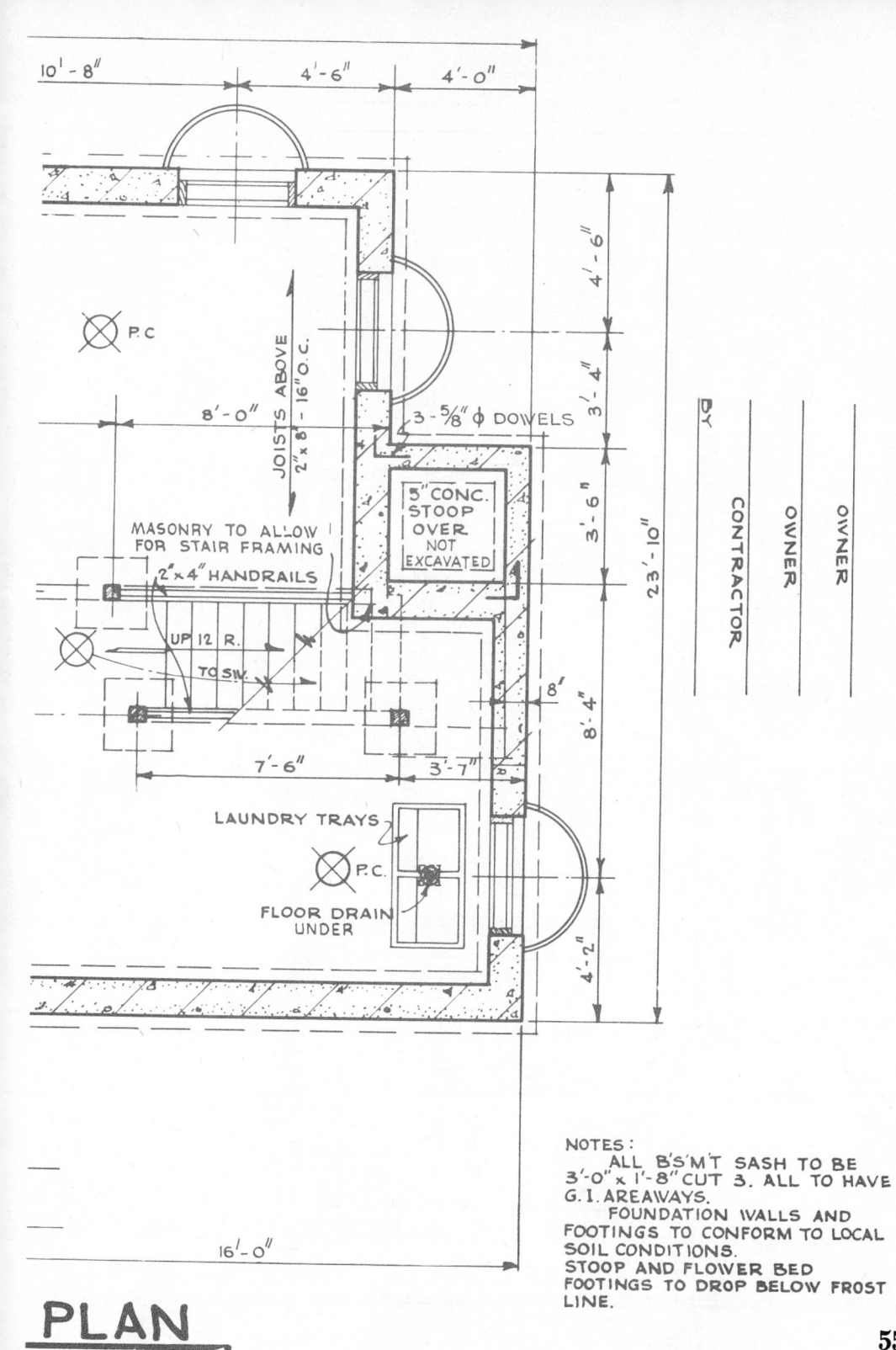

10' - 8"   4' - 6"   4' - 0"

4' - 6"

P.C

3' - 4"

3-5⁄8" ⌀ DOWELS

JOISTS ABOVE
2" x 8" - 16" O.C.

8' - 0"

3' - 6"

5" CONC.
STOOP
OVER
NOT
EXCAVATED

MASONRY TO ALLOW
FOR STAIR FRAMING
2"x 4" HANDRAILS

23' - 10"

UP 12 R.

TO SW.

8'

8' - 4"

7' - 6"   3' - 7"

LAUNDRY TRAYS

P.C.

4' - 2"

FLOOR DRAIN
UNDER

BY

CONTRACTOR

OWNER

OWNER

APPROVED

16' - 0"

NOTES :
    ALL B'S'M'T SASH TO BE
3'-0" x 1'-8" CUT 3. ALL TO HAVE
G.I. AREAWAYS.
    FOUNDATION WALLS AND
FOOTINGS TO CONFORM TO LOCAL
SOIL CONDITIONS.
STOOP AND FLOWER BED
FOOTINGS TO DROP BELOW FROST
LINE.

PLAN

ELEVATIONS

FRONT

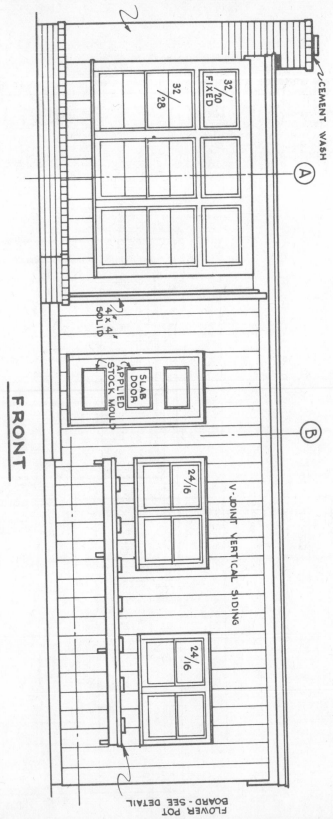

COMMON BRICK

CEMENT WASH

32/20 FIXED

32/28

A

4" x 4" SOLID

SLAB DOOR

APPLIED STOCK MOULD

B

24/16

V-JOINT VERTICAL SIDING

24/16

FLOWER POT BOARD - SEE DETAIL

LEFT SIDE

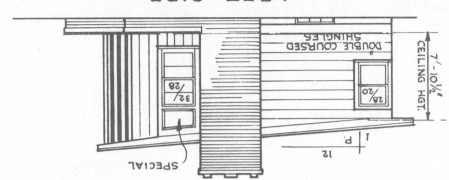

DOUBLE COURSED SHINGLES

32/28

28/20

CEILING HGT.

7'-10½"

SPECIAL

12

P

1

REAR

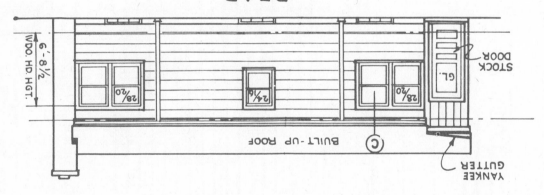

6'-8½"
WDO. HD. HGT.

28/20

24/16

28/20

GL.

STOCK DOOR

BUILT-UP ROOF

C

YANKEE GUTTER

RIGHT SIDE

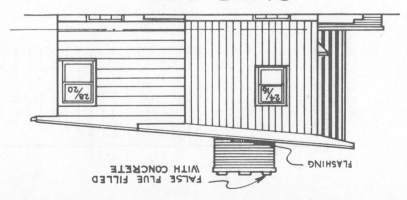

28/20

24/16

FLASHING

FALSE FLUE FILLED
WITH CONCRETE

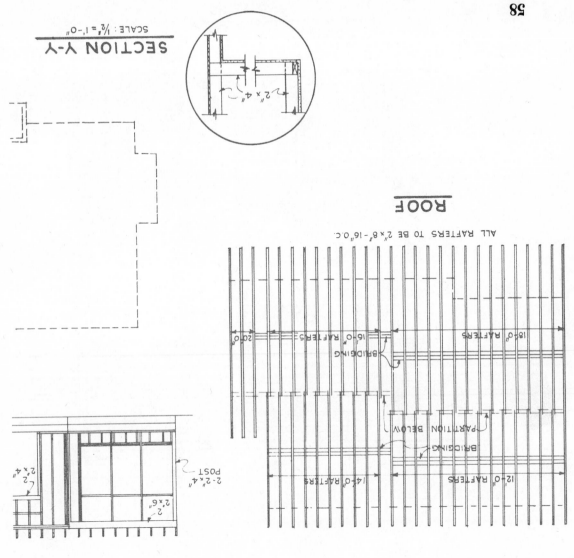

SECTION Y-Y
SCALE: 1/2" = 1'-0"

ROOF

ALL RAFTERS TO BE 2"×8"-16" O.C.

20'-0' · 16'-0' RAFTERS · 18'-0' RAFTERS

BRIDGING

PARTITION BELOW

BRIDGING

14'-0' RAFTERS · 12'-0' RAFTERS

2 2"×4"
2-2"×4" POST
2 2"×6"

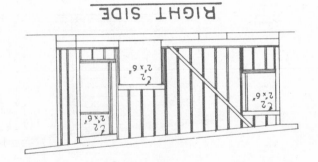

RIGHT SIDE

2 2"×6"
2 2"×6"
2 2"×6"

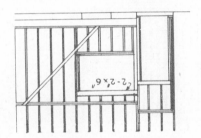

2-2"×6"

FRAMING

SCALE: 1/8" = 1'-0"

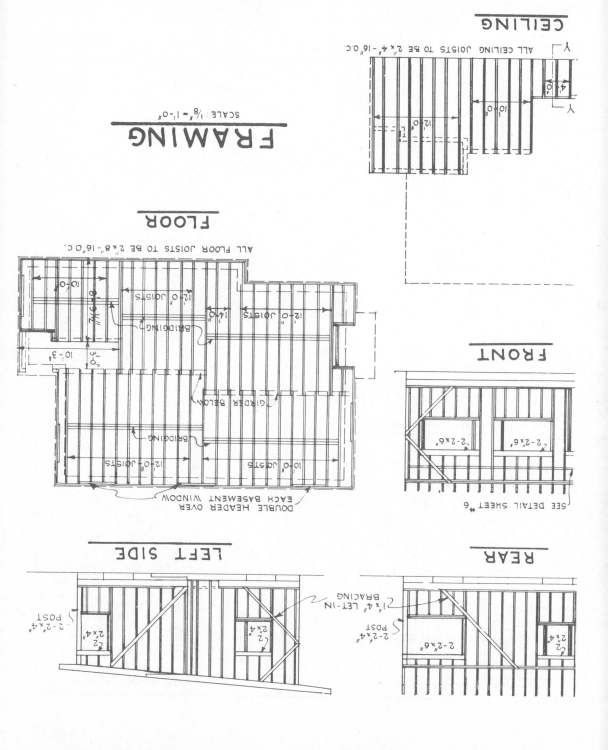

CEILING

ALL CEILING JOISTS TO BE 2"x 4"-16"O.C.

FLOOR

ALL FLOOR JOISTS TO BE 2"x 8"-16"O.C.

12'-0" JOISTS
BRIDGING
12'-0" JOISTS
14'-0"
10'-0"
7'-0" JOIST
10'-3"
3'-0"
GIRDER BELOW
BRIDGING
10'-0" JOISTS
12'-0" JOISTS
DOUBLE HEADER OVER
EACH BASEMENT WINDOW

FRONT

2-2"x 6"
2-2"x 6"
SEE DETAIL SHEET #6

REAR

2-2"x 4"
POST
2-2"x 6"
1"x 4" LET-IN
BRACING
2 2"x 4"

LEFT SIDE

2-2"x 4"
POST
2 2"x 4"

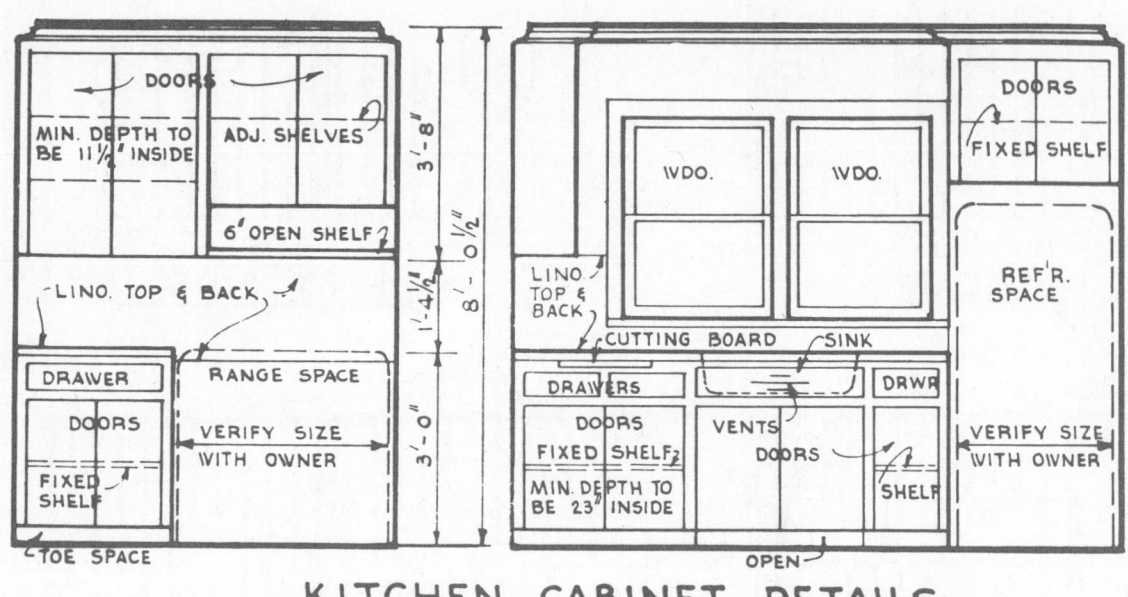

KITCHEN CABINET DETAILS
SCALE: 3/8" = 1'-0"

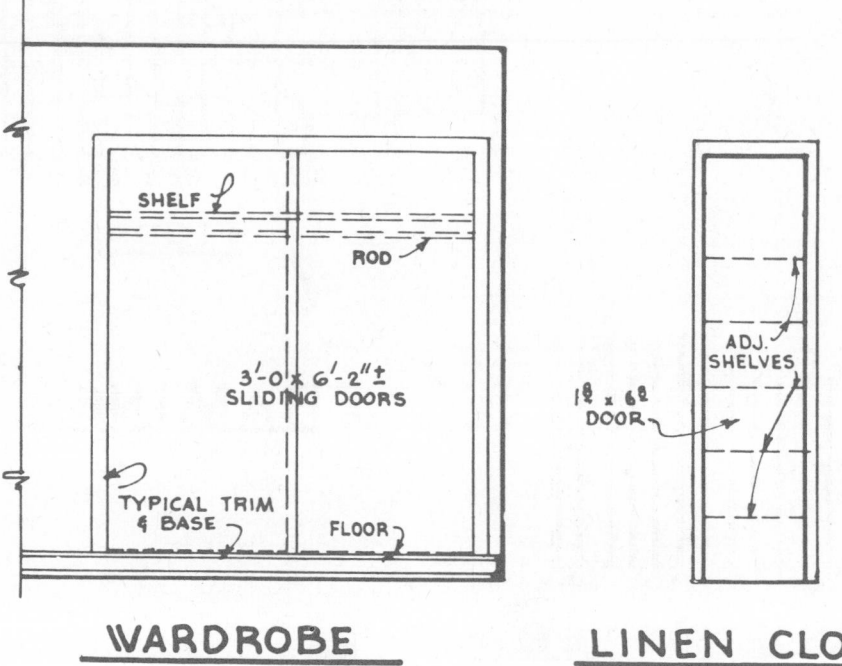

WARDROBE
SCALE: 3/8" = 1'-0"

LINEN CLOSET
SCALE: 3/8" = 1'-0"

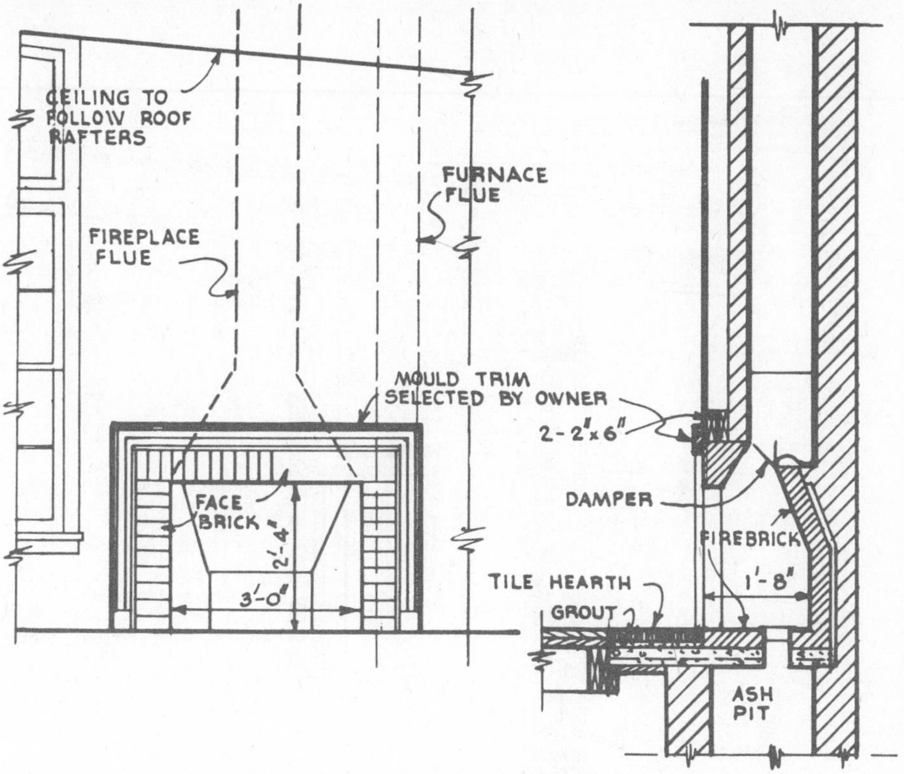

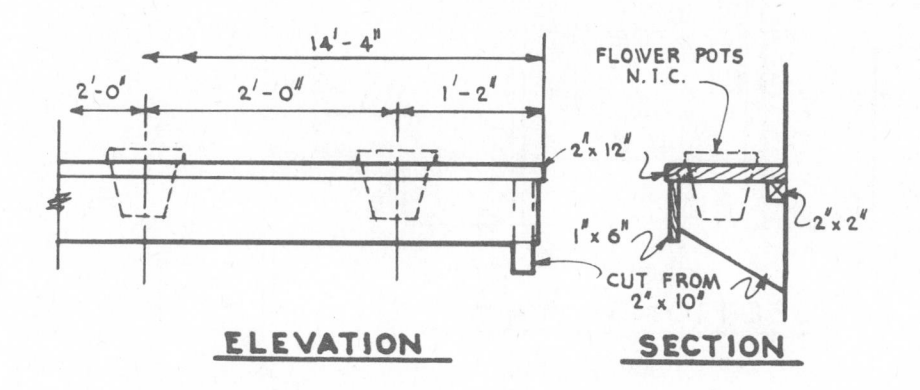

FIREPLACE DETAILS

SCALE: $3/8'' = 1'-0''$

CEILING TO FOLLOW ROOF RAFTERS

FURNACE FLUE

FIREPLACE FLUE

MOULD TRIM SELECTED BY OWNER

$2 - 2'' \times 6''$

FACE BRICK

$2'-4''$

$3'-0''$

DAMPER

FIREBRICK

TILE HEARTH

$1'-8''$

GROUT

ASH PIT

FLOWER BOX DETAIL

SCALE: $3/4'' = 1'-0''$

$14'-4''$

$2'-0''$ $2'-0''$ $1'-2''$

FLOWER POTS N.I.C.

$2'' \times 12''$

$1'' \times 6''$

$2'' \times 2''$

CUT FROM $2'' \times 10''$

ELEVATION

SECTION

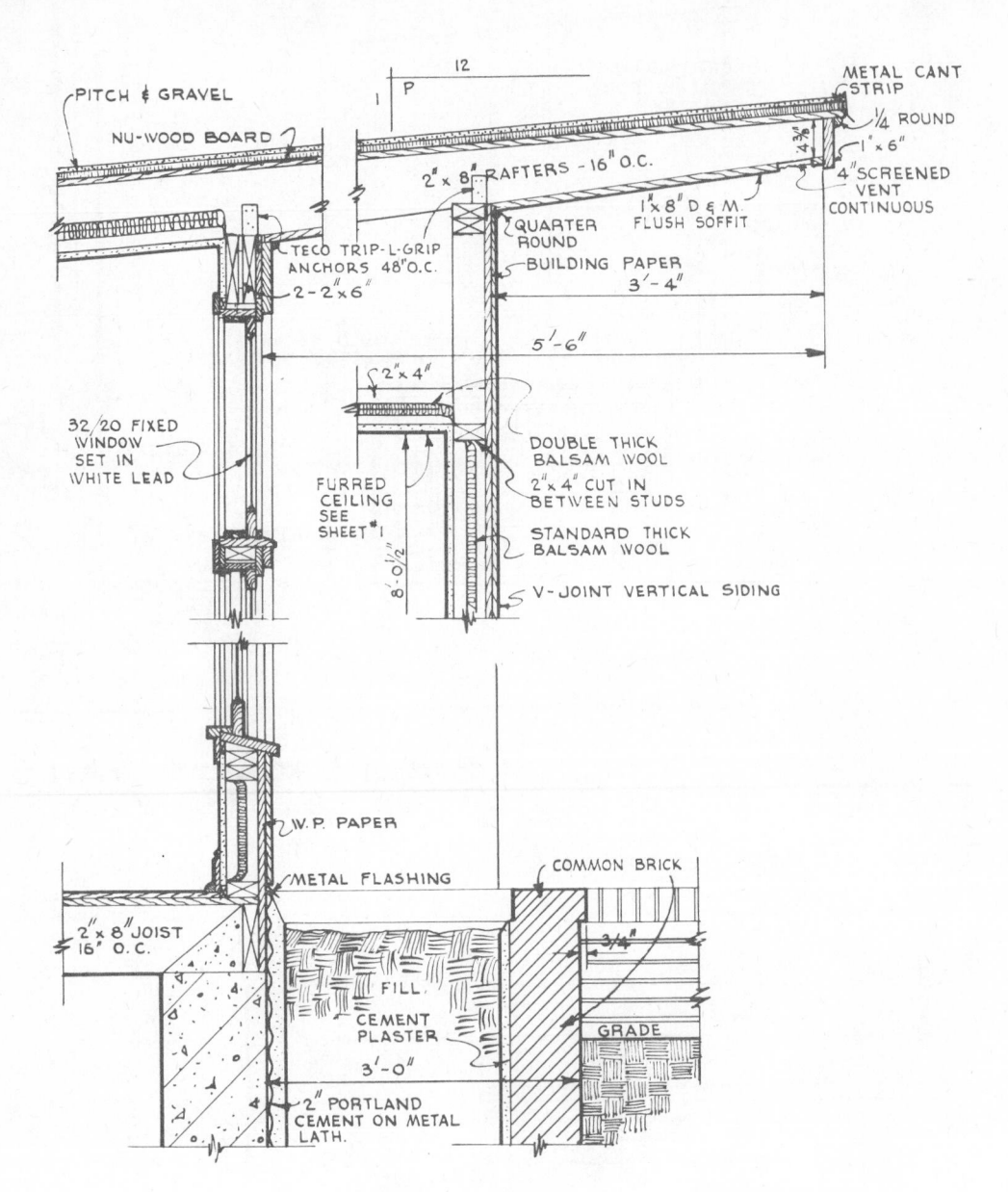

PITCH & GRAVEL

NU-WOOD BOARD

12
1 P

METAL CANT STRIP
¼ ROUND
1" x 6"
4" SCREENED VENT CONTINUOUS

2" x 8" RAFTERS - 16" O.C.

1" x 8" D & M FLUSH SOFFIT

QUARTER ROUND

TECO TRIP-L-GRIP ANCHORS 48" O.C.

2 - 2" x 6"

BUILDING PAPER
3'-4"

5'-6"

32/20 FIXED WINDOW SET IN WHITE LEAD

2" x 4"

DOUBLE THICK BALSAM WOOL

2" x 4" CUT IN BETWEEN STUDS

STANDARD THICK BALSAM WOOL

V-JOINT VERTICAL SIDING

FURRED CEILING SEE SHEET #1

8'-0½"

W.P. PAPER

METAL FLASHING

COMMON BRICK

2" x 8" JOIST 16" O.C.

¾"

FILL

GRADE

CEMENT PLASTER

3'-0"

2" PORTLAND CEMENT ON METAL LATH.

SECTIONS A & B

DETAILS

SCALE: ¾" = 1'-0"

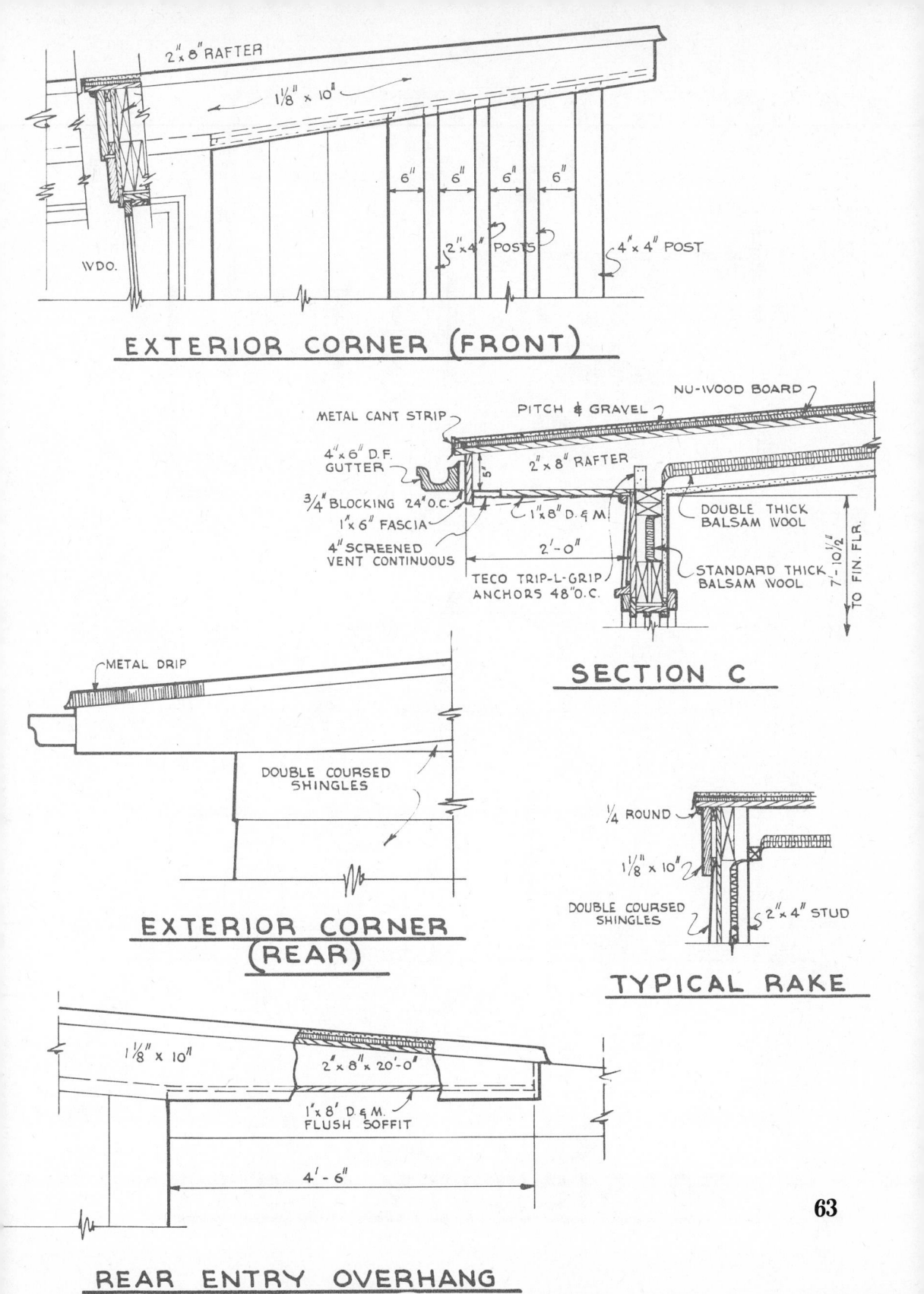

EXTERIOR CORNER (FRONT)

2" x 8" RAFTER

1⅛" x 10"

6" 6" 6" 6"

2" x 4" POSTS

4" x 4" POST

WDO.

SECTION C

METAL CANT STRIP

PITCH & GRAVEL

NU-WOOD BOARD

4" x 6" D.F. GUTTER

2" x 8" RAFTER

¾" BLOCKING 24" O.C.

1" x 6" FASCIA

1" x 8" D. & M.

DOUBLE THICK BALSAM WOOL

4" SCREENED VENT CONTINUOUS

2'- 0"

STANDARD THICK BALSAM WOOL

TECO TRIP-L-GRIP ANCHORS 48" O.C.

7'-10½" TO FIN. FLR.

5

EXTERIOR CORNER (REAR)

METAL DRIP

DOUBLE COURSED SHINGLES

TYPICAL RAKE

¼ ROUND

1⅛" x 10"

DOUBLE COURSED SHINGLES

2" x 4" STUD

REAR ENTRY OVERHANG

1⅛" x 10"

2" x 8" x 20'-0"

1" x 8' D. & M. FLUSH SOFFIT

4'- 6"

63

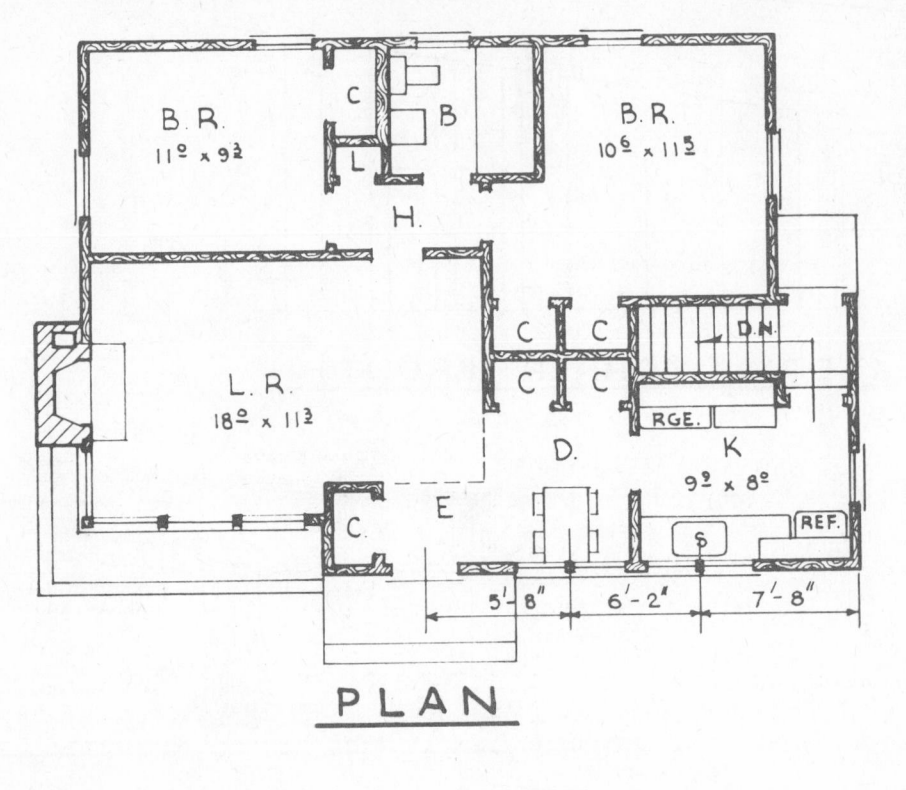

PLAN

FRONT

SCALE: $\frac{1}{8}" = 1'-0"$

POSSIBILITY NO. 1

64

POSSIBILITY NO. 2

PLAN WITH NO FIREPLACE

THIS PLAN MAY BE USED WITH EITHER EXTERIOR

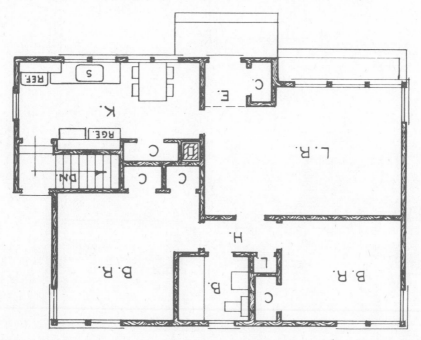

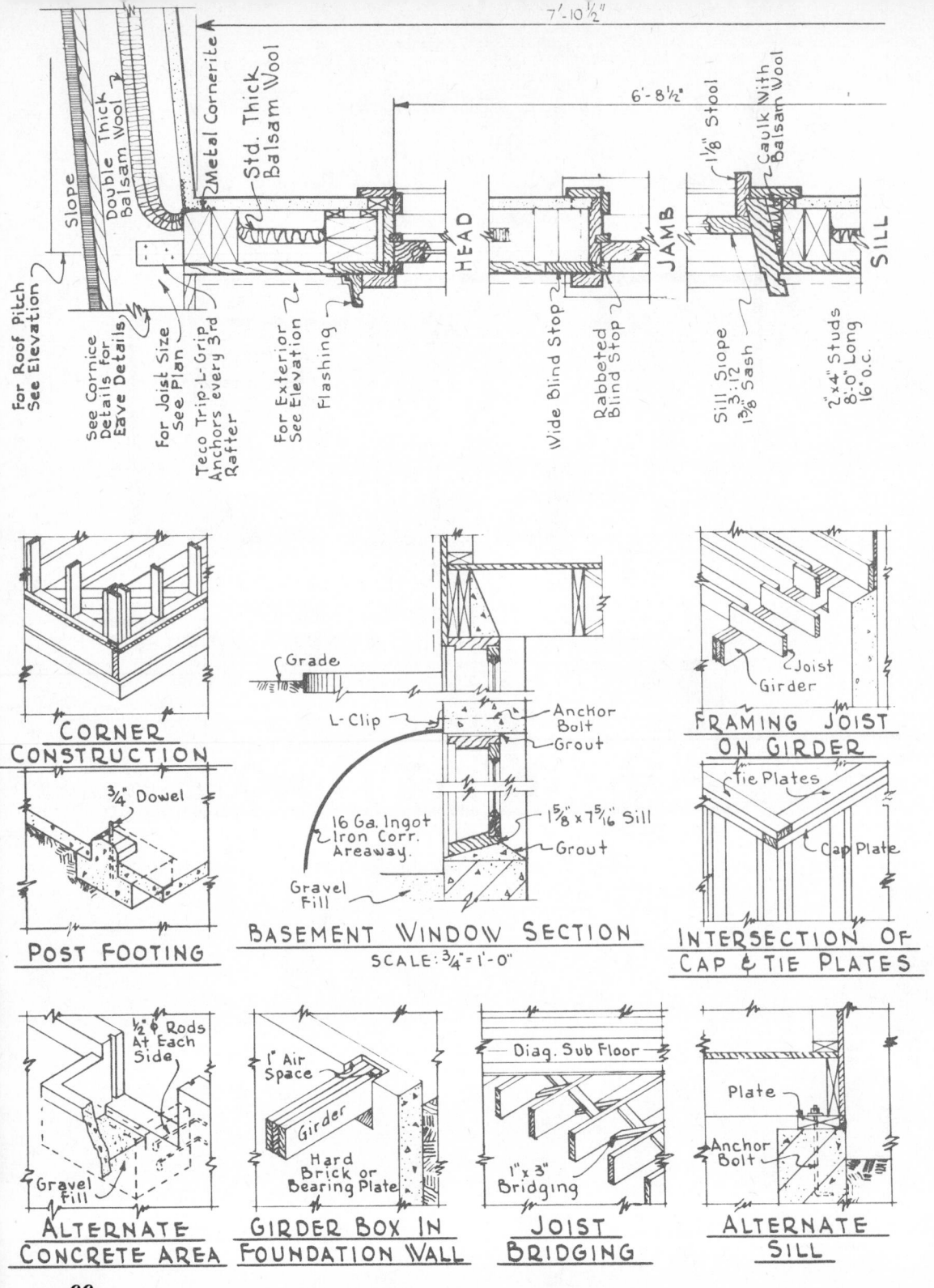

7'-10½"

6'-8½"

For Roof Pitch See Elevation

Slope

Double Thick Balsam Wool

Metal Cornerite

Std. Thick Balsam Wool

HEAD

JAMB

SILL

1⅛" Stool

Caulk With Balsam Wool

See Cornice Details for Eave Details

For Joist Size See Plan

Teco Trip-L-Grip Anchors every 3rd Rafter

For Exterior See Elevation

Flashing

Wide Blind Stop

Rabbeted Blind Stop

Sill Slope 1⅜:12

1⅜ Sash

2"x4" Studs 8'-0" Long 16" o.c.

CORNER CONSTRUCTION

POST FOOTING

¾" Dowel

Grade

L-Clip

Anchor Bolt

Grout

16 Ga. Ingot Iron Corr. Areaway.

Gravel Fill

1⅝" x 7⁵⁄₁₆" Sill

Grout

BASEMENT WINDOW SECTION
SCALE: ¾"=1'-0"

FRAMING JOIST ON GIRDER

Joist

Girder

Tie Plates

Cap Plate

INTERSECTION OF CAP & TIE PLATES

ALTERNATE CONCRETE AREA

½"Ø Rods At Each Side

Gravel Fill

GIRDER BOX IN FOUNDATION WALL

1" Air Space

Girder

Hard Brick or Bearing Plate

JOIST BRIDGING

Diag. Sub Floor

1"x 3" Bridging

ALTERNATE SILL

Plate

Anchor Bolt

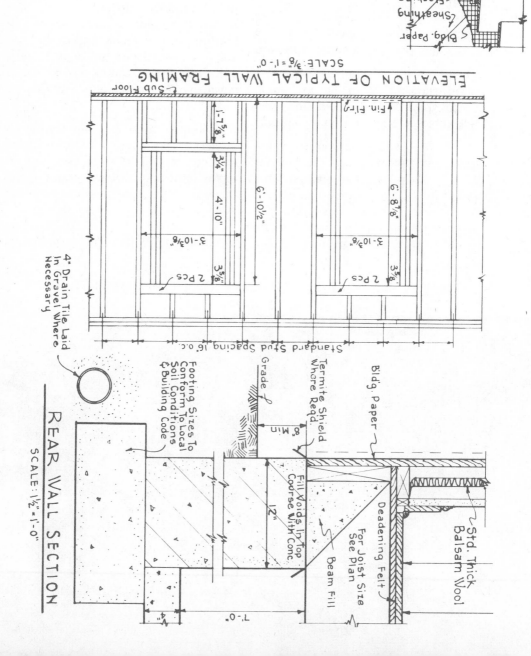

DRIP CAP FLASHING

Drip Cap

Sheathing Flashing

Bldg. Paper

ELEVATION OF TYPICAL WALL FRAMING
SCALE 3/8" = 1'-0"

⅊ Sub Floor

Fin. Flr.

1'-7⅝"

3¼"

4'-10"

6'-10½"

6'-8⅞"

3'-10⅜"

3'-10⅜"

3⅝"

3⅝"

2 Pcs

2 Pcs

Standard Stud Spacing 16" o.c.

4" Drain Tile Laid
In Gravel Where
Necessary

Footing Sizes To
Conform To Local
Soil Conditions
& Building Code

Grade

Termite Shield
Where Reqd.

8" Min.

Bldg. Paper

Fill Voids In Top
Course With Conc.

12"

Deadening Felt

For Joist Size
See Plan

Beam Fill

Std. Thick
Balsam Wool

4"

1'-0"

REAR WALL SECTION
SCALE: 1½" = 1'-0"

4–6b.   This is the finished house shown in the drawings on pages 52 through 67.

electrical wiring and plumbing, may be included.

Framing Plans. These plans show the size, number, location, and spacing of structural members that make up the framework of the house. Separate framing plans are usually shown for the floor, roof, ceiling, and walls.

Elevations. Elevations are external views of the house made from the front, rear, right, and left sides. They are picture-like views of the building that show exterior materials, height and width of doors, windows, and other items.

Sectional Views. Sectional views or sections show very important information on height. They show how a house would look if it could be cut vertically. Sectional views are like elevations in that they show vertical views. They are usually drawn to a larger scale than the elevations. *Typical sections* are used to show a cross section of a wall or portion of a wall, while *detail sections* show a cross section of a structural part of the house, other than a wall.

Details. Details are larger scale drawings that show specific parts of the home, for instance, the construction of kitchen cabinets or roof frame.

Symbols. Because of the small scale of drawings, symbols are used to give important information not given by the dimensions. Symbols indicate materials such as concrete, brick, or wood. *Figs. 4–7 and 4–8.* Other symbols are used for millwork such as doors, windows, and stairs. There are still other symbols for electrical circuits, plumbing, and heating. *Figs. 4–9 and 4–10.*

68

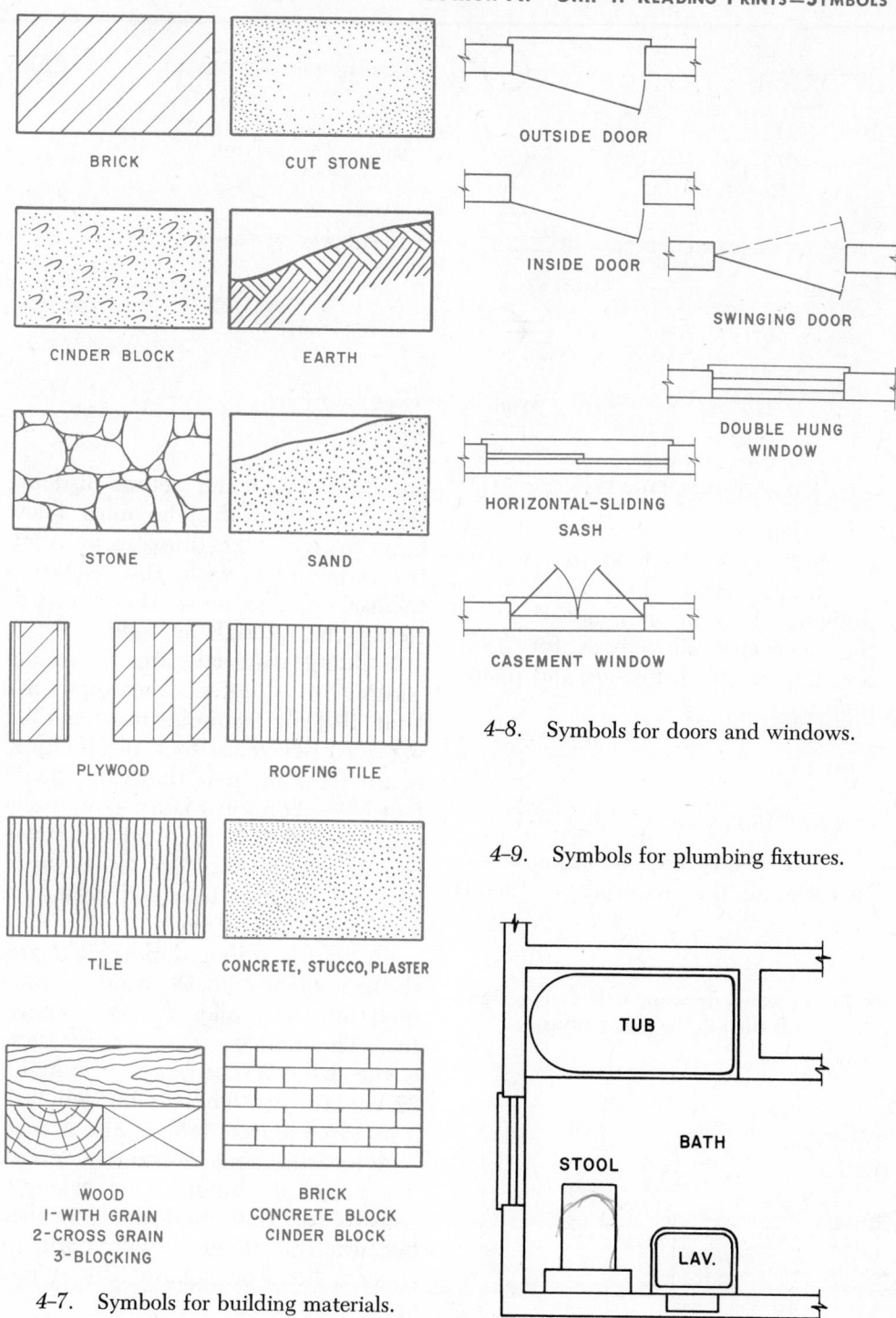

BRICK

CUT STONE

OUTSIDE DOOR

CINDER BLOCK

EARTH

INSIDE DOOR

SWINGING DOOR

STONE

SAND

DOUBLE HUNG WINDOW

HORIZONTAL-SLIDING SASH

PLYWOOD

ROOFING TILE

CASEMENT WINDOW

4–8.   Symbols for doors and windows.

TILE

CONCRETE, STUCCO, PLASTER

4–9.   Symbols for plumbing fixtures.

WOOD
1—WITH GRAIN
2—CROSS GRAIN
3—BLOCKING

BRICK
CONCRETE BLOCK
CINDER BLOCK

TUB

BATH

STOOL

LAV.

4–7.   Symbols for building materials.

69

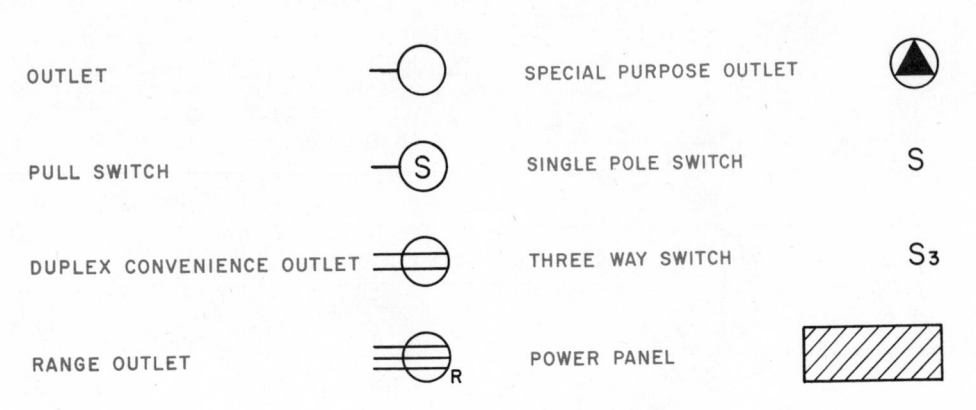

OUTLET		SPECIAL PURPOSE OUTLET
PULL SWITCH		SINGLE POLE SWITCH S
DUPLEX CONVENIENCE OUTLET		THREE WAY SWITCH S₃
RANGE OUTLET		POWER PANEL

4–10. Symbols for electrical wiring.

PATTERN DRAWINGS

Working drawings for patternmaking are made to standards used in the metal trades. *Fig. 4–11.* These drawings may or may not show all the necessary allowances for draft, machine finish, shrinkage, and distortion.

Boat drawings are discussed in Unit 43.

ESTIMATING AND PLANNING

Every woodworker must know how to estimate the materials he needs, and how to plan the method of doing the job. To do this, he must know how to read the drawing or print, be acquainted with the materials themselves, and know the standards by which materials are sold.

Building materials are priced according to different measures. See Unit 10. For example, most lumber is priced per board foot, per hundred board feet, or per thousand board feet (M). You must know how to figure *board feet* in order to determine how much to purchase. Other wood materials such as trim and siding are sold by the *linear foot*.

Plywood, hardboard, particle board, sheathing, wallboard, and similar materials are sold by the *square foot*. The most common size for these is the 4′ by 8′ sheet which contains 32 square feet. The *square*, which is a hundred square feet, is also a common measurement for some materials. A square of shingles, for example, consists of four bundles, so called because this amount will normally cover a hundred square feet of roof area.

4–11. Pattern drawing follows the standards used in the metal industry.

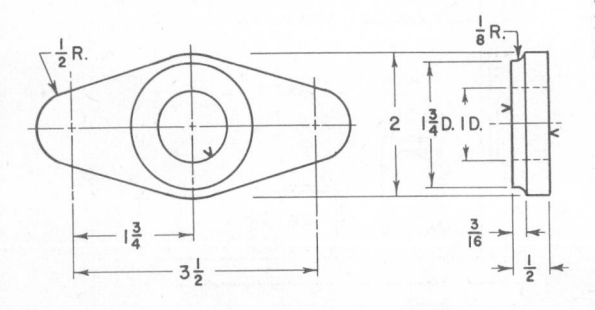

Bill of Materials or Materials List.
This is a tabulated list of the materials required for a particular job. *Fig. 4–13.* It shows in detail the quantity, size, grade or species, price, and purpose of the items needed. A bill of materials for a piece of furniture might be slightly different from one for a house but would include all the information necessary to the ordering of materials.

Estimating in Wood Construction.
The number and kinds of materials needed can be learned from the print. In furniture construction you must check the print for the size of each part and then list this on the bill of materials. These are the finished sizes; therefore an extra amount as waste allowance must be added for thickness, width, and length to find the *cut-out* size. To the finished sizes, add about $\frac{1}{16}''$ to $\frac{1}{8}''$ for thickness, $\frac{1}{8}''$ to $\frac{1}{4}''$ for width, and $\frac{1}{2}''$ for length.

In house construction, the method of estimating is slightly different. This usually involves calculating how many pieces of each length are to go into the house framing.

• Joists, for example, are usually spaced 16″ on center (O.C.). In this case it is relatively simple to find the number needed. Multiply the total distance around the house, in feet, by $\frac{3}{4}$; add one (1) to the results, and one (1) for every double joist and you will find the approximate number needed.

• To figure the large sheets required, such as sheathing, find the number of square feet in the area to be covered and then divide by the number of square feet in each piece. Remember that most large materials come in the standard size 4′ x 8′, or 32 square feet.

• To find the length of narrower wood materials needed to cover a certain area, keep in mind that it takes 1.5 feet of 8-inch material or 1.2 feet of 10-inch material to cover one square foot. To determine the footage required to cover a given area, multiply the footage needed for a square foot by the number of square feet in the area.

• To estimate the quantity of shingles to buy, first determine the ground area of your house, including eaves and cornice overhang in square feet. Add to this amount: for $\frac{1}{4}$ pitch 12 per cent, for $\frac{1}{3}$ pitch 20 per cent, and for $\frac{1}{2}$ pitch, 42 per cent. Divide the above total by 100. The answer is the number of shingle "squares" you should order to cover your roof. Add one square for every 100 lineal feet of hips and valleys.

4–12a.   A planter end table.

71

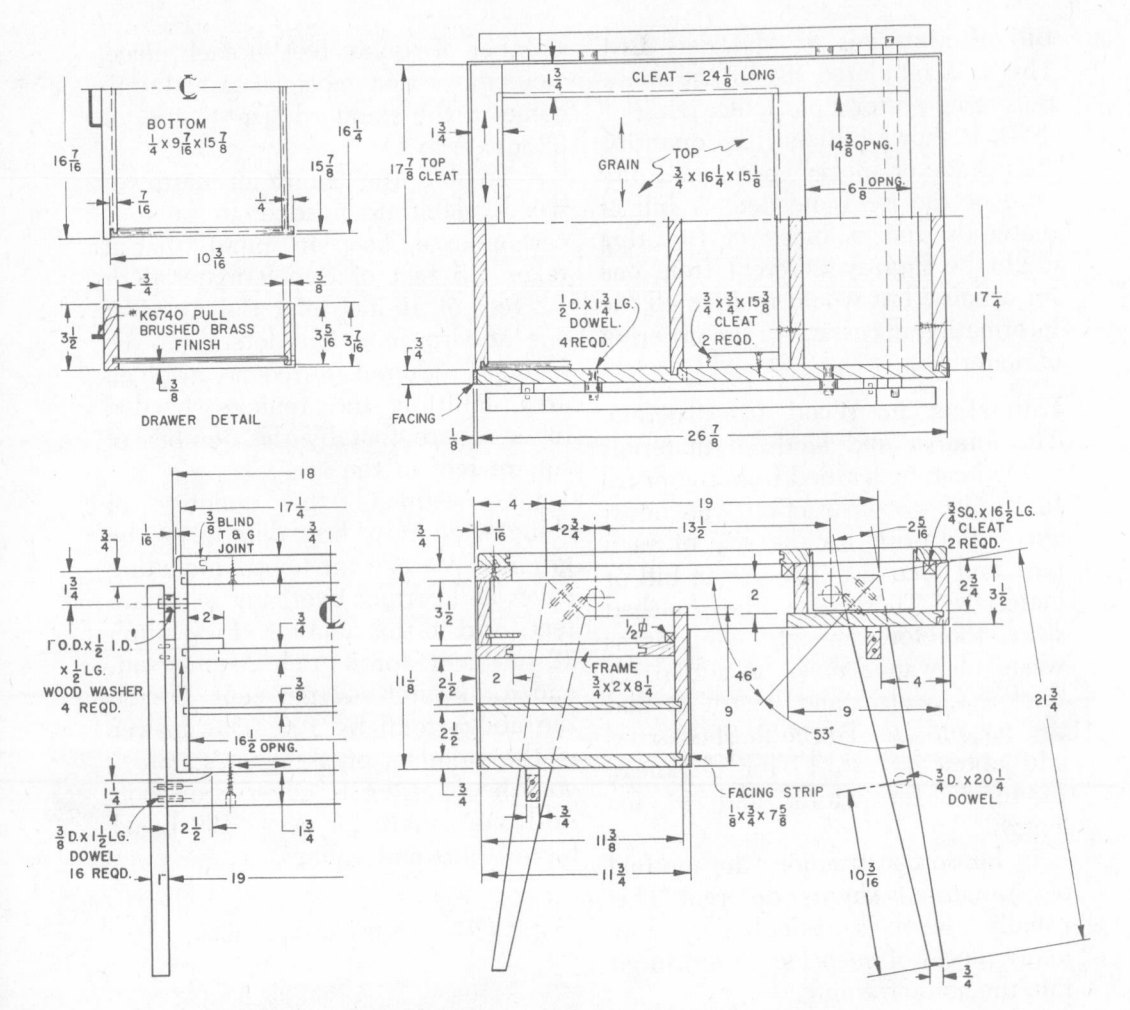

4-12b. Working drawing of the planter end table.

• For rafters on 16″ center, do the following: to ¾ of the length of the building, add 1; for example, for a building 16′ x 32′, take ¾ of 32 which equals 24, then add 1, making 25. This is the number of rafters required for *one side* of the building.

Planning Your Work. Before beginning the construction of any product, such as a furniture piece, wood pattern, boat, or built-in, you should have the following:

• A drawing or print of the product.

• A bill of materials or a materials list.

• A plan of procedure. This is a list of steps for making each part, assembling the product, and finishing

4–12c. BILL OF MATERIALS FOR THE PLANTER END TABLE

Important: All dimensions listed below are FINISHED size.

No. of Pieces	Part Name	Thickness	Width	Length	Material
4	Legs	1″	2⁵⁄₁₆″	21¾″	White Oak
2	Side Rails	1″	2″	19″	White Oak
2	Stretchers	¾″	1¾″	19″	White Oak
1	Stretcher	¾″ dia.		20¼″	White Oak
2	Cabinet Sides	¾″	26⅞″	11⅛″	Comb Grain White Oak Plywood S1S
1	Center Panel	¾″	17¼″	9″	Comb Grain White Oak Plywood S1S
1	Back Panel	¾″	17¼″	3½″	Comb Grain White Oak Plywood S1S
1	Top	¾″	16¼″	15⅛″	Comb Grain White Oak Plywood S1S
1	Bottom Shelf	¾″	11⅜″	17¼″	Comb Grain White Oak Plywood S1S
1	Center Shelf	⅜″	11⅜″	17¼″	Comb Grain White Oak Plywood S1S
1	Drawer Front	¾″	3½″	16⁷⁄₁₆″	Comb Grain White Oak Plywood S1S
3	Top Rail and Drawer Frame Front and Back	¾″	2″	17¼″	White Oak
2	Drawer Frame Sides	¾″	2″	8¼″	White Oak
2	Top Cleats	¾″	1¾″	17⅞″	White Oak
1	Top Cleat	¾″	1¾″	15⅛″	White Oak
2	Top Cleats	¾″	1¾″	24⅛″	White Oak
1	Planter Support	¾″	9″	17¼″	Any Wood
1	Center Rail	¾″	2¾″	16½″	Any Wood
2	Cleats	¾″	¾″	16½″	Any Wood
2	Cleats	¾″	¾″	15⅜″	Any Wood
2	Facing Strips	⅛″	¾″	11⅛″	White Oak
2	Facing Strips	⅛″	¾″	7⅝″	White Oak
2	Facing Strips	⅛″	¾″	3½″	White Oak
1	Facing Strip	⅛″	¾″	16½″	White Oak
1	Facing Strip	⅛″	⅜″	16½″	White Oak
4	Dowels	½″ dia.		1¾″	Hardwood
16	Dowels	⅜″ dia.		1½″	Hardwood
4	Wood Washers	1″ dia.		½″	White Oak
2	Drawer Sides	⅜″	3⁷⁄₁₆″	10³⁄₁₆″	Solid Oak
1	Drawer Back	⅜″	3⁵⁄₁₆″	15⅞″	Solid Oak
1	Drawer Bottom	¼″	9⁷⁄₁₆″	15⅞″	Birch Plywood
2	Drawer Stops	½″ sq.		2″	Hardwood
1	No. K6740 Drawer Pull				
27	No. 8 x 1¼″ F. H. Wood Screws				
4	No. 8 x 1¾″ F. H. Wood Screws				
1	Planter Liner	26 ga.	13⅛″	21⅜″	Sheet Copper or Galv. Steel

it. *Fig. 4–12.* In furniture manufacture, the construction of each part is planned on a *route sheet*. This sheet includes a sketch of the piece, the number needed, a list of the operations to be performed, and other pertinent information. See Unit 41.

In building construction the contractor, architect, and client need the following:

• A complete set of prints or working drawings. This should include the plans, the elevations, the details, and the sections.

• A complete and detailed materials list or bill of materials. *Fig. 4–13 and 4–14.*

• Complete specifications. These are detailed, written instructions used as an agreement between the client and the builder. They cover all items such as general conditions of construction, excavation and grading, masonry, framing and carpentry, sheet metal, lath and plaster, electrical wire, plumbing, heating and air conditioning, painting and finishing, and any other items that are included in the building contract.

Section A

CHECK YOUR KNOWLEDGE

1. Name some of the values of wood as a building material.

2. Wood, coal, iron ore, and petroleum are important natural resources. Describe the advantages wood has over the others.

3. Tell of the importance of the forests to the early development of this country.

4. Before the new model of a car is built, a wood model of it is made to full size. Give the reasons why wood is commonly used in making the model or mock-up of an object.

5. Name five musical instruments that are made primarily of wood.

6. Name the wood that might be the best for making baseball bats.

7. The paper of this book is made from wood. Name five other things you use every day that are made of wood, but that you no longer recognize as wood.

4-12d. PLAN OF PROCEDURE FOR THE PLANTER END TABLE

1. Lay out and cut cabinet sides on circular saw. Grain of wood should run up and down on side panels.

2. Cut to size all remaining pieces of cabinet on circular saw.

3. Set up dado head on circular saw and cut required grooves in all cabinet panels, top cleats, drawer frame members, front, back, and sides. Also, cut tongues on bottom shelf, drawer frame members, top cleats, top rail, planter support, and center, back, and top panels.

4. Locate and bore dowel holes in side panels. Drill screw holes in top rail and cleats.

5. Assemble cabinet, top, and drawer.

6. Cut all pieces for leg assembly on circular saw.

7. Taper legs with taper jig on circular saw.

8. Miter legs and top rails on circular saw.

9. Lay out and cut notch on ends of stretchers on band saw or jig saw.

10. Mount round stretcher on lathe and cut shoulder on each end, or insert ⅜″ dowel in ends of stretcher. Also, turn wood washers on lathe.

11. Locate and bore all dowel holes in rails, legs, and stretchers, except those in top rails for joining leg assemblies to cabinet. Drill and counter bore screw holes in stretchers.

12. Glue up legs and top rails.

13. Assemble legs and stretchers but *don't* glue. Set cabinet into place and then locate dowel holes in top rails and the screw holes in bottom of cabinet. Disassemble and drill dowel and screw holes.

14. Glue leg assemblies and stretchers.

15. Insert dowels through sides of cabinet and put wood washers in place. Set cabinet in position and drive dowels into place from inside of cabinet. Install screws through stretchers.

16. Mount top on cabinet.

17. Apply modern grey oak finish.

18. Lay out, cut, bend, and solder planter.

8. List three good reasons for taking a course in woodwork.

9. Describe a vocationally competent worker in woodworking.

10. Name three professional occupations in which a knowledge of woodwork is important. Identify the following: the largest skilled trade in woodworking; the area of woodworking most closely related to the metalworking field; the number of people in the United States who work in the retail lumber business.

11. Describe the correct way to dress in the shop.

12. List woodworking operations that require eye protection.

13. Tell what is the greatest danger in using hand tools.

14. A portable electric drill can be dangerous. Name the safety rules that should be followed when you use one.

15. List the special safety precautions you should practice when using a machine.

16. Describe the correct way of lifting heavy lumber.

17. Describe the proper storage of oily rags and the reason for this.

18. Name some of the kinds of design in woodwork.

19. Give the three keys to good design.

20. Name some elements of design, including the two kinds of balance. Give an example of each.

21. Name the three most popular styles of American furniture.

22. Define structural design. Give an example of it.

23. Clip out examples of good design from a magazine and tell in which ways they are pleasing.

24. Discuss the selection of a project design for the beginner.

25. Name the kinds of drawings a carpenter must be able to read.

26. Name three ways in which woodworking drawings differ from metalworking drawings.

27. Name the four kinds of drawings used in cabinetmaking and furniture construction.

28. Name the kinds of drawings in a set of working drawings for a home.

29. Define scale.

30. Give the purpose of a sectional view of a house.

31. Tell why pattern drawings follow the standards of the metalworking industry.

32. Name the major problems in making a drawing for a boat.

33. Describe a bill of materials or materials list.

34. Identify the measure that is used in selling plywood.

35. Tell how to figure the number of joists needed for a home.

36. Name the three items needed by the contractor, architect, and client before a new home is started.

THINGS TO DO

1. Report on the development of transportation vehicles, showing how changes were made in the kinds of materials used.

2. Find out if a new public building is being erected in your area, and if a scale model of this building has been built. See if you can bring the model to class, and discuss its value in construction.

3. Write a detailed report about one of the occupations in woodworking. Read all you can and, if possible, visit with someone who is now in that occupation.

4. As a class, draw up a set of safety standards for your woodshop.

5. Visit a furniture store and examine the design and construction of several pieces of furniture. Write a report on what you found.

6. Find a design for a piece of furniture that you would like to build; make a bill of materials and a plan of procedure.

7. Get a set of blueprints for a home and study them.

8. Write a report on one of the leading furniture designers in the United States.

9. Keep a scrapbook of design ideas in woodworking.

10. As a class, set up an organization along the lines of industry, with management, design, engineering, production, accounting, and sales departments. Carry out a mass-production job, with each department doing its part.

MATERIAL LIST

FOR

HOME No. 4144

ITEM	GRADE & SPECIES	LUMBER PCS.	SIZE	LENGTH	F.B.M.	PRICE	AMT.
FRAMING							
Posts	#1 D.F.	3	6x6	14'-0"	126		
	"	3	2x4	10'-0"	20		
	"	1	4x4	10'-0"	14		
Girders	"	6	2x8	16'-0"	128		
	"	3	2x8	8'-0"	32		
1st Floor Joists	"	4	2x8	14'-0"	75		
	"	30	2x8	12'-0"	480		
	"	22	2x8	10'-0"	294		
1st Floor Joist Headers	"	2	2x8	16'-0"	43		
	"	3	2x8	12'-0"	48		
	"	2	2x8	10'-0"	27		
	"	3	2x8	8'-0"	32		
Flower Pot Support	"	1	1x6	16'-0"	8		
	"	1	2x12	14'-0"	28		
	"	1	2x2	14'-0"	5		
	"	1	2x10	4'-0"	7		
Ceiling Joists	"	8	2x4	12'-0"	64		
	"	6	2x4	10'-0"	40		
	"	3	2x4	4'-0"	8		
Rafters	"	3	2x8	20'-0"	80		
	"	15	2x8	18'-0"	360		
	"	10	2x8	16'-0"	214		
	"	10	2x8	14'-0"	187		
	"	15	2x8	12'-0"	240		
Studs - Exterior	#2 D.F.	94	2x4	10'-0"	627		
	"	33	2x4	8'-0"	176		
Studs - Partition	"	5	2x6	10'-0"	50		
	"	134	2x4	10'-0"	893		
Plates	"	1	2x6	14'-0"	14		
	"	9	2x4	16'-0"	96		
	"	9	2x4	14'-0"	84		
	"	21	2x4	12'-0"	168		
	"	12	2x4	10'-0"	80		
	"	9	2x4	8'-0"	48		
Lintels (Wdo. & Door)	#1 D.F.	6	2x6	14'-0"	84		
	"	2	2x6	12'-0"	24		
	"	5	2x4	8'-0"	27		
Diagonal Braces	#3 P.P.	4	1x4	12'-0"	16		
	"	2	1x4	14'-0"	9		
Stair Horses	#1 D.F.	3	2x10	12'-0"	60		
Bsmt. Stair Treads	"	3	2x10	12'-0"	60		
Handrail	"	2	2x4	10'-0"	13		
Grounds	#3 P.P.	1220 L'	1x1	Random	102		
Bridging	"	380 L'	1x3	"	95		
SHEATHING							
Sub-Flooring	#2 D.F.Shiplap		1x8	Random	940		
Wall Sheathing	#3 P.P.Shiplap		1x8	"	1456		
Roof Sheathing	"		1x8	"	1267		

4–13.   Part of the materials list for the house shown in *Fig. 4–6.*

SPECIFICATIONS FOR HOME No. 4144

The house is to be built for_____Owner,

residing at (Number)_____(Street)_____

_____
(City or Town)   (County)   (State)

and is to be built upon the Owner's property located as described below:

_____

_____

LOCATION OF HOUSE ON LOT — The location of the house shall be as shown and dimensioned on the Plot Plan included in the Working Drawings.

GENERAL CONDITIONS OF THE SPECIFICATIONS

GENERAL DESCRIPTION OF THE WORK—The Contractor shall supply all labor, material, transportation, temporary heat, fuel, light, equipment, scaffolding, tools and services required for the complete and proper shaping of the work in strict conformity with the Drawings and Specifications. All work of all trades included in the Specifications shall be performed in a neat and workmanlike manner equal to the best in current shop and field practice.

BIDS—In receiving bids for the work specified herein, the Owner incurs no obligations to any bidder and reserves the right to reject any and all bids.

CONTRACT DOCUMENTS—The Contract Documents consist of the Drawings, Specifications, Plot Plan and the Agreement. The Contract Documents are complementary and what is called for by one shall be as binding as if called for by all. The intent and purpose of the Contract Documents is to include all labor, material, equipment, transportation and handling necessary for the complete and proper execution of the work.

PERMITS AND INSPECTIONS—The Contractor shall give all notices, secure and pay for all permits and inspections and shall comply with all laws, ordinances and regulations governing construction, fire prevention, health and sanitation bearing on the conduct of the work.

PROTECTION—The Contractor shall fully and continuously protect all parts of the work from damage, and shall protect the Owner against all loss or injury arising in connection with the execution of the Contract. He shall protect adjacent property as required by law, and shall provide and maintain all passageways, guard fences, lights and other facilities for protection as required by public authority or local conditions. The Contractor shall protect all trees, shrubs, walks and curbs from damage during building operations. The Owner shall provide adequate fire and tornado insurance during construction.

CONTRACTOR'S LIABILITY INSURANCE—The Contractor shall insure himself against claims under Workmen's Compensation Acts and from all other claims for damage for personal injury, including death, which may arise from operations under this Contract, whether such operations be by himself or by any Sub-Contractor or by anyone directly or indirectly employed by either of them. Certificate of such insurance shall be furnished and shall be subject to the Owner's approval for adequacy of protection.

CASH ALLOWANCES—All cash allowances specified shall be included in the Contract sum. If the Owner's selections total more or less than the allowances specified, the Contract sum shall be adjusted accordingly.

EXTRA WORK—Work shall not be started on any item not included in the Plans, Specifications and Contract until the Owner and Contractor agree in writing to the specific quantity and quality intended and to the cost of the extra work. Owner and Contractor shall operate in strict conformity with this requirement for their mutual protection.

CLEANING—The Contractor shall at all times keep the premises free from accumulations of waste materials and rubbish, and at the completion of the work all rooms and spaces shall be left broom clean.

WORK NOT INCLUDED—The following items of work are excluded from the Contract, however, may be included if noted under "Special Items Included."

Blasting	Furniture and Furnishings
Sub-soil Drain	Venetian Blinds
Waterproofing	Window Shades
Driveways and Walks	Refrigerator
Finished Grading, Planting	Cooking Range
and Landscaping	Bathroom Accessories
Fences	Weatherstripping

EXCAVATION AND GRADING

The General Conditions of the Specifications apply to this Section.

WORK INCLUDED—The work under this Section shall consist of furnishing all equipment and performing all necessary labor to do all excavating and rough grading work shown or specified. Excavate to dimensions one foot greater in size than the outside dimensions of the masonry and to the depth required or to solid formation suitable for the foundation. The top soil removed from the excavation shall be stored on the site. Sufficient excavated materials shall be retained to bring the grade up to the necessary level to receive the top soil. If additional earth is required for the rough grading, the Contractor shall furnish it as specified under Special Items Included. Excavation shall be kept free from standing water at all times.

BACK FILLING—The Contractor shall back fill against all walls to the grade line with clean earth well tamped and wetted.

MASONRY

The General Conditions of the Specifications apply to this Section.

WORK INCLUDED—The work under this Section shall consist of furnishing and installing all material and equipment and performing all necessary labor to do all masonry work shown or specified.

FOOTINGS—Footings shall be of concrete mixed in the proportion of 1 part Portland cement, 3 parts of clean, coarse, sharp sand free from loam or vegetable matter, and 5 parts of ¾" gravel. Concrete shall be machine mixed with clean water to the proper consistency and shall be placed immediately after mixing and thoroughly puddled into the forms. Contractor shall check bearing power of soil in all cases and construct footings of sufficient size to conform to local soil requirements and building code.

4-14. Specifications for the house shown in *Fig. 4-6*. This is the first of four pages. Other main topics covered are Miscellaneous Iron, Framing and Carpentry, Sheet Metal, Lath and Plaster, Painting and Finishing, Electric Wiring, Plumbing, and Heating.

Section B

WOOD MATERIAL TECHNOLOGY

Here is the raw material for homes, furniture, paper, plastics, and many other products you use every day. The more you know about it the better you will be able to work with it. Wood is unlike any other building material. Each log has a distinct character all its own.

Unit 5: KINDS OF WOODS

Can you identify common species of wood? Do you know what kinds are best for building a boat, a bookshelf, or the frame of a house? Knowledge of this kind is valuable because wood is one of the most common and useful of substances.

Often, any one of several species is suitable for a specific use. Other species, however, may be entirely unfit for that use. Of those suitable, some are better than others because they are stronger, perhaps, or more attractive, or hold paint better. Others may be superior because they are harder, shrink less, resist decay, or are more easily cut and joined. It follows, then, that correct identification is essential to insure selection of the right wood for a given job.

In the great majority of day-to-day transactions, wood identification is a relatively simple problem. By acquiring a little know-how, lumbermen, dealers, builders, manufacturers, consumers, students, and home-workshop hobbyists can solve their identification problems on the spot.

In this chapter, the uses of 34 species are described. Obviously, many others could have been included. Those chosen are the ones most commonly found in retail lumber yards.

For information on botanical differences among species, such as the shape of leaves, pattern of bark, and form of fruit, the reader is referred to the U. S. Dept. of Agriculture Yearbook for 1949. Anyone who has difficulty in identifying different species can get all the help he needs from the official wood identification agency of the United States Government, the Forest Products Laboratory at Madison, Wisconsin. Each year this laboratory identifies thousands of wood specimens for people in other branches of the government, industry, and the general public. This laboratory has been called upon to identify wood from tombs of Egyptian Pharaohs, sunken pirate ships, pre-historic forests, and the beam that supports the Liberty Bell. Remember, then, that if you have a problem in identifying a certain kind of lumber, send a small sample of it to:

Wood Identification Service
Forest Products Laboratory
Madison, Wisconsin

HARDWOODS

(Broad-Leafed Species)
American Beech (Fagus grandifolia)

Uses. American beech is used for

lumber and veneer for furniture, and is especially suitable for food containers, since it does not impart taste or odor. (Properties are listed on page 85).

American Sycamore (Platanus occidentalis)

Uses. The principal uses of American sycamore are for lumber and veneer. Products made from the lumber include cheaper grades of furniture, boxes, flooring, scientific instruments, handles, and butchers' blocks.

Rock Elm (Ulmus thomasii)

Uses. Rock elm lumber is used principally for containers and furniture, especially the bent parts of chairs.

American Elm (Ulmus americana)

Uses. Very similar to rock elm.

Black Walnut (Juglans nigra)

Uses. The outstanding uses of black walnut are for furniture, gunstocks, and interior finish. In the furniture industry, it is used either as solid wood cut from lumber or as veneer and plywood.

Black Cherry (Prunus serotina)

Uses. Nearly all the black cherry that is cut is sawed into lumber. Much goes into furniture. Other uses include burial caskets, woodenware, and novelties.

Hickory (Carya)

Uses. Hickory goes into tool handles, athletic goods, and lawn furniture.

White Ash (Fraxinus americana)

Uses. By far the most common use of white ash is in making handles. The wood is also used in the manufacture of furniture, and almost exclusively employed for many types of sports equipment, such as long oars and baseball bats.

American Basswood (Tilia americana)

Uses. Large amounts of basswood are used for crates and boxes, for manufacture of sash, doors, and general millwork, and for core material overlaid with high-grade furniture veneers, such as walnut and mahogany.

Sweetgum (Liquidambar styraciflua)

Uses. The principal uses of sweetgum are for lumber, veneer, and plywood.

Black Tupelo (Nyssa sylvatica)

Uses. Black tupelo is used mainly for lumber and veneer. The lumber goes largely into shipping containers and furniture.

White Oak (Quercus)

Uses. Most white oak is made into lumber for flooring, furniture, general millwork, boxes, and crates. It is the outstanding wood for tight barrels, kegs, and casks because of the nonporous heartwood. It has long been the leading wood for the construction of ships and boats.

Red Oak (Quercus)

Uses. Most of the red oak cut in this country is converted into flooring, furniture, millwork, boxes and crates, coffins, agricultural implements, boats, and woodenware. Considerable red oak lumber is also used in building construction. The hardness and wearing qualities of red oak have made it an important flooring wood for homes.

Yellow Birch (Betula alleghaniensis)

Uses. Because of its pleasing grain pattern and ability to take a high polish, yellow birch is widely used in the furniture industry. Spools, bobbins, and other turned articles are also important products.

Sugar Maple (Acer saccharum)

Uses. Sugar maple is used principally for lumber and veneer. Probably 90 per cent of the lumber is manufactured into such products as flooring, furniture, boxes and crates, handles, woodenware, and novelties. It is especially suitable for bowling alleys, dance floors, and other flooring that is subjected to hard use.

Yellow Poplar (Liriodendron tulipifera)

Uses. The principal uses of yellow poplar are for lumber and veneer. The lumber goes mostly into furniture, boxes and crates, interior finish, siding, fixtures, and musical instruments. The veneer is used extensively for finish, furniture, and various forms of cabinetwork.

Cottonwood (Populus)

Uses. A large proportion of the annual output of cottonwood is cut into lumber and veneer, and then remanufactured into containers and furniture.

Mahogany, Authentic—African (khaya ivorensis), Cuban (swietenia mahogoni), and Tropical American (swietenia macrophylla)

Uses. This wood is used primarily in fine furniture and for paneling and veneer stock. It is also used for accessories and art objects. Some of the more practical uses include boats and wood patterns.

Mahogany, Philippine — Tanguile (Shorea polysperma) and Red Lauan (Shorea negrosensis) among others

Uses. The majority of the species known as Philippine mahogany are ideal for cabinetwork and casework The wood is very popular for furniture, paneling, trim, and many other building uses. NOTE: These species are not true mahogany. Tanguile, for instance, resembles African mahogany, but is coarser in grain, more variable in color, and lacks the tiny glistening dark deposits in the pores that give depth and character to the true mahoganies. A sample of tanguile is shown on page 180.

Butternut (Juglans cinerea)

Uses. This wood has traditionally been used for fine American cabinetwork. Its natural warmth and interest-

81

ing grain make it suitable for impressive woodwork installations. It is used to some extent for interior finishes of houses. This wood, which resembles walnut in many respects, is shown on page 176C.

Pecan (Carya illinoensis)

Uses. The principal use of this southern hardwood is as a veneered product for interior cabinetry and paneling. Because of its hardness and strength it has had wide-spread use in furniture. Perhaps due to its growing availability in ¼" prefinished panel form, its use in architectural woodwork is increasing. See page 178 for an illustration.

SOFTWOODS

(Cone-Bearing Species)

Redwood (Sequoia sempervirens)

Uses. Probably from one-half to two-thirds of the redwood lumber produced is used for planks, dimension lumber, boards, joists, and posts. Much of the remaining lumber is remanufactured into house siding, sash, blinds, doors, general millwork, outdoor furniture, and tanks. Richly colored redwood paneling provides pleasing interior effects.

Western Red Cedar (Thuja plicata)

Uses. The principal uses of western red cedar are for shingles, lumber, poles, posts, and piling. The lumber goes largely into exterior siding for houses, interior finish, greenhouse construction, flumes, and structural timbers, with smaller amounts being used in the manufacture of ships, general millwork, and utility poles.

Shortleaf Pine (Pinus echinata)

Uses. Shortleaf pine lumber is used principally as building material, such as interior finish, ceiling, frames, sash, sheathing, subflooring, and joists, and for boxes and crates, caskets, furniture, woodenware, and novelties.

Ponderosa Pine (Pinus ponderosa)

Uses. Ponderosa pine is used principally for lumber and, to a lesser extent, for piling, poles, posts, and veneer. For cabinets and millwork, the clearer, softer material is used, while the manufacture of boxes and crates consumes the lower grade lumber. Knotty ponderosa pine has come into wide use as paneling for interior finish.

Sitka Spruce (Picea sitchensis)

Uses. The greater part of the lumber is remanufactured into various products such as furniture, planing-mill products, sash, doors, blinds, and general millwork. Specialty uses include aircraft, ladder rails, and piano sounding boards.

Engelmann Spruce (Picea engelmannii)

Uses. A large proportion of the lumber goes into building construction and boxes. Much of it is used for subflooring, sheathing, and studding.

Sugar Pine (Pinus lambertiana)

Uses. Sugar pine is used almost entirely for lumber in buildings, boxes and crates, sash, doors, frames, general millwork, and foundry patterns. It is suitable for all phases of house construction, with the high-grade material going into interior and exterior trim, siding, and paneling, while the lower grade material is used for sheathing, sub-flooring, and roof boards.

Western White Pine (Pinus monticola)

Uses. Practically all of the western white pine that is cut is sawed into lumber. About three-fourths of this lumber is used in building construction. The lower grades are used for subflooring and wall and roof sheathing, while the high-grade material is made into siding of various kinds, exterior and interior trim, partition, casing, base, and paneling. Other uses of western white pine include match planks, boxes, and millwork products.

Western Larch (Larix occidentalis)

Uses. Western larch is used principally in building construction as rough dimension lumber, small timbers, planks, and boards. Some of the high-grade lumber is made into interior finish, flooring, sash, doors, blinds, and other products.

Douglas Fir (Pseudotsuga menziesii)

Uses. The principal uses of Douglas fir are for lumber, timbers, piling, and plywood. Remanufactured lumber goes mostly into sash, doors, general millwork, railroad-car construction and repair, boxes, and crates. Plywood is now in wide use for sheathing, concrete forms, prefabricated house panels, millwork, ships, and other structural forms.

Western Hemlock (Tsuga heterophylla)

Uses. Western hemlock is used primarily for pulpwood and construction lumber and, to a limited extent, for containers and plywood core stock.

White Fir (Abies)

Uses. White fir is used principally for lumber and pulpwood. The lumber goes largely into building construction, planing-mill products, boxes and crates, sash, doors, frames, and general millwork.

Cypress (Taxodium distichum)

Uses. Tidewater red cypress, once a premier wood for exterior applications, is now virtually extinct. However, other species, including yellow cypress and southern cypress are still commercially important. Though less decay resistant than tidewater red cypress, the species currently available are still used for some exterior applications. More generally they are utilized for paneling, where the strong, bold grain is best displayed. See the illustration on page 176E.

Further discussion of the kinds of woods, and specifically the scientific methods of identifying woods, will be found in Unit 13.

Unit 6: PROPERTIES OF WOODS

To select wood wisely you must know two things: (1) the properties of the woods you are considering; (2) the wood properties which are important for the job you are planning. For example, siding for a house requires good nailing and weather-resistant qualities rather than high strength. For joists, the most important qualities are stiffness, the ability to stay in place, and minimum tendency toward shrinkage. For certain pieces of sports equipment, such as a baseball bat, toughness or the ability to withstand sudden shock is the most important quality. Sometimes two products will have almost identical uses, but the wood that is best for one will not be best for the other. Ash is in common use for college and professional baseball bats; southern yellow pine is also used for bats, but usually for ones that will be subjected to less shock, as in softball or in games among small boys.

In furniture construction, attractive appearance and desirable wood grain are prime requirements. Wood selected for furniture projects must be hard enough to resist denting. Some woods which are strong and of good enough quality for the exposed parts of furniture lack necessary hardness. On the other hand, the hardness of such woods as oak or teak makes them difficult to work, especially by hand woodworking processes.

In furniture construction, several things must be considered. First of all, the wood must be relatively hard so that it will not dent easily. This eliminates such woods as basswood, cottonwood, chestnut, and willow. Second, the wood must have a good appearance and take a fine finish. Some woods otherwise suitable for furniture construction do not possess attractive color or figure. Third, furniture woods should have minimum tendency toward warpage, excessive shrinking, and swelling. For these reasons, mahogany and walnut are considered two very desirable furniture woods.

Woods for the framing of a house are different from those for interior finish because of the physical characteristics required. A good understanding of these characteristics is very helpful in making intelligent choices for each type of wood construction. *Fig. 6–1,* shows the common kinds of woods and classifies them for each property. In this table,

6-1. WOOD PROPERTIES

	Relative Hardness	Comparative Weight	Freedom from Shrinkage and Swelling	Freedom from Warping	Hand Tool Working	Nail Holding Power	Comparative Bending Strength	Stiffness	Compression Strength	Toughness	Resistance to Decay	Amount of Figure	Ease of Finishing
HARDWOODS													
American Beech	High	Heavy	Poor	Low	Hard	High	High	High	High	High	Low	Medium	Easy
American Sycamore	High	Heavy	Poor	Low	Hard	Medium	Medium	Medium	Medium	Medium	Low	Medium	Easy
Rock Elm	High	Heavy	Poor	Low	Hard	High	High	High	High	High	Medium	High	Medium
American Elm	High	Medium	Poor	Medium	Hard	High	Medium	Medium	Medium	High	Medium	High	Medium
Black Walnut	High	Heavy	Medium	High	Medium	Medium	High	High	High	Medium	High	High	Medium
Black Cherry	High	Medium	Medium	High	Medium	Medium	High	High	High	Medium	Medium	Medium	Medium
White Ash	High	Heavy	Poor	Medium	Hard	High	High	High	High	High	Low	High	Easy
True Hickory	High	Heavy	Poor	Medium	Hard	High	High	High	High	High	Low	Medium	Easy
Sugar Maple	High	Heavy	Poor	Medium	Hard	High	High	High	High	High	Low	Medium	Medium
Yellow Birch	High	Heavy	Poor	High	Hard	High	High	High	High	High	Low	Medium	Medium
Red Oak	High	Heavy	Poor	Medium	Hard	High	High	High	Medium	High	Low	High	Medium
White Oak	High	Heavy	Medium	Medium	Hard	High	High	High	High	High	Medium	High	Medium
Black Tupelo	High	Medium	Poor	Low	Medium	Medium	Medium	Medium	Medium	Medium	Low	Medium	Medium
Sweet Gum	Medium	Medium	Poor	Medium	Medium	Medium	Medium	Medium	Low	Medium	Low	Medium	Medium
Basswood	Low	Light	Poor	High	Easy	Low	Low	Low	Low	Low	Low	Low	Poor
Yellow Poplar	Low	Medium	Medium	High	Easy	Medium	Medium	Medium	Low	Low	Low	Low	Easy
Cottonwood	Low	Medium	Poor	Low	Medium	Low	Low	Low	Low	Medium	Low	Low	Poor
Mahogany	Medium	Medium	Good	High	Medium	Low	Medium	Medium	Medium	Low	High	High	Medium
Mahogany, Philippine	Medium	Medium	Good	High	Easy	Medium	Medium	Medium	Medium	Medium	Medium	High	Medium
Pecan	High	Heavy	Poor	Medium	Hard	High	High	High	High	High	Low	Medium	Medium
Butternut	Medium	Light	Medium	High	Easy	Low	Medium	Medium	Low	Low	Medium	High	Easy
SOFTWOODS													
Redwood	Medium	Medium	Good	High	Medium	Medium	Medium	Medium	Medium	Medium	High	Medium	Medium
Western Red Cedar	Low	Light	Good	High	Easy	Low	Low	Low	Low	Low	High	Medium	Medium
Shortleaf Pine	High	Heavy	Medium	Medium	Hard	High	High	High	High	Medium	Medium	High	Medium
Ponderosa Pine	Low	Medium	Medium	High	Easy	Low	Low	Low	Low	Low	Low	Medium	Medium
Sitka Spruce	Low	Medium	Medium	High	Medium	Medium	Medium	High	Low	Medium	Low	Low	Medium
Engelmann Spruce	Low	Medium	Medium	High	Medium	Low	Low	Low	Low	Low	Low	Low	Medium
Sugar Pine	Low	Light	Good	High	Easy	Low	Low	Low	Low	Low	Low	Low	Poor
Western White Pine	Low	Light	Good	High	Easy	Low	Low	Low	Low	Low	Low	Low	Poor
Western Larch	High	Heavy	Medium	Medium	Hard	High	High	High	High	Medium	Medium	High	Medium
Douglas Fir	Medium	Medium	Medium	Medium	Hard	High	High	High	High	Medium	Medium	High	Medium
Western Hemlock	Medium	Medium	Medium	Medium	Medium	Medium	Medium	High	Medium	Medium	Low	Medium	Medium
White Fir	Low	Light	Medium	Medium	Medium	Medium	Medium	Medium	Medium	Low	Low	Low	Poor
Cypress	Medium	Medium	Medium	Medium	Medium	Medium	Medium	Medium	Medium	Medium	High	Medium	Medium

it is assumed that the woods are equal in size, dryness, and strength, and equally free from knots and other defects. Hardwoods differ greatly from softwoods in some of their uses and properties. In general, hardwood species are not only harder but also heavier and tougher than softwoods, and have a tendency to shrink more. Hardwoods and softwoods are very similar in stiffness, which means that on a weight-for-weight basis the softwoods are stiffer. Softwoods are used primarily in house construction, whereas hardwoods are more popular for furniture, sports equipment, and many industrial uses.

HARDNESS

Hardness means that the wood is solid or firm and that the surface does not dent, scratch, or cut easily. *Fig. 6-2.* In general, the harder woods resist wear better and are less subject to scratches, nicks, and dents. *Fig. 6-3.* They also take an excel-

6-3. Children and their toys are hard on furniture. There will be fewer dents in pieces made of hard woods such as oak or maple.

lent polish. The main disadvantage of hard woods is the difficulty of cutting them with tools. They are harder to nail and are much more likely to split. Teak, which is a very fine furniture wood, is extremely hard and abrasive, and requires machining by carbide-tipped tools. Hardness is of great value when selecting woods for flooring, fine furniture, and tool handles. There is a definite difference in hardness between springwood and summerwood. For example, in southern yellow pine or Douglas fir, the summerwood is denser and has a darker color at the annular growth ring. Maple, on the other hand, has no pronounced spring or summerwood characteristics, and therefore has a hardness of surface that is quite uniform. One thing to remember is that classification of woods by species into hardwoods and softwoods does not mean actual hardness. Many softwoods cut from evergreen trees are actually harder than some hardwoods cut from broad-leaf trees.

6-2. This attractive dining room furniture is made of maple, one of the harder woods.

86

In building construction, particularly framing, woods that have softness and uniformity are preferred to those that are harder. Such woods as ponderosa pine, sugar pine, and white pine can be cut, sawed, and nailed with relative ease.

WEIGHT

The weight of wood is an important consideration in many types of construction. Weight is a good indicator of the relative strength of wood. A heavy piece of dry wood will be stronger than one of the same size that is light in weight. We think of balsa as an extremely lightweight wood. A few woods such as quebracho are so heavy that they will not float in water. The relative weights of wood given in *Fig. 6–1* are based on kiln-dried samples.

FREEDOM FROM SHRINKING AND SWELLING

Like any other plant material, wood tends to shrink as it dries and to swell as it takes on moisture. Everyone has had experience with drawers and doors that stick during and immediately after rain. Wood shrinks and swells almost twice as much *in width* if it is flat grained as it does if it is quarter sawed or edge grained. For this reason, many woods for flooring are edge grained or quarter sawed. *Fig. 6–4.* All woods shrink or swell very little *in length*. See Unit 8. Most of the shrinkage and swelling is eliminated when wood is properly air-dried or kiln-dried before being put to use. This is especially true of lumber that is properly

cared for during processing and after it is in use.

Woods that have relatively low total shrinkage may dry so slowly that they get into use before all the shrinkage has been taken out. This happens sometimes with such woods as western larch and redwood. As a result they give more trouble than you might expect. Make sure that such woods are properly dried before using them. The best way to check moisture content is with a moisture meter.

FREEDOM FROM WARPING

Warping is described as any variation from a true or plane surface. A warp may be a bow, crook, cup, or twist. Warping causes much waste of lumber in construction and manufacturing. As with shrinkage, warping can be reduced to a minimum by the use of dry, quarter-sawed materials. There must be a minimum of warping and shrinkage if wood is to stay in place. This means that desirable woods remain flat and straight, and

6–4. Even with quarter-sawed flooring, a gap of $\frac{1}{8}$" between the boards will appear if the moisture content changes from 20 to 8 per cent.

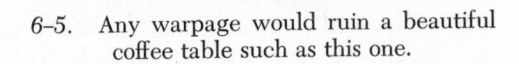

6–5. Any warpage would ruin a beautiful coffee table such as this one.

do not change in size. This is especially important in cabinetmaking and furniture production. *Fig. 6–5.*

EASE OF WORKING WITH HAND TOOLS

Many woods are relatively easy to cut, shape, and fasten together with hand tools. Others, such as oak and maple, are difficult. Other things being equal, ease of working with hand tools is extremely important in house construction. *Fig. 6–6.* In most manufacturing operations, machines can work the various woods with almost equal ease. A good car-

6–6. This carving is being done on western white pine. Is this wood easy or hard to work with hand tools?

penter working with well-seasoned lumber can get good results with even the harder woods. The beginner, however, should choose woods that are easy to work. Of course, the sharpness of cutting edges is very important. Dull tools give trouble on any kind of wood, but particularly on the harder ones. Woods that are easy to work have a soft, uniform texture, and finish to a smooth surface. The hard-to-work woods are either hard or not uniform in texture.

NAIL-HOLDING POWER

Fasteners, including nails, are the weakest part of any construction. The

6–7. The nail-holding power of wood is especially important in carpentry where most of the structural parts are joined by nails.

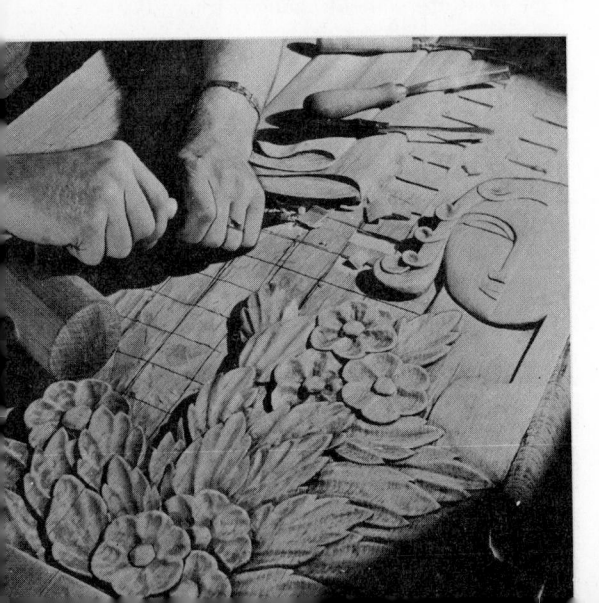

88

resistance that wood offers to the withdrawal of a nail is an important quality. *Fig. 6–7.* Woods that are dense and hard usually have the best nail-holding power. Size, type, and number of nails all have a definite effect on the strength of a joint.

The resistance to withdrawal of nails increases directly with nail diameter. Of the three common types of nails—namely, plain, cement-coated, and barbed—the cement coated nail usually holds best in wood that has been properly seasoned. Several of the more specialized types of nails described in Unit 36 provide better nail-holding qualities. Wood should never be nailed if the moisture content is too high since nails lose much of their holding power as wood dries. Of course, if wood splits as it is nailed, holding power is greatly reduced, even if the split is only a slight one.

BENDING STRENGTH

Bending strength is the ability of lumber to be bent without breaking. *Fig. 6–8.* It is particularly important for members which are used in a horizontal position and rest on two or more supports, such as beams in plank-and-beam construction. A small increase in the height of the beam aids bending strength far more than does a similar increase in width. For example, an increase of one inch in the height of a 10-inch beam will increase its bending strength by 21 per cent, whereas a similar increase in width will add only about 10 per cent to the bending strength. Laminated construction and hollow beams

6–8. Bending strength is important for structural members such as beams.

are other methods of obtaining bending strength.

Although some woods are low in bending strength, they can still be used for joists, beams, and girders; however, a larger size is needed. Because of their lower cost, softwoods are generally used for construction. Therefore their relative bending strengths are very important.

STIFFNESS

Stiffness is the quality that resists bending under loads. *Fig. 6–9.* This is particularly important in house construction in selecting the correct kind and size of floor joists and studding. Height and length have great effect on stiffness. For example, a change of 1/32 of an inch in the thickness of a standard 25/32″ board produces a change of 12 per cent in the stiffness of the board. Another example: A 10″ joist has only about one-fourth more wood in it than an 8″ joist, yet, when it is set on edge in a building, it is more than twice as stiff. Stiffness is not much affected by

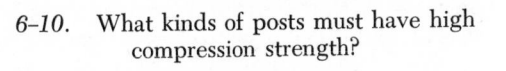

6-9. Stiffness is necessary for a good spring board. Most of them are made of laminated construction. Why?

such defects as knots, checks, or shake. (These defects are explained in Unit 9. See *Figs. 9–2 and 9–4.*) Therefore in home construction the material that is sound though knotty can be used very well for such structural members as joists and studs.

COMPRESSION STRENGTH

Compression strength means the ability of a piece of lumber to resist being mashed or squeezed together by weight applied against its ends. A supporting post is an example of a structural member that must have good compression strength. *Fig. 6–10.* This is particularly important in home construction by the plank-and-beam method. Even when it is important to have compression strength, woods in the low or medium class can be used if the cross-sectional area is made larger.

TOUGHNESS

Toughness means that the wood can withstand sudden shock loads. Tough wood must be highly resistant

to repeated shocks, jars, jolts, or blows. *Fig. 6–11.* Heavier woods such as hickory, birch, oak, maple, and ash are high in shock resistance. *Fig. 6–12.* Generally, the hardwoods are used when a good, tough wood is needed. None of the softwoods is high in toughness. The best of all woods for toughness is hickory. Tough woods are excellent for posts and beams that must carry heavy weight because they give warning of failure by cracking rather than completely splintering, and can be reinforced. Some of the

6-10. What kinds of posts must have high compression strength?

softwoods, especially those with several defects, break without warning.

RESISTANCE TO DECAY

All materials, including metals and plastics, will deteriorate under undesirable conditions. In wood this is known as *decay*. Sometimes it is called *dry rot*, although this is not an accurate description. Wood will last almost indefinitely if it is kept thoroughly dry. It will decay only when there is too much moisture present, particularly when it is in contact with the ground. Wood decays through the growth of certain fungi. A fungus, however, requires warmth, oxygen, food, and moisture for survival. Unless wood has excess moisture, fungi die for lack of the water necessary for growth. The proper kiln drying of lumber kills any fungi that exist in wood. Wood can also be treated with certain preservatives to prevent fungi from developing.

6-11.   Would basswood be a good material for a baseball bat? Why?

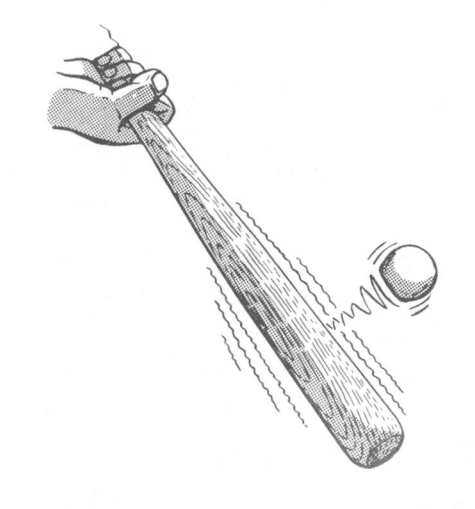

6-12.   This machine is used for testing the toughness of wood.

SURFACE APPEARANCE OR FIGURE

Most woods purchased for use in furniture, interior trim, or in any other place where a natural finish is applied should be selected on the basis of appearance or figure. The figure is caused by different things in different woods. Maple, walnut, and birch, for example, have good figure because of the wavy or curly grain; red gum has a coloring matter that gives it fine appearance. In oak and beech, the flakes or rays (*Fig. 7–3*) provide the distinctive quality. In general, wood has a better grain appearance when plain sawed than when quarter sawed. The color of wood has a definite influence on the figure. Stains and fillers can be applied to bring out the figure in the natural wood.

EASE OF FINISHING

Finishing and painting are very important steps in the completion of any wood product. Paint-holding qualities are particularly important in woods used for the exterior of homes. *Fig. 6-13.* Wood is painted for three reasons:

• To provide decoration, especially color, and to brighten the surface for better lighting.

• To provide a covering that will protect the wood from direct exposure to weather.

• To reduce the porousness of the wood surfaces.

Woods vary considerably in their ability to hold paint. In general, paints hold better on edge-grained or quarter-sawed than on flat-sawed lumber. Finishes are applied to wood to decorate it and to keep it from quickly absorbing liquids which would stain or spot it. Remember, however, that wood does not have to be painted for protection; it is the only material that has *its own natural, weathered surface.* Weather will cause the surface of wood to wear away only about twenty-five thousandths of an inch in a century. Wood does weather, but it will not decay by being exposed to the elements. Most paint failures are due to improper venting; the interior moisture of a house cannot escape without going through the walls.

Other problems include a paint film that is too thick, painting too frequently, or an inadequate paint film. Particular care must be taken when painting over knots in both white and yellow pines.

6-13. Comparing types and qualities of painted surfaces on redwood.

92

Unit 7: NATURE OF WOOD

To understand fully how to machine, sand, and finish wood, and how to avoid the difficulties of shrinking and swelling, it is absolutely necessary to understand the cellular structure of wood. *Fig. 7–1.* Wood is, of course, the hard substance under the bark of trees and shrubs. *Fig. 7–2.* If you look at the cross section of a tree you see several

7–1. This mahogany tree is typical of the raw material of the wood industry.

7–2. Parts of a tree and how it grows. A tree makes its food by taking in carbon dioxide from the air and water from the earth. Sunlight is required by the leaves for the preparation of this food. The process by which the leaves give off moisture is called transpiration.

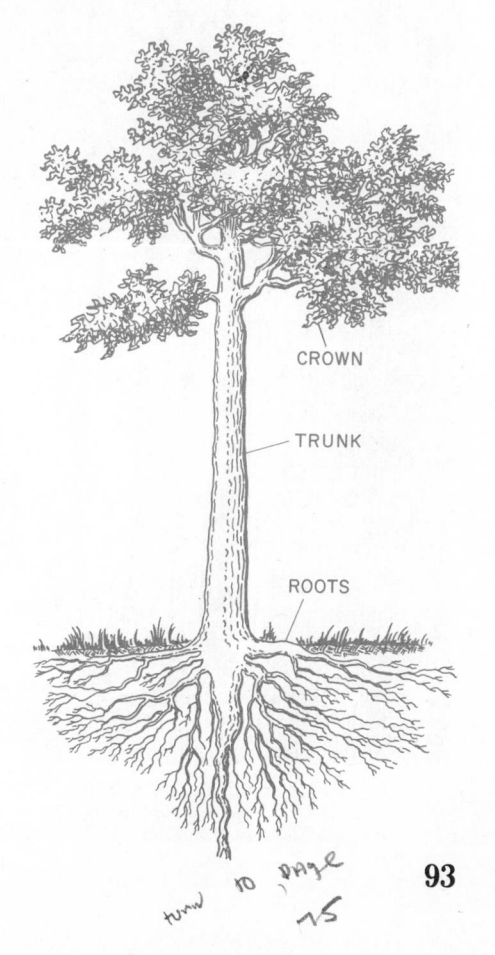

CROWN

TRUNK

ROOTS

turn to page 75

93

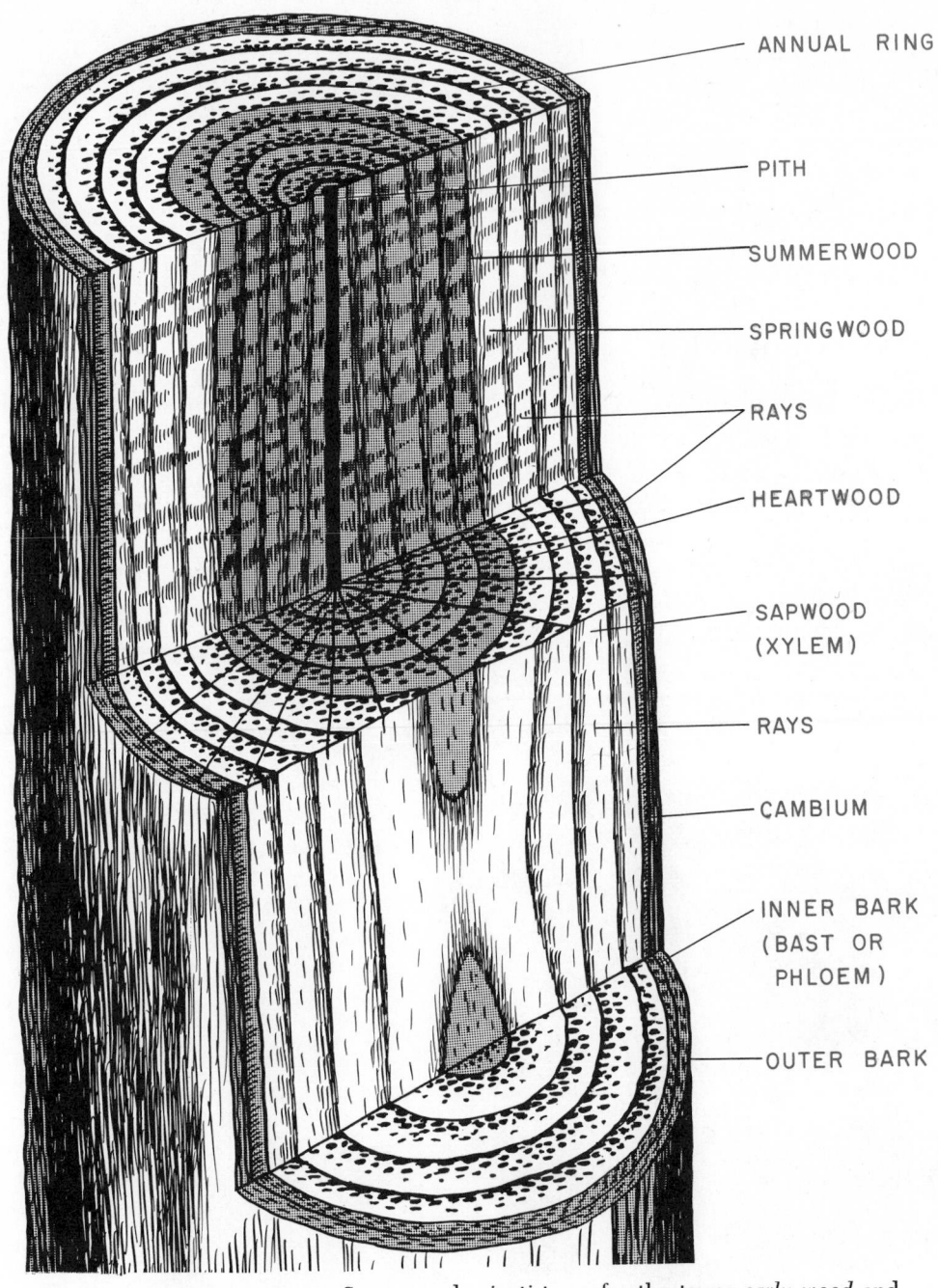

ANNUAL RING

PITH

SUMMERWOOD

SPRINGWOOD

RAYS

HEARTWOOD

SAPWOOD
(XYLEM)

RAYS

CAMBIUM

INNER BARK
(BAST OR
PHLOEM)

OUTER BARK

7-3.   Cross section a tree. Some wood scientists prefer the terms *early wood* and *late wood* rather than *springwood* and *summerwood*.

well defined features from the outside toward the center as follows: *Fig. 7–3.*

• The *outer bark* (protecting the tree) is the dead, corky part that varies in thickness with the kind of tree and its age. The *inner bark* (bast or phloem) carries the food made in the leaves down to branches, trunk, and roots.

• The *cambium* is the narrow layer of cells which repeatedly divide to form more wood on the inside and bast on the outside.

• The *wood* itself is the part of the tree used to make lumber. It is divided into sapwood and heartwood. The sapwood is the newer growth, usually lighter in color. It is actually the growing part of the tree. It carries the sap from roots to leaves. The heartwood is generally darker in color because of the presence of resin and other materials. The heartwood is dead as far as the

7-4. An enlarged view of a tiny piece of wood, showing the tube structure. Here you can see that wood has pores and cells.

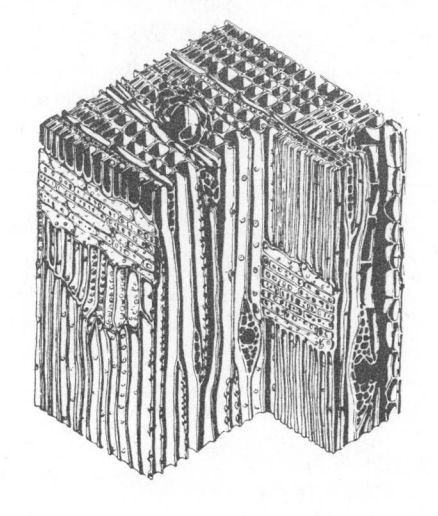

growth of the tree is concerned. This will be explained further in the discussion of cells.

• The *pith* is the small, center core. This represents the primary growth formed when the woody stem or branch elongates.

• Radiating out from the center of a tree are *medullary rays*. These ribbon-like groups of cells form horizontal passageways for the food which nourishes the tree.

CELL STRUCTURE

Like all other plant and animal tissues, wood is composed of cells, tiny living units. *Fig. 7-4.* If you look at a piece of wood through a microscope, you see that it is made up of long, narrow tubes or cells. *Fig. 7-5.* The larger ones are known as *tracheids* (windpipes). Greatly magnified, these would appear as long, hollow cigars. Some cells in hardwoods are not pointed at the ends, but are more like sections of drain pipe. These are called *vessels*. Generally much wider than tracheids, they give the hardwoods a more open grain. All the cells are tightly grown together and, in cross section, have the appearance of a honeycomb. In living sapwood these cells consist of an enclosed cell wall and a cavity filled with *protoplasm*. Protoplasm is mainly a solution of proteins in water. No cells in the heartwood contain protoplasm, but some types of cells in the sapwood do.

7-5. Enlarged view of a wood cell (from softwood).

Most of the cells are arranged in a vertical fashion, which gives wood its straight grain. At frequent intervals the medullary rays thread their way between the vertical cells. The rays run at right angles to the vertical cells from the pith out to the bark, and are important in the movement and storage of food in the sapwood. Food storage cells are generally arranged in the medullary rays. They store plant food between growing seasons. The walls of wood cells are made up of several layers of tightly wound threads called fibrils. These fibrils are made up of long cellulose molecules wound together like wire rope.

Water exists in green wood in two conditions: as free water in the cell cavities and as water absorbed in the cell wall. Particularly in the sapwood there is a great deal of water, much of which is in the form of free water inside the cells. There is also a certain amount of water between the fibrils in the cell walls. When wood contains just enough water to saturate the cell walls it is said to be at *fiber saturation point*. Water in excess of this cannot be absorbed by the cell walls and becomes free water. Removal of the free water from the cell cavities has no influence on the properties of wood except to reduce its weight.

The water in the cell walls is known as *hygroscopic* water. Wood can absorb and retain within itself a certain amount of this type of moisture and can actually pick it up from the surrounding atmosphere. Therefore the amount of water within the cells, even of seasoned wood, depends

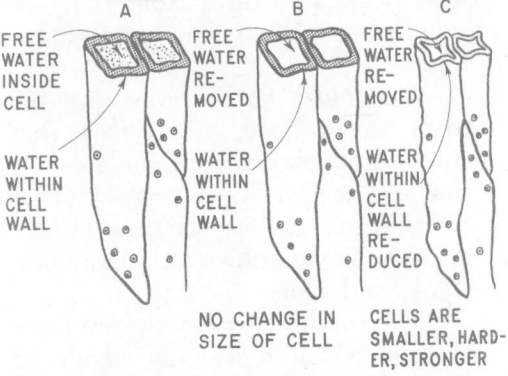

7-6. How wood cells change as water is removed. *a.* Green wood. *b.* Fiber saturation point. *c.* Kiln dried.

on the relative humidity of the area to which the piece is exposed. The amount of water also depends to some extent on whether the wood is sapwood or heartwood. At the same humidity, sapwood usually has a higher moisture content than does heartwood. Remember, removal of free water from the cell cavities does not affect the properties of wood. Since free water evaporates first, shrinkage does not begin until the fiber saturation point is reached. This point varies from about 23 to 30 per cent moisture content. When a piece of wood is exposed to air, evaporation takes place and continues until there is a balance between the water in the wood and the moisture in the air. After the fiber saturation point has been reached, the cell walls begin to give up their moisture. They shrink in all directions, although not uniformly. *Fig. 7-6.* The cause of shrinking is the contraction of the cell walls due to the drying. More will be said about this in the unit on seasoning woods.

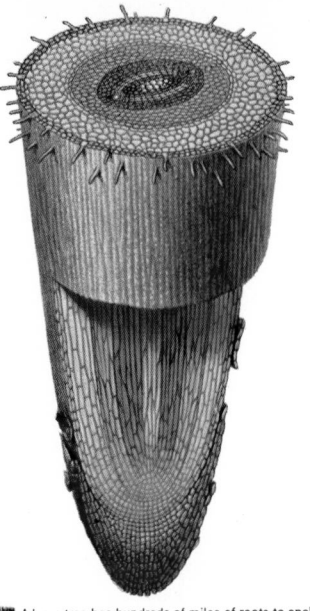

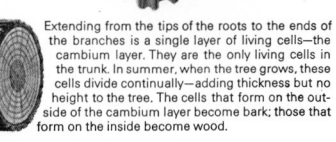

A large tree has hundreds of miles of roots to anchor it to the soil. But most of that length is dead, woody matter. At the very tips of the roots are living, growing cells that push a protective cap of dead cells through the soil. Just behind the tip are the root-hairs, tiny, single-cell projections that absorb water and dissolved minerals from the soil, and start it on its way up to the leaves.

Extending from the tips of the roots to the ends of the branches is a single layer of living cells—the cambium layer. They are the only living cells in the trunk. In summer, when the tree grows, these cells divide continually—adding thickness but no height to the tree. The cells that form on the outside of the cambium layer become bark; those that form on the inside become wood.

Only about one percent of a living tree is actually alive. The living parts are the very tips of the roots, the leaves, the buds, the flowers, the·seeds, and a single thin layer of cells that sheathes (encases) the entire tree from the root tips to the buds on the ends of the smallest branches. Still, this tiny amount of living matter accounts for the growth of our forest giants, sometimes to more than a hundred feet.

The leaves—or needles, in coniferous trees—make sugar out of water passed up from the roots and carbon dioxide in the air. In doing this they utilize the energy of light, with the aid of chlorophyll. The sugar is passed back to the other living cells of the tree so that they can breathe—that is, combine the sugar with oxygen to create energy for the infinite processes of life which enable them to grow and develop.

The leaf buds on the twigs are alive, too. It is their growth that gives a tree height, and extends its branches. Cells at the base of the bud divide and elongate, building a new twig behind the developing leaf. This growth is coordinated with the growth in the cambium layer, so that as a tree grows in height, its trunk and its branches are all growing in thickness at the same time.

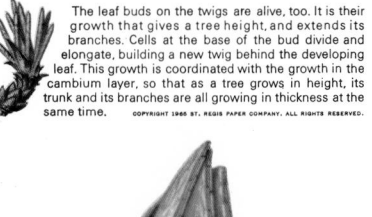

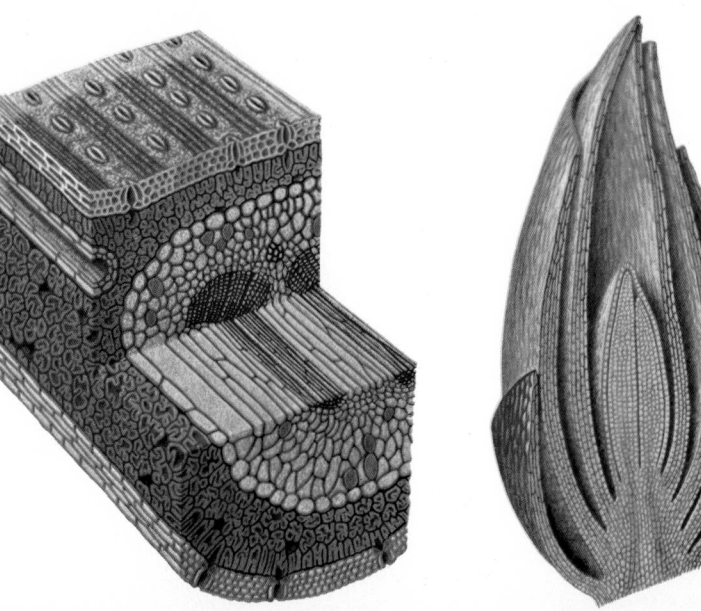

96 A

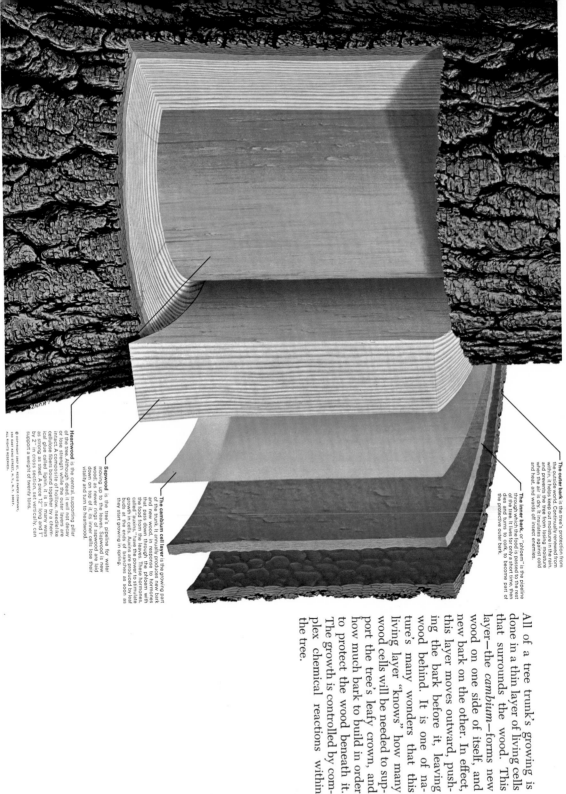

All of a tree trunk's growing is done in a thin layer of living cells that surrounds the wood. This layer—the *cambium*—forms new wood on one side of itself, and new bark on the other. In effect, this layer moves outward, pushing the bark before it, leaving wood behind. It is one of nature's many wonders that this living layer "knows" how many wood cells will be needed to support the tree's leafy crown, and how much bark to build in order to protect the wood beneath it. The growth is controlled by complex chemical reactions within the tree.

The outer bark is the tree's protection from the outside world. Continually renewed from within, it helps keep out moisture in the air, and prevents the tree from losing moisture when the air is dry. It insulates against cold and heat, and wards off insect enemies.

The inner bark, or "phloem," is the pipeline through which the food is passed to the rest of the tree. It lives for only a short time, then dies and turns to cork, to become part of the protective outer bark.

The cambium cell layer is the growing part of the trunk. It annually produces new bark and new wood, in response to hormones that pass down through the phloem with the food from the leaves. These hormones, called "auxins," have the power to stimulate growth in cells. Auxins are produced by leaf buds at the ends of branches as soon as they start growing in spring.

Sapwood is the tree's pipeline for water moving up to the leaves. Sapwood is new wood. As newer rings of sapwood are laid down on top of it, its inner cells lose their vitality and turn to heartwood.

Heartwood is the central, supporting pillar of the tree. Although dead, it will not decay or lose strength while the outer layers are intact. A composite of hollow, needlelike cellulose fibers bound together by a chemical glue called lignin, it is in many ways as strong as steel. A piece 12" long and 1" by 2" in cross section, set vertically, can support a weight of twenty tons.

B 96

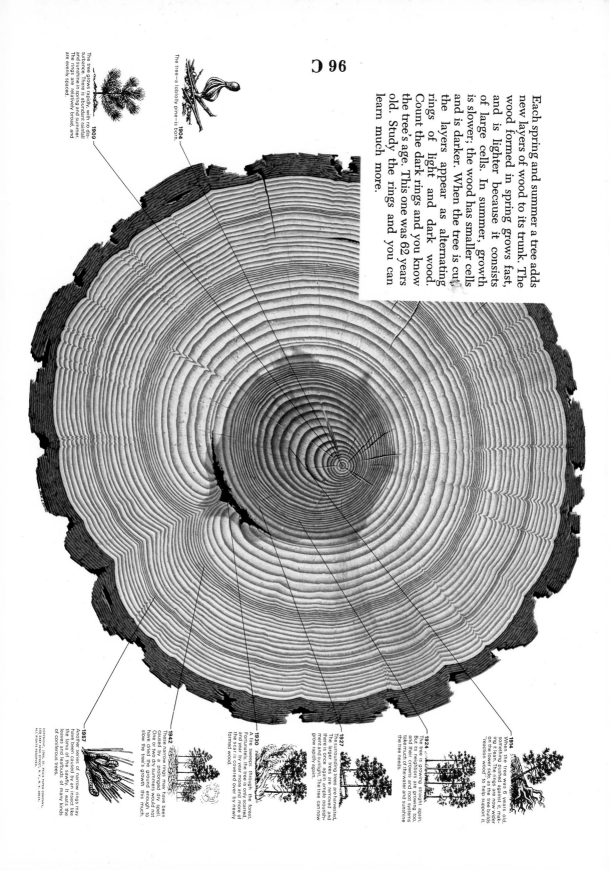

Each spring and summer a tree adds new layers of wood to its trunk. The wood formed in spring grows fast, and is lighter because it consists of large cells. In summer, growth is slower; the wood has smaller cells and is darker. When the tree is cut the layers appear as alternating rings of light and dark wood. Count the dark rings and you know the tree's age. This one was 62 years old. Study the rings and you can learn much more.

1904
The tree—a loblolly pine—is born.

1909
The tree grows rapidly, with no disturbance. There is abundant rainfall and sunshine in spring and summer. The rings are relatively broad, and are evenly spaced.

1914
When the tree was 6 years old, something pushed against it, making it lean. The rings are now wider on the lower side, as the tree builds "reaction wood" to help support it.

1924
The tree is growing straight again. But its neighbors are growing too, and their crowns and root systems take much of the water and sunshine the tree needs.

1927
The surrounding trees are harvested. Fortunately, the tree is not scarred. The larger trees are removed and there is once again ample nourishment and sunlight. The tree can now grow rapidly again.

1930
A fire sweeps through the forest. Fortunately, the tree is only scarred, and year by year more and more of the scar is covered over by newly formed wood.

1942
These narrow rings may have been caused by a prolonged dry spell. One or two dry summers would not have dried the ground enough to slow the tree's growth this much.

1957
Another series of narrow rings may have been caused by an insect like the larva of the sawfly. It eats the leaves and leafbuds of many kinds of coniferous trees.

America's demand for lumber and paper grows by about four percent each year. Good forest management helps meet this demand, but it is also highly important to make full use of each log. At one time it was not uncommon for fifty percent of some logs to go unused. Now, as shown here, waste is kept to a minimum in the sawmill.

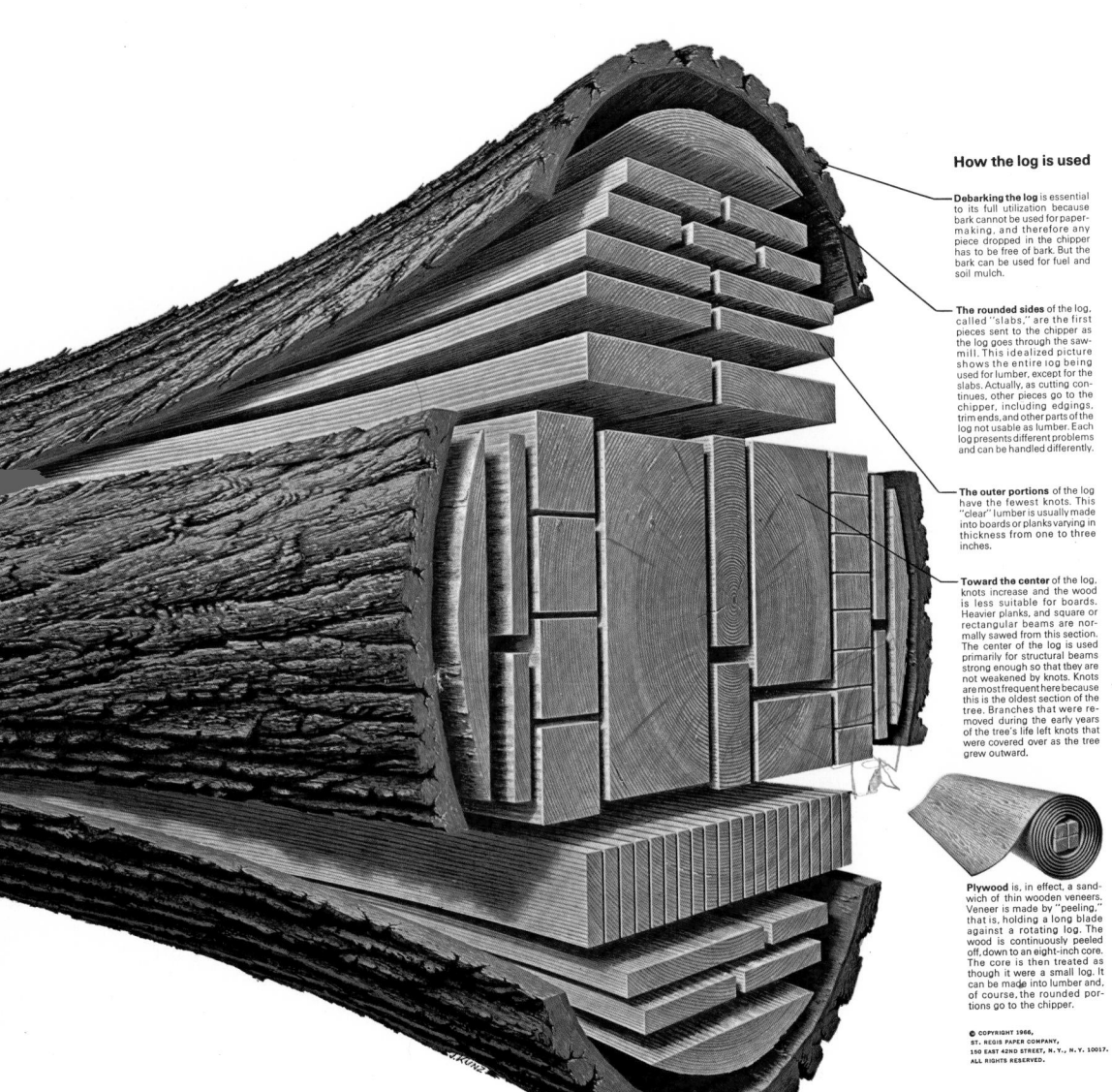

How the log is used

Debarking the log is essential to its full utilization because bark cannot be used for paper-making, and therefore any piece dropped in the chipper has to be free of bark. But the bark can be used for fuel and soil mulch.

The rounded sides of the log, called "slabs," are the first pieces sent to the chipper as the log goes through the sawmill. This idealized picture shows the entire log being used for lumber, except for the slabs. Actually, as cutting continues, other pieces go to the chipper, including edgings, trim ends, and other parts of the log not usable as lumber. Each log presents different problems and can be handled differently.

The outer portions of the log have the fewest knots. This "clear" lumber is usually made into boards or planks varying in thickness from one to three inches.

Toward the center of the log, knots increase and the wood is less suitable for boards. Heavier planks, and square or rectangular beams are normally sawed from this section. The center of the log is used primarily for structural beams strong enough so that they are not weakened by knots. Knots are most frequent here because this is the oldest section of the tree. Branches that were removed during the early years of the tree's life left knots that were covered over as the tree grew outward.

Plywood is, in effect, a sandwich of thin wooden veneers. Veneer is made by "peeling," that is, holding a long blade against a rotating log. The wood is continuously peeled off, down to an eight-inch core. The core is then treated as though it were a small log. It can be made into lumber and, of course, the rounded portions go to the chipper.

96 D

GROWTH RINGS

Between the bark and the wood itself is a layer of thin, living cells, called cambium, in which the growth in thickness of the bark and wood develops by cell division. Wood that is already formed does not grow either in diameter or in length. New growth always takes place by the addition of new cells at the cambium, mostly in the spring and summer months in the temperate zones. It is this seasonal growth that produces well marked, annual growth rings. As a matter of fact, the age of a tree can be determined by counting the number of these rings. In the tropics the growing season is not so precise; thus many tropical woods either have no visible growth rings or the rings may be formed at any time of year. In all cases, as the tree grows larger in diameter, the bark is pushed outward. This causes the bark layers to stretch, crack, and become rigid. In some kinds of trees, there is a great difference in the wood formed early and that formed later in the growing season; the result is very pronounced annual growth rings. *Fig. 7-7.*

Springwood and Summerwood. Growth rings in trees are made up of springwood and summerwood. The portion formed early in the growing season is called springwood (early wood) and that which is formed later is called summerwood (late wood). Springwood has larger cell cavities and thinner walls. In some woods the change from springwood to summerwood may be gradual while in others it is abrupt. It de-

pends on the kind of wood and the growing conditions when the wood is formed. Certain kinds of trees such as maple, gum, and yellow poplar show little difference in the appearance of the springwood and summerwood. In such trees as yellow pine and certain hardwoods such as ash and oak, growth rings are very prominent. In these trees the springwood is very different from the summerwood; it is lighter in weight, softer and weaker than summerwood. Springwood shrinks less across grain and more lengthwise along the grain.

Sapwood and Heartwood. Sapwood is the part of the tree just inside the cambium. Its functions are to allow water and nutrients (food materials) to move from the roots upwards in the stem to the crown, and to store food for tree growth. Sapwood is usually

7-7.   Cross section of a log showing the annual growth rings. Each light ring is springwood (early wood), each dark ring summerwood (late wood):

turn to page A

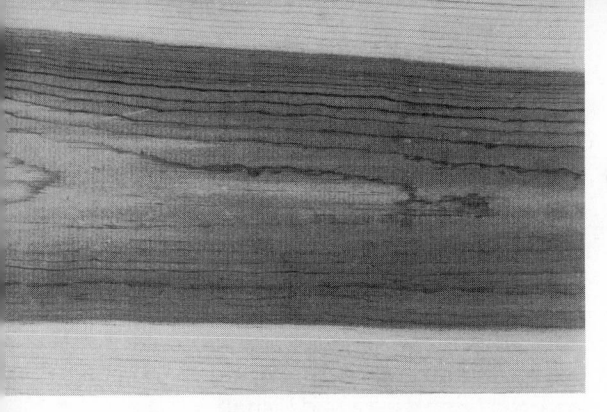

7-8. This cut board shows the difference in color between sapwood and heartwood. Sapwood is lighter in color.

7-9. When a board is cut from straight grain stock the edge looks like A. When a board is cut from cross grain stock it appears as in B.

lighter in color. *Fig. 7-8.* Sapwoods usually vary in radial thickness from 1½ to 2 inches but may be much more or less. Heartwood is made up of inactive cells that have already performed their functions for sap conduction and other life processes of the tree. Heartwood sometimes contains deposits of materials that give it a darker color. All heartwoods are not dark colored, however. The materials in the cells make heartwood lumber more durable for out of doors. There is no great difference in weight and strength between heartwood and sapwood when dry. **Grain Pattern of Wood.** Wood grain is determined by the arrangement of the cells or fibers. Straight grain wood is that in which the cells and fibers have grown parallel to the center of the tree. *Fig. 7–9.* Sometimes the fibers show a wavy or curly pattern due to difference in the size of the cells. When the fibers are not straight, the board is said to have cross grain. *Fig. 7–10.* In cross grain, the fibers usually follow a spiral pattern during the growth of the tree. Another cause for cross grain may be that the saw mill did not cut the board parallel to the bark.

METHODS OF CUTTING BOARDS FROM LOGS

There are two common ways of cutting boards. *Fig. 7–11.* The first is called *plain sawed* (when it is hardwood) or *flat grained* (when softwood). The log is squared and sawed lengthwise (tangent to the annual growth rings). The second method is called *quarter sawed* (when hardwood) or *edge grained* (when softwood). This lumber is not cut parallel to the grain, but sawed so that its rings form angles of forty-five to ninety degrees with the surface.

Plain-sawed lumber is usually cheaper. A knot will extend through

7-10 How to measure cross grain. The cross-grained slope in these illustrations is 1:12. That means that the grain lines slope down 1″ in a 12″ segment of the wood.

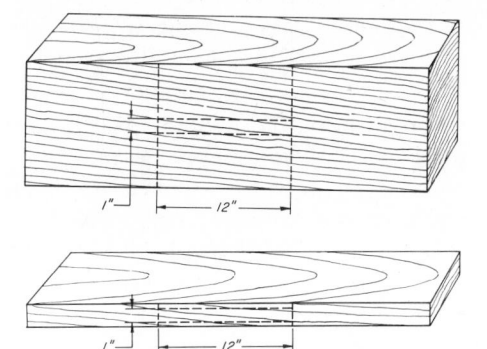

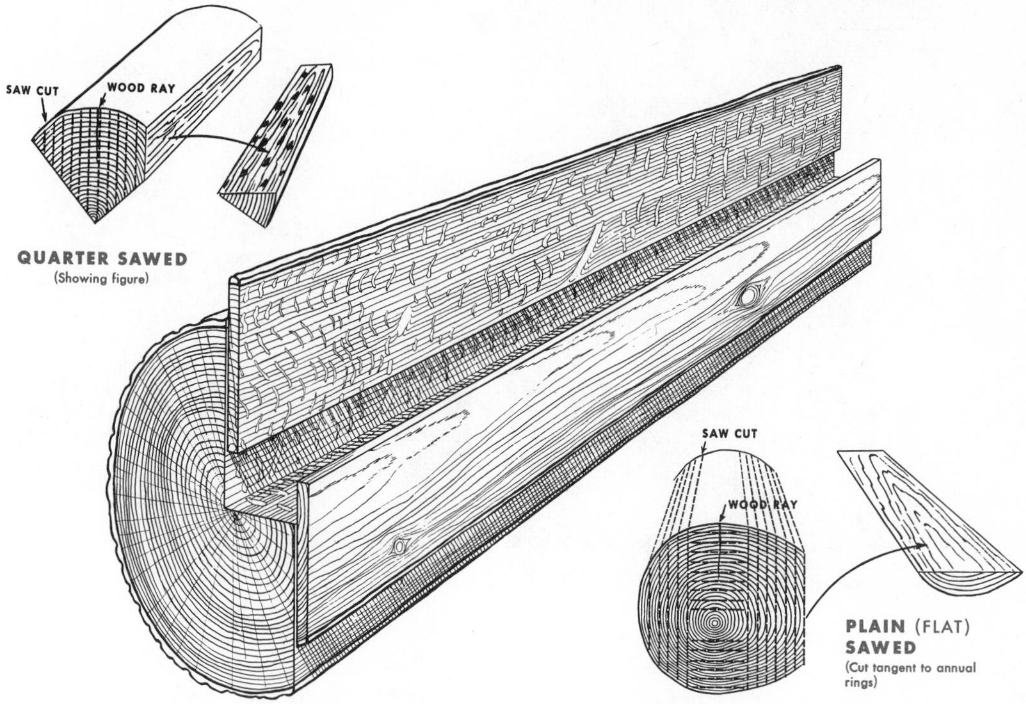

7–11.   Common methods of cutting lumber.

more boards in plain sawed lumber than in quarter sawed. It is also easier to kiln dry, and produces greater widths. However, it has a high tendency to shrink and warp.

Quarter-sawed lumber has low tendency to warp, shrink, and swell, provides a more durable surface, does not tend to twist or cup, and holds paints and finishes better. *Fig. 7–12.*

SOFTWOODS AND HARDWOODS

Although lumber is usually specified as either soft or hard, these terms do not refer to the actual softness or hardness of the wood itself. Softwoods come from evergreens,

(cone-bearing) or needle-bearing trees. Some common ones used in construction are pine, fir, cedar, and

7–12.   Lumber ready for use in building construction.

7-13a.   A common softwood.

7-14a.   A typical hardwood.

redwood. *Fig. 7–13.* Hardwoods are cut from broad-leaf, deciduous trees. (Deciduous means that they shed their leaves annually.) *Fig. 7–14.* Some common ones are birch, maple, oak, walnut, cherry, and mahogany. You will soon find that some softwoods are actually harder than

some hardwoods. For purposes of use, woods are grouped according to their actual hardness and other properties. See Unit 6, PROPERTIES OF WOODS.

7-14b.   Leaves of some common hardwoods.

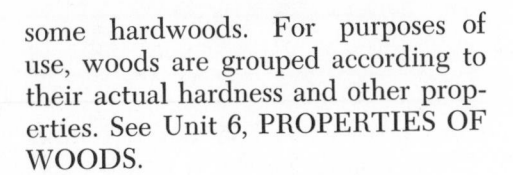

cherry   mahogany   birch

7-13b.   Many softwoods belong to the pine family. *Conifer* simply means cone bearing.

SOFTWOOD
(Conifers)

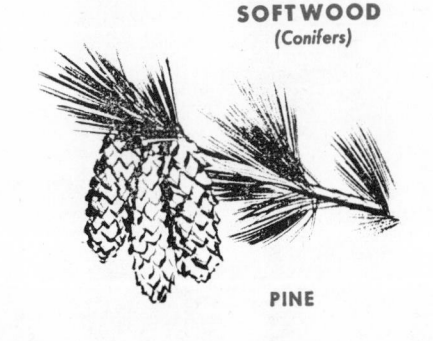

PINE

maple   walnut   oak

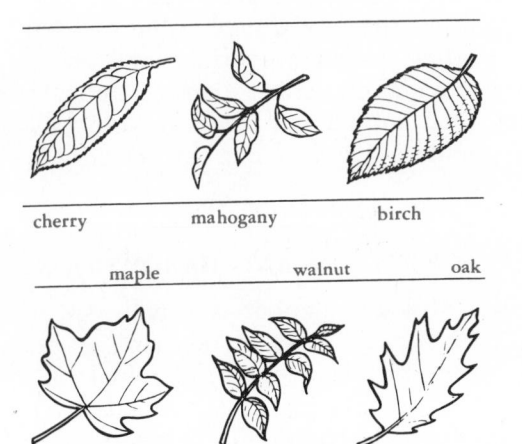

Chemicals in Wood. The four major chemical materials obtained from wood are *cellulose, hemicellulose, lignin* and *extractives. Fig. 7–15.* The percentage of each material in wood varies with each species but particularly between the hardwoods and softwoods. An average hardwood consists of 45 per cent cellulose, 25 per cent hemicellulose and 23 per cent lignin plus some 7 per cent of other materials. On the other hand, the average softwood contains about 42 per cent cellulose, 25 per cent hemicellulose, 30 per cent lignin and about 3 per cent other materials. These basic materials in wood can be separated one from the other by chemical processes and the resulting materials used in the production of many items. Cellulose, for example, is the basic ingredient in products you use every day such as the rayon fiber in rubber tires and the clothing you wear. *Fig. 7–16.* It is also used as one part of the fuel for solid-fuel rockets. A few other uses for cellulose are in photographic film, cosmetics, sponges, and plastics.

The hemicellulose of hardwoods can be used to produce a carbon

7–16.   All of the items shown here are made of wood, including the curtains.

sugar which in turn can be processed into molasses or yeast for cattle feed. It also can be converted into a material called *furfural*—a chemical used in the manufacture of nylon, paper, and many solvents.

Lignin, the "wood glue" that holds the other materials together, can be converted into vanillin or into a chemical material used in foundry molds; it can be made into tanning agents for leather, or used for many other purposes. *Fig. 7–17.* Today, the full chemical utilization of wood is quite limited. In the future, chemicals

7–15.   Here are some common materials obtained from a tree.

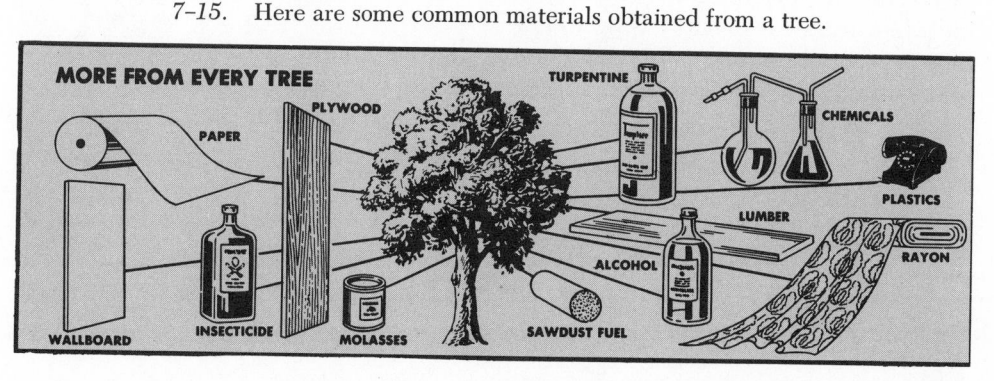

MORE FROM EVERY TREE

PAPER   PLYWOOD   TURPENTINE   CHEMICALS   PLASTICS   LUMBER   RAYON   ALCOHOL   SAWDUST FUEL   MOLASSES   INSECTICIDE   WALLBOARD

7–17. The siding of this house is made of hardboard, one of the man-made building materials in which lignin is the "wood glue" that holds the materials together.

from wood will be used in making tasty foods for humans, attractive clothing, fuels for a trip to the moon, plastic construction materials for homes, and in thousands of other ways. It will truly be the most versatile of all of our natural resources.

Extractives such as oils, fats, and coloring materials are not actually a part of the wood itself.

Unit 8: SEASONING

The amount of moisture in lumber is an important factor in its usability. *Moisture content* is given as a percentage—the lower the figure the drier the wood.

Because of the change in size of wood cells, lumber shrinks as it dries and swells as moisture is added. If lumber holds too much moisture (over 20 per cent) over an extended period of time, a fungus may develop which will cause the wood to deteriorate. You will recall that this process, often called decay or dry rot, was mentioned in Unit 6.

When a tree is first cut down, all of the wood is green. From 30 to 300 per cent of its weight is moisture as compared with an oven-dried piece of wood which contains practically no moisture.

It is important to remember the main points about moisture in wood, discussed in Unit 7. Here is a brief review.

Moisture in green wood exists in two conditions: as free water in the cell cavities, and as water absorbed in the cell walls. When all of the free water is removed and the wood contains just enough water to saturate the cell walls, it is said to be at *fiber saturation point*. The removal of free water has little effect upon the properties of wood except to reduce its weight. However, as water in the cell walls evaporates, the walls contract and wood begins to shrink. Free water is removed first. Therefore shrinkage does not really begin until the fiber saturation point has been reached.

At the fiber saturation point, wood has approximately 23 to 30 per cent moisture content. The shrinkage that occurs after the fiber saturation point is about proportionate to the amount of moisture lost. For a one per cent loss in moisture below the fiber saturation point the wood shrinks about 1/30th. For example, wood dried to 15 per cent moisture content has attained about one half its total shrinkage. Cell walls shrink in all directions, although not uniformly. *Fig. 8–1.* The diameter of the cells is reduced, and they draw closer together.

During drying, the outer parts of wood are reduced in moisture content sooner than the inner parts. Reduction in the size of the cells causes some shrinkage in wood that is quarter sawed or edge grained and a greater amount in wood that is plain

103

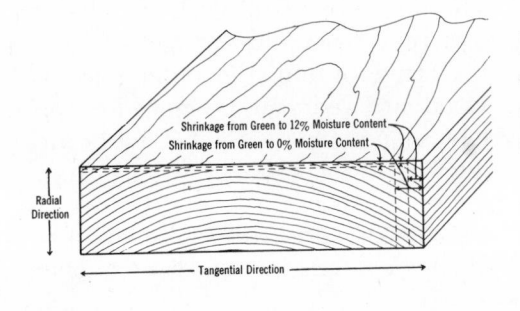

8–1. The shrinkage and distortion of flats, squares, and rounds as affected by the direction of the annual rings. Tangential shrinkage is about twice as great as radial.

sawed or flat grained. Generally speaking, the shrinkage is about twice as great across a plain-sawed face as it is across an edge-grained face. Wood shrinks most in the direction of the annual growth rings, and about half as much across these rings. *Fig.*

8–2. Notice the difference between shrinkage in the tangential direction and in the radial direction.

8–2. Wood shrinks very little in length along the grain—so little, in fact, that end-to-end shrinkage is generally not considered.

Medullary rays, you will recall, are groups of cells which radiate out from the center of the tree. The stiffening effect of these rays keeps wood from shrinking less when cut edge grained or quarter sawed than when cut plain sawed or flat grained.

As a user of wood products you are interested in wood shrinkage. Your main concern is with changes in the size of the wood as you process it in the shop and after it is part of a finished article.

Although no method has been devised to keep wood products absolutely free from shrinking and swelling, certain things can be done to reduce this trouble to a minimum.

METHODS OF DRYING LUMBER

Wood increases in strength, hardness, and stiffness as it dries. There are two common methods of drying lumber: namely, *air drying* and *kiln drying*. Both are entirely satisfactory, depending on the particular use for the lumber. For some purposes lumber is first *air dried* and then *kiln dried*. In other cases it is all air dried or all kiln dried.

In air drying or seasoning, rough lumber is stacked in layers with crossers or spacers between, so that air can circulate freely. *Fig.* 8–3. Circulating air performs three functions:

• It carries heat to the lumber pile to aid evaporation.

• It carries the moisture out of the pile as the water evaporates.

8–3.   Air drying or seasoning lumber.

8–5a.   Loading stacks of lumber into a kiln.

• It breaks up the film of still air that surrounds each board, thus reducing the humidity at that point and helping to remove more of the water vapor from the wood.

Important factors in proper air drying are the location of the air drying yard, the method of stacking the lumber, and the problems of temperature, humidity, and wind. After

8–4.   The correct stacking of lumber for kiln drying or for storage.

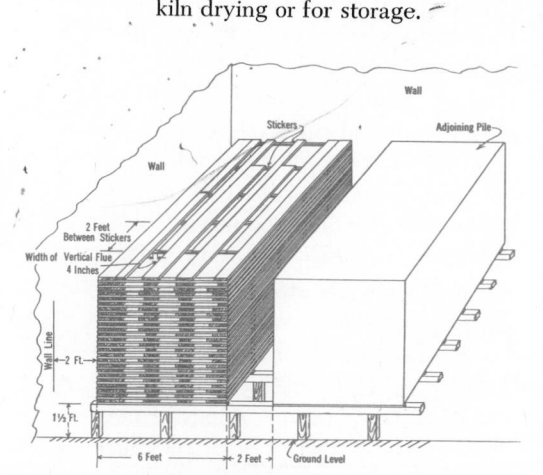

exposure to air for an adequate length of time, usually from one to three months, the moisture content of wood should be a minimum of about 12 to 15 per cent. Lumber at 20 per cent or less is immune to decay.

In kiln drying, lumber is stacked in piles and placed in a kiln (oven) in which air volume and temperature are carefully controlled. *Fig. 8–4.* Here the moisture content of the lumber is reduced to a specified amount. *Fig. 8–5.* The advantages of kiln drying are:

• Moisture content can be reduced to a definite amount and can be lowered farther than through air drying.

• Kiln drying takes a much shorter time than air drying.

• Kiln drying tends to kill the decay fungi and insects in the wood.

• If properly done, kiln drying usually results in fewer imperfections than does air drying.

In this procedure, steam is usually sprayed on the lumber to moisten it uniformly and then it is dried until

105

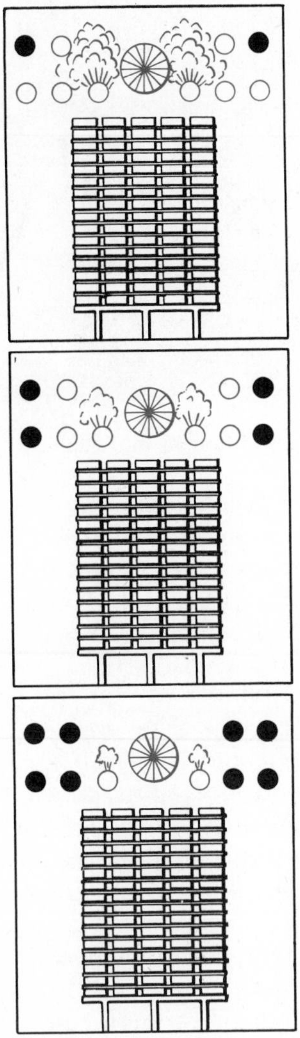

STEP 1

HIGH STEAM

LOW HEAT

GREEN WOOD

STEP 2

STEAM REDUCED

HEAT INCREASED

WOOD DRYING

STEP 3

LITTLE STEAM

HIGH HEAT

WOOD SEASONED

8-5b. Kiln drying.

the moisture content is about 4 to 12 per cent. Green, one-inch lumber can be dried to 6 to 12 per cent in three or four days in a modern kiln. Moisture content can be checked during the drying process with a moisture meter. *Fig. 8-6.*

In both kinds of drying, seasoning

causes some defects that downgrade the quality of the lumber. Among the most common are checks, honeycombs, warps, loosening of knots, and cracks caused by unequal shrinkage. Lumber for furniture should be kiln dried to less than 10 per cent. Construction lumber is usually dried to about 12 to 19 per cent.

STORING LUMBER

In the Yards. Lumber stored in lumber yards should be indoors under covered sheds or protected for outer storage by covering with plastic or waterproof paper. If the sides, top, and ends of lumber are properly covered, it will not absorb too much moisture out of doors even in damp, rainy, or humid weather. In indoor storage, moisture content can be controlled by regulating the temperature in the storage shed.

On the Job. Lumber received on the job for house construction should be stored carefully to prevent shrinking and swelling. It should be off the ground and piled carefully with little crosspieces of wood, called stickers, between each layer. *Fig. 8-7.* It should then be covered with waterproof material until used.

Lumber kept indoors will pick up or lose moisture until it reaches a balance with the moisture of air in the room. In *Fig. 8-8,* you see a map of the United States which shows the proper moisture content for wood to be used in the interior parts of heated buildings. Even if lumber, when delivered, has a lower moisture content than is indicated, it will pick up additional moisture until it balances

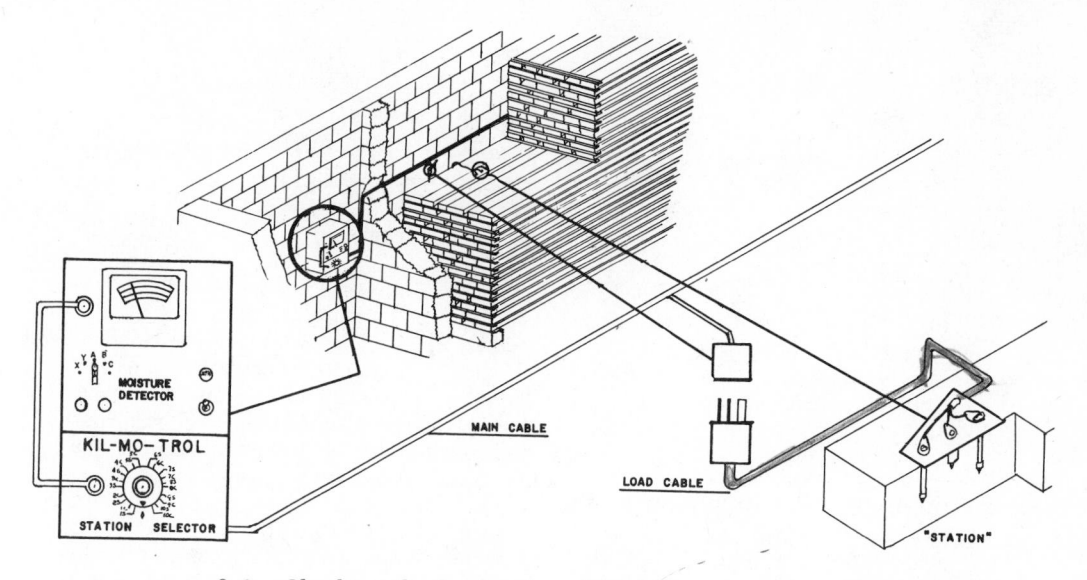

8-6.   Checking the lumber in a kiln with a moisture meter.

with that in the air. *Fig. 8–9.* Even paint does not keep wood from absorbing moisture since it does not completely seal the wood.

Checking Moisture Content (M.C.)
There are two common ways of determining the moisture content. One is by oven-drying methods and the other is by using a moisture meter. In the oven-drying method sample pieces are cut which are about one inch long in the direction of the grain. Samples should be weighed immediately. They should then be placed in an oven at about 214-221 degrees F.

8-7.   Are good practices being used here in storage of lumber on the job?

8-8.   Recommended moisture content averages for interior finishing of woodwork in various parts of the United States.

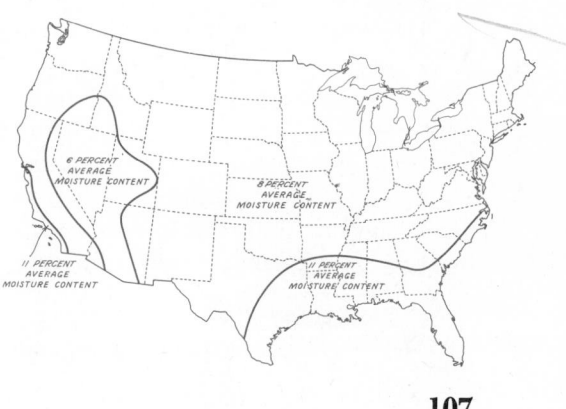

8–9a. Water in a cubic foot of wood at 60 per cent relative humidity. (Bottles in these two illustrations are quart-size.)

8–9b. Water in a cubic foot of wood at 10 per cent relative humidity. Relative humidity is simply an expression of the amount of moisture actually present in air as compared to the maximum amount the air could hold at a given temperature. Wood takes on or gives off a surprising quantity of moisture as the air surrounding it varies. When wood finally stops absorbing or giving off moisture, at any given temperature and relative humidity, it is said to have reached its Equilibrium Moisture Content (EMC).

and kept there until they stop losing weight. Then the amount of moisture can be figured by this formula: Percentage of moisture content equals *weight when cut* minus *oven dry weight* over *oven dry weight* times *100*.

$$\text{Pct. moisture content} = \frac{\text{weight when cut} - \text{oven dry weight}}{\text{oven dry weight}} \times 100$$

For example, if a small piece of wood weighs 12 oz. when cut and 10 oz. after drying, its moisture content would be determined as follows:

$$\text{Pct. moisture content} = \frac{12 \text{ oz.} - 10 \text{ oz.}}{10 \text{ oz.}} \times 100.$$

Pct. moisture content = 20

In modern practice, however, a moisture meter is used to determine moisture content. While the moisture meter readings do not show the same accuracy as those obtained with an oven sample, they do give a much better check than any guess or estimate. These meters provide the only means of checking moisture content rapidly as lumber is being processed

through a manufacturing plant or in home building.

There are two types of moisture meters. One is supplied with needles which pierce the lumber and measure the electrical resistance of current flow through the wood. *Fig. 8–10.* The other is a capacity type that mea-

8–10. Using a needle-type moisture meter to check the moisture content in a stack of lumber.

8–11. The best moisture content for wood used in homes ranges from about 8 per cent for interior trim to about 19 per cent for framing materials.

sures the relation between moisture content and a constant setting. This second type can be recognized by the plates or shoes which are applied to the lumber surface. The accuracy of most meters is within the range of plus or minus 1 per cent of the true figure. Accuracy is based on the assumption that moisture content is uniform throughout the thickness of a board. However, when lumber is dried rapidly in a kiln, higher moisture is found in the center of the piece than on the outside. A more accurate reading can be obtained by cutting off the end of a board and inserting the needles in the end grain near the center of the piece. Meters should never be used on foggy days or when the air is excessively humid. Top boards or outside pieces that have been exposed to the weather for some time may be above or below the average of the lumber pile.

Moisture content is extremely important to any kind of good woodworking. In house construction, such things as the prevention of plaster cracks and the fitting of drawers and doors depend on the use of lumber with proper moisture content. *Fig. 8–11.* In furniture construction, the moisture content is even more important. The fitting of joints, the quality of glue joints, and again the effective operation of doors and drawers, all depend on proper moisture content. *Figs. 8–12 and 8–13.*

109

SELECTION OF LUMBER

Here are some suggestions for selecting and preparing lumber and using it in a finished product.

• Before the lumber is machined, make sure moisture content of the pieces is uniform and correct. Lumber that is too wet will shrink. If it is too dry, it will swell.

• Never store flooring or finish lumber in a house that has just been plastered, because the lumber will pick up the moisture from the walls.

• If shrinkage across the grain is likely to be serious, use edge-grained stock.

• The moisture content of a finished article should be about the same as that in the place where it is to be used. While many types of protective coatings help, they do not keep out all of the moisture. Protec-

tive coatings help to prevent a difference in moisture distribution between the surface and the interior.

• After an article has been built, try to protect the wood from great extremes of humidity. It is very important that a woodworking shop or storeroom be equipped with humidity-control apparatus and a ventilating system.

8–13. Shrinkage in width of 2″x10″ framing lumber at various moisture contents. At 19% M.C. (which is average for the building industry) the shrinkage is 6/32″, but at 6% M.C. the shrinkage is more than ½″.

8–12. Quality furniture cannot be produced if there is too much or too little moisture in the wood. Furniture factories have humidity-controlled rooms in which the lumber and partly completed furniture are stored.

Unit 9: GRADING LUMBER

Since lumber is produced from a living and growing material, it cannot be classified according to the same uniform standards as metals or plastics. Instead, lumber must be divided into many different grades based on the number of defects found in it. A tree grows much like an onion, adding a new layer each year. When the tree is small, the limbs are low to the ground. As it grows larger, the lower limbs drop off and additional material fills out the tree's diameter. Each limb that drops causes a knot to be formed, but as a tree increases in diameter, the growth covers these knots. Because of this, the best quality lumber is found in the lower part of the trunk near the outside.

Lumber is classified according to grades so that the purchaser can know the quality of the wood he buys. In the grading process, a lumber piece must meet the lowest requirements for its grade. Wide differences in quality are found in the same grade because some lumber is much better than the minimum for its grade, but not quite good enough for a higher classification. In the saw mill, the sawyer attempts

to cut each log into pieces of the best possible grade. This is done by turning the log a quarter turn or more as necessary after each cut. The actual grading of the lumber is done by specialists. *Fig. 9–1.* While the wood is still in the rough, these men must determine the grade in which each board belongs. In some cases a defect may not appear until after the board has been surfaced. However, the board remains in its grade group; the divisions are not perfect and are subject to human error.

LUMBER DEFECTS

Defects in lumber are the faults which detract from the quality of the piece, either in appearance or utility. The prevailing idea that lumber full

9–1. These men must have a complete knowledge of grading rules. Many associations sponsor classes for the men who work as lumber graders.

111

of knots is seriously defective is wrong. In ordinary use, a sound, tight-knotted piece loses little of its value. The exception to this is lumber which should not have a knotty appearance for reasons other than actual soundness. The same is true of stain, which should not be regarded as a serious defect.

The defining of various defects is difficult. A light or small defect in one piece is often a medium or large defect in another. In better grades of lumber the defects are light, small, or serious, depending upon the size of the piece and on the way they come into combination with other defects.

A *bark pocket* is a patch of bark partially or wholly enclosed in wood. A *check* is a crack in the wood structure of a piece, usually running lengthwise. *Fig. 9–2.* A *roller check* is caused when a piece of cupped lumber is flattened as it passes between the machine rollers. A *peck* consists of a channeled or pitted area or pocket. Wood tissues between pecky areas remain unaffected in ap-

pearance and strength. Peckiness occurs only while the tree is still alive.

Decay is disintegration of wood fiber. It shows in various stages from barely perceptible to soft and very evident. *Fig. 9–3. Rot* and *dote* mean the same as decay. *Heart pith* is the pith or spongy center of the tree which appears on the surface of a piece of lumber. *Shake* is a crack between and parallel to the rings of annual growth. It produces a defect in the lumber noticeably different from heart pith.

Stain is a discoloration that penetrates the wood fiber. It can be any color other than the natural color of the piece in which it is found. It is classed as light, medium, or heavy and is generally blue or brown. Light stain is often barely perceptible.

A *pin wormhole* is not over $\frac{1}{4}''$ in diameter; worm holes bigger than $\frac{1}{4}''$ are classed as *large. Torn grain* is a roughened area. This sometimes happens during the surfacing of lumber

9–3. Decay.

9–2. A check in the wood surface.

112

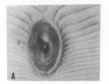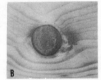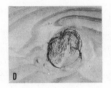

9–4.   Common kinds of knots: *a*. Intergrown; *b*. Encased; *c*. Spike; *d*. Decayed; *e*. Knot hole.

when the machine tears out bits of the wood. A *skip* is an area that the planer failed to surface. In a *slight skip* the area was not surfaced smooth. In a *heavy skip* the planer knife did not touch the area at all. A *machine burn* is a darkening of the wood due to overheating of the machine knives.

A *knot* in a piece of sawed lumber is a portion of a branch or limb of the tree. *Fig. 9–4.* If a board has more than one knot, the average diameter of the largest and the smallest knots determines the measurement, unless otherwise stated. A *branch knot* is one that has been sawed at an angle parallel, or nearly parallel, to the direction of the limb growth. A *spike knot* is a branch knot that runs to the edge of the piece of lumber, growing larger as it approaches the edge.

A *pin knot* is one not over $\frac{1}{2}''$ in diameter. A *small knot* is one between $\frac{1}{2}''$ and $\frac{3}{4}''$ in diameter. A *medium knot* is one over $\frac{3}{4}''$, but not over $1\frac{1}{2}''$ in diameter. A large knot is one over $1\frac{1}{2}''$ in diameter.

A *red knot* results from live branch growth in the tree; it is firmly grown into the wood structure. An *intergrown knot* is partly or wholly grown together with the fiber of the surrounding wood. A *black knot* results from a dead branch which the wood

growth of the tree has surrounded.

A *sound knot* is free from decay. An *unsound knot* has some decay; it may vary in degree from incipient (just the first traces) to pronounced. A *tight knot* is one so fixed by growth or position in the wood structure that it firmly retains its place in the piece. A *not-firm knot* under ordinary conditions will hold its place in a dry board; yet under pressure it can be started but not easily pushed out of the piece. A *loose knot* is one that cannot be relied upon to remain in place in the piece.

Pitch is an accumulation of resinous material. It may be *light, medium,* or *heavy,* as shown by its color and consistency. *Massed pitch* is a clearly defined accumulation of solid pitch. A *pitch pocket* is a well-defined opening in the wood fiber which holds, or has held, pitch. A *very small pitch pocket* is one not over $\frac{1}{8}''$ wide and not over 2″ long. A *small pitch pocket* is one not over $\frac{1}{8}''$ in width and not over 4″ in length, or not more than $\frac{1}{4}''$ in width nor over 2″ in length. A *medium pitch pocket* is one not wider than $\frac{1}{4}''$ nor longer than 8″, or not over $\frac{3}{8}''$ in width nor over 4″ in length. In a *large pitch pocket* the width or length exceeds the maximum for a medium pitch pocket.

113

Wane is the presence of bark or absence of wood on corners of a piece of lumber. *Warp* is any variation from a true or plane surface, including crook, bow, cup, twist, or, more frequently, any combination of these. *Bow* and *crook* are similar. Both are deviations from a straight line drawn from one end of a piece of lumber to the other. If you were to place a lath on its *thin edge* and draw the corners back toward you, this would give you an idea of bow. By placing the lath on its *flat side* and bending the corners toward you, you get the effect of crook.

HARDWOOD GRADING

The grades of hardwood lumber are designed primarily for use by the furniture industry, since this is where most good hardwood is required. Hardwood grades are summarized in *Fig. 9–6*. In general, the first two grades are sold as a group and are called firsts and seconds or FAS. Look at this chart to find some of the standards. *Firsts* and *seconds* must be graded from the poor side of the board; when the grading is done, the poorest side is examined. In the case of *firsts*, the boards must be six inches or more in width and must range in length from eight to sixteen feet.

The first step in grading a board for *firsts* is to determine the *surface measure*. This is the number of square feet in the board. For a board containing from 4 to 9 square feet, $91\frac{2}{3}$ per cent of the board must be clear (without defects) by taking only one cut. For example, suppose

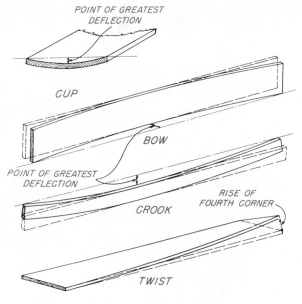

9–5. Warp.

a board 6 inches wide and 8 feet long has a small defect at one end. If this could be cut off and $91\frac{2}{3}$ per cent of the material retained, would the board meet the grade standard? For *seconds*, $83\frac{1}{3}$ to $91\frac{2}{3}$ per cent of surface measure must yield clear-face cuttings. Both firsts and seconds require that pieces be not less than 6 inches wide and 8 feet long. In the next grade, *select*, the minimum width is 4 inches while the minimum length is 6 feet. This is followed by No. 1 Common and No. 2 Common. A complete set of hardwood lumber grades is available from the National Hardwood Lumber Association. Hardwood flooring is graded by different standards following the rules of the Maple Flooring Manufacturers Association, or the rules of the National Oak Flooring Manufacturers Association.

9–6.   STANDARD HARDWOOD GRADES[1]

Grade and lengths allowed (feet)	Widths allowed	Surface measure of pieces	Amount of each piece that must work into clear-face cuttings	Maximum cuttings allowed	Minimum size of cuttings required
Firsts:[2]	Inches	Square feet	Percent	Number	
8 to 16 (will admit 30 percent of 8- to 11-foot, ½ of which may be 8- and 9-foot).	6+	4 to 9	91⅔	1	4 inches by 5 feet, or 3 inches by 7 feet.
		10 to 14	91⅔	2	
		15+	91⅔	3	
Seconds:[2]		4 and 5	83⅓	1	
8 to 16 (will admit 30 percent of 8- to 11-foot, ½ of which may be 8- and 9-foot).	6+	6 and 7	83⅓	1	Do.
		6 and 7	91⅔	2	
		8 to 11	83⅓	2	
		8 to 11	91⅔	3	
		12 to 15	83⅓	3	
		12 to 15	91⅔	4	
		16+	83⅓	4	
Selects:					
6 to 16 (will admit 30 percent of 6- to 11-foot, 1/6 of which may be 6- and 7-foot).	4+	2 and 3	91⅔	1	Do.
		4+	(3)		
No. 1 Common:		1	100	0	
		2	75	1	
		3 and 4	66⅔	1	
4 to 16 (will admit 10 percent of 4- to 7-foot, ½ of which may be 4- and 5-foot).	3+	3 and 4	75	2	4 inches by 2 feet, or 3 inches by 3 feet.
		5 to 7	66⅔	2	
		5 to 7	75	3	
		8 to 10	66⅔	3	
		11 to 13	66⅔	4	
		14+	66⅔	5	
No. 2 Common:		1	66⅔	1	
		2 and 3	50	1	
		2 and 3	66⅔	2	
		4 and 5	50	2	
4 to 16 (will admit 30 percent of 4- to 7-foot, ⅓ of which may be 4- and 5-foot).	3+	4 and 5	66⅔	3	3 inches by 2 feet.
		6 and 7	50	3	
		6 and 7	66⅔	4	
		8 and 9	50	4	
		10 and 11	50	5	
		12 and 13	50	6	
		14+	50	7	

[1] Inspection to be made on the poorer side of the piece, except in Selects.
[2] Firsts and Seconds are combined as 1 grade (FAS). The percentage of Firsts required in the combined grade varies from 20 to 40 percent, depending on the species.
[3] Same as Seconds.

SOFTWOOD GRADING

The National Bureau of Standards of the Department of Commerce has established American Lumber Standards for softwood lumber. These standards are intended as guides for the different associations of lumber producers, each of which has its own grading rules and specifications. Most of the major associations, such as the Western Wood Products Association, Redwood Inspection Service, Southern Pine Inspection Bureau, and many

Class	Category	Type	Subtype	Grades
Softwood lumber (this classification applies to rough or dressed lumber; sizes given are nominal)	Yard lumber (lumber less than 5 inches thick, intended for general building purposes; grading based on use of the entire piece)	Finish (less than 3 inches thick and 12 inches and under in width)		A select B select C select D select
		Boards (less than 2 inches thick and 2 inches or over in width). Strips (under 8 inches in width)		No. 1 boards No. 2 boards No. 3 boards No. 4 boards No. 5 boards
		Dimension (2 inches and under 5 inches thick and 2 or more inches in width)	Planks (2 inches and under 4 inches thick and 8 inches and over wide)	No. 1 dimension No. 2 dimension No. 3 dimension
			Scantling (2 inches and under 5 inches thick and under 8 inches wide)	No. 1 dimension No. 2 dimension No. 3 dimension
			Heavy joists (4 inches thick and 8 inches or over wide)	No. 1 dimension No. 2 dimension No. 3 dimension
	Structural material (lumber 2 inches or over in thickness and width, except joist and plank; grading based on strength and on use of entire piece)	Joist and plank (2 inches to 4 inches thick and 4 inches and over wide)		
		Timbers classified as beams, stringers, posts, caps, sills, girders, purlins, etc. must be 5 or more inches nominally in least dimension		
	Factory and shop (grading based on area of piece suitable for cuttings of certain size and quality)	Factory plank graded for door, sash, and other cuttings 1 inch to 4 inches thick and 5 inches and over wide	Factory clears upper grades	Nos. 1 and 2 clear factory No. 3 clear factory
			Shop lower grades	No. 1 shop No. 2 shop No. 3 shop
		Shop lumber graded for general cut up purposes	1 inch thick (northern and western pine, and Pacific coast woods)	Select Shop
			All thicknesses (cypress, redwood, and North Carolina pine)	Tank and boat stock, firsts and seconds, selects No. 1 shop No. 2 shop, box

others participated in developing these grading rules. If you are working with just a few kinds of lumber most of the time, you should obtain grading rules from the associations involved and become fairly well acquainted with them. One of the main ideas of these standards is to divide all softwood lumber for *grading purposes* into two groups:

• Dry lumber that is seasoned or dried to a moisture content of 19 percent or less.

• Green lumber, which has moisture content in excess of 19 percent. Complete standards are available from the National Bureau of Standards, Department of Commerce, under Federal Register Volume 34, Number 233.

Softwood lumber is classified according to use and extent of manufacture as follows:

Use Classifications. *Fig. 9-7. Yard lumber.* Lumber of those grades, sizes, and patterns which are generally intended for ordinary construction and general building purposes.

Structural lumber. Lumber that is 2″ or more in nominal thickness and width, for use where working stresses are required. (NOTE: Nominal sizes are somewhat larger than actual size. This is explained in the next unit.)

Factory and shop lumber. Lumber that is produced or selected primarily for remanufacturing purposes.

Yard lumbers are cut for a wide variety of uses. They are divided into two grade qualities — finish (select) and common grades.

Finish (select) grades are further classified. Grade A is practically clear wood and is used for such items as finish flooring, ceilings, partitions, and siding. Grade B has very few imperfections. It may include small checks or stain marks. Grades C and D have increasingly more imperfections, but are still suitable for a good paint finish.

The common grades of boards are those that are suited for general utility and construction purposes. The major differences between the grades are in the number of knots and amount of pitch. These range from Nos. 1 and 2 which can be used without waste to Nos. 3, 4, and 5 which involve a limited amount of waste.

Manufacturing Classifications. *Rough lumber.* Lumber which has not been dressed (surfaced) but which has been sawed, edged, and trimmed at least to the extent of showing saw marks in the wood on the four longitudinal surfaces of each piece for its overall length.

Dressed (surfaced) lumber. Lumber that has been dressed by a planing machine, for smoothness of surface and uniformity of size. Lumber may be dressed on one side (S1S), two sides (S2S), one edge (S1E), two edges (S2E), or a combination of sides and edges (S1S1E, S1S2E, S2S1E, S4S).

Worked lumber. Lumber which, in addition to being dressed, has been matched, shiplapped, or patterned. *Matched lumber* has been worked with a tongue on one edge of each piece and a groove on the opposite edge to provide a close tongue-and-groove joint by fitting two pieces together; when end-matched, the tongue and groove are worked in the ends also. *Shiplapped lumber* has been worked or rabbeted on both edges of each piece to provide a closelapped joint by fitting two pieces together. *Patterned lumber* is shaped to a pattern or to a molded form, in addition to being dressed, matched, or shiplapped, or any combination of these workings.

Unit 10: BUYING LUMBER

It is important to learn how to purchase lumber for furniture and home construction. The lumber has to serve the particular purpose for which it is intended. You should not buy lumber of a better quality than needed, nor should you be satisfied with poor or incorrect lumber.

BUYING FROM A LUMBER YARD

In addition to yard lumber, a retail lumber yard may carry one or two kinds of hardwood in grades suitable for finishing cabinetwork and flooring. Hardwood of all types can be ordered from the retail lumber yard or from yards specializing in hardwood.

In general, trim items (moldings, *Fig. 10-1*) are cut to size in standard patterns at the millwork plant and sold by retail yards. Cabinets of hardwood and hardwood plywood are often made by the millwork plant ready for installation by the carpenter. Hardwood flooring is a mill product. The

10-1. Common patterns of molding.

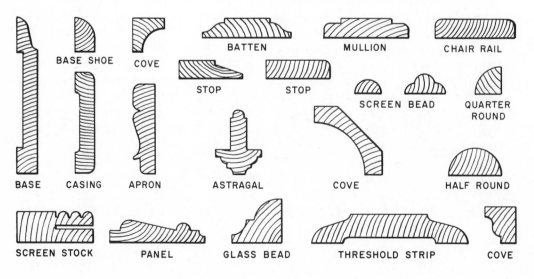

BASE SHOE   COVE   BATTEN   MULLION   CHAIR RAIL

STOP   STOP   SCREEN BEAD   QUARTER ROUND

BASE   CASING   APRON   ASTRAGAL   COVE   HALF ROUND

SCREEN STOCK   PANEL   GLASS BEAD   THRESHOLD STRIP   COVE

10-2. COMMONLY USED LUMBER ABBREVIATIONS

AD—Air dried
ALS—American Lumber Standards
AV—Average
B&B or B&Btr—B and better
BD—Board
BD FT—Board feet
BEV—Bevel
BM—Board measure
BTR—Better
C/L—Carload
CLG—Ceiling
CLR—Clear
COM—Common
CSG—Casing
DF—Douglas fir
DIM—Dimension
DKG—Decking
D/S, DS—Drop siding
D&M—Dressed and matched; center matched unless otherwise specified
D&CM—Dressed and center matched
D&SM—Dressed and standard matched
E—Edge
EB1S—Edge bead one side
EG—Edge (vertical) grain
FAS—Firsts and seconds
FG—Flat or slash grain
FCTY—Factory lumber
FLG—Flooring
FT—Foot
FT BM or FBM—Feet board measure
FT SM—Feet surface measure
GR—Green
HDWD—Hardwood

HRT—Heart
HRTWD—Heartwood
IN—Inch or inches
JTD—Jointed
KD—Kiln dried
LBR—Lumber
LGTH—Length
LIN—Lineal
M—Thousand
M BM—Thousand (ft.) board measure
MC—Moisture content
MLDG—Moulding or molding
N—Nosed
OC—On center
OG—Ogee
P—Planed
PC—Piece
QTD—Quartered, when referring to hardwoods
RDM—Random
REG—Regular
RGH—Rough
R/L, RL—Random lengths
RND—Round
R/W, RW—Random widths
SAP—Sapwood
SD—Seasoned
SDG—Siding
SEL—Select
SF—Surface foot; that is, an area of 1 square foot
SG—Slash grain
SM—Surface measure
SPA—Southern Pine Association
SQ—Square
SQRS—Squares
STD—Standard

STD M—Standard matched
STK—Stock
STRUCT—Structural
SYMBOLS
  ″—Inch or inches
  ′—Foot or feet
  x—By, as 4 x 4
  $\frac{4}{4}$, $\frac{5}{4}$, $\frac{6}{4}$, etc.— thickness expressed in fractions of an inch
S&E—Side and edge
S1E—Surfaced one edge
S2E—Surfaced 2 edges
S1S—Surfaced one side
S2S—Surfaced two sides
S4S—Surfaced four sides
S1S&CM—Surfaced one side and center matched
S2S&CM—Surfaced two sides and center matched
S4S&CS—Surfaced four sides and caulking seam
S1S1E—Surfaced one side, one edge
S1S2E—Surfaced one side, two edges
S2S&SM—Surfaced two sides and standard matched
TBR—Timber
T&G—Tongued and grooved, center matched unless otherwise specified
VG—Vertical (edge) grain
WCLA—West Coast Lumbermen's Association
WPA—Western Pine Association
WTH—Width

species of softwood carried by a yard often depends largely on geographic location. For example, a lumber yard in a western state would be certain to carry Douglas fir, ponderosa pine, redwood, and spruce.

When ordering lumber it is important to know the standard abbreviations. The common abbreviations are given in *Fig. 10-2*. Familiarity with these abbreviations will help you throughout your woodworking experience. This is useful consumer information, which can save you money when it comes time to make a lumber purchase.

Lumber classifications discussed in the previous unit are important when buying lumber as well. For explanation of such terms as boards, dimension lumber, and timbers, review *Fig. 9-7*.

Other key terms include:

• *Roughdry size.* This is the size of lumber before dressing and at the moisture content specified for sea-

119

soned lumber. Roughdry lumber is slightly larger in thickness and width than minimum-finished dry lumber.

(Following is the exact definition of *roughdry* from the March 1970 revision of American Lumber Standards for Softwood Lumber, set forth by the Department of Commerce, National Bureau of Standards: "The minimum roughdry thickness of finish, common boards, and dimension of sizes 1 or more inches nominal thickness shall not be less than ⅛ inch thicker than the corresponding minimum finished dry thickness, except that 20 percent of a shipment may be not less than ³⁄₃₂ inch thicker than the corresponding minimum-finished dry thickness. The minimum roughdry widths of finish, common strip, boards, and dimension

shall be not less than ⅛ inch wider than the corresponding minimum-finished dry width.")

• *Dressed sizes.* Dressed sizes of lumber, such as siding, *Figs. 10-3 and 10-4*, and finish, flooring, ceiling, partition, and stepping, *Fig. 10-5*, shall equal or exceed the minimum sizes shown in the accompanying charts.

LUMBER SIZES

Softwood lumber is classified as either green or dry. Dry lumber has 19 percent or less moisture and green has moisture in excess of 19 percent. *Fig. 10-6.* All hardwood and most softwood lumber is dried before it is dimensioned (run through a surfacer at the mill). Dressed or surfaced (actual) size is smaller than nominal size.

10-3. NOMINAL AND MINIMUM-DRESSED DRY SIZES OF SIDING AT 19 PERCENT MAXIMUM-MOISTURE CONTENT

(The thicknesses apply to all widths and all widths to all thicknesses)

Item	Thicknesses		Face widths	
	Nominal[1]	Minimum dressed	Nominal	Minimum Dressed
		Inches		*Inches*
Bevel siding	½	⁷⁄₁₆ butt, ³⁄₁₆ tip	4	3½
	⁹⁄₁₆	¹⁵⁄₃₂ butt, ³⁄₁₆ tip	5	4½
	⅝	⁹⁄₁₆ butt, ³⁄₁₆ tip	6	5½
	¾	¹¹⁄₁₆ butt, ³⁄₁₆ tip	8	7¼
	1	¾ butt, ³⁄₁₆ tip	10	9¼
			12	11¼
Bungalow siding	¾	¹¹⁄₁₆ butt, ³⁄₁₆ tip	8	7¼
			10	9¼
			12	11¼
Rustic and drop siding (shiplapped, ⅜-in. lap)	⅝	⁹⁄₁₆	4	3
	1	²³⁄₃₂	5	4
			6	5
Rustic and drop siding (shiplapped, ½-in. lap)	⅝	⁹⁄₁₆	4	2⅞
	1	²³⁄₃₂	5	3⅞
			6	4⅞
			8	6⅝
			10	8⅝
			12	10⅝
Rustic and drop siding (dressed and matched)	⅝	⁹⁄₁₆	4	3⅛
(tongue and groove)	1	²³⁄₃₂	5	4⅛
			6	5⅛
			8	6⅞
			10	8⅞

[1] For nominal thicknesses under 1 inch, the board measure count is based on the nominal surface dimensions (width by length). With the exception of nominal thicknesses under 1 inch, the nominal thickness and widths in this table are the same as the board measure or count sizes.

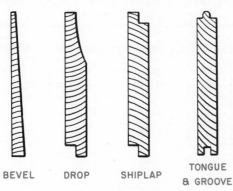

BEVEL   DROP   SHIPLAP   TONGUE & GROOVE

10-4. Common kinds of siding.

Lumber sizes are indicated by the nominal dimensions. For example, a 2″ x 4″ (softwood) that is dried will measure 1½″ x 3½″, while a green 2″x4″ will measure $1\frac{9}{16}$″ x $3\frac{9}{16}$″. Hardwood lumber dimensions are given in dry sizes only. For example, a 1″ hardwood piece, when surfaced, is reduced to $1\frac{3}{16}$″, while the dressed 1″ piece becomes $\frac{25}{32}$″ or ¾″.

In lumber dimensions, the first figure is always the thickness, the second

10-5. NOMINAL AND MINIMUM-DRESSED DRY SIZES OF FINISH, FLOORING, CEILING, PARTITION, AND STEPPING AT 19 PERCENT MAXIMUM-MOISTURE CONTENT

(The thicknesses apply to all widths and all widths to all thicknesses except as modified.)

Item	Thickness		Face Widths	
	Nominal	Minimum dressed	Nominal	Minimum dressed
		Inches		Inches
Finish	⅜	$\frac{5}{16}$	2	1½
	½	$\frac{7}{16}$	3	2½
	⅝	$\frac{9}{16}$	4	3½
	¾	⅝	5	4½
	1	¾	6	5½
	1¼	1	7	6½
	1½	1¼	8	7¼
	1¾	1⅜	9	8¼
	2	1½	10	9¼
	2½	2	11	10¼
	3	2½	12	11¼
	3½	3	14	13¼
	4	3½	16	15¼
Flooring	⅜	$\frac{5}{16}$	2	1⅛
	½	$\frac{7}{16}$	3	2⅛
	⅝	$\frac{9}{16}$	4	3⅛
	1	¾	5	4⅛
	1¼	1	6	5⅛
	1½	1¼		
Ceiling	⅜	$\frac{5}{16}$	3	2⅛
	½	$\frac{7}{16}$	4	3⅛
	⅝	$\frac{9}{16}$	5	4⅛
	¾	$\frac{11}{16}$	6	5⅛
Partition	1	$\frac{23}{32}$	3	2⅛
			4	3⅛
			5	4⅛
			6	5⅛
Stepping	1	¾	8	7¼
	1¼	1	10	9¼
	1½	1¼	12	11¼
	2	1½		

In tongued-and-grooved flooring and in tongued-and-grooved and shiplapped ceiling of $\frac{5}{16}$-inch, $\frac{7}{16}$-inch, and $\frac{9}{16}$-inch dressed thicknesses, the tongue or lap shall be $\frac{3}{16}$-inch wide, with the over-all widths $\frac{3}{16}$-inch wider than the face widths shown in the table above. In all other worked lumber of dressed thicknesses of ⅝-inch to 1¼ inches, the tongue shall be ¼-inch wide or wider in tongued-and-grooved lumber, and the lap ⅜-inch wide or wider in shiplapped lumber, and the over-all widths shall be not less than the dressed face widths shown in the above table plus the width of the tongue or lap.

10-6. NOMINAL AND MINIMUM-DRESSED SIZES OF BOARDS, DIMENSIONS, AND TIMBERS

(The thicknesses apply to all widths and all widths to all thicknesses.)

Item	Thicknesses			Face widths		
	Nominal	Minimum dressed		Nominal	Minimum dressed	
		Dry	Green		Dry	Green
		Inches	Inches		Inches	Inches
Boards	1	¾	²⁵/₃₂	2	1½	1⁹/₁₆
	1¼	1	1¹/₃₂	3	2½	2⁹/₁₆
	1½	1¼	1⁹/₃₂	4	3½	3⁹/₁₆
				5	4½	4⅝
				6	5½	5⅝
				7	6½	6⅝
				8	7¼	7½
				9	8¼	8½
				10	9¼	9½
				11	10¼	10½
				12	11¼	11½
				14	13¼	13½
				16	15¼	15½
Dimension	2	1½	1⁹/₁₆	2	1½	1⁹/₁₆
	2½	2	2¹/₁₆	3	2½	2⁹/₁₆
	3	2½	2⁹/₁₆	4	3½	3⁹/₁₆
	3½	3	3¹/₁₆	5	4½	4⅝
				6	5½	5⅝
				8	7¼	7½
				10	9¼	9½
				12	11¼	11½
				14	13¼	13½
				16	15¼	15½
Dimension	4	3½	3⁹/₁₆	2	1½	1⁹/₁₆
	4½	4	4¹/₁₆	3	2½	2⁹/₁₆
				4	3½	3⁹/₁₆
				5	4½	4⅝
				6	5½	5⅝
				8	7¼	7½
				10	9¼	9½
				12	11¼	11½
				14	....	13½
				16	....	15½
Timbers	5 and thicker.	...	½ off	5 and wider.	...	½ off

10-7. STANDARD THICKNESSES OF SURFACED LUMBER — HARDWOODS

Thickness (Widths vary with Grades)

Nominal (Rough)	Surfaced 1 Side (S1S)	Surfaced 2 Sides (S2S)
⅜″	¼″	³/₁₆″
½″	⅜″	⁵/₁₆″
⅝″	½″	⁷/₁₆″
¾″	⅝″	⁹/₁₆″
1″	⅞″	¹³/₁₆″
1¼″	1⅛″	1¹/₁₆″
1½″	1⅜″	1⁵/₁₆″
2″	1¹³/₁₆″	1¾″
3″	2¹³/₁₆″	2¾″
4″	3¹³/₁₆″	3¾″

the width, and the third the length. *Fig. 10-7* shows both the rough or nominal thickness and the dressed or surfaced thickness and width for hardwood. Softwoods are cut to standard thickness, width, and length. Nominal widths are 4″, 6″, 8″, 10″, and 12″. The standard lengths of softwoods are from 8′ to 20′ increasing at intervals of 2′. Hardwood lumber is generally available in standard thicknesses, but because of its high cost it is cut to whatever widths and lengths are most economical and convenient.

How Lumber is Sold. Most lumber is sold by the board foot. A *board foot* is a piece 1″ thick by 12″ wide by 12″ long. Stock that is less than 1″ thick is figured as 1″. There are three common ways of figuring board feet. These are as follows:

• Board feet equal thickness in inches times width in inches times length in feet divided by 12. For example, a board that measures 2″ by 4″ by 12′ contains 8 board feet. Using the formula above:

$$\text{Bd. Ft.} = \frac{\text{T (inches)} \times \text{W (inches)} \times \text{L (feet)}}{12}$$

$$\text{Bd. Ft.} = \frac{2 \times 4 \times 12}{12} = 8$$

• Board feet equals thickness in inches times width in feet times length in feet. For example, a piece of white pine 2″ thick by 12″ wide by 6′ long would be 12 board feet.

$$\text{Bd. Ft.} = \text{T (inches)} \times \text{W (feet)} \times \text{L (feet)}$$

$$\text{Bd. Ft.} = 2 \times 1 \times 6 = 12$$

• Board feet equals thickness in inches times width in inches times length in inches divided by 144. For example, a board measuring 2″ x 4″ x 7.5′ would contain 5 board feet.

$$\text{Bd. Ft.} = \frac{\text{T} \times \text{W} \times \text{L}}{144} \quad \text{(inches)}$$

$$\text{Bd. Ft.} = \frac{2 \times 4 \times 90}{144}$$

$$= \frac{720}{144} = 5$$

A board under 1″ in thickness is figured as one inch. Remember that there are 144 cubic inches in one board foot. Lumber is sold by the board foot, by the 100 board feet, or by the 1,000 board feet (M). For example, if lumber sells at $450 per (M) it costs $45 for 100 board feet and $.45 for one board foot. In ordering softwood lumber, consider:

• *Quantity*: feet, board measure, number of pieces that are a definite size, and length.

• *Size*: Thickness in inches, nominal width in inches, length in feet.

• *Grade*: as indicated by the correct grading rules.

• *Kind of wood*: southern pine, Douglas fir, etc.

• *Product*: flooring, siding, boards, etc.

• *Condition of seasoning*: green or kiln dried.

• *Surfacing*: rough (rgh), surfaced two sides (S2S), or surfaced four sides (S4S).

• *Grading rules*: Southern Pine Association, Western Pine Association, other.

WRITING HARDWOOD LUMBER SPECIFICATIONS

When ordering hardwood for furniture, specify *quantity, thickness, kind of wood, grade, surface, condition of seasoning,* and *widths and lengths.* Here is a typical order (with explanation added in parentheses).

500 Bd. Ft. (board feet), 1″ *or* ¼ (thickness is expressed in inches or in fractions of an inch), African mahogany, FAS (firsts and seconds, explained in *Fig. 9–6,* page 115), Rgh (rough), KD 5–8% (kiln dried to a

123

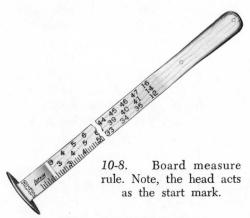

10-8.   Board measure rule. Note, the head acts as the start mark.

specific percentage), RW & RL (random widths and lengths).

Remember these points when ordering:

· Be thorough. Omit nothing important.

· Use standard terms and abbreviations.

· Order lumber rough if a surfacer or planer is available. Otherwise order it surfaced two sides (S2S).

· Indicate the percentage of moisture content, not just "kiln dried."

· If the job permits, order random widths and lengths, as this costs less. *Fig. 9–6* lists minimum dimensions of each grade.

CHECKING DELIVERED LUMBER

After the lumber has been delivered, you should check to make sure you have received the correct species, grade (this may be difficult), and amount. Check the amount as follows:

Board Measure. Board measure is the way of determining the amount of board feet in a piece or a pile of lumber. Sometimes you will be able to calculate this easily. You know, for

example, that for any board 1″ thick and 12″ wide, the number of board feet is the same as the length of the board in feet. If a piece is 1″ thick, 12″ wide, and 8′ long, you know immediately that it contains 8 board feet.

For harder problems, use a measuring device called a *board rule*, sometimes called a *lumberman's board stick. Fig. 10-8* Follow these directions: (1) Determine the length of the board. (2) Place the rule across the width of the board, with the "start" mark exactly even with the left edge of the board. (3) On the rule find the row of figures based on the length of the board. (4) Follow this row to the extreme right edge of the board. The number which appears there indicates board feet.

For instance, suppose a 1″ thick board is 8′ long and 6″ wide. Place the rule across the stock, with the "start" mark lined up with the left edge. Find the row of figures marked *8′ Lengths* and follow it across to the right edge of the board where the number 4 appears. *Fig. 10-9.*

The *Essex board measure table* on the framing or rafter square can also be used to determine board feet quickly. *Fig. 10–10.* A board 12″ wide and 1″ thick will contain the number of board feet equal to the number of linear feet in its length. The figure 12, therefore, on the outer edge, represents a 1″ board 12″ wide. Suppose you are checking a board that is 1″ thick, 12″ wide, and 8′ long. You know immediately that it contains 8 board feet. Look at the column of figures under the 12 on the square until you reach the figure represent-

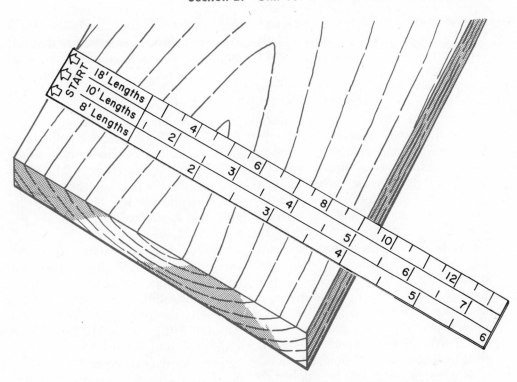

10-9.   Using a board measure rule to find the number of board feet surface measure in a piece of lumber.

ing the length of the board in feet; this gives you the same answer.

Let's take another example. Suppose the board is 8″ wide and 14′ long. You again look under the 12 and move your eye down the column until you reach the figure 14 (the length). Then follow along this line to the left until you reach a point directly under the figure 8 (width in inches) on the edge graduations. Here you find 9 to the left of the cross-line and 4 to the right of the the same line. This tells you there are 9 and $\frac{4}{12}$ (or $9\frac{1}{3}$) board feet in a 1″ board. If the board were 2″ in thickness the total would be twice this amount. If the board is wider than

12″, the answer will be found to the right of the 12″ mark.

In checking the number of board feet in a piece or a pile of lumber, remember these points:

• In tallying random widths and lengths, no record is made of the size of each individual piece. Tallies list only the thickness, the kind of lumber, the grade, and the footage con-

10-10.   Essex board measure table on a framing square.

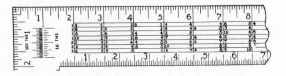

tent of all pieces of a given thickness.

• The board rule measures only the surface area of lumber 1″ thick or thinner, which is actually sold on a square foot basis. Thickness greater than 1″ is measured according to the surface areas and a fraction is added to the total tally. For example, suppose you are measuring $1\frac{1}{4}″$ lumber and you have two pieces, each 5 board feet by surface measure, or a total of 10 board feet. You also have two pieces, each of which has 7 board feet surface measure or a total of 14 board feet. Add these together and you have 24 board feet. Add one quarter for the $1\frac{1}{4}″$ stock and the total is 30 board feet. If the material had been $1\frac{1}{2}″$ thick, 50 per cent more would have been added.

• Don't bother about fractional lengths. Each piece should be added as if it contained a whole number of board feet. For example, pieces falling between $4\frac{1}{2}$ and $5\frac{1}{2}$ on the board rule are recorded as 5. Pieces that fall between $8\frac{1}{2}$ and $9\frac{1}{2}$ are recorded as 9. Pieces that fall directly on the half mark should be dropped to the next lower foot on one and extended to the next higher foot on the next.

• When tallying short length stock, such as walnut cut to 4- and 5-foot lengths, use a double scale. In other words, read 4-foot lengths as 8′, 5-foot lengths as 10′, etc. When the tally has been completed, divide the total by 2.

• Some woods contain odd measurements such as 9 and 11. These off lengths are not shown on a standard board rule, but they can be tallied mentally. For example, if you have a 9-foot length, use the 18 board foot length rule and divide by 2.

• If the board is sawed with a taper, measure at a point one third distant from the narrow end.

Unit 11: PLYWOOD AND VENEERS

Plywood is a most versatile building material. It can be used in nearly every step of home building, in furniture construction, built-ins, cabinets, fixtures, boat building, and for many other commercial purposes. *Figs. 11–1, 2,* and *3.*

DESCRIPTION

Plywood consists of glued wood panels made from layers, or plies, of veneer or veneer and wood. The grain of the layers is at an angle, usually at right angles, to the grain of the other plies. *Fig. 11–4.* The outer plies are called *faces,* or *face* and *back.* The center ply or plies are called the *core.* The plies just under the face and back at right angles are called *crossbands.*

Veneer is a very thin sheet of wood that is sawed, peeled, or sliced from a log. The grain of each veneer sheet or ply runs at right angles to the adjacent ply; the grain of the outer plies always runs in the same direc-

11–1. Both the exterior and interior of this home are of plywood.

11-2. Most built-ins for homes are constructed of plywood.

tion. Softwood plywoods are made entirely of veneer of three, five, or seven plies. Hardwood plywoods may be made entirely of veneer (in which

11-3. Most of the exterior parts of this chest are of plywood construction. Many consumers do not realize that plywood is used in the very best and most expensive construction. They have the mistaken idea that solid wood is better than plywood. The best furniture makers use solid wood for certain structural parts and plywood (which they make themselves) for other parts. Note the specially selected and matched swirl-mahogany-veneered drawer fronts and doors.

11-4. Veneer core plywood construction.

case they are called *veneer core* plywoods), or of veneer bonded to solid or glued-up lumber core, (called *lumber core* plywood). *Fig. 11-5.*

The wood grain and figure pattern of face veneers are determined largely by three things: (1) the part of the tree from which the veneer is cut (crotch, burl, or stump); (2) the method of cutting; and (3) the species of tree (walnut, mahogany, or Douglas fir).

METHODS OF CUTTING

Veneers for plywood vary according to panel thickness, the kind of wood, and the ways the panels are used. For example, a quarter-inch panel of good hardwood has two

11-5. Lumber core plywood.

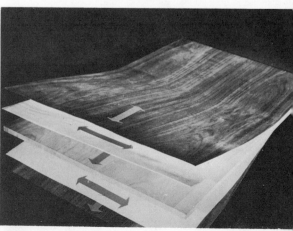

faces of ⅛" veneer, with a core of ¾₆"
veneer. This is slightly more than ¼"
for the three panels.

Veneers for plywood are cut either
on a giant lathe or on a slicer. The
cutting is done by bringing the log
against the razor-sharp blade as the
veneer is peeled or sliced off. There
are three common methods of cutting
veneer for plywood: *rotary cutting,
flat slicing,* and *quarter slicing. Fig.
11–6. Rotary cutting* is the most common. It is used for all fir plywood and
certain types of hardwood plywood.
In this method, a log is placed in a
large lathe. *Fig. 11–7.* When the wood
rotates against the sharp knife, the
veneer peels off the log much the
same as wrapping paper is pulled
from a roll. Rotary-cut veneer has a
wide grain marking because the cutting is done along the arc of the
annual growth rings. *Fig. 11–8.* The
chief advantage of this method is
that it produces wide, long sheets of
veneer. Birch is one of the hardwoods

11–7.   Cutting fir plywood veneer on a
large lathe.

usually cut by the rotary method.
Flat slicing is the method of cutting
veneer from wood much as a potato
is sliced. The log is first sawed into
hexagonal (six-sided) shape and then
split in half. Each half, called a
flitch, is held in the vice-like clamps
of the slicer. The flitch moves up and

11–6.   The three common ways of cutting
veneer: rotary, plain or flat, and quarter
slicing.

11–8.   Note the wide grain markings on
this fir plywood.

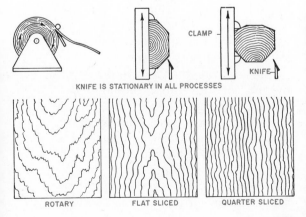

CLAMP

KNIFE

KNIFE IS STATIONARY IN ALL PROCESSES

ROTARY   FLAT SLICED   QUARTER SLICED

129

11-9. Flat slicing the veneer.

down against a sharp blade and the veneer is cut off on the down stroke. *Fig. 11-9.* In flat slicing, the grain pattern is determined by the angle at which the knife cuts through the growth rings. The veneer usually has a striped effect at the edges, with a larger, rather wide grain towards the center. Walnut is one of the hardwoods usually cut by this method. *Quarter slicing* is the most costly method of veneer cutting and is similar to flat slicing. It is done on the same slicing machine. In quarter slicing, however, the hexagonal log is quartered rather than halved before the veneer is cut. Quarter slicing is done on most finer, imported woods on which definite striped effects are desirable. Mahogany is a good example.

PLYWOOD PRODUCTION

All plywood is produced in approximately the following manner:

The outer bark of the log is removed. Then the log or flitch is softened or tenderized in a hot-water or steam bath. (This is not necessary for all species.) Temperatures are controlled according to the kind of wood in order to obtain veneer with the smoothest possible surface.

The logs are then cut into veneer by one of the three methods described above.

Huge steam dryers remove moisture from the wet veneer, after which it is carefully checked for quality and moisture content.

Veneers that have been quarter or flat sliced are trimmed and sorted.

The veneer sheets are put through an edge jointer and permanently bonded together at the edges in a tapeless splicer to make sheets of the required width.

If the plywood panels are to be made with a solid lumber core, called *lumber core plywood,* select kiln-dried lumber is planed and trimmed with smooth uniform surfaces and edges. Then glue is applied to the edges to form the larger panel. If the plywood is to be made of *veneer core plywood,* various pieces of veneer are used.

In assembling the panel, the crossband veneers are put through a glue spreader that distributes the adhesive uniformly on both sides. The kind of adhesive depends on the future use of the plywood. The trend today is to choose some kind of waterproof resin adhesive. Crossbands are then laid with the plies at right angles to the core.

The assembled wood "sandwich" is placed in a giant hot press where the pressure and controlled heat of the metal plates permanently set the adhesive, bonding the layers together into a single, strong panel. *Fig. 11–10.*

After the bonded plywood leaves the press it is carefully trimmed to size with precision equipment and then sanded. In some cases, additional steps produce a pre-finished plywood panel.

Plywood must be manufactured with care to avoid the stresses of shrinking and swelling that cause warping. Most problems can be eliminated when plywood is manufactured by balanced construction. This means that the plies on either side

11–10. Gluing up the plywood. The veneer has been coated with glue and arranged with the grain of each ply at right angles to the one above and below it. These are then placed in a hot press, where the combination of heat and pressure welds the plies together.

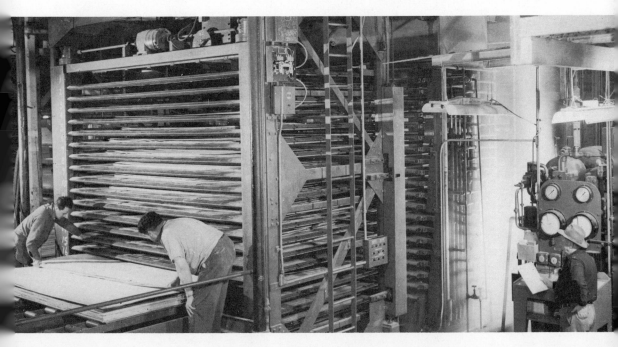

11–11a. Selecting the veneer for fine furniture.

of the core are arranged in pairs. Each pair is composed of two plies that are opposite, similar, and parallel. The greater the thickness of the panel, the more nearly equal are its strength and shrinkage properties both across it and along its length. Also, the greater the number of plies, the greater is the resistance to splitting. For example, a 5-ply, $\frac{3}{8}''$ panel is better than a 3-ply, $\frac{3}{8}''$ panel. With lumber core plywood, the face and back plies may be of different woods, such as a mahogany face and a birch back. However, this sometimes creates a problem; if the back and face of thin, 3-ply panels are different, there can be a good deal of warpng.

Making Plywood in Furniture Manufacture. Furniture manufacturers make their own hardwood lumbercore plywood. The manufacturer buys the raw materials including the stock for the core, crossbands, and veneer. The veneer varies in thickness from

$\frac{1}{60}''$ to $\frac{1}{28}''$. Standard American veneer is $\frac{1}{28}''$ thick. Some companies use $\frac{1}{24}''$ veneer. Those imported from other countries are thinner, usually $\frac{1}{60}''$. *Fig. 11–11a.*

The core is cut from a less expensive material such as poplar or basswood. The pieces are cut to widths from 2″ to 4″ and to the length needed for the furniture piece. The face and edges are surfaced and then the core is glued up. Solid lumber of the same material as the veneer is glued (banded) to the outside edges whenever a molding cut or an irregular surface must be

11–11b. The construction of a plywood door for a cabinet.

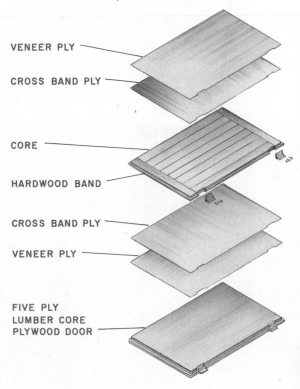

VENEER PLY

CROSS BAND PLY

CORE

HARDWOOD BAND

CROSS BAND PLY

VENEER PLY

FIVE PLY
LUMBER CORE
PLYWOOD DOOR

machined. *Fig. 11–11b.* After the core is dry, it is planed to thickness. For example, if the final plywood is to be ¾″ thick, the stock will be surfaced to about ½″ to ⁹⁄₁₆″. Crossbanded material should be cut slightly larger than is actually needed. It is made of stock ½₀″ to ⅛″ thick and is cut especially for this purpose. A very important step before the face veneers are added is the *matching*, that is, selecting plies that are nearly identical in thickness, moisture content at time of gluing, and grain direction. The art of matching veneers has been developed to a high degree of perfection. Because face veneers are thin, adjacent sheets have similar grains or figure marks. By utilizing this duplication of pattern, all sorts of designs are possible.

After the face veneers for the particular furniture piece have been chosen, they are carefully re-dried. Depending on design, the veneers are matched in one of several ways: *Fig. 11–12.*

• In the *book match*, two adjacent sheets of veneer are opened up like a book and then taped side to side.

11–12b.   Soft diamond.

• *End match* is similar to book match except that the ends, not the sides, of the two sheets of veneer are joined.

• Other kinds of matching include *diamond match, reverse diamond, slip,* and various other effects. In many cases the veneer cutter works out a design in two or more kinds of veneer. *Fig. 11–13a.* This is hand cut and matched before it is added to the plywood. A good illustration is the table shown in *Fig. 11–13b.* After the pieces have been cut, the edges must be smoothed, then glued and fastened with long masking tape to

11–12.   Common methods of matching veneers: *a.* Book matched.

11–12c.   Slip matched.

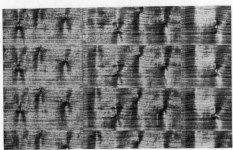

11-13a. Matching the veneer for the front of a chest.

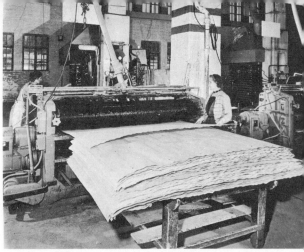

11-14a. Gluing the surface of the veneer.

hold them in place until the veneer is added to the plywood. If the veneer is not wide enough, two or more pieces are taped together.

The final step is to apply glue to the core, crossband, and one face of the veneer. *Fig. 11-14a.* Plywood, you remember, consists of a core, two pieces of crossbanding material, the face veneer, and the back veneer. The whole unit is clamped in a press and cured. *Fig. 11-14b.*

11-13b. Notice the beautiful veneer matching on the top of this table. Designs such as this are cut from contrasting veneers.

Veneering in the School Shop. You can follow the procedure of the furniture manufacturer in making your own lumber-core plywood. There are many materials available that make a good ready-made core, requiring only the face and back veneer. These materials include fir plywood and hardboard. Particle board, which is also in common use, usually requires crossbands to avoid "telegraphing" of the particle surface through the veneer. If you do not wish to use these materials as a core you can

11-14b. Plywood clamped in a batch press.

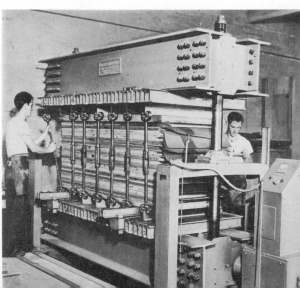

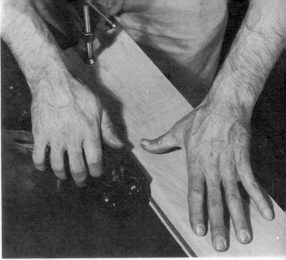

11-15. Veneering in the school shop. *a.* Matching the grain.

11-15b. Planing.

make or purchase the lumber core. You can also purchase the crossbanding and the veneer. Crossbanding stock is available in thicknesses of ¹⁄₂₀″, ¹⁄₁₀″, and ⅛″. Standard American veneers, you will remember, are ¹⁄₂₈″ thick and are sold by the square foot. They are available in a wide variety of American and foreign hardwoods. To do the veneering follow these easy steps:

1. Select the veneer that you will use for the face surface. Match the grain, using as many pieces as you need to cover the panel. Always allow a little extra for trimming. You must also have a back veneer, but this does not have to be matched as carefully. *Fig. 11–15a.*

2. Clamp the two adjoining pieces together between straight hardwood stock, and plane the edges true. This can be done with a hand plane or on the jointer. Repeat for each two adjoining pieces of veneer. *Fig. 11–15b.*

3. Place the pieces on a flat table and fasten them together with masking tape. Reverse the sheet, and

check for any cracks. If you see any imperfections, take the joint apart and rework it until you have a perfect joint. Then retape the front surface. *Fig. 11–15c.*

4. Turn the sheet over on the bench or table. Bend open the joints, and edge-glue the pieces together. *Fig. 11–15d.* Use a good, white glue. Wipe off the excess glue, and then tape the back side of the joints together. *Fig. 11–15e.* Allow the sheet of veneer to dry overnight. Remove the masking tape from the back side of the veneer.

11-15c. Taping the front.

135

11–15d. Gluing the edges.

5. If the veneer is to be glued directly to the plywood, particle board, or hardboard, then apply contact cement to both surfaces of the core stock and one surface of both pieces of veneer. Place the veneer over the core stock. Use a veneer roller to roll the surface both with and across the grain. *Fig. 11–15f.* Repeat on both surfaces. Remove the masking tape and go over the surface again with the roller.

6. If the plywood is to consist of a lumber core, crossbands, and veneers, then you will need a small veneer press. *Fig. 11–16.* For this job

any good grade of glue can be used. (See Unit 35.) Cover both surfaces of the core, crossbanding material, and one surface of the veneer. Assemble the plywood, making sure that each layer is at right angles to the next. Place a sheet of wax paper in the press, then the plywood, then another sheet of wax paper, and finally a piece of heavy plywood, slightly larger than the piece being glued. Apply even pressure and then allow to dry overnight.

ADVANTAGES OF PLYWOOD

• Plywood is *strong* because it utilizes good wood, but more important, because of the method of construction. Solid wood is relatively strong along the grain but weaker across it; in plywood, the plies are crossbanded. When they are placed with opposing grain directions, this natural strength is applied to both length and breadth.

• Plywood *retains its dimensions.* Wood tends to shrink across grain. In plywood, this is minimized because of the crossbanding.

11–15e. Taping the back.

11–15f. Using a veneer roller.

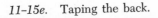

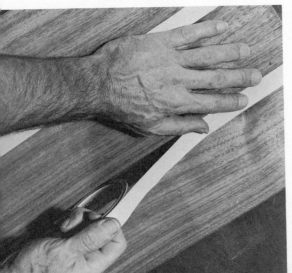

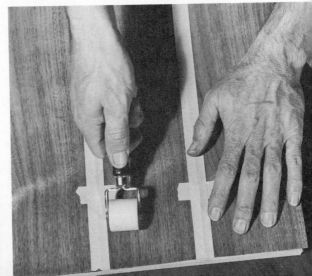

• It has a *smooth surface.* In most cases plywood surfaces are pre-sanded.

• It is *easy to use* and saves time because the large, uniform sheets can be cut to size or shape before they are installed.

• It *can be bent* around curved surfaces. The radius of the curve to which plywood can be bent is determined by the thickness. *Fig. 11–17,* shows the radius to which plywood can be bent dry. If waterproof glue has been used and the plywood is soaked or steamed, the bending radius can be reduced as much as one half.

Limitations. A strip of plywood is not as strong in tension or compression as a strip of solid wood of the same size. This should be apparent when you recall that the plies which run at right angles to the direction of stress add only a fraction to the tension and compression strength, as compared to a similar area of solid wood. Plywood strength is about equal in all directions because every

11–16. A small, shop-made veneer press.

11–17. BENDING PROPERTIES

The following table indicates radii to which birch and mahogany veneer core plywood panels can be bent in a dry condition. (Source: "Plywood" by Louis H. Meyer.) Values are for dry bending. Type I (waterproof) panels soaked or steamed average approximately 50% greater flexibility.

	Thickness	Lengthwise of panel	Crosswise of panel
Birch	1/16″	7.6″	4.1″
(Poplar core)	1/8″	13.3″	8.3″
	1/4″	28.0″	20.9″
	3/8″	39.6″	34.4″
Mahogany	1/16″	5.9″	4.1″
(Poplar core	1/8″	10.2″	8.3″
crossband)	1/4″	21.5″	20.9″
	3/8″	30.3″	34.4″

other ply is at right angles. While plywood, weight for weight, is stronger than steel, it is not as strong under certain conditions as a piece of solid wood.

GRADE STANDARDS

Hardwood Plywood

Faces and Backs

PREMIUM GRADE. Includes special selections and types (produced by individual mills), architectural veneers, and matched grain panels for special uses.

GOOD GRADE. For natural finish; face of tight, smoothly cut veneer. If matched, joints do not have sharp contrasts in color and grain.

SOUND GRADE. For smooth paint surfaces; face is free from open defects. May show stains, streaks. Veneer not matched for grain and color.

UTILITY GRADE. Discoloration, knotholes up to 3/4″ diameter, minor open joints, small areas of rough grain, but no shake or similar defects.

137

BACKING GRADE. Unselected for grain or color. Limited knotholes and splits, as detailed in the grading standards. Small defects permitted, not to impair panel strength.

Types

TYPE I. Fully waterproof bond, to withstand full weather exposure.

TYPE II. Weather-resistant bond, to retain practically all of its strength when occasionally subjected to a thorough wetting and drying.

TYPE III. Two-cycle bond, suitable for use where panels will not be subjected to water, continuous dampness, or continuous high humidity.

Dimensions

Panels are commonly available in widths from 24″ to 48″ in 6″ breaks, and in lengths from 36″ to 96″ in 12″ breaks. Wider panels and lengths of 10′ to 12′ are available from many distribution warehouses.

Thickness

Veneer core construction panels in plies of 3, 5, 7, and 9 are generally available in the following thicknesses:

$$3 \text{ ply}-\tfrac{1}{8}″, \tfrac{3}{16}″, \tfrac{1}{4}″$$
$$5 \text{ ply}-\tfrac{5}{16}″, \tfrac{3}{8}″, \tfrac{1}{2}″$$
$$5 \text{ and } 7 \text{ ply}-\tfrac{5}{8}″$$
$$7 \text{ and } 9 \text{ ply}-\tfrac{3}{4}″$$

Unless otherwise stated, all hardwood plywood panels are sanded both sides.

Core Constructions

VENEER CORE construction is preferred for Type I plywood, for bending and molding, exterior purposes or where subjected to moisture. The number of plies required depends on how the panel will be used; as a general rule, the more plies, the more stable the panel will be and the more uniform its strength.

LUMBER CORE construction is generally used for furniture, built-ins, store fixtures, and when edge treatment of wood is desired, or where butt hinges are used. The core is made of narrow solid wood strips arranged to equalize stress and edge-glued together. Panels with face wood banded on edges are available.

Checklist

Does your order show these specifications?

1. Number of pieces.
2. Width, length, and thickness (finished).
3. Number of plies.
4. Core construction (lumber or veneer).
5. Species of wood.
6. Grade.
7. Type (adhesive requirement).

Softwood Plywood

Softwood plywood is manufactured in accordance with federal specifications. (*Product Standard PS-1-66 for Softwood Plywoods — Construction and Industrial* is the title of the regulation which governs this process.) Two grading systems are applied to plywoods. *Appearance grades* are based on how a piece of plywood looks. This is important when one or both sides will be exposed to view. *Fig. 11-18. Engineered grades* are based more on such properties as strength and moisture resistance. *Fig. 11-19.* Grade markings on backs and edges make it easy to identify the various grades of plywood. *Figs. 11-20 and 11-21.* Appearance grades are largely deter-

Use these symbols when you specify plywood	Description and Most Common Uses	Typical Grade-trademarks (2)	Veneer Grade			Most Common Thickness (inch) (3)						
			Face	Back	Inner Plys	1/4	5/16	3/8	1/2	5/8	3/4	1
Interior Type												
N-N, N-A, N-B, N-D INT-DFPA	Natural finish cabinet quality. One or both sides, select all heartwood or all sapwood veneer. For furniture having a natural finish, cabinet doors, built-ins. Use N-D for natural finish paneling. Special order items.	N-N · G-1 · INT-DFPA · PS 1-66 ; N-A · G-2 · INT-DFPA · PS 1-66	N	N,A B or D	C or D	■					■	
A-A INT-DFPA	For interior applications where both sides will be on view. Built-ins, cabinets, furniture and partitions. Face is smooth and suitable for painting.	A-A · G-3 · INT-DFPA · PS 1-66	A	A	D	■		■	■	■	■	■
A-B INT-DFPA	For uses similar to Interior A-A but where the appearance of one side is less important and two smooth solid surfaces are necessary.	A-B · G-4 · INT-DFPA · PS 1-66	A	B	D	■		■	■	■	■	■
A-D INT-DFPA	For interior uses where the appearance of only one side is important. Paneling, built-ins, shelving, partitions and flow racks.	A-D GROUP 1 INTERIOR	A	D	D	■		■	■	■	■	■
B-B INT-DFPA	Interior utility panel used where two smooth sides are desired. Permits circular plugs. Paintable.	B-B · G-3 · INT-DFPA · PS 1-66	B	B	D	■		■	■	■	■	■
B-D INT-DFPA	Interior utility panel for use where one smooth side is required. Good for backing, sides or built-ins. Industry: shelving, slip sheets, separator boards and bins.	B-D GROUP 3 INTERIOR	B	D	D	■		■	■	■	■	
DECORATIVE PANELS	Rough-sawn, brushed, grooved or striated faces. Good for interior accent walls, built-ins, counter facing, displays and exhibits.	DECORATIVE · B-D · G-1 · INT-DFPA	C or btr.	D	D		■	■	■			
PLYRON INT-DFPA	Hardboard face on both sides. For counter tops, shelving, cabinet doors, flooring. Hardboard faces may be tempered, untempered, smooth or screened.	PLYRON · INT-DFPA			C & D				■	■	■	
Exterior Type												
A-A EXT-DFPA (4)	Use where the appearance of both sides is important. Fences, built-ins, signs, boats, cabinets, commercial refrigerators, shipping containers, tote boxes, tanks and ducts.	A-A · G-4 · EXT-DFPA · PS 1-66	A	A	C	■		■	■	■	■	■
A-B EXT-DFPA (4)	For use similar to A-A EXT panels but where the appearance of one side is less important.	A-B · G-1 · EXT-DFPA · PS 1-66	A	B	C	■		■	■	■	■	■
A-C EXT-DFPA (4)	Exterior use where the appearance of only one side is important. Sidings, soffits, fences, structural uses, boxcar and truck lining and farm buildings. Tanks, trays, commercial refrigerators.	A-C GROUP 2 EXTERIOR	A	C	C	■		■	■	■	■	■
B-B EXT-DFPA (4)	An outdoor utility panel with solid paintable faces for uses where higher quality is not necessary.	B-B · G-1 · EXT-DFPA · PS 1-66	B	B	C	■		■	■	■	■	■
B-C EXT-DFPA (4)	An outdoor utility panel for farm service and work buildings, box car and truck linings, containers, tanks, agricultural equipment.	B-C GROUP 3 EXTERIOR	B	C	C	■		■	■	■	■	■
HDO EXT-DFPA (4)	Exterior type High Density Overlay plywood with hard, semi-opaque resin-fiber surface. Abrasion resistant. Painting not ordinarily required. For concrete forms, signs, acid tanks, cabinets, counter tops.	HDO · A-A · G-1 · EXT-DFPA · PS 1-66	A or B	A or B	C Plugged			■	■	■	■	
MDO EXT-DFPA (4)	Exterior type Medium Density Overlay with smooth, opaque resin-fiber overlay heat-fused to one or both panel faces. Ideal base for paint. Highly recommended for siding and other outdoor applications. Also good for built-ins, signs and displays.	MDO · B-B · G-2 · EXT-DFPA · PS 1-66	B	B or C	C			■	■	■	■	
303 SPECIAL SIDING EXT-DFPA	Grade designation covers proprietary plywood products for exterior siding, fencing, etc., with special surface treatment such as V-groove, channel groove, striated, brushed, rough sawn.	303 SIDING 16 o c GROUP 4 EXTERIOR	B or btr.	C	C			■	■	■		
T 1-11 EXT-DFPA	Exterior type, sanded or unsanded, shiplapped edges with parallel grooves 1/4″ deep. 3/8″ wide. Grooves 2″ or 4″ o.c. Available in 8′ and 10′ lengths and MD Overlay. For siding and accent paneling.	T1-11 GROUP 1 EXTERIOR	C or btr.	C	C					■		
PLYRON EXT-DFPA	Exterior panel surfaced both sides with hardboard for use in exterior applications. Faces are tempered, smooth or screened.	PLYRON · EXT-DFPA			C				■	■	■	
MARINE EXT-DFPA	Exterior type plywood made only with Douglas fir or Western larch. Special solid jointed core construction. Subject to special limitations on core gaps and number of face repairs. Ideal for boat hulls. Also available with overlaid faces.	MARINE · A-A · EXT-DFPA · PS 1-66	A or B	A or B	B	■		■	■	■	■	■
SPECIAL EXTERIOR	Premium Exterior panel similar to Marine grade but permits any species covered under PS 1-66.	A-A · G-2 · SPECIAL · EXT-DFPA · PS 1-66	A or B	A or B	B	■		■	■	■	■	■

Notes: (1) Sanded both sides except where decorative or other surfaces specified. (2) Available in Group 1, 2, 3, or 4 unless otherwise noted. (3) Standard 4 x 8 panel sizes, other sizes available. (4) Also available in Structural I (face, back, and inner plies limited to Group 1 species).

11-18.   Grade-use guide for appearance grades of plywood.[1]

Interior/Exterior Type	Use these symbols when you specify plywood (1)(2)	Description and Most Common Uses	Typical Grade-trademarks	Veneer Grade			Most Common Thickness (inch) (3)							
				Face	Back	Inner Plys	1/4	5/16	3/8	1/2	5/8	3/4	7/8	1-1/8
Interior Type	STANDARD INT-DFPA (4)	Unsanded Interior sheathing grade for floors, walls and roofs. Limited exposure crates, bins, containers and pallets.	STANDARD 32/16 DFPA INTERIOR	C	D	D		■	■	■	■	■	■	
	STANDARD INT-DFPA (4) (with Exterior glue)	Same as Standard sheathing but has Exterior glue. For construction where unusual moisture conditions may be encountered. Often used for pallets, crates, bins, etc. that may be exposed to the weather.	STANDARD 32/16 DFPA INTERIOR EXTERIOR GLUE	C	D	D		■	■	■	■	■	■	
	STRUCTURAL I and STRUCTURAL II INT-DFPA	Unsanded structural grades where plywood strength properties are of maximum importance. Structural diaphragms, box beams, gusset plates, stressed skin panels. Also for containers, pallets, bins. Made only with exterior glue. Structural I limited to Group 1 species for face, back and inner plys. Structural II permits Group 1, 2, or 3 species.	STRUCTURAL I 32/16 DFPA INTERIOR EXTERIOR GLUE	C	D	D			■	■	■	■	■	
	UNDERLAYMENT INT-DFPA (4)	For underlayment or combination subfloor-underlayment under resilient floor coverings, carpeting. Used in homes, apartments, mobile homes, commercial buildings. Ply beneath face is C or better veneer. Sanded or touch-sanded as specified.	UNDERLAYMENT GROUP 1 DFPA INTERIOR	C Plugged	D	C & D	■		■	■	■	■		
	C-D PLUGGED INT-DFPA (4)	For utility built-ins, backing for wall and ceiling tile. Not a substitute for Underlayment. Ply beneath face permits D grade veneer. Also for cable reels, walkways, separator boards. Unsanded or touch-sanded as specified.	C-D PLUGGED GROUP 2 DFPA INTERIOR	C Plugged	D	D		■	■	■	■	■	■	
	2-4-1 INT-DFPA (5)	Combination subfloor-underlayment. Quality base for resilient floor coverings, carpeting, wood strip flooring. Use 2-4-1 with Exterior glue in areas subject to excessive moisture. Unsanded or touch-sanded as specified.	2-4-1 GROUP 2 DFPA INTERIOR	C Plugged	D	C & D								■
Exterior Type	C-C EXT-DFPA (4)	Unsanded grade with waterproof bond for subflooring and roof decking, siding on service and farm buildings. Backing, crating, pallets, pallet bins, cable reels.	C-C 32/16 DFPA EXTERIOR	C	C	C		■	■	■	■	■	■	
	C-C PLUGGED EXT-DFPA (4)	Use as a base for resilient floors and tile backing where unusual moisture conditions exist. For refrigerated or controlled atmosphere rooms. Also for pallets, fruit pallet bins, reusable cargo containers, tanks and boxcar and truck floors and linings. Sanded or touch-sanded as specified.	C-C PLUGGED GROUP 4 DFPA EXTERIOR	C Plugged	C	C	■		■	■	■	■	■	
	STRUCTURAL I C-C EXT-DFPA	For engineered applications in construction and industry where full Exterior type panels made with all Group 1 woods are required. Unsanded.	STRUCTURAL I C-C 32/16 DFPA EXTERIOR	C	C	C		■	■	■	■	■	■	
	PLYFORM CLASS I & II B-B EXT-DFPA	Concrete form grades with high re-use factor. Sanded both sides. Edge-sealed and mill-oiled unless otherwise specified. Special restrictions on species. Also available in HDO.	B-B PLYFORM CLASS I DFPA EXTERIOR	B	B	C					■	■		

Notes:

(1) All Interior grades shown also available with exterior glue.
(2) All grades except Plyform available tongue and grooved in panels 1/2" and thicker.
(3) Panels are standard 4x8-foot size. Other sizes available.
(4) Available in Group 1, 2, 3 or 4.
(5) Available in Group 1, 2, or 3 only.

11-19. Grade-use guide for engineered grades of plywood.

mined by the grade of veneer used for the face and back of the panel. *Fig. 11-22.* Veneer grade and type of glue are important in determining engineered grades.

Type. Plywood is manufactured in two types — *Exterior,* with 100 percent waterproof glue, and *Interior,* with highly moisture-resistant glue. Veneers in inner plies of Interior type plywood may be of lower grade than those in Exterior type. For all applications that will be exposed to the weather, Exterior type should be used. Although Interior type plywood does not have a permanently waterproof bond, it may be used any place where it will not subject to continuing moisture or extreme humidity.

Group. Plywood is manufactured

140

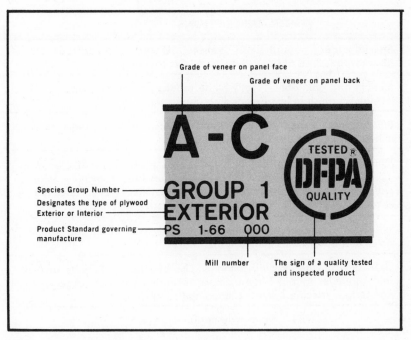

11-20. Typical back-stamp.

11-21. Typical edge-mark.

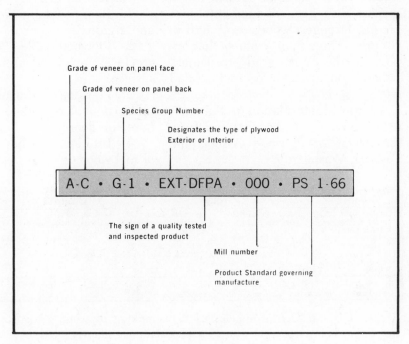

VENEER DESCRIPTIONS	
N	Special order "natural finish" veneer. Selected all heartwood or all sapwood. Free of open defects. Allows some repairs.
A	Smooth and paintable. Neatly made repairs permissible. Also used for natural finish in less demanding applications.
B	Solid surface veneer. Circular repair plugs and tight knots permitted. Can be painted.
C	Minimum veneer permitted in Exterior type plywood. Knotholes to 1″. (Occasionally knotholes ½″-larger permitted providing total width of all knots and knotholes within a specified section does not exceed certain limits.) Limited splits permitted.
C plugged	Improved C veneer with splits limited to ⅛″ in width and knotholes and borer holes limited to ¼″ by ½″.
D	Used only in Interior type for inner plys and backs. Permits knots and knotholes to 2½″ in maximum dimension and ½″ larger under certain specified limits. Limited splits permitted.

11-22. Veneer descriptions.

from some 30 different species of wood. On the basis of stiffness these species have been divided into four groups. Strongest woods are found in Group I. The *Group Number* that appears in the DFPA grade-trademark is based on species used in face and back. *Fig. 11-23.*

Additional information on the engineered grades can be obtained from the American Plywood Association, Tacoma, Washington.

Uses of Softwood Plywood in Home Construction. *Fig. 11-24.*

1. Roof decking adds strength and rigidity.

2. Plywood gable ends and soffits create a smooth, clean, easy-to-paint surface.

3. Plywood subfloors and the underlayment provide a firm, smooth base for flooring.

4. Interior walls have the warmth of real wood.

Group 1	Group 2	Group 3	Group 4
Douglas fir 1	Cedar, Port Orford	Hemlock, Western	Cedar
Larch, Western	Douglas fir 2	Lauan	Incense
Pine, Southern	Fir	Red	Western red
Loblolly	California red	White	Fir, subalpine
Longleaf	Grand	Pine, Western white	Pine, sugar
Shortleaf	Noble	Spruce, Sitka	Poplar, Western
Slash	Pacific Silver		Spruce, Engelmann
Tanoak	White		
Douglas fir 1 — Washington, Oregon, California, Idaho, Montana, Wyoming, British Columbia, Alberta.			
Douglas fir 2 — Nevada, Utah, Colorado, Arizona, New Mexico.			

11-23. Classification of species used in making plywood, according to strength. Strongest woods are in Group 1.

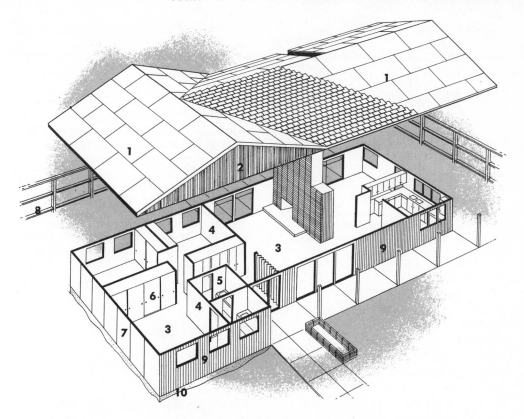

11-24. Use of plywood in home construction, as explained in numbered paragraphs in the text.

5. Plywood gives a smooth, flat, and durable base for tile, cork, and decorative walls.

6. Plywood built-ins can be planned for beauty, convenience, and need.

7. Sheathing produces walls that are warm, strong, and rigid.

8. Plywood fences, windbreaks, and patio screens provide privacy and comfort.

9. Plywood exteriors are smart and modern, fitting any home styling.

10. Plywood used for concrete forms can be re-used for sheathing.

WORKING WITH PLYWOOD

Storage to Avoid Warpage. The best method of storing plywood is to lay the sheets flat. If this is not possible, they should be stored on edge with the sheets supported in a vertical position. Never lay plywood at an angle, especially the thinner panels, as it will warp.

Cutting Plywood to Avoid Splintered Edges. When hand sawing, always place plywood with the good face up and use a saw that has at least 10 to

143

11–25. Notice the low angle of the saw. This reduces splitting out the underside. If you put a piece of scrap lumber underneath, and saw it along with the plywood, you will find it easier to keep the saw at the correct angle.

15 points to the inch. *Fig. 11–25.* Make sure that the panel is supported firmly so it will not sag. Hold the saw at a low angle when cutting and, if possible, place a piece of scrap stock underneath. When using the circular saw, install a sharp combination blade or one with fine teeth. The blade should be adjusted so that the teeth just clear the top of

11–26. A power hand saw should be used with the good side down. Tack a strip of scrap lumber to the top of each sawhorse and you can saw right through it without damaging the horse.

the stock. Always place the plywood on the table saw with the good side up. When cutting with a portable, power handsaw, place the good face down. *Fig. 11–26.*

Selecting the Correct Type of Plywood. Never attempt to use interior plywood for exteriors. This is especially important when making furniture and in home construction. Excessive dampness or moisture will cause the plies to separate.

Planing Ply Edges. It is seldom necessary to plane the edges of plywood, but when it must be done, always work from both ends toward the center. This prevents any tearing out of the plies at the end of the cut. *Fig. 11–27.* Use a plane with a sharp blade and take shallow cuts. When using a jointer, adjust it to a very thin cut.

Treating the Edges of Plywood. There are several ways to finish the edges of plywood. The most common is to use an edge-banding material of the same veneer as the face. In some cases this material has an

11–27. Planing the plywood edges.

adhesive on it; all that is required is to peel off the backing paper and apply the edge banding to the plywood edges. In other cases it is necessary to use a contact cement since some edge bands have fabric backing but no adhesive. Laminated plastic materials may also be applied with contact cement to the edges of tables. *Fig. 11–28.* Some of the more common edge treatments are shown in *Fig. 11–29.* If plywood is to be painted, the edge-end grain can be filled with wood putty.

Using Nails and Screws in Plywood. Nails or screws do not hold well in the edge of plywood. It is important to remember this, especially when attaching hinges. Whenever possible, hinges for plywood doors should be the kind that attach to the face surface rather than to the edge.

When nailing plywood, always choose nail size in terms of panel thickness. Nails should be selected as follows: for $\frac{3}{4}''$ plywood, 6d casing nails or 6d finishing nails; for $\frac{5}{8}''$, 6d or 8d finishing nails; for $\frac{1}{2}''$, 4d or 6d; for $\frac{3}{8}''$, 3d or 4d; and for $\frac{1}{4}''$ use $\frac{3}{4}''$ or

11–28.   Applying a laminated plastic surface to the edges of tables. Apply to edges first, then to the counter or table top. A thicker, more massive effect can be obtained by nailing a 1″ by 1$\frac{1}{4}$″ stringer all around underneath the edge.

1″ brads. For very careful installations, pre-drill to keep the nails from splitting out at the edge. *Fig. 11–30.* The drill should be slightly smaller in diameter than the nail. Space nails about six inches apart for most work. Closer spacing may be necessary only when nailing thin plywood to avoid buckling between the joints. Nails and glue together produce a strong joint. Flathead wood screws are needed

11–29a and b.   Other methods of treating the edges of plywood.

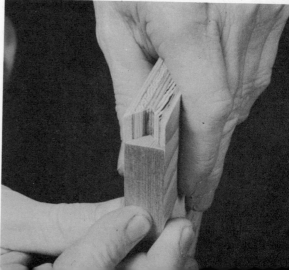

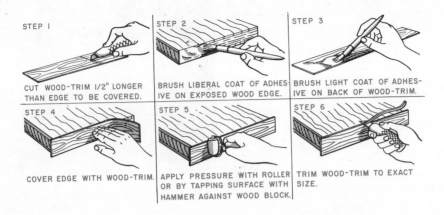

STEP 1	STEP 2	STEP 3
CUT WOOD-TRIM 1/2" LONGER THAN EDGE TO BE COVERED.	BRUSH LIBERAL COAT OF ADHESIVE ON EXPOSED WOOD EDGE.	BRUSH LIGHT COAT OF ADHESIVE ON BACK OF WOOD-TRIM.
STEP 4	STEP 5	STEP 6
COVER EDGE WITH WOOD-TRIM.	APPLY PRESSURE WITH ROLLER OR BY TAPPING SURFACE WITH HAMMER AGAINST WOOD BLOCK.	TRIM WOOD-TRIM TO EXACT SIZE.

11-29c. Gluing thin veneer on the edge of plywood.

when nails will not provide adequate holding power. Glue should also be used whenever possible.

The following gives plywood thicknesses, diameter, and the length of the smallest screws recommended: (Use longer screws when the work permits).

$\frac{3}{4}$" plywood—No. 8—$1\frac{1}{2}$"
$\frac{5}{8}$" plywood—No. 8—$1\frac{1}{4}$"
$\frac{1}{2}$" plywood—No. 6—$1\frac{1}{4}$"
$\frac{3}{8}$" plywood—No. 6—1"
$\frac{1}{4}$" plywood—No. 4—$\frac{3}{4}$"

11-30. Nailing plywood.

Screws or nails should be countersunk and the holes filled with wood dough, putty, or plugs. *Fig. 11-31.* Apply filler until it is slightly higher than the plywood surface and then sand it level after it is dry.

Drilling Plywood. If the back side of plywood is going to show, chipped

11-31. Covering the heads of screws or nails.

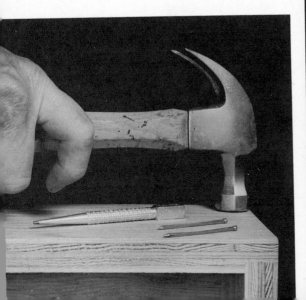

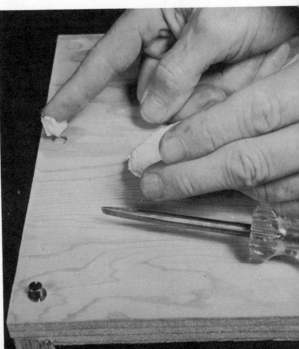

11–32. Butt joints like the one at the left are simple to make. For thinner panels, install a reinforcing block (shown at right) or nailing strip to make a stronger joint. In both cases, glue will make the joint many times stronger than if it were made with nails and screws alone.

11–33. Rabbet joints are neat and strong. Notice the dado joint for installing shelves.

edges can be eliminated by placing a wood block under the back when drilling.

Selection of the Correct Kind of Corner Joints. Because of the construction of plywood, it is extremely important to select the correct kind of corner joint both for strength and appearance. For elementary construction in which the surfaces are to be painted, butt joints can be used. Frame construction with butt joints makes it possible to use thinner plywood. *Fig. 11–32.* Rabbet joints are simple to make and are excellent for many types of drawers, buffets, chests, or cupboards. *Fig. 11–33.* The only problem is that the

plies show where the face surfaces meet. One method of eliminating this is to cut the rabbet from one piece of the plywood and then to cut the entire stock away from the other member, leaving only the face veneer which overlaps the second member. The best joint for plywood corners is the miter joint or some adaptation of it. The more difficult miter joints are the rabbet miter and lock miter. See Unit 34.

Chipping of the Face Veneer. In working plywood, it is important not to chip off the expensive face veneer, especially in hardwoods. This can happen at an exposed edge or corner. After stock is cut, the face corners can be protected by fastening tape to them during the construction process.

147

11–34. Here is a good example of the excellent furniture that can be made of fir plywood.

Care in Sanding. Since most good face veneers are only ⅟₂₈″ thick, it is very important not to sand the surface too much. *Fig. 11–34.* Good hardwood plywoods come with a super-fine sanded surface to which a finish can be applied directly. The greatest care in sanding must be taken when plywood is used in combination with solid lumber. It is easy to over-sand plywood surfaces, especially with a portable or stationary belt sander.

Removing Nails and Screws. Plywood resists splitting much more than ordinary woods; therefore nails and screws can be fastened close to the edges. Plywood has equal strength both along and across the sheet. It also resists splitting because of cross-band construction. In removing nails from plywood, pull straight out rather than at an angle. You may splinter the outside ply if you pull or draw out the nails at an angle.

Unit 12: PROCESSED-WOOD AND PLASTIC MATERIALS

Two man-made materials used extensively in all kinds of wood construction are hardboard and particle board. Both of these materials are unlike any other in their characteristics and uses.

HARDBOARD

Hardboard is an all-wood panel manufactured from wood fibers. Logs are cut into small wood chips which are reduced to fibers by steam or a mechanical process. These fibers are refined (*Fig. 12–1*) and then compressed under heat and pressure in giant presses to produce a sturdy, quality building material.

Some of the advantages of hardboard are these: exceptional strength; superior wear resistance; does not split, crack, or splinter; high abrasive resistance; permanent resistance to moisture; easy to work with ordinary tools; easy to fasten and bend.

Hardboard has many uses, both in the interior and exterior of new and remodeled homes, for such things as walls, ceilings, doors, siding, partitions, and built-ins. *Fig. 12–2*. In furniture manufacture, hardboard is excellent for door and drawer parts, table tops, and for the backs of bookcases, cabinets, and chests. *Fig. 12–3*.

Hardboard is also used in the manufacture of automobiles, house trailers, boats, airplanes, and buses. *Fig. 12–4*. In business and industry, it is used for signs, displays, partitions, fixtures, and countless other purposes.

Kinds of Hardboard. Hardboard is made in two types: standard (Type I) and tempered or treated (Type II). *Fig. 12–5*. Standard hardboard is divided into two classes on the basis of strength. Class one has greater strength than class two. Both can be used where there will be no unusually hard wear or extreme humidity. Tempered or treated hardboard is stronger than standard because it has been impregnated with a special tempering compound and baked to increase its strength. It has high resistance to abrasion and to changes in temperature and humidity. It is designed for all weather exterior, interior, and special industrial uses. Some tempered hardboards are made with the addition

149

12-1. Steps in the

1. LOG HANDLING

2. DEFIBERING

3. REFINING

4. FORMING THE MAT

Manufacture of Hardboard

1. Logs are conveyed from storage yards to huge chippers which reduce the wood to clean, uniformly sized chips.
2. The chips are then reduced to individual wood fibers by either the steam or the mechanical defibering processes.
3. Fibers are put through certain mechanical processes varying with the method of manufacture, and small amounts of chemicals may be added to enhance the resulting board properties.
4. The fibers are interlocked in the felter into a continuous mat and compressed by heavy rollers.
5. Lengths of mat, or "wetlap," are fed into multiple presses where heat and pressure produce the thin, hard, dry board sheets.
6. Leaving the press, moisture is added to the board in a humidifier to stabilize it to surrounding atmospheric conditions.
7. The board is trimmed to standard specified dimensions, wrapped in convenient packages, and readied for shipment.

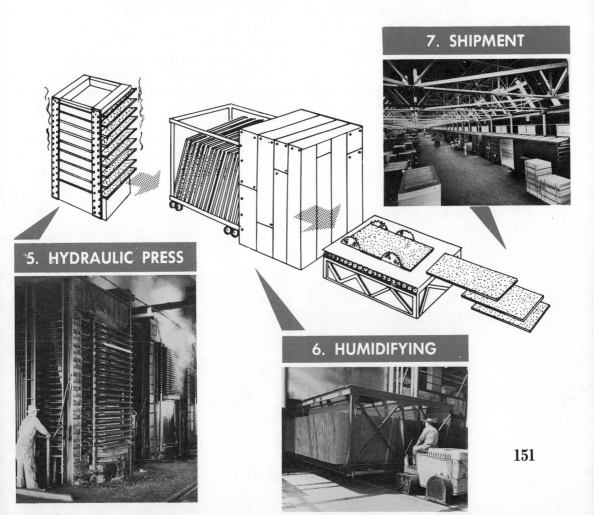

7. SHIPMENT

5. HYDRAULIC PRESS

6. HUMIDIFYING

151

12-2.   The exterior of this home is of hardboard.

of black dye for use as table and counter tops, kick plates, and blackboards. Both standard and tempered hardboards are manufactured with two types of surfaces. The screen back, S1S, has one smooth surface; the back is rough and looks like screening. In the other variety, S2S, both surfaces are very smooth. Hardboards are made in thicknesses from $\frac{1}{12}''$ to $\frac{5}{16}''$; the most common thicknesses are $\frac{1}{8}''$, $\frac{3}{16}''$, and $\frac{1}{4}''$. Panels are 4' wide and come in standard lengths of 6', 8', 10', 12' and 16'.

Special Hardboards. Hardboards are made into many special decorative surfaces. *Fig. 12–6.* Some of the most popular patterns are tiled, embossed and striated. Many hardboards have printed and pre-finished surfaces with wood grain, simulated leather, or other coatings. A very popular and useful kind is perforated hardboard. This has closely spaced, punched or drilled holes which can be used with various fixtures for flexible and decorative wall mountings and for storage. *Fig. 12–7.*

12-3.   Hardboard is an excellent material for drawer bottoms because of its dimensional stability.

12-4.   Stamping out hardboard parts for the interior of a car door.

PLAYSKOOL

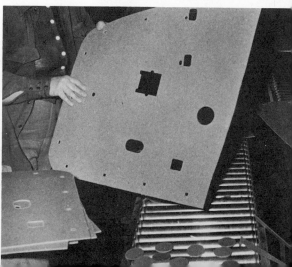

12-5.   Standard sheets of hardboard.

12-6.   A few of the various design patterns available in hardboard.

Working with Hardboard. When ordering hardboard, specify the type, class, thickness, S1S or S2S, and special surfaces.

Since hardboard is man-made, it does not behave quite the same as lumber. Here are some things you should know about it:

• All regular woodworking tools can be used for working with hardboard. However, if quantity production is to be done, it is better to use carbide-tipped tools.

• Cutting should be done with the exposed surface up. Install a combination or crosscut blade on the

12-7.   An economical "storage wall" hardboard paneling for utility rooms, children's rooms, garages, and other areas where versatile wall storage and attractive appearance must be combined. This hardboard has perforations for pegboard hooks and accessories in two thirds of the panel, while the bottom third is solid "wainscoted."

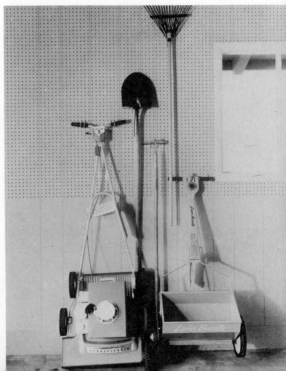

12-8. Precision cut wood shavings are used in particle board. Some manufacturers use larger shavings in the center of the board and smaller ones toward the surface to provide a better surface finish.

circular saw. Use a fine-toothed hand saw.

• Machining. Hardboard may be machined the same as other wood products. For shaping, routing, planing, and cutting, very sharp tools should be used. Absence of grain allows uniformly fine machining without splintering.

• Sanding. Only edges that have been sawed require sanding. Follow regular sanding techniques. Face or surface sanding is not recommended.

• Gluing. Use casein glue to fasten hardboard to studding, and nails to hold panels in place until the adhesive sets. For counter tops, contact cement is practical.

• Bending can be done in one direction only; never attempt to make a compound bend. Whenever possible, hardboard should be bent around a form and then fastened in place.

154

• Join the edges of panels with a loose fit, leaving a slight gap at all joints. The edge can be neatly beveled or rounded for better appearance; decorative trim or molding can also be used.

• Fastening. Hardboard can be fastened in place with any wood fastenings, such as nails, staples, screws and bolts. If nails are used, always choose 3d galvanized finish nails for interior hardboards. Nails should be spaced about 8″ apart throughout the panel and 4″ apart at the edges. Joints should be made only where solid support is available. For exteriors, use galvanized nails (casing or box), at least 5d, or hardened siding nails. Never attempt to toenail hardboard. Also, do not nail closer than $\frac{3}{8}$″ to the edge.

• Finishing hardboard panels is easy with paint, enamel, varnish, lacquer, shellac, wax, or latex-base paint. Since hardboard is grainless and has a smooth, glassy-hard surface, it takes a beautiful finish.

PARTICLE BOARD

Particle board is made by combining wood chips, scraps, flakes, or other wood fragments with an adhesive to form a large board. This material is one of the results of research in wood technology. It combines the better utilization of wood with new developments in adhesives and glues. The manufacture of particle board has come about almost entirely since 1948. Now, however, it is a major building material for both furniture and home construction.

Particle board is real wood in a

blended form. Its properties can be changed by varying such things as the kind and amount of adhesive, the pressure, the size and shape of the chips, and the methods of forming it.

How Particle Board is Manufactured. The basic process for manufacturing particle board varies with the manufacturer although most follow a similar procedure. The first step in the process is to cut the particles, chips, or flakes of wood. *Fig. 12–8.* Special machines slice the wood into the size shavings specified by the manufacturer. Many different kinds of wood are used as the basis. Some of the most common are Douglas fir, poplar, pine, hemlock, alder, and aspen. A few manufacturers use some harder woods. These fine particles of wood are then mixed with a special adhesive. For particle board to be used for interior construction, a synthetic resin glue is required; for external application of particle board, a phenolic resin glue is used. *Fig. 12–9.*

Most particle board is manufac-

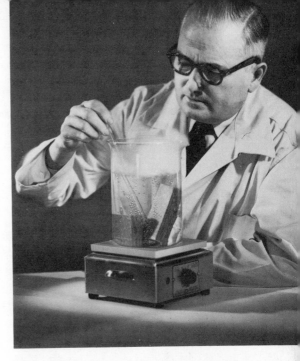

12–9. This scientist is testing particle board. When made with phenolic resin glues, this material will not disintegrate even when kept in boiling water for an hour or more. It can be used for exterior construction, cabinets, partitions, and even boats.

tured by pressing the mixture of wood particles and adhesive in a conventional, multi-platen, hot press. This mat of wood shavings is bonded together. A few manufacturers form

12–10.   Notice the compactness and smoothness of particle board.

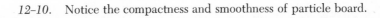

12-11.   Common uses for particle board. *a*. Walls in home building.

the particle board by forcing the mixture through an extrusion press. (Extrusion means forcing bulk material through small openings.) To complete the process, the edges are trimmed and the surface planed and/or sanded. *Fig. 12–10.*

Particle board is made in various standard panel sizes. The most common are sheets 4′ x 8′ and 5′ x 8′. It is available in thicknesses from ⅛″ to 1⁷⁄₁₆″.

The physical properties of particle board vary greatly. Particle board is used extensively as core stock in furniture and cabinetwork. *Fig. 12–11.* The face and edges of particle

12–11b.   Furniture construction.

board may be covered with laminated plastic or a veneer. Some of the many other uses include sporting goods, toys, house trailers, paneling, siding, musical instruments.

Particle board is made by many different manufacturers under their own trade names. A lumber dealer can tell you the commercial names. Particle board is also molded into such products as luggage and carrying cases, stool and chair seats, trays, and dishes.

WORKING WITH PARTICLE BOARD

Particle board is easy to work with standard wood tools. Because it has no grain, there are no hard or soft spots. It saws, routes, rabbets, and drills with greater ease than plywood.

Store particle board and all veneers or lumber to be glued to it under identical moisture conditions; maintain moisture content below 10 percent. Panels should be kept in flat, even stacks in a clean, dry location, away from hot pipes and out of the direct path of heaters. Stacking sticks should be of uniform thickness and should extend the full width of the material. They should be placed no more than

12-13. Filling the edges with plastic wood.

24 inches on centers, not over 6 inches from panel ends and should be aligned vertically to prevent bowing.

Sawing, Drilling and Routing. High speed, carbide tipped cutting tools are recommended for large volume cutting. Regular wood working tools produce equally good cuts but require more frequent sharpening. *Fig. 12-12.* Torn or ragged edges are usually the result of dull tools, eccentric (off-center) arbors, or lack of positive feed. Saws, drills, and routers should be checked regularly for sharpness and eccentricity. Saw arbors more than half of one thousandth inch off-center will cause rough edges. Saw teeth should be checked for alignment. Saws with teeth more than several thousandths of an inch out of line will leave ragged cuts.

Surface Gouges. Although particle board panels leave the manufacturer's mill with a smooth, flat surface, occasionally they are gouged, scratched or damaged in shipping or handling. Plastic wood or wood dough will repair most damaged areas. *Fig. 12-13.*

12-12. Cutting particle board on the circular saw.

157

12-14. Adding a metal edge to particle board that has been covered with plastic laminates.

Edge Filling. Considerable time can be saved by filling the edges of an entire stack of identical parts at one time. Fillers may be applied to the edge of a stack with a brush, rag, or squeegee, or by spraying. If care is taken to leave a well-filled smooth edge, only minimum sanding is required prior to final finishing.

Applying veneers and plastic laminates. With the improved surface qual-

12-15. Here are some of the world's straightest studs manufactured of finger-jointed lumber. These spliced members are now being used in home construction. They pass every test of government-insured projects.

ities of many particle boards, it is not necessary to add crossbands. This permits relatively simple three-ply construction. Veneers and plastic laminates are applied to the core with contact cement. *Fig. 12-14.* Both the veneer and the particle board should have approximately 6 to 8 percent moisture content. Wood veneers can be bonded in either a hot or a cold press.

FINGER JOINT

One of the most important single developments in the lumber industry in recent years has been the development of satisfactory methods of joining wood to make wider and longer pieces of solid lumber. The key to this development is the use of the finger joint and powerful, wood-welding adhesives. Standard-dimension lumber such as the 2″ x 4″ is made of spliced members. *Fig. 12-15.* These have been tested and found to be equal to solid pieces for studs, trimmers, plates, and other structural parts of a house. Lumber can also be joined on both edge and end to form one-piece boards as wide as needed. These are ideal for counter tops, shelving, cabinets, and many other trim parts of a house. *Figs. 12-16* and *12-17.*

12-16. This wide board is a manufactured product. Pieces of solid lumber can be made any width or length.

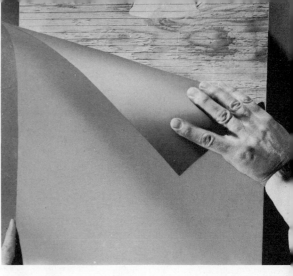

12-17. The finger joint is the key to the manufacture of this product.

SHEETBOARD OR PLY-VENEER, AND INSULATION BOARD

Sheetboard or *ply-veneer* is a sheathing product made from lower grades of lumber to which is glued a wet-strength kraft paper. *Fig. 12-18.* This material combines the insulating advantages of lumber with the convenience of larger panels. *Fig. 12-19.*

Insulation board is a pre-formed, rigid panel manufactured from fibers of wood, cane, or other vegetable matter. Although it is made from materials similar to hardboard, it is softer and of a lower density. It is

12-18b. Ply-veneer. Note that heavy kraft paper covers the wood core, adding strength.

also commonly known as fiberboard or wallboard.

Insulation board is not painted when used as sheathing, shingle backing, or in other places where it is not visible or exposed to the weather. Extra asphalt is added to some types to increase strength and moisture resistance. Other types are

12-18a. The construction of sheetboard.

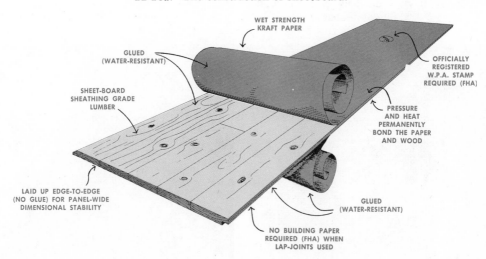

WET STRENGTH KRAFT PAPER

GLUED (WATER-RESISTANT)

SHEET-BOARD SHEATHING GRADE LUMBER

OFFICIALLY REGISTERED W.P.A. STAMP REQUIRED (FHA)

PRESSURE AND HEAT PERMANENTLY BOND THE PAPER AND WOOD

LAID UP EDGE-TO-EDGE (NO GLUE) FOR PANEL-WIDE DIMENSIONAL STABILITY

GLUED (WATER-RESISTANT)

NO BUILDING PAPER REQUIRED (FHA) WHEN LAP-JOINTS USED

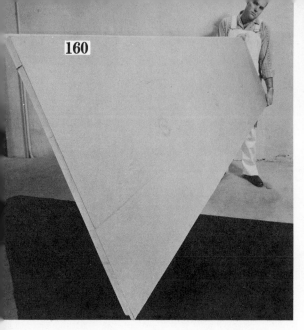

12-19a. This board is strong and rigid.

12-20. Installing ceiling tile by fastening with an adhesive.

covered on either side with a thin sheet of aluminum. When insulation board forms the exterior surface of a building, it is painted for protection as well as decoration.

Following are some of the more common types of insulation board:

12-19b. A wardrobe made of sheetboard material. It saws and nails with the workability of lumber.

• *Structural insulation board* is a low-density panel made from wood or vegetable fibers which are held together with a bonding agent. Other materials may be added to this board to give it properties required for specific uses.

12-21. Using building board for interior construction.

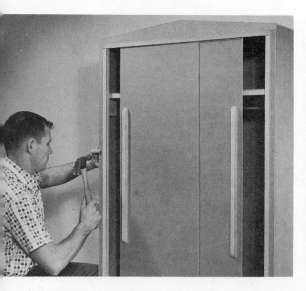

12-22.   The walls of this room are interior finish board in a panel form.

• *Acoustical board* is a low-density, sound-absorbing, structural insulation board. It has a factory-applied finish which increases its sound absorption and is also decorative. It is usually made in the form of tiles. *Fig. 12-20.*

• *Building board* is a natural-finish, multi-purpose structural insulating board. *Fig. 12-21.*

• *Insulating roof form board* is a specially fabricated insulating board designed as a permanent form for roof construction.

• *Interior finish board* is structural insulation board with a factory-applied paint finish. It is made in the form of plane board, panels, or tiles for interior use. *Fig. 12-22.*

• *Sheathing*, a structural insulating board for use in building construction, may be treated, impregnated,

or coated to give it additional water resistance. *Fig. 12-23.*

• *Roof insulation board* is a structural board for deck roof insulation.

12-23.   Exterior sheathing under the siding.

INSULITE
BILDRITE
SHEATHING

161

12-24. Note the construction of this sandwich panel.

SANDWICH CONSTRUCTION

Sandwich construction is layer construction made by bonding thin facings to a thick core. *Fig. 12-24.* The thin facings are usually made of some strong material such as veneer, hardboard, or plastic laminate. The top of the desk you see in *Fig. 12-25* is a good illustration of sandwich construction. The center layer of the top is a honeycomb-core made of plastic-impregnated paper. Even by itself this core is so strong that a man can jump on it without crushing it. The top facing is a plastic laminate while the lower face is veneer.

In the manufacture of sandwich panels a light core material such as paper, balsa wood, or plastic foam is used. The facings consist of some stiff, sturdy material such as plywood, veneer, hardboard, metal, or

12-25. The top of this desk is sandwich construction.

plastic laminate, and are bonded to the core in a hot press. This produces rather lightweight material with a very sturdy surface.

PLASTIC AS A BUILDING MATERIAL

Plastic is a man-made material that has enjoyed wide usage in the furniture and building industries. Plastics are of two types, *thermoplastic* (which softens when heated); and *thermosetting* (which cannot be reshaped).

Thermoplastics. *Vinyl* is a tough material with excellent wear resistance. Although hard and rigid when cold, it can be made soft and flexible by heat. A great many floor tiles are vinyl. *Fig. 12-26.*

Polyethylene is a tough, translucent material, made in flexible as well as rigid varieties. It is highly resistant to stains and excellent for outdoor use. Often it is used as a film-type vapor barrier for insulation and also for temporary covering of lumber, doors, windows, and similar items.

Acrylic is hard, rigid, and very clear. It is available in various colors, or colorless. It is commonly used in domed skylights.

Thermosetting. *Phenolic,* an inexpensive plastic, is hard and opaque. It will withstand heat even though it is quite brittle. A common use is in electrical outlets and covers.

Melamine-amino has an extremely hard, durable surface that resists stain, heat, water, and scratches. It is available in a wide range of bright

12-26.   Installing vinyl tile.

colors and also in wood-grain patterns. More and more it is being used in the building industry for wall surfaces, and it is especially popular for tops of furniture pieces. *Fig. 12-27.*

12-27.   This desk top is melamine-amino plastic.

163

Polyester is a stiff, flexible material, usually reinforced with glass fibers to make it harder and stiffer. It is used for wall panels, covering for partitions, and many other building purposes. *Fig. 12-28.*

Plastic Products. Of all the plastic products used in home and furniture construction, the two most common are Fiberglas and plastic laminates (melamine). *Fig 12-29.*

Fiberglas is available in flat, corrugated sheets in a wide variety of colors. It is commonly used for patio covering or room dividers. *Fig. 12-30.* It can be cut, drilled, and shaped with ordinary wood tools. Liquid Fiberglas is used to cover boats, water skis, surfboards, and similar wooden items. This gives the product a hard, smooth, waterproof surface.

12-28. This chair seat is Fiberglas.

12-29. The tops of all these kitchen cabinets and the freezer front are plastic laminates.

12-30. This patio cover is Fiberglas.

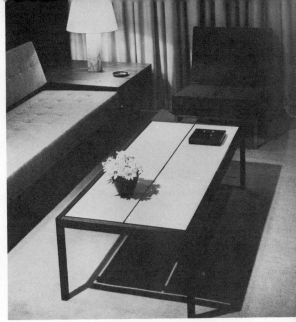

12-31. A coffee table with a split, white, plastic-laminate top. Legs and rails are oil-finished solid walnut, dovetailed at the corners.

A *plastic laminate* is a series of layers of material, pressed together under high pressure. It consists of kraft paper impregnated with phenolic resin and a surface of rayon papers that are impregnated with melamine resin. The laminates are subjected to heat of about 300 degrees F. and to very great pressures. The heat makes the resin in each sheet flow and combine with the resin in the other sheets while under pressure to form a homogeneous mass. Most of the plastic laminates are made to a standard 1/16″ thickness. All high-pressure laminates have some sort of decorative surface. These consist of plain colors, decorative patterns, or wood grains made to match natural, finished wood surfaces. A piece of furniture made of wood and matching laminate has a look of unity.

Most case-goods manufacturers are using high-pressure, decorative laminates for the tops of their furniture, since this protects the surface. *Fig. 12-31.*

Because of their thinness, laminates do not possess great strength by themselves. They usually need some material such as plywood or particle board as the core. If plywood is used, it should be at least 3/4″ thick with five or more plies. Softwood plywood should have a B face or better. If particle board is used, it is very important that the surface be smooth and uniform in thickness. It, too, must be 3/4″ thick or more.

For making furniture, plastic laminates may be purchased already glued to some core material such as plywood, particle board, or hardboard. However, in home construction, plastic laminates are usually applied on the job.

165

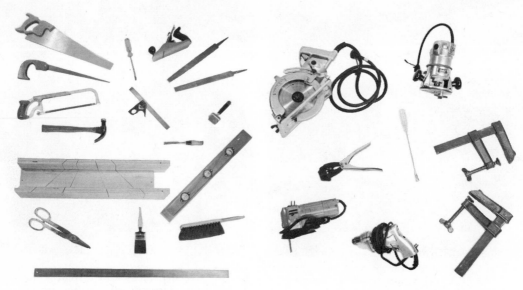

12-32. Hand tools needed to install plastic laminates.

12-33. Portable power tools that are useful for installing laminates.

INSTALLING PLASTIC LAMINATE

The following is a recommended method of installing plastic laminate on kitchen cabinet tops.

Cutting the Plastic Laminate. Basic hand tools can be used, but the work is done more easily and quickly with portable power tools. *Fig. 12-32.* Laminate can be cut easily with any of the saws shown in *Fig. 12-33.* However, it is better to use a carbide-tipped saw. Cut plastic laminate with the face or decorative side up. There is one exception to this: Cut with the face down when using a cut-off or portable electric circular saw. When cutting with a hand saw, keep the blade at a low angle and cut on the down stroke. Move the blade with even strokes. Always support the material firmly as close to the line of cut as possible. *Fig.*

12-34. When using a hand jig saw or saber saw, always hold the saw firmly against the material to prevent chattering. A good cutting method is to sandwich the material together with C clamps. Lay the material face up on a piece of plywood or lumber. Cut a strip of plywood or lumber and place it on the top side of the material. If the strip has a straight edge and is properly positioned, it will act as a template and will also guide the saw. *Fig. 12-35.* The material may chip slightly when sawed. In order to have clear, smooth edges, allow enough material for surfacing after sawing.

Applying and Spreading the Cement. The cement can be applied with a brush, fiber roller, or spreader. Spread the contact cement in a thin, uniform film, being sure to get complete coverage. Two coats should be

12-34.   Using a cut-off saw. Note that the face side is turned down.

12-35.   Using a hand jig saw to cut the material. Here the face side is turned up.

applied to the core material and one to the covering material. Dull spots that appear after drying indicate insufficient cement. Usually 15 minutes at least must be allowed after each coat, and both surfaces must be completely covered with a glossy surface. Spread enough cement to avoid having any dull spots. After drying, there should be a high gloss all over the surface. Poor bonds are caused by one or more of the following: inadequate adhesive spread; under- or over-drying; improper rolling; inadequate pressure; or working at temperatures lower than 70 degrees F. For spreading on horizontal surfaces, use the metal spreader usually furnished with each can of contact cement. *Fig. 12-36.* Hold the spreader teeth at 90 degrees when applying cement to a low, soft-density, or uneven material such as fir or Philippine mahogany-faced plywood. In applying the laminate to hard, high-density, and smooth surfaces, hold the spreader teeth at 45 degrees. *Fig. 12-37.* An animal-

hair brush can be used for vertical surfaces.

Positioning the Laminate. When the contact cement has dried sufficiently, you are ready to bond it to the surface being covered. To test dryness, tamp a small piece of brown paper on the cemented surface. When paper will not stick, the cement is ready for bonding. *Warning*: Once the two contact-cemented surfaces touch, there is an immediate bond; and no further positioning is

12-36.   Applying the contact cement.

167

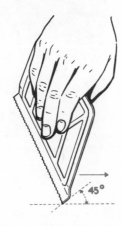

12-37. Correct method of holding the spreader.

Applying Pressure with a Roller. Roll from the center to the edges, paying particular attention to the edges. A roller 3″ long and of small diameter is very satisfactory. *Fig. 12-39.* For hard-to-reach areas, pressure should be applied by holding a block of wood on the material and tapping with a hammer. Room temperature of 70 degrees F. or more must be maintained. If there is a bond failure due to inadequate pressure, improper rolling, bonding at a temperature below 70 degrees F., or over-drying, follow this corrective procedure. Use a hand electric iron at the temperature for silk. Heat a small area of the top until you can touch the material, but cannot hold your hand on it. Heat will reactivate the cement films so that a permanent bond can be made by either rolling the area until cool, or by clamping the heated area until it cools entirely. Correct a bond failure due to under-drying as follows: Remove the laminate with the contact cement solvent. Allow to dry completely. Re-cement both surfaces and bond as recommended.

possible. Therefore, to properly align the laminate to the plywood, place heavy sheets of brown wrapping paper (not newspaper) between the plywood and the material. Cut slip sheets in two or three pieces and overlap them for easy removal. Center the plastic laminate and move the first sheet a few inches at a time, pressing the material by hand as you go. *Fig. 12-38.* Then remove the remaining slip sheets.

12-38. Placing the material in position.

12-39. Rolling the surface.

12-40. Trimming the edge.

12-41. Cutting out a sink opening.

Finishing the Edges. An electric-powered router saves much time and effort. *Fig. 12-40*. If plywood has been edged with a plastic laminate, use a carbide-tipped bevel trimming bit with a 20- to 25-degree angle for exposed edges to be finished. If a router is not available, the excess overhang can be taken down with a block plane and then finished off with a smooth file. Hold the plane at a 20- to 25-degree angle for bevel finishing. If the edge is to be finished with overlapping metal molding, use a router with a flush cutting, a saber saw, or a block plane.

Making a Sink Cutout. The best method for cutting out a kitchen sink area is to make the cut after the laminate has been bonded to the base material. This eliminates any possible breakage. Another method is to cut the material and the base separately. In either case the cutout can be made by this method: Measure for positioning of the cutout; use the outside edge of the clamp-on frame as a template for marking the laminate for cutting; drill a hole large enough to insert a saber saw blade on the inside of the line mark-ing, and make a rough cutout with the saber saw. *Fig. 12-41*. Another method is to drill a hole, insert a key-hole saw to make a start, and cut straight sections either with a key-hole saw or carpenter's saw. Make the rough cutout and then finish with a medium rasp.

EDGE-BANDING WITH PLASTIC LAMINATES

Generally the same procedure applies for edge-banding with plastic laminate as for covering main areas. There are, however, some differences and precautions.

• A plastic laminate edge band has a more pleasing appearance if the edge of the plywood is built up by adding a strip for thickness. Glue or nail the strip to the top for the desired thickness on the drop edge. *Fig. 12-42*. C clamps will hold the strip in place while nailing.

• Make sure all surfaces are free of dust, dirt, and grease. Prime coat all edges of the core to be self-edged and allow to dry. *Fig. 12-43*. The adhesive coat is then applied to the core edges and the plastic laminate.

• Plastic laminate strips used for

169

12-42. Adding a double thickness for the edge.

12-44. Placing the edge banding on the edge.

edge-banding should be $\frac{1}{8}''$ to $\frac{1}{4}''$ larger than the core edges. This is to allow for trimming and positioning of the strips on the core. When positioning or bonding the strips to the core, start at one end and work to the other. *Fig. 12-44.*

• Use a router with a carbide-tipped bit to trim overhang. Use a flush cutting bit on a top edge which is to be lapped with plastic laminate covering the top. Use a bevel trimming bit for an underneath edge which is exposed. Then finish with a fine or smooth file. *Fig. 12-45.* Another method is to use a plane and file. Plastic laminate edge-banding strips can be bent to a radius of 9'' without heating, and to a $2\frac{1}{2}''$ radius when heated. Tools needed are an electric hand iron, an infrared lamp or electric stove, and a temperature-indicating crayon. To prepare for bending, turn the iron upside down or use the stove or lamp. Set for highest temperature and allow to heat. On the back of the plastic laminate, with the crayon, mark the area to be bent. Put on heat-resisting gloves. Place the plastic laminate with the decorative side on the iron. When the crayon melts, the laminate is ready to be bent. Form or bend the laminate around the piece to which it is to be bonded. Hold it on the form until it cools and can be handled without gloves. A formed piece should be kept on the form until the laminate is bonded to the core, since the material has a tendency to flatten out. When the edge-banding strip is to go around corners, there must be at least 6'' of flat surface on either side.

12-43. Applying the contact cement to the edge.

12-45. Trimming the edge.

170

Unit 13: WOOD SCIENCE

Wood science is a study of the physical and chemical properties of wood. This unit will help you understand the scientific approach to identifying woods, thus increasing the knowledge you gained from Unit 5. Learning about wood science will also give you a better understanding of the nature of wood and its value in manufacturing and construction. *Fig. 13-1.* Too often, people who work with wood do not understand it. They misuse or abuse it with the result that the end product is poor. The fault is not in the material but rather with the worker who lacks knowledge of wood's characteristics and working qualities.

IDENTIFICATION OF WOODS

The structure of wood offers the most reliable means for its identification. Color, odor, weight, and hardness also help in identifying woods but, as a rule, such qualities are too variable to be used singly in distinguishing a large number of woods. This drawback applies particularly to color, which not only varies in the natural wood but is modified by such things as treatment, paints, stains, and decay.

There are three common ways of identifying wood species based on their structure. Easiest (but least reliable) is simply to look at the wood, with the unaided eye. A better method is to use a hand lens which enlarges the surface ten to twenty times. *Fig. 13-2.* This is often satisfactory, especially for large boards. The third and surest method is to place thin sections of wood between glass slides and view them through a microscope. *Fig. 13-3.* The microscope usually enlarges the cell structure 70 to 100 times.

Wood can be cut in three distinct

13-1. Inspecting a bore sample of a telephone pole to determine the penetration of chemical preservative.

13-2. Using a hand lens to inspect a wood surface.

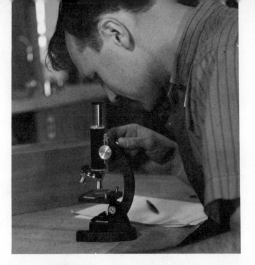

13-3. Studying wood samples under a microscope. Very inexpensive microscopes are available that will do a good job in the lab.

planes with respect to the annual rings. *Fig. 13-4.* The end of a piece of wood shows a cross section of the annual layers of growth. This is also known as the *transverse surface* or *cross-sectional face*. It shows the size and arrangement of the cells better than any other surface. The illustrations shown are all reproductions of photographs of cross sectionals. When wood is cut lengthwise through the center or pith of the tree, the surfaces exposed are known as the *radial faces* or *quartered surfaces*. A longitudinal surface which does not pass through the center is known as the *tangential face* (or *tangential surface*). Technically a tangential surface is at right angles to the radius.

Preparing Wood for Microscope Examination. As mentioned, the most accurate way of identifying wood is to cut thin slices of the wood in various directions — end grain, radial grain, and tangential grain — and view them under a microscope. It is important to examine a representative piece of the wood. If the wood is freshly cut, a thin slice can usually be cut off without any other preparation. Kiln-dried wood must be softened so a very thin slice can be cut off. One way is to put the wood in boiling water until it becomes waterlogged.

Another way that is particularly good for hardwoods is to soak the wood in equal parts of glycerin and alcohol.

The best way to slice the wood is with a fixture like the one in *Fig. 13-5.* It must have a very sharp knife. Do not sand or otherwise polish the surface of the wood, as this would change its character. The sample should be washed three times in pure alcohol, then placed in *clove oil* for five minutes. After this, place the sections in cedarwood oil for one minute and then transfer to clear 1″ x 3″ glass slides. Add a few drops of hot glycerin jelly to the section and place a warm glass over it. Heat the slide until bubbles appear and then hold tight with spring clothes pins until cool.

Structure of Hardwoods. *Pores.* Pores are hollow tubes composed of comparatively large cells with open ends, set one above the other. *Fig. 13-6.* Technically, they are known as *vessels*. Pores are confined almost entirely to hardwoods, or woods from broadleafed trees. For this reason, hardwoods are also called *porous woods*. *Fig. 13-7.* In conifers, the cells are all closed at the ends and do not form vessels. Thus, conifers are classed as *nonporous woods*.

In coarse-textured or so-called "open-grain" woods, such as oak and

172

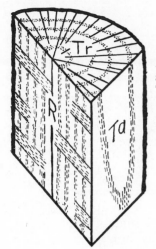

13-4. A block of wood showing three surfaces: Tr — Transverse, cross-sectional, or end surface. R—Radial face or quartered surface. Ta— Tangential surface.

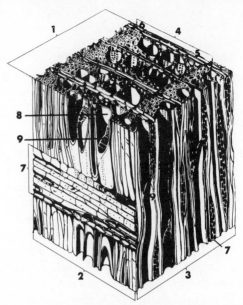

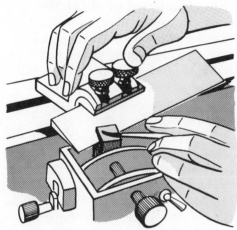

13-5a. Fixture for cutting specimens for microscope inspection.

13-5b. Simple wood fixtures that can be made for cutting specimens. A groove is cut in a block of wood, and a stop controls the length of cut. Use a sharp knife to cut the specimen.

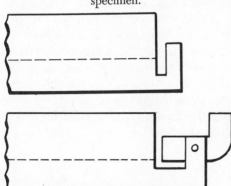

13-6. Hardwood. This is an enlargement of a $\frac{1}{32}''$ cubic section of yellow poplar. Numbered items are: 1. Cross-sectional face. 2. Radial face. 3. Tangential face. 4. Annual rings. 5. Springwood (early wood). 6. Summerwood (late wood). 7. Wood rays. 8. Vessel or pore. 9. Sieve or perforation plate—a small grid at the end of each vessel segment.

13-7. Hardwood pore arrangements. *a.* Ring-porous, with radial pore arrangement in summerwood. *b.* Ring-porous, with wavy tangential pore arrangement in summerwood. *c.* Ring-porous, without definite pore arrangement in summerwood. *d.* Diffuse-porous wood.

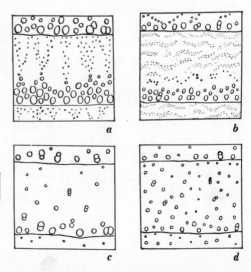

walnut, some of the pores are plainly visible to the unaided eye; but in finer-textured woods, such as beech, maple, and basswood, they are visible only with a good hand lens.

In some hardwoods the pores are comparatively large at the beginning of each annual ring and they decrease in size more or less abruptly toward the summerwood, thus forming a distinct porous ring in the springwood. Such woods are classed as *ring-porous* woods. Oak, pecan, and walnut are examples of this class. In other hardwoods the pores are almost uniform in size throughout the annual ring, or decrease slightly toward the outer portion of the summerwood. Such woods are known as *diffuse-porous* woods. Birch, cherry, mahogany, and maple are examples of this class. Pores in the summerwood of ring-porous woods are variously arranged.

Tylosis (tī-lō'-sĭs). The pores of some woods, except those in the outer sapwood, are filled with frothlike growth called tylosis (plural: tyloses). These are formed by ingrowths from neighboring cells and fill the pores somewhat like toy balloons crowded into an air shaft. Tyloses are especially abundant in the white oak group.

Wood Fibers. Most of the denser, harder part of hardwoods is composed of very narrow, comparatively long, thick-walled cells known as *wood fibers.* As a rule, these fibers are too small to be separately distinguished with a hand lens. Conifers have no true wood fibers.

Wood Parenchyma Cells (pả-rĕn'-kĭ-mȧ). These are comparatively short, usually thin-walled cells, too small to be seen individually without a compound microscope. Collectively, they may be recognized on the cross section by the *light-colored* tissue they form. In some hardwoods the parenchyma cells are so scattered that they are not noticeable—for example, in elm and maple.

Pith Flecks. These are abnormal groups of parenchyma cells appearing on the end surface of some woods as small, discolored spots. Pith flecks appear as darkened streaks on the longitudinal surface. These abnormal cells are caused by insect larvae which burrow into the young wood under the bark, the passages being later filled up by parenchyma cells. Pith flecks are very abundant in cherry, maple, and a few other species.

Medullary Rays. These were discussed in Chapter 7. To review briefly, medullary rays, also known as pith rays, are narrow bands of cells extending radially in a tree. Some of the rays in the oaks are comparatively wide and conspicuous, giving quartered oak its beautiful "silver grain." They are also very plain in maple and cherry. In some woods they are so fine that they are hardly noticeable on the radial face and not visible at all on the end (cross-sectioned) surface except through a lens.

In some woods rays are arranged in tiers or stories, one above the other, appearing on the tangential surface as very fine bands running across the grain. Moistening the surface brings out these bands more clearly in some woods. This arrangement is known as *storied rays.*

174

Structure of Conifers (Softwoods). Conifers have no pores and no true wood fibers. They do have a radial arrangement of the fibrous cells (tracheids), and in some groups of conifers there are resin ducts or resin cells. In all of these ways conifers are different from hardwoods. *Figs. 13-8 and 13-9.*

Tracheids (trā′-kē-ĭds). Most wood from conifers is made up of *tracheids* —elongated cells that occur in softwoods instead of the pores and wood fibers found in hardwoods. The tracheids are narrower in cross section than most pores and wider than most wood fibers. With a good hand lens, a smoothly cut end surface and good light, the tracheids can be seen in most coniferous woods. They are practically uniform in tangential diameter and are arranged in definite radial rows. In the outer part of each annual ring the tracheids become somewhat flattened radially and thicker walled, producing a harder and darker band of summerwood. In the hard pines, larches, and Douglas fir, the summerwood is very conspicuous and, because of its density, adds greatly to the strength of the wood.

Resin Ducts. The wood of pine, spruce, larch, and Douglas fir contains *resin ducts,* which are more or less continuous passages within the tree. Some of the ducts are vertical, and are parallel to the grain. Others, which are within certain medullary rays, run at right angles to the grain and are horizontal in the tree. The vertical resin ducts may be seen with a lens (and in some of the pines usually without a lens) on a smoothly cut end surface, where they appear as darker or lighter colored specks or small pores. They should not be confused with the pores or vessels of hardwoods which are much more numerous and serve an entirely different purpose. The horizontal resin ducts are smaller than the vertical ducts and are not easily seen with a hand lens.

Pitch pockets, resin streaks, and exudations of resin on an end surface are a positive indication of the presence of resin ducts, and do not occur in cedar, cypress, redwood, and the true firs. The absence of such accumulations of resin, however, does not necessarily mean the *absence of resin ducts* in the wood.

Resin will not exude, as a rule, on cuts made after the wood is seasoned. Warming pieces in an oven will usually cause enough resin to exude to indicate the presence of resin ducts.

Wood Parenchyma or Resin Cells. Wood parenchyma in conifers is scarce. It forms a layer of one or two cells around the resin ducts but is inconspicuous and not used in making identifications without a high-power microscope.

In redwood, parenchyma cells (usually referred to as *resin cells)* containing a brownish gum, are scattered throughout the annual rings. In redwood they are not easily noticed because of the dark color of the wood. Resin cells are usually more scattered when found in the cedars.

Medullary Rays. The rays in conifers are very narrow, excepting those containing horizontal resin ducts, which are slightly wider. These wider rays are termed *fusiform rays* and are found only in pines, spruces, larches,

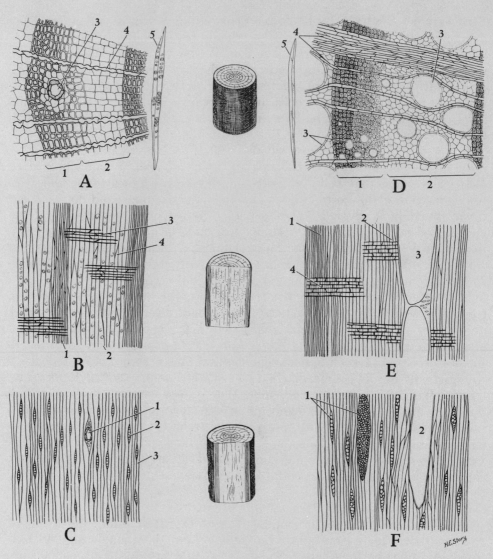

Courtesy CCM: General Biological Inc., Chicago

13-8. The enlarged views at left show features of white pine and those at right show redwood. The smaller views (center) show the part of the log from which the sections were taken. *A1.* Summerwood (late wood). *A2.* Springwood (early wood). *A3.* Resin duct. *A4.* Ray. *A5.* Tracheids. *B1.* Summerwood (late wood). *B2.* Springwood (early wood). *B3.* Ray. *B4.* Tracheids. *C1.* Resin duct. *C2.* Ray. *C3.* Tracheids. *D1.* Summerwood (late wood). *D2.* Springwood (early wood). *D3.* Early wood vessel. *D4.* Large and small seriate rays. *D5.* Fiber. *E1.* Summerwood (late wood). *E2.* Springwood (early wood). *E3.* Vessel. *E4.* Rays. *F1.* Ray. *F2.* Vessel.

EASTERN WHITE PINE — An important tree in Colonial America, for homes and for the masts and spars of ships. It is still an important timber tree, and one source of knotty pine decorative paneling.

DOUGLAS FIR — Averaging 150 to 200 feet in height, the Douglas fir is considered the most important timber tree in the world. It is used principally for construction lumber and plywood, and for telephone poles.

LONGLEAF PINE — Found throughout southeastern U.S., this tree is a major source of turpentine, pitch, and resin; its lumber is also widely used in building construction, and in railroad cars.

WESTERN HEMLOCK — A tall, graceful tree, the western hemlock is important for timber and is also a prime source of pulpwood; and tannin, used in tanning leather, can be extracted from its bright red inner bark.

BALSAM FIR — The most popular of all Christmas trees; used extensively for pulp and for wooden boxes and crates. It is also the source of a very clear oil called Canada Balsam, used in high power microscopy.

PONDEROSA PINE — A tall, straight tree found in many parts of western U.S.; second only to Douglas fir as a timber tree. Its wood is used for lumber, railroad ties, telephone poles, posts, and mine timbers.

WHITE SPRUCE — Spruces are the major pulping trees of eastern U.S., and Canada. White spruce has strong, resilient wood widely used for lumber and, because of its resonant qualities, for many musical instruments.

WHITE OAK — The oaks have always been our most important hardwood timber trees. Early American mansions, public buildings, and ships' hulls, were of oak. White oak was the traditional wood for whiskey barrels.

SWEET GUM — The sweet part of the sweet gum is a sticky substance that oozes from cuts in the trunks and branches. The strong, light wood is widely used in furniture. Also an important pulping tree.

SHAGBARK HICKORY — Tough hickory lumber supplied spokes for the wheels that crossed the continent and the ax handles that cleared the wilderness. Hickory smoke is used for curing ham.

YELLOW POPLAR — The yellow poplar, the tallest hardwood in the east, is a favorite ornamental tree, and an important source of wood for musical instruments, television cabinets, and other furniture.

SUGAR MAPLE — This is the tree that maple syrup and maple sugar come from. But it is also an important source of fine hardwood, prized for furniture. It grows in the eastern half of the U.S., and Canada.

The colors on the map, and the matching dot next to each tree, show the principal areas where it grows.

Trees are one of America's leading natural resources. Twelve of the most important species are shown on this page. The next seven pages show wood samples of some of these and other key varieties. The samples include three hardwoods — white ash, butternut, and yellow poplar; and four softwoods — cypress, Douglas fir, ponderosa pine, and redwood. The lower portion of each sample shows natural wood grains; the upper portions show two stained finishes. Many other finishes can be applied. This page is used with permission of *St. Regis Paper Company*. The seven pages of samples are used with permission of the *Architectural Woodwork Institute*. Full-color samples of sixteen other wood species can be found in the textbook CABINETMAKING AND MILLWORK, also by Dr. John L. Feirer.

176 A

White ash.

176 B

Butternut.

176 C

Yellow poplar.

176 D

Cypress.

176 E

Douglas fir.

176 F

Ponderosa pine.

176 G

Redwood.

176 H

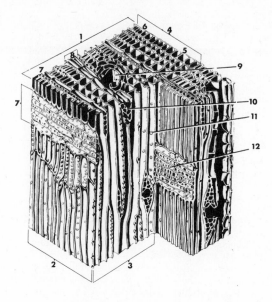

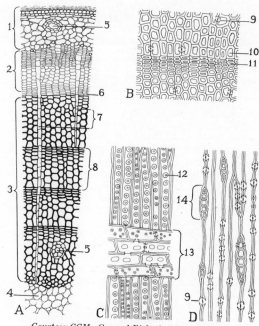

Courtesy CCM: General Biological Inc., Chicago

13-9a. Softwood. This is an enlargement of a ⅟₃₂″ cubic section. Numbered items are: 1. Cross-sectional face. 2. Radial face. 3. Tangential face. 4. Annual ring. 5. Springwood (early wood). 6. Summerwood (late wood). 7. Wood ray. 8. Fusiform ray. 9. Vertical resin duct. 10. Horizontal resin duct. 11. Border pit. 12. Simple pit.

13-9b. Pine stem. 1. Cortex. 2. Phloem. 3. Xylem. 4. Pith. 5. Resin duct. 6. Cambium. 7. Rays. 8. Annual ring. 9. Pith pit. 10. Springwood (early wood). 11. Summerwood (late wood). 12. Border pit. 13. Long ray. 14. Rays.

Resinous

1. Douglas fir	4. Sugar pine
2. Southern yellow pine	5. Ponderosa pine
	6. Western larch
3. White pine	7. Engelmann spruce

Non-Resinous

1. Red cedar	2. Redwood

and Douglas fir. The fusiform rays occasionally help to determine the presence of resin ducts, especially in the spruces and larches, in which the vertical resin ducts are sometimes not easily found. On the radial surface the horizontal resin ducts may often be recognized as brownish lines, especially in the pines.

Procedure for Identifying Woods.
First, determine whether the sample is softwood (nonporous) or hardwood (porous). If softwood, does it have resin ducts? This will indicate whether it is in the resinous or nonresinous group.

If it is a hardwood, is it in the ring-porous or diffuse-porous group? Check the distinguishing characteristics that can be seen with the eye, a hand lens, or a microscope, and compare with the description given here. If it is not one of the more common woods, identification can be made by consulting a good reference book or by sending a sample to the Forest Products Laboratory.

1. White-Oak Group. *Fig. 13-10.*

Pores. In springwood, the pores are large and easily visible to the unaided eye, forming a porous ring one or two rows wide, or in broad rings. The pores decrease in size more or less abruptly toward the summerwood, where they are grouped in V-shaped radial bands. In the summerwood they are somewhat angular and so small and numerous that it is exceedingly difficult to count them even with the aid of a good hand lens.

The large pores in the springwood are usually plugged with tyloses except in the outer portion of the sapwood.

Rays. Some of the rays are very broad and conspicuous, and from ½″ to 4″ high (i.e., measured with the grain), while others are so fine as to be barely visible with a lens. The broad rays appear as conspicuous streaks where the bark has been removed.

Parenchyma. Plainly visible with a lens as light-colored tangential lines and also as a lighter-colored area surrounding the pores of the summerwood.

Annual rings. Mostly from moderately wide to narrow; occasionally wide.

Sapwood. From one to several inches in thickness, often discolored by tannin and other material.

Heartwood. Grayish brown, usually without reddish tinge.

2. Red-Oak Group. *Fig. 13-11.*

Pores. In springwood, the pores are large and easily visible without a lens, forming a porous ring that may be two, three, or even four rows wide. They decrease in size more or less abruptly, or in wide rings somewhat gradually, toward the summerwood where they are grouped in radial bands, often branching or widening toward the outer limit of the annual ring. The pores in the summerwood are well rounded and very distinct under a lens; occasionally barely visible without a lens. They are not too numerous or crowded and can be easily counted with the aid of a magnifying glass.

Rays. Some of the rays are very broad and conspicuous; others are so fine as to be barely visible with a lens and are easily overlooked. In height (i.e., measured with the grain) the large rays range from ¼″ to 1″ or occasionally more, averaging somewhat less than in the white oaks. They appear as conspicuous darker streaks where the bark has been removed.

Parenchyma. Plainly visible as light-colored tangential lines in the summerwood and as a lighter area surrounding the smaller pores.

Annual rings. Mostly from moderate in width to wide.

Sapwood. Highly variable in thickness, from 1″ to 3″.

Heartwood. Mostly brown with reddish tinge, especially in the vicinity of knots. Exceptional pieces resembling white oak in color may be found.

3. Pecan (Hickory) Group. *Fig. 13-12.*

Pores. Plainly visible with the unaided eye in the springwood, forming a ring one, two or three pores wide, decreasing in size somewhat gradually toward the summerwood, in which they are smaller but still occasionally visible without a lens. In summerwood pores are not numerous and are isolated or in radial groups of two or three.

Most of the larger pores except those in the outer sapwood are filled with tyloses.

Rays. Rather fine, not distinct without a lens.

Parenchyma. In numerous fine, light-colored, tangential lines, not widening out and encircling the pores as in ash, but usually extending between the pores or passing around them on one side; very plain under a lens and sometimes visible without a lens.

Annual rings. Clearly defined; highly variable in width.

13-10. White Oak. *13-11.* Red oak. *13-12.* Pecan.

(The end or cross-sectional views in these and the following illustrations are enlarged *ten* times except where otherwise indicated.)

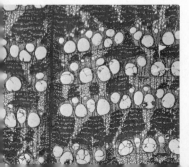
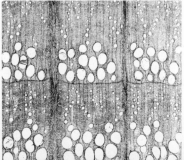
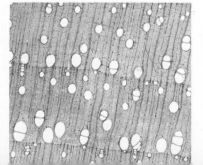

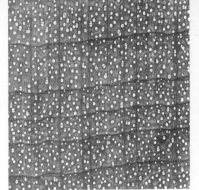

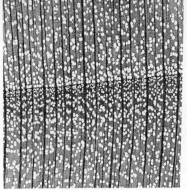

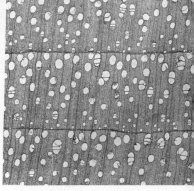

13-13.   Sugar maple.   13-14.   Cherry.   13-15.   Black walnut.

Sapwood. From 1″ to 2″ and occasionally as much as 3″ wide.

Heartwood. Brown to reddish brown.

4. Maple Group. *Fig. 13-13.*

Pores. Small, not visible with the unaided eye; round, nearly always isolated, rarely in radial rows of two or three; practically uniform in size throughout the growth ring; not crowded.

Rays. Two kinds: some very distinct without a lens, fully as wide as the largest pores except near the center of a tree, and conspicuous on a radial cut as small, reddish brown "flakes;" others very fine, barely visible with a lens.

Parenchyma. Not noticeable.

Annual rings. Not very distinct; defined by a reddish brown line. Pith flecks rarely present.

Sapwood. Several inches wide; white with slight reddish brown tinge.

Heartwood. Light reddish brown.

5. Cherry Group. *Fig. 13-14.*

Pores. Small, not visible with the unaided eye, evenly distributed or gradually decreasing in size and number toward the end of each annual ring; isolated or in irregular groups of two to four; numerous, occupying one-third or slightly more of the space between the rays.

Rays. Very distinct on end and radial surfaces; as wide or almost as wide as the largest pores.

Parenchyma. Not noticeable.

Annual rings. Fairly distinct; defined by an abrupt difference in the size of the pores in the summerwood and succeeding springwood; much more pronounced in some samples than in others. Pith flecks occasionally present but inconspicuous because the color is the same as that of the surrounding wood.

Sapwood. Narrow, usually less than 1″.

Heartwood. Reddish brown in varying shades from moderately dark to very dark.

6. Black Walnut. *Fig. 13-15.*

Pores. Comparatively large and easily visible with the unaided eye, especially in the spring-wood, and gradually decreasing in size toward the outer portion of each annual ring. (Although at first sight some pieces may give the impression of being ring-porous, they are not classed as such because the large pores in the beginning of each annual ring do not form a definite zone beyond which they decrease abruptly in size.) Tyloses are present but do not fill the pores completely.

Rays. Very fine and inconspicuous; not distinct without a lens.

Parenchyma. Present in the form of several lighter-colored, irregular tangential lines readily visible in the sapwood but obscure in the heartwood.

Annual Rings. Distinct; marked by an abrupt difference in the size of the pores in the summerwood and succeeding springwood, and by a fine, light-colored line.

Sapwood. Narrow, mostly less than 1″ wide, but occasionally up to 3″; white, or discolored to yellowish or purplish brown.

Heartwood. Rich chocolate-brown with lustrous surface.

7. Birch. *Fig. 13-16.*

Pores. Usually not distinct to the unaided eye but clearly visible in some pieces; not crowded, occupying less than one-third of the total area between the rays except in very narrow rings; occasionally in radial rows of two to four. Tyloses absent.

Rays. Fine, not distinctly visible without a lens; appearing on the radial surface as very fine reddish brown "flakes."

Parenchyma. Not noticeable.

Annual rings. Not distinct to the unaided eye

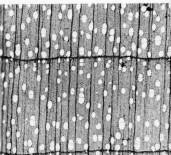

13-16.   Yellow birch.

179

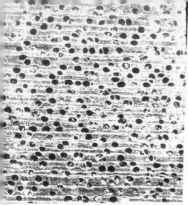

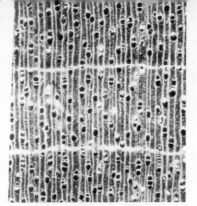

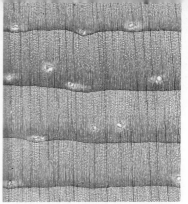

13-17.   Philippine mahogany.
(Enlarged 7½ times.)

13-18.   True mahogany.
(Enlarged 7½ times.)

13-19.   Western white pine.

except in specimens showing rapid growth; defined by a fine line and a slight decrease in pore size at the end of each year's growth. Pith flecks usually absent.

Sapwood. Several inches in width, but extremely variable in different pieces.

Heartwood. Reddish brown.

8. Mahogany, Philippine (tanguile and red lauan). *Fig. 13-17.*

Pores. Plainly visible without a lens, evenly distributed and fairly uniform in size. Slightly smaller on the average in tanguile than in red lauan. Pores contain glistening tyloses which are hardly visible without a lens.

Rays. Not distinctly visible without a lens. On quarter-sawed surfaces, the rays though not large are very conspicuous because of their reddish color.

Annual rings. Not well defined, although white tangential lines of varying lengths are present which are from ⅛″ to several inches apart.

Sapwood. Very pale grayish or reddish brown in color.

Heartwood. Varies in color from pale to dark reddish brown. Tanguile usually has a slight purplish tinge.

9. Mahogany, True. *Fig. 13-18.*

Pores. Plainly visible, fairly uniform in size and evenly distributed. May contain dark reddish brown gum. Occasionally, especially in the heavier grades, the pores contain white deposits.

Rays. Very fine but distinctly visible without a lens. Very distinct on quarter-sawed surfaces

where they may appear lighter or darker than the wood fibers.

Annual rings. Defined by light-colored lines.

Sapwood. Narrower than heartwood and from white to light brown.

Heartwood. Reddish brown in various shades, but each piece fairly uniform in color except for differences in the reflection of light. Becomes darker on exposure to light.

10. White Pine. *Fig. 13-19.*

Resin Ducts. Scattered haphazardly throughout the annual ring. Openings plainly visible with a lens and, under favorable conditions, even without a lens.

Rays. Mostly very fine, some (containing horizontal resin ducts) slightly wider and more conspicuous under a lens.

Annual rings. Distinct, moderate in width, the soft springwood passing very gradually into the slightly harder and darker summerwood which does not offer much more resistance in cutting than the springwood.

Sapwood. Mostly from 1″ to 2″ in width, occasionally 3″.

Heartwood. Cream to light reddish brown.

11. Engelmann Spruce. *Fig. 13-20.*

Resin Ducts. Present; comparatively few; mostly isolated, less frequently two adjacent, and occasionally many in a tangential row; inconspicuous, easily overlooked, often visible only as white specks in the summerwood, their presence also indicated by occasional wider medullary rays which contain the horizontal resin ducts.

Rays. Very fine, except as indicated above.

Annual Rings. Moderate in width; summerwood narrow, not much denser or darker than the springwood; transition from springwood to summerwood gradual.

Sapwood. Not distinctly defined, but noticeable on green timbers because of its higher moisture content; variable from ¾″ to 2″ in width.

13-20.   Engelmann spruce.

180

12. Redwood. *Fig. 13-21.*

Resin Ducts. Normally absent, present only as result of injury and then in a tangential line at point of injury only.

Rays. Narrow; uniform in width; easily visible with a lens because lighter colored than the surrounding wood.

Annual Rings. Moderate and regular in width; very distinct because of the summerwood which is more pronounced than in the cedars. The dark specks are cells containing resin. They are numerous in this species but, on account of the dark color of the wood, are not easily seen on the end sufADDCUNCE. On split surfaces the resin cells are often quite distinct under a lens, appearing as dark lines running with the grain.

Sapwood. One to several inches in width; almost white.

Heartwood. Uniform deep reddish brown.

13. Red Cedar. *Fig. 13-22.*

Resin Ducts. Absent.

Rays. Very narrow and inconspicuous; uniform in width.

Annual Rings. Distinct, moderately narrow, with a thin but dense band of summerwood.

Sapwood. From ¼″ to 1″ in width.

Heartwood. Brown, usually with a reddish hue.

Physical Properties. The wood is light, straight-grained, and easily split. It has a distinct odor characteristic of cedar shingles, and the heartwood has a spicy bitter taste.

14. Douglas Fir. *Fig. 13-23.*

Resin Ducts. Present; small and inconspicuous; occasionally visible without a lens as elongated whitish specks, especially in the summerwood; the openings not visible without a lens; often in tangential rows of from 2 to 20 or more.

Rays. Mostly very fine, a few (containing horizontal resin ducts) slightly wider and more conspicuous under a lens.

Annual Rings. Very distinct; variable from narrow to wide; summerwood always conspic-

uous as a denser and darker band but variable from very narrow in slow growth to wide and hard in trees of rapid growth.

Sapwood. About 1″ wide in Rocky Mountain forms, and several inches wide in Pacific Coast forms.

Heartwood. Mostly orange reddish to red, the springwood as well as the summerwood being colored; sometimes yellowish in old Pacific Coast trees.

SPECIFIC GRAVITY

Broadly speaking, the strength of wood depends upon its weight when dry. For a given moisture content, the higher the specific gravity, the greater the strength of the wood. To compare the weight of various woods, therefore, they must all be equally dry. *Specific gravity* is commonly used for an accurate comparison of the relative weight of woods.

A simple way of determining the specific gravity of a piece of wood is by the flotation method. Essentially, the method consists of determining the proportion of a piece of wood with parallel sides that is submerged when it is floated in water. The test specimen should be 1″ square in cross section and 10″ long, marked into 10 equal divisions of 1″. When the piece is floated upright in a cylinder of water, its specific gravity at current moisture content can be determined by observing how much of the piece is submerged. *Fig. 13-24.* For example,

13-21. Redwood.

13-22. Red cedar.

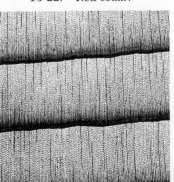

13-23. Douglas fir.

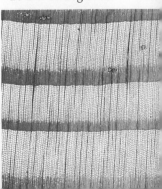

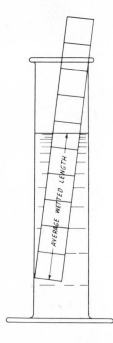

AVERAGE WETTED LENGTH

13-24. Checking specific gravity.

EFFECT OF MOISTURE CONTENT ON WEIGHT AND DIMENSION

if six divisions of the piece are under water, the specific gravity is 0.6, while if it sinks to the seventh mark, the specific gravity is 0.7. When the water level reaches a point somewhere between two dividing marks on the piece, specific gravity may be visually estimated with reasonable accuracy; a water level halfway between 6 and 7, for example, would be 0.65. This is the specific gravity of the entire wood—that is, the cell walls and the spaces in the cells. This value varies for different woods because some woods have more air space or more cell wall material than others. The weight, or density, of the cell wall is the same for all woods. While this value is constant the amount of cell wall material in a given volume of wood varies considerably.

Because specific gravity is a measure of the amount of cell wall material in wood, it is a useful indicator of strength properties and of suitability for various uses. Heavy woods such as Douglas fir or oak are used for heavy construction, while lighter ones (white pine, for example) are better when load bearing is not the prime consideration.

To use the oven drying method of determining moisture content, the oven must be capable of maintaining a constant temperature of 100° to 105°C. (214° to 221°F.) and the balance scale must be accurate to within 1/10″. *Figs. 13-25 and 13-26.* Cut specimens of solid wood at least one foot from the end of the piece. These specimens should be 1″ long with the grain 4″ wide. The wood block must be cut so that the growth rings appear as in *Fig. 13-27.* Plywood specimens can be any convenient size but should not be cut from the edge of the piece. Trim off all the loose splinters and carefully weigh the specimen on the scale. Also, measure the thickness of the piece at three points across the board, using a 1″ micrometer. Measure the width across the board to the closest $\frac{1}{32}$″. Record the data for the dimensions and weight as shown in *Fig. 13-28.* Dry the specimens for 24 hours in an oven at 100° to 105° C. and weigh and measure immediately. Difference in weight of the piece before and after being dried, divided by weight when dry, gives the moisture content of the piece before drying; this is expressed in percentage of the oven-dry weight multiplied by 100. Also measure the piece after drying. Various comparisons can be made by using pieces of the same species from different sections of the lumber pile, or by using different species.

Expansion and Contraction. The effect of moisture on the size of wood can be illustrated by cutting a series

13-25. Electric oven for making dry test.

13-26. Weighing samples on a scale.

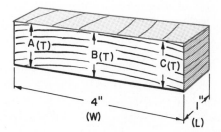

13-27. Method of cutting wood for checking changes in sizes and weights. A, B, and C indicate measurement points across the thickness (T).

WEIGHT

Before	
After	
% Change	

13-28. Sample charts for recording changes in oven-dried wood specimens. (Do not write in this book.)

SIZE

Measurement	Thickness			Length	Width
	A	**B**	**C**		
Before					
After					
% Change					

183

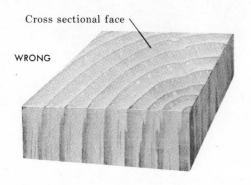

Cross sectional face

WRONG

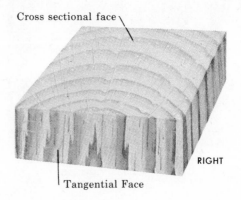

Cross sectional face

RIGHT

Tangential Face

13-29. Incorrect and correct methods of cutting wood for checking expansion and contraction.

of 2″ x 2″ x 1″ wood blocks, with the 1″ length parallel to the grain and the other two directions being true radial and tangential directions as shown in *Fig. 13-29.* Place one piece in the fixture with the dial gauge as shown and add moisture to the end grain. *Fig. 13-30.* Note how the wood expands. Place the second piece in the fixture and record the measurement. Place the specimen in the oven to dry and then remeasure. Make this comparison with different kinds of wood. You will note that wood with high specific gravity tends to shrink and swell more.

PEG for Stabilizing Wood. In construction, when species or pieces with different specific gravity are to be combined in a single product, the differences in shrinkage and swelling may cause splitting or warping. Therefore users of wood have long wanted a way to prevent wood from shrinking and swelling with variation in moisture content. The Forest Products Laboratory at Madison, Wisconsin, has developed a chemical that has

shown the greatest promise and is now widely used in processing wood products. This white waxlike material, resembling paraffin, is called polyethylene glycol-1000 (PEG for short). This chemical is non-toxic, dissolves readily in water, and does not discolor wood. When a piece of green, nondried wood is soaked for an appropriate period in a 30-50 per cent water solution of PEG, the wood does not shrink appreciably when it dries. Because there is little or no change in dimension, treated wood has less tendency to warp and is usually free of checks and splits that so frequently develop in wood, especially thick stock, during the drying period. Equally important, the treated wood, when dried, swells very little when exposed to high humidities. PEG attacks the problem of change in wood dimension by bulking the microscopic, lacelike structure of the individual wood fiber walls. Heavily treated wood is thus permanently kept from shrinking, swelling, or warping regardless of the atmospheric humidity.

184

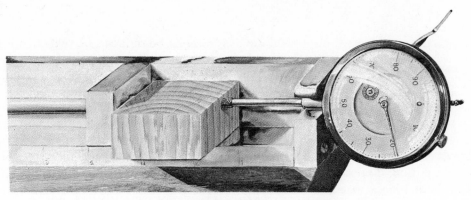

13-30. Fixture for checking expansion and contraction.

Treatment with PEG permits efficient processing of green or partially dry wood. It is ideally suited for such items as solid bowls, serving trays, candlesticks, art carvings, gun stocks, and similar products that normally require thick pieces of the highest and most expensive grades of kiln-dried hardwood. If the PEG treatment is to be used for projects such as lamp posts, bowls, and bases, then it is better to rough turn the items ¼″ to ⅜″ oversize before they are treated.

To treat the wood, it is necessary to have some kind of watertight container. The best type is a plywood box that has been treated on the inside with fiberglass to make it waterproof. *Fig. 13-31.* In constructing the box or tank, it is important that the corners be made with good joints that will support the liquid adequately. While the soaking can be done in 30 per cent solution for three to five weeks at room temperature, it is better to heat the liquid to speed the treatment. Treating time can be reduced to one or two weeks by increasing the temperature of the solution to 140 to 160° F. For this reason, it is a good idea to equip

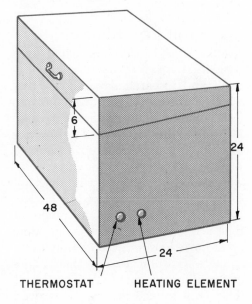

13-31. Box for treating wood with PEG.

the soaking tank with a heating element and thermostat. After the wood parts have been soaked they should be slowly dried to 8 to 10 per cent moisture content. This can be done in a simple conditioning room, maintaining a temperature of about 75° F., with 30 per cent relative humidity. However, if a small kiln is available, the items can be dried in about seven

185

days. After treatment, the wood can be worked to finish size. To finish, use one or two coats of polyurethane varnish, the only finish that can be used satisfactorily.

To determine the value of the PEG treatment, turn two identically shaped bowls from green wood. Treat one in PEG solution; do nothing to the other. Dry both pieces to 8 per cent moisture content, then compare the weight of the pieces and inspect for checks and splits.

FIRE RETARDATION

Many people think of wood as a basic fuel for fire; however, experiment and research have shown that wood can be used to protect man from fire. Wood resistance to fire is particularly good in large buildings where big timbers or laminated beams or arches provide the framework. Because wood burns slowly and does not soften or become weakened by intense heat, large timbers retain much of their original strength for many hours after fire exposure. Wood frequently is more resistant to fire than many non-combustible materials. This is well illustrated by the fire that destroyed Chicago's huge McCormick Place in January, 1967. There the contents caught on fire and the intense heat caused the non-combustible structural members to fail. The roof then collapsed and the building was completely destroyed. In contrast, wood structural members will hold a roof long enough to permit fire fighters to attack and extinguish fire within a structure.

The combustibility (burnability) of wood can be reduced by two chemical methods. The most common consists of injecting solutions of fire retardant salt into wood under pressure; in the other, paints containing fire retardant chemicals are applied to the wood surface. Certain paints are also used on wood that is already installed in structures to make it less combustible. Experiments show that when flames are not present, treated wood will stop burning immediately.

Section B

CHECK YOUR KNOWLEDGE

1. Name five common hardwoods.
2. Name at least five of the more important softwoods.
3. Give a good source of information on the botanical differences among species.
4. Tell where you can obtain information on identification of woods.
5. Give the principal uses of walnut.
6. Name the two major kinds of oak. Point out the differences between them.
7. Name the two kinds of mahogany.
8. Name a good wood for house construction in an area where termites are a problem.
9. Name one of the principal uses of Douglas fir.
10. Tell why it is important to know the properties of wood.
11. Discuss some of the differences between hardwood and softwood species.
12. Discuss the differences between the hardness of softwoods and hardwoods.
13. Balsa wood is sometimes used in life preservers; tell why.
14. Wood shrinks or swells more when it is cut flat grain. State the reason for this.
15. Explain why oak is a poor project choice when only hand tools are available.
16. Name the weakest part of any wood construction.
17. Describe what happens when wood with too high moisture content is nailed.

186

18. Tell which is better for increasing bending strength of a beam—adding to the height or the width of a beam.

19. Name the wood that makes the best baseball bat. Explain.

20. Tell the conditions under which wood decays.

21. Tell how woods get their figure patterns.

22. Give the reasons why wood is painted.

23. Define wood.

24. Describe the cross-section parts of a tree.

25. Explain the purpose of medullary rays.

26. Water exists in green wood in two conditions. Explain.

27. Tell how to determine the age of a tree.

28. Summerwood is sometimes called late wood. Explain.

29. Tell where new growth takes place in a tree.

30. Describe the two common methods of cutting boards.

31. Softwoods are not always soft and hardwoods are not always hard. Explain.

32. Name the four major chemical materials of wood.

33. Tell how much moisture a tree contains when it is first cut down.

34. Describe what is meant by fiber saturation point.

35. Describe the two common methods of drying lumber.

36. Tell which drying method is best for woods that will go into furniture.

37. Describe two methods of learning the moisture content of wood.

38. Give some practical suggestions for controlling the problem of moisture content of wood.

39. Discuss uniform standards of wood as opposed to metal.

40. Explain the difference in lumber quality in different grades, such as select and common in softwoods.

41. Name and describe some of the major lumber defects.

42. Hardwood grading is designed primarily for the furniture industry. Discuss the reason for this.

43. Explain the difficulty of grading softwood lumbers.

44. Explain the variation in the application of American Lumber Standards by the many different lumber associations in establishing their grading standards.

45. Name the three main classes of softwood lumbers.

46. Explain why it is important to know how to purchase lumber.

47. Give the class of lumber that is intended for further cutting in the manufacture of doors and sash.

48. State the minimum thickness of structural lumber.

49. Name some of the common shapes of siding.

50. Name the two hardwoods widely used for flooring.

51. Tell how most lumber is sold.

52. Describe a board foot of lumber.

53. Tell how to determine the board measure in a piece of wood.

54. Explain the use of the Essex board measure table.

55. Describe plywood and the difference between veneer-core plywood and lumber-core plywood.

56. Describe the three common methods of cutting veneer for plywood.

57. Define flitch.

58. Describe the manufacture of plywood.

59. Give a description of the grading for softwood and hardwood plywoods.

60. State the advantages of plywood over solid wood.

61. Describe some of the special plywoods.

62. List the places where plywood is found in home construction.

63. Tell how veneering can be done in the school shop.

64. Describe the treatment of plywood edges to give a finished appearance.

65. Describe the best way of storing plywood to avoid warpage.

66. Describe the correct method of cutting plywood.

67. List the similarities and differences between hardboard and particle board.

68. Name the two kinds of hardboard.

69. Name the tools that should be used

on hardboard if quantity production and machining is to be done.

70. Explain how hardboard can be bent.

71. Name some of the woods used in making particle board.

72. Explain how particle board is made.

73. Describe sheetboard.

74. Name the wood joint that is used to increase the width and length of lumber.

75. Name the materials used to make insulation board.

76. Describe sandwich construction.

77. Name the two major classifications of plastics.

78. Describe Fiberglas and tell where it is used.

79. Plastic laminates are used on counter tops and in bathrooms. Give the reason.

80. Name the best cutter bits to use on plastic laminates.

81. Describe how laminates can be bent.

82. Name the three common ways of identifying wood species based on their structure.

83. What is the difference between a ring-porous and a diffuse-porous hardwood.

THINGS TO DO

1. Make a sample display board of common woods in your area of the country.

2. Obtain samples of three or four unusual woods and attempt to identify them. If you have difficulty, contact the Forest Products Laboratory. Write a report.

3. Make a picture collection of furniture and home construction, and indicate the woods used in each illustration.

4. Design a piece of equipment for testing one of the properties of wood. Then test several samples of different woods.

5. Get a cross-section of a tree trunk and label the parts.

6. Make a chart showing the differences between hardwood and softwood. Include in this an enlarged view of the wood surface showing the pores.

7. Check the moisture content of some sample pieces of newly cut wood using the oven-drying method.

8. Visit a kiln drying plant and write a report on this seasoning process.

9. Check your local lumber yard to find the common lumbers that are available.

10. Write up an order for the lumber you will use in one of your projects.

11. Make a model or mock-up of the rotary method of cutting plywood.

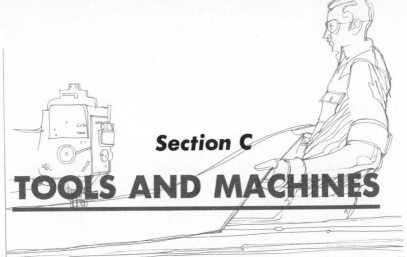

Section C
TOOLS AND MACHINES

With "know-how" you can change the raw material into useful products. You will need tools and machines to fashion the wood. Learn to handle them correctly and safely and you will acquire skills that will be valuable to you all your life.

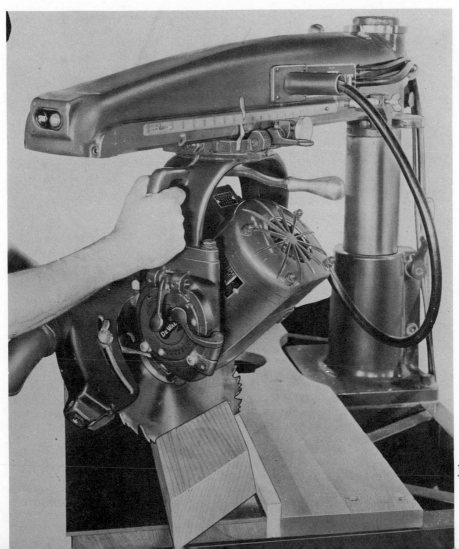

Unit 14: LAYOUT, MEASURING, AND CHECKING DEVICES

TOOL	DESCRIPTION	USES
Bench Rule *Fig. 14–1.*	A 12-inch or one foot rule. One side is divided into eighths, the other into sixteenths.	1. To make simple measurements. 2. To adjust dividers. *Caution.* Never use as a straightedge.
Zig-Zag Rule *Fig. 14–2.*	A folding rule of six- or eight-foot length.	1. To measure distances greater than 2′, place the rule flat on the stock. 2. To measure less than 2′, it is better to use the rule on edge. (This instrument is good for inside measurement, since the reading on the brass extension can be added to the length of the rule itself.)

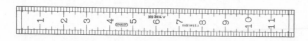

14–1.

14–2.

Flexible Tape Rules *Fig. 14–3.*	A flexible tape that slides into a metal case. Comes in lengths of 6′, 8′, 10′, 12′, 50′, and 100′. The steel tape has a hook on the end that adjusts to true zero.	1. To measure irregular as well as regular shapes. 2. To make accurate inside measurements. (Measurement is read by adding 2″ to the reading on the blade.)
Try Square *Fig. 14–4.*	A squaring, measuring, and testing tool with a metal blade and a wood or metal handle.	1. To test a surface for levelness. 2. To check adjacent surfaces for squareness. 3. To make lines across the face or edge of stock.

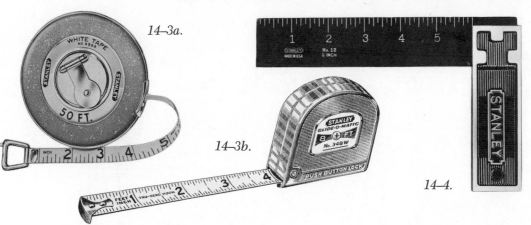

14–3a.

14–3b.

14–4.

TOOL	DESCRIPTION	USES
Combination Square *Fig. 14–5.*	Consists of a blade and handle. The blade slides along in the handle or head. There is a level and a scriber in the handle.	1. To test a level or plumb surface. 2. To check squareness—either inside or outside. 3. To mark and test a 45-degree miter. 4. To gauge-mark a line with a pencil.
Sliding T Bevel *Fig. 14–6.*	A blade that can be set at any angle to the handle. Set with a framing square or protractor.	1. To measure or transfer an angle between 0 and 180 degrees. 2. To check or test a miter cut.
Dividers *Fig. 14–7.*	A tool with two metal legs. One metal leg can be removed and replaced with a pencil. To set the dividers, hold both points on the measuring lines of the rule.	1. To lay out an arc or circle. 2. To step off measurements. 3. To divide distances along a straight line.

14–5.

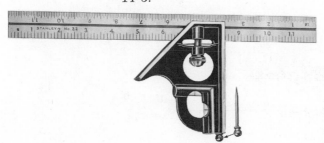

14–6.

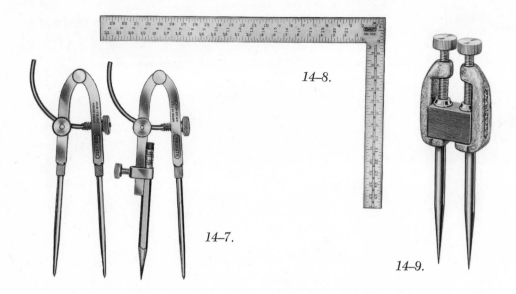

14–8.

14–7.

14–9.

TOOL	DESCRIPTION	USES
Framing or Rafter Square *Fig. 14–8.*	A large steel square consisting of a blade, or body, and a tongue.	1. To check for squareness. 2. To mark a line across a board. 3. To lay out rafters and stairs.
Trammel Points *Fig. 14–9.*	Two metal pointers that can be fastened to a long bar of wood or metal.	1. To lay out distances between two points. 2. To scribe arcs and circles, larger than those made with dividers.
Carpenter's Level *Fig. 14–10.*	A rectangular metal or wood frame with several level glasses.	To check whether a surface is level or plumb.
Scratch Awl *Fig. 14–11.*	A pointed metal tool with handle.	1. To locate a point of measurement. 2. To scribe a line accurately.

14–10.

14–11.

14-12.

14-13.

TOOL	DESCRIPTION	USES
Marking Gauge *Fig. 14–12.*	A wood or metal tool consisting of a beam, head, and point.	To mark a line parallel to the grain of wood.
Plumb Bob and Line *Fig. 14–13.*	A metal weight with a pointed end. The opposite end has a hole for attaching the cord.	1. To determine the corners of buildings. 2. To establish a vertical line.

Unit 15: SAWING TOOLS

TOOL	DESCRIPTION	USES
Back Saw *Fig. 15–1.*	A fine-tooth, crosscut saw with a heavy metal band across the back to strengthen the thin blade.	1. To make fine cuts for joinery. 2. To use in a miter box.
Crosscut Saw *Fig. 15–2.*	A hand saw in lengths from 20″ to 26″ with from 4 to 12 points per inch. A 22″, 10 point saw is a good one for general purpose work.	1. To cut across grain. 2. Can be used to cut with the grain. *Caution:* Never cut into nails or screws. Never twist off strips of waste stock.
Rip Saw *Fig. 15–3.*	A hand saw in lengths from 20″ to 28″. A 26″, 5½-point saw is good for general use.	To cut with the grain. *Caution:* Support the waste stock. Never allow end of saw to strike the floor.
Compass Saw *Fig. 15–4.*	A 12″ or 14″ taper blade saw.	1. To cut gentle curves. 2. To cut inside curves.
Keyhole Saw *Fig. 15–5.*	A 10″ or 12″ narrow taper saw with fine teeth.	To cut small openings and fine work.

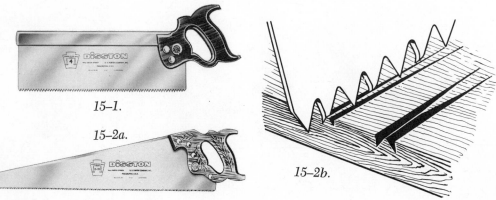

15–1.

15–2a.

15–2b.

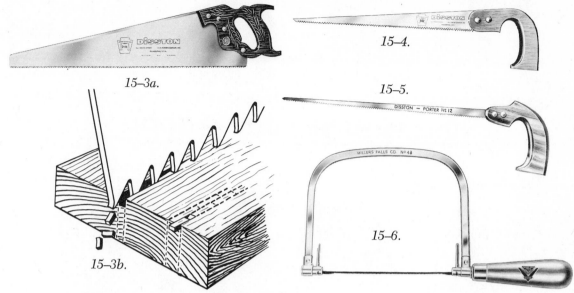

15–3a.

15–4.

15–5.

15–3b.

15–6.

TOOL	DESCRIPTION	USES
Coping Saw *Fig. 15–6.*	A U-shaped saw frame permitting $4\frac{1}{2}''$ or $6\frac{1}{2}''$ deep cuts. Uses standard $6\frac{1}{2}''$ pin-end blades.	1. To cut curves. 2. To shape the ends of molding for joints. 3. For scroll work.
Miter Box Saw *Fig. 15–7.*	A longer back saw (24" to 28").	Used in a homemade or commercial miter box for cutting miters or square ends.
Dovetail Saw *Fig. 15–8.*	An extremely thin blade with very fine teeth.	For smoothest possible joint cuts.
Hacksaw *Fig. 15–9.*	A U-shaped frame with handle. Uses replaceable blades.	To cut metal fasteners and hardware.

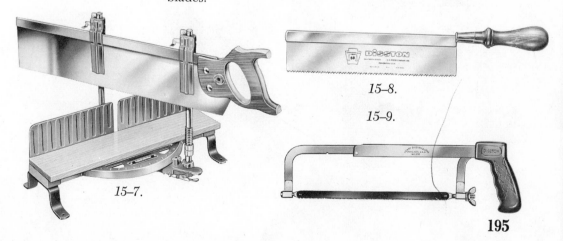

15–7.

15–8.

15–9.

195

Unit 16: EDGE CUTTING TOOLS

TOOL	DESCRIPTION	USES
Smooth Plane Fig. 16–1.	A 7″ to 9″ plane.	1. For general use. 2. For smaller work.
Jack Plane Fig. 16–2.	A 14″ or 15″ plane.	1. Ideal for rough surfaces where chip should be coarse. 2. Also used to obtain a smooth, flat surface.
Fore Plane Fig. 16–3.	An 18″ plane.	For fine flat finish on longer surfaces and edges.
Jointer Plane Fig. 16–4.	A 22″ or 24″ plane.	1. To smooth and flatten edges for making a close-fitting joint. 2. For planing long boards such as the edges of doors.

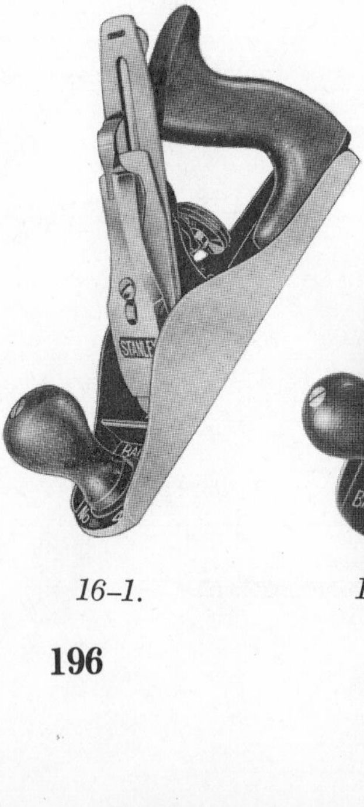

16–1. 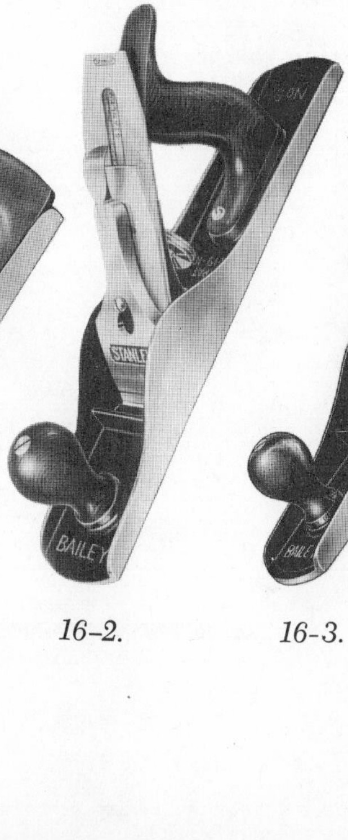   16–2. 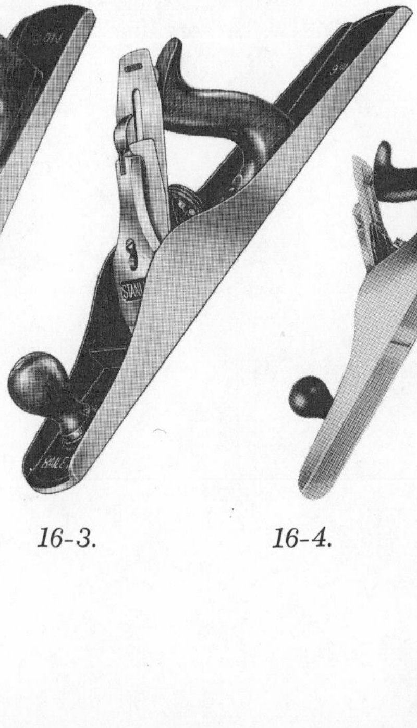   16-3.    16-4.

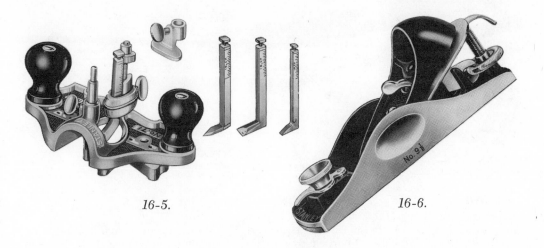

16-5.   16-6.

TOOL	DESCRIPTION	USES
Router Plane *Fig. 16–5.*	A cutting tool with several cutters.	To surface the bottom of grooves and dadoes.
Block Plane *Fig. 16–6.*	A small plane with a single, low-angle cutter with the bevel up.	1. To plane end grain. 2. For small pieces. 3. For planing the ends of molding, trim, and siding.
Chisels *Fig. 16–7.*	A set usually includes blade widths from $\frac{1}{8}''$ to $2''$.	To trim and shape wood.
Draw Knife *Fig. 16–8.*	An open-bevelled blade with handles on both ends.	To remove much material in a short time.
Surform Tool *Fig. 16–9.*	Available in file, plane type. Also round, or block-plane types. A blade with 45-degree cutting teeth.	For all types of cutting and trimming.

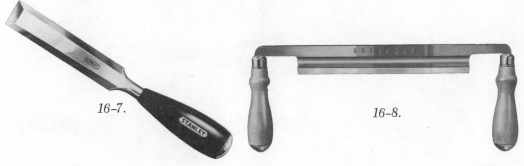

16-7.   16-8.

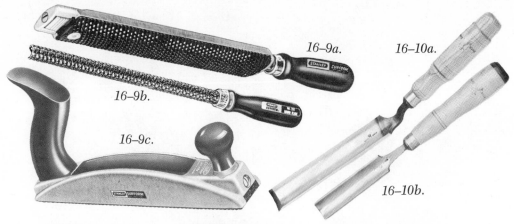

16–9a.

16–10a.

16–9b.

16–9c.

16–10b.

TOOL	DESCRIPTION	USES
Gouges *Fig. 16–10.*	A chisel with a curved blade. Sharpened on the inside or, more commonly, on the outside.	To cut grooves or to shape irregular openings.
Hatchet *Fig. 16–11.*	A cutting tool with a curved edge on one side and a hammer head on the other. Has hammer-length handle.	To trim pieces to fit in building construction. For nailing flooring.
Spokeshave *Fig. 16–12.*	A small plane-like tool.	To form irregularly shaped objects.
Hand Scraper *Fig. 16–13.*	A blade-like tool.	To scrape the surface of open-grain wood.
Cabinet Scraper *Fig. 16–14.*	A blade in a holder.	To scrape the surface of furniture woods.

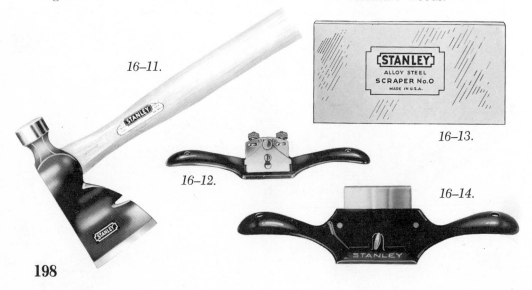

16–11.

STANLEY
ALLOY STEEL
SCRAPER No.0
MADE IN U.S.A.

16–13.

16–12.

16–14.

Unit 17: DRILLING AND BORING TOOLS

TOOL	DESCRIPTION	USES
Auger Bit *Fig. 17–1.*	May be either single-twist or double-twist bit. Comes in sizes from No. 4 ($\frac{1}{4}''$) to No. 16 (1'').	1. To bore holes $\frac{1}{4}''$ or larger. 2. Single twist bit is better for boring deep holes.
Dowel Bits *Fig. 17–2.*	A shorter bit with a sharper twist.	To bore holes for making dowel joints.
Expansion Bit *Fig. 17–3.*	A bit that holds cutters of different sizes. Sometimes this tool is called an expansive bit.	1. To bore a hole larger than 1''. 2. One cutter will bore holes in the 1'' to 2'' range. 3. A second cutter will bore holes in the 2'' to 3'' range.
Brace *Fig. 17–4.*	Two common types—the plain for a full swing, and the ratchet for close corners.	To hold and operate bits.

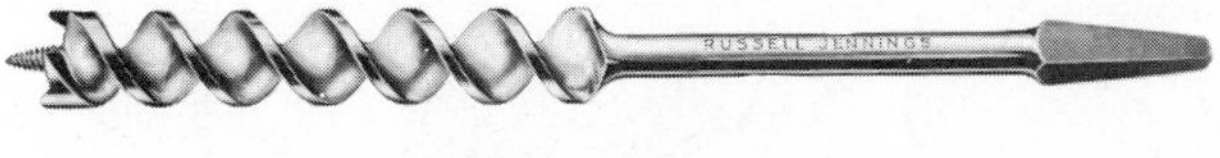

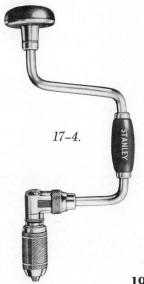

17–4.

17–1.

17–2.

17–3.

TOOL	DESCRIPTION	USES
Foerstner Bit Fig. 17–5.	A bit with a flat cutting surface on the end.	1. To bore a shallow hole with a flat bottom. 2. To bore a hole in thin stock. 3. To bore a hole in end grain. 4. To enlarge an existing hole.

17–5.

Bit or Depth Gauges Fig. 17–6.	Two types—one is a solid clamp, the other a spring type.	To limit the depth of a hole.
Twist Drill (*a*) or Bit Stock Drill (*b*) Fig. 17–7.	A fractional-sized set from $\frac{1}{64}''$ to $\frac{1}{2}''$ is best.	To drill small holes for nails, screws, etc.
Hand Drill Fig. 17–8.	A tool with a 3-jaw chuck.	To hold twist-drills for drilling small holes.
Automatic Drill Fig. 17–9.	A tool with drill points and handle. Size of drill points are: #1 = $\frac{1}{16}''$; #2 = $\frac{5}{64}''$; #3 = $\frac{3}{32}''$; #4 = $\frac{7}{64}''$; #5 = $\frac{1}{8}''$; #6 = $\frac{9}{64}''$; #7 = $\frac{5}{32}''$; #8 = $\frac{11}{64}''$.	To drill many small holes.

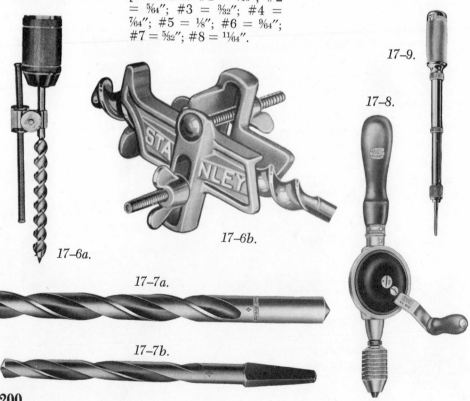

17–9.

17–8.

17–6a.

17–6b.

17–7a.

17–7b.

Unit 18: TOOL SHARPENING

Sharp cutting tools are the key to successful woodworking. Most tool sharpening must be done by the person who uses the equipment, but it is better to have some done professionally.

ABRASIVE STONES

There are two classes of sharpening stones—natural and artificial. Natural stones are very dense and hard. They "cut" or sharpen slowly but produce very fine edges. They are available in several grades of hardness. Artificial stones sharpen faster. The two common types are silicon carbide and aluminum oxide. (See Unit 38, Abrasives and Sanding.) Silicon-carbide stones are made in many shapes and are used primarily for high-carbon tool and knife sharpening. The harder and tougher grit of aluminum oxide makes these stones ideal for sharpening hard tool steels. Some kind of lubricating oil should be used on sharpening stones for the following reasons: (a) to get a faster sharpening job, (b) to get a finer edge, and (c) to prevent clogging or loading of the stone with metal chips. The lubricating oil

should be light and free-flowing. A new stone should be soaked in oil for a few hours before using it. The stone should be wiped clean after using. Occasional cleaning can be done with gasoline or ammonia.

HAND TOOLS

Plane Irons. In general the sharpening of plane irons involves two steps. First, the edge must be ground to the proper angle (between 20 and 30 degrees) on a grinder. *Fig. 18–1.* (If the edge is in good shape this is not

18–1. Using a grinding attachment to grind the bevel on a plane-iron blade.

201

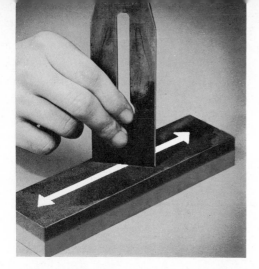

18–2. Squaring the edge. Use a square to check the blade edge. If the edge needs truing, one common method is to hold the blade vertical and rub back and forth over the stone until the edge is square.

18–4. Honing the cutting edge by moving it back and forth in a straight line.

necessary). If grinding must be done, hold the tool at a constant angle to give it a true, straight bevel. *Fig. 18–2.* Move the tool from left to right across the face of the wheel. Dip the tool frequently in water. Friction heats the tool, and the cutting edge loses its hardness if allowed to get too hot. Second, the edge is honed, whetted, or stoned to keen sharpness on an oilstone. Use a medium to fine stone. Hold the bevel flat. Then raise the end slowly until the blades make an angle of about 30 to 35 degrees with the stone.

Hone, using a figure eight or a long, straight motion. *Figs. 18–3* and *18–4.* Occasionally reverse the blade and lightly hone the face, holding it absolutely flat. Test for sharpness on your finger nail. The tool should bite the nail. Try the cutting edge on a soft piece of wood.

Chisel. Grind and hone to an angle of 25 degrees in the same way as for a plane iron.

18–3. Honing the cutting edge using the figure-eight pattern.

18–5. Place the blade at the proper bevel angle to the stone and move the blade from one end to the other. If it has a curved edge, use a rocking motion so that the full edge gets equal honing.

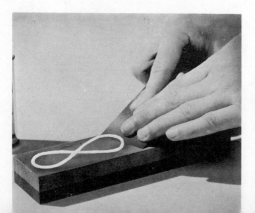

18-6. This is one of the few tools on which both sides must be honed equally. Hold it so that it can be reversed without changing your grasp on the handle. Lay the blade flat on the stone and then raise the back slightly and stroke the edge across the stone. Turn the blade on its back and reverse the motion.

18-7. Hold the draw knife, as shown, at the correct angle to the surface of the stone and draw it across diagonally so that all parts of the edge are equally honed.

18-8. Hone the upper side of the cutting edges, being careful to retain the original bevel angle.

Hatchet. The hatchet must be wedge shaped and fairly heavy. The angle of both the edge and the blade bevel should be decidedly obtuse so that, in use, it splits off chips and frees itself for the next stroke. *Fig. 18–5.*

Pocket Knives. Pocket knives should be ground to an angle of about 25 degrees. Place the blade flat on the stone in a diagonal position, then tip the back of the blade up about 25 degrees. *Fig. 18–6.*

Draw Knife. Hold the draw knife by its handle at the correct angle to the surface of the stone. Draw it across diagonally so that all parts of the edge are equally honed. *Fig. 18–7.*

Auger Bit. Use a small, flat, auger-bit file or auger-bit stone. Sharpen the upper side of the cutting edges, being careful to retain the original bevel angle. Sharpen the inside of the spurs only. *Fig. 18–8.*

Countersink. Sharpen the face of the cutting edge. *Fig. 18–9.*

Screw Driver. Rounded edges on a screw driver cause slipping and burring. The end of the screw driver should be flat. Keep the two faces of the blade parallel. *Fig. 18–10.*

18-9. Hone the face of the cutting edges, using a fine stone.

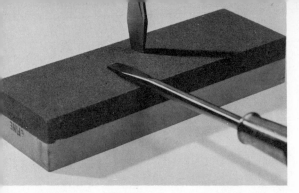

18–10. Round edges on a screw driver cause slipping and burred screw slots. These edges can be quickly restored by shaping on a coarse stone. Keep the two faces of the blade parallel and carefully shape the bottom of the blade until it is square.

18–11. Sharpening a gouge.

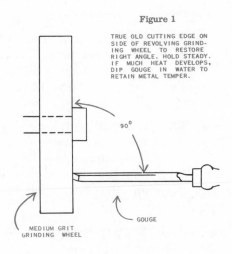

Figure 1

TRUE OLD CUTTING EDGE ON SIDE OF REVOLVING GRINDING WHEEL TO RESTORE RIGHT ANGLE. HOLD STEADY. IF MUCH HEAT DEVELOPS, DIP GOUGE IN WATER TO RETAIN METAL TEMPER.

90°

GOUGE

MEDIUM GRIT GRINDING WHEEL

Figure 2

RESTORE ORIGINAL BEVEL ANGLE AS ESTABLISHED BY TOOL MANUFACTURER. ROTATE GOUGE AT STEADY RATE FROM POINT TO POINT, AS HEAT DEVELOPS, DIP GOUGE IN WATER TO RETAIN METAL TEMPER.

MEDIUM GRIT GRINDING WHEEL

ABOUT 30°

GOUGE

Figure 3

DEBURR NEW CUTTING EDGE BY PLACING CONCAVE FACE OF GOUGE FLAT ON CONVEX FACE OF INDIA GOUGE SLIP. RUB BACK AND FORTH GENTLY. THIS BREAKS OFF THE FINE WIRE EDGE THAT DEVELOPS WITH EACH NEW STONING. THE GOUGE SHOULD NOW BE READY FOR USE.

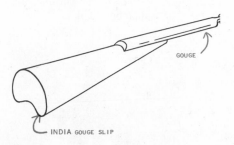

GOUGE

INDIA GOUGE SLIP

Figure 4

SET NEW CUTTING ANGLE WITH INDIA GOUGE SLIP. APPLY CONVEX EDGE OF GOUGE TO CONCAVE FACE OF SLIP SO THAT BEVEL HEEL IS CLEAR OF STONE. SHARPEN BY PUSHING GOUGE FORWARD AND ROTATE AT SAME TIME FROM POINT TO POINT.

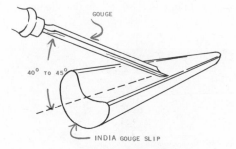
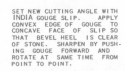

GOUGE

40° TO 45°

INDIA GOUGE SLIP

204

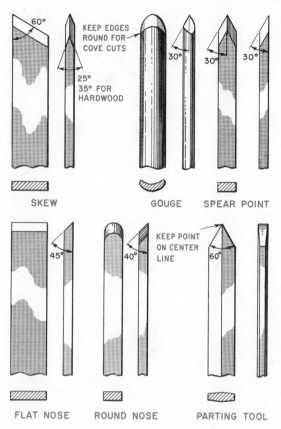

SKEW   GOUGE   SPEAR POINT

FLAT NOSE   ROUND NOSE   PARTING TOOL

18–12.   The correct angles for sharpening turning tools.

18–13.   Methods of grinding jointer knives.
a. On drill press, using wood jig and cup wheel.

Wood-turning Tools. Sharpen these tools in the same manner as chisels. The method of sharpening a gouge is shown in *Fig. 18–11*. The correct grinding angle for each tool is shown in *Fig. 18–12*.

Hand Saws. Hand saws of all types should be sent out to be sharpened.

MACHINE TOOLS

All machine tools should be touched up frequently with an oilstone to keep them sharp. They should be ground as little as possible.

Planer Knives. A grinding attachment is either standard equipment on the machine or an accessory bought for it. Most surfacers or planers come with complete instructions in manufacturers' manuals on how to grind the knives.

Jointer Knives. A wood jig can be made so that the jointer knife can be ground to an angle of 36 degrees. Several methods of grinding the blades are shown in *Fig. 18–13*. When

18–13b.   On circular saw, using wood jig and flat-edge wheel.

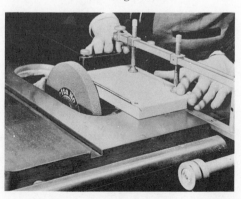

mounted in the cutter head, the rear edge of the bevel should be about ¹⁄₁₆″ from the surface of the cutter head. Jointer knives should be honed often. Partly cover a fine oilstone with wax paper so that it will not scratch the table. Place it on the front table as shown in *Fig. 18–14.* Turn the cutter head until the stone rests flat on the bevel. Hold the head in this position, then stroke the bevel by moving the stone to right and left. Repeat the same number of strokes on each knife.

Circular and Band Saw Blades. These should be sent out for grinding. If the blades are carbide-tipped, grinding will need to be done much less frequently.

Shaper Cutters. Hold the face of the shaper cutter against an oilstone and work the tool back and forth. *Fig. 18–15.* A slipstone can be used on the bevelled cutting edge, but care must be taken not to change the shape of the cutter.

Mortising Chisel. Grind the mortising chisel with a conical-shaped grinding wheel held in the chuck of a drill press as shown in *Fig. 18–16.*

18–14.   Honing a jointer knife.

18–15.   Honing a shaper cutter.

18–16.   Sharpening a mortising chisel.

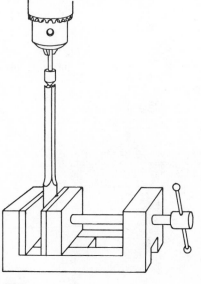

18–13c.   Grinding a jointer knife on a grinder.

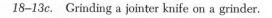

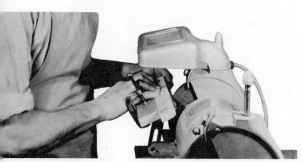

206

Unit 19: COMMON OPERATIONS AND PRINCIPLES

Woodworking machinery is used for cutting, surfacing, shaping, jointing, and smoothing. It is employed in every step from the cutting and processing of raw materials to the completion of the wood product. Lumbering, building construction, furniture making, millwork, boat building, manufacturing plywood and similar man-made board materials—these are among the many important industries which make use of woodworking machinery.

COMMON CUTS

Some of the common cuts made on machines are: *Fig. 19–1.*
• *Groove,* or *plough*—a rectangular recess cut with the grain of wood.
• *Dado*—a rectangular recess cut across grain.
• *Rabbet*—an "L"-shaped slot cut at the end or edge of a board.
• *Chamfer*—a slanted surface cut only part way down an edge, usually at an angle of 45 degrees.
• *Bevel*—a sloping edge for fitting two pieces together to form a "V" shape.
• *Miter*—a straight cut at an angle, usually 45 degrees.

• *Taper*—an angle that makes the stock gradually smaller toward one end. Tent pegs, the legs of chairs, tables, and stools are often tapered. Sometimes all four sides are tapered; at other times only two sides.
• *Mortise*—a rectangular-shaped opening in a piece of wood.

19–1.   Common cuts.

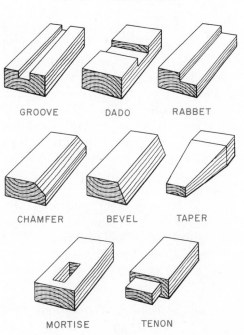

GROOVE   DADO   RABBET

CHAMFER   BEVEL   TAPER

MORTISE   TENON

207

• *Tenon*—a rectangular shape cut at the end of a board, made to fit into a mortise.

MACHINING OF WOOD

In machining all kinds of woods, you need to know four things:
  • The characteristics of the wood.
  • The characteristics of the machine you are using.
  • The correct setup.
  • The operation of the machine (such as the actual cutting, shaping, or surfacing).

The previous section dealt with the characteristics of wood and wood products. We will now consider detailed information on the care and operation of machines.

In machining woods, there are three principal objectives:
  • How can you obtain maximum surface quality?
  • How can you maintain maximum control over the dimension? Each piece should be machined accurately. Of course, the accuracy needed in rough carpentry is much different from that required in fine furniture construction.
  • How can you get the best results with the fewest operations and lowest cost? In industry, there must be concern not only for completing the product but for doing it as rapidly, efficiently, and inexpensively as possible. This should also be true to a large extent in your own work.

Some of the operations most commonly performed in woodworking will be described here.

Surfacing. Important questions that must be asked are: What is good planing, and how can you judge whether you are getting a well planed surface? This, of course, depends to some extent on the kind of product. If you could look at a planed surface under a microscope, you would see that it consists of a series of waves which are actually knife marks made as the lumber is fed under or over the revolving cutting head. These waves are at right angles to the direction of feed. The best way to judge the quality of a planed surface is by the number of knife marks per inch (the more, the better) and by the height of the wave marks (the lower, the better). This can be done both by feeling the wood and by looking at it closely. Good planing usually results when as many knives as possible, of equal length and sharpness, make the cuts. In a well planed surface the wood cells must not be crushed, glazed, or beaten. Otherwise they will not absorb stain, glue, or other finish. If knives are dull, a scraping cut will be made that crushes the wood fibers.

Ordinarily, the rate of feed is one of the most easily controlled factors affecting the quality of planed work.

19–2a. Knife marks: R—radius of cutting circle. W—Distance between knife marks. D—Wave height.

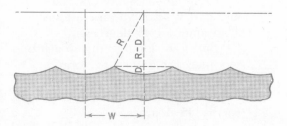

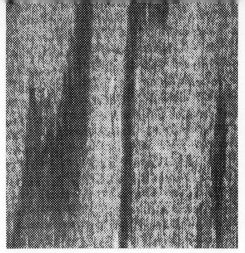
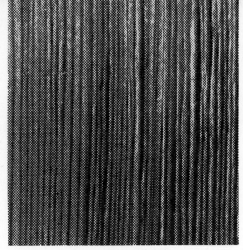

19–2b.   Satisfactory surfacing—flat grain and vertical grain.

This control should result in the correct number of knife marks per inch. Note, in *Fig. 19-2a,* that *D* represents the depth of cut and the height of the wave marks on the lumber, *W* the distance between each successive knife cut, and *R* the radius of the cutting circle. It is good to keep *D* as small as possible. This can be done by decreasing the rate of feed, by increasing the radius of the cutting circle, or by increasing either the number of knives or the speed of the head. Usually, however, the only one that can be varied is the feed. In general, the feed should be adjusted so that, on dry lumber, there are about 10 or 12 knife marks per inch. On extremely cross-grained or curly-grained work, it is better to have 15 or more knife marks per inch. *Fig. 19–2b.*

Problems in Planing a Surface. The most common troubles encountered in surfacing lumber are the following:

• *Raised grain.* This is usually caused by dull knives, having head speed too slow, cutting too light, or feeding too slow. *Fig. 19–3.*

• *Torn or chipped grain.* This is the result of machining cross grain lumber against the grain, or of having feed speed that is too high. Torn or chipped grain sometimes results when the chip breaker on the surfacer is too far away from the knives. *Fig. 19–4.*

19-3.   Raised grain.

19-4.   Chipped grain.

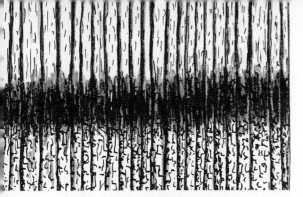

19-5. Machine burn.

• *Fuzzy grain.* This appears particularly when very dry lumber has been surfaced and then allowed to absorb moisture.

• *Machine burn.* This occurs most often when lumber sticks in the machine. Knife burns are more common than roller burns. *Fig. 19-5.*

• *Chip marks.* These happen when the blower system is not working properly. The chips drop back onto the wood surface and are crushed into it by the rollers. *Fig. 19-6.*

Sawing. Resawing should be done on dry lumber with a rip saw or a good combination saw. The speed should be about 70 to 100 feet per minute. Finish sawing or trimming should be done with a hollow-ground saw.

Sanding. The important things in sanding are to have the correct grade of sandpaper and to apply proper pressure. Because of the difference in density, summerwood has a great-

19-6. Chip mark.

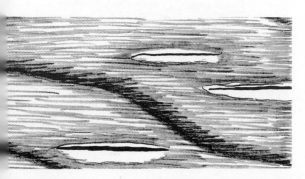

er tendency to show scratches than springwood when the sandpaper is too coarse. On the other hand, if the paper is too fine and excessive pressure is applied, you can burn the wood surface, with the result that it will not take a good finish. If the wood pieces are wide, it is very important to sand both sides to eliminate any warpage. As soon as the pieces have been given a finish sanding, a primer coat should be applied to keep the lumber from absorbing too much moisture and developing a raised grain.

Machining. Machining end grain should be done with a jointer, spindle shaper, or router. It is important that the cutter-head speed be high so the wood will not tear out.

CARBIDE-TIPPED TOOLS

Carbide is the name given to several different alloys of carbon and such metallic elements as tungsten, titanium, or tantalum. *Fig. 19-7.* It is exceptionally hard, almost as hard as diamond. It maintains a sharp cutting edge under conditions that would cause other cutting tools to burn. One of the major developments in wood production is the use of carbide-tipped cutting tools. The tool has a piece of carbide brazed to its tip to form the cutting edges. Some of the major advantages of carbide-tipped tools are:

• They give a smoother cut or surface. For example, when carbide-tipped saws are used, the edges of wood do not have to be jointed for gluing. This often eliminates several steps in construction.

210

• They last longer and will do a very good cutting job, lasting up to ten times longer than ordinary cutting tools before resharpening is needed.

• They are the only satisfactory cutting tools for certain materials. Teakwood, for example, will rapidly dull an ordinary cutting tool because of its abrasive nature. Also, in the machining of decorative laminate materials such as Formica and Pan-elyte, carbide-tipped tools give a smoother edge and do not dull.

The disadvantages are that carbide-tipped tools cost a great deal more than ordinary cutting tools, and they must be resharpened on special equipment.

Carbide-tipped tools are available for all kinds and sizes of woodworking machinery including those frequently used in the school shop. They are most commonly used on the surfacer, jointer, circular saw, radial arm saw, shaper, and router.

POWER MECHANICS

The carpenter or cabinetmaker of the past depended upon his own muscle power. Today, the builder has both portable and stationary machines to do much of his work. Power mechanics is all around you in the woodshop. Think about these basic ideas and how they affect you every day. A *machine* is a device used to make work easier or to perform work; it applies force to good advantage. *Work* is done when a force is moved through a distance to make something move or stop moving. *Force* is the push or pull that

19–7a.   A carbide-tipped blade.

19–7b.   Another style of carbide-tipped blade.

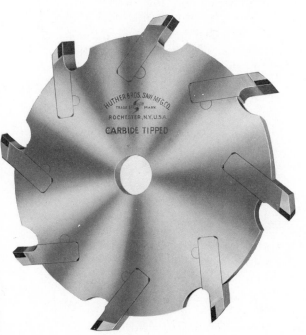

can do work. A machine helps you work by multiplying forces. By the exertion of force on a machine in one place, the machine can exert force at another place and, in many cases, in another direction. It is true, however, that you can never get more out of a machine than you put into it. In fact, some force is actually lost through friction. In addition, no machine can increase both force and distance at the same time.

While the machines you see in a wood shop appear to be complicated, they actually are made up of the six simple, basic machines. *Fig. 19–8.* To operate, the woodworking machine needs a supply of energy delivered to it by an external force. Electrical motors provide that energy. The electrical motor on a woodworking machine is designated by its horsepower rating and by the type of electricity on which it operates. For example, a home workshop machine may have a one-half horsepower motor that operates on 115-volt, single-phase current. A machine in a furniture factory may have a two- or three-horsepower motor that operates on 220 or 440 volt, three-phase current. It is important to have a motor of the correct size for each machine. The transmission of energy may be accomplished through several devices such as friction drive, reciprocating or oscillating drive, linkage gears, V belts, or direct drive. In all cases, drive serves one of two purposes:

1. It makes the machine operate at a higher rpm (revolutions per minute) than the power source does, thus gaining *speed*.

2. It reduces the rpm of the machine, causing a gain in *power* through mechanical advantage.

Belts and Pulleys. Most woodworking machines have belts and pulleys which transmit power and provide a means of changing the speed of the machine tool. When two pulleys are linked together with a belt, one pulley is always the *driver* (the one on the motor), and the other is the *driven* (the one on the machine). *Fig. 19–9.* The relationship of size and speed between driver and driven pulleys must be understood. If both driver and driven pulleys are the same size or diameter, both run at the same speed or rpm. For example, if the motor operates at 1,725 rpm, the driven pulley likewise operates at 1,725 rpm. If, however, the driver pulley is twice the size of the driven pulley, then the driven (or smaller) pulley turns at twice the speed of the larger or driver pulley. The amount of power transmitted between driver and driven pulleys also depends on pulley sizes. If a small driver pulley and a larger driven pulley are used, then more power is produced on the machine.

The two most common pulley arrangements on wood machines are V belts and pulleys, and variable speed pulleys. V pulleys have a V-shaped groove cut around their circumference; a V-shaped belt fits accurately into the groove. V belts are endless, made in one piece. Therefore they run more quietly than flat belts. They are generally installed on machinery requiring high speeds. Some woodworking ma-

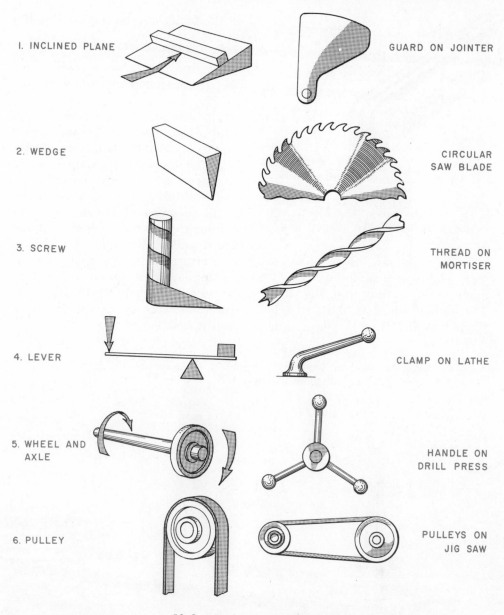

1. INCLINED PLANE   GUARD ON JOINTER

2. WEDGE   CIRCULAR SAW BLADE

3. SCREW   THREAD ON MORTISER

4. LEVER   CLAMP ON LATHE

5. WHEEL AND AXLE   HANDLE ON DRILL PRESS

6. PULLEY   PULLEYS ON JIG SAW

19–8.   Six basic machines.

chines that operate at a single speed have only one V belt and a single set of pulleys. Good examples of these are the circular saw, band saw, and jointer. Other single-speed machines have double belts and pulleys for better transmission of power. On such machines as the drill press,

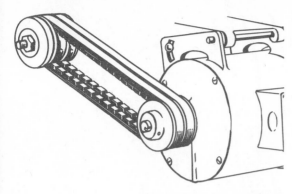

19–9. The driver pulley (at right end of belt) is on the motor. The driven pulley (upper left) is attached to the machine.

on the motor and on the small pulley on the driven unit.

To determine pulley sizes or speeds for setting up machines, use one of the following simple formulas:

• If you know the speed of the motor, the diameter of the driver pulley, and the diameter of the driven pulley, and you want to know the speed of the driven pulley, do this: Multiply the speed of the motor by the diameter of the driver pulley and divide by the diameter of the driven pulley. *Example*: A 2″ motor pulley turns at 1,725 rpm to drive a 4″ pulley on a jigsaw. How many strokes a minute will the jigsaw make? Multiply 1,725 by 2, divide by 4. Result: 862.5 rpm.

lathe, and jig saw, there is often a four- or five-step pulley on both the motor and operating unit. *Fig. 19–10.* The highest speed is obtained when the belt is placed on the large pulley

19–10. At this position the spindle speed is the same as the motor speed because both pulleys have exactly the same diameter.

• If you know the speed of the motor, the diameter of the driver pulley, and the required speed of the machine, and you need to find the diameter of the driven pulley, do this: Multiply the speed of the motor by the diameter of the driver pulley and then divide by the required speed. *Example*: Suppose you know that there is a 3″ diameter pulley on a motor that operates at 1,725 rpm and you want the jointer head to operate at 2,550 rpm. What size driven pulley do you need? Multiply 1,725 by 3, divide by 2,550. Result: about 2″.

• If you know the required speed of the machine, the diameter of the driven pulley, and the speed of the motor, and you want to find the diameter of the driver pulley, do this: Multiply the required speed of the machine by the diameter of the driven pulley and divide by the speed of the motor. *Example*: Suppose a shaper must operate at 3,600 rpm and it has a driven pulley that measures 2″ in diameter. The motor operates at 1,725 rpm. What diameter pulley should you use on the motor? Multiply 3,600 by 2, divide by 1,725. Result: about 4″.

Variable-speed pulleys make it possible to change the speed without stopping either pulleys or machine. *As a matter of fact, the speed must be changed only while the machine is running*. The pulleys of a variable-speed drive are made of two parts having V-shaped sides. By means of an adjusting screw attached to a crank wheel, (*Fig. 19–11*) one

19–11. Notice that the spindle speed can be changed from a low of 500 rpm to a high of 4,500 rpm. The higher speeds are for shaping and routing.

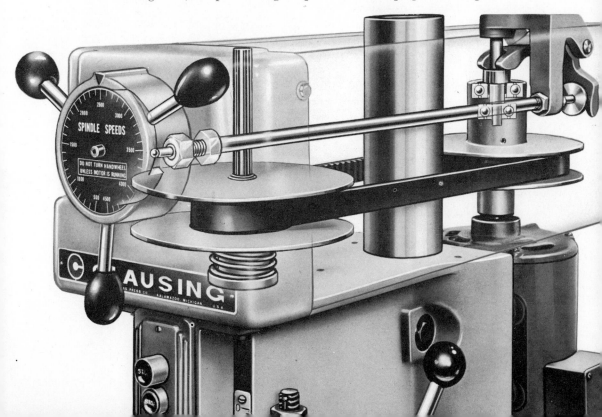

equipped with *direct-drive* mechanisms. This is true, for example, of some electric drills and cut-off saws. The tool operates at only one speed.

Many modern woodworking machines are *gear- or chain-driven.* A gear-driven feed mechanism provides positive drive (without slippage) which is very important in

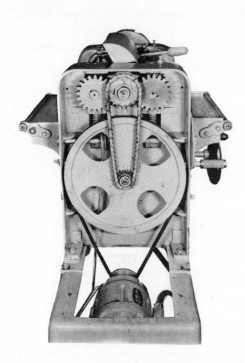

19–12. The feed mechanism of this modern planer has three types of driving mechanisms. They are: belt and pulleys for reducing speed and increasing power; sprockets and chain for operating the cutter head; and gears for driving the infeed and outfeed rolls.

19–13. Note the mechanism on the head of a drill press. The pulley rotates the spindle. The spindle quill is moved up and down through the pinion attached to the handle that meshes with the rack.

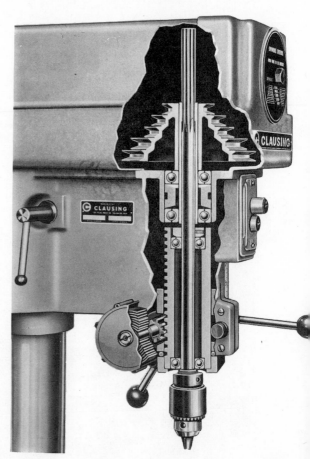

side of the driver may be opened or spread apart. As it spreads, the belt moves inward toward the smaller diameter, producing slower speed in the driven pulley that has closed to make a larger pulley. As the sides of the driver pulley are brought together, the belt is forced outward toward the larger diameter; this increases the speed of the driven pulley that opens to make a smaller pulley.

Other Power Transmission Methods. Some portable power tools are

216

such tools as the modern planer. *Fig. 19–12.*

Reciprocating drive is usually combined with rotating drive. It is found in such machines as the hollow chisel mortiser, the boring machine, and the drill press. *Fig. 19–13.* When a tool moves forward and backward, retracing its path upon arrival at either end, the tool has a motion of reciprocation. If there is also a rotating motion, it has rotating reciprocation.

MAINTENANCE OF MACHINES

The life and usefulness of any machine depends on the care given to it. Some of the most important maintenance jobs are these:

• Proper lubrication according to the specifications of the manufacturer is highly important and should be done on a regular schedule.

• All working parts should be kept free of dust and other materials that would have an abrasive action on the parts. *Fig. 19–14.*

19–14. The mechanism of the table saw must be kept free of sawdust if it is to operate easily. Can you tell which handle tilts the saw blade and which raises and lowers the blade?

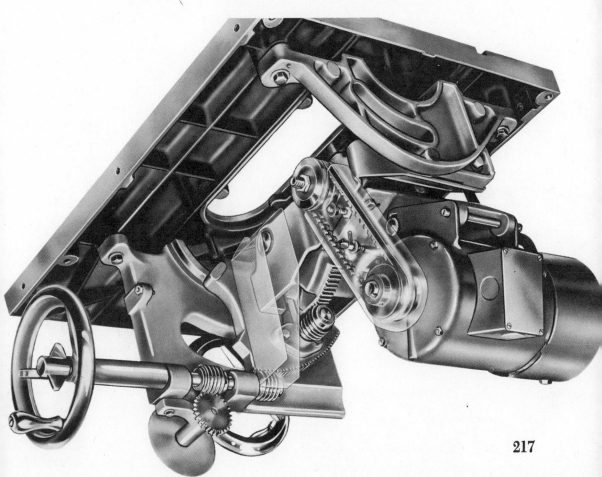

217

• All machined surfaces such as the top of the saw, jointer, and planer bed should be kept free of rust and corrosion and should be coated with a no-rust product.

• All knives and cutting tools should be sharpened or ground so that they are kept in their very best cutting condition.

• All safety devices should be kept in good condition. Any defective part should be replaced immediately.

• V belts should be maintained as follows: Avoid oil, grease, or any other substance that will ruin rubber; keep belts snug but not tight; make sure the belts fit the pulleys.

• Pulleys generally are secured to the shafts with a key and set screw. It is important to keep all pulleys in line. If it is necessary to true a pair of pulleys, cut a narrow board with a double bevel on one edge. Place this bevelled edge in the V pulleys to align them.

• There are many kinds of bearings but the most common are roller or ball-bearings. *Figs. 19–15.* These must be greased or oiled as needed.

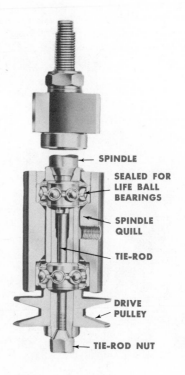

19–15. This cutaway shows the parts of the shaper head. Note that the spindle rotates on two ball-bearings.

SPINDLE

SEALED FOR LIFE BALL BEARINGS

SPINDLE QUILL

TIE-ROD

DRIVE PULLEY

TIE-ROD NUT

Unit 20: RADIAL ARM SAW

The radial arm saw is an upside-down saw which can do all types of cutting. *Fig. 20–1.* For certain operations it is quicker and much more convenient than a circular saw. The motor and blade move back and forth under a long, radial arm that is fastened above the table and at-

20–1. Parts of a radial arm saw.

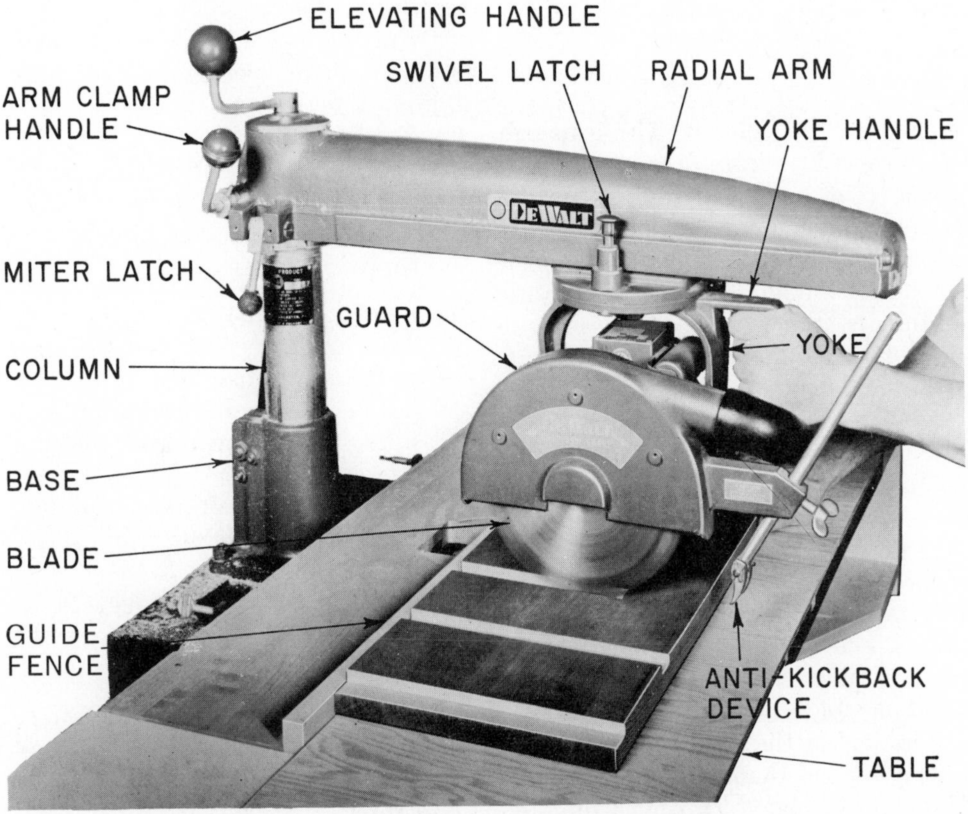

ELEVATING HANDLE

SWIVEL LATCH   RADIAL ARM

ARM CLAMP
HANDLE

YOKE HANDLE

MITER LATCH

GUARD

YOKE

COLUMN

BASE

BLADE

GUIDE
FENCE

ANTI-KICKBACK
DEVICE

TABLE

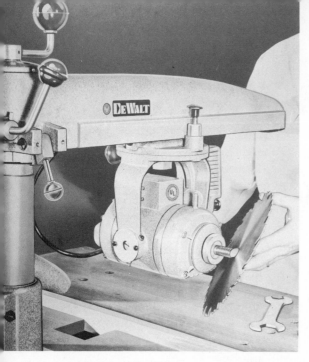

20-2. Attaching the correct type of saw blade on the arbor.

tached to the column. The arm can be turned in a complete circle. The yokes that hold the motor can be turned 360 degrees horizontally. Motor and blade can be tilted in an arc of 180 degrees. With these adjustments, the saw has the advantage of three-dimensional movement.

For crosscutting, mitering, cross-bevelling, dadoing, and similar operations, the work is held firmly to the table and the blade pulled through the lumber. For operations such as ripping and grooving, the blade is locked in position and the lumber fed into the revolving blade. This saw is extremely popular with carpenters and builders because of its great flexibility.

The *size* of the radial saw is determined by the diameter of the blade and the horsepower rating. Common

sizes range from 8 to 14 inches. The overall size of the table and the length of the overarm also vary with the size of the saw. It is possible, however, to obtain any size of saw with a standard length radial arm, a medium, or an extra long. The longer overarm makes it possible to cut wider stock.

USING THE SAW

When both radial arm and circular saws are available, the radial arm saw is better for the following operations:

• Rough cutting stock to length. If this is done often, the saw should be equipped with extension tables to handle the longer stock.

• Cutting several pieces of lumber (duplicate parts) at the same time to the correct length.

• Cutting stock to finish lengths.

• Cutting straight and angle dadoes.

• Cutting miters and bevels.

• Ripping stock.

Common Adjustments.

• Raise or lower the saw by turning the elevating handle.

• Rotate the overarm by holding the miter latch down and pushing the arm.

• Turn the yoke through a 360-degree circle by releasing the swivel clamp latch.

• Tilt the motor 90 degrees in either direction by releasing the bevel latch.

Safety. Follow the general safety practices for all woodworking machines, listed in Unit 2. Also observe these rules.

• Use the correct saw blade.

• Mount the saw on the arbor so that the blade turns towards the operator.

• Always keep the safety guard and the anti-kickback device in position.

• Make sure that clamps and locking handles are tight before turning on the machine.

• When crosscutting, adjust the anti-kickback device to clear the top of the work by about one-eighth inch. This acts as a guard to keep your fingers from coming near the revolving saw.

• For crosscutting, dadoing, and similar operations, hold the work firmly to the table and pull the saw into the work. Cut on the forward stroke.

• Always return the saw to the rear of the table after each cut. Make sure that the saw is as close to the column as possible before starting a new cut.

• When cutting long stock to length, make sure that the ends are supported so that the stock will not tip when the cut is completed.

• For ripping, make sure that the blade is rotating towards you. Use the anti-kickback device to hold the work firmly against the table and guide fence. Feed the stock from the end opposite the anti-kickback device.

• Keep your hands away from the danger area—*the path of the saw blade.*

Crosscutting.

• Mount a crosscutting or combination saw blade on the arbor so that the teeth point toward you. *Fig. 20–2.*

• Adjust the radial arm to zero (at right angles to the guide fence).

• Adjust the motor so the blade will be at right angles to the table top and then lock the radial arm with the arm clamp handle.

• Turn the elevating handle down until the teeth are about one-sixteenth inch below the surface of the wood table. The blade should follow the saw kerf already cut in the table.

• Adjust the anti-kickback device about one-eighth inch above the wood surface.

• Place the stock on the table with the layout line in the path of the saw. Make sure that the stock is held firmly to the table.

• Turn on the power and allow the saw to reach full speed. Grasp the motor yoke handle and pull the saw firmly but slowly through the work. *Fig. 20–3.*

• When the cut is complete, push the saw back beyond the guide fence and turn off the power.

20–3. It's easy to crosscut 2″ x 4″ stock with one simple, straight-line saw motion.

221

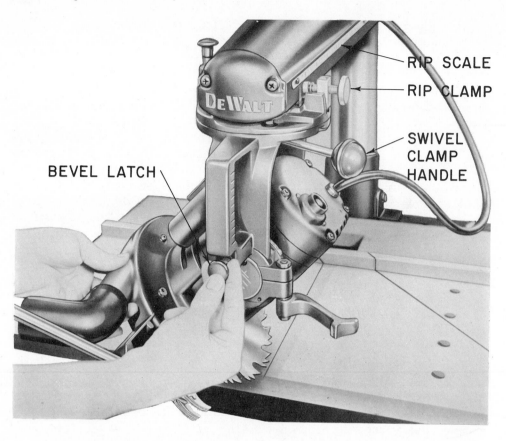

RIP SCALE

RIP CLAMP

SWIVEL CLAMP HANDLE

BEVEL LATCH

20–4.   To tilt the motor to 45 degrees, pull out on the bevel latch.

20–5.   A bevel cut is simple with the motor tilted to the correct angle.

20–6.   With the motor at 45 degrees the bevel cut-off operation is easy, even when five pieces are cut at the same time.

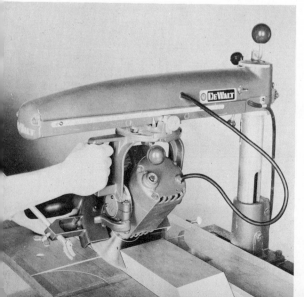

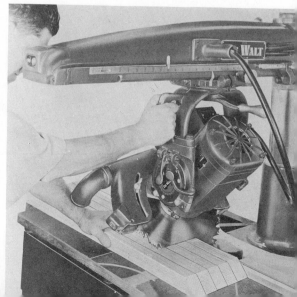

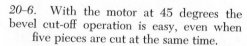

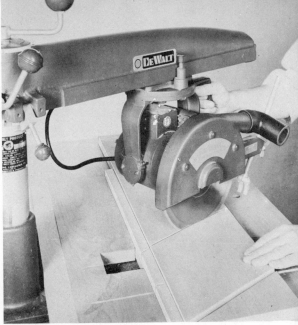

20–7. To swing the radial arm for a miter cut, release the arm clamp handle and move the arm to the desired angle.

20–8. Simply lock the arm at a 45-degree position and then make a perfect-fitting miter cut without moving the stock.

Cutting Stock to Exact Lengths.

• Square the best end of each piece, allowing as much waste material for the other end as possible.

• Use a hand clamp as a stop. Fasten this to the guide fence at the correct distance. Place the stock on the table with the first edge against the hand clamp. Cut to exact length. This technique can also be followed for cutting duplicate parts to length.

• To make a bevel cut, turn the motor to a 45-degree bevel. *Figs. 20–4, 20–5,* and *20–6.*

• To make a miter cut, move the arm to a 45-degree position. *Figs. 20–7* and *20–8.*

• To make a hopper cut, (compound bevel and miter cuts) turn the motor to the correct angle and move the arm to the correct angle. *Fig. 20–9.* (A chart for these settings is shown in *Fig. 34–68.*)

20–9. The compound miter (hopper cut) is easy to make. Swing the arm to the correct angle and tilt the motor the correct amount. This is excellent for making jack rafter cuts.

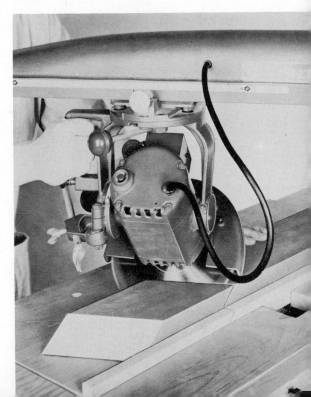

20–10. For dadoing, simply remove the saw blade and replace with a dado head. A cut of any width can be made by moving the lumber after each pass.

Cutting Dadoes and Gains Across the Stock.

• Mount a dado head on the arbor shaft. Install the necessary blades and cutters to obtain the correct width.

• Mark the location of the dado on the face of the stock.

20–11. Pull up on the swivel latch to turn the motor and yoke for ripping.

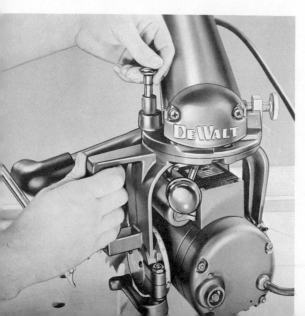

• Adjust for the depth of cut. Turn the elevating handle until the dado head touches the work. Then remove the work and continue to lower the dado head to the desired depth. Each turn of the handle lowers it one-eighth inch.

• Make sure that the stock is marked correctly for the dado. This is especially important when cutting dadoes on the inside of a chest. Make sure that the right and left parts are marked properly. You must be especially careful when cutting a stop dado to mark the part correctly. It is often helpful to first try a dado on a scrap piece of stock.

• Place the stock to be cut on the table, with the layout line directly under the dado head. Cut by pulling the saw blade completely across the stock. *Fig. 20–10.*

• An angle dado can be cut by locking the radial arm at the desired angle.

Ripping.

• Mount a combination or ripping blade. Pull the entire motor to the front of the arm. Release the swivel clamp latch and rotate the yoke 90 degrees clockwise until the blade is parallel to the guide fence. *Fig. 20–11.*

• Move the motor along the radial arm until the correct width is shown on the rip scale. Tighten the rip clamp and lower the saw until the blade just touches the wood table. Check with a rule to make sure the correct width will be cut.

• Adjust the guards so that the infeed end clears the work by about one-eighth inch. Adjust the anti-

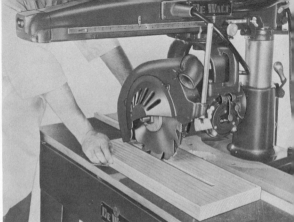

20–12. To rip stock, first make sure the arm is in the crosscut position. Turn the motor and yoke at right angles to the arm. The built-in rip scale instantly measures the correct width. Rip the stock by pushing it through the saw.

20–14. To cut a groove (or plough), use the same set-up as for ripping. Just replace the blade with a dado head and set for the correct depth.

kickback device so the points rest on the wood and hold it firmly against the table.

• Make sure that the saw is rotating upward and towards you. Turn on the power.

• Hold the stock against the guide fence and the table, and feed it slowly into the revolving blade. If it is long stock, it is a good idea to have someone help at the other end. Never feed the work from the anti-

kickback end. Whenever necessary, use a push stick to complete the cut. *Fig. 20–12.*

• Bevel ripping can be done by adjusting the blade to the correct angle and lowering it until the teeth just touch the surface of the table. *Fig. 20–13.*

• Grooving can be done with a dado head. *Fig. 20–14.*

• For cutting the tongue in a tongue-and-groove joint, proceed as shown in *Fig. 20–15.*

20–13. Any bevel rip job is handled as easily as straight ripping. Simply tilt the motor and lock to the correct angle.

20–15. A dado head with a spacer can be used to cut the tongue for a tongue-and-groove joint.

Unit 21: PLANER OR SURFACER

The planer, or surfacer, is made in a variety of sizes ranging from 12″ to 52″ in bed width. The size of the planer is indicated by the capacity of work it will handle. A medium-sized planer will surface stock 8″ thick and 30″ wide. *Fig. 21–1*. There are two general types of planers. The more common is the *single surfacer* used primarily to bring material to thickness after any warp or wind has been removed. With the single surfacer, the piece must be straightened on the jointer before being fed through the machine. The *double surfacer* planes both surfaces

21–1.   This is a single-surface, 4-roll planer with a capacity of 30″ x 8″.

at the same time, and some can straighten the material as well. (See *Figs. 41–2 and 3.*)

PARTS

The planer has a heavy frame and includes an adjustable table, planer head, feed-driving mechanism, table raising and lowering mechanism, and a depth-of-cut or thickness scale indicator.

Planer Head Parts. The planer head has the following parts: *Fig. 21–2.*

One or two *lower infeed (table) rolls* and one or two *upper infeed rolls* move the stock. The upper roll has a corrugated surface and is usually made in sections. This roll feeds the rough stock into the planer.

A *chip breaker* is a heavy casting

that presses on the wood. On large surfacers it is made in sections. The chip breaker is placed between the cutter head and the infeed rolls to prevent the knives from chipping the wood surface.

The *cutter head* is similar to that on a jointer. It is mounted on top of the frame between the feed rolls. It contains three, four, or more knives depending on the size of the machine.

Just back of the cutter head is the *pressure bar.* It exerts pressure on the finished surface of the board, holding it firmly against the table.

One *upper* and one *lower outfeed roll* (both smooth) move the smooth surface of the board through the planer. Most planers are equipped with grinding attachments.

21–2a.   Parts of the planer head.

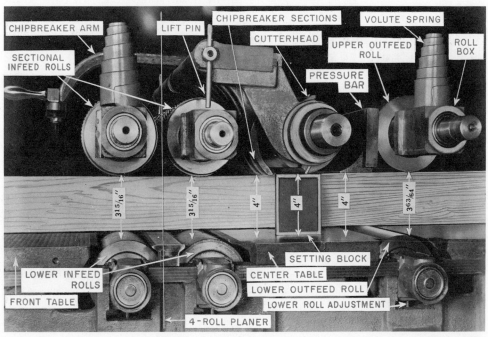

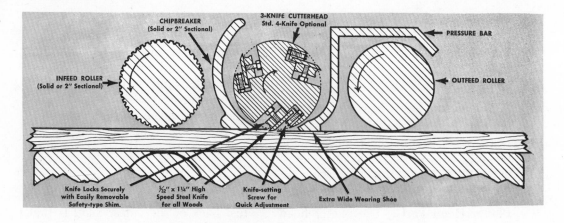

21–2b. Cutting-roller assembly (side view)

CHIPBREAKER
(Solid or 2″ Sectional)

3-KNIFE CUTTERHEAD
Std. 4-Knife Optional

← PRESSURE BAR

INFEED ROLLER
(Solid or 2″ Sectional) →

← OUTFEED ROLLER

Knife Locks Securely
with Easily Removable
Safety-type Shim.

5/32″ x 1¼″ High
Speed Steel Knife
for all Woods

Knife-setting
Screw for
Quick Adjustment

Extra Wide Wearing Shoe

USING A PLANER

• Before planing a board that has warp, plane one face on the jointer.

• Adjust the planer to a thickness of about ⅟₁₆″ less than the thickness of the stock.

• Adjust to correct feed and then turn on the motor.

• Always stand to one side of the machine to avoid the possibility of injury from kickback.

• If the stock is long, get someone to help you or place a "dead man" (roller) at the other end of the long stock.

• Determine the grain direction of each piece; place pieces conveniently near the infeed end with the grain in the proper direction.

• Never feed stock that is shorter than the distance between the infeed and outfeed rolls.

• Place the jointed side down

21–2c. Upper sectional infeed roll.

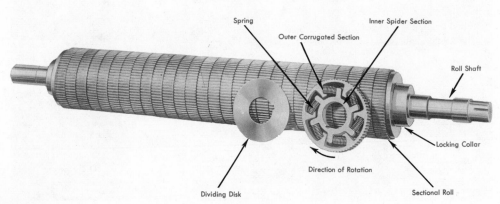

Spring

Inner Spider Section

Outer Corrugated Section

Roll Shaft

Locking Collar

Sectional Roll

Direction of Rotation

Dividing Disk

228

against the table and push it into the infeed rolls, keeping it straight. *Fig. 21-3.*

• When a short piece is run through the planer, make sure that another piece butts against it.

• If the stock should stick as it goes through the machine, lower the table and then turn off the power.

• After stock has been glued up to make a large surface such as a table top, it is impossible to true or face it on the jointer. To do this on the planer, remove all glue from the surface. Then adjust the machine to slow feed speed, and light cut. Place the best face on the bed of the planer and true one side. Then reverse the stock, readjust for the thickness, and plane the second surface smooth.

• Never plane varnished or painted stock. In fact, used lumber of any kind should never be run through a planer.

Reducing Flat Stock to Thickness. Make sure that one surface of the stock is a true working surface. If there is any warp defect in the stock this should be removed on the jointer. Measure the thickness of the stock. If several pieces of similar thickness are to be surfaced, always measure the thickest piece. Adjust the depth control wheel until the thickness-scale indicator shows a setting of $\frac{1}{16}''$ less than the thickest piece. Arrange the pieces with the working face down. Also try to surface the pieces so that the cut will be made "with the grain." Feed the stock into the surfacer by applying some hand pressure to the end of the

21-3.   Feeding stock into a planer.

board nearest you. As soon as the infeed roll grips the stock, remove your hands from it. Feed each successive piece into the planer at a different location on the bed to avoid uneven wear on the knives. After the stock has been run through the first time, check the thickness. If more material must be removed, reset the machine for the next cut. If a large amount of material must be removed, it is a good idea to take cuts from either face to equalize the strain and reduce the chance of warpage. The final cut should leave the piece slightly thicker than the specified size, ($\frac{1}{64}''$ to $\frac{1}{32}''$) to allow for finish hand work including sanding.

Squaring up Legs on a Planer. One of the most common uses for the planer is to square up stock for legs and other furniture parts. After the stock has been cut to rough size, use the jointer to give the pieces a working face and edge. Mark these surfaces so they can be easily identified. Arrange each piece so that the jointed face will be against the planer table and the jointed edge to your right. Adjust the planer for thickness of cut. Turn on the power and run all pieces through the machine.

Return the pieces to the infeed end and turn each piece one quarter turn clockwise (to the right). *Don't change the thickness setting.* Feed the stock through the planer the second time. Measure the size of the stock. If necessary, reset the machine and repeat the two steps until the stock is planed to size.

Planing Thin Stock. For stock less than $\frac{3}{8}''$ thick it is a good idea to surface it on a thicker support board. Select a true piece of squared-up stock that is at least $\frac{3}{4}''$ thick. The piece should be slightly wider and longer than the thin stock. Adjust the depth-of-cut to slightly less than the combined thickness of the two pieces. Place the thin stock over the support board and then feed it into the planer as you would thicker material.

Unit 22: CIRCULAR SAW

The circular saw is used for many types of cutting and for joinery (making joints to fasten pieces of wood together). Saws range in size from 8″ bench models to 16″ production machines. Circular saws are not all alike. These variations in features are common:

• Either the table tilts or the arbor and blade tilt. *Fig. 22–1a.*

• The saw may have one arbor called a *variety saw,* or two arbors, called a *universal saw,* on which two different blades can be mounted.

• The work is fed into the blade either by hand or by power. *Fig. 22–1b.*

• The saw may be a small bench model or a large production type. The saw in most common use is the hand-fed 10″ floor-type with tilting arbor. *Fig. 22–2.* This is described in this unit.

PARTS

The saw has a base or frame on which an arbor and table are mounted. *Fig. 22–3.* The blade protrudes through an opening in the table. The blade can be raised or lowered and tilted to an angle up to 45 degrees. A *fence* guides the stock for ripping. There is a *miter gauge* against which the wood is held for crosscutting. Saws also come equipped with a *guard,* a *splitter,* and an *anti-kickback device.*

Adjustments. *To raise or lower the blade,* loosen the lock on the elevating hand wheel and turn it up or down. Be sure to lock the blade in

22–1a.   A heavy-duty saw that can accommodate a 16″ or 18″ saw blade.

22–1b.   Roll-feed rip saw.

position after it is set to correct height.

To tilt the blade, turn the tilt hand wheel until the correct angle is shown on the graduated dial.

To move the fence, loosen the fence lock and push it forward or along the fence guard bar. A wheel on the fence slide allows easy adjustment for fine corrections. The fence is usually placed to the right of the blade.

To adjust the miter gauge, loosen the lock on the top and turn it to the desired angle. A plunger knob at the front provides for quick indexing at 90-degree and 45-degree positions. The miter gauge can be used in the slot on either side of the saw blade.

SAW BLADES

There are many kinds of saw blades including special-purpose blades such as the one designed especially for cutting plywood. The most common include:

• The *rip saw* which is used primarily for cutting stock in the direction of the grain. *Fig. 22–4.*

• The *crosscut* or *cutoff saw* used primarily for cutting across the grain. *Fig. 22–5.*

22–2.   A 10″ circular saw equipped with an excellent guard. Some illustrations in this section show cutting operations without a guard. This is only so that you can see the work being done. USE A GUARD WHENEVER POSSIBLE.

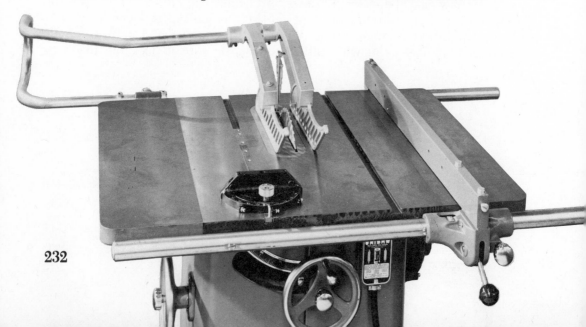

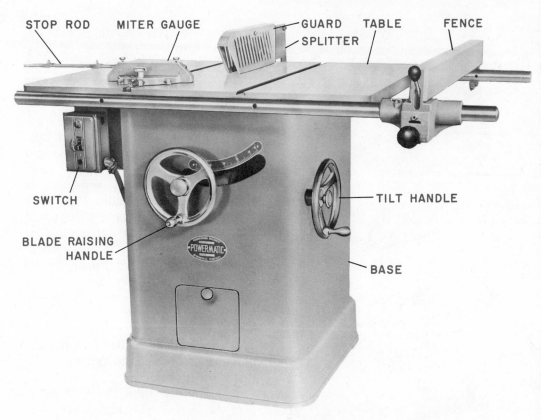

STOP ROD   MITER GAUGE   GUARD   TABLE   FENCE
SPLITTER

SWITCH

BLADE RAISING
HANDLE

POWERMATIC

TILT HANDLE

BASE

22–3.   Parts of a circular saw.

22–4.   Rip saw blade.   22–5.   Crosscut saw.

233

22-6.   Combination.

22-7.   Hollow ground combination.

• The *combination* saw for both ripping and crosscutting. *Fig. 22-6.* Sometimes the combination type is hollow ground for clearance so that the saw will not tend to overheat. *Fig. 22-7.*

• *Carbide-tipped* blades are used for higher production, for cutting wood, hardboard, and other composition materials. A carbide-tipped

blade makes a smooth finish cut without burning, streaking, or glazing. These blades are available in many tooth styles. They give many additional hours of smooth cutting with less sharpening. *Fig. 22-8.*

Removing and Replacing a Blade.

1. Press on the rear of the insert plate to remove it.

2. Force a piece of wood against the front of the blade. *Fig. 22-9.* Some saw arbors have a lefthand thread; to loosen the nut it must be turned to the right (or clockwise). Other saws have a righthand thread and the nut must be turned to the left (or counter-clockwise) to loosen.

3. Select a correct size wrench and loosen the nut.

4. Remove the collar and the old blade. Then clean the sawdust from the arbor and collar.

5. Carefully slide the new blade over the arbor threads. Make sure that the tips of the teeth point to-

22-8.   Carbide-tipped woodcutting saws.

22-9.   Removing a blade.

SAFETY

To work safely, *check for two—The machine and you!* Make safety a habit.

• Follow all the general safety instructions in Unit 2.

• Use a blade guard whenever it is practical.

• Make certain that the gauge is square with the blade. *Fig. 22–10.*

• Check to see that the fence is in line with the saw before starting to work.

• Concentrate on what you are doing. Avoid distractions. Then you will avoid accidents.

• Never stand directly in front of the saw blade. Stand to one side so you are out of the way if the work kicks back.

• Always use a sharp blade. It is safer.

• Turn off the power when not using the saw.

• Stop the motor when making any adjustments, when removing pieces from the table, and when cleaning the table.

• Keep the blade tight on the arbor.

• Adjust the blade so that it is about $\frac{1}{8}''$ above the stock being sawed. The only exception to this is when you are using a concave-ground saw. This saw blade should project well up through the cut.

• Use *all possible safety devices.*

• Hold stock firmly when cutting.

• Never try to saw "freehand." You are sure to get hurt.

• Never clear away scraps close to the saw with your fingers. To remove them, push them away with a long wooden stick.

ward the operating position, and that the manufacturer's name stamp is uppermost. Then replace the washer and nut.

6. Lock the blade by working a piece of wood against the back of the blade and the opening of the table, and tighten the arbor nut. Replace the insert plate.

7. Rotate the blade by hand to make sure it clears the table.

SUGGESTIONS FOR CUTTING

• Always let the blade do the cutting. Never force the stock into the blade.

• Don't feed with jerky action or twist the work.

• Get the "feel" of the speed at which the blade will handle the kind of work you are doing. Feed the stock into the blade with a firm, even motion.

• Keep the blade sharp and set correctly.

• Wipe some kerosene on the blade before cutting wood with considerable pitch. This helps the blade to cut freely.

22-10. Checking the miter gauge and blade with a square.

• Never attempt to cut cylindrical stock on the saw without a jig.

• Make sure the miter gauge clears the tilted saw.

• Keep fingers clear of the saw's track.

• Fasten a stop block to the fence when cutting off a piece of stock to length.

USING THE SAW

Crosscutting. Crosscutting is sawing wood across the grain. Mount a crosscut or combination blade on the arbor. Place the stock on the table against the blade and raise or lower until the blade is $\frac{1}{8}''$ above the stock. Place the work against the miter gauge. Check to see that the gauge is set at 90 degrees for a right-angle cut. Here are several ways of crosscutting stock to length:

1. To cut a single piece or a few pieces, mark the length on the edge of the stock. The gauge is usually used in the left slot or groove. Hold the stock on the table against the gauge. Move the stock back and forth until the cutoff line is in line with the blade. *Fig. 22–11.* Turn on the power and then push the stock forward to cut off the waste stock.

2. To cut many short pieces, place the fence on the table and clamp a clearance or stop block to the front end of the fence. *Fig. 22–12.* The clearance block will prevent the pieces from being pinched between the blade and the fence, which would result in dangerous kickback. Set the fence to the correct distance, allowing for the thickness of the clearance or stop block. Hold the edge of the stock against the miter gauge and square the end. Then push the square end against the

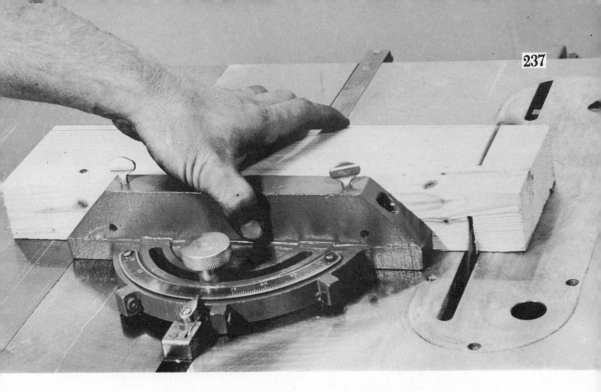

22–11. *Crosscutting to length.

clearance block. Hold it firmly against the gauge and move it past the blade to cut off the first length. Turn off the power and check the length of this piece. Then cut as many as needed. Never reach across the saw to catch cut-off pieces. Let them

*Illustrations marked with asterisk show the guard removed only so details can be seen. *You should use this guard.*

22–12. *Using a stop block to cut identical pieces to length.

22–13. *Using a stop rod to cut a lap joint.

22–15. *The open position is sometimes more convenient.

fall to the floor or catch them in a box. *Caution: Never use the fence itself for this operation without a clearance block.* Fig. 22–12.

3. To cut to length, use the stop rod. Use the stop rod that fits into the miter gauge. *Fig. 22–13.* Square the end of all pieces first. Then adjust the stop on the rod to the correct length. Cut to length.

Cutting Flat Miters. Miters are cut in much the same way as a square end, except that the gauge is adjusted to the correct angle. The gauge can be used in either a closed or open

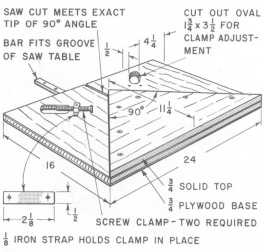

22–16a. Using a mitering jig on the circular saw.

22–16b. Drawing of the mitering jig.

22–14. *The closed position for cutting a flat miter is best because the stock can be held more firmly to the miter gauge.

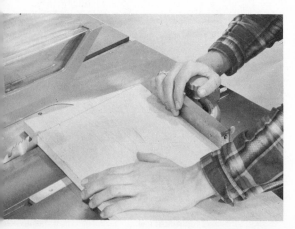

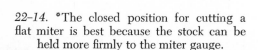

SAW CUT MEETS EXACT TIP OF 90° ANGLE

CUT OUT OVAL $1\frac{3}{4}$ x $3\frac{1}{2}$ FOR CLAMP ADJUSTMENT

BAR FITS GROOVE OF SAW TABLE

$\frac{1}{2}$ $4\frac{1}{4}$

90° $11\frac{1}{4}$

16

24

$\frac{3}{4}$ SOLID TOP

$\frac{3}{4}$ PLYWOOD BASE

$2\frac{1}{8}$ $\frac{1}{2}$

SCREW CLAMP — TWO REQUIRED

$\frac{1}{8}$ IRON STRAP HOLDS CLAMP IN PLACE

238

position. *Fig. 22–14* or *Fig. 22–15.* Since all miter cuts tend to creep during cutting, it is important to hold the work securely against the gauge. A mitering jig is a handy device to use, especially if picture-frame molding must be cut. This jig will produce a perfect 45-degree right- and lefthand miter every time. It holds the material to be mitered securely, eliminating the tendency for the work to "creep" toward or away from the saw blade. *Fig. 22–16.*

Cutting a Bevel or Edge Miter. Tilt the saw blade to the correct angle, usually 45 degrees. Check the angle on the tilt gauge or, for more accurate work, use a sliding T bevel. When the blade is tilted for angle cuts, the miter gauge or the fence can be used to guide the work. *Fig. 22–17.*

Grooving for a Spline Miter Joint. To cut a groove or kerf for a spline, tilt the blade to 45 degrees and then move the fence towards the saw and lock in position so that the cut will be made very close to the middle of the bevel or miter where the stock is

22–17b.   Another example of cutting a bevel or edge miter.

thick. Set the saw for the desired depth of cut. The miter gauge can be used to help guide the narrow stock. *Fig. 22–18.*

22–18.   Cutting a groove or kerf for a spline.

22–17a.   °Cutting a bevel or edge miter.

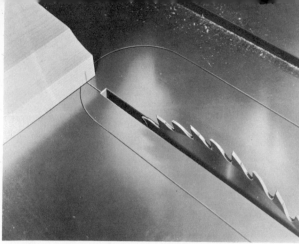

22–19. *Making a compound miter cut.

22–21. Using a marked line on the stock to check for width of cut.

Making a Compound Miter Cut. The compound miter cut is used for making shadow boxes, picture frames, and some frame parts of modern furniture. This joint is sometimes called a hopper joint and it can be made with a butt corner or a miter corner. Let's suppose you wish to make a picture frame with a slope (work angle) of 45 degrees, with the frame having a miter corner. Check the table for compound miter cuts, *Fig. 34–68,* Unit 34. Look down the column under "Tilt of Work" to 45 degrees. Note that the blade must be

22–20. Measuring for cutting to width.

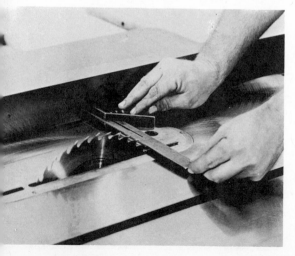

tilted to an angle of 30 degrees and the miter gauge set to an angle of 54¾ degrees. Make the settings and then cut one end with the compound miter. Then turn the board over for the next cut. *Fig. 22–19.*

Ripping. Ripping is sawing wood with the grain, using the fence to guide the stock. Use a ripping or combination blade.

Ripping Short Pieces to Widths of More than 6″. 1. Make sure that the stock has one planed edge and face.

2. Adjust the ripping fence to width, using a rule, the scale on the saw, or sample stock. *Fig. 22–20.* Another method is to mark the stock and then hold it against the fence until the mark lines up with the blade. Test by cutting into the stock. Make corrections as needed. *Fig. 22–21.*

3. Clamp the fence in position.

4. Adjust the blade until it is about ⅛″ above the stock. Use the splitter, anti-kickback dogs, and guard.

5. Stand to one side of the saw and hold the stock with both hands.

240

6. Turn on the power. Hold the planed edge against the fence and feed the stock into the saw with firm, even pressure. Be sure your hands are out of the line of cut. *Fig. 22–22.* NOTE: If the blade heats or smokes, remove the stock by lifting upward quickly. Keep the saw running until the blade cools Turn off the power and examine the blade to see if it is dull.

7. Never reach over the saw to catch the piece that has been ripped. Let sawed-off stock fall to the floor or into a box.

Ripping Long Pieces of Stock. On long pieces, get a helper (called a tail-off man) to hold the board *level* and *against the fence.* Make sure he does not pull the stock. Another method is to use a roller support (called a dead man) as shown in *Fig. 22–23.*

Ripping Narrow Stock. Never feed the stock between the blade and the fence with your hand. Always use a push stick as shown in *Fig. 22–24a.*

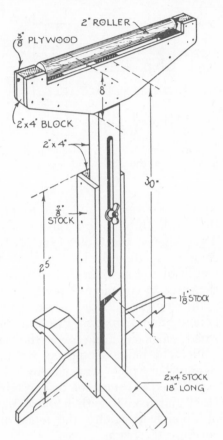

22–23.　Roller support.

22–22.　°Apply side pressure with your left hand to hold the stock against the fence.

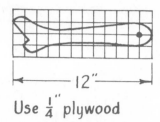

Use $\frac{1}{4}''$ plywood

22–24a. Use ¼″ plywood for push stick. The thinner the stick, the less chance of kick-out.

This device not only helps to push the work through but also holds it down against the table. *Fig. 22–24b.* Another method is to rip half the length of the stock and then reverse the piece to complete the cut.

Ripping Very Thin Stock. Use a hollow-ground blade. Place a plywood auxiliary table over the saw blade. The blade should cut through the auxiliary table without any other cut. Place the thin stock on the table. Hold and feed it with a thick piece of wood held against the fence and covering the blade.

Cutting Plywood. Use a combination crosscut blade without much set. Allow the blade to protrude above the plywood just the height of the teeth. Place the plywood on the table with the good side up. *Fig. 22–25.* Cutting large panels can be a one-man job if you have an extension support on the table. *Fig. 22–26.*

Resawing. Resawing means to saw a thick board or plank into two or more thinner boards. Stock can be resawed on the table saw only if the width is not more than twice the capacity of the saw. For example, if the maximum cut of the saw is $3\frac{1}{4}''$, the widest board that can be handled is $6\frac{1}{2}''$. Cuts can be made from either edge on wider boards and then the resawing completed on the band saw or by hand.

1. Raise the blade until it is about $\frac{1}{4}''$ more than half the width of the stock. When resawing hardwoods, it is a good idea to make one shallow cut and then raise the blade again.

22–24b. *Using a push stick.

22–25. Cutting plywood.

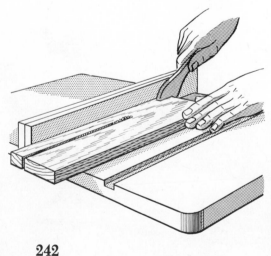

242

2. Adjust the fence to the thickness of the board.

3. Clamp a feather board to the table. *Fig. 22–27.* This will hold the stock firmly against the fence. Place the feather board so that the far edge projects a little beyond the front of the saw. *Fig. 22–28.*

4. Make the first cut. Then turn the stock end over end and make a cut from the other edge. Remember to keep the same side of the board against the ripping fence for both cuts.

5. Be especially careful, since the guard cannot be used for this operation.

Cutting a Rabbet. Mark the width and depth of the rabbet on one end or edge of the stock. There are

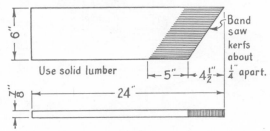

22–27.   A feather board.

several ways of making the cut; two are described here:

One method is to set the fence and saw depth to the mark for the first cut as shown in *Fig. 22–29.* Then make this cut. Readjust the fence and saw height for the second cut to clean the corner. With this method the waste piece sometimes shoots out between the saw and the fence with

22–26.   An extension table makes cutting plywood a one-man job.

22-28. *Resawing.

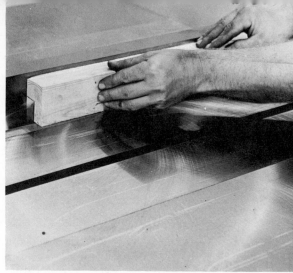

22-29b. *Note that the first cut has been made and that this cut will clean out the corner.

22-30a. Second method of cutting a rabbet.

22-29a. *First method of cutting a rabbet.

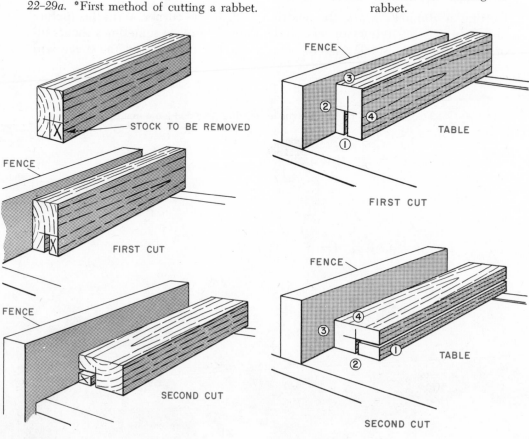

STOCK TO BE REMOVED

FENCE

FIRST CUT

FENCE

SECOND CUT

FENCE

① ② ③ ④

TABLE

FIRST CUT

FENCE

① ② ③ ④

TABLE

SECOND CUT

22-30b. *Making the first cut.

great force. *Always stand to one side, never directly behind the saw.*

The second method is to make the first cut from the face surface. *Fig. 22–30.* Make the first cut a little less than the required depth. Then make the second cut with the opposite face against the fence and the edge against the table top. In this method the final cut removes the supporting stock. Make sure that enough stock remains to keep the piece firmly supported so it will not tip or drop into the table insert.

Using the Dado Head. The dado head can be used to cut grooves, dadoes, rabbets, tenons, and for similar operations. The head consists of two outside cutters ($\frac{1}{8}$″ in thickness) together with several inside chippers of different thicknesses. *Fig. 22–31.* With the proper combination, you can cut grooves from $\frac{1}{8}$″ to $1\frac{3}{16}$″, increasing by $\frac{1}{16}$″. For example, to cut a $\frac{7}{16}$″ groove, use the two outside cutters or saws ($\frac{1}{8}$″ plus $\frac{1}{8}$″) and two inside chippers, one $\frac{1}{8}$″ and one $\frac{1}{16}$″. To enlarge the grooves slightly more than specified, use paper washers. Always use the chippers between the blades, never alone. Other adjustable types can be set to different widths. *Fig. 22–32.*

Making the Setup. 1. Remove the insert plate, blade guard, and splitter.

2. Place the first blade on the arbor, then the chippers, then another blade, the collar, and the nut.

3. Distribute the inside chippers around the saw. Place the inside chippers with the two cutting edges in line with the bottom of the gullets or spaces between the groups of blade teeth. This is necessary because the inside chippers or cutters are swaged (bent) thicker near their cutting edges. This swaged part must be allowed to enter the gullet. If this is not done, it will cut oversize grooves and also damage the cutters.

22–31.   Parts of a dado head—outside cutters and inside chippers.

245

22–34a. *Cutting dadoes with a dado head.

4. Always use the special insert plate that comes with the unit.

5. Turn the dado head by hand to make sure it does not strike any part of the saw itself.

Cutting with the Dado Head. To cut grooves, adjust for the correct height and then use the fence as a guide. *Fig. 22–33.*

To cut dadoes, use the fence as a stop without a stop block. Hold the work firmly against the miter gauge. *Fig. 22–34.*

To make a tenon, use the dado head as shown in *Fig. 22–35.* For example, if a tenon ⅜″ thick is to be cut on the end of a ¾″ piece, adjust the dado head to a height of ³⁄₁₆″. Set the fence a distance from the left-

22–32a. Adjustable dado head.

22–32b. Another type of dado head.

22–34b. Another example of cutting dadoes with a dado head.

22–33. *Cutting grooves with a dado head.

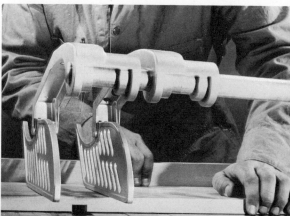

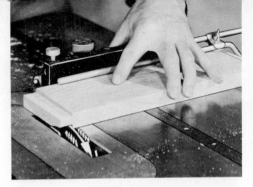

22–35. °Cutting a tenon with a dado head.

22–37. Using a commercial type tenoning jig.

hand side of the dado head equal to the length of the tenon. Set the miter gauge square and then cut the test dado with the end of the work against the fence. After the first cut, move the stock and make several more to complete half the tenon. Turn the piece over and cut the other half. It is a good idea to cut a trial piece to make sure the tenon fits the mortise correctly.

When dadoing across the end of work, slow the feed at the end of the cut to avoid splintering.

For a stopped dado or gain, clamp a stop block to the fence or directly to the table top. *Fig. 22–36.*

Cutting a Tenon. There are several ways of cutting a tenon. One of the best methods is to use the dado head described above and shown in *Fig. 22–35.* Another good method is to use a tenoning jig. The commercial type fits into one of the grooves in the table top to take stock up to $2\frac{3}{4}''$ thick and any width within the capacity of the saw. *Fig. 22–37.*

Cutting a tenon without a jig. (Never attempt to do this unless the rail is at least 4″ wide.)

Method A. Adjust the saw height for the thickness of the tenon on one side. Adjust the fence so that the length from the left side of the blade to the fence is equal to the length of the tenon. Hold the stock against the miter gauge and the end against the fence. Make both the shoulder cuts. *Fig. 22–38.* Readjust the height of the saw equal to the length of the tenon, and adjust the fence to make the cheek cut. Clamp a simple jig or feather board near the saw blade so that it will keep your hand from dropping into the blade. *Fig. 22–39.* Hold the stock firmly on edge and feed it through the saw to make the cheek cut. *Fig. 22–40.*

22–38. °Making the shoulder cuts.

22–36. Cutting a stopped dado or gain.

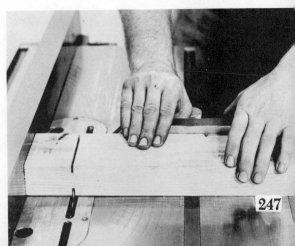

22–39. Making the cheek cut, using a feather board as a safety device.

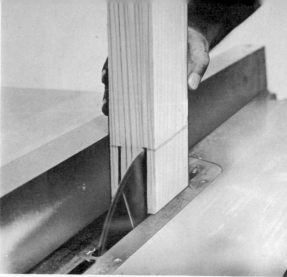

22–41. *Making the cheek cuts first.

METHOD B. Some woodworkers like to reverse the procedure in cutting tenons because they feel it is safer to make the cheek cuts first. Adjust the fence so that the cheek of the tenon away from the fence will be cut. Adjust the blade height to equal the length of the tenon. Always check the cut with a scrap piece

22–40. *This is a dangerous operation. Special care must be taken when making the cheek cut freehand. Hold the stock firmly against the fence with the end flat against the table. Never rock the work as you feed it.

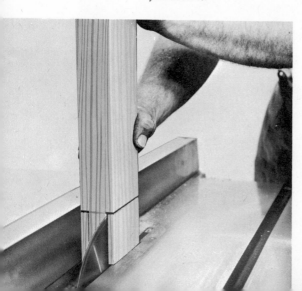

before cutting the actual tenons. Make the first cut and then reverse the stock before making the second cut. With this method, waste stock gives end support even when you make the second cut. *Fig. 22–41.* Then place the stock flat in position for the shoulder cut. Clamp a clearance or stop block to the fence. Adjust the fence for the shoulder cut, and make the height of the blade equal to the thickness of waste material to be removed. Make the two shoulder cuts.

Cutting Tapers. Three simple jigs are used for sawing: the solid jig for wedge cutting, the stepped jig for double tapering, and the adjustable jig.

Wedges. 1. Make the jig from a board about 5″ wider and about 6″ longer than the wedge to be cut. *Fig. 22–42.*

2. Lay out and cut the length and taper of the wedge from one edge of the board. Cut the wedge shape on the band saw.

248

3. Place the work in the notch and set the jig against the ripping fence. Adjust to the correct width.

4. Cut one wedge. Then reverse the stock end for end and cut the next wedge.

Taper with Stepped Taper Jig or Guide Board. To taper with a stepped taper jig or guide board, make a guide board as shown in *Fig. 22–43.*

Taper with Adjustable Jig. 1. Make an adjustable jig, *Fig. 22–44,* of two pieces of hardwood about 1″ x 4″ x 40″. Add a stop block, hinge, and slotted adjustment strap. Lay off and mark a line 12″ from the hinged end.

2. Figure the amount of taper and then adjust the jig to the correct taper per foot.

22–42. Cutting wedges.

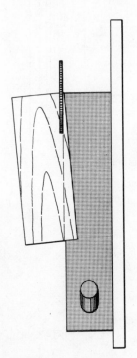

22–43. Notice that the notch block is made equal to the amount of the taper on one side of the stock. The block is located on the guide board so that the distance is equal to the length of the taper.

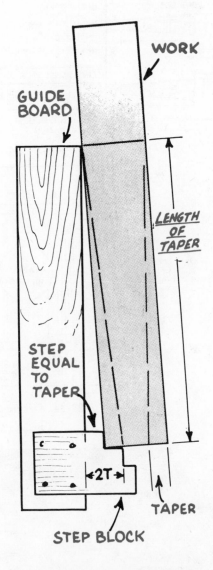

WORK

GUIDE BOARD

LENGTH OF TAPER

STEP EQUAL TO TAPER

2T

STEP BLOCK

TAPER

TAPER RIPPING

249

3. Place the jig against the fence and line up the tapered surface with the saw blade. *Fig. 22–45.* Make the first cut. Then readjust the fence and make the second cut.

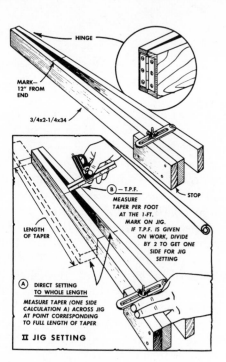

HINGE

MARK— 12" FROM END

3/4x2-1/4x34

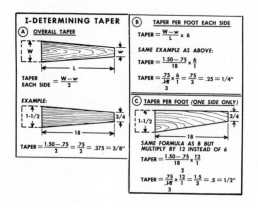

I–DETERMINING TAPER

(A) **OVERALL TAPER**

$$\text{TAPER}_{\text{EACH SIDE}} = \frac{W-w}{2}$$

EXAMPLE:

$$\text{TAPER} = \frac{1.50-.75}{2} = \frac{.75}{2} = .375 = 3/8''$$

(B) **TAPER PER FOOT EACH SIDE**

$$\text{TAPER} = \frac{W-w}{L} \times 6$$

SAME EXAMPLE AS ABOVE:

$$\text{TAPER} = \frac{1.50-.75}{18} \times \frac{6}{1}$$

$$\text{TAPER} = \frac{.75}{18} \times \frac{6}{1} = \frac{.75}{3} = .25 = 1/4''$$

(C) **TAPER PER FOOT (ONE SIDE ONLY)**

SAME FORMULA AS B BUT MULTIPLY BY 12 INSTEAD OF 6

$$\text{TAPER} = \frac{1.50-.75}{18} \times \frac{12}{1}$$

$$\text{TAPER} = \frac{.75}{18} \times \frac{12}{1} = \frac{1.5}{3} = .5 = 1/2''$$

LENGTH OF TAPER

(B) – T.P.F.
MEASURE TAPER PER FOOT AT THE 1-FT. MARK ON JIG. IF T.P.F. IS GIVEN ON WORK, DIVIDE BY 2 TO GET ONE SIDE FOR JIG SETTING

STOP

(A) DIRECT SETTING TO WHOLE LENGTH
MEASURE TAPER (ONE SIDE CALCULATION A) ACROSS JIG AT POINT CORRESPONDING TO FULL LENGTH OF TAPER

II JIG SETTING

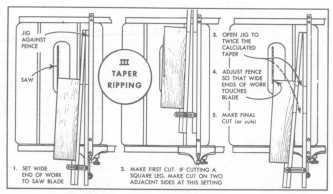

JIG AGAINST FENCE

SAW

III TAPER RIPPING

1. SET WIDE END OF WORK TO SAW BLADE

2. MAKE FIRST CUT. IF CUTTING A SQUARE LEG, MAKE CUT ON TWO ADJACENT SIDES AT THIS SETTING

3. OPEN JIG TO TWICE THE CALCULATED TAPER

4. ADJUST FENCE SO THAT WIDE ENDS OF WORK TOUCHES BLADE

5. MAKE FINAL CUT (or cuts)

22–44.   Using an adjustable taper jig.

22–45.   Cutting a taper.

Unit 23: BAND SAW

The band saw is used primarily for cutting curved edges. The size is measured in terms of wheel diameter and ranges from a small 10″ machine to the largest with wheels up to 7′ or more in diameter. These larger ones, called *band mills*, have double cutting blades about 16″ or more in width. They are used in lumbering to cut logs into planks and timbers.

Another type is the *band resaw* used in lumber yards and mills for resawing thick stock to thinner widths.

PARTS AND CONTROLS

The band saw is a relatively simple machine. *Fig. 23–1.* It consists of a frame on which are mounted two large wheels. The upper wheel is adjustable and can be tilted. The

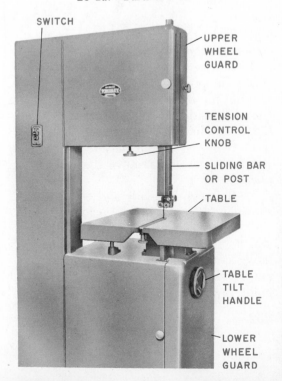

23–1a. Parts of a band saw.

SWITCH

UPPER WHEEL GUARD

TENSION CONTROL KNOB

SLIDING BAR OR POST

TABLE

TABLE TILT HANDLE

LOWER WHEEL GUARD

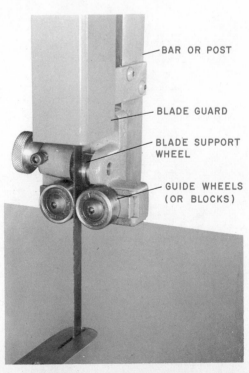

23–1b. Upper guide.

BAR OR POST

BLADE GUARD

BLADE SUPPORT WHEEL

GUIDE WHEELS (OR BLOCKS)

lower, or driving, wheel is connected to a motor with a belt and pulley. The work is held on a table. A sliding bar moves up and down; to it is attached guide blocks and guide wheels. The wheels and most of the blade are covered with guards. *Fig. 23–2* shows the controls with corresponding numbers: (1) tension control knob, (2) tilt adjusting screw, used to tilt the upper wheel, (3) the sliding bar which controls the vertical position of the saw guide bracket, (4) table-tilt handle used to control the table tilt; the table can be tilted and locked securely in any angle from 0 to 45 degrees in one direction and, in some cases, a few degrees in the other direction, and (5) guard covers that can be loosened to remove the blade.

Replacing a Blade. 1. With the power off, remove or open the wheel guards.

23–3a.   Removing the blade from the saw.

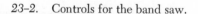

23–2.   Controls for the band saw.

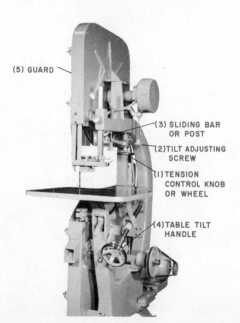

(5) GUARD

(3) SLIDING BAR
OR POST

(2) TILT ADJUSTING
SCREW

(1) TENSION
CONTROL KNOB
OR WHEEL

(4) TABLE TILT
HANDLE

2. Turn the tension control knob to release the blade tension.

3. Release the upper and lower blade support wheels so that they will not interfere with the tracking of the new blade. Also loosen the guide blocks or wheels.

4. Remove the pin or screw from the table slot and remove the throat plate.

5. Remove the blade and coil it as shown in *Fig. 23–3.*

6. Select the correct blade for the job. Pass the new blade through the table slot and over the upper and lower wheels. Make sure the teeth point towards the table.

252

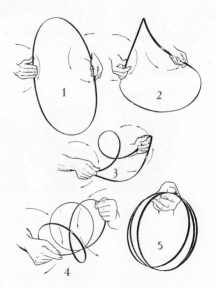

23–3b.   Folding or coiling a blade.

7. Turn the tension control knob until there is slight tension on the blade.

8. Replace the throat plate and screw or table pin. Check with a level until the table top is in one plane.

9. Revolve the wheel by hand to see if the blade stays on. If necessary, tilt the upper wheel by means of the tilt adjusting screw until the blade is tracking on the center of the wheel. *Fig. 23–4.*

10. Adjust the blade tension. This is a matter of feel. The blade should have a slight "give" when pressed between the fingers. There should be less "give" with a wider blade than with a narrower one.

11. Move the upper and lower blade support wheels forward until they almost, but not quite, touch the saw blade. They should run free when the machine is idling. Move the guide blocks or wheels until the

teeth of the blade clear the front. Insert a piece of heavy wrapping paper between the guide blocks or wheels and the blade, and push them together. Then tighten the guide blocks or wheels.

SUGGESTIONS FOR SAFE OPERATION

• Make sure that the stock is free of nails before doing any cutting.

• Check the saw blade to make sure it has proper tension and that the teeth point downward.

• Lower the blade guide so that it is not more than $\frac{1}{4}''$ above the work. This will keep the blade from twisting.

• Make sure that all guards are securely fastened and that the throat plate is clear of sawdust.

• Feed the work evenly and slowly so that you don't twist or crowd the blade.

• Never back the saw out of long cuts because this may pull the blade off the wheels.

23–4.   Note that the blade should stay in the center of the wheel.

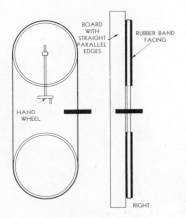

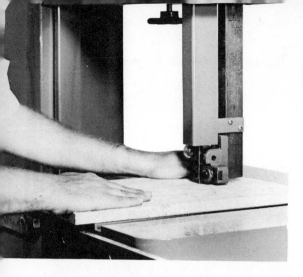

23–5a. Straight cutting on the band saw.

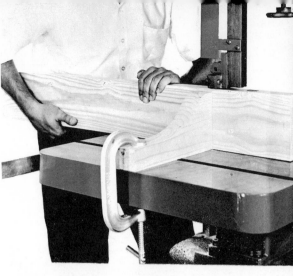

23–7a. Resawing, using a pivot block.

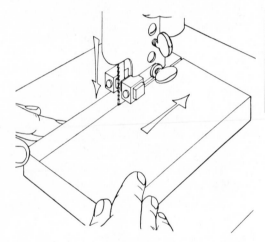

23–5b. Correct method of straight cutting.

23–6. Resawing, using a fence.

- Never try to cut a curve of small radius with a wide blade unless you make relief cuts.
- Apply beeswax to the blade when cutting hardwood or wood that has quite a bit of pitch.

USING THE SAW

Straight Cutting. Stand to the left of the work and the blade. Guide the stock with your right hand and use your left hand to hold the work

23–7b. Making diagonal cuts.

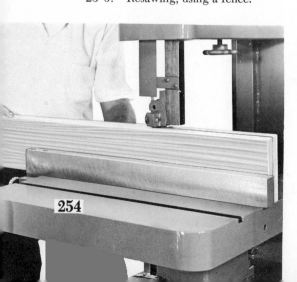

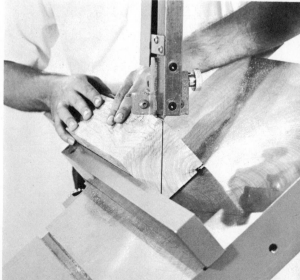

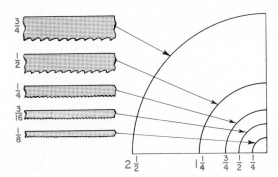

23-8. Correct blade widths for cutting arcs without making relief cuts. For example, a ¼″ blade can cut an arc with a ¾″ radius, or a 1½″ circle.

steady. *Fig. 23-5.* When doing straight cutting you should be in line with the blade. Sometimes due to a factor called "lead," the blade pulls to one side or the other. If this happens, you must adjust the feed, guiding it from one side to the other. "Lead" is due to improper adjustment of the guides or to an improper set of the blade itself.

Resawing. Boards are resawed to reduce their thickness. In some cases you may first want to pre-cut from either edge on the circular saw. However, if all the resawing is done on the band saw, there will be less waste of stock due to the narrower kerf. Always use the widest blade available since this will make it easier to follow the cutting line. Make sure the lower edge is planed true and then mark the cutting line on top. Follow one of these cutting techniques:

• If the blade is in near-perfect condition so that it does not "lead," clamp the fence at the proper distance from the blade and resaw. *Fig. 23-6.*

255

• Fasten a pivot block to the table for the correct thickness. You can then move the stock in either direction to correct for "lead." *Fig. 23-7a.*

• Hold a right-angle block against the side of the stock with one hand and regulate the feed with the other. This allows for a change of end angle if the board is warped a little.

• Diagonal ripping can be done by tilting the table and using the fence as a guide. *Fig. 23-7b.*

Cutting Curves. The minimum arc that can be cut with a ⅛″ blade has a ¼″ radius. A ⅜″ blade can cut a 2″ diameter circle. *Fig. 23-8.* If a wide blade must be used for short curves, either break up the curve into a series of tangent cuts, or make a series of relief cuts up to the layout line before cutting the curve. *Fig. 23-9.*

23-9. Eliminate the twisting strain by using a series of radial cuts.

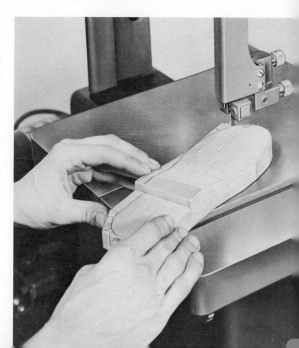

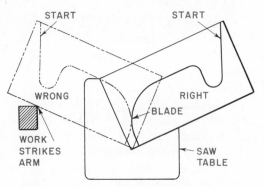

START   START

WRONG   RIGHT

BLADE

WORK
STRIKES
ARM

SAW
TABLE

23–10. Remember to watch the feed direction so that the work will not bind against the upper arm.

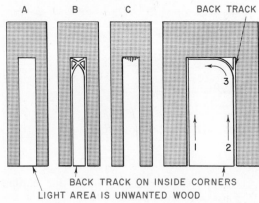

A   B   C   BACK TRACK

BACK TRACK ON INSIDE CORNERS
LIGHT AREA IS UNWANTED WOOD

23–12. Steps in cutting a square opening.

Think through the pattern of cutting before you begin. If you don't, you may find the stock swinging against the arm of the saw and preventing you from continuing the cut. *Fig. 23–10.*

Cut through the waste stock when it is impossible to continue a cut. Don't back out of a cut unless there is no other possible way.

Drill or bore turning holes in the waste stock whenever possible. *Fig.*

23–11. Always make short cuts first and then longer cuts. To cut a narrow slot, first drill or bore a hole at the end of the square opening. Cut a larger rectangular opening as shown in *Fig. 23–12.*

Tilt the table to cut a bevel. Use a wooden fence to hold the stock in place when bevel ripping.

Break up a combination or complicated cut to simplify the sawing. *Fig. 23–13.*

23–11. Use turning holes.

23–13. Whenever possible, break up complex cuts into several simpler cuts.

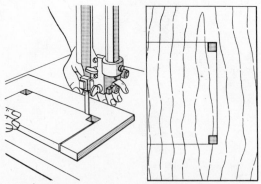

TURNING HOLES MADE WITH MORTISING CHISEL

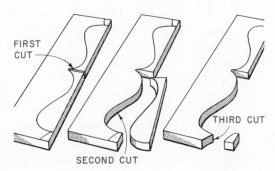

FIRST
CUT

SECOND CUT

THIRD CUT

When sawing several pieces to the same shape, nail them together in the waste stock and then cut them as one piece.

A good way to cut circles is by using an extension bar type of circle jig. *Fig. 23–14.*

23–14.   Using a circle-cutting jig.

Unit 24: JIG OR SCROLL SAW

The jig or scroll saw is used to cut inside and outside curved parts. It does the same kind of cutting as the hand coping saw. *Fig. 24-1.* It has limited use in most of the occupational fields except patternmaking, but it is used by hobbyists, sign makers, and model makers for cutting intricate designs. *Fig. 24-2.*

24-1. A jig or scroll saw.

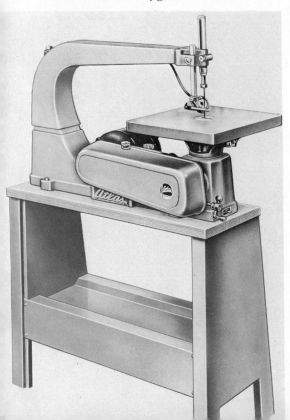

The machine can be used for cutting not only wood but also rubber, plastic, metal, and other materials. The size of the jig saw is determined by the distance from the blade to the inside of the overarm. The portable jig saw, or saber saw, has greater value to the carpenter than the stationary type. See Unit 26.

There are no set rules for speed; however, the two medium speeds are usually for hard wood. Use high speeds on soft woods when a very smooth curve is needed. Use the slowest speed for metals.

BLADES

Install the largest blade with the coarsest teeth that will cut the stock cleanly and still follow the layout line. *Fig. 24-3.* Three teeth should be in contact with the stock at all times. Thickness and width of blades should vary with the sharpness of the curve. A sharper curve requires a narrower and thinner blade.

Mounting the Blade. 1. Remove the insert plate and insert the blade in the lower chuck. Move it back as far as it will go between the stationary

258

24–2. Cutting pattern parts on a jig saw.

and floating jaw. Make sure the teeth point towards the table.

2. Place the blade in a vertical position and then tighten the jaws; for greater accuracy, use a square block of wood to position the blade.

3. Turn the pulley over by hand until the blade is at the top of the stroke.

4. Loosen the blade-tension knob and lower the unit. Insert the blade about ⅜″ in the upper chuck, then tighten.

5. Raise the upper shaft housing until you have the proper tension. Tighten the lock nut. The tension should be just enough to hold the blade straight during cutting. Too much tension will cause the blade to break; too little will buckle the blade.

6. Replace the throat plate.

Adjusting the Blade Guides and Work Hold-down. Adjust the blade guide and work hold-down as shown in *Fig. 24–4.* The slotted blade guide should be open just the thickness of the blade and in position so that the front edge is even with the bottom of the blade teeth. The hold-down should just touch the work; the support wheel should just touch the back of the blade.

Adjusting the Table. Loosen the knob to tilt the table to the correct angle. The table tilts from 0 to 15 degrees to the left and from 0 to 45

24–3.   Chart for selecting the correct blade.

Material Cut	Thick In.	Width In.	Teeth Per Inch	Blade Full Size	Material Cut	Thick In.	Width In.	Teeth Per Inch	Blade Full Size
Steel • Iron Lead • Copper Aluminum	.020	.070	32		Wood Veneer Plus Plastics Celluloid • Hard Rubber Bakelite • Ivory Extremely Thin Materials	.008	.035	20	
Pewter • Asbestos Paper • Felt	.020	.070	20			.019	.050	15	
Steel • Iron • Lead	.020	.070	15		Plastics • Celluloid Hard Rubber	.019	.055	12	
Copper • Brass Aluminum	.020	.085	15		Bakelite • Ivory Wood	.020	.070	7	
Pewter • Asbestos Wood	.020	.110	20			.020	.110	7	
Asbestos • Brake Lining • Mica Steel • Iron • Lead Copper • Brass Aluminum Pewter	.028	.250	20		Wall Board • Pressed Wood Wood • Lead Bone • Felt • Paper Copper • Ivory • Aluminum	.020	.110	15	
					Hard and Soft Wood	.020	.110	10	
						.028	.187	10	
Wood Panels and Veneers	.010	.048	18			.028	.250	7	
Plastics • Celluloid Hard Rubber Bakelite • Ivory Wood	.010	.070	14		Pearl • Pewter Mica Pressed Wood Sea Shells Jewelry • Metals Hard Leather	.016	.054	30	
	.010	.055	16			.016	.054	20	
	.010	.045	18			.020	.070	15	
						.020	.085	12	

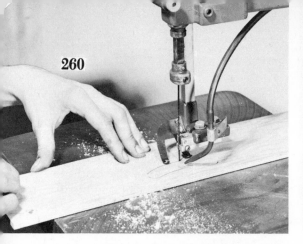

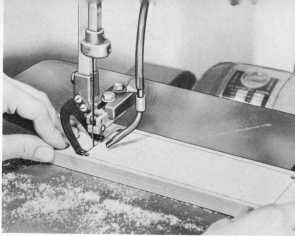

24-4. The blade guide and work hold-
down is adjusted correctly.

24-6. Cutting an internal opening.

degrees to the right. The table can be swivelled to handle angular cutting on long stock.

OPERATING THE JIG SAW

Let the blade do the cutting; do not force the stock into the blade or twist the work sharply. Feed directly into the blade. To start the blade in the stock at an angle, apply light side pressure. Cut through the waste stock when you cannot continue the cut. Back up only as a last resort. Fig. 24-5.

For cutting internal curves and designs:

• Drill a relief hole through the waste stock. The hole should be slightly larger than the blade. Fig. 24-6.

• Remove the insert plate and loosen the upper part of the blade. Lower the chuck.

• Put the blade through the hole and then fasten the other end to the upper chuck.

• Adjust the blade guides of the hold-down.

The upper and lower chucks can be turned 90 degrees to cut long stock. Fig. 24-7.

24-7. Note that the chucks are rotated 90 degrees so that the blade is at right angles to the overarm. Then a side feed is used for cutting long work.

24-5. Completing an external or outside cut.

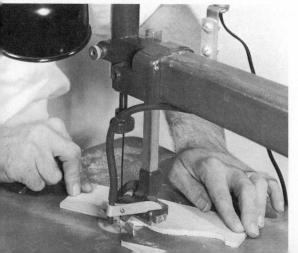

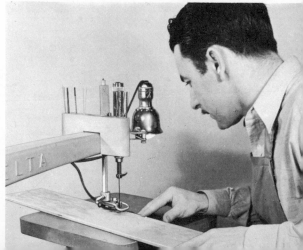

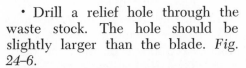

Unit 25: CUT-OFF SAW

The electric cut-off (power, hand, or circular) saw is designed primarily for on-the-job sawing, especially for carpentry and general woodshop work. It can be used for pre-cutting of lumber or for trimming off uneven ends of boards in forms already nailed in place.

Electric hand saw blades range in size from 4″ to the heavy duty 10″ or 12″. *Fig. 25–1.* The saw is rated principally by blade size which determines its maximum depth of cut. The 8″ size, which is the most popu-

lar, will cut to a depth of $2\frac{3}{4}''$. Most saws have a friction clutch that allows the motor to run even though the blade is held stationary in the wood. This protects the saw and tends to minimize accidents.

SAFETY

• Make sure that the work is safely supported and is in a position where you can work comfortably.

• Support the work so the cutting can be done without sawing the support itself. Scrap strips can be nailed to the support to protect it from the saw. When plywood and other light materials are to be sawed, place the material on a table with a 1″ or 2″ space underneath.

• Install the blade best suited for the work. A crosscut or combination blade is best for cutting across grain.

• Connect the saw properly to the power source. Make sure that the ground-wire slip is attached to a ground connection. If an extension cord must be used, make sure that it has 12-gauge wire or larger for lengths up to 100 feet, and 10-gauge or larger for lengths up to 150 feet.

• Lubricate the saw regularly and keep the air passages clean.

25–1. Parts of the saw.

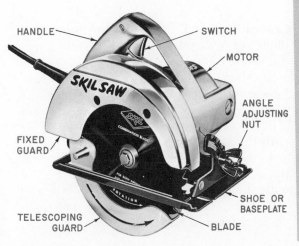

HANDLE

SWITCH

MOTOR

ANGLE ADJUSTING NUT

FIXED GUARD

SHOE OR BASEPLATE

TELESCOPING GUARD

BLADE

25-2. Crosscutting with the saw.

USING THE SAW

General Suggestions. Always rest the front of the baseplate or shoe on the work before turning on the switch. Allow the blade to come to full speed before starting the cut. If the saw

25-3. Cutting off the ends of sheathing after it has been nailed in place.

slows down or stalls, back it out. Don't turn off the switch.

Never put your hand directly in front or in back of the saw blade. Whenever possible, use both hands on the saw itself. Keep a sharp blade on the saw at all times. *When cutting plywood, always cut with the best face down.*

Crosscutting. 1. Adjust the saw blade to protrude about $\frac{1}{8}''$ below the work.

2. Mark a guide or layout line indicating where the cut is to be made.

3. Place the work over sawhorses with the layout line outside.

4. Place the shoe or baseplate on the work with the line of cut matched with the guide line.

5. Turn on the power and cut along the guide line. *Fig. 25-2.*

This saw has a distinct advantage in that sawing can be done after the work has been nailed in place. *Fig. 25-3.* For example, roofing boards can be nailed and then the edges trimmed. This saves time and labor.

Ripping. 1. Mark a line showing the location of the cut.

2. Place the work over sawhorses so that the cut can be made continuously.

3. Whenever possible, use the rip guide and adjust for the correct width of cut. *Fig. 25-4.*

4. Start the cut and then slowly walk along with the saw. Another method is to cut a short distance, then stop and pull the saw back in the kerf. Walk forward to a new position and then resume the cutting.

Bevel Sawing. 1. Adjust the shoe to the correct angle on the graduated scale on the front of the saw. *Fig. 25-5.*

2. Adjust for correct depth of cut.

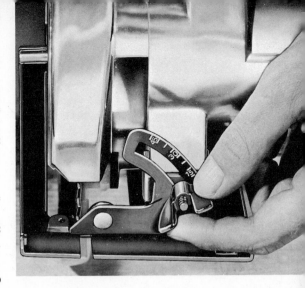

25-5.   Adjusting the shoe to the correct angle, using the bevel gauge.

Remember that the depth possible with the saw set at bevel angle is less than that for a straight cut.

3. Make the bevel cut, guiding the saw to the outside of the mark or the long side of the bevel. The blade tilts under the baseplate and the short side will be at the bottom of the cut. *Fig. 25-6.*

25-4.   Ripping stock, using a ripping guide.

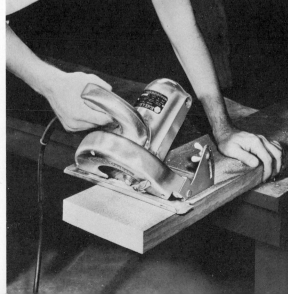

25-6.   Making a bevel cut.

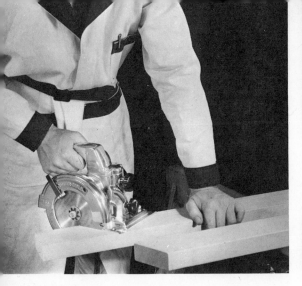

25-7.   Making a miter cut without a guide.

25-8.   Starting a pocket cut. Note how the guard must be held out of the way to start the cut.

Making Miter Cuts. A miter cut is an ordinary straight cut across a board at an angle, usually 45 degrees. This can be done either freehand or with the saw guide. *Fig. 25-7.*

To use a guide, place the slide bar along the edge of the work. Set the guide to the correct angle and then move the saw along the straightedge.

Pocket Cutting. A pocket cut is an opening in the middle of a wide piece of work.

1. Adjust the blade at maximum depth to minimize the length of the clearing cut.

2. Swing the guard out of the way and pivot the front edge of the baseplate on the work. *Fig. 25-8.*

3. Start the saw and slowly lower the blade into the stock. Make sure that you start far enough forward from one corner so that the saw does not cut beyond the corner line. The saw can be backed slightly to bring it to the corner.

4. Be sure to release the switch and let the saw stop before lifting it out of the work. After making the cut, clean out the corners with a hand saw.

Unit 26: HAND JIG, SABER, OR BAYONET SAW

The hand jig (saber or bayonet) saw is ideal for many on-the-job cuts. It can cut straight and curved lines as well as internal openings for such things as electrical outlet boxes or heating ducts. The tool is much like a floor-type jig saw except that it is portable.

26–1.   Hand jig saw.

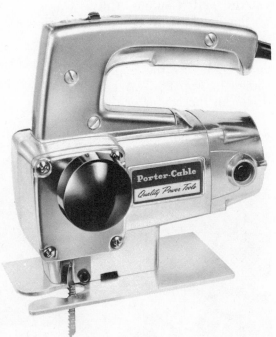

The exact design of the saw varies with the manufacturer. However, all consist of a motor, a handle, a mechanism to change rotary action to up-and-down action, and a baseplate or shoe. *Fig. 26–1.* On some types the base can be tilted for making bevel cuts. *Fig. 26–2.* Blades are available to cut wood, plywood, light metal, plastics, and many other materials. *Fig. 26–3.* The blades are held in place by two or more set screws or by a small lock clamp.

26–2.   Notice that the base can be tilted for bevel cutting.

26-3. SELECTING THE CORRECT BLADE

Heavy cuts 2″ x 4″ at 45°	6 teeth per inch
General cutting	7, 10
Smooth cuts	12
Plywood	12
Hardboard	12
Cardboard	Knife
Leather	Knife

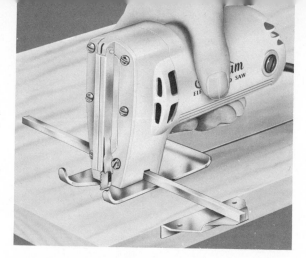

26–5. Using a guide for ripping along a straight line.

USING THE SAW

Straight Cutting. 1. Install the blade with the teeth facing forward and pointing upward. The cutting is done on the up-stroke.

2. Clamp the work rigidly because if it vibrates it will break the expensive blade. Leave space beneath the layout line.

3. Start the motor and allow it to come up to full speed. Hold the saw *firmly* on the work; then move it along slowly. *Fig. 26–4.* Do not force the cutting. Use only enough pressure to keep the saw moving at all times. The saw is held in the right hand and the left can be used to steady the work or the saw.

Crosscutting and ripping can be done by following the line freehand; however, for more accurate straight cutting, a ripping fence should be used. *Fig. 26–5.* If the saw does not have a ripping guide, clamp a board to the work as a guide for one edge of the baseplate.

Curves and Contour Cuts. Curve cutting is done freehand. Hold the saw firmly on the work and carefully follow the layout line. *Fig. 26–6.* To cut a circle, use the ripping guide as shown in *Fig. 26–7.* A nail must be driven in the center of the circle.

26–4. Freehand straight cutting.

26–6. Cutting irregular curves.

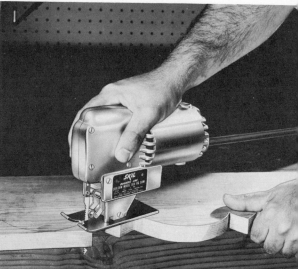

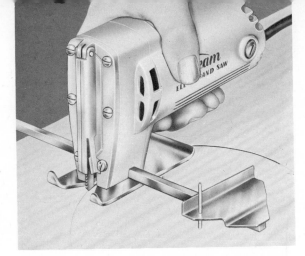

26-7. Cutting a perfect circle, using the
rip guide.

Bevel Cutting. Most of the saws have a shoe that can be adjusted from 0 to 45 degrees for bevel cutting.

Inside Cuts. Whenever possible, drill a small starting hole in the waste stock to begin the inside cut. However, it is possible to make inside cuts without first drilling a hole. This is called plunge cutting. To do this, rest the saw on the shoe at an angle of about 45 degrees and turn on the power. *Fig. 26-8.* Slowly rock the saw back and forth until the blade cuts through the waste stock. Then cut up to the finish line.

26-8. Plunge cutting an opening for an
electrical outlet box.

267

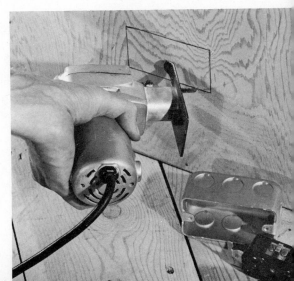

Unit 27: JOINTER

The jointer is used to plane a surface, an edge, or an end, and to square stock. It does the work of a hand plane although it operates in a different way. The jointer has a circular cutter head with three, four, or more high-speed steel knives. These knives make a rotary or revolving cut into the wood. The smoothness of the cut depends on the number of knives, the speed of rotation, and the feed. The size of the jointer is indicated by the length of the knives, and varies from a small 4″ bench machine to large production machines with knives as long as 36″. *Fig. 27–1.*

PARTS AND CONTROLS

The jointer consists of a heavy frame with two tables, cutter head, guard, and fence. *Fig. 27–2.* The *rear, or outfeed, table* is adjusted infrequently. The *front, or infeed, table* controls the depth of cut. The *fence,* similar to that found on a circular saw, can be tilted in either direction about 45 degrees from a right-angle position. It can also be adjusted crosswise over the table. The *guard* covers the cutter head and swings either out or up as stock is run over the tables. When the stock is passed over the knives, the

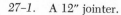
27–1. A 12″ jointer.

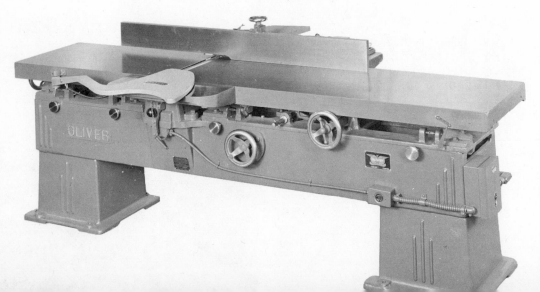

spring returns the guard to its original position. *Except when cutting a rabbet, tenon, or taper, never remove the guard.*

Adjusting the Rear or Outfeed Table. Once this table is adjusted, it is not moved except for cutting a recessed groove. This table should be exactly the same height as the knives at the highest point. Rotate the cutter head until one knife is at the top position. Then place a straightedge over the rear table as shown in *Fig. 27–3*, and raise or lower the table until both are in the same plane. If the table is too high, it will cut a taper. *Fig. 27–4.* If it is too low, it will cut a "snipe," a small, concave cut, at the end of the stock. Always lock the rear table after adjustment. On some jointers, the rear table is fixed, and the cutter head must be raised or lowered.

Adjusting the Front Table. Loosen the lock nut and then turn the knob beneath the front table to raise or lower it for the correct depth of cut. When lowering the table, bring it down just a little bit below the depth required and then raise it to

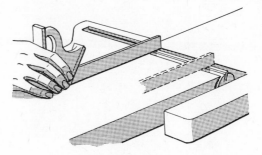

27-3. Using a straightedge to adjust the rear table to the correct height.

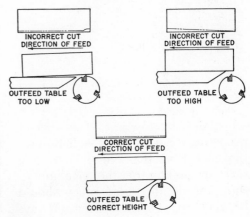

27-4. Notice that the jointer cuts a taper when the outfeed table is too high. A "snipe" is cut at the end of the stock when the outfeed table is too low.

27-2. Parts of a jointer.

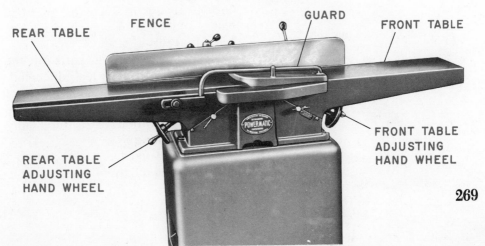

269

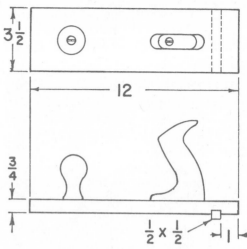

27-6b.   Push block.

27-5.   Checking the fence with a try square.

the correct height. This will remove the slack from the screw. There is a scale or pointer on the machine to show the depth. Its accuracy should be checked every so often. Always lock the table after adjusting it for depth of cut.

Adjusting the Fence. Loosen the fence lock and, with a try square, set the fence perpendicular to the table. You can use the scale and pointer on

27-6a.   Using a push block.

the machine for adjusting the fence to other angles, but, for greater accuracy, set with a sliding T bevel or try square. *Fig. 27–5.* The fence can be moved back and forth over the cutter head.

SAFETY

Remember the danger of getting your fingers too close to the revolving cutter head. This makes it very important always to keep the guard in place, and to keep your hands away from the cutter head.

Make sure that all parts of the machine are securely locked, including the table and fence. Be sure that the knives are sharp. If one of the following conditions exists, the blades need sharpening:
  • Planed wood has a fuzzy look.
  • The stock chatters when cutting.

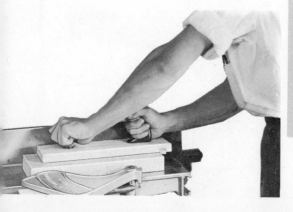

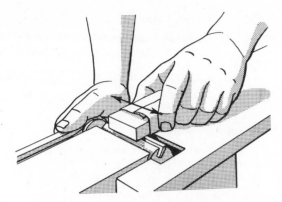

27-7.   Honing the knives to keep the cutting edge sharp.

• It seems difficult to feed the stock across the knives. Honing is usually all that is necessary.

When face jointing (surfacing) short pieces, use a push block. *Fig. 27-6.* Never try to surface a piece shorter than 12″. Stop the jointer before cleaning and making adjustments. Examine the stock carefully before surfacing to make sure it is free of knots and nails.

Feed the stock slowly and take a cut of ½₂″ or less for a very smooth finish.

HONING THE BLADES

1. Lock the front table about ⅛″ below the cutting edge of the knives.

2. Cover about two thirds of a large abrasive stone with paper so it won't scratch the table. *Fig. 27-7.*

3. Remove the fence and guard from the machine.

4. Turn the cutter head until the stone is resting flat on the bevel of the blade and the remainder of it is on the front table.

5. Hold the cutting head in this

position and rub the stone crosswise with equal pressure until the blade is sharp.

6. Turn to the next blade and do the same.

USING THE JOINTER

Face Planing. Adjust for the correct depth of cut. Consider the width of the stock, the crookedness of the grain, and the hardness of the wood. If the stock is warped, place the concave side down and take several light cuts.

With both hands hold the work over the front table. Place your left hand on the front of the stock as soon as it rests firmly on the rear table. When the right hand approaches the blade, hold the work firmly with the left hand and place the right hand on the stock over the rear table. *Fig. 27-8.* For thin stock or short pieces, use a push block.

Jointing an Edge. To make a square joint, adjust the fence to a 90 degree angle.

Apply equal pressure to the stock to hold it firmly against both fence

27-8.   Face planing stock.

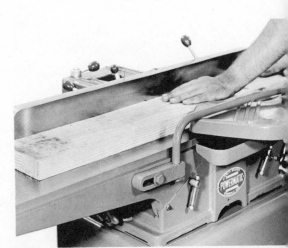

271

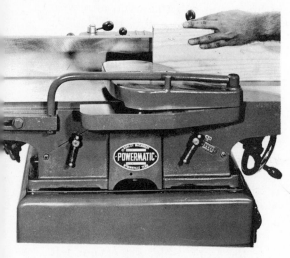

27–9. Jointing an edge, when done correctly, is a simple operation. *a.* Hold the best face side against the fence.

and table. Then feed the stock slowly over the cutter head. *Fig. 27–9.*

If considerable jointing must be done, move the fence occasionally to distribute the wear on the blade.

End Jointing. 1. Adjust for a very light cut. Care must be taken to pre-

27–9b. As the work is pushed over the cutter head . . .

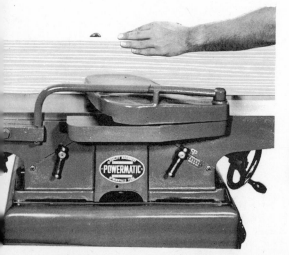

vent the wood from splitting out on the edges. Never end plane stock that is less than 10″ in width. *Fig. 27–10.*

2. Make a short cut about ¹⁄₁₆″ deep and about ½″ long at one end; then reverse the stock and feed from the opposite direction.

Fig. 27–11 shows the steps in squaring up stock on the jointer.

When planing the edges of plywood, move the fence as far to the right as possible and adjust for a very thin cut.

Beveling and Chamfering. 1. Tilt the fence and check it with a sliding T bevel. The fence can be tilted in or out. It is safer with the fence tilted in.

2. Take medium cuts until the chamfer or bevel is nearly the desired shape. *Fig. 27–12.*

3. Finish by taking several very light cuts.

Taper Cutting. The jointer should be used to cut a taper with a depth less

27–9c. . . . pressure is exerted so that the newly formed surface makes perfect contact with the rear table.

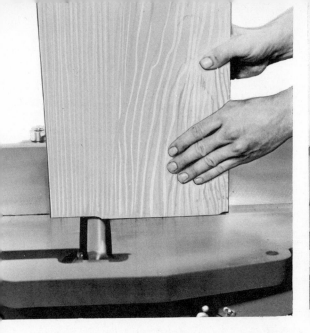

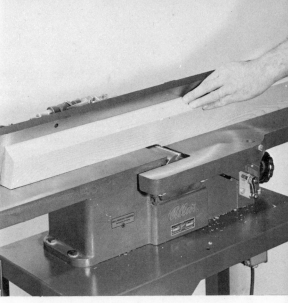

27-10. *Always make a very light cut to prevent chipping when end jointing.

27-12. *Cutting a bevel or chamfer.

than $\frac{1}{2}''$ and a length less than that of the infeed table. It can also be used for a longer and deeper taper.

Shallow Tapers. 1. Lower the front table about $\frac{1}{32}''$ less than the full depth of the taper you want. Place the stock against the fence, and position it with the line where the taper starts over the lip of the outfeed table. Lower the other end and make a cut.

2. Lower the table to a setting of

$\frac{1}{32}''$ and take a light finishing cut across the full length. Keep safety in mind as you work. Review the principles discussed in Unit 2.

Short Tapers. 1. Lower the front table the desired amount. Clamp a stop block to the fence over the front table for the correct length of taper.

2. Place the stock against the stop block. Lower it and then pull the stock across the cutter head.

Long Tapers. 1. Divide the stock into a number of equal parts. Each part must be slightly less than the length of the front table. The depth of cut must also be divided into the same number of equal parts. For example, if a 36″ board is to be tapered $\frac{3}{8}''$, divide the board into two equal parts, since the table length is usually at least 18″. *Fig. 27–13.*

27-11.   Steps in squaring up stock.

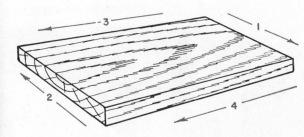

*On these pictures the guard has been removed so the operation can be seen clearly. Use the guard when you do these processes.

273

274

2. Adjust the front table to a ³⁄₁₆″ depth of cut. Then you must make two cuts.

3. Cut the rear part first by placing the board over the blade at the center mark. *Fig. 27–14* shows the first cut being made.

4. Then make the second cut starting at the beginning of the taper, and make a full length cut.

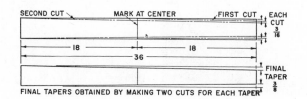

27–13. When stock is longer than the front table, divide it into equal sections. Start the first cut at the middle of the stock.

27–14. *Making the first cut on a long taper.

Unit 28: HAND OR POWER PLANE

The electric plane is an important labor-saving tool, especially for the carpenter. It is highly useful in planing long edges, as in fitting a door. *Fig. 28–1.* Some models are designed only for edge planing while on others many types of cutting can be done.

ELECTRIC HAND PLANE

The size of this tool ranges from $\frac{1}{2}$ to $1\frac{1}{4}$ horsepower. The plane consists of a frame with a handle, a motor, and a spiral-shaped cutter. A grinding attachment is also supplied.

The frame has a bevel adjustment for making angular cuts. Depth of cut can be kept uniform throughout an operation, or varied. The location of the cutter is adjustable in relationship to the shoes (the base of the frame). Front and rear shoes are always in alignment when the depth adjustment is at zero.

POWER BLOCK PLANE

The power block plane is designed to do many operations, such as trimming the edges of doors, rabbeting cabinet doors, beveling countertop edges, planing shingles, and fitting drawers. *Figs. 28–2 and 28–3.* It is a lightweight tool that can be con-

28–1. Using an electric hand plane for trimming the edge of a two by four.

28–2. The power block plane can be used for planing the edge of a door.

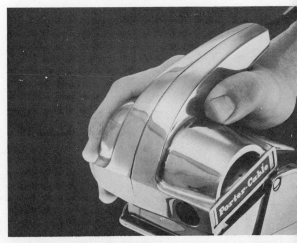

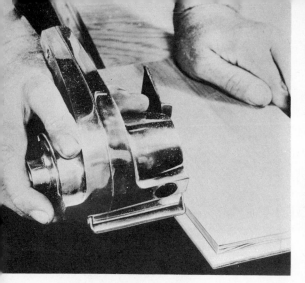 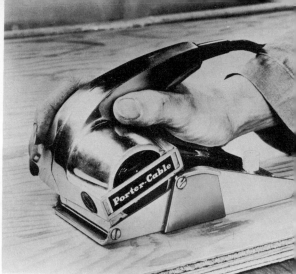

28–3. Cutting a rabbet on a lip door with the power block plane.

28–4. Using the tool as a surface plane.

trolled with one hand, making it ideal for overhead work. It can plane 2″ dressed lumber with a maximum cut of ¼₄″ on each pass. A high-speed steel cutter is used for all wood surfaces. With a carbide cutter, the plane can be used on the toughest building materials, including plastic laminates, hardboard, and even aluminum.

The power block plane is easily converted to a surface plane by removing the 90-degree fence held in place by thumbscrews. *Fig. 28–4.*

Unit 29: ROUTER

The portable hand router can perform many cutting, shaping, and routing jobs. *Fig. 29–1.* One good example of its usefulness is in the cutting of gains for installing hinges on doors, a long and tedious job by hand. With a portable router and a hinge-mortising template, hinges can be installed quickly and easily.

The router consists basically of a motor and a base. A collet (or split) chuck is attached to the end of the motor to hold the cutting tools. *Fig. 29–2.* The work that can be done with the router depends on the kinds of cutters, fixtures, and attachments. *Fig. 29–3* shows the common shapes of router bits. Router cutters can be used singly or in combination. In the furniture industry and in manufacturing doors and windows, a larger, floor-type router is needed. *Fig. 29–4a.* This machine performs many routing operations. *Fig. 29–4b.*

29–2. The router.

29–1. Using a portable router to cut an edge on a table top.

STRAIGHT BITS ONE PIECE

RABBETING BITS

CORNER ROUNDING BITS

BEADING BITS

ROMAN OGEE BITS

DOVETAIL BITS

CHAMFER BITS
45° Bevel

SASH BEADING BITS

SASH COPING BITS

COVE BITS

"V" GROOVING BIT

CORE BOX BITS

29–3.   Router bits are made of high-speed tool steel or carbide steel. Here are a few of the common shapes.

29–4a.   Floor-type router used in industry.

OPERATING INSTRUCTIONS

Select the correct shape of cutter or bit for the work to be done. Insert the shank of the bit or the cutter arbor in the collet to a depth of about $\frac{1}{2}''$. Then tighten the nut or nuts holding the cutter firmly to the collet.

Depth of cut is regulated by moving the motor up and down in the base. On some types of routers the motor screws into the base; on others it is raised or lowered by a simple gear and rachet. Many routers have a depth dial on the motor housing to

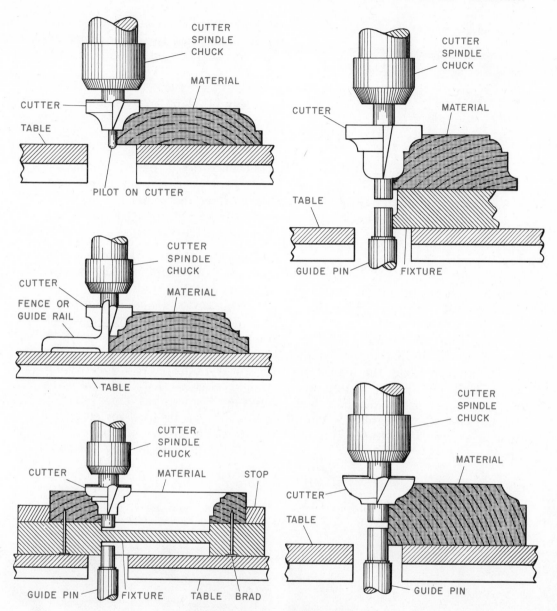

29–4b.   Methods of routing.

make it simple to set the depth of cut. Loosen the lock nut on the base and then raise or lower the motor until correct depth is reached. If the motor screws into the base, each complete revolution equals ¹⁄₁₆″. After the correct depth has been obtained, lock the base to the motor.

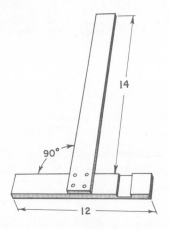

29-5. A simple device for guiding the router.

Do not feed the router too slowly, for this will cause the bit or cutter to burn the wood. Feeding too fast will produce excessive wear on bits or cutters. For extremely heavy cuts, you should learn to recognize the sound and feel of the motor when it is operating correctly. Never force the bit; let it cut freely.

For very deep cuts, it is a good idea to cut to partial depth first and then to reset the router for the total depth. This is especially true when working on hardwoods.

Always check the cutting action of the router on scrap stock of the thickness that you will use.

When using the router, hold the base firmly to the flat surface of the wood. Always move the tool from left to right for straight cutting, at a rate slow enough to maintain high motor speed. For irregular or circular cutting, move the router counterclockwise.

Guiding the Router. There are five main ways of controlling the sidewise movement of the router:

• *Using a home-made guide block or T-square guide.* A straight piece of stock can be clamped to the work to limit the sidewise movement of the router. A better device for making straight cuts on flat surfaces is to build a T-square as shown in *Fig. 29-5*. This can be used for cutting a rabbet, dado, groove, or spline.

• *Using a straight and circular*

29-6. Using a guide for routing along a straight edge.

29-7a. Using the guide for routing a curved edge.

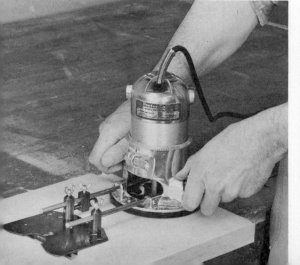

29-7b. Using the guide for routing to a corner to cut a rabbet on a frame.

29-8. The pilot edge of a cutter will control the depth of cut.

guide. A commercial guide can be attached to the base of the router; for straight cutting, the straightedge is used. This edge is adjusted to the correct distance from the cutter so that it will ride along the edge or surface of the stock. *Fig. 29–6.* The guide can also be used for shaping in corners or along irregular edges. *Fig. 29–7.*

• *Using a cutter with a pilot end.* Many router cutters are made with a small, cylindrical pilot just below the cutting end. When the bit reaches the desired depth, the pilot contacts the stock and prevents a deeper cut. (In *Fig. 29–3* the rabbeting, corner rounding, beading, Roman ogee, chamfer, and cove bits have pilots.) A pilot end is especially useful for beading, rounding over, and making cove cuts and moldings. *Fig. 29–8.*

• *Using a template.* A template of the correct shape can be made on a jigsaw from ¼" plywood or hardboard. Tack the template to the stock with small brads in a part of the work that will not show or will be

removed. If the routing must go completely through the stock, place scrap wood underneath. Use a straight bit for sharp corner recesses, or a rounding-over bit for rounded corners.

• *Freehand routing.* This work is done without the use of any guide devices. Quality is determined by the operator's skill. Raised letters can be made with a recessed background, or the letters themselves can be cut out of a flat surface. *Fig. 29–9.* The routing is first done by making a pencil layout on the wood. Hold the base at a slight angle to the work and then turn on the machine. Lower the router bit into the wood and then carefully guide it along the layout lines. A router can be used to do preliminary shaping for bowls and trays, to get them ready for final carving.

Making Joint Cuts. *Cutting a Groove or Dado.* Select a straight bit that has the same diameter as the groove or dado you must cut. If a bit with the exact diameter you need is not

281

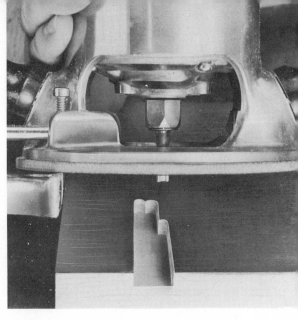

29–9a. Freehand routing is done without any guides. The quality of work depends on the operator's skill.

29–10. This shows how a narrower bit can be used to cut a wider dado with two or more passes.

available, a narrower bit can be used by making two or more passes. *Fig. 29–10.* Use a guide or a straightedge to control the position of the cut. *Fig. 29–11.*

   Making a Spline Joint. Since most splines are made of $\frac{1}{8}''$ or $\frac{1}{4}''$ ply-

wood, use a straight bit. *Fig. 29–12.* Lay out the location of the spline and then use a guide board or straightedge to control the position of the cut.

   Mortise-and-Tenon Joint. While a mortise and tenon can be cut by

29–9b. A sub base has been added to the router base to shape this mahogany tray. This is necessary because the permanent base is too small.

29–11. Using a guide to cut equally spaced dadoes.

29-12.   The recess for the spline has been cut with the router.

hand, it is much more efficient to use power tools such as the circular saw, the mortising attachment of the drill press, or the mortiser.

Dovetail Joint. This joint is best made with a router and dovetail attachment. *Fig. 29–13.*

Hinge Butt Routing. A special bit is available for hinge butt routing or hinge mortising, along with a metal template to control the size and location of the hinge opening, or gain. Because bits leave a slight curve at the corner of cuts, it is necessary to square out the corner with a chisel if square corner hinges are to be installed. *Fig. 29–14.*

29-13.   Using a router and a finger template to cut the edges of two boards that are to be joined by a dovetail. This will insure a perfect fit.

29-14.   Using a router and a template to cut the gain or opening for the hinge. The template can be used on both the door itself and the door frame.

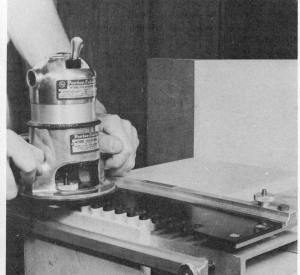

Unit 30: SHAPER

The shaper is used to cut the edges and ends of stock for molding, decorative effects, and joints. It is a dangerous machine unless precautions are taken before and during its operation. The high speed of rotation and the very nature of the work make adequate guards difficult to arrange.

The shaper is a simple machine. It consists of a spindle that projects through the table top, a heavy steel base, a motor and drive mechanism, and a fence. *Fig. 30–1.* There is a groove in the table top for a miter gauge. On most shapers the spindle can be moved up and down to position it, and on some the table can be raised and lowered. For smooth cutting, the shaper must operate at a speed of 7,200 to 8,500 rpm.

There are several kinds of shaper cutters. The safest is the three-lip, solid type which is recommended for all basic operations. *Fig. 30–2.*

30–1a. Parts of a shaper.

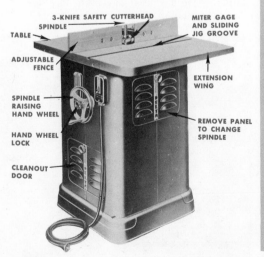

TABLE

3-KNIFE SAFETY CUTTERHEAD
SPINDLE

MITER GAGE
AND SLIDING
JIG GROOVE

ADJUSTABLE
FENCE

EXTENSION
WING

SPINDLE
RAISING
HAND WHEEL

REMOVE PANEL
TO CHANGE
SPINDLE

HAND WHEEL
LOCK

CLEANOUT
DOOR

SAFETY

• Make sure the cutter is locked securely to the spindle.

• See that the spindle is locked at the correct height.

• Always feed the stock into the cutter in the direction opposite to cutter rotation.

• Always position the left fence so it will support the work after it passes the cutter. Keep the fences locked securely.

• Use a depth collar when shaping irregular work.

• Never shape through a loose knot or through stock that is cracked or split.

• Never attempt to back stock into the knives.

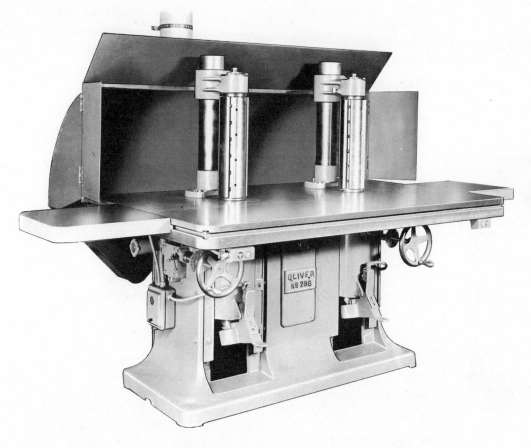

30–1b. A double spindle shaper of the type used in the furniture industry.

30–2. These solid, three-lip shaper cutters are commonly available in high-speed steel or with carbide tips.

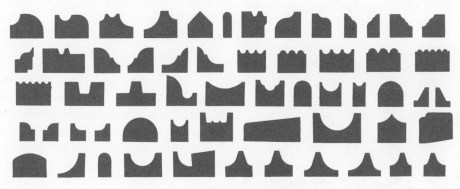

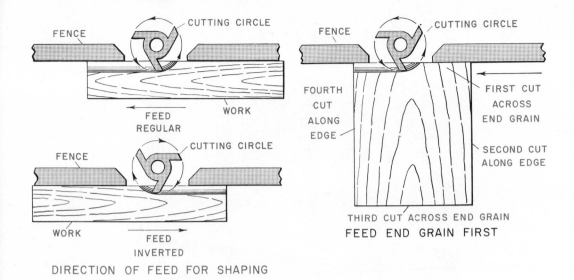

FENCE — CUTTING CIRCLE

WORK

FEED
REGULAR

FENCE — CUTTING CIRCLE

WORK — FEED
INVERTED

DIRECTION OF FEED FOR SHAPING

FENCE — CUTTING CIRCLE

FOURTH
CUT
ALONG
EDGE

FIRST CUT
ACROSS
END GRAIN

SECOND CUT
ALONG EDGE

THIRD CUT ACROSS END GRAIN
FEED END GRAIN FIRST

30–3. Make sure that the cutter is revolving in the correct direction. Always shape end grain first.

USING THE SHAPER

Straight Shaping. 1. Select a cutter of the correct shape and lock it on the spindle with the keyed washer

30–4a. Cutting an edge, using the fence as a guide.

and hex nut. The spindle can be locked or held securely with a wrench while tightening the nut.

2. Check to make sure the cutter rotates *towards the work to be cut* and that the feed is against the revolving cutter. *Fig. 30–3.*

3. Adjust the table or spindle as necessary to make the cut at the correct location.

4. Position the fence for the depth of cut. For molding operations where the entire edge is shaped, the two rear fences must be moved forward to support the work after the cut is made. *Fig. 30–4.*

5. Whenever possible, use the spring hold-down clip or clips to hold the stock against the fence and table. Do not set them too tight.

6. Make a trial cut on a scrap piece of the same thickness as the

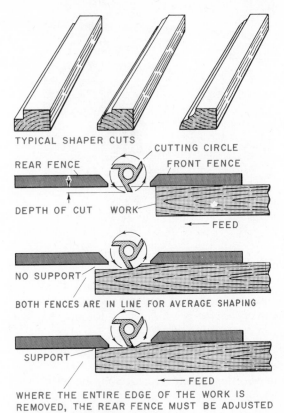

TYPICAL SHAPER CUTS

REAR FENCE

CUTTING CIRCLE

FRONT FENCE

DEPTH OF CUT   WORK

← FEED

NO SUPPORT

BOTH FENCES ARE IN LINE FOR AVERAGE SHAPING

SUPPORT

← FEED

WHERE THE ENTIRE EDGE OF THE WORK IS
REMOVED, THE REAR FENCE MUST BE ADJUSTED
TO FORM A SUPPORT

30–4b. Note how the rear fence supports
the work after the total edge is shaped.

30–5. Using a miter gauge for shaping
end grain.

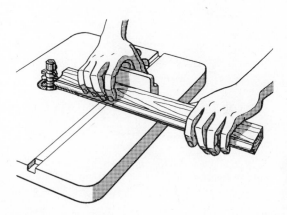

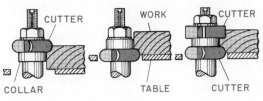

CUTTER   WORK   CUTTER

COLLAR   TABLE   CUTTER

30–6. Limiting the depth of cut by using
a depth collar.

stock. Hold the stock firmly against
the fence and table with your left
hand and feed it slowly with your
right hand. Check the depth and position of cut.

7. The miter gauge should be inserted in the table slot to hold work
when shaping the end of narrower
stock. *Fig. 30–5.*

Irregular Shaping. 1. Remove the
fence.

2. Select a cutter of the correct
shape, and the collar that will give
the correct depth of cut. The collar
can be used above, below, or between
two cutters. If possible, have the
collar below the cutter. *Fig. 30–6.*

3. Lock the collar and cutter to
the spindle.

4. Insert the small guide pin into
the table top a few inches from the
spindle. Place it in the correct one of
the two holes next to the table opening. Use the right one if the cutter
rotation is clockwise, and the left
one if it is counterclockwise.

5. Check the stock to see that the
edge that bears against the collar
has no irregularities in it.

6. Start the machine. Use the
guide pin as a fulcrum to support
the work until it has been fed into the
collar. *Fig. 30–7.* If the stock has

287

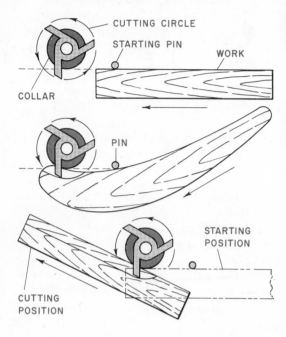

30–7. Use a starting pin to help in shaping an edge on irregular stock.

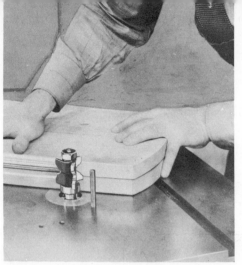

30–9a. Shaping with a pattern.

square corners, cut the end grain first.

7. As the edge is shaped, hold the stock steady against the collar, and shape only against the direction of spindle rotation. Swing the work

30–8. Cutting a tenon. Notice the high wood fence that acts as a guard. An auxiliary wood table is attached to the miter gauge.

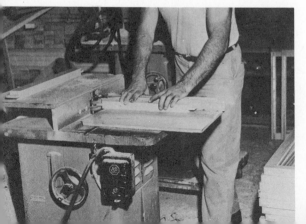

away from the pin after the shaping is started.

Tongue-and-groove Joints. Select a pair of matched cutters—a male to cut grooves or dadoes, a female to cut tenons. *Fig. 30–8.* Use a high, auxiliary wood fence for greater safety.

Shaping with Patterns. Shaping with a pattern is similar to shaping against collars. The differences are that the pattern and not the work rides

30–9b. Attaching the blank stock to the pattern.

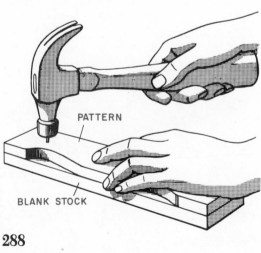

288

against the collar, (*Fig. 30–9a*) and the entire edge of the stock can be shaped. The shape of the pattern must exactly match that of the work to be formed, and its edges must be smooth and clean. The pattern is fastened to the work with brads, nails, or screws that project about ¼". *Fig. 30–9b.*

Shaping of most kinds can also be done on the drill press, provided that speeds of at least 5,000 rpm can be obtained. *Fig. 30–10.*

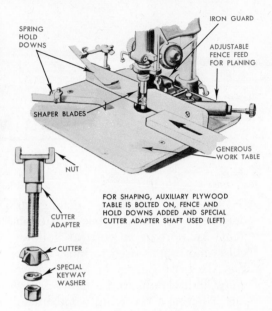

30–10.   Shaping on a drill press.

Unit 31: MORTISER

A mortiser cuts the rectangular opening for a mortise-and-tenon joint. An upright or vertical hollow-chisel mortiser is used in most shops. *Fig. 31-1.* It has a square, hollow chisel that clamps to the motor housing. There is a revolving wood bit in the center of the chisel. When the combination of bit and chisel is

31-1.   A vertical, hollow-chisel mortiser.

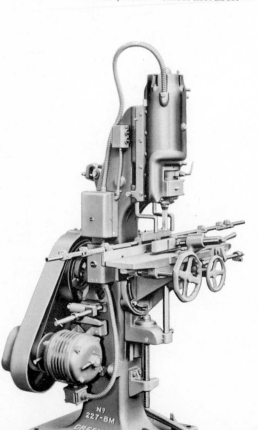

forced into the wood, the bit bores a hole almost as large as the chisel. The sharp edge of the chisel itself cuts a square opening. A mortising attachment for a drill press can also be used. This is described at the end of this unit. In sash-and-door manufacturing, a chain-saw mortiser is used; this has a continuous saw that cuts a square opening with a rounded bottom. *Fig. 31-2.*

PARTS OF THE MACHINE

The mortiser consists of a heavy, cast-iron column, a horizontal table, and a chisel ram attached to a motor. The table itself can be moved vertically (up and down), transversely (in and out), and longitudinally (back and forth). On some types of mortisers, the table does not move back and forth; therefore you must move the work; on others the table can be tilted 45 degrees to the right or left. The head is moved up and down on the column by depressing a foot lever. At the lower end is a chuck for holding the bit and the chisel.

Mortising chisels are available in sizes from $\frac{1}{4}''$ to $1\frac{1}{4}''$ at intervals of $\frac{1}{16}''$. Common sizes are $\frac{1}{4}''$ and $\frac{3}{4}''$.

290

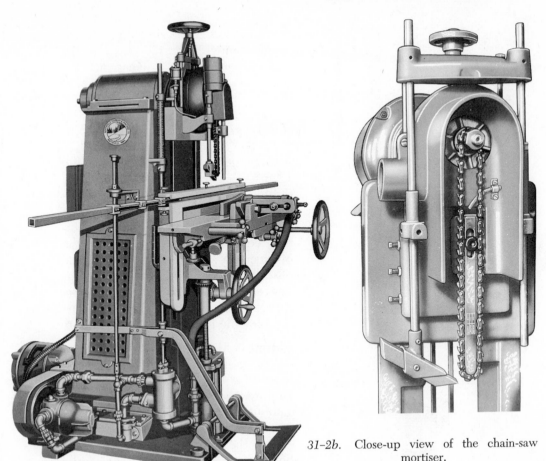

31-2b. Close-up view of the chain-saw
mortiser.

31-2a. A chain-saw mortiser.

Boring bits to match these chisels
are available. Split bushings are also
needed. *Fig. 31–3.*

USING A MORTISER

1. Square up the stock to size and
lay out the location for *one* mortise
on each side of the leg. Then mark
all other legs as shown in *Fig. 31–
4.* L.F. means *left front* and R.F.
right front. The mortises on the other
parts will then be in the proper posi-

tion when the table has been correctly set. When cutting mortises on
two sides of a piece, always check
the location of each.

2. Select the correct size of chisel
and bit. For example, use a $\frac{1}{2}''$ bit
and chisel for a $\frac{1}{2}''$ mortise. Also
select the correct size bushing for the
chisel. These split bushings are all
the same diameter on the outside,
with varying inside dimensions to
hold chisels of different sizes.

3. Insert the bushing for the chisel
and then install the chisel itself. The

291

31–3. Mortising chisels and bits.

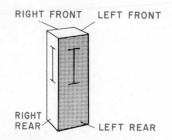

RIGHT FRONT   LEFT FRONT

RIGHT
REAR   LEFT REAR

31–4. Right front and right rear indicate
that the top of the leg is against the right
stop when cutting this mortise.

31–5. Checking to see that the chisel is
square with the fence.

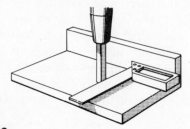

chisel opening provides an escape
for the chips. Place the chisel in the
socket, with a slight clearance between its shoulder and the face of
the socket. This clearance should be
$\frac{1}{32}''$ for chisels up to $\frac{3}{4}''$ and $\frac{1}{16}''$ for
chisels larger than $\frac{3}{4}''$.

4. To align the chisel, hold a
square against the side of it and
against the fence. *Fig. 31–5.* Then
tighten the set screws that hold the
chisel in place. Next, insert the bit
until the lips are flush with the cutting edge of the chisel. Fasten the
bit securely. Loosen the socket and
push the chisel up so that the should-
der rests against the face of the chisel
socket. This will give proper clearance for the bit to run free. *Fig. 31–6.*

Cutting a Mortise. 1. Place the stock
on the table with a mark on the end
indicating the depth of the mortise.
Depress the foot pedal its maximum
amount. Turn the screw adjustment
on the table until the chisel, at the
end of the stroke, is in line with the
bottom of the mortise. Release the
foot pedal.

2. Place the end of the stock under the chisel and move the table in
or out until the chisel is directly over
the layout. Move the work until the
mortising chisel is over the extreme
right end of the mortise. Place a
stop against the end of the stock so
that other identical pieces will be located automatically. Also adjust the
stop on the table. Now move the
table until the chisel is at the left end
of the mortise and adjust the stop.
There are two holddown clamps that
can be used to keep the work in
place.

292

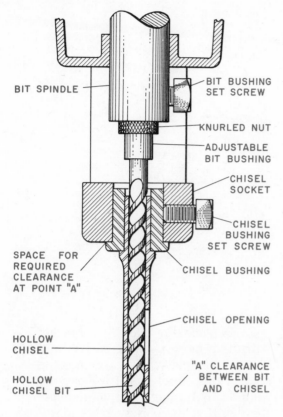

BIT SPINDLE

BIT BUSHING
SET SCREW

KNURLED NUT

ADJUSTABLE
BIT BUSHING

CHISEL
SOCKET

CHISEL
BUSHING
SET SCREW

SPACE FOR
REQUIRED
CLEARANCE
AT POINT "A"

CHISEL BUSHING

CHISEL OPENING

HOLLOW
CHISEL

HOLLOW
CHISEL BIT

"A" CLEARANCE
BETWEEN BIT
AND CHISEL

3. Move the table back to the starting position, with the chisel at the left end of the mortise. Turn on the machine, depress the pedal, and cut to full depth. *Fig. 31–7.* Move the table to the right and cut to full depth. Then move along the mortise layout, skipping a space between each cut. These alternate strokes are used to equalize pressure by cutting on four sides with the first passes, and on two sides on the final passes. Make sure that you center the chisel on the final passes. *Fig. 31–8.*

4. Cut all identical mortises. Then reset the machine for mortises in a different location. The cutting of matched mortises, such as on table legs, requires that the entire setup be reversed before the second mortise of the pair is cut. The righthand stop block should be placed on the left and vice versa. Check each setup carefully with a sample piece.

31–6.   Note that the bit must extend beyond the chisel a little so that the bit will cut the hole before the chisel squares it up.

31–7b.   Here is how it looks up close when you are cutting the mortise.

31–7a.   Cutting the mortise.

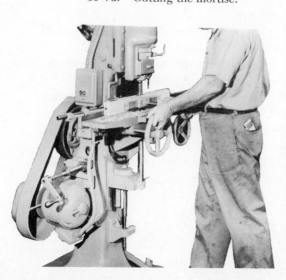

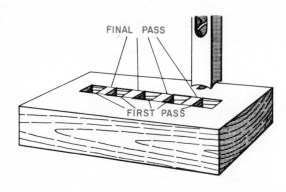

31–8. Correct method of making an oblong mortise up to $\frac{1}{2}''$ in width. Note that you *do not* make consecutive cuts.

MORTISING ATTACHMENT

A mortising attachment will convert most drill presses into mortisers. It consists of a fence to keep the work in line, and a mortise-chisel holder that can be clamped to the quill of the drill press. On most machines, the bit is held in the chuck. In some cases an adapter must be used. *Fig. 31–9.*

Using the Mortising Attachment.
1. Remove the chuck and the feed-stop bracket from the quill.

31–9a. Mortising attachment on a drill press.

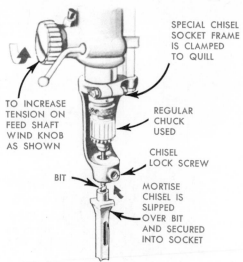

31–9b. Set up for cutting a mortise.

2. Replace the feed-stop bracket with the mortise-chisel socket and clamp it in place. Use a depth-stop stud in this chisel socket to keep the quill from turning, and to regulate the depth of the chisel cut.

3. Replace the drill chuck and install an adapter.

4. Fasten the fence to the table so that it clears the chisel and is in about the final position. This can be moved in and out to locate the mortise.

5. Install the correct chisel and bit in the socket.

6. Revolve the chuck by hand to see that the bit does not scrape.

7. Adjust the drill press to a speed of about 1,000 rpm.

8. Cut the mortise. Stop blocks can be clamped to the table top to regulate the length of movement.

294

Unit 32: POWER DRILLING AND BORING

Power drilling is usually done with a portable electric drill or with a drill press. In the furniture industry the horizontal or vertical spindle boring machine is the device most frequently used for all types of dowel joints, whether the pieces are to be joined butt, miter, or at compound angle. *Figs. 32–1 a and b.*

DRILLS, BITS, AND SPECIAL-PURPOSE CUTTING TOOLS

Twist Drills. Twist drills are used both in the portable electric drill and

32–1a. Using a horizontal boring machine to bore dowel holes in table rails. This shows the machine in use in a furniture factory. Three holes, $\frac{7}{8}''$ center to center, can be bored on this machine at the same time.

in the drill press. *Fig. 32–2a.* Carbon steel drills, for use only on wood, are available in diameter sizes from $\frac{1}{32}''$ to $\frac{3}{4}''$ at intervals of $\frac{1}{64}''$. High-speed steel drills, which may be used on metal as well as on wood, are available in diameters from $\frac{1}{64}''$ to $\frac{1}{2}''$ at intervals of $\frac{1}{64}''$. For general-purpose work, drills should be high-speed steel. The proper point angle depends on the material to be drilled. For general work in both metal and wood, the twist drill should have an included angle of 118 degrees. *Fig. 32–2b.* Some twist drills are made in larger sizes but with a $\frac{1}{4}''$ shank so they can be used in a $\frac{1}{4}''$ portable

32–1b. Using a multiple-spindle, vertical boring machine to bore dowel holes.

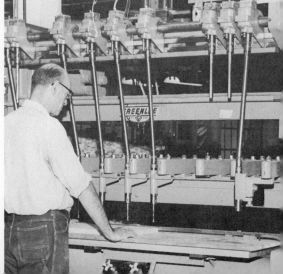

32–2a. A twist drill with a taper shank. Use only drills with straight shanks in a chuck.

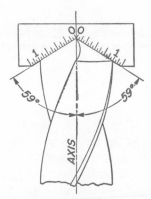

32–2b. This included angle is best when both wood and metal drilling must be done.

32–3. Spur machine bits.

electric drill. A *spur machine bit* is one of the cleanest and fastest-cutting styles. It looks like a combination twist drill and auger bit. *Fig. 32–3.*

Auger Bits. An auger bit for power drill and drill press should have a straight shank and a brad point *Fig. 32–4.* Never try to use a bit with a tang in the power drill. The common auger bits are made either with a solid center or as double-twist bits. Common power shank sizes are from No. 4 ($\frac{1}{4}''$) to No. 16 (1''). Dowel bits are shorter than standard auger bits.

Power or Speed Bits. Flat power bits or speed bits are made by several different manufacturers. *Fig. 32–5.* Typical sizes are from $\frac{1}{4}''$ to 1'', increasing in 16ths, with a $\frac{1}{4}''$ shank. Some types are made with changeable cutter heads.

32–4. Power auger bit with straight shank and brad point.

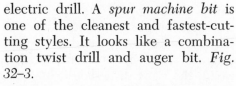

32–5. Flat power bit.

32–6. Masonry drill.

Masonry Drills. Masonry drills with carbide tips should be used at slow speeds and with heavy pressure. The sizes vary from $\frac{1}{8}''$ to $\frac{1}{2}''$ for $\frac{1}{4}''$ chucks and to $1\frac{1}{2}''$ for $\frac{1}{2}''$ chucks, increasing by 16ths in both cases *Fig. 32–6.*

296

32–8. Plug cutter.

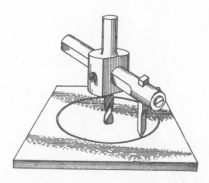

32–9. Circle and hole cutter.

32–7. Rotary saw hole cutter.

Rotary-Saw Hole Cutters. Different makes of rotary-saw hole cutters vary in size and depth of cut. This tool cuts large-diameter holes in wood, metal, and plastics. *Fig. 32–7.*

Plug Cutters. A plug cutter is used to make matching wood plugs to conceal screw heads. *Fig. 32–8.*

Circle and Hole Cutters. Circle and hole cutters are made in a wide variety of styles and sizes, *Fig. 32–9,* to cut holes in wood from $\frac{5}{8}''$ to 8" in diameter. These tools are best used on the drill press.

32–10. A Foerstner bit is used for pattern-making and other intricate woodworking. It is guided by the rim of the tool, not by the center. This permits boring an arc of a circle in any direction, regardless of grain, to cut oval and curved openings, squared corners, or round holes with flat bottoms, polished sides, and sharp edges.

Foerstner Bits. The Foerstner bit bores in end grains, through knots, and in cross-grain. It is also good for boring a flat-bottom hole. Sizes are from $\frac{1}{4}''$ to 2". *Fig. 32–10.*

297

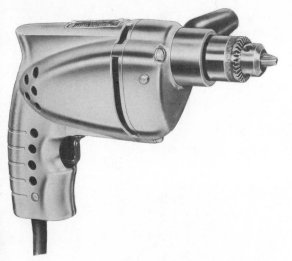

32–11a.   Portable electric drill—$\frac{1}{4}$" size.

PORTABLE ELECTRIC DRILL

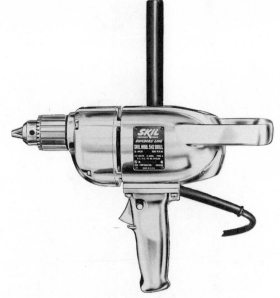

32–11b.   Portable electric drill—$\frac{1}{2}$" size.

Portable electric drills vary as to size and various horsepower rating. The most common sizes, however, are those that take bits of $\frac{1}{4}$" and $\frac{1}{2}$" diameter. *Fig. 32–11.* Drills are equipped with a trigger-type switch. Press the trigger for power; release it and the power turns off. Most types have a locking pin that will hold the trigger "on" until disengaged. Two types of chucks are available, but most drills have the (Jacobs) geared type, which is the best. It requires a special key to open and close it. The other type, called the *hex-key chuck*, requires an Allen wrench to open and close it.

The portable electric drill can be used for many jobs including drilling holes in masonry, wood, and metal, driving screws with a screw-driver attachment, cutting, sanding, buffing, and grinding. Adapters are available for many of these operations.

Some electric drills have a two-speed switch; they can be used at higher speeds for wood and plastics and with lower speeds for metal. Another type is battery-operated, requiring no cord. This frees the drill for use anywhere, such as on a boat where 110-volt electric current is not available.

Suggestions for Using. 1. Lay out the wood carefully. Mark the correct center of each hole with the center punch.

2. Open the chuck as far as possible and insert the drill until it is at the bottom of the chuck. Tighten it securely so that all three jaws hold the bit or drill.

3. Make sure that thin work is backed up with a solid piece of wood.

298

4. Grasp the control handle firmly and point the drill as you would a pistol. *Fig. 32–12.* Use your left hand to control the feed as necessary.

5. Make sure that the tool is straight. Always start with the power off. Place the point on the location of the hole.

6. Turn on the switch, and guide the tool into the work. If necessary, support the drill with your left hand. Any sidewise movement will break a small tool.

DRILL PRESS

The drill press is a very versatile tool. It can be used for drilling and boring and, with attachments, as a mortiser, router, shaper, or planer. The drill press comes with step pulleys or variable-speed pulleys. Variable-speed pulleys are extremely valuable in the wood shop, since they provide a wide range of speeds from

500 to 4,500 rpm. The higher speeds are necessary for shaping, routing, and planing. Use speeds from 1,200 to 3,000 rpm for drilling and boring wood.

The drill press is made either as a bench or floor model. Size is indicated by the largest diameter of stock through which a hole can be drilled. For example, a 15" drill press measures 7½" from the center of the chuck to the column. *Fig. 32–13.*

32–13.   Drill press with variable-speed pulleys.

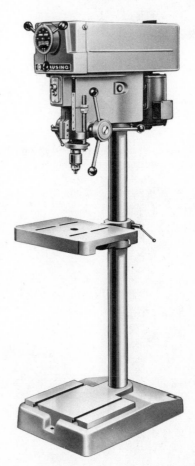

32–12.   Using a small, electric drill to cut holes for installing screws.

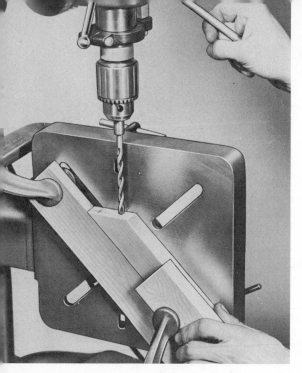

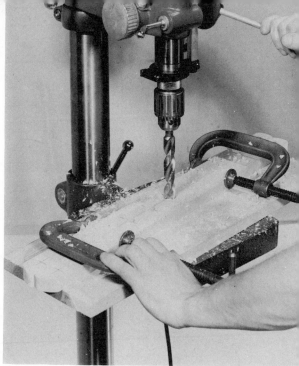

32–14.   Drilling dowel holes for a miter joint.

32–16.   Here's a way of cutting round notches by clamping two pieces of stock together and drilling a hole, half in one piece and half in the other.

32–17.   Using a wood guide clamped to the table to position the hole. This is a good idea when making duplicate parts, each requiring a hole in the same location.

32–15.   Boring a larger, flat-bottom hole with a Foerstner bit.

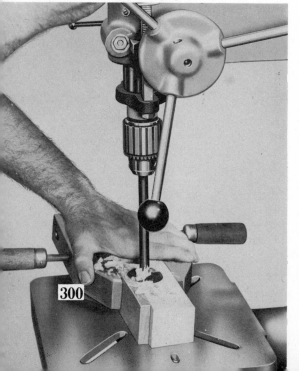

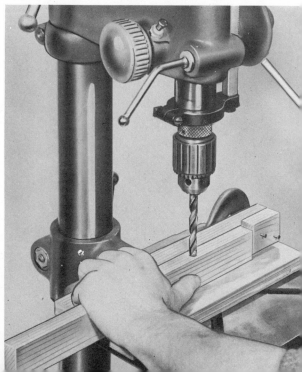

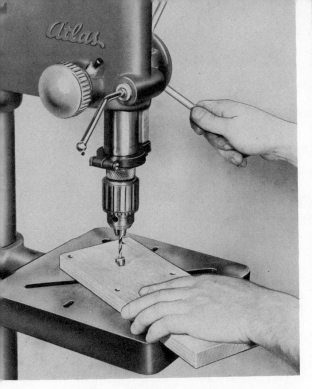 

32-18. Drilling and countersinking holes for installing screws. The countersink is fastened to the drill so that both operations are done at the same time.

32-19. Drilling holes for a dowel joint in the ends of a rail.

Both twist drills and bits can be used in the drill press. If the machine is to be used as a boring tool for making miter dowel joints, a guide should be clamped to the table. *Fig. 32-14.* Some of the more common uses of the drill press are shown in *Figs. 32-15 to 32-19.*

Unit 33: WOOD LATHE

The wood lathe is used to turn rounded furniture accessories, such as legs, and utility items, such as wood patterns. The machine combines power with the ability to perform delicate operations. Good examples of wood lathe work can be found in the turned parts of most Early American and Colonial furniture. *Fig. 33–1.* The skilled cabinetmaker must be proficient in the use of the lathe, and the patternmaker also needs some ability in its use. Most turned parts in furniture manufacture are made on the *automatic* wood lathe. *Fig. 33–2.*

On the automatic lathe, the stock is moved against several pre-set knives, so that the part is shaped in one operation; or, the lathe follows a pattern fastened to it, cutting an exact duplicate. The setup of the knives requires a skilled craftsman, but to operate this machine a worker needs little skill, because this is primarily a feeding operation.

SIZE AND PARTS

Lathe size is designated by the largest diameter it will turn and by bed length. A typical size is a 10″

33–1. Many of the parts for this product were turned on an automatic wood lathe.

33–2. Automatic wood lathe used in furniture manufacture.

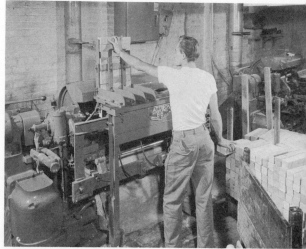

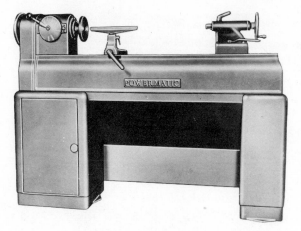

33–3a.   Wood-turning lathe with motor in the head.

The *headstock* is permanently mounted on the left end of the bed; it has a hollow spindle, threaded on both ends. A *spur* center can be inserted in the spindle for turning between centers, or a *faceplate* can be attached to either end of the spindle for faceplate turning. The *tail stock* is movable and can be locked at many positions along the bed. It also has a hollow spindle in which the *cup* center is inserted. The *tool rest* consists of a base that clamps to the bed, and the tool rest itself that clamps to this base. Tool rests come in several lengths. Measuring and marking tools needed are a rule, pencil, dividers, inside caliper, and outside caliper. *Fig. 33–4.*

Turning Tools. *Fig. 33-5.* The *gouge* is used to rough out stock to a round shape. A bevel is ground on the con-

diameter with a 36″ bed. A lathe can be either belt-driven or equipped with a direct-drive motor. Speeds range from about 600 rpm to 3,400 rpm. Parts are shown in *Fig. 33–3.*

33–3b.   Parts of a lathe.

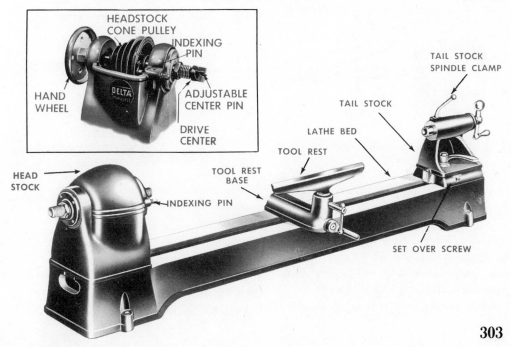

303

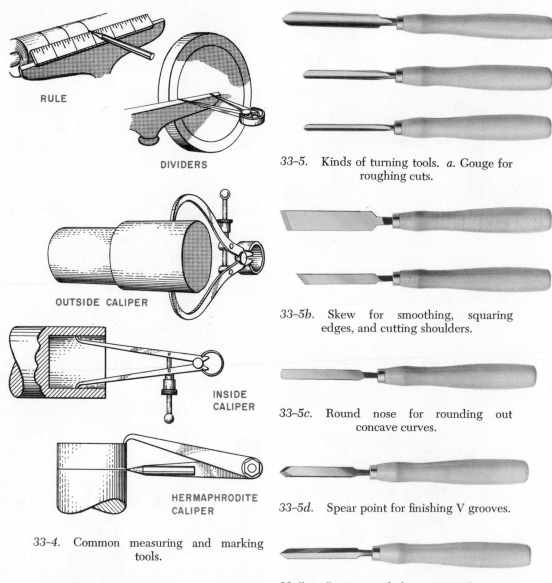

RULE

DIVIDERS

OUTSIDE CALIPER

INSIDE CALIPER

HERMAPHRODITE CALIPER

33–4. Common measuring and marking tools.

33–5. Kinds of turning tools. *a*. Gouge for roughing cuts.

33–5*b*. Skew for smoothing, squaring edges, and cutting shoulders.

33–5*c*. Round nose for rounding out concave curves.

33–5*d*. Spear point for finishing V grooves.

33–5*e*. Parting tool for cutting diameter grooves and cutting off stock.

vex side at an angle of about 30 degrees. Usually two gouges are needed, a $\frac{1}{2}''$ and a $1''$ or $1\frac{1}{2}''$.

The *skew* is used for smooth cuts to finish a surface. It is also needed for cutting shoulders, trimming ends, and for cutting V's and beads.

The *parting tool* is needed to cut a recess or groove with straight sides and a flat or square bottom.

The *round nose* is used for rough turning and for forming concave recesses, coves, and circular grooves. It is used for many scraping operations in faceplate turning.

The *diamond point* or spear is used to finish the insides of recesses or square corners.

SAFETY

• Roll up your sleeves snugly and remove tie, if any, before beginning to use the lathe.

• Use the correct spindle speed. A speed of about 1,800 rpm is best for most spindle turning. If the pieces are larger than 2″, use a slower speed until the piece has been rounded. Use a speed of about 600 rpm for faceplate work.

• Be sure tools are sharp, and hold them firmly on the tool rest.

• Make sure that the tail stock is securely fastened when turning between centers.

• Always remove the tool rest when sanding between centers.

• Stop the lathe before making any adjustment.

• If pieces vibrate, always stop the machine to check the reason.

METHODS OF TURNING

The two basic methods of wood turning are scraping and cutting. Scraping is simpler and easier to learn, and patternmakers use it because it is more exact; therefore it will be emphasized in this unit.

In the scraping method, tools scrape or wear away the wood fibers. Thus, all flat surfaces are shaped with the gouge or skew, the square nose, and the spear point or diamond chisel. All concave surfaces are turned with the round-nose chisel.

Spindle Turning. Spindle turning is done with the work held between the live (or moving) center and dead (or non-moving) center. This includes straight turning, making shoulder cuts, cutting tapers, and cutting convex and concave surfaces and grooves.

1. Select the correct kind of wood, slightly larger than the diameter to be turned and 1″ longer than needed. If the stock is larger than 3″ square, cut it to an octagon shape on the band saw.

2. Draw lines diagonally across the ends. The intersection of the lines is the approximate center.

3. Mark the center with a prick punch or scratch awl. If the wood is extremely hard, drill a small hole at the center and cut shallow saw kerfs across the corners. *Fig. 33–6.*

4. With a spur center in position over one end of the stock, strike it several times with a mallet to drive it into the wood. Now, place the stock over the spur center. Move the tail stock to about ¼″ from the end and clamp it to the bed. Turn the tail stock spindle until the cup center is seated in the center hole at the end of the stock. Then release the pressure and apply a little beeswax or oil. Re-tighten the tail stock until there is a little tension on the hand wheel, and then lock it in position.

5. Move the tool rest to within ⅛″ of the work, with the top of the rest about ⅛″ above the center. If the stock is quite long, adjust the tool rest with one end even with the tail stock end of the stock.

6. If the stock is from 1″ to 2″ in

305

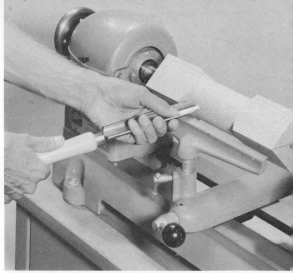

33-7. Notice that the left hand is under the gouge.

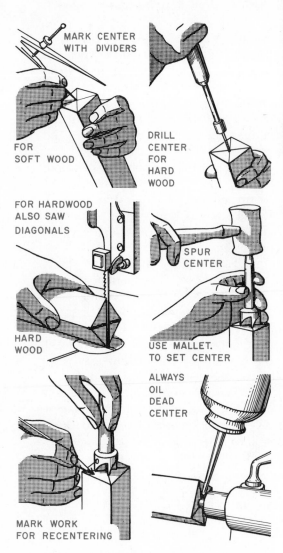

MARK CENTER WITH DIVIDERS

FOR SOFT WOOD

DRILL CENTER FOR HARD WOOD

FOR HARDWOOD ALSO SAW DIAGONALS

HARD WOOD

SPUR CENTER

USE MALLET TO SET CENTER

ALWAYS OIL DEAD CENTER

MARK WORK FOR RECENTERING

33-6. Preparing spindle work for mounting.

the stock to a cylinder shape. Hold the gouge blade securely in the left hand and the handle in the right hand. *Fig. 33-7.* Steady the gouge with the left hand by placing the heel of the palm against the front of the tool rest. Hold the palm on top of the tool for heavy cutting, and under the tool for fine cutting. To cut with a gouge, bring the turning tool against the wood and twist it slightly

33-8a. Roll the gouge slightly to help in the cutting.

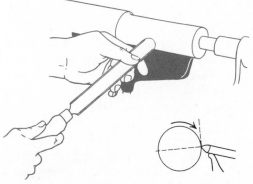

diameter, use the fastest speed; from 2″ to 3″, one of the middle speeds; above 3″, the slowest speed.

7. Turn the lathe over by hand once or twice to make sure everything clears.

8. Use the gouge to cut or scrape

33–8b. Hold the gouge straight for scraping.

rest as the work progresses, keeping about $\frac{1}{8}''$ clearance. To scrape with a gouge, hold it as shown in *Fig. 33–8*.

Finish Turning. When the stock has been reduced to the approximate diameter, use the skew for smooth cuts. *Fig. 33–9* shows how to scrape a cylinder to size. Start the scraping some distance in from the end to prevent the tool from catching and splitting the wood. When using the skew, always place the chisel on the tool rest before bringing it against the work. The *parting tool, Fig 33–10*, can be used as a scraper to cut a cylinder to length and to cut a shoulder. It also can be used to cut recesses, tapers, and complex parts. Hold the parting tool on edge over the tool rest with your right hand, and hold a caliper in your left. Force the parting tool into the revolving stock. At the same time, hold the points of the caliper on the cylinder until they just slip over.

Scraping a Shoulder. Set the outside caliper to the smaller diameter. Use a parting tool to cut a groove perpendicular to the layout line in the waste

to the right, forcing it into the revolving stock until the cutting begins. The beveled edge should be tangent to the cylinder. *Fig. 33–8*. Then move the tool slowly towards the tail stock. After each cut, move the gouge several inches more toward the headstock and repeat. When the cylinder is formed to within about 2″ of the headstock, twist the tool to the left and push it toward the headstock. Continue to cut until a cylinder is shaped. Check the diameter frequently with a caliper that is set about $\frac{1}{8}''$ over finished diameter. Move the tool

33–9. Using a skew for a scraping tool.

33–10a. Using a parting tool.

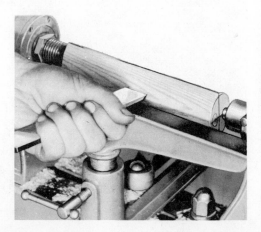

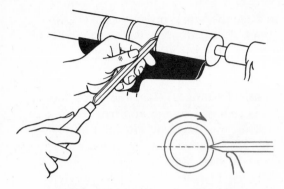

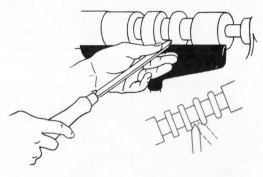

33–10b. This tool is particularly useful in faceplate turning. It is slowly pushed into the work with the point slightly above the center. As the tool advances into the work, the handle should be raised slightly until the desired diameter is secured.

33–11. A diamond-point or spear-point chisel is used for cutting V-grooves and beads. To get better control of the chisel, the back of the left forefinger is placed against the tool rest while the fingers support and guide the chisel. The cutting is done with the point which should cut slightly above the center of the stock.

stock. The groove should be cut to the caliper measurement. Use a square-nosed tool or skew and scrape to the smaller diameter. Use a parting tool to cut stock to length. Hold the diamond-point tool flat to cut a V in the wood. *Fig. 33–11.* Cut coves by using a round-nose tool. *Fig. 33–12.* Swing the tool from one side to

the other, using the tool rest as a fulcrum point.

Faceplate Turning. Replace the spur center with a faceplate. Mount stock less than 4″ in diameter and 2″ thick on a chuck that has a screw permanently fastened in its center. Mount larger objects on a standard face-

33–10c. The diameter can be checked as the cut is made.

33–12a. The round nose is used for rounding out concave curves after the diameter cut has been made with a parting tool.

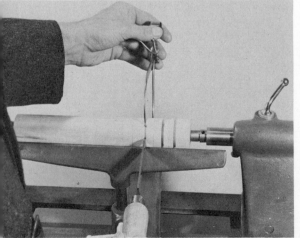

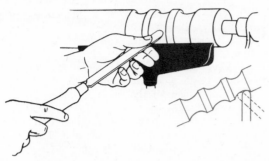

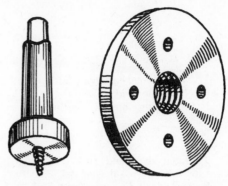

33–12b. Another view showing use of the round-nose chisel. Correct movement of the blade when the tool is swung from side to side is shown at lower right.

33–13. Two types of faceplates. Single screw center (left) and standard faceplate (right).

plate, using three or four small wood screws to hold it in place. *Fig. 33–13.* All turning on the faceplate is done by the scraping method. The tool rest may be used parallel to the sides or swung 90 degrees for turning on the face of the work. *Fig. 33–14.* Use the same tools and techniques for face turning as for spindle turning. Smooth finished work by holding a piece of 3/0 or 4/0 sandpaper lightly against the work with the lathe running at medium or high speed.

33–14a. Turning work on a faceplate.

33–12c. To make the cut, hold the chisel flat and level on the tool rest. Push the chisel against the stock easily, keeping the edge a little above center. As the cut gets deeper, move the chisel from side to side and gradually work down to the bottom of the cut made by the parting tool.

33–14b. Another view of turning work on a faceplate.

33–14c. A third illustration of turning work on a faceplate.

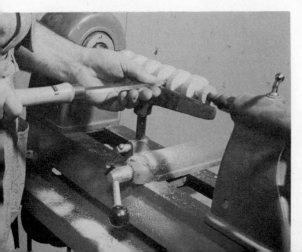

Section C

CHECK YOUR KNOWLEDGE

1. Name three common kinds of rules.
2. Name the kind of rule that would be used for laying out a house or large building.
3. Name four uses for the combination square.
4. Name the hand saws that can be used for cutting irregular curves.
5. Tell why a hacksaw is needed in the woodshop.
6. Name the kind of plane you would use for trimming the edge of a house door.
7. Tell how the size of an auger bit is measured.
8. Give the common uses for a Foerstner bit.
9. Describe the way a plane iron is sharpened.
10. Give the correct angle for grinding a skew.
11. Tell the difference between a groove and a dado.
12. Name some of the problems in planing a surface.
13. Describe what can happen when too fine a grade of sandpaper is used.
14. Describe a carbide-tipped tool and give its advantages and disadvantages.
15. Describe two common pulley arrangements used on wood machines.
16. A shaper requires extremely high speed; tell how this can be obtained by installing pulleys of different sizes on the motor and on the spindle.
17. A variable speed pulley has an advantage. Name it.
18. Describe the general maintenance of any one machine.
19. Tell in what way a radial arm saw differs from a circular saw.
20. Describe crosscutting on a radial arm saw. Tell how this differs from ripping.
21. Name the more common uses for the radial arm saw.
22. Give the reasons carpenters like the radial arm saw.
23. Tell how to do ripping on a radial arm saw.
24. Give another name for the planer.
25. Tell how the size of a planer is indicated.
26. Describe squaring up legs on a planer.
27. Give the reasons the circular saw is the most basic woodworking machine.
28. Name some of the common kinds of circular saw blades.
29. List the safety precautions that should be observed in using a circular saw.
30. Tell how crosscutting is done on the circular saw.
31. Describe two methods of cutting a rabbet.
32. List some of the common uses for a dado head.
33. Describe the way a tenon is cut on the circular saw.
34. Tell the primary use for a band saw.
35. Describe how to replace a blade on a band saw.
36. List safety suggestions for using the band saw.
37. Describe how to cut curves on a band saw.
38. Describe the jig saw and its uses.
39. Tell why an electric cut-off saw is valuable in carpentry.
40. Name some safety suggestions for using the cut-off saw.
41. If you were selecting a single portable tool to buy for home construction, one would be the natural choice. Name it and give the reasons for this choice.
42. Tell why an electrician finds a hand jig saw a valuable tool.
43. Tell why it is important to hold the hand jig saw firmly on the work.
44. Describe the method of cutting inside curves.
45. Tell how the size of a jointer is indicated.
46. Name or describe the following: the table that must be adjusted for depth of cut; the most common use for the jointer; the precaution that should be taken when cutting end grain on a jointer.
47. Describe two types of portable electric planes and name the craftsmen who would find the greatest use for them.
48. Describe the kind of work that can be done with a portable hand router.

49. Name five ways of guiding a router.

50. Tell why the shaper is a dangerous machine.

51. List safety precautions for using the shaper.

52. Tell how shaping is done.

53. Tell what it means to shape with a pattern.

54. Explain the usefulness of a mortiser in chair and table construction, and tell about the correct way of using a mortiser.

55. Describe a boring machine and tell where it is used.

56. List the major kinds of drills and bits used for power drilling.

57. Name some of the common uses for the drill press.

58. Describe the making of turned parts in furniture manufacturing.

59. Name the occupations in which the wood lathe is used the most.

60. Describe the two methods of turning.

61. Name the method of turning that is always followed when working on a face-plate.

THINGS TO DO

1. Write a history of one of the machine tools.

2. Select one of the machine tools and make a display panel showing the kinds of work that can be done on it.

3. Write a report on the science of planing wood.

4. Compare the advantages and disadvantages of a circular saw and a radial arm saw. Write a report.

5. Visit a furniture factory to discover the machines that are used.

6. Make a list of the operations that can be performed on two or more woodworking machines.

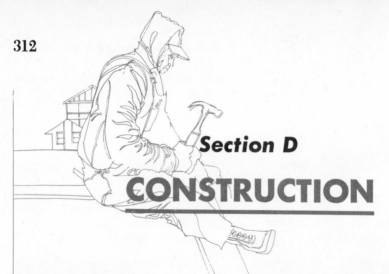

Section D

CONSTRUCTION

There are correct techniques for every construction operation, even such a simple thing as nailing. What kind of nails? How many? Where to drive them? All these are questions every craftsman must be able to answer.

Unit 34: JOINERY

Joinery is the art and skill of assembling and fastening together two or more pieces of wood. You will find many good illustrations of joinery throughout this book.

SQUARING UP STOCK BY MACHINES

When making duplicate parts, you should perform the same operation on all parts before starting a new step. Most hardwood stock for furniture is purchased rough, so first you must get the stock and square it up. The steps needed to bring it to fin-

ished size are described here. For most cabinetmaking, stock is brought to correct thickness and width by planing and jointing, and to correct length by sawing. If end grain is exposed, it may be necessary to plane the ends. Before stock is rough cut to length, it should be checked for the following:

Warp. Warp is any variation from a true or plane surface. Review the detailed discussion in Unit 9. *Figs. 34-1 and 34-2.*

Grain direction. Always plane or

34-2.   These two sticks, placed at the ends of a piece of stock, will show twist.

34-1.   Note the cupping caused by uneven shrinkage.

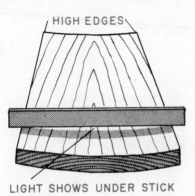

LIGHT SHOWS UNDER STICK

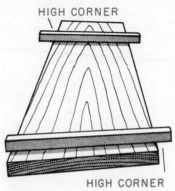

STICKS DO NOT LIE LEVEL

313

DIRECTION OF GRAIN

34-3.   Grain direction.

surface a board *with the grain. Fig. 34-3.* Planing against the grain roughens the surface. It may be difficult to see grain direction on a rough board; however, jointing will make it easier to see.

The following are steps in squaring up stock. *Fig. 34-4.*

1.   True up and joint the working face of each piece.

2.   True up one edge. Place the working face against the jointer fence and joint the working edge. Mark the surface and edge.

3.   Plane to thickness. Adjust the planer to about 1/16" less than the thickest stock. Run all of the pieces through.

4.   Cut and plane to finished width. Adjust the circular saw to about 1/16" or 1/8" over finished width and rip.

34-4.   Steps in squaring up stock by machine.

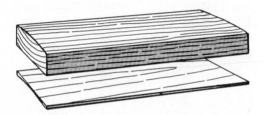

STEP I: THE FACE SURFACE

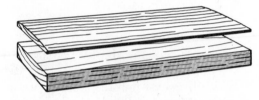

STEP 3: THE SECOND FACE

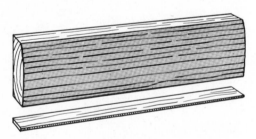

STEP 2: THE FIRST EDGE

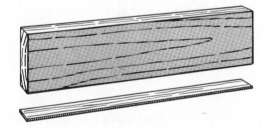

STEP 4: THE SECOND EDGE

STEP 5: THE ENDS

314

Then plane to finished width on the jointer.

5. Cut one end square on a circular saw or a radial arm saw. Lay out the correct length and cut to finished length. Remember to allow enough for joints. If end grain must be exposed, cut one end square and surface it on the jointer. Then cut the other end ¹⁄₁₆″ over length, and surface to exact length on the jointer.

Some cabinetmakers like to square up stock the same way as for hand planing. This means doing the following:

1. Joint the working face.
2. Joint the working edge.
3. Cut one end square. Plane if necessary.
4. Cut to length. If necessary, plane the second end.
5. Cut and plane to finished width.
6. Plane to thickness.

JOINERY DESCRIPTION

There are well over a hundred different kinds of wood joints used in house construction, furniture manufacturing, boatbuilding, and pattern-making. All can be grouped into nine basic types. It is very important to select the correct kind of joint for the work or job to be done. Some joints are simple to make, while others require a good deal more time and elaborate equipment. A good rule to follow is to choose the simplest joint that will do the job. You should consider its final appearance and its strength or durability. The butt joint, for example, is used commonly in house construction because it is very

34–5. The screen above is a simple framework made with butt joints forming a pattern of smaller squares.

simple to make. *Fig. 34–5.* In drawer construction, many kinds could be used. The thing to remember about a drawer is that you usually apply stress as you open it; this tends to pull the front of the drawer away from the sides. Therefore, for drawers, the best joint is the dovetail; however, this requires special equipment. *Fig. 34–6.* The legs and rails of a table or chair have a tendency to spread out. For this reason, the best method to join them is with mortise-and-tenon joints. *Fig. 34–7.* Here again, a good deal of time is required unless special equipment is available. A good substitution for the mortise-and-tenon is the butt joint reinforced with dowels and corner blocks. This is employed widely by furniture manufacturers.

Strengthening Joints. Most joints are permanently fastened with glue, nails, and/or screws. There are sev-

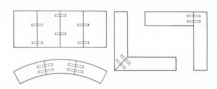

34–8a. Several kinds of dowel joints.

34–8b. Dowel pins usually have a spiral groove which helps the glue to flow and helps to lock the two pieces together.

34–6. If you examine the drawer construction in good-quality furniture, such as this chest of drawers, you will find that a dovetail joint is used to join the front and sides of the drawers.

eral additional ways in which a joint can be strengthened.

Dowel. A dowel is a pin or peg of wood that fits into two matching holes to strengthen the joint. *Fig. 34–8.* Dowel rod is usually made of birch in diameters from $\frac{1}{8}''$ to $1''$ in 3′ lengths. They are cut about $\frac{1}{8}''$ or $\frac{1}{4}''$ shorter than the combined depth of the two holes. Small dowel pins are made with spiral grooves and

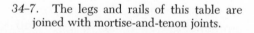

34–7. The legs and rails of this table are joined with mortise-and-tenon joints.

pointed ends; the spiral groove helps the glue to flow and adds to the strength of the joint. Dowel centers are small metal pins used for spotting the location of holes on two parts of a joint. Their use is explained in caption 34–8. A dowel sharpener is used to point the ends of dowels. Dowels are commonly used to strengthen

34–8d. Dowel centers are useful in locating adjoining holes. The location for dowels is marked on the first pieces and drilled. Then the dowel centers are put in place. When the two pieces are held together, the dowel centers show the hole locations on the second piece.

316

34-9. Here two shorter splines are to be used to strengthen a miter joint.

edge joints, miter joints, and butt joints. Many manufacturers prefer the dowel joint for fastening legs and rails in chair construction. The diameter of the dowel should be no more than half the thickness of the stock.

Spline. A spline is a thin piece of wood or metal inserted in the groove between two parts of a joint. *Fig. 34-9.* A groove or slot is cut in each part of the joint. Then a thin piece of wood with grain at right angles to the edge is inserted and glued in place. One-eighth inch plywood or hardboard makes a good spline. Many furniture manufacturers place a metal spline on the corner of all miter joints. This holds the four corners firmly and keeps the joints from spreading open.

Key. A key is a small piece of wood inserted in one or both parts of a joint to hold it firmly together. A key is often placed across the corner of a miter joint and is sometimes used as a wedge lock in a mortise-and-tenon joint. *Fig. 34-10.*

Glue block. A glue block is a small, triangular-shaped piece of wood used to strengthen and support two pieces of wood joined at an angle. *Fig. 34-11.* It is frequently used to strengthen the corner of butt, rabbet, or dado joints. You will also find them under drawer bottoms and inside chests and cabinets.

Corner block. A corner block is a larger, triangular piece of wood or metal used for added strength at the corners of frames or where legs and rails join. *Fig. 34-12.* These are glued and/or screwed in place.

Gussets. Plywood or metal gussets are triangular or trapezoid

34-10.   A key is another method of locking two pieces together.

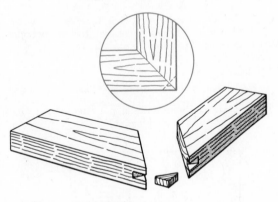

34-11.   Glue blocks are used generously in good furniture to help strengthen adjoining surfaces.

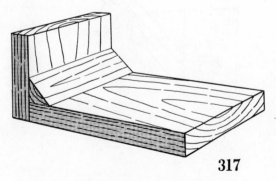

317

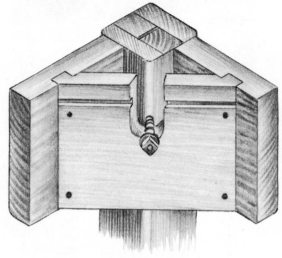

34–12a. A corner block is needed for all chairs and tables to stiffen the connection between the leg and the two rails.

34–12c. Here is a type of corner block used in heavy, commercial furniture.

34–12b. Sometimes a patented metal corner block is used.

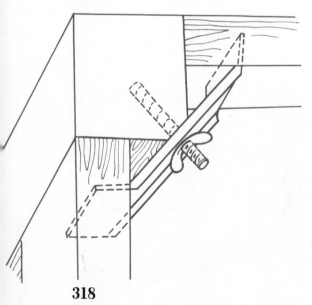

shapes made of $\frac{1}{4}''$ plywood or metal and fastened to the exterior of the joint. *Fig. 34–13.* In house construction these are commonly used where appearance is not important, such as in truss roof framing.

KINDS OF JOINTS

End Joints. It is almost impossible to make an *end-butt joint* that will be strong and permanent by itself. *Fig. 34–14.* Even with the best gluing, not more than 25 per cent of the tensile

34–13. A gusset is commonly used in carpentry, especially when truss roof framing is used for roof construction.

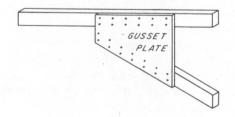

GUSSET
PLATE

34-14.   End butt.

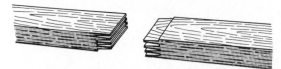

34-15. Scarf joint. This is sometimes strengthened with dowels or by nailing a strip on either side.

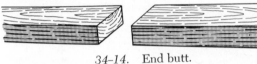

34-16. The finger joint is considered the most important industrial joint.

strength of the original solid wood can be retained in the end-butt joint but it can be strengthened by the use of dowels. The *scarf* joint should be cut at a very shallow angle (1 to 12 degrees is best) and fastened with

34-17. Note the precision cut and fit of this finger joint used in the manufacture of 2" x 4" lumber.

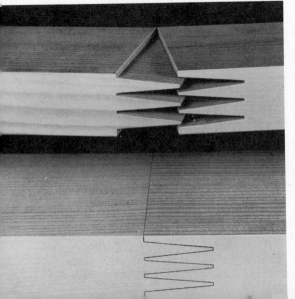

glue. It is used to extend the length of a board such as in laminated construction. *Fig. 34-15.* The most important industrial joint for end-grain work is the *finger joint. Fig. 34-16.* This joint is used extensively in making wide boards, in extending the length of dimension lumber, and in laminated construction. *Fig. 34-17.* It is cut on a shaper or a special, finger-joint molding machine. This joint, along with the new adhesives, has opened an entirely new era in the manufacture of man-made wood products. *Fig. 34-18.* When glued properly, the finger joint is as strong as the original solid wood.

Butt Joints. The butt joint is the simplest and easiest to use. It is commonly found in all house construction, especially framing, and in simple box construction. *Fig. 34-19.* The square end of one member fits against the flat surface or edge of the second member. *Fig. 34-20.* It is a rather

34-18. Wide boards such as this solid lumber are joined on the sides and ends with a finger joint.

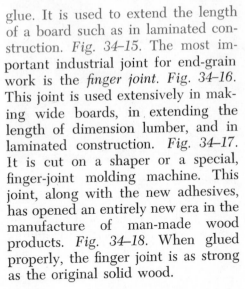

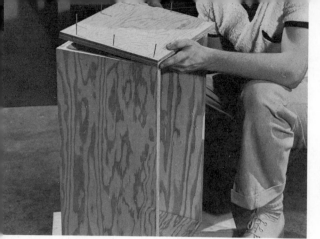

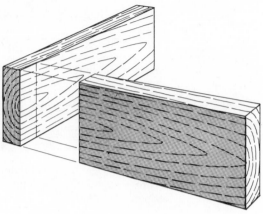

34–19a. Building a box with simple butt
joints.

weak joint since the end grain is the
weakest part of the wood for joining
purposes. In house framing, butt
joints are toenailed to strengthen
them. *Fig. 34–21.* In cabinetmaking,
the butt joint is often reinforced with
a corner glue block. *Fig. 34–22.*
Added strength can be obtained by
placing dowels at each joint and
then reinforcing with corner blocks.
Fig. 34–23. Many chairs, tables, and
benches have this kind of joint as a
substitute for the mortise-and-tenon
joint. *Fig. 34–24.*

The *middle-rail butt with dowels*
is used to install dividers in furniture
and casework. *Figs. 34–25, 34–26, 34–
27.* The *frame butt with dowels* is

34–19b. Assembling with nails.

34–20a. Butt joint on edge.

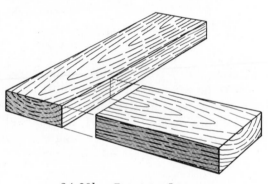

34–20b. Butt joint flat.

34–21. Butt joints are used in most house
framing. However, the adjoining surfaces
are strengthened by fastening material
both to the inside and outside of the frame.

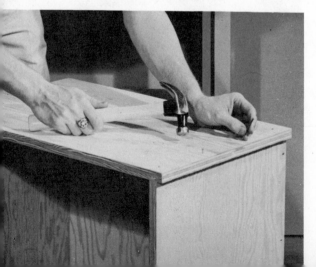

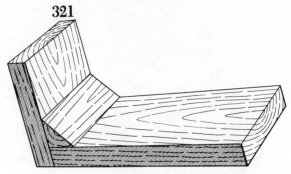

34-22.   Corner butt with glue block.

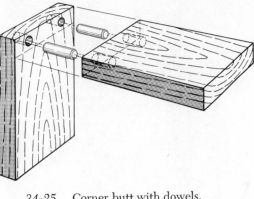

34-25.   Corner butt with dowels.

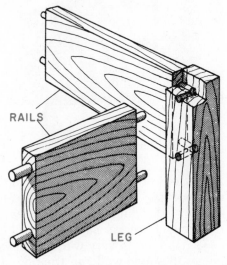

RAILS

LEG

34-23.   Dowels used to join the leg to rail
in chair construction.

34-24.   The legs and rails of this chair are
strengthened with dowels and corner blocks.

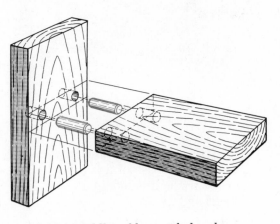

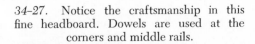

34-26.   Middle rail butt with dowels.

34-27.   Notice the craftsmanship in this
fine headboard. Dowels are used at the
corners and middle rails.

34–28. The base and the frame dividers of this fine chest are joined with dowels.

34–30. Here you see tongue-and-groove roof boards being installed.

used for making a frame that might serve as the base of a furniture piece or the frame dividers in a chest. *Figs. 34–28* and *34–29.*

Edge Joints. This type of joint is used to make up larger surfaces such

34–29. Frame butt with dowels.

as the tops of tables and desks. House construction flooring, decking, and interior paneling are made with *tongue-and-groove edge joints. Fig. 34–30.* In fact, in very warm climates, homes of single-wall construction are built of vertical pieces of paneling joined by tongue-and-groove. In this single-wall construction, *Fig. 34–31,* there are no studs or other supports for the roof and ceiling; the exterior walls are made of one-inch, tongue-and-groove redwood. Most house construction in Hawaii is of this type. The edge can also be strengthened with a dowel, a spline, or by cutting a rabbet on both edges. *Figs. 34–32* through *36.*

Rabbet Joints. The rabbet joint is made by cutting an "L" groove across the edge or end of one piece and fitting the other piece into it.

34–34. Rabbet edge. This is also called ship lap when used in siding.

34–31. Redwood paneling in the wall construction of this home is of tongue-and-groove type.

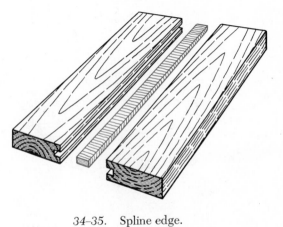

34–35.   Spline edge.

34–36.   Dowel edge.

34–32.   Plain edge.

34–33.   Tongue-and-groove.

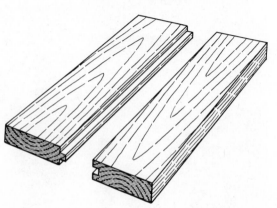

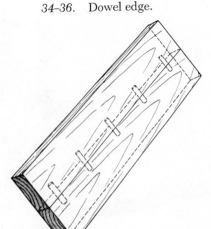

323

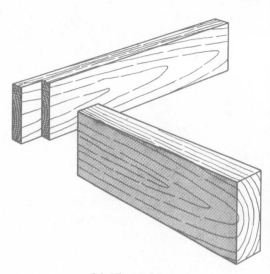

34–37.   Rabbet joint.

34–38.   Using a rabbet joint in box construction.

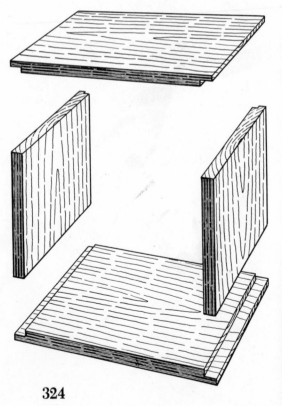

34–39.   Here a rabbet joint is used on the corners and a dado joint for the divider.

34–40.   The back panel of this china cabinet is installed with a rabbet joint.

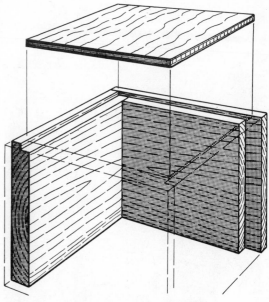

34-41. The standard method of applying backs to cabinets calls for a rabbet joint.

34-42. Back panel for box or case.

Cut the rabbet to a *width* equal to the thickness of the material, and to a *depth* of one-half to two-thirds the thickness. *Fig. 34-37.* This is commonly used in drawer and box construction and in making cabinet built-ins and similar items. *Figs. 34-38 and 34-39.* The rabbet joint conceals one end grain and also curbs the twisting tendency of the joint. The backs of most cabinets, bookcases, and chests are joined with the end grain facing the back. This is called a *back-panel rabbet joint. Figs. 34-40* through *34-42.* Simplest ways to cut the rabbet are with the dado head on the circular saw, jointer, shaper, or router. Of these, the easiest is on the circular saw.

Dado Joints. A *dado* is a groove cut across grain to receive the butt end of a second piece. *Fig. 34-43.* It is used primarily for installing shelves, partitions, and steps, and in dividers

34-43. A simple dado joint. The groove is cut to a width equal to the thickness of the second piece and to a depth of about one half the thickness of the first piece.

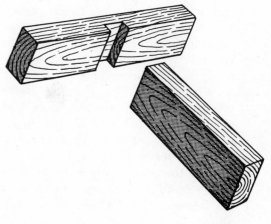

325

34-44. The dividers of this wall shelf are joined to the sides with exposed joints.

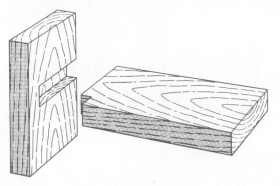

34-45. Blind dado.

34-46. The shelves of this Early American cabinet are joined to the sides with a blind dado joint.

for bookcases and chests. *Fig. 34-44.* This joint provides a supporting ledge and makes it possible to fit pieces together with gluing only. A *stop or blind dado* is cut only part way across the first piece. *Fig. 34-45.* A corner is cut from the second piece to fit into it. *Fig. 34-46.* The *dovetail dado* gives added strength and locks the pieces together. *Fig. 34-47.* The dovetail must be cut across grain, and a notch or tenon must be cut in the end of the second piece to fit into this dovetail. It is a good joint to use in drawer construction. The *half*

326

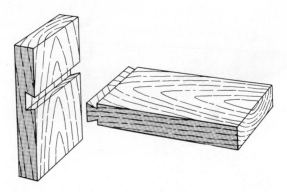

34-47.   Dovetail dado.

34-49.   Dado and rabbet joint.

dovetail joint is much easier to cut and has good holding power. *Fig. 34–48.* The *dado and rabbet joint* is also good in drawer construction. The dado is cut to a width equal to one-half the thickness of the stock, and to a depth equal to one-half to two-thirds the thickness. The rabbet is cut to fit. This joint is frequently used for joining the back to the sides of drawers. *Fig. 34–49.* The best method of cutting the dado joint is with the dado head on the circular or radial arm saw. *Fig. 34–50.* Other machines that can be used are the shaper, drill press, or router.

Lap Joints. This joint is used in both home and furniture construction. The

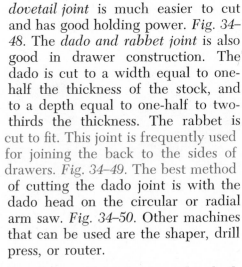

34-48.   Half-dovetail dado.

plain lap, the simplest, is made by laying one piece over the other and then fastening the two pieces with screws, nails, and glue. This type is only as strong as the fasteners used. The *cross lap* or *middle half lap* is used for joining two cross pieces with flush faces. *Fig. 34–51.* The pieces may cross at right angles or any other angle. *Fig. 34–52.* Each piece is dadoed half its depth or width. It can be used for making egg-crate or grid designs. The *edge lap* is very similar except that it is crossed on edge. *Fig. 34–53.* The *middle lap* can be used to join bracing members between frames or for forming a strong

34-50.   Cutting a dado using a dado head on a radial arm saw.

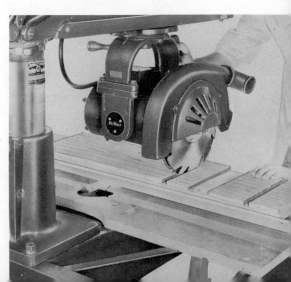

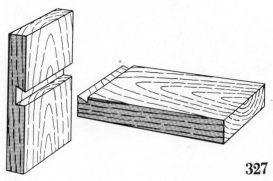

327

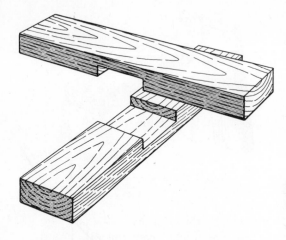

34–51. Cross lap or middle half lap.

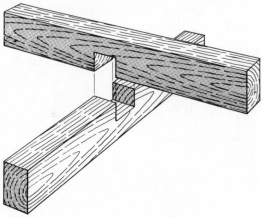

34–53. Edge lap.

"T" joint. *Fig. 34–54.* To make a *middle half lap,* cut an end lap on one member and then cut a middle lap on the other. The miter half lap can be cut on corners so that it will hide one end-grain face. It will make a neat 45-degree angle on the face lap surface. The *end lap* is commonly used in making window frames, screen doors, and storm-window frames. *Fig. 34–55.* It is a good corner joint if made properly. Of course, it does expose the end grain in both corners. All lap joints are best cut

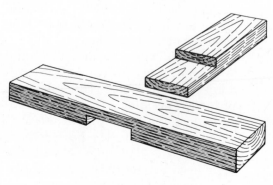

34–54. Middle lap or T lap.

34–55. End lap.

34–52. Cutting a cross-lap joint at an angle to join the legs of a piece of outdoor furniture.

34-56. A miter joint is used to join the corners of this chest.

with the dado head on the circular saw. They can be cut on a band or jig saw, however.

Miter Joints. The miter is an angle joint that hides the end grain of both pieces. *Fig. 34–56.* It is a rather weak joint unless strengthened with a dowel, spline, or key. It is commonly used for making picture and door frames, moldings such as those around doors and windows, and for corner joints on cabinets and casework. *Fig. 34–57.* The miter joint is usually cut at 45 degrees to form a 90-degree angle. However, a miter may be cut at other angles such as in house framing. *Fig. 34–58.* A simple miter can be strengthened by using a spline, dowel, or key. *Figs. 34–59 through 34–65.* The *lock miter joint* is excellent because it requires no other reinforcement. It can be cut on the circular saw. *Fig. 34–66.* A com-

34-57.   The grill work in this room divider has miter joints to form the rectangular open boxes.

34-58.   A miter cut must be made at the ends of the rafters in roof framing. The angle depends on the pitch of the roof.

pound miter or hopper joint is used to make picture frames and shadow boxes, and for roof framing. *Fig. 34-67. Fig. 34-68* shows how to set the circular saw for cutting various compound miter or hopper cuts. *Fig. 34-69.* The *miter with rabbet* combines the features of the rabbet with the miter joint. It is a very good corner

34-62.   Flat miter with dowels.

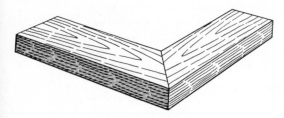

34-59.   Flat miter. This may be held together by nails, screws, or other metal fastener.

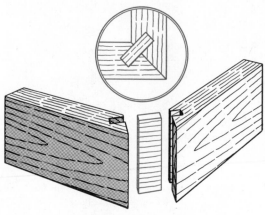

34-63.   Edge miter with spline. Note that the spline is placed closer to the inner corner for strength. Also, the grain of the spline runs at right angles to the grain of the wood.

34-64.   Edge miter with dowel.

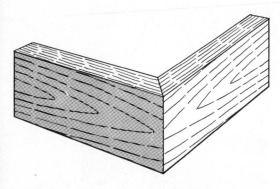

34-60.   Edge miter.

34-61.   Flat miter with spline.

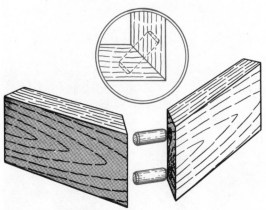

joint for plywood cabinets and cases since it helps to hold the corner square and also provides plenty of gluing surface. *Fig. 34–70.* The miter with end lap combines the strength of a lap joint with the neat appearance of the miter joint. Notice that the end grain shows from only one side of the frame. *Fig. 34–71.*

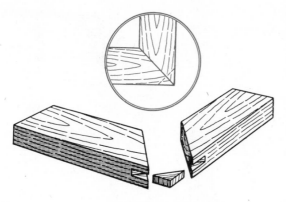

34–65.   Flat miter with key or feather.

34–68.   Use this table to find the correct setting for cutting a hopper or compound miter joint.

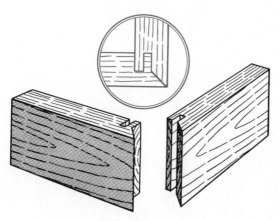

34–66.   Lock miter.

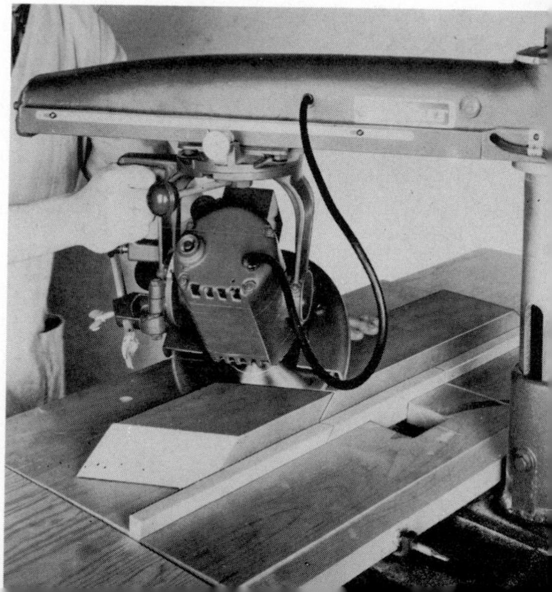

34–67.   Compound miter or hopper joint.

Tilt of Work	4-Side Butt		4-Side Miter	
	Blade Tilt	Miter Gauge	Blade Tilt	Miter Gauge
5 degrees	½	85	44¾	85
10 degrees	1½	80¼	44¼	80¼
15 degrees	3¾	75½	43¼	75½
20 degrees	6¼	71¼	41¾	71¼
25 degrees	10	67	40	67
30 degrees	14½	63½	37¾	63½
35 degrees	19½	60¼	35¼	60¼
40 degrees	24½	57¼	32½	57¼
45 degrees	30	54¾	30	54¾
50 degrees	36	52½	27	52½
55 degrees	42	50¾	24	50¾
60 degrees	48	49	21	49

a radial arm saw.

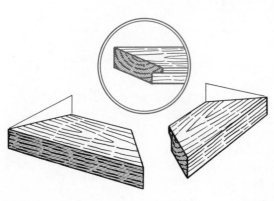

331

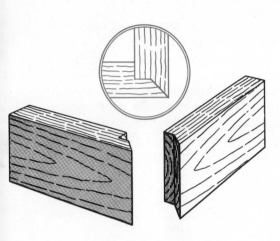

34-70. Miter with rabbet.

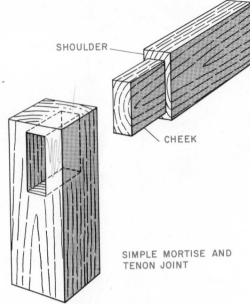

SHOULDER

CHEEK

SIMPLE MORTISE AND TENON JOINT

34-73. The blind or simple mortise-and-tenon.

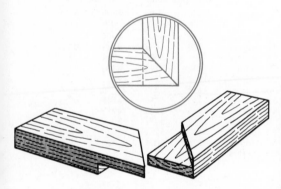

34-71. Miter with end lap.

34-72. The legs and rails of this table are joined with mortise-and-tenon joints. A dowel peg through the leg and rail locks the joint in place.

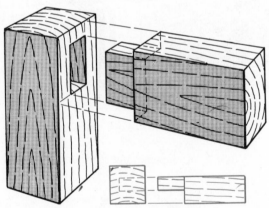

34-74. Bare-faced mortise-and-tenon.

Mortise-and-Tenon Joints. These are found in good leg-and-rail construction such as for making tables, chairs, and benches. *Fig. 34-72.* It is also used in better quality frame construction. Most common is the blind mor-

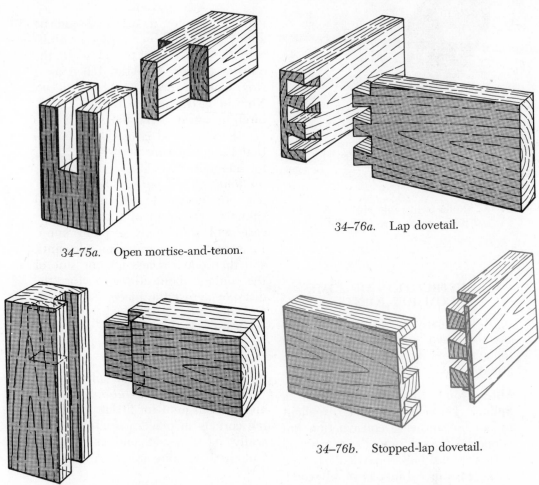

34–75a.   Open mortise-and-tenon.

34–76a.   Lap dovetail.

34–75b.   Haunched mortise-and-tenon.

34–76b.   Stopped-lap dovetail.

tise-and-tenon. *Fig. 34–73.* In this, a rectangular opening called the mortise is cut in one piece, and a tenon is cut at the end of the other piece. The tenon should be about one half the thickness of the stock. The *bare-faced mortise-and-tenon* is used where the leg and rail surface must be flush. *Fig. 34–74.* The *open mortise-and-tenon* is commonly used in frame construction. *Fig. 34–75a.* In the *pin mortise-and-tenon* a dowel

rod is installed through the mortise-and-tenon to strengthen it; the dowel is inserted in offset holes that will pull the tenon tight. The *haunched mortise-and-tenon* is used in frame construction for added strength. *Fig. 34–75b.*

Dovetail Joint. The *dovetail joint* is found in the very best drawer-and-box construction. *Fig. 34–76.* It is primarily a fine furniture joint, made only when dovetailing equipment is available.

333

34-77. Miter with full spline. See *Fig. 34-63* for another example of this.

CONSTRUCTION OF SOME COMMON JOINTS

Of the many different joints that can be used in construction, the following require special care and attention:

Miter Joint Strengthened with a Spline. The miter joint is excellent for all box-and-case construction but is relatively weak unless strengthened with a spline. This is particularly true if the case or cabinet is of plywood.

Miter joint with a full spline. Cut a plain miter for all joints. Adjust the blade to an angle of 45 degrees and set the miter gauge to 90 degrees. A

34-78. Blind splined miter offers a neat, strong joint with an attractive appearance on casework front.

good recess for a spline should be about ⅛″ wide by ¼″ deep. Make sure the cut is not too close to the outside corner. Use the fence as a stop. Cut the recesses on both pieces. Now make the spline from ⅛″, 3-ply birch plywood or hardboard. *Fig. 34-77.* If solid wood is used, make sure that the grain runs across the corner for adequate strength.

Blind splined miter. On fine cabinetwork, it is better to use a blind spline so the front of the cabinet or case will show only a plain miter. First, cut a plain miter for all joints, and then cut a recess for one side of the miter about three-fourths the distance across the piece. *Fig. 34-78.* Cut the other half by backing the stock into the saw. This is necessary in order to make the pieces match. Use stop blocks to control the length of cut. Cut and trim the spline to fit.

Miter joint with a rabbet. This is an excellent joint for fitting and holding corners in place. *Fig. 34-79.* It is really part rabbet and part miter. Cut piece A. Lay out a rabbet that

34-79a. Miter joint with rabbet.

is a depth of one-half the thickness of the stock and a width equal to the thickness. Cut the rabbet. Make a miter cut across the tail of the rabbet. Cut piece *B*. Lay out a rabbet that has a depth and a width equal to one-half the thickness of the stock. Cut the rabbet. Make a miter cut across the tail of the rabbet. This cut should be made with the tail side down against the table. A second way is to make only the first cut of the rabbet, then reverse the stock and make the miter cut.

34–79b. Steps in cutting a miter joint with a rabbet.

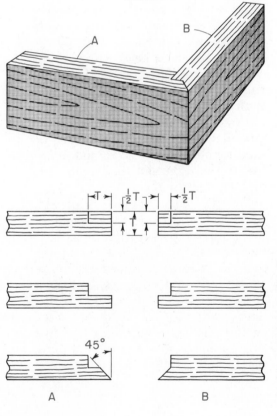

A   B   45°   B

Mortise-and-Tenon Joint. A good mortise-and-tenon joint is ideal for strength and durability. A tenon should be about one-half the thickness of the stock and about ½″ to ¾″ narrower than the total width. *Fig. 34–80.* It should also be at least 1″ long. The mortise should be at least ⁵⁄₁₆″ from the outside face and must be made at least ⅛″ deeper than the tenon.

Cut the mortise on a mortiser or drill press. There are usually eight mortises to be cut for a chair or table. Lay out the location of two of the mortises on one leg. Mark a line on the end of the leg to show the correct depth. Mark one mortise *LR* (left rear) and the other mortise *RR* (right rear). Then mark *LR* and *RR* on all other pieces at the correct location of the mortise as shown on the drawing. A complete layout does not have to be made for the other legs. Adjust the machine for the correct mortise and cut all similar ones, then readjust for the second mortise and

34–80. Layout for a mortise-and-tenon joint.

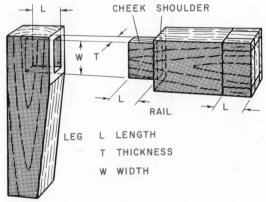

CHEEK   SHOULDER

W   T

L

RAIL

LEG   L   LENGTH
      T   THICKNESS
      W   WIDTH

335

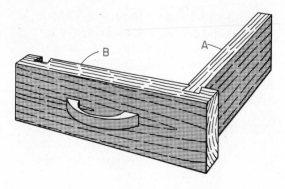

34-81.   Layout for a dovetail-dado joint.

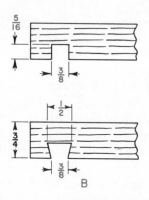

34-83.   Cutting the dovetail. (Piece B of
Fig. 34-81.)

cut all of those. Cut the tenon to fit
as described in Unit 22.

Dovetail Dado Joint. This is a good
joint for front drawer corners and for
leg-and-rail construction. It is especially good for drawers on which the
front extends beyond the side. *Fig.
34-81* shows a well-proportioned joint
in which the front is made of ¾"
stock and the sides of ½" material.
Always cut the mortise first.

34-82.   Steps in cutting the tenon or tail
for a dovetail-dado joint. (Piece A of *Fig.
34-81.*)

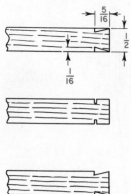

A

Cut the mortise. (Piece B of *Fig.
34-81.*) The mortise can be cut with
the dovetail bit on a portable router
or on a drill press. To cut a mortise
on a circular saw, first cut a dado
⅜" wide and ⁵⁄₁₆" deep. *Fig. 34-83.*
Replace the dado head with a crosscut blade. Adjust the blade to an
angle of 15 degrees and make the
angle cut on either side to clear out
the mortise. A blade with the teeth
ground off at 15 degrees can be
used for this. Place the ripping fence
first to the right and then to the left
to do the cutting.

Cut the tenon. (Piece A of *Fig.
34-81.*) Set the blade to a height of
¹⁄₁₆", with ⁵⁄₁₆" between the fence and
the left side of the blade. Make the
two shoulder cuts. Adjust the blade
to an angle of 15 degrees, and set it
at a distance of ½" to the left of the
fence. *Fig. 34-82.* Hold one face
against the fence and make the first
cut; then reverse the stock and make
the second.

336

Unit 35: ADHESIVES AND GLUING

An adhesive is any glue, cement, or mucilage that is used to bond materials together. The term *adhesive* is used because it is more inclusive than the word glue. *Fig. 35–1.*

Adhesives are some of the most important materials in modern wood technology. The future of wood in the space age is dependent to a large degree on the success of bonding wood to wood, or to other materials. Glued-up stock is used in almost every kind of wood construction. *Fig. 35–2.* The skills involved in gluing and clamping are also important. *Fig. 35–3.*

35–1. This "animal" illustrates the use of modern adhesives in joining various materials. The materials include wood, metal, plastics, and ceramics.

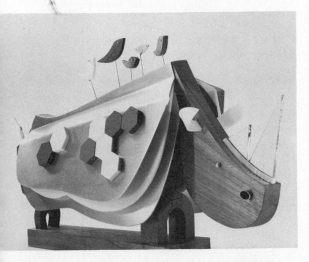

PROBLEMS IN GLUING

Problems in gluing and bonding wood must be understood in order to do a good job. Some of these are:

Recognizing the Characteristics of Wood. Wood differs from other materials such as metal or plastics in that it is porous. It is much stronger *with the grain* than across it. Wood varies in cell structure. It also varies in the amount of moisture it contains, in its extracts, and in its machining qualities. All of these things have an effect on the type of adhesive to choose and on the method of bonding to follow.

Gluing End Grain. Gluing stock face to face or edge to edge produces a very strong bond. The joints are durable and may be stronger than the wood itself. *Gluing of end grain,* however, is difficult. Because of the thousands of cut-off ends of strong, hollow fibers, it is difficult to achieve a sturdy, durable bond. Even when gluing end grain to edge or face grain, additional adhesive must be applied.

Moisture Content. The amount of moisture in wood affects both the

337

35–2. Most of the construction materials in this home are wood and adhesives. The exterior siding is hardboard, the sheathing is insulating board, and the interior is plywood. All the windows and doors are glued-up millwork. Adhesives literally hold much of this house together. Some experimental homes are completely glued together; there are no nails or screws.

rate at which adhesive dries and the strength of the finished joint. When wood takes on too much moisture after gluing, it swells and shrinks; this may result in failure of the wood or of the bond.

35–3. To make good furniture and other wood products you must know how to glue up stock and parts.

Well Fitted Joints; Gap-Filling Properties. Some adhesives will not work well except on a carefully fitted joint. Other types have good gap-filling properties and do a good job even though the fit is not too accurate.

Method of Applying. Some adhesives require rapid assembly of parts and adequate pressure to provide a a good bond. Others can be applied slowly and require no special pressure.

Curing Qualities. The rate at which adhesives dry varies greatly.

Machined Surfaces. The quality of the machined surface affects the adhesive joint. A smooth, unsanded surface is usually required. The use of certain carbide-tipped blades may eliminate the need for jointing wood before bonding.

338

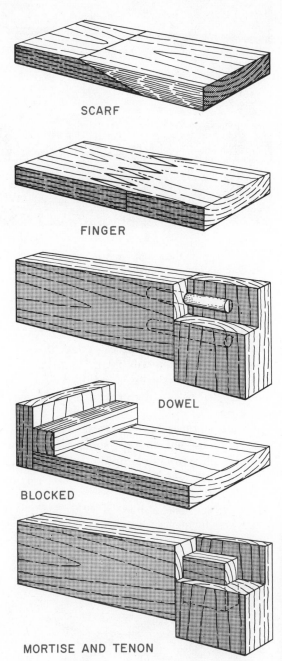

SCARF

FINGER

DOWEL

BLOCKED

MORTISE AND TENON

35–4. Common kinds of joints that require gluing.

339

THE GLUE JOINT

Because of its cellular structure, wood can be glued much more easily than most other materials. *Fig. 35–4.* In general, the lighter the weight of wood, the easier it is to glue. Glue does not penetrate the cell walls but fills only the cell cavities or pores. There are five important keys or links that make a good glue joint. These are:

• The glue-to-wood surface bond on the first piece.

• The glue anchored in the cell cavities of the first piece.

• The glue-to-glue bond between the wood surfaces.

• The glue anchored in the cell cavities of the second piece.

• The glue-to-wood surface bond on the second piece.

Kinds of Clamps. *Hand screws* are used when gluing face to face, for clamping small parts, and for holding work as it is cut or formed. *Fig. 35–5.* The range of sizes is as follows:

35–5. Using hand screws to hold parts together.

340

No.	5/0	4/0	3/0	2/0	0
Length, jaws	4″	5″	6″	7″	8″
Jaw opening	2″	2½″	3″	3½″	4½″
No.	1	2	3	4	5
Length, jaws	10″	12″	14″	16″	18″
Jaw opening	6″	8½″	10″	12″	14″

C clamps are used for clamping face to face, for repair work, and for holding parts together. *Fig. 35–6.* C clamps should be used with blocks or scraps to keep from marring the wood surfaces. The sizes are as follows:

Opening	3″	4″	5″	6″
Depth	1⅞″	2¹⁄₁₆″	2½″	2¾″
Opening	8″	10″	12″	
Depth	3¼″	3⅜″	3⅝″	

35–7a. Clamp the joint tightly together with bar clamps as shown. Note the blocks of wood under the jaws which protect the wood surface from damage.

35–6. Using C clamps to clamp a miter joint on a cabinet. Here triangular blocks are glued to the corners with paper under them for easy removal. (The paper is glued to the blocks and the wood surface.) Apply glue to mitered ends and pull together in alignment with clamps. Remove the clamps after the glue has set, and pry the blocks away. Sand off the paper.

Bar or cabinet clamps are used for clamping larger surfaces edge to edge. These are available in lengths from 2 to 10 feet or longer. *Fig. 35–7.* The 3- to 5-foot lengths are most common.

Other Clamps and Presses. There are many special clamps, such as the speed clamp, miter clamp, and spring

35–7b. Using bar clamps to hold door frame parts together.

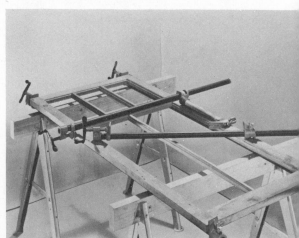

35–8. Here both bar clamps and speed clamps are used to hold the glued-up parts. Notice the block placed across the stock to assure a level surface.

clamp. *Figs. 35–8 and 35–9.* In industry, *clamp carriers* are often used for gluing. *Fig. 35–10.* In addition, there are *continuous presses* and *batch presses.* The continuous press operates with the stock constantly moving. *Fig. 35–11.* The batch press is used when the stock is moved into place and stopped during the appliltion of heat and/or pressure. *Figs. 35–12 and 35–13.* In many millrooms, the glue line is cured by means of high-frequency heat. *Fig. 35–14.*

KINDS OF GLUE

Until recently, only two types of glue—starch or vegetable and protein or animal glue—were used as adhesives in the woodworking industry. Today, however, there are many kinds. They can be grouped first on the basis of their origin or composition. These include:

• Starch, sometimes called vegetable glue.

35–9a. Special clamps frequently save work and help you do a better job. Here are various types of edge clamps used to glue wood or laminated plastic edging to plywood. Bar clamps or quick clamps grip the panel which is protected by scrap wood. Then edge-clamping fixtures are inserted to bear against the edgebanding materials while the glue sets.

• Protein, including hide or animal glue, casein, soybean, and blood glue.
• Synthetic resins, including the formaldehyde combinations of urea, melamine, phenol, resorcinol, and the resin emulsions.

35–9b. Stacking clamps for use in production.

341

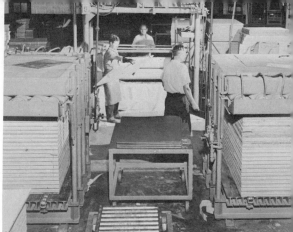

35–10. Revolving clamp carriers. These are used in both small and large millrooms.

35–12. A batch press used to glue up stock. This is a cold press which utilizes air to apply the pressure. Other types utilize electricity or hydraulics.

Another way to group glues is according to their resistance to water:

• *Waterproof.* The cured glue line will withstand more severe conditions than the wood itself. Glues in this group are recommended for the most severe exposure such as exterior and marine use.

• *Water-resistant.* The cured glue line will stand repeated soaking and drying without failure. These glues

may be used for exterior exposure in which there will be some protection from the elements.

• *Low water-resistant.* The cured glue line will not withstand frequent contact with water or high humidity. These glues are not recommended for any type of exterior exposure.

The following are the common types of glues. They are described

35–11. Here is a rotary press used to laminate plies of dissimilar materials when bonding with contact cement or other pressure-sensitive adhesives.

35–13. Here a hot press is used in gluing. A combination of heat and pressure speeds the curing.

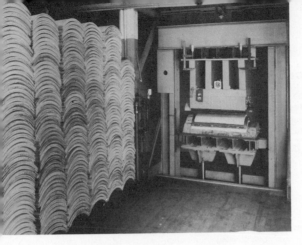

35–14. Using a high-frequency heat unit to speed the curing of glue.

White Liquid Resin. The white liquid resin glues, or polyvinyls, offer ease of handling since no mixing is required. They give a colorless glue line and rapid curing time at room temperatures. They do not resist moisture, however, and are easily affected by temperature.

Resorcinol. Resorcinol glues form a very good bond that will stand the most extreme exposure to moisture and water. These glues can be used for all types of curing operations since the addition of certain catalysts changes the assembly and curing time. The great difficulty is that resorcinol creates a dark glue line.

in some detail in *Figs. 35–15 and 35–16.*

Liquid Hide Glue. Liquid hide glue is one of the very best for interior furniture. It should not be used on wood which has a moisture content of over 10 per cent. It is relatively easy to use although less sensitive than hot hide glue.

Powdered Resin Glue. Powdered resin glue is a light tan-colored, cold-setting, resin adhesive in powdered, water-soluble form. It sets hard, producing a very strong, water-resistant

Fig. 35-15. FASTENING WOOD WITH ALL TYPES OF ADHESIVES

Glue Type	Room Temperature	How to Prepare	How to Apply	70° Clamping Time Hardwood	Softwood
Liquid Hide	Sets best above 70°. Can be used in colder room if glue is warmer.	Ready to use.	Apply thin coat on both surfaces; let get tacky before joining.	2 hours	3 hours
White Liquid Resin	Any temperature above 60°. But the warmer the better.	Ready to use.	Spread on and clamp at once.	1 hour	1½ hours
Resorcinol	Must be 70° or warmer. Will set faster at 90°.	Mix 3 parts powder to 4 parts liquid catalyst.	Apply thin coat to both surfaces. Use within 8 hours after mixing.	16 hours	16 hours
Powdered Resin	Must be 70° or warmer. Will set faster at 90°.	Mix 2 parts powder with ½ to 1 part water.	Apply thin coat to both surfaces. Use within 4 hours after mixing.	16 hours	16 hours
Powdered Casein	Any temperature above freezing. But the warmer the better.	Stir together equal parts by volume glue and water. Wait 10 minutes and stir again.	Apply thin coat to both surfaces. Use within 8 hours after mixing.	2 hours	3 hours
Contact Cement	70° or warmer.	Ready to use.	Apply thin coat. Dry for five minutes. Apply second coat.	No clamping. Bonds instantly.	
Epoxy Cement	Any temperature.	Resin and hardener mixed in amounts stated on container.	Apply with stick or brush.	No clamping. Drys faster with heat.	

Fig. 35-16. WHICH ADHESIVE FOR THE JOB?

	Liquid Hide Glue	Polyvinyl White Liquid Resin Glue	Resorcinol	Plastic Powdered Resin
Especially good for:	First choice for furniture work and wherever a tough, lasting wood-to-wood bond is needed. A favorite for cabinetwork and general wood gluing.	A fine all-around household glue for mending and furniture making and repair. Excellent for model work, paper, leather, and small assemblies.	This is the glue for any work that may be exposed to soaking: outdoor furniture, boats, wooden sinks.	Use it for woodworking and general gluing where considerable moisture resistance is wanted.
Not so good for:	Because it is not waterproof, do not use it for outdoor furniture or for boat building.	Not sufficiently moisture-resistant for anything to be exposed to weather. Not so strong and lasting as Liquid Hide Glue for fine furniture work.	Not good for work that must be done at temperatures below 70°. Because of dark color and mixing, not often used unless water-proof quality is needed.	Do not use with oily woods or with joints that are not closely fitted and tightly clamped. Must be mixed for each use.
Advantages:	Very strong because it is raw-hide-tough and does not become brittle. It is easy to use, light in color, resists heat and mold. It has good filling qualities, so gives strength even in poorly fitted joints.	Always ready to use at any temperature. Non-staining, clean and white. Quick-setting qualities recommend it for work where good clamping is not possible.	Very strong, as well as waterproof. It works better with poor joints than many glues do.	Very strong, although brittle if joint fits poorly. Light-colored, almost waterproof.
Source:	From animal hides and bones.	From chemicals.	From chemicals.	From chemicals.

	Powdered Casein	Contact Cement	Epoxy Cement
Especially good for:	Will do most woodworking jobs and is especially desirable with oily woods: teak, lemon, yew.	Laminate plastics to plywood or particle board; veneer edges to solid wood; fasten plywood panels to walls.	Will bond wood to metal or other dissimilar materials. Use in combination with wood, tile, metal, glass, etc. Will not shrink or swell during hardening. Water proof, oil proof, and non-inflammable.
Not so good for:	Not moisture resistant enough for outdoor furniture. Will stain acid woods such as redwood. Must be mixed for each use.	Edge or end gluing.	Not good for fastening wood to wood in large products. (Must be used in well-ventilated room. Avoid getting into eyes.)
Advantages:	Strong, fairly water-resistant, works in cool locations, fills poor joints well.	No clamping. Bonds instantly.	Can be painted, sanded, filled, drilled, or machined. Can fill large holes.
Source:	From milk curd.	Rubber base.	From chemicals.

bond. It is especially good for its durability under sheer loading.

Casein. Casein glues are excellent gap-filling glues which can be used for poorly surfaced materials. Casein glues will bond wood through a wide range of moisture contents from 2 to 20 per cent. Two difficulties with casein glues are their abrasive effect on cutting tools and their wood-staining characteristics.

Contact Cement. Contact cement is a neoprene-based resin, rubber-type adhesive. The adhesive is applied to both surfaces and allowed to dry, and then the surfaces are brought

344

into contact. The bond is immediate and therefore no clamping, nailing, or holding down is required. This makes contact cement particularly useful in applying plastic laminates such as countertops. *Fig. 35-17.*

Epoxy Resins. Epoxy resins are a two-part adhesive consisting of resin and a hardener. When mixed together, a chemical action takes place which provides an ideal adhesive material. These can be used to join wood to wood or to almost any other material.

PREPARING WOOD FOR GLUING

Controlling Moisture Content. A good glue joint must develop the full strength of the wood under all conditions of stress. To obtain this result, it is necessary to control the gluing operation as well as the condition of the material. *Fig. 35-18.* Under conditions that exist in most school shops, it is impossible to control the specific moisture content of wood. However, the moisture content before gluing should be as close as possible to a certain point which, when increased by moisture of the glue, will nearly equal the average moisture content of the article in use.

The average moisture content of interior woodwork is about 8 per cent for the United States. It ranges, however, from 4 per cent in the northern states in winter and desert states, to 13 per cent along the coasts in summer. Exterior woodwork has about 12 to 19 per cent average moisture content, but varies widely. (See *Fig. 8-8.*)

It is important that the wood parts being glued be at or near the same moisture content at the time of gluing. In furniture manufacturing, this is achieved by storing wood in a room where temperature and humidity are carefully controlled. If moisture content is too high, the glue which penetrates the cell cavities is thinned. Curing is delayed and a weak joint results. On the other hand, if moisture content is too low, the dry wood absorbs water from the glue, preventing an even spread and full penetration into the cell cavities. High-quality glue joints cannot be made on wet wood.

35-17. Decorative plastic laminates are usually applied with contact cement.

35-18. In furniture manufacture, the moisture content of lumber is checked with electrical meters through each step of manufacture.

35–19. This huge hot press is used to produce plywood panels. Plywood rolls continuously and automatically out of this press.

Uniformity of moisture content is an all-important factor. If woods of different moisture content are glued together, there will be shrinking and swelling which cause stresses; these may result in warpage or cracked glued joints.

Preparing the Surface for Gluing or Machining. A good gluing surface is smooth, uniform, true, free from loose and crushed fibers, and clean. The best way to prepare a glue joint is to surface the wood on a planer or jointer that has sharp knives and correct adjustment. The surface may also be prepared by hand planing with a plane, chisel, or spokeshave. If the wood is machined on a surfacer, distinct wave marks must be avoided as they prevent good contact and cause a varied glue line from thick to thin. Also avoid the burnished surface that results from dull knives.

A sawed surface, particularly one that is made with a blade with carbide tips, can be used for certain kinds of glued joints. The surface should be even and solid without any loose splinters or torn grains. The two surfaces to be glued should be checked frequently to make sure they fit properly. When gluing plywood surfaces together, it may sometimes be necessary to sand lightly because plywood has a glazed surface caused by compression during manufacture. However, only light sanding should be done since the face ply is very thin.

TYPES OF CONSTRUCTION

All types of joints can be glued together. The edge grain is the simplest and should result in a good surface. Face gluing is also fairly easy; surfaces with grain running parallel are glued together. This is sometimes called *laminating. Crossbanding* is gluing such as that done in making plywood. *Fig. 35–19.* A *veneer surface* is often glued to a solid core at right angles to the surface. With this type of gluing, it is extremely important that there be equal pressure over the entire surface. *End gluing* is the most difficult, as explained earlier, because the pores tend to absorb the glue. Glued end joints usually are not made with square-edged surfaces

346

because the strength is low. When gluing end grain to end grain, the scarf or finger joint is used.

STEPS IN GLUING

Mixing the Glue. Several glues such as liquid hide glue and polyvinyl resin emulsion glue (frequently referred to as just white liquid glue) are available in tubes or plastic squeeze bottles, ready for use. This eliminates the problem of mixing. Many other glues, however, must be mixed just before use. Most are mixed by hand. *Fig. 35–20.* It is extremely important that the ingredients be measured accurately and mixed properly. The directions on the can should be followed. The amount of water or other solvents should be checked. Because it is so porous end grain requires a high glue-to-water ratio.

Powdered glues should be mixed as needed, following the directions on the can. Never mix more glue than can be used at one time. Stir the glue briskly, and allow it to stand for at least fifteen minutes. Then mix it again for at least one minute until the glue is about as thick as whipping cream.

Resorcinol glue comes in two separate cans: a powdered catalyst or hardener, and the liquid resin. Mix according to the directions on the can.

Spreading the Glue. A uniform spread of glue is important. If part of the surface has too little glue, the strength of the joint will be greatly reduced. On the other hand, if too much glue is used, an excessive amount squeezes out and is wasted.

Too much glue can also cause a heavy glue line which has lower strength and durability than a normal one. Glues can be spread with a stick, a clean brush, a roller, or a mechanical spreader. *Figs. 35–21 and 35–22.* Roll-type glue spreaders, such as those shown in *Fig. 35–23,* may be used with many kinds of glue. Glue may be spread on only one surface (called single spreading) but double spreading results in much better gluing. When gluing end grain, always apply one thin coat, let it become tacky, and then apply a second coat before joining the parts. Heavier spreads are required for casein glues than for cold-setting, resin glues. Glues that squeeze out should never be wiped off with a wet cloth, as this adds moisture content to the wood You know that the correct amount of glue has been used when there are small, regularly spaced beads of glue along the glue line.

35–20.   Here is a cold glue mixer of a type that might be used in a small furniture factory

BLACK

347

35-23a. Small, roll-type glue spreaders can be used with many kinds of glue. They distribute the glue evenly.

35-21. Applying liquid hide glue with a stick. End grain absorbs glue so quickly that it is best to apply a preliminary coat. Allow to soak in for a few minutes, then apply another coat before joining the parts.

Assembling the Parts. On furniture or cabinetwork, always make a trial assembly before applying glue. Assembly time is the time between spreading the glue and applying the pressure. *Fig. 35-24.* Some glues have a longer assembly time than others. This time can be divided into two

steps. Open-assembly time is the time between spreading the glue and bringing the pieces to be glued into contact with each other. Closed-assembly time is the time the pieces are in contact before pressure is applied. At normal room temperature it is important that the assembly time be relatively short so that the glue is still fluid when the pressure is applied.

Applying Pressure. Most new joints must be placed under pressure after assembly in order to get a good glue

35-22. Using a small hand roller to spread white glue.

35-23b. A small, roll-type glue spreader in use.

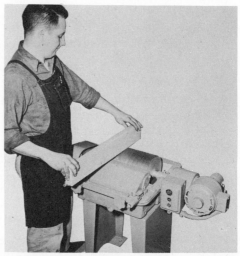

35-24a. Assemble parts immediately after spreading glue.

35-25. Alternate the clamps—one above, the next below.

joint. However, the amount of pressure should not be so great that it will squeeze out much of the glue and result in a starved joint. Both adequate and equally distributed pressure are important. Pressure helps to spread the glue to form a continuous, thin layer between the two surfaces. It also brings the surfaces in close contact and holds them in position while the glue sets or cures. Almost any method can be followed to hold the parts together. The ones

most common to the school shop, however, involve the use of various clamps. When gluing edge to edge, place a clamp every 15 to 18 inches. When gluing a furniture piece, it is important to place protective blocks against the smoothly sanded surfaces to keep the metal clamps from making dents. Always alternate clamps on either side of the work to equalize the pressure. *Fig. 35–25.* Check the parts to make sure they are level and square. *Fig. 35–26.*

35-24b. **PRESSURES THAT CAN BE OBTAINED BY THE USE OF BAR CLAMPS.**

35-26. Use a straightedge and a square to check the parts. If necessary, loosen the clamps and strike the parts with a wooden mallet. *a.* Using the straightedge.

Tightened with one hand easy — clamp will develop 200-400 pounds pressure.

Tightened with one hand hard — clamp will develop 400-800 pounds pressure.

Tightened with both hands easy — clamp will develop 800-1200 pounds pressure.

Tightened with both hands hard — clamp will develop 1200-1600 pounds pressure.

349

Industry utilizes many mechanical devices for clamping surfaces together. Some of these include the revolving clamp carrier, cold presses, hot presses, and rotary presses.

Curing or Setting the Glue. After gluing, the assembled article must be allowed to dry until it has developed sufficient strength to withstand internal stresses that tend to spread the parts. In most cases, the glue should be kept at room temperature for the stated length of time. In manufacturing, the use of high frequency heat, or hot presses which combine heat and pressure, may reduce the assembly time to a few minutes. *Fig. 35–27.*

Allow the assembly to cure or dry

35–27.   A small, school-type high-frequency electronic gluing machine.

turn to page 550 pussy

35–26b. Using the square.

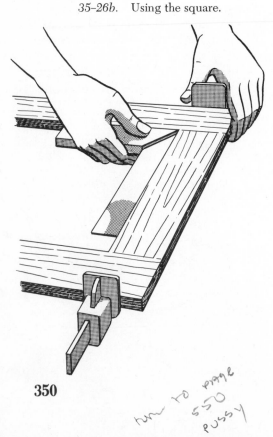

thoroughly. When dry, remove any bits of glue with a chisel or knife. Never try to remove glue by planing or sanding. If there is glue stain around the joint, always bleach it before applying the finish.

Checking the Glue Joints. If the glue joint has been properly made, it will be stronger than the wood itself. In industry it is important to check glued joints by using every possible test. Some of these include the shear test, tensile test, and breaking test. *Fig. 35–28.* A joint can be opened for examination by placing a blunt chisel at the glue line and striking it with a hammer. Some of the conditions that make a weak joint are:

• *Starved joint,* a joint with too little glue.

• *Chilled joint,* a joint in which the glue has chilled to a jelly at the glue

350

line, either before or after the application of pressure. It most frequently happens with animal glue.

• *Dried joint,* a joint in which the glue has dried without bonding at the glue line either before or after pressure is applied.

TIPS FOR GOOD GLUING

Check the following to get good glued joints:

• Are all the parts of the assembly at the proper moisture content and temperature? Moisture content should not vary more than 3 per cent.

• Are the gluing surfaces smooth, free of irregularities, and as even as possible? Does the joint fit properly?

• Has the glue been selected to give the correct kind of service? For exterior use, make sure a waterproof glue is used.

• Has the glue been stored and mixed properly? Do not use over-aged glue or glue that has been thinned too much.

• Are the wood and the room at the proper temperature for gluing? Usually between 70 and 80 degrees is right.

• Is the glue spread evenly and in the correct amount?

• Have all joints been placed under equal pressure?

• Is the pressure well distributed and continuous throughout?

• Has the assembly been under pressure long enough to allow the glue to dry properly?

• Has excess glue been removed before machining?

35–28.   Block-shear testing the quality of glue joints.

351

Unit 36: WOOD FASTENERS

The strength and stability of many products, such as homes, boats, built-ins, and some furniture, depend to a large degree upon the metal fasteners that hold the parts together. One of the reasons why wood is such a versatile building material is that wood pieces can be joined with a variety of fasteners such as nails, screws, bolts, pins, and commercial metal connectors of various shapes. *Fig. 36-1.* It is important to choose the cor-rect kind of fastener for the job to be done.

NAILING TOOLS

Claw Hammer. This tool is made with either a wood or metal handle. Most carpenters prefer a wood handle because it does not vibrate very much. *Fig. 36-2.* Hammers are designated by weight and vary from 5 to 20 ounces. A 16-ounce hammer is a good one for routine carpentry.

Nail Set. This is a small metal punch with a cupped end which prevents it from slipping off the head of the nail.

36-1. Driving nails may look like a simple operation but it is not. You must know how to select the right nails and how to drive them correctly. For example, a coated or aluminum nail is essential for exterior siding if you are to eliminate rust spots. If too many nails are used, the board may crack.

36-2. The correct-size claw hammer is important. Use one to suit the work—a heavy one for framing, a lighter one for cabinetwork.

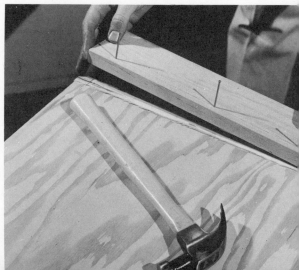

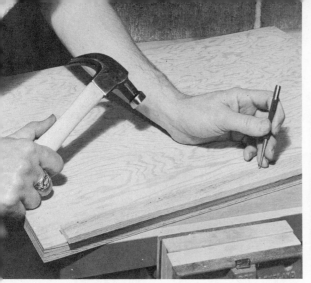

36–3. For cabinetwork, drive the nail until it is just about, but not quite, flush with the surface. Then use a *nail set*.

36–5. Here you see men assembling the components of a pre-cut home, using a nailing machine.

This tool is used to sink the heads of casing and finishing nails below the wood surface. *Fig. 36–3.*

Stapling Tools. A hand-operated stapling tool is commonly used to install insulation board, including acoustical tile. *Fig. 36–4.* A *portable nailing* or *stapling machine* is used in the assembly of homes done on a production basis. This machine is used to prefabricate component parts in the factory and also, on the job,

to assemble the units. Most of these machines are air-operated. *Fig. 36–5.*

Nailing Machines. Stationary nailing machines are made in a wide variety of sizes and in single or multiple units. The nails or staples for these machines must be specially designed. *Fig. 36–6.*

36–4. Using a hand stapler to install ceiling tile.

36–6. A nailing machine in use in a factory.

353

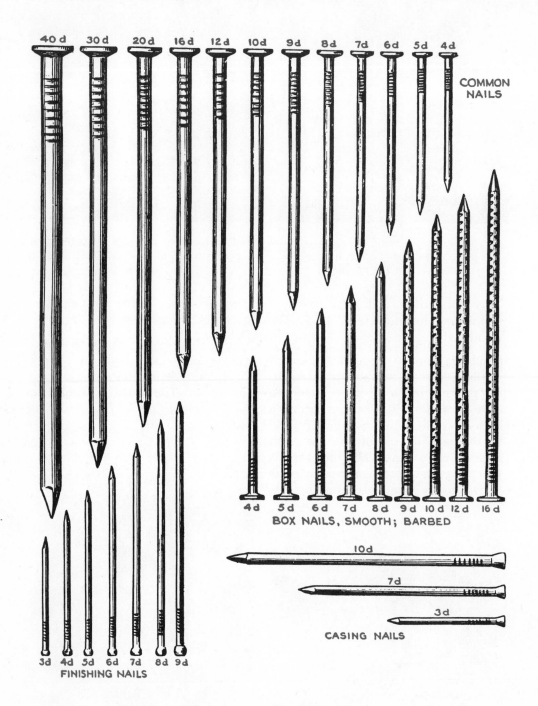

40 d 30 d 20 d 16 d 12 d 10 d 9 d 8 d 7 d 6 d 5 d 4 d

COMMON NAILS

BOX NAILS, SMOOTH; BARBED

4d 5d 6d 7d 8d 9d 10d 12d 16d

3d 4d 5d 6d 7d 8d 9d

FINISHING NAILS

10d

7d

3d

CASING NAILS

36–7a. Kinds and sizes of general-purpose nails.

NAILS

To meet every fastening condition, metallurgists and engineers have developed many kinds of nails. The most common are general-purpose nails which include *common, box, casing,* and *finishing. Fig. 36–7a.* These are made of mild steel or aluminum. For interior work, bright steel nails are chosen. For exterior construction, aluminum nails or hot-dipped, galvanized nails should be specified. Common nails are used for rough construction such as carpentry. Box nails are slender yet stiff; they are the best for fences, trellises, flower boxes, lawn furniture, and ornamental exterior woodwork of all types. Casing nails are excellent for window and door frames, cornices, corner-boards, and similar projects. Finishing nails are ideal for cabinetwork, trim, and other work on which the head of the nail should not show.

Nail sizes are given by the old English term *penny,* for which the symbol "d" is used, such as two penny (2d), or four penny (4d). These terms probably go back to the days when 100 nails of a size cost 2 pence or 4 pence. Today the term represents the length of the nail measured from the head to the point. Nail sizes start at 2d, which is 1" long, and range to 60d which is 6" long. *Fig. 36–7b.* While an 8d common and an 8d finishing nail are both $2\frac{1}{2}$" long, the common nail is larger in diameter. In addition to general purpose nails, many different kinds are made for use with other building materials.

Special-Purpose Nails. Some special-purpose nails are:

• *Flooring nails* made with a cement-coated surface or with a spiral or annular thread. They are designed to provide good holding power. *Fig. 36–8.*

• *Drywall nails* designed with an annular thread to eliminate the nuisance of popping. *Fig. 36–9.*

• *Wood-shake nails* which are ideal for fastening cedar shingles or shakes in place. *Fig. 36–10.*

36–7b. COMPARATIVE NAIL SIZES.

Size	Length In Inches	American Steel Wire Gauge Number		
		Common	Box and Casing	Finishing
2d	1	15*	15½	16½
3d	1¼	14	14½	15½
4d	1½	12½	14	15
5d	1¾	12½	14	15
6d	2	11½	12½	13
7d	2¼	11½	12½	13
8d	2½	10¼	11½	12½
9d	2¾	10¼	11½	12½
10d	3	9	10½	11½
12d	3¼	9	10½	11½
16d	3½	8	10	11
20d	4	6	9	10
30d	4½	5	9	
40d	5	4	8	

*Note: The decimal equivalent of common gauge numbers is:

15 = .072	12 = .106	9 = .148	6 = .192
14 = .080	11 = .121	8 = .162	5 = .207
13 = .092	10 = .135	7 = .177	4 = .225

36–8. Flooring nail.

36–9. Drywall nail.

36–10. Wood-shake nail.

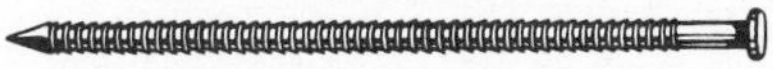

355

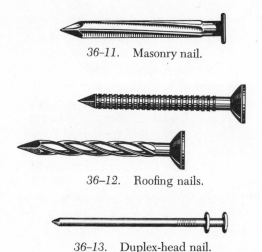

36–11.   Masonry nail.

36–12.   Roofing nails.

36–13.   Duplex-head nail.

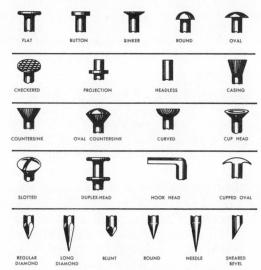

36–14.   Kinds of nail heads and points.

• *Masonry nails* made of hardened steel and with knurled body. *Fig. 36–11.*

• *Roofing nails* made with annular thread body or as a spiral thread. *Fig. 36–12.*

• *Duplex-head nails* designed for temporary installation. The lower head is driven home for a strong, tight fastening. The regular head is spaced for easy removal. *Fig. 36–13.*

• *Escutcheon pins* which are small brass nails with round heads.

• *Wire brads* which are small, flat-headed, mild-steel nails with sharp points. They come in lengths from ½″ to 1½″ in gauge numbers from 20 to 14.

Special-purpose nails vary in the following ways:
   • *Length as specified by d.*
   • *Diameter.*
   • *Kind of nail head.*
   • *Kind of point, Fig. 36–14.*
   • *Kind of material.*
   • *Kind of coating.*
   • *Kind of body.*

Nails are made of soft or mild steel, hard steel, aluminum alloy, copper, brass, commercial bronze, silicon bronze, Monel metal, and stainless steel. In boatbuilding, nails of monel metal are superior to all others. *Fig. 36–15.* Nails may be covered with cement, or they may be hot-dipped galvanized nails, enameled, or zinc-plated. The nail body is made with spiral thread, annular thread, or screw thread. *Fig. 36–16.* All of these surfaces increase nail-holding power.

METHODS OF NAILING

There are two common methods of nailing in building construction, namely, *straight driving* and *toenailing*. Straight driving is used for most wood assembly. However, it is found that if nails are driven at a very slight slant, they have better holding power. *Figs. 36–17 and 36–18.* If nails are driven completely through two pieces

STYLE	TYPE	AVAILABLE IN					
		Copper	Brass	Comm'l Bronze	Silicon Bronze	Monel	Stainless Steel
	"COMMON" NAILS Available in Annular Thread (as shown), in Spiral Thread, or Smooth.	✔	✔	✔	✔	✔	✔
	ROOFING/SLATING NAILS Available in Spiral Thread (as shown), in Annular Thread, or Smooth.	✔	☆	☆	☆		☆
	BOAT NAILS Available in Annular Thread (as shown) in Spiral Thread, or Smooth.	✔	✔	✔	✔	✔	☆
	SIDING NAILS Available in Annular Thread (as shown), in Spiral Thread, or Smooth.		✔			☆	✔
	ESCUTCHEON PINS Available in Annular Thread (as shown), or Smooth.	☆	✔	☆	☆	☆	✔
	SQUARE NAILS Barbed (as shown), or Smooth. Measured diagonally; higher count than round nails.	✔	☆	✔	✔	☆	☆

✔ **Regular items.**   ☆ **Available on request.**

36–15. Materials of which nails are made, in addition to mild steel and aluminum.

of wood, they should be clinched by bending them cross-grain since this gives better holding power. Toe-

36–16. Three kinds of nails. Left to right: spiral, screw, and annular thread.

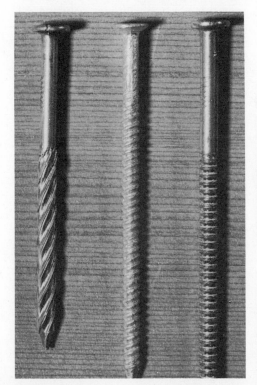

nailing is the common way of joining end grain to face grain in such wood construction as house framing. *Figs. 36–19 and 36–20.* Toenail joints, or course, are strongest when a nail that will not cause splitting is used. For toenailing, the angle should be about 30 degrees. The full shank of

36–17. Starting a nail for straight nailing.

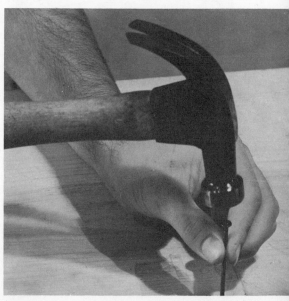

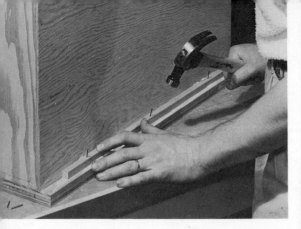

36–18. Note that the nails are being driven at a slight angle. This is still called straight nailing.

36–19a. Toenailing.

36–19b. This cutaway view shows the holding effect of toenailing.

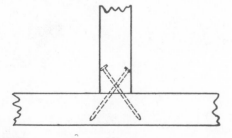

36–20. Toenailing a rafter to the ridge board.

the nail should be buried without excessive damage to the wood from hammer blows.

Good Nailing Practices. Choose the nail with the smallest possible diameter for the job. Although holding power increases as nail diameter increases, there is greater tendency toward splitting. Laboratory tests show that the box nail reduces splitting 74 per cent over the common nail used in general construction, while holding power is reduced only 10 per cent.

Use a blunt-pointed nail to avoid splitting. A long, sharp, tapered point has the action of a splitting wedge. The short, blunt, tapered point has a shearing action, pushing the fibers ahead. This causes some loss in holding power, but much less than that caused by splitting. Carpenters have found that blunting the point of standard nails lessens splitting. Several types of blunt-point nails are now available.

Nails readily split wood when driven close to the edge. Small-diameter or blunt-pointed nails can be used to reduce splitting in such locations. Another way is to pre-bore a lead hole. This also applies to drilling hardwood. *Fig. 36–21.* The pre-bored hole should be slightly smaller in diameter than the nail shank.

Warped or crooked lumber is difficult to nail without splitting. This lumber should be used in positions where splitting is not too objectionable.

Splitting occurs much more rapidly on dense woods than on lighter woods. Small-diameter nails hold just as well in dense woods as larger nails hold in lighter woods.

Cement-coated nails have up to 100 percent greater holding power than uncoated nails. This increase is only temporary, however, and a short time after installation, the holding power of cement-coated nails is about the same as uncoated nails.

Non-ferrous nails should be used when rusting or corrosion is a problem. Nails made of softer metals such as aluminum should be larger in diameter than the same length steel nails in order that withdrawal strength will be about the same. Non-ferrous metals should not be allowed to come in contact with dissimilar metals since corrosion may take place.

Hardened steel nails, smaller in diameter than common nails of the same length, can be used to advantage sometimes, especially when nailing hardwood flooring.

New nail designs should be selected when maximum holding power and minimum splitting potential are required. These include the new drive nails and angular and spiral-threaded groove nails.

36–21.   Drilling a small hole to eliminate the danger of splitting.

Do not try to drive nails home with one blow when nailing cupped or twisted boards. Nails should be driven partway in and set later.

If a nail bends, do not try to straighten it by striking it on the side. Always remove the nail and take a new one.

For plywood, nail size should be determined primarily by the thickness of the plywood. Used with glue, all nails shown will provide a strong joint: for ¾″ plywood, 6d casing or 6d finishing nails; for ⅝″, 6d or 8d finishing nails; for ½″, 4d or 6d; for ⅜″, 3d, or 4d; for ¼″ use ¾″ brads or 3d finishing nails. For backs on which there is no objection to visible heads, use 1″ lath nails. You can substitute casing for finishing nails wherever you want a heavier nail. *Fig. 36–22.*

36–22. This series of plywood panels is shown with the types of nails to be used with each thickness.

Nail rabbeted bevel siding about 1″ above the lower edge. Nails should penetrate 1½″ into the studs or, as in *Fig. 36–23*, into the stud and wood sheathing combined for greater holding power. Note how expansion clearance of about ⅛″ has been left in the rabbet.

36–23. Here you see the correct way of nailing siding. Remember to use a coated nail or one of aluminum to prevent rust spots.

WOOD SCREWS

Wood screws are usually used to fasten one-inch-thick or lesser material to heavier pieces. *Fig. 36–24.* They may be used to fasten side grain to side grain or to end grain. When both pieces are surfaced or smooth sawed, the strength of the joint can be increased considerably by gluing the adjoining surfaces and then setting the screws while the glue is wet. Wood screws have much greater holding power than nails of similar sizes. They are widely used in attaching fixtures and hangers to wood, and in light structural members.

The common head shapes are the *flat, round,* and *oval. Fig. 36–25.* Screws are made with either *slotted*

36–24. In cabinetwork, the screw is one of the best methods of fastening parts together.

or *recessed* (Phillips) heads. *Fig. 36–26*. Materials include mild steel, aluminum, copper, brass, and monel metal. Roundhead screws of mild steel are made with a blue finish. Flathead screws have a bright finish. Ovalhead screws are usually plated with cadmium or chromium and are used to install hinges, hooks, and other hardware. Screws come in lengths form $\frac{1}{4}''$ to 6″ and in gauge sizes from 0 (smallest) to 24 (largest). *Fig. 36–27*. The gauge tells the diameter. Each screw length comes in three to ten different gauge numbers. The smallest, 0, has a diameter of .060″; the diameter of each succeeding number is .013″ larger. For example, a number 5 screw is .125 (.060 + [.013 × 5]) or $\frac{1}{8}''$ in diameter. A number 11 screw would be 0.203 or $^{15}\!/_{64}''$ in diameter. Generally, the lower gauge numbers are for thinner woods. Screws are packed in the factory in boxes of one gross.

Tools for Installing Screws. There are two types of *screw drivers*. The *plain screw driver* is used with slotted head screws. Size depends on the length and diameter of the blade. *Fig. 36–28*. The screw driver tip should be equal in width to the largest diameter of the screw head. *Fig. 36–29*. The recessed (Phillips) screw driver comes in several diameters and lengths. The *spiral-type screw driver* is usually sold in a set with three sizes of screw-driver bits. *Fig. 36–30*. In addition, a No. 2 Phillips screwdriver bit is available. This provides an easy way to drive screws quickly. Care must be taken not to damage the wood. Correct size shank and pilot holes are important.

An *82-degree countersink* is needed for flathead screws that will be flush

36–25. Common types of screws.

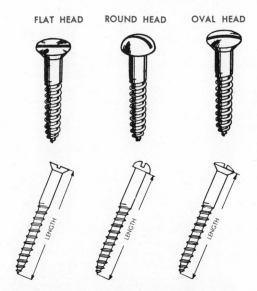

FLAT HEAD   ROUND HEAD   OVAL HEAD

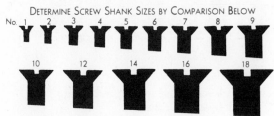

DETERMINE SCREW SHANK SIZES BY COMPARISON BELOW

No. 1 2 3 4 5 6 7 8 9

10 12 14 16 18

36–26. A recessed (Phillips) head screw.

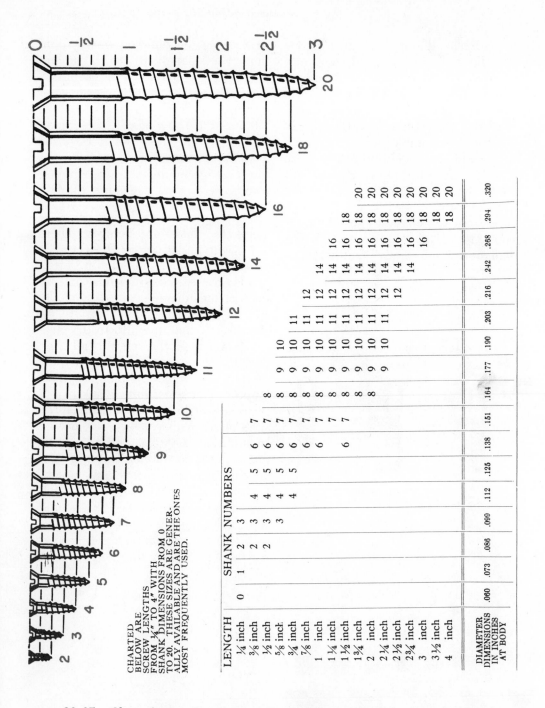

36–27. Chart of common screw sizes. Screws are also available in gauges 22 and 24, with lengths from 4½″ to 6″, but these are not common.

36–28a.   Plain screw drivers for slotted head screws.

36–30a.   Spiral-type screw driver.

36–28b.   Recessed or Phillips head screw driver.

with the surface. *Fig. 36–31.* This countersink is made in two types, one to be used in a brace and the other in a hand drill or drill press.

The *screwdriver* bit can be used in a brace for setting screws. *Fig. 36–32.*

A *screw-mate drill countersink* is a good tool to use for installing flathead screws. *Fig. 36–33.* It will do four things: drill to the correct depth,

36–29.   Select the correct width of blade for installing slotted head screws: (left) too small; (center) correct; (right) too large.

36–30b.   Using a spiral-type screw driver.

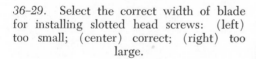

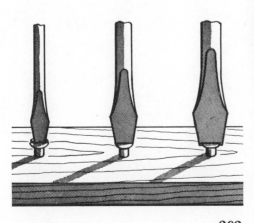

363

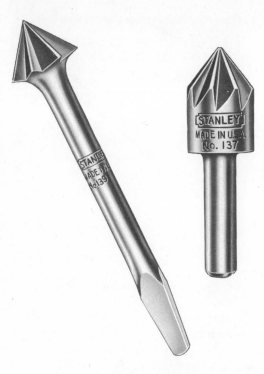

36–32b. Screw-driver bit being used to install screws.

36–33. Screw-mate drill and countersink. The chart shows common combinations of length and gauge number.

Screw Size	Screw Size	Screw Size
½″ x #5	1¼″ x #8	1½″ x #14
¾″ x #6	1¼″ x #9	1¾″ x #8
¾″ x #7	1¼″ x #10	1¾″ x #10
¾″ x #8	1¼″ x #12	1¾″ x #12
1″ x #6	1¼″ x #14	2″ x #10
1″ x #7	1½″ x #8	2″ x #12
1″ x #8	1½″ x #10	2″ x #14
1″ x #10	1½″ x #12	2½″ x #12

36–31. Two types of countersinks: (left) countersink for brace; (right) countersink for hand drill or drill press.

36–32a. Screw-driver bit.

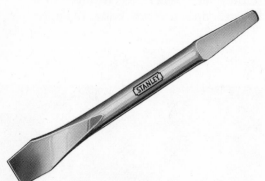

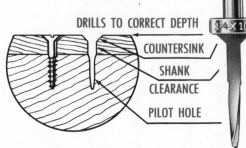

DRILLS TO CORRECT DEPTH

1/4 X 10

COUNTERSINK

SHANK

CLEARANCE

PILOT HOLE

countersink, make the correct shank clearance, and make the correct pilot hole. The tool is stamped with the length and gauge number. For example, a tool stamped 1¼ x 10 would be used for a flathead screw 1¼″ long and No. 10 gauge size. A *counterbore screw-mate* will do all the operations performed by the screw-mate plus drilling holes for wood plugs. *Fig.*

Screw Size	Plug Size	Screw Size	Plug Size
1" x #8	3/8" x 3/8"	1½" x #12	½" x ½"
1" x #10	3/8" x 3/8"	1¾" x #10	3/8" x 3/8"
1¼" x #8	3/8" x 3/8"	1¾" x #12	½" x ½"
1¼" x #10	3/8" x 3/8"	2" x #14	½" x ½"
1½" x #10	3/8" x 3/8"	2" x #18	5/8" x 5/8"

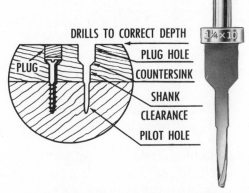

DRILLS TO CORRECT DEPTH

PLUG

PLUG HOLE
COUNTERSINK
SHANK
CLEARANCE
PILOT HOLE

1/4 x 10

36–34. Screw-mate counterbore. The chart shows width and depth of plugs for use with common-size screws.

36–34. There are several other patented devices for doing this kind of work.

If a large number of screws must be installed, such as in boatbuilding, use a *screwdriving attachment* on a portable drill. *Fig. 36–35.* There are also portable electrical tools which are designed exclusively for driving the screws.

Installing Screws. To obtain the maximum strength, holes for screws must be *pre-bored*. Two holes are needed, one for the shank of the screw, and the other for the threaded portion called the pilot or anchor hole. Screw joints are subject to two types of loads, the *lateral* or *sideways* load, and the *direct withdrawal* load. For both types the drill size for the

36–35. Screw-driving attachment for a portable drill.

shank hole should be seven-eighths the diameter of the screw. For lateral loads, the pilot hole for the screw should be 60 per cent of the threaded portion; for withdrawal loads, it should be slightly less than one-half.

1. Choose a screw long enough to go two-thirds its length into the second part. Another good rule to follow is that the threaded part should go into the second member. *Fig. 36–36.* The diameter of the screw should

36–36. Make sure the threaded portion goes all the way into the second member.

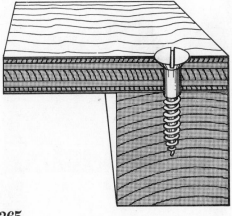

Screw Gage No.	0	1	2	3	4	5	6	7	8	9	10	11	12	14	16	18	20
Shank Hole Hard & Soft wood	$1/16$	$5/64$	$3/32$	$7/64$	$7/64$	$1/8$	$9/64$	$5/32$	$11/64$	$3/16$	$3/16$	$13/64$	$7/32$	$1/4$	$17/64$	$19/64$	$21/64$
PILOT HOLE SOFT WOOD	$1/64$	$1/32$	$1/32$	$3/64$	$3/64$	$1/16$	$1/16$	$1/16$	$5/64$	$5/64$	$3/32$	$3/32$	$7/64$	$7/64$	$9/64$	$9/64$	$11/64$
PILOT HOLE HARD WOOD	$1/32$	$1/32$	$3/64$	$1/16$	$1/16$	$5/64$	$5/64$	$3/32$	$3/32$	$7/64$	$7/64$	$1/8$	$1/8$	$9/64$	$5/32$	$3/16$	$13/64$
Auger Bit Sizes For Plug Hole			3	4	4	4	5	5	6	6	6	7	7	8	9	10	11

36–37. Drill sizes for screws.

be chosen according to the thickness of the wood. For thinner woods, use small-diameter screws.

2. Drill the shank hole to the correct diameter. The drill sizes shown in *Fig. 36–37* are for general-purpose work.

36–38. Steps in installing a flathead screw: *a.* Drill the shank hole. *b.* Drill the pilot or anchor hole. *c.* Countersink. *d.* Check the amount of countersink with the screw head. *e.* Install the flathead screw. *f.* Screw properly installed.

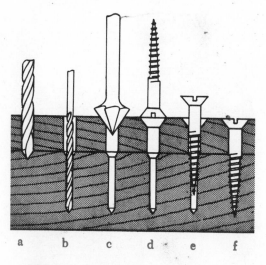

a   b   c   d   e   f

3. Place the first piece over the second and punch a hole with a scratch awl.

4. Drill the pilot or anchor hole to the depth that you want the screw to penetrate. You can use a chart to determine the size of the hole, or you may judge this by holding the drill behind the screw.

5. For flathead screws, countersink so the screw will be flush with the surface. *Fig. 36–38.*

6. Screws should be driven by turning with a screw driver. The head should not be hammered into the hole. Hammering destroys the contact between the threads and wood and greatly reduces both lateral and withdrawal resistance.

7. If the screwhead must be plugged, cut a plug (bung in boatbuilding) with a plug cutter or fill the hole with plastic wood.

36–39. Lag screw.

When using flathead screws for plywood, choose sizes as shown below. These sizes show the minimums. Use a longer screw if the work permits:

¾" plywood — No. 8 screw — 1½" long

⅝" plywood — No. 8 screw — 1¼" long

½" plywood — No. 6 screw — 1¼" long

⅜" plywood — No. 6 screw — 1 " long

¼" plywood — No. 4 screw — ¾" long

Heavy Screws and Bolts. Heavy screws and bolts are used to fasten wooden members together, side grain to side grain, and to fasten metal members to wood side grain. Since they are available in such a wide variety of sizes, there is no limit to the parts that can be assembled. All standard bolts, nuts, and screws for metal assembly can be used. Some of the most common are:

Lag screws—similar to wood screws, but larger in diameter, longer, and with a square head. *Fig. 36–39.* They range in size from ³⁄₁₆" to 1¼" in diameter and from 1" to 16" long. They are used in places where the presence of a nut on the surface would be objectionable. The lead hole for the shank of the lag screw should be of the same diameter as the shank and should have the same depth as the unthreaded shank. The pilot hole should have a diameter equal to 60 to 75 per cent of the

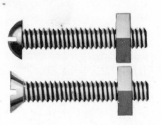

36–41.   Stove bolts.

thread diameter. Install the lag screw with a wrench.

Carriage bolts—used in framing and in fastening metal and wood parts together. *Fig. 36–40.* They have a crown head and a short, square section under the head which keeps the bolt from turning when the nut is tightened. They are made of galvanized steel, bronze, or monel metal. Carriage bolts are used with washers and the correct size nut.

Stove bolts—made with a threaded shank with round or flat heads. *Fig. 36–41.* Square nuts come with the bolts.

Machine bolts—made with square or hexagon heads. They are available in a wide range of shank diameters and lengths. Square or hexagon head nuts are also available. *Fig. 36–42.*

Using Bolts. The strength of wood parts connected with bolts is determined to a large degree by the size and type of the bolt hole. The hole should be smooth and just large enough so that the bolt will slip in

36–40.   Carriage bolt.

36–42.   Machine bolts.

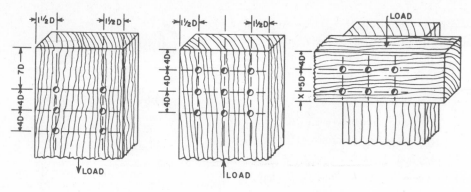

36–43. Spacing of holes for installing bolts.

under slight pressure or with a light tap of the mallet. If the hole is too small, driving it in may split the wood. If the hole is too large, the assembly will be loose. The bolt spacing should be as shown in *Fig. 36–43*.

Timber Connectors. There are several types of metal connectors that provide superior joint efficiency. They are used primarily in truss roof construction. (See Unit 47.)

Wall Fasteners. There are several kinds of fastening devices for attaching cabinets, built-ins, and other items to walls. The following are useful fasteners for attaching a piece to a drywall, plaster wall, or a hollow masonry wall:

Toggle Bolts. A toggle bolt is made with either a spring head or a solid head. *Fig. 36–44.* Holding power increases with the size. A hole must be drilled large enough for the bolt to slip through. *Fig. 36–45.* In masonry walls, a star drill or carbide-tipped bit must be used.

Molly Bolts. The molly bolt is made in several lengths and diam-

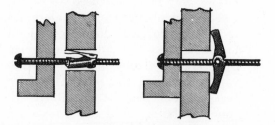

36–44a. Spring head toggle bolt.

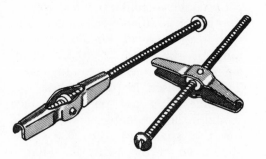

36–44b. Solid head toggle bolt.

36–45. Installing a toggle bolt.

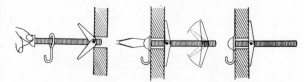

368

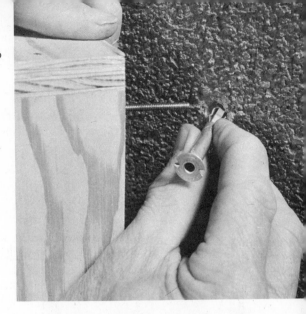

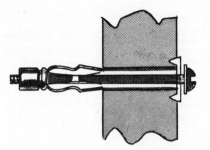

36–46a.   Molly bolt inserted.

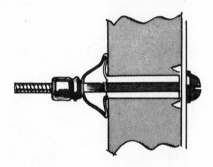

36–46b.   Molly bolt secured.

36–47.   Installing a molly bolt.

eters. *Fig. 36–46.* This fastener has several advantages: The anchor shank completely fills the hole giving a more durable, secure anchoring, and the supported material can be removed and replaced without loss of the anchor. *Fig. 36–47.*

Anchor Bolts. An anchor bolt with perforated plate can be used on solid masonry walls. *Fig. 36–48.* Fasten the base to the wall with black mastic or epoxy cement, letting it squeeze through the hole.

When items must be attached to a solid masonry wall, the following anchors are useful:

A *rawl plug* is an anchor designed for use with wood, sheet metal, or lag screws. *Fig. 36–49.* Installation of

rawl plugs is very simple. Drill the proper size hole, insert the rawl plug, then put the fixture in place and drive the screw.

A *lead screw anchor* can be used with a lag or wood screw in masonry walls. *Fig. 36–50.* Many other types of expansion holders are also available.

Miter Joint Fasteners. Two types of metal fasteners commonly used on

36–48.   Installing a cabinet after the anchor plate is secured to the cement wall.

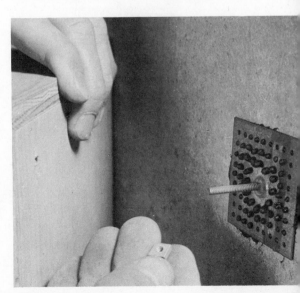

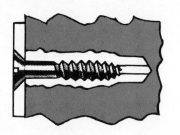

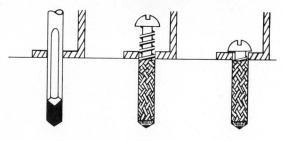

36–49. Installing a rawl plug.

36–50a. Using a lead screw anchor.

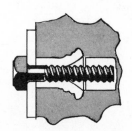

36–50b. Ackerman plug.

36–50c. Lead shield.

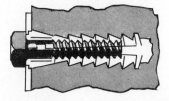

miter joints are *chevrons*, designed to draw wood together to make a tight joint, and *corrugated fasteners*, used for holding a miter and other kinds of joints. *Fig. 36–51.*

Household Fasteners. Some common household screw devices include:

• The *cup hook*—usually made of brass in sizes $\frac{1}{2}''$, $\frac{5}{8}''$, $\frac{3}{4}''$, $1''$, $1\frac{1}{4}''$, and $1\frac{1}{2}''$. *Fig. 36–52.*

• *Screw hooks*—made in lengths from $1\frac{1}{4}''$ to $2\frac{1}{2}''$.

• *L* or *square-bent* or *utility* hooks —available in lengths from $1''$ to $2\frac{1}{2}''$.

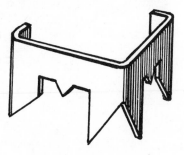

36–51a. Chevrons.

36–51b. Corrugated fasteners.

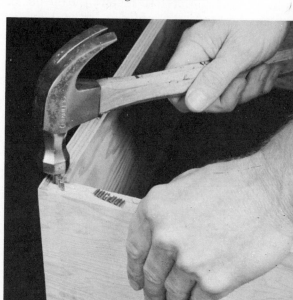

• *Screw eyes*—made of light or heavy wire with small or medium eyes, in many different sizes.

Repair Plates. Repair and mending plates come in many sizes and shapes. *Fig. 36–53.* A *mending plate* is used to strengthen a butt or lap joint. The *flat-corner* iron is used to strengthen corners of frames such as screen doors or windows. The *bent corner* can be applied to shelves and the inside corners of tables, chairs, and cabinets. It can also be used to hang cabinets and shelves. *T plates* are used to strengthen the center frame of a rail.

36–52.   Household fastening devices.

36–53.   Repair plates.   *a.* Mending.   *b.* Flat corner.   *c.* Bent corner.   *d.* T plate.

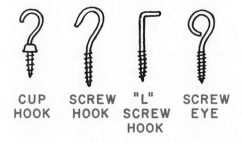

CUP HOOK   SCREW HOOK   "L" SCREW HOOK   SCREW EYE

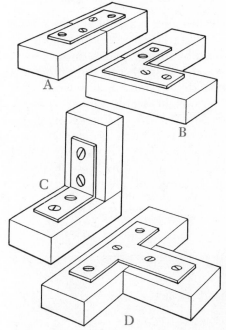

Unit 37: LAMINATING AND BENDING

Laminating and bending may be done separately but are often combined.

LAMINATED WOOD

Laminating is one of the processes for making large pieces of wood. It is done by gluing two or more layers of wood together with the grains approximately parallel. (Plywood has the grains at right angles to each other.) *Fig. 37–1.* Pieces may be glued edge to edge or face to face to form large areas for many wood products, from walnut gun stocks to huge beams and arches. *Fig. 37–2.*

37–1. The frame of this chair is made of laminated wood.

The process is widely used in furniture manufacture, especially for bent parts of tables and chairs. *Fig. 37–3.* The development of this process in the building industry is one of the more important achievements of recent years. *Fig. 37–4.* Larger beams and arches contribute both sound structure and beauty to churches, auditoriums, commercial buildings, and homes. The ends of the laminated pieces may be joined with a butt joint, but for greater strength a scarf or finger joint is usually used.

Advantages. Glued, laminated wood members have all the advantages of wood plus the following additional features:

37–2. Laminated walnut gun stocks glued from 1″ stock using low temperature phenol resin.

37–3. This chair shows the use of solid wood for the arms and legs and laminated material for the back.

• The best materials can be used for maximum strength and appearance.

• All checks and other defects can be eliminated.

• Larger cross sections, wider widths, and greater lengths can be obtained than are possible with solid lumber.

• The process can produce arches and other large members that can be used to make a most efficient framing system.

• Smaller pieces of lumber can be utilized so there is little waste.

• Complex shapes can be produced by lamination.

• Laminated structures are not subject to as much shrinkage or checking as solid lumber.

The Process for Arches and Beams. Glued, laminated arches and beams can be produced in any dimension or length using kiln-dried lumber of nominal thickness 2″ or less. Straight beams are usually built up of 1⅝″ laminations (2″ nominal). Arches

and curved beams are fabricated of either 1″ or 2″ nominal lumber. The key steps in producing beams and arches are as follows:

37–4. The arches for this church form the framework for construction and at the same time add beauty of design. This would not be possible without laminated construction.

373

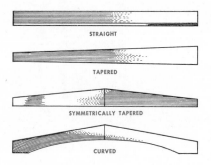

37–5. Types of beams.

37–7. Assembling the laminated arches using metal plates, bolts, and nuts.

1. Individual boards are cut to length and planed. The ends are bevelled or scarfed so they can be lapped and glued end-to-end to produce the desired length.

2. Each piece of lumber making up the beam goes through a glue spreader that applies an even coat of glue to both sides. Interior members are covered with a water-resistant casein glue while exterior members are coated with a waterproof-phenol, resorcinol, or melamine-resin glue.

3. The pieces are then placed in jigs that shape them. There are three basic types of beams: straight, tapered, and curved. *Fig. 37–5.* Common shapes of arches are the high "V", the parabolic, and the circular segment. However, many other shapes are possible. *Fig. 37–6.*

4. The laminated structure is clamped tight in the press and allowed to dry.

5. The beam or arch is machined again on a surfacer that will handle a variety of shapes and sizes.

6. The completed beam or arch is given a surface finish and holes are drilled, notches cut, and other shaping done as may be required.

7. The beams or arches are then covered with protective paper and shipped to the site of construction. *Fig. 37–7.*

Points to Remember.

• The material should be all the same kind of lumber to avoid interior stress.

37–6. Types of arches.

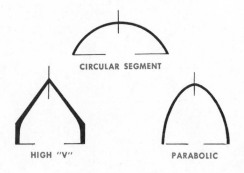

• Material should have no more than 3 per cent variation in moisture content.

• Choose the correct glue and gluing method. A waterproof-resin glue is best for most jobs. The glue should be applied with some kind of glue spreader.

• If end grains must be joined, use the correct end joint—a scarf or finger joint.

• Douglas fir and southern pine are the most commonly used materials for laminating. For smaller products any kind of wood can be used.

BENDING WOOD

Curved parts for furniture can be produced either by band sawing or bending. However, band sawing is wasteful, and sawed parts have crossed grains and end grains along the surface of the curve. Bending, therefore, is a much better method of producing parts that require sharp curvature such as in manufacturing furniture, boats, and sports equipment. The best materials for bending are white oak, elm, hickory, ash, beech, birch, maple, and walnut.

The comparatively low toughness of softwoods makes them difficult to bend, although yew and Alaska cedar can be used. Douglas fir and southern yellow pine, cedars, and redwoods can be bent moderately after steaming. *Fig. 37–8.* The Forest Products Laboratory has recently found that when bending hardwood squares ¾″ in size on a 20″ radius without end pressure or any support on the outside of the bend and without selection beyond excluding knotty,

decayed, or checked pieces, the percentage of breakage was as follows:

Oak, white	9 per cent
Oak, red	14 per cent
Birch	22 per cent
Elm	28 per cent
Ash	36 per cent
Beech	40 per cent
Poplar, yellow	51 per cent
Maple, hard	51 per cent
Gum, black	55 per cent
Cottonwood	69 per cent
Sycamore	84 per cent
Basswood	95 per cent

The correct amount of steaming and the way in which pressure is applied are important factors in bending. Also, some kinds of woods must be handled more carefully than others. Low bending breakage is a very important quality in selecting woods for building boats and certain kinds of furniture. Types of bending breakage are shown in *Fig. 37–9.*

There are several ways of bending wood. All methods require a mold or form in the shape of the finished product.

Bending Solid Wood by Steaming or Soaking. The best method of making wood pliable for bending is to steam or soak it in boiling water until it contains from 12 to 20 per cent moisture. The amount of moisture needed

37–8.   Bending to shape.

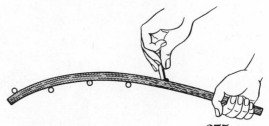

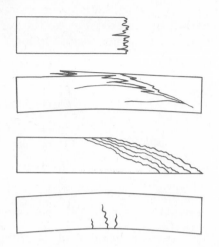

37–9. Common breaks caused by bending (from top to bottom): Brash, Tension, Cross grain, and Compression.

37–10. Steam heating solid stock for bending.

37–11. This rim-type bending machine will bend a chair part through an arc of 180 degrees.

37-12a. A small bench-type glue spreader.

37-12b. An industrial-type glue spreader in operation.

depends on the sharpness of the curve and the methods to be used in drying and holding the bent parts. *Fig. 37-10.* The dry wood should be steamed or boiled about one hour for each inch of thickness. After steaming, the stock should be placed in the mold, form, or jig. *Fig. 37-11.* The piece should be cooled and dried until it holds its curved shape. The best method in most shops is to hold the bent piece in a form and place it in a drying room.

Producing Laminated Pieces without Moisture. The best method of producing laminated pieces without moisture is to bend and glue them together in one step. Use dry material and cut and/or plane it very thin, ⅛" or ¹⁄₁₆", so that it will bend easily when dry. Both hard and soft woods can be laminated by this method. Glue is applied to both surfaces with a hand or machine spreader. *Fig. 37-12.* Place the pieces in a form or mold, and clamp them in place until dry. *Fig. 37-13.*

MOLDED PLYWOOD

Curved and molded plywood can be produced by bending and gluing in one operation or bending previously glued, flat plywood. Light, molded plywood parts are made in a manner similar to laminating. *Fig. 37-14.* Layers of wood, glued with grains at right angles, are placed in metal forms. *Fig. 37-15.* The forms

37-13a. Fastening stock in a form or mold for a school-shop job.

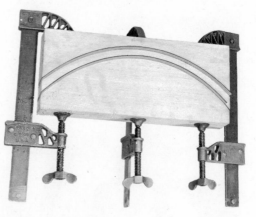

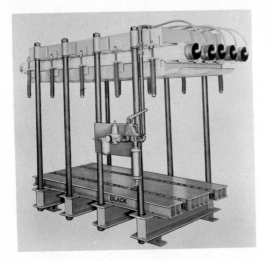

37–13b. Here is an air-operated laminating cold press of the kind used in industry.

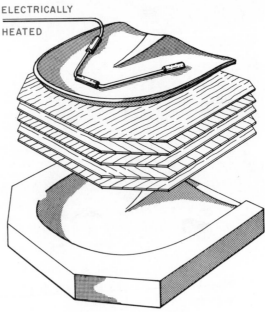

ELECTRICALLY

HEATED

37–15. These metal forms are used in molding the plywood.

are clamped together and heat applied with a hot press In a few minutes the layers are solidly glued together in the desired shape. Molded plywood chair seats and backs are made in this way. Usually heat is applied so that the glue will set rapidly and hold the unit shape. *Fig. 37–16.*

Flat plywood can be bent to a moderate curvature without heat or moisture. *Fig. 11–17.* The amount of the bend depends on the thickness of the plywood and the kind of veneer. Sharper bends can be made by ap-

37–14. The chair seat and back are made of molded plywood.

37–16. A hot press in which heat and pressure are used for shaping plywood.

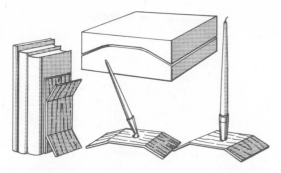

37–17. Several small projects made by laminating. The mold (top), made from a heavy piece of birch or maple, can be used to form the laminated parts for all of these projects.

plying moisture and heat to the plywood, then bending it. When this is done, however, be sure the plywood has been made with waterproof glue.

LAMINATING AND BENDING IN THE SCHOOL SHOP

Laminating with Dry Stock. Examples of this shown in *Fig. 37–17* are book ends, a note holder, a candle stick, and a pen holder. Other good examples are a fishing net, a salad server, and the shaped leg of a chair.

Make a mold of the desired shape. For example, the mold or form for the fishing net was made from a piece of band iron bent to shape and welded. *Fig. 37–18.* The stock can be held with spring metal clamps or strips of heavy rubber cut from an inner tube. The mold for the salad serving set and note holder was cut from a thick piece of maple or birch. *Fig. 37–19.* The molds for the chair legs are much more complicated. *Fig. 37–20.*

$\frac{1}{8}$" x 1" BAND IRON

37–18. The form or mold for making a laminated fishing net frame and other project ideas.

Cut very thin pieces to width and length, $\frac{1}{28}$" to $\frac{1}{16}$". You can use standard veneer stock of teak, walnut, oak, maple, or other hardwoods. Make sure the surfaces are smooth. If a scarf joint is needed for increasing the length of the stock, this can be cut by hand or on a machine. The scarf should be cut at a very shallow angle of not more than 8 degrees, and 6 degrees is even better. It can be cut on either thin veneer or solid wood on any one of several machines. With a special jig, the jointer will

379

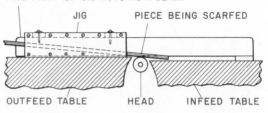

JIG   PIECE BEING SCARFED

OUTFEED TABLE   HEAD   INFEED TABLE

37–21. Cutting a scarf joint on the jointer.

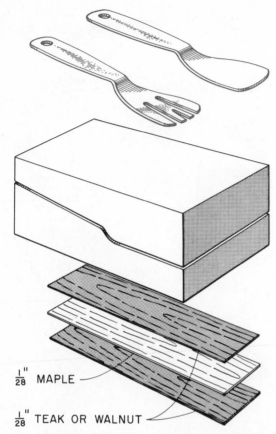

$\frac{1}{28}$" MAPLE

$\frac{1}{28}$" TEAK OR WALNUT

37–19. The form or mold for making a salad-serving set. The form can be lined or covered with thin rubber for more even pressure.

37–20. The parts of this chair are made of laminated materials. Here you see the mold used to form the legs.

cut an accurate scarf joint on solid wood. *Fig. 37–21.* With a similar jig, the surfacer or planer can be used to produce a scarf joint on solid stock or veneer. Another way of scarfing thin and narrow stock is on a vertical spindle shaper with a special jig. *Fig. 37–22.* The scarf can also be cut with a hand plane if the stock is held in a jig. Apply a thin coat of glue to one or both surfaces to be joined. Place wax paper between the laminated stock and the mold or form. Use a roller for applying the glue. Place the laminating material between the forms; begin to clamp near the center of the piece and work toward the outside.

37–22. Cutting a scarf joint on the spindle shaper. (View is from the top.) The length of the cut surface should be about 7 times the thickness.

APPROXIMATELY 7 × THICKNESS

SHAPER HEAD   HOLD DOWN BAR

SURFACE OF
ROUGHING
CUT

T

JIG   "C" CLAMP

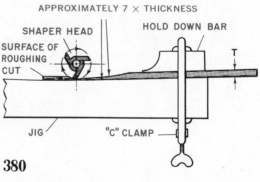

380

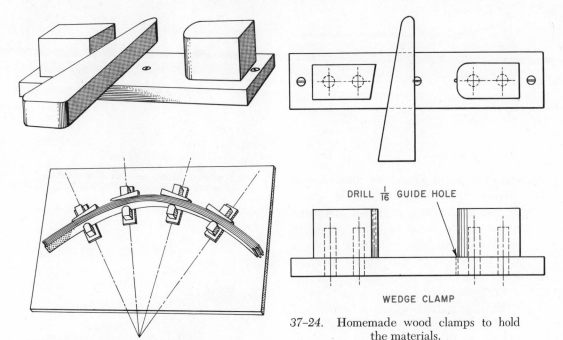

DRILL $\frac{1}{16}$ GUIDE HOLE

WEDGE CLAMP

37-24. Homemade wood clamps to hold the materials.

37-23. A form or mold for laminating simple, curved materials.

Using Wedge Clamps. Another method of making laminated wood for curved work is first to lay out the shape of the piece on $\frac{3}{4}''$ plywood. *Fig. 37-23.* Fasten metal pins or nails on the curved lines at intervals of 5" or 6". Make a series of wood clamps similar to those shown in *Fig. 37-24.* Place the clamps over the metal pins so each drops into a guide hole. Glue the thin pieces together and apply the wedge clamps. Apply C clamps between the wood clamps.

Bending the Ends of Water or Snow Skis. Make a bending jig or mold similar to that shown in *Fig. 37-25.* On the band saw, edge rip the end to be bent to a depth of 13" to 15". Cut the sheets of veneer slightly

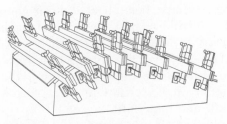

37-25. Mold for bending water skis.

larger than the saw kerfs. Apply good waterproof glue to both surfaces and slip into place. Place the ski on the bending jig or mold, and clamp the tip first; then continue to clamp until it is in shape and completely tightened down. Tighten each clamp a little at a time until all are tight. Allow the ski to remain in the jig until the glue is thoroughly dry. Shape the ends of the ski by band sawing. *Fig. 37-26.*

381

37–26a. Preformed planks can be purchased for making water skis.

Bending Solid Wood by Steaming or Soaking. This procedure is sometimes used to form parts for furniture, or for sports items such as toboggans or skis. Make sure a form or mold of the desired size and shape is available. Select wood carefully and cut it to approximate dimensions. Soak or steam the part as much as is needed. *Fig. 37–27.* Cut a thin piece of sheet metal, preferably stainless steel, the same width as the stock. When the pieces have been heated until they are pliable, clamp one end of each piece to the form with the sheet metal directly over the outside of it. Continue to draw the stock around the form or mold, clamping each piece a little at a time until the stock is firmly held against the form. *Fig. 37–28.* The exterior of the wood cannot be stretched very much (less than 1 or 2 per cent). The interior can be compressed as much as 25 per cent. Therefore, if you try to form the wood too rapidly, it will split out on the exterior side. Allow the pieces to dry at least 24 hours on the form.

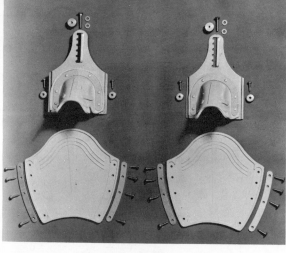

37–26b. Hardware for making water skis.

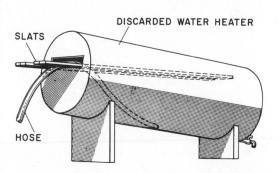

SLATS

HOSE

DISCARDED WATER HEATER

37–27. A way of bending with hot steam. An old hot-water tank can be used as a container. Steam from the heating plant can be used. Another method is to fill the tank with water and apply heat as the wood is soaked.

37–28. Fasten the wood to a mold, form, or jig. This one can be used for building a toboggan.

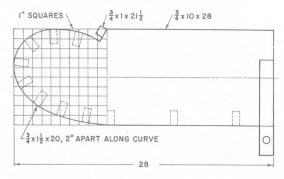

1" SQUARES $\frac{3}{4}$ x 1 x 2$\frac{1}{2}$ $\frac{3}{4}$ x 10 x 28

$\frac{3}{4}$ x 1$\frac{1}{2}$ x 20, 2" APART ALONG CURVE

28

Unit 38: ABRASIVES AND SANDING

Abrasives are hard materials that will wear away the surface of another material. When abrasives are used for smoothing wood, the process is called *sanding. Figs. 38–1 and 38–2.* In most woodworking plants sanding is classified in three ways: sanding before finishing, sanding of intermediate coats, and wet sanding of finish coats.

38–1. This man realizes the value of good sanding. He has wisely elevated his work so he does not need to bend, and has allowed himself plenty of "elbow room." What other good practices does he demonstrate?

COATED ABRASIVES

There are three things to know about the coated abrasives you use: the *minerals,* the *backing,* and the *bond.*

Minerals. Five kinds of materials are used for abrasives. *Flint, emery,* and *garnet* are natural minerals, while *silicon carbide* and *aluminum oxide* are man-made, or synthetic.

• *Flint,* which is quartz, is white

38–2. Without careful, thorough sanding, the handsome finish of this desk would not have been possible.

38-3. Common kinds of abrasive papers used in woodwork. From back to front: garnet, flint, aluminum oxide, and silicon carbide.

in color and very similar in appearance to white sand.

• *Emery,* dull black in color, is hard, and rocky in structure.

• *Garnet,* which is reddish-brown,

is of medium hardness with a good cutting edge.

• *Silicon carbide* is shiny black in color and, because of its brittle qualities, it fractures into sharp, sliver-like wedges.

• *Aluminum oxide* is grey brown and is extremely tough and resistant to wear. It is capable of penetrating almost any surface. *Figs. 38–3 and 38–4.*

Backing. The four common backings used for abrasives are:

• *Paper,* which is available in four different weights—"A", which is light paper stock, "C" and "D" which are intermediate weight papers commonly known as cabinet papers, and "E" which is a strong and durable paper used in belt and roll abrasives.

• *Cloth,* which comes in two weights. "J" is lightweight and flexible, and "X" is durable and strong. *Fig. 38–5.*

• *Fiber,* which is made from rag

38-4a. SANDPAPERS FOR WOOD

NAME	GRIT SIZES					AVAILABLE IN	USES
FLINT Paper	Extra Coarse	Coarse	Medium	Fine	Extra Fine	9" x 10" Sheets (See Note)	For hand sanding common woodwork, removing paint, varnish, etc. Also for small miscellaneous jobs.
GARNET Paper	Very Coarse 30-D(2½)	Coarse 50-D(1)	Medium 80-D(0)	Fine 120-C(3/0)	Very Fine 220-A(6/0)	9" x 11" Sheets	Good all-around paper for hand sanding good woodwork, furniture, etc., dry.

NOTE: Flint paper is also available in packs containing an assortment of coarse, medium and fine grits in 4½" x 5" sheets.

38-4b. SANDPAPERS FOR WOOD AND METAL

NAME	GRIT SIZES					AVAILABLE IN	USES
Paper (Aluminum Oxide)	Very Coarse 30-D(2½)	Coarse 50-D(1)	Medium 80-D(0)	Fine 120-C (3/0)	Very Fine 220-A(6/0)	9" x 11" Sheets	For hand or machine sanding of hardwoods, metals, plastics and other materials.
Cloth (Aluminum Oxide)	Very Coarse 30-X(2½)	Coarse 50-X(1)	Medium 80-X(0)	Fine 120-X (3/0)		Belts for all popular belt sanders. X-weight	Strong cloth-backed belts for sanding wood, metal, plastics and other materials with stationary or portable belt sanders.
Paper-Waterproof (Silicon Carbide)			Very Fine 220-A	Extra Fine 320-A	Super Fine 400-A	9" x 11" Sheets	Best paper for wet sanding by hand or machine, primers and between coats on wood, metal or other materials. Can be used with water, oil or other lubricants.

stock paper that has been condensed and hardened. Strong, tough, flexible, and relatively hard, it has much more body than other backings. It is used for discs and for drum sanding materials.

• *Combination.* There are two common combinations—paper and cloth laminated together, and fiber and cloth laminated together. The paper-and-cloth type is used mainly in high-speed drum sanders while the fiber-and-cloth type is used for discs.

Bonds. Coated abrasives have a bond, or adhesive, that locks the material to the backing. There are two bond layers. The first is called the "bond coat" and the second the "size coat." Five different types of bonds are:

• *Glue.* Animal-hide glue can be used for both the bond and the size coat.

• *Glue and filler.* A hide glue, with filler added, produces a bond that is durable and strong. This is used both for the bond and the size coat.

• *Resin over glue.* The combination of pure hide glue for the bond coat and a synthetic resin for the size coat makes an abrasive that is extremely resistant to heat.

• *Resin over resin.* This is a synthetic resin used for both the bond and the size coats. It is not only heat-resistant, but also withstands moisture and humidity.

• *Waterproof.* This is a synthetic resin type used for the bond and the size coats on a waterproof backing. With this it is possible to use water and other liquids with coated abrasives.

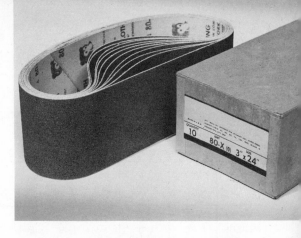

38-5. This is an aluminum oxide abrasive belt, with an "X" weight cloth backing, in a medium (80) grit. This would be used on a portable belt sander.

GRIT SIZES

Abrasives used in sandpaper originally come in chunks which are mechanically crushed. The broken particles are then sifted into certain grit sizes by passing them over a series of very accurately woven silk screens. The mesh of these screens (or number of openings per inch) ranges from very fine to very coarse. Mesh numbers are used to designate grit sizes. For example, grits that pass through a screen with 80 openings per linear inch are called grit size 80. The more openings per inch in a mesh, the smaller the opening. Therefore, grit sizes get finer as the number goes up.

In earlier years, an old grit size number system was arbitrarily adopted for sandpaper. This system is still used to some extent. For example, if you want a fine garnet paper, you would ask for garnet paper 120-C or garnet paper 3-0. Either request would get you the same paper. The letters A, C, D, and E after the grit

	Grit No.	0 Grade	Gen. Uses
VERY FINE	400 360 320 280 240 220	10/0 — 9/0 8/0 7/0 6/0	For polishing and finishing after stain, varnish, etc., has been applied.
FINE	180 150 120	5/0 4/0 3/0	For finish sanding just before staining or sealing.
MEDIUM	100 80 60	2/0 1/0 ½	For sanding to remove final rough texture.
COARSE	50 40 36	1 1½ 2	For sanding after very rough texture is removed.
VERY COARSE	30 24 20 16	2½ 3 3½ 4	For very rough, unfinished wood surfaces.

38–6.   Table of grit sizes. The 0 grade of grit No. 80 can be listed as either 1/0 or 0.

sizes designate the weight of the backing.

It is important to select the correct grit size for the work to be done. *Fig. 38–6* shows the range.

Kinds of Sanding in Relation to Grit Size. *Roughing.* This is a heavy sanding operation in which a maximum

38–7.   Sanding a duck decoy on a disc sander.

amount of material is removed with a coarse grit abrasive.

Blending. This is an operation in which medium grits are used for removing less stock and roughing, and for *general smoothing.*

Finishing. Finishing is done with finer grits. Its purpose is the removal of scratch patterns formed by the coarser grits.

Polishing or Rubbing. This is a burnishing action which removes or blends the fine scratch patterns of the finishing operation. Polishing or rubbing requires extremely fine grits, generally used with some kind of lubricant such as oil or water.

FORMS OF ABRASIVES

Abrasives are made in sheets, rolls, discs, and belts. The *sheets* are used for hand sanding and for oscillating sanders. They are available in almost every size, but the most common is 9″x11″. Smaller sizes are made to fit various brands of finishing sanders.

Rolls are used for drum sanding and spindle sanding. Narrower sizes are used for light clean-up jobs on a spindle sander; wider ones are used on high-speed drum sanders.

Discs are used for both portable and stationary grinders. They come in almost every diameter. Common sizes are 7″ and 9⅛″ diameters for portable electric grinders. The larger diameters are glued to the faceplate of a stationary grinder. *Fig. 38–7.*

Belts are used on belt sanders and are made in sizes to fit all machines from small portable grinders to large industrial equipment.

386

Selecting Coated Abrasives. Before selecting the coated abrasive, consider these four points:

• *What kind of material* is to be sanded? Is it a hard hardwood (such as birch), a soft hardwood (such as mahogany), softwood, plastic laminate, or still another material? Some ideas for selecting the correct abrasives for various woods are shown in *Fig. 38–8.*

• *Size, shape, and condition.* Is the piece easily handled, or is it large and bulky? Is the surface flat, or is it contoured? Will the product require maximum stock removal, or merely blending and polishing?

• *Equipment.* Is the item to be sanded by hand or will a machine be used?

• *Finish.* What should the finish be—rough, finish, polish, or a high lustre? This has much bearing on the grit or grit sequence to choose.

HAND SANDING

Hand sanding of wood is usually done with flint or garnet paper. In some cases, a sanding block is used, with a rubber back to which an abrasive is attached. The sanding block

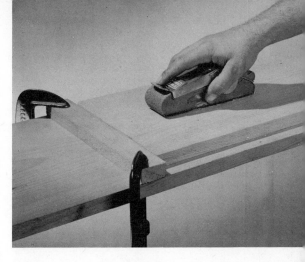

38–9. Using sheet sandpaper in a commercial holder. A better job can be done with less effort if the work is set up so that you can work freely and in comfort.

may be homemade or a commercial product. *Fig. 38–9.* If homemade, it should be the right size to hold one-fourth or one-sixth of a sheet of paper.

In hand sanding remember to do all sanding *with the grain.* When sanding end grain, always sand in one direction. *Fig. 38–10.* Apply just enough pressure to make the sand-

38–10. To sand end grain square, clamp the piece between scrap wood with edges flush.

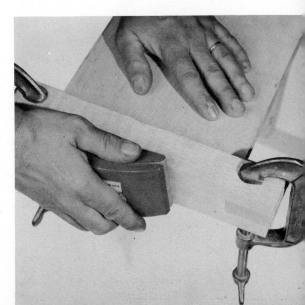

38–8. ABRASIVE CHART FOR USE WITH PORTABLE SANDER

Woods	Roughing	Blending	Finishing
Oak	2½ to 1½	½ to 1/0	2/0 to 5/0
Maple	2½ to 1	½ to 1/0	2/0 to 5/0
Birch	2½ to 1	½ to 1/0	2/0 to 5/0
Walnut	2½ to 1½	½ to 1/0	2/0 to 5/0
Mahogany	2½ to 1½	½ to 1/0	2/0 to 4/0
Gum	2½ to 1½	½ to 1/0	2/0 to 4/0
Curly Maple	2½ to 1½	½ to 1/0	2/0 to 5/0
Cypress	2½ to 1½	½ to 1/0	2/0

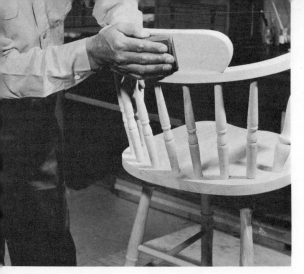

38–11. Made of resilient rubber, this sanding block is ideal for sanding curved surfaces such as the back of this captain's chair.

paper cut. Do not press so hard that it makes scratches. Clean off the sandpaper and the surface often with a brush. Do not sand surfaces that are to be glued because sawdust will fill the pores and prevent glue from holding. Never attempt to sand off pencil or knife marks; always plane them or use a scraper.

388

Most curved or irregular surfaces must be sanded by hand. Usually such surfaces are already quite smooth and can be finished with a very fine grade of sandpaper. Because of its flexibility, abrasive cloth is best for sanding deep cuts and curved work. Whenever possible, the sanding block should conform to the shape of the work. *Fig. 38–11.* A dowel of the right size sometimes serves as a good backing for sanding concave work.

MACHINE SANDING

Stationary Machines. *Belt-and-disc sanders* are the most common machines for sanding small parts that can be brought to the machine. Sometimes belt and disc are combined into one machine. *Fig. 38–12.* Both belt and disc types are equipped with a table so that a guide can be used. The disc sander is used to sand complex bevels, curves, and other small surfaces, and is especially useful in pat-

38–12. A combination belt and disc sander.

38–13. Parts of a disc sander.

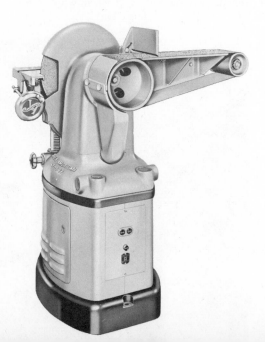

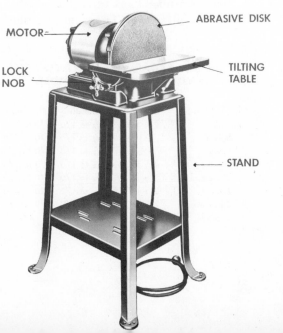

MOTOR

ABRASIVE DISK

LOCK NOB

TILTING TABLE

STAND

ternmaking. *Fig. 38–13.* The belt sander is used in sanding flat surfaces and edges. *Figs. 38–14 and 38–15.*

The belt sander can be located in a vertical, horizontal, or slant position by loosening the hand lock and moving the entire unit.

To install a new belt, first remove the drum guard. Release the tension on the belt, slip the old one off, and replace with a new one. Apply a slight amount of belt tension and then rotate the belt by hand to see if the belt stays on center. To track the belt, loosen the knob which controls the tilt of the idler arm, and tilt in one direction or the other. When the belt tracks properly, tighten and add belt tension.

To install a new sanding disc, first remove the old paper. If glue was

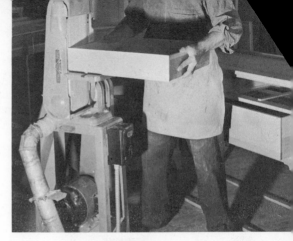

38–15.   Sanding the side of a drawer on a belt sander.

used, soak the disc in water to remove the old glue. If rubber cement or stick cement was used, turn on the machine and hold a hardwood stick against the disc. This will heat the disc and loosen the old adhesive. Then use some kind of adhesive (glue, rubber cement, or commercial stick cement) to apply a new disc. Apply the adhesive and put the new disc in place. Allow it to dry for a short time. *Fig. 38–16.*

38–16.   Installing a new disc on a disc sander. *a.* Applying the cement while the disc rotates.

38–14.   Parts of a belt sander.

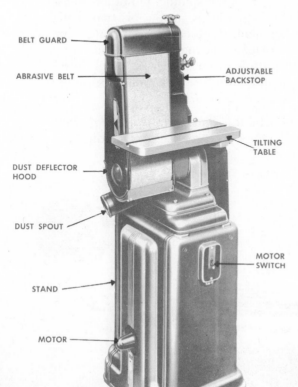

BELT GUARD

ABRASIVE BELT

ADJUSTABLE BACKSTOP

DUST DEFLECTOR HOOD

TILTING TABLE

DUST SPOUT

MOTOR SWITCH

STAND

MOTOR

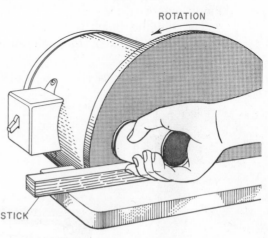

ROTATION

STICK

389

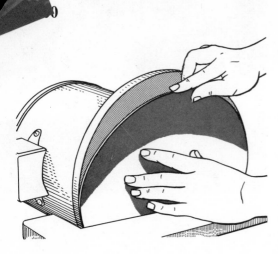

38–16b. Applying the new abrasive disc.

Hand-stroke or block-belt sanders have a long, continuous belt that moves around two drums. *Fig. 38–17.* A movable table rolls back and forth under the belt. A sanding block that may be attached to a metal arm or held freehand is used to apply the pressure for sanding. *Fig. 38–18.* This machine is used to sand large surfaces, such as table tops and the sides and tops of cabinets. In using this machine, the piece is laid on the movable table and the sanding is done in one of two ways:

• The sanding block is held lightly against the back of the belt and moved back and forth along the total length of the stock. Then the work is moved to a new position; or,

• You can sand all the way across one end of the stock and then move slowly toward the other end. There will be no excessive abrasive line if the cross movement is slow.

In either method, moldings and other irregular shapes can be sanded by using a special-shaped sanding block.

Spindle sanders have a revolving spindle on which the abrasive paper is fastened. *Fig. 38–19a.* The spindle moves up and down slowly to spread the wear and also to prevent the wood from burning. This machine is used primarily to sand edges and irregular-shaped curves. To replace the abrasive paper or cloth on a drum sander, remove the worn paper. Sometimes a wedge on one side holds the paper on the spindle. On other types, the spindle is made of two half-segments that can be separated for replacing the new paper. The large, multiple-drum sander is widely used in the furniture and millwork industries. *Fig. 38–19b.*

Portable Sanders. *Portable belt sanders* are excellent for sanding as-

38–17. A hand stroke or block belt sander.

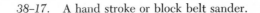

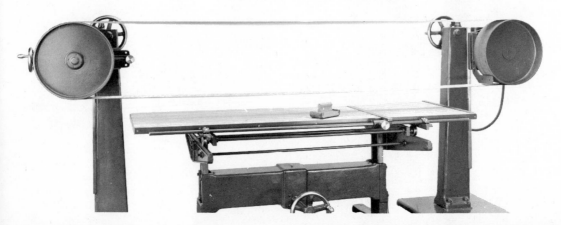

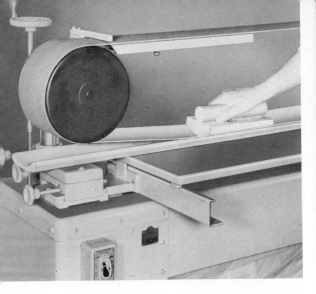

38–18. Sanding a concave surface, holding the sanding block freehand.

38–19b. Using a large drum sander to sand furniture parts.

sembled cabinet work. Heavy duty types are made for floor sanding. *Fig. 38–20*. Machine size is determined by the width and length of the belt. Common sizes are 2″ x 21″, 3″ x 24″ and 3″ x 27″. The belt should be spliced and installed on the sander

38–19a. A spindle sander. Notice that the table can be tilted.

so that a splice runs off the work. You will find an arrow stamped on the back of each belt which indicates the way in which the splice should run. When the belt has been placed on the pulleys, it can be made to run straight by adjusting the set screws. The belt should not rub along the left side of the machine. In using a portable sander, the following techniques should be followed:

38–20a. A portable belt sander.

391

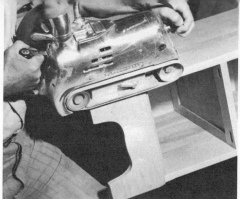

38–20b.   A belt-type floor sander.

38–22.   Portable belt sanders are great time and labor savers.

1. Place the cord over your right shoulder and hold the machine firmly in both hands.

2. Turn on the switch and then lower the sander so that the heel touches the work first. Then move the sander back and forth in straight lines. Never allow the sander to stand still for any length of time, since this will cut deep grooves in the wood.

3. When sanding fir or similar woods with hard and soft spots in them, always cross-sand a little first. If you always sand with the grain on these woods, the softwood will be cut out, leaving ridges on the surface. *Fig. 38–21.*

38–21.   Correct method of using a portable belt sander.

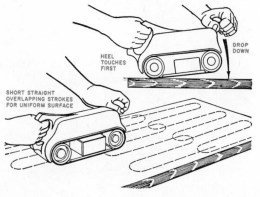

HEEL TOUCHES FIRST

DROP DOWN

SHORT STRAIGHT OVERLAPPING STROKES FOR UNIFORM SURFACE

4. When using a portable belt sander, work slowly and evenly.

5. In sanding a door, always sand the rails first, and then the stiles. *Fig. 38–22.*

Rotary-type sanders are excellent for fast, rough sanding. *Fig. 38–23.* They work well in corners where other sanders cannot reach. Never attempt to use the entire abrasive surface at once. This will cause the sander to bounce and gouge the surface. Make use of approximately the outer third of the circular sanding sheet, holding it as flat to the work as you can without touching more. Hold the sander firmly in both hands. Keep it moving in an even stroke to avoid scratching or gouging. Start at the outer edge of the disc and work in toward the center in long, sweeping strokes. Be especially careful at the edges of stock to keep from rounding them over.

There are many kinds of *finishing sanders,* but they all operate in one or more of the three ways shown in Fig. 38–24. The most common types are *orbital action* and *straight-line action.* Orbital action is good for rapid sanding, but straight-line action

38–23a. The portable disc sander is tipped slightly for most effective use of the abrasive.

is ideal for very fine finishing or for the last sanding.

These machines are relatively easy to use. *Fig. 38–25.* Clip a pad of paper or abrasive cloth to the base of the machine. Lower the pad to the surface, and work back and forth slowly. Again, be careful not to round the edges or ends of stock.

COMMON PROCEDURES IN SANDING

· Select the grade of abrasive, according to the kind of surface you want.

· Do all cutting operations before sanding.

· In general, sand with the grain when doing finish sanding. Use a "skimming" motion to guide the sander. Crossgrain sanding can be done to smooth the surface.

38–23b. Using a heavy-duty disc sander for sanding the edge of a hardwood floor.

· Sand surfaces, edges, and ends square.

· Sand all edges very slightly to prevent splintering.

· Always begin with the finest grit paper that will do the job. Coarse paper will scratch; finer papers are needed to get a really smooth job.

· Always come up to edges squarely without permitting the tool to overhang. If you are trying to round the edge, support some of the sander weight with your hands to prevent a too-fast cutting action. It is better to make several light passes rather than one heavy one.

· Use an open-coated paper to remove old paint or varnish. Select the grit coarseness to match the thickness of the paint.

38–24. The three kinds of action possible with a finishing sander. Orbital action is used for coarser sanding. Straight-line action produces a fine, satin-smooth finish.

 ORBITAL ACTION   STRAIGHT LINE ACTION   MULTI MOTION ACTION

38–25. A double-action finishing sander. This sander can be switched to either orbital or straight-line action. With this machine, work can be done ten times faster than by hand.

Unit 39: INSTALLING HARDWARE

The selection and installation of such items as hinges, handles, pulls, catches, and locks are very important because a home or a piece of furniture greatly depends on its hardware. *Fig. 39–1*. These items are manufactured in such a wide variety of sizes and kinds that only a few examples can be covered in this unit. Much hardware is too specialized to be available in the average hardware store or lumber yard and must be ordered from companies dealing specifically in these items.

Hardware has much effect on the final appearance of furniture and the home; therefore it should be of the correct design and quality. For example, in a colonial kitchen, the knobs, pulls, and cabinet hinges must carry out the colonial design. *Fig. 39–2*. Decorative hardware can be purchased in early American or colonial, traditional, and modern or contemporary styles.

39–1. Quality furniture should have quality hardware. This chest, made of solid pecan, select butternut, and rare myrtle burl veneers, has custom-designed, gold-washed hardware.

39–2. The hardware for this kitchen matches its colonial design.

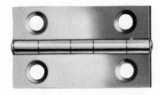

39–3. Butt hinges: *a.* Loose-pin hinge.

39–3*b.* Solid-pin hinge.

COMMON HARDWARE ITEMS

Hinges. The *butt hinge* is used for hanging most house doors and also many cabinet and furniture doors. For exterior doors, a ball-bearing hinge is best. Hinges for interior doors have either a loose or solid pin and are made of steel or brass. *Fig. 39–3.* Most hinges are swaged; that is, they have a slight offset at the barrel which permits the leaves to come closer together. A gain must be cut in both the jamb or frame of the door and in the edge of the door itself. In good home construction, three hinges should be installed on each door. The third hinge permits the butt-edge of the door to stay in alignment and prevents warping, which is a considerable problem when working with lightweight doors such as interior, screen, and combination. A warped door cannot be properly locked. *Fig. 39–4* gives a general rule for determining hinge size. The location of hinges for house doors is shown in *Fig. 39–5.*

39–5. LOCATION OF HINGES ON DOORS

Top hinge 5″ from jamb rabbet to top edge of barrel.

Bottom hinge 10″ from bottom edge of barrel to finished floor.

Third hinge centered between top and bottom hinges.

The above is the U.S. Standards procedure.

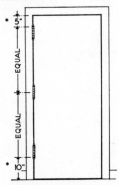

* certain western states use as standard 7″ from top and 11″ from bottom

39–4. RULES FOR DETERMINING PROPER SIZE OF HINGE

Door Thickness (Inches)	Width of Doors (Inches)	†Height of Hinges (Inches)
3/4 to 1 1/8 cabinet	to 24	2 1/2
7/8 and 1 1/8 screen or combination	to 36	3
1 3/8	to 32	3 1/2
	over 32	4
1 3/4	to 36	*4 1/2
	over 36 to 48	*5
	over 48	*6
2, 2 1/4 and 2 1/2	to 42	5) Extra
	over 42	6) Heavy

*Extra heavy hinges should be specified for heavy doors and for doors where high frequency service is expected.

†Width of hinges as necessary to clear trim.

NOTE: Height of hinge is always first dimension not including tips.

39-6. Surface hinges are quickly mounted. They require no gain, add an ornamental touch, and come in many styles. A pair of H or H-L hinges will do for most doors. For larger doors use a pair of H-L plus one H. T or strap hinges help prevent sag in larger doors.

Surface hinges are easy to install since they fasten directly to the front of the door and frame. They vary from simple strap hinges for storage units to decorative hinges in different styles. *Fig. 39–6.*

Cabinet hinges must be chosen according to the kind and style of door.

Semi-concealed hinges for lip doors are made in several styles such as contemporary or colonial, and for different door thicknesses. *Fig. 39–7.* To install them, first mark the location for the hinge on the inside of the door and fasten the hinge to the door itself. *Fig. 39–8.* Hold the door with the hinge against the frame. Mark the location of the screws, do the drilling, and install the hinge.

Semi-concealed *loose-pin hinges* offer the same appearance when the door is closed as ordinary butt hinges, since only the barrel shows. They are much better for flush plywood doors because screws go into flat plywood grain. *Fig. 39–9.*

Pivot hinges are inconspicuous. They are often used for fitting doors to cabinets without frames. *Fig. 39–10.* Pivot hinges are particularly useful on plywood and particle-board doors. Only the pivot shows from the

39-7. Two styles of semi-concealed hinges: *a.* Modern.

39-7b. Matched set of traditional hardware.

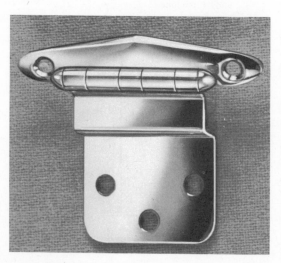

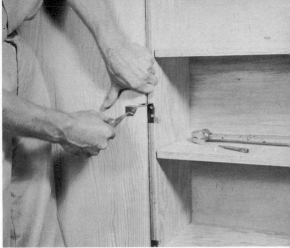

39-8. Overlapping doors (lip doors) are neatly hung with semi-concealed hinges. They are excellent for plywood since screws go into flat grain. These hinges have $\frac{1}{2}''$ inset, and are made for doors of $\frac{3}{4}''$ plywood rabbeted to leave $\frac{1}{4}''$ lip. Such hinges are made in many styles and finishes.

front when the door is closed. These units come in pairs for small doors, or three (called a pair and a half) for larger doors.

The *piano hinge* is continuous hinge material that can be cut to correct length. *Fig. 39-11.* This hinge is especially good for desks or cabinets with tops that can be lowered.

39-9. . Semi-concealed, loose-pin hinges.

39-10a. Pivot hinges give a neat, modern appearance to flush doors. They mount directly onto the cabinet side or top. Construction is simplified because no face frame is necessary. Only the pivot is visible from the front when the door is closed. Use a pair for small doors, three (called a pair and one half) for larger doors.

39-10b. Enlarged view of pivot hinge.

39-11a. Continuous (piano) hinge.

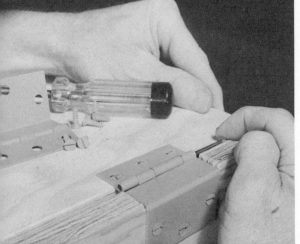

39–11b. Installing a piano hinge on a vanity chest.

39–12. One type of door support.

One of several types of supports is then used to hold the top in position when it is open. *Fig. 39–12.*

Double-acting butt hinges are installed on folding screens and doors so that the unit can be folded in either direction or flat. *Fig. 39–13.*

39–13. Installing double-acting butt hinges.

39–14. Concealed hinge.

Concealed or invisible hinges are installed on fine furniture when a flush door should not show but, instead, appear to be a flush panel. *Fig. 39–14.*

A dropleaf table hinge is designed with an offset so that the table leaf will not hang below the top of the table. *Figs. 39–15 and 39–16.*

Drawer Pulls and Handles. These come in a wide variety of designs and shapes. *Fig. 39–17.* It is important to purchase handles and knobs that match not only the styling, but the quality of the furniture or home. In

39–15. Two pairs of table-leaf hinges and two table-leaf supports are needed for this table.

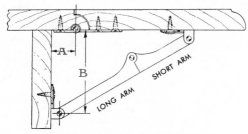

Dimension A (inches)	Dimension B (inches)		
	6″ Size	8″ Size	10″ Size
½	3½	3½	5
1	3¼	3³⁄₁₆	4¹¹⁄₁₆
1½	2¹³⁄₁₆	2⅞	4⁷⁄₁₆
2	2½	2½	4
2½	2⅛	2⅛	3⁹⁄₁₆

39–16. Table-leaf hinge and table-leaf support.

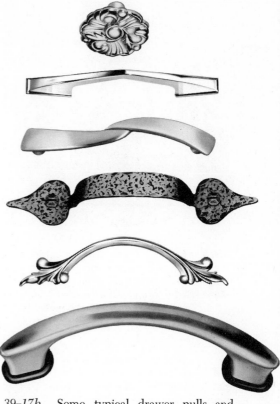

other words, choose first the style, and then choose a quality to match the cabinet or the furniture piece. A very good way to judge a piece of furniture in a showroom or store is by the quality of its hardware. Good furniture pulls and handles are made

39–17b. Some typical drawer pulls and handles.

39–17a. Drawer pulls and door handles come in a wide variety of styles and designs.

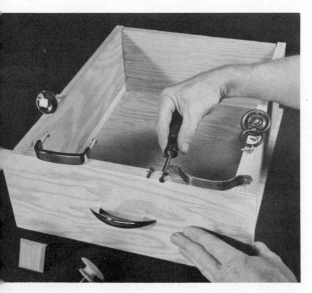

of solid brass. Some are silver or gold plated.

Door Trim and Accessories. Smaller cabinet sliding doors may have commercial *upper and lower guides* of aluminum, wood, or plastic. These doors are usually equipped with some kind of *finger cups. Fig. 39–18.* For larger doors, the cups are usually rectangular in shape. For larger sliding doors such as those in closet openings, complete sets of hardware can be purchased including track, hangers, trim, and accessories. *Fig. 39–19.*

The common kinds of *door catches* are friction, "snap grip," roller, mag-

399

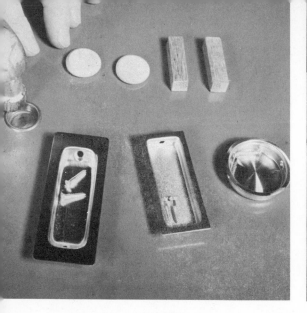

39–18. Sliding doors are equipped with finger cups. For large doors, use rectangular cups or large, round ones. A round pull, shown at the top, is suitable when clearance between the doors is adequate.

39–20. Two metal brackets are fastened to the top of each door with a pair of screws. Nylon wheels with ball bearings roll in a double-lipped track fastened to the door frame with screws. Single-lipped track is also made for single doors.

39–19. Rolling or sliding doors for closets and large storage units may have rollers mounted either at the top or bottom. Top-mounted hardware usually is smoother in operation.

netic, and ball. *Figs. 39–21 and 39–22.* There is also a hook-type catch which will hold one side of a double door closed while the other is pulled open.

There are many types and qualities of *lock sets* and *latches* found in the home. Some outside doors have locks with key slots and with both a latch bolt and a dead bolt. The dead bolt can be turned from the inside for added security. *Fig. 39–23.* Other types have a locking device on the inside (but no key) for use on bathroom and bedroom doors. Still others have no locking device at all.

Most door locks are installed by boring two holes: a large one from one side to the other and a smaller one from the edge into the larger hole. Other types require a notch or cut-out in the door before installation.

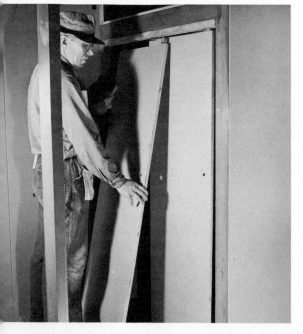

400

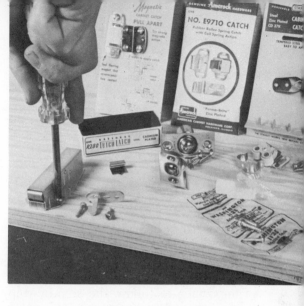

39–21. Common kinds of catches: *a.* Friction.

39–22. Catches come in many varieties besides the conventional friction catch shown at the extreme right. Touch type, being installed here, lets the door open at a touch. Magnetic catches, which have no moving parts, are the most popular for good-quality furniture and kitchen cabinets. Roller catches and the ones made of plastics work better than simple steel friction catches.

39–23. Several types of door lock sets and latches. *a.* Entrance key lock.

39–21b. Magnetic catch.

39–23b. Passage lock.

401

39–23c.   Privacy lock.

For furniture and cabinets, small locks can be purchased. Complete instructions for installation are packed in the box by the manufacturer. It is important to follow the step-by-step procedure. *Fig. 39–24.*

Other Hardware. There is an endless variety of specialty hardware for the home. This includes items for closets, kitchens, garage doors, exterior hardware for screens and storm windows, gate hardware, and many others.

39–24.   Cabinet locks: *a.*   Cylinder-cam type.

39–24b.   Surface-mounted,   with   plate tumbler.

39–24c.   Surface   mounted   with   lever tumbler.

39–24d.   Wardrobe with barrel key.

Section D

CHECK YOUR KNOWLEDGE

1. Describe joinery.
2. Tell how to square up stock by the machine method.
3. Woodworkers do not agree on the exact procedure for squaring up stock on machines. Explain the possible reason for this.
4. Give the approximate number of wood joints.
5. Name four ways of strengthening a wood joint.
6. Name the most important end joint and give the reason for its importance.
7. Give the primary use of butt joints.
8. Tell where the rabbet joint is most commonly located in case construction.
9. Name the kind of dado joint to use when it should not show from the front.
10. Name three kinds of lap joints.
11. Tell how a miter joint can be strengthened.

12. Many people confuse the mortise with the tenon; describe each part of this joint.
13. Tell why a miter joint with a rabbet is a good one for plywood.
14. Tell how to lay out a dovetail dado joint.
15. Describe the terms "adhesive" and "glue."
16. Name some of the common problems in gluing wood.
17. Name the clamps that you would use to glue up a table top.
18. Name the clamps that can be used

402

without any protective scrap blocks on a finished surface.

19. Tell how to prepare wood for gluing.

20. Describe one type of glue.

21. Name the kind of glue that you would select for boat work.

22. Tell how to check for good gluing.

23. Describe laminating.

24. Tell why laminating is so important in building construction.

25. Name the points that should be remembered in laminating wood.

26. Describe several methods of bending wood.

27. Explain the difference between laminated stock and plywood.

28. Describe a shop method of bending and laminating.

29. Name four kinds of wood fasteners.

30. Name the kind of tool used in assembling parts for a pre-fabricated home.

31. Name the four kinds of general-purpose nails.

32. Name four special-purpose nails.

33. Give five ways in which nails differ.

34. Describe two common methods of nailing in building construction.

35. Tell where non-ferrous metal nails should be used.

36. Tell how splitting of wood can be minimized when nailing.

37. Name the common shapes of wood screws.

38. Describe a Phillips-head screw driver and name the kind of screw head for which it is designed.

39. Tell, in thousandths, the size or diameter of a number seven screw.

40. Describe the particular value of a spiral-type screw driver.

41. Tell how to install a flathead wood screw.

42. Describe a molly bolt and tell where it is used.

43. Name some common household fasteners.

44. Define an abrasive.

45. Name the five common materials used for abrasives.

46. Name three materials that are used for the backing of abrasives.

47. Explain how grit size of abrasives is indicated.

48. Compare the old grit-size number system with the present system.

49. Name three forms in which abrasives are available.

50. Describe how you should select the correct type of coated abrasive.

51. Compare the action of a belt sander and a disc sander.

52. Explain the three operating principles of finishing sanders.

53. Describe how a rotary type sander should be used.

54. Name five kinds of cabinet hardware.

55. Explain the matching of hardware to the style of furniture.

56. Name three kinds of catches.

THINGS TO DO

1. Visit a furniture store and see how many different kinds of joints you can find on the furniture. Make a report.

2. Make a sample of at least one kind of joint.

3. Glue several small pieces of wood together with different kinds of glues. Test them.

4. Write a report on one of the synthetic glues.

5. Study the history of nails. Find out when the first metal nails were used.

6. Make a display board of as many different kinds of nails as you can find.

7. Visit a house now under construction. Find out how many different kinds of metal fasteners are being used.

8. Make a survey of your area to find a building in which laminated beams or arches are used. Find out why this kind of structural material was used in place of steel or cement.

9. Make a project of laminated construction.

10. Write a report on the manufacture of silicon carbide and aluminum oxide.

11. Make a display panel of different kinds of hardware.

403

Section E

MAJOR PRODUCTION AREAS

Almost all production areas in woodwork were needed to make this vacation dreamhouse possible. The house itself was the work of carpentry and related building trades. The furniture and built-ins were the result of applying cabinet-making techniques to furniture production. Painting and finishing protect and beautify it. Even patternmaking played its part. The plumbing fixtures and some of the hardware for the home and furniture started out as wood patterns.

Unit 40: CABINETMAKING

Cabinetmaking deals not only with the making of cabinets, as the name might imply, but also with the construction of furniture, doors, windows, built-ins, and other finished wood products. This work is done in in cabinet shops where furniture and cabinets are made to specifications, in furniture manufacturing plants, in mill rooms of lumber yards, in factories where doors, windows, and other stock items for the building trade are made, and by the carpenter or cabinetmaker who does finished work on the job. *Fig. 40–1.* This section describes some of the common standards of joinery, assembly, and workmanship. There are many other special situations in which the work must follow the specifications and drawings that have been laid out by the designer or architect. The methods described here are accepted by most craftsmen.

FURNITURE AND BUILT-IN CONSTRUCTION METHODS

There are five basic ways in which furniture and built-ins are put together. Sometimes these methods are combined.

Skeleton or Leg and Rail. This is found in most standard chairs, tables, and benches. *Fig. 40–2.* It usually consists of four legs and four or more rails. The structural parts are solid wood while the others are lumber core plywood. The rails are joined to the legs with dowels and corner blocks. Some cabinet shops still produce the mortise-and-tenon joint; however,

40–1. A small cabinet shop specializing in kitchen cabinets.

40–2.   Both the table and the chairs illustrate leg-and-rail construction.

with modern glue, the dowel-and-corner block is just as strong.

Box. A box consists of four sides with the grain running in the same direction, and a bottom. *Fig. 40–3.* The corners are joined with any satisfactory joint, ranging from a simple butt joint to a fine box or dovetail joint. The bottom of the box may be fastened against the sides, rabbeted into it, or installed in a groove around the inside. The box may or may not have a cover. A drawer is an example of a simple box.

40–3.   The top of this interesting sewing table is really a box with interior dividers and a cover.

40-4.   This small night stand is a good example of case construction.

40–6a.   Use of frame construction makes it possible to utilize thinner plywood and other panel materials.

Case Construction. This is really a box turned on its side or end. It is found in chest construction, bookcases, cabinets, and most built-ins. *Fig. 40-4.* The back is usually made by cutting a rabbet around the inside. The front may be trimmed with molding and/or with doors that are fastened in the opening. The shelves may be fixed or adjustable.

Carcass. The carcass is an enclosed cabinet, usually having doors and drawers. *Fig. 40-5.* Frequently, it is made of panel construction. The difference between case and carcass construction is largely that case work involves fewer internal details.

Frame with Cover. In constructing some built-ins, cabinets, closets, and similar storage units, a light frame is built. Then the exterior is covered with plywood, hardboard, or similar panel stock. *Fig 40-6.*

40–5.   A beautiful cabinet made of French walnut and cherry, illustrating carcass construction.

40–6b.   Building a storage unit.

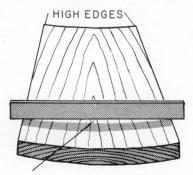

HIGH EDGES

LIGHT SHOWS UNDER STICK

40-7.   How wide boards will cup.

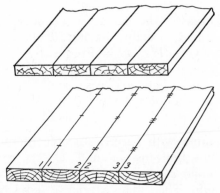

40-8.   The proper arrangement of pieces before gluing. Fit the pieces together. Then mark or number the adjoining surfaces so you won't make a mistake when gluing up.

40-9a.   Applying veneer edging material.

MATERIAL FOR LARGE AREAS OR SURFACES

There are three common ways of covering large areas or surfaces in furniture and cabinetmaking.

Glued-up Stock. When a large area of solid wood is needed for such things as table tops, the material must be glued up. One of the problems encountered in working with large surfaces of solid wood is warping. Wide boards tend to cup as snown in *Fig. 40-7*. To avoid this, stock that is eight or more inches in width is usually cut into narrower widths, about four to six inches. The surfaces and edges are dressed so you can find out the quality of the surface. Then the pieces are arranged in such a way that: *Fig. 40-8*.

• The grain runs in the same direction in all pieces.

• The color and grain match as well as possible.

• The joined pieces are placed with the annular rings on the ends in opposite directions. This is done to compensate for the warping tendency.

• The pieces fit properly.

After this is done, the pieces are glued together with a plain edge joint. If necessary, the edges may be strengthened with dowels or splines.

Plywood, Particle Board, and Hardboard. Plywood and other man-made materials to a large extent have replaced solid glued-up stock for use in large surfaces and areas. Lumber core plywood is commonly used in furniture construction, while that used for built-ins is veneer-core plywood. The major problem in using

408

plywood is treating or covering the edges, which are unattractive if left exposed. The most common procedure today is to apply commercial edging material made of thin veneer. *Fig. 40–9a.* To install it, the cloth backing strip is removed and the edge attached to the plywood with contact cement. Manufactured parts of furniture, such as the tops of tables and chests, are made with an edge of solid wood to match the veneer. Several methods of treating edges of plywood are shown in *Fig. 40–9b.*

Panel or Frame Construction. Panel or frame construction is used for large areas of doors, drawers, desks,

40–10. The sliding doors on the front of this cabinet are of panel construction.

40–9b. Several methods of covering the edges of plywood.

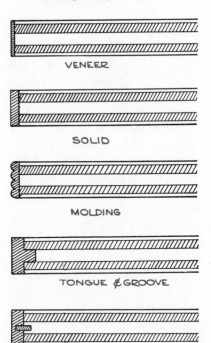

VENEER

SOLID

MOLDING

TONGUE & GROOVE

SPLINE

and other case and carcass work, both for structural and design purposes. *Fig. 40–10.* The chief advantage is that there is less warping than with solid pieces. A frame is made of vertical parts called *stiles* and horizontal members called *rails.* *Fig. 40–11.* There may be two or more rails, depending on how many panels are to be installed in a single unit. The center rails are called intermediate or lock rails.

In making a frame, the rails are joined to the stiles with one of several types of joints (*Fig. 40–12*): dowel, open mortise-and-tenon, stub mortise-and-tenon, or haunched mortise-and-tenon. A groove or a rabbet is cut around the inside of the frame to receive the panel. *Fig. 40–13.* This panel may be plywood, hardwood, glass, metal, or any other suitable material. *Fig. 40–14.* Panels are made as follows:

1. Measure the overall size of the frame. Cut the stiles and the rails to correct length to provide for the necessary joint.

409

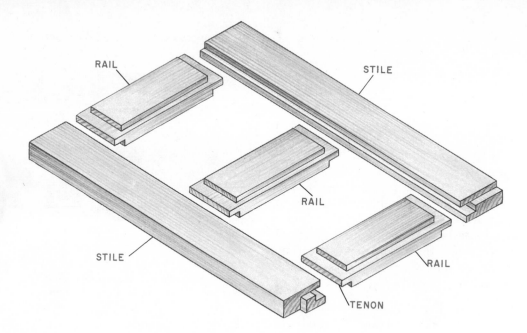

RAIL

STILE

STILE

RAIL

RAIL

TENON

40–11. Parts of a typical panel or frame.

40–12. Kinds of joints used in making a panel or frame.

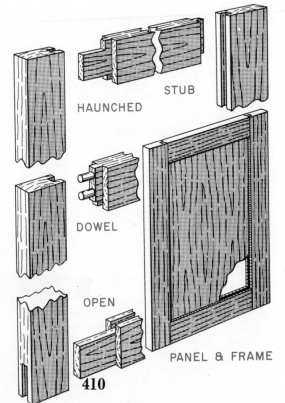

HAUNCHED

STUB

DOWEL

OPEN

PANEL & FRAME

410

2. Square up the stock.

3. Join the rails to the stiles. In making a stub mortise-and-tenon, the thickness of the tenon is the same as the width of the groove, and the length of the tenon is the same as the depth of the groove. In making a haunched mortise-and-tenon joint, the thickness of the mortise should be the same as the width of the groove. The mortise should be started far enough away from the ends of the stiles to prevent breaking out. The width and depth of the mortise should be about two-thirds the width of the rail. The length of the tenon should be equal to the depth of the mortise plus the depth of the groove. Cut a notch in the tenon so that the long part will fit into the mortise opening, and the short part into the groove.

4. Lay out and cut a groove or a rabbet on all edges on which the panel is to fit. The groove or rabbet

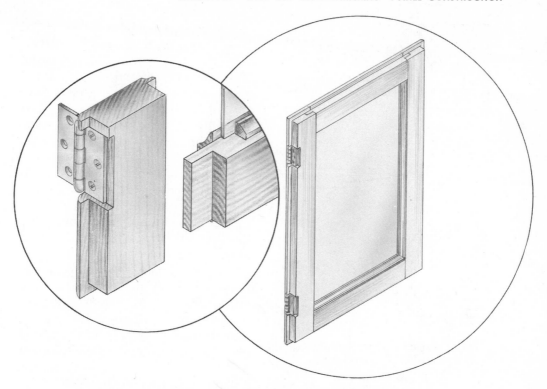

40–13.   This panel door has a rabbet cut around the inside to receive the glass.

should be as deep as or slightly deeper than it is wide. If the inside of the frame is to be decorative, both the groove and the decorated edge can be cut on the shaper. *Fig. 40–15.*

5. Make a trial assembly of the panel in the frame. Then take it apart and wax the edge of the panel. In gluing up the panel, apply the glue to the joint itself but never to the groove. In some cases, panel construction is done with a rabbet cut around the inside edge of the frame; in this way, the back side of the panel may be flush or recessed. In this construction, the panel must be glued or fastened in place.

411

40–14.   Note that the center of these door panels is of specially designed metal grill work.

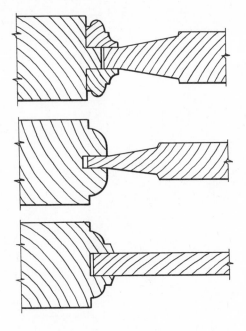

40–15. Decorative edges installed on the inside edge of a panel surface.

Some doors really can be called panels because, as in panel construction, the door consists of two stiles and a number of rails and mullions which surround panels of wood, glass, and other materials. *Fig. 40–16.* A stile-and-rail door should be made with either a blind mortise-and-tenon or a doweled corner. If dowels are used, the length of the dowel should be approximately the same as the width of the stiles. The diameter of the dowels should be about one-third the thickness of the stiles. In blind mortise-and-tenon construction, the tenon should be approximately three-fourths of the rail width. The inside edges of the stiles and rails should be shaped (called *sticking*) as shown in *Fig. 40–17.* The sticking may be made for flat panels, raised

40–16a. Panel door construction with glass.

412

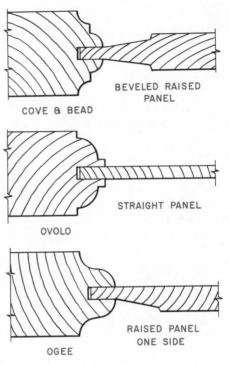

COVE & BEAD

BEVELED RAISED PANEL

OVOLO

STRAIGHT PANEL

OGEE

RAISED PANEL ONE SIDE

40–16b. Panel door construction with solid center.

40–17. Standard stickings are the Cove and Bead, the Ovolo, and the Ogee.

panels on one side, or raised panels on both sides. All mullions (intermediate rails) should be doweled into the adjoining stiles and rails.

LEG-AND-RAIL CONSTRUCTION

There are several ways in which legs can be joined to cross rails. It is important to take great care in attaching legs to rails since, in this kind of construction, there is a tendency for the legs to spread apart. When weight is added a great deal of strain is put on the joint. One method is to use a blind mortise-and-tenon joint: the corner can then be strengthened with a wood or metal corner block. *Fig. 40–18.* The most common construction in furniture manufacture is dowels and a corner block in place of the mortise-and-tenon. *Fig. 40–19.* A third common way is to use open mortise-and-tenon joints. *Fig. 40–20.* These are somewhat simpler to make since the open mortise can be cut on a circular saw.

CASE CONSTRUCTION

In constructing a box or case, the first problem is to decide on the kind of corner joints to have. For exposed corners, the best are the rabbeted miter and the blind spline miter. De-

413

tails on cutting and fitting these joints are described in Unit 34. In case work, all solid partitions or dividers (such as drawer frames) should be dadoed into the other members. *Fig. 40–21.* Use either a plain dado or a blind dado. If the case or box is to have a back, a rabbet should be cut around the back sides. The rabbet should be cut just deep enough to take the plywood or hardboard panel. However, if the unit is to fit against the wall, the rabbet should be cut as deep as $\frac{1}{2}''$ to $\frac{3}{4}''$. The remaining lip can then be trimmed, if necessary, to get a good fit against the wall. *Fig. 40–22.*

In constructing the case work for a desk or chest (carcass construction), you must decide if the frames

or dust panels between the drawers are to be exposed at the front or if the drawers are to cover these panels. If the frame is to be exposed, the front of the frame should be made of

40–19a. Leg-and-rail construction using dowels.

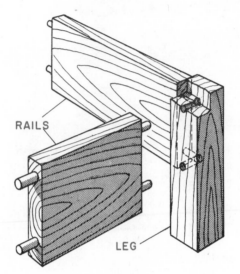

RAILS

LEG

40–18. A mortise-and-tenon with a corner block used in leg-and-rail construction.

40–19b. A commercial corner block or brace.

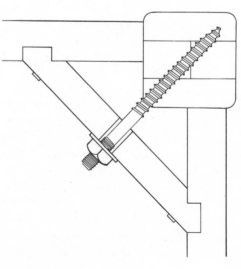

414

the same wood as the case itself. *Fig. 40–23*. If the drawer front will cover the edge of the frame then a less expensive wood can be used. *Fig.*

40–20. An open mortise-and-tenon joint for leg-and-rail construction.

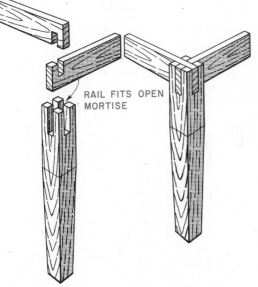

RAIL FITS OPEN MORTISE

40–21. Case construction with dividers that are dadoed into the case.

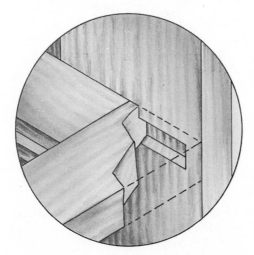

40–24. In the best furniture construction, thin plywood or hardboard is used in each frame (panel construction) to keep the dust out. An open frame is often used in less expensive construction. A frame edge (molding or facing) is often attached to the front of case work. The corners

40–22. Fitting a simple case against a wall.

40–23. Note that in this chest the dust panels or frames are exposed; therefore the front must be made of the same material as the case exterior.

should be made with miter joints. *Fig.
40–25.* Whenever two adjoining
members meet at right angles, construction can be strengthened by use
of *glue blocks*. These are small, triangular pieces of wood that are glued
and/or nailed in place on the inside
or back of the case, where they will
not interfere with appearance or
function.

CARCASS CONSTRUCTION

As has been indicated before, a
carcass consists of a case in which
there are drawers and/or doors. The
case itself may be solid wood, plywood, or panel construction. Most
furniture manufacturers prefer plywood.

Fitting Doors. (Review Unit 39 on
Installing Hardware.) There are
many kinds of doors that can be
made to cover an enclosure. Before
construction is started, it is important
to decide on the kind of door and

40–24a. A chest in which the frames are
covered by the drawer fronts.

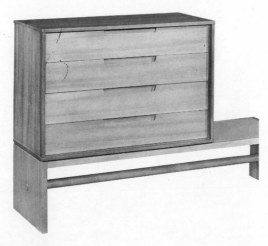

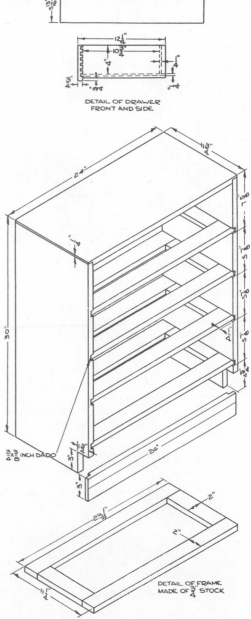

DETAIL OF DRAWER
FRONT AND SIDE

40–24b. Another chest showing internal
construction of the frames in the case
Here, too, the drawers cover the frames.

416

40-25. Fitting an edge molding on a case.

hinge to be used. Some of the most popular kinds of doors are:

Flush Door in Frame. If the front of the case or carcass has a frame, the door may fit flush into it. Then, butt hinges or surface hinges can be used. *Fig. 40–26.* Most fine furniture has butt hinges for better appearance, but

40-26. Note the flush doors on this corner cupboard.

this requires that a gain be cut both in the door and in the frame. Very careful fitting is necessary. Surface hinges are much easier to use. They require no mortising and they can add a decorative touch since they come in many styles. If a double door is to be hung in the opening, the two may join at center so that either can be opened. In other words, each door has a straight edge. A wood or metal stop will keep the doors from closing too far. A rabbet stop can be cut so that the right door must be opened first. *Fig. 40–27.* For good appearance,

40-27. A commercial-type case with a rabbet stop. This cabinet has a lip door.

417

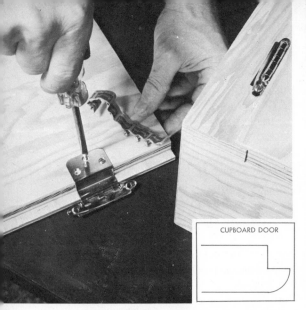

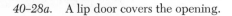
CUPBOARD DOOR

40–28a.   A lip door covers the opening.

40–28b.   Fitting a lip door to a cabinet.

and to take care of any shrinkage in the door, a groove can be cut on the adjoining edges of the two doors.

1. Check the opening of the frame with a square. Sometimes the opening is slightly "out of square," in which case the door must be carefully cut to fit.

2. Measure the inside height of the door frame at several points and cut off the top and bottom of the door so that it will slip into the frame. It may be necessary to hold the door up to the opening several times and plane off a little to get it to fit.

3. Measure the width of the opening at top and bottom. Transfer this measurement to the door and cut to fit.

4. Place the door in the frame opening and check it carefully. The lock side is frequently cut at a slight bevel so that, when the door swings open or closed, the inside edge will not strike the frame and yet the door will be tight when closed.

418

Lip Door. A lip door is easier to fit since it covers the frame of the door itself. *Fig. 40–28.* A rabbet is cut around the four edges of the door, and the outer edge is rounded. It can be hung with either butt or semi-concealed hinges. Semi-concealed hinges are excellent for plywood since the screws go into the face grain. The hinges should be purchased before the lip door is cut because the depth of the rabbet cut determines the hinge dimensions. The ones shown in *Fig. 39–8* have a $\frac{1}{2}''$ insert and are made for $\frac{3}{4}''$ plywood doors that are rabbeted to leave a $\frac{1}{4}''$ lip.

Doors without Frames. Sometimes the door itself covers the edges of the case or carcass. *Fig. 40–29.* Pivot hinges are used. A slightly angular cut is made at the top and another at the bottom of the door so that the hinge itself does not show when the door is closed. This gives flush doors a neat, modern appearance. They are mounted directly on the cabinet sides. Construction is simplified because no face frame is necessary. Only the pivot is visible from the front when the door is closed. You can use a pair for small doors, a pair and a half for larger ones.

Drop Door. A drop door is one which opens from the top and drops down to form a flat surface. *Fig. 40–30.* This can be used for a desk or any other writing surface. Almost any kind of hinge can be installed along the bottom edge although a piano hinge is best. Several types of support hardware can be purchased to hold the door open at right angles to the case.

Sliding Doors. Sliding doors are commonly used when space is limited or when a regular door would take up too much room. *Fig. 40–31.* Sliding

40–30. Using a piano hinge to add a drop door to this cabinet.

doors are also commonly used with glass for safety reasons.

There are several ways of making a sliding door. The simplest is shown

40–29. This compact storage unit has a door without frames.

40–31. This medicine cabinet is a good illustration of the useful sliding door.

40–32a. This sliding door is made by attaching some cleats to the inside of the cabinet unit.

in *Fig. 40–32.* Another simple method is to cut two grooves in the top and two more in the bottom edges of each door. Then a rabbet is cut on the back of the front door and the front of the back door. This leaves the

40–32b. Grooves for sliding doors.

doors almost touching; there will be only a small gap for dust. If the doors are made of plywood, seal all the edges. To make the doors removable, cut the groove at the top twice as deep as the one at the bottom. Then the door may be inserted by pushing it up into the extra space in the top groove and dropping it into the bottom. Special track made of wood, metal, or plastic can be purchased for doors of wood, glass, or hardboard. *Fig. 40–33.* In some cases, this track is designed in such a way that the doors roll on ball bearings.

40–33. Sliding doors in a commercial cabinet.

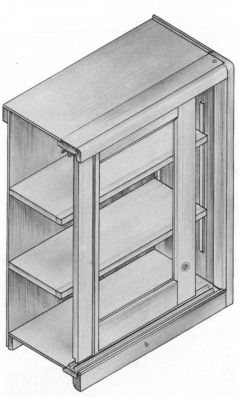

40-34. The door is held up with small wedges while the location of the hinges is marked.

Installing Butt Hinges. Usually a door is hung by two hinges; however, if it is to support great weight, a third is installed at the middle. The butt hinges should be proportioned to the size of the door. A 1″ butt hinge, for example, would be satisfactory for a 1- to 2-foot door, a 2″ hinge for a 2- to 4-foot door, and a 3″ hinge for doors that support considerable weight. See Unit 39.

1. Place the door in the opening and put small wedges below one or both sides to hold the door in place. Measure up from the bottom and down from the top, and mark the door and frame to indicate tops and bottoms of the two hinges. *Fig. 40-34.* Remove the door from the opening.

2. With a try square, continue the line across the edge of the frame and the door to indicate the position of the hinge.

3. Place the hinge over the edge of the door and determine how far it is to extend beyond the door. Draw a line to indicate the depth of the hinge. Do this on both door and frame.

4. Measure the thickness of one leaf of the hinge and set a marking gauge to this amount. Mark the door and the frame to indicate this depth.

5. A gain (the opening for the hinge) is usually cut by hand with a chisel, as shown in *Fig. 40-35.* Outline the gain and then cut small notches in the stock to be removed. Trim out the gain. *Fig. 40-36.* If a portable router is available, this job can be done quickly. See Unit 29.

6. Place the hinge in the door edge, drill pilot holes for the screws, and attach the hinge.

40-35. The gain has been partly chiseled out. Next, cut away excess stock to form the opening.

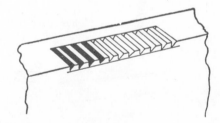

40-36. A gain ready to receive the hinge.

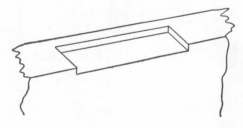

421

40–37a. Simple methods were used in making this drawer.

7. Hold the door against the frame, mark the position of one hole on either hinge, and drill a pilot hole. Insert one screw in each hinge.

8. Check to see if the door operates properly. If the door stands away too much from the frame side, it may

be necessary to trim the gains a little more. This should be done toward the front edge of the frame. If the door binds on the hinge side, cut a little piece of cardboard to go under the hinge. When the door operates properly, install the other screws.

DRAWERS

There are many kinds of drawers but the three most common are: flush drawer in a frame, lip drawer, and flush drawer without a frame. The simplest drawer has a rabbet joint that fastens the front to the side, and a butt, rabbet, or rabbet-and-dado joint that holds the back to the side. *Fig. 40–37.* The bottom of the drawer can be nailed to a rabbet that has been cut out of the sides and front; or it can be fastened in a groove that has been cut in the sides and front. *Fig. 40–38.* Better joints for fastening the front of the drawer to the side are the drawer corner joint (sometimes called a rabbet-and-groove joint) and the dovetail joint.

40–37b. This drawing shows easy techniques commonly used in drawer-making.

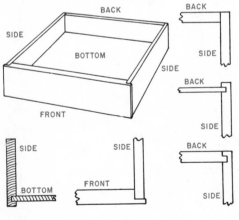

40–38. Sliding the bottom of the drawer into the grooves cut in the sides and front of the drawer.

422

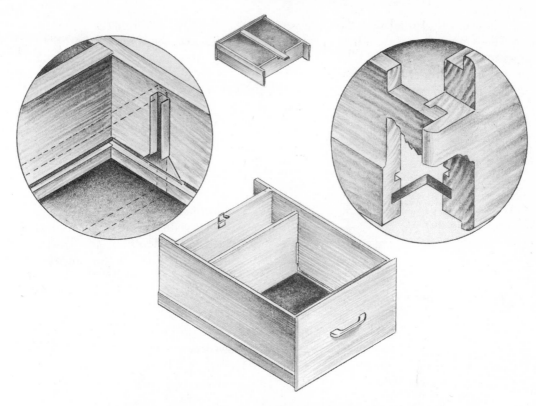

40–39a.   Commercial drawer construction on a lip drawer.

40–39b.   The dovetail joint used in drawer construction.

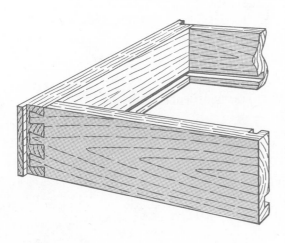

Fig. 40–39. The dovetail joint is found in the best furniture. The back can be joined to the sides with either a dado or a rabbet-and-dado joint. Drawer fronts can be made with the front covering the dust-panel frame or with the dust-panel frame exposed.

Determine the Size of the Drawer. Measure the opening (both height and width) into which the drawer will fit. There should be a clearance of about ⅟₁₆″ on either side and ⅟₁₆″ for height. Also measure the depth of the drawer. *Fig. 40–40.*

423

Choose the Wood for the Drawer. The front should match the rest of the project and should be as thick as or slightly thicker than the other parts. Usually the front is ¾″ thick. The sides and back should be about ½″ thick in a clear lumber such as pine, willow, oak, or maple. The drawer bottom is most often made of ⅛″ or ¼″ plywood or hardboard.

Joints. The four most common joints for fastening the front to the sides are the rabbet, the drawer-corner joint (rabbet and groove), the dovetail, and the dovetail dado.

The *rabbet* is made by cutting a recess on the inside of either end of the front. The depth of the rabbet should equal two-thirds the thickness of the front. The width should be slightly more than the thickness of the sides to allow for clearance.

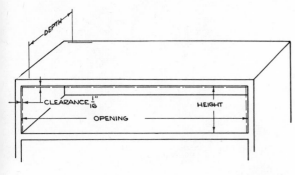

40-40. Measuring the size of the drawer front.

40-41a. Steps in making a drawer corner joint.

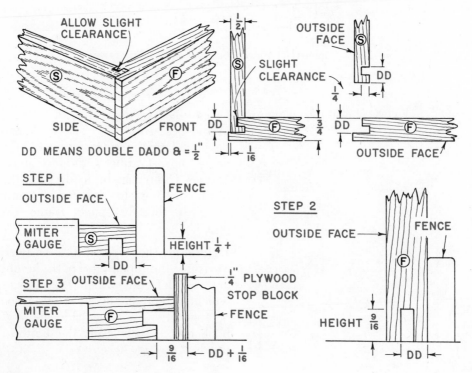

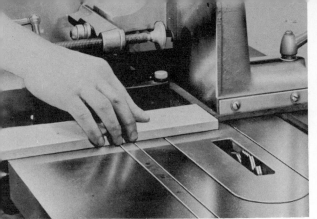

40–41b. Cutting dado in sides.

The *drawer-corner joint* is often used to fasten the sides to the front because it is strong and easy to make on the circular saw. *Fig. 40–41* shows this joint made with a ¾″ drawer front and ½″ sides. A clearance of ¹⁄₁₆″ is allowed for the front to extend beyond the sides. The steps in making this joint are as follows:

1. Use a dado head that is ¼″ wide. Adjust the dado head to a height of slightly more than ¼″. Set the ripping fence to a distance of twice the width of the dado head measured from the left edge of the blade (double dado), or ½″. Cut dadoes on the inside face of the sides at the front end.

2. Set the height of the dado head to an amount equal to the thickness of the sides plus ¹⁄₁₆″ (for front overlap), or ⁹⁄₁₆″. With the inside face of the front held against the fence, cut a dado across both ends of the front.

3. Set the dado head to a height of slightly more than ½″. Adjust the fence to a distance of ⁹⁄₁₆″ from the left edge of the dado head. Use a piece of ¼″ plywood for a stop block. Place the inside face against the

table and trim off ⁵⁄₁₆″ from the inside tenon of the drawer front. The joint should slide together easily. Sometimes the joint is made with a narrow dado and a thin tenon.

Make a *dovetail joint* by using the portable router. (See Unit 29.)

The *dovetail-dado joint* (not to be confused with the dovetail joint) is used to join the sides to the front when the case is made without a frame. The front of the drawer overlaps the sides of the case to cover them. *Fig. 40–42.* The method of cutting this joint is described in Unit 34, *Joinery.*

Decide on the Back Drawer Joints. The back can be joined to the sides with a butt joint, a dado, or a rabbet-and-dado. If the dado joint is used,

40–41c. Cutting dado in front.

425

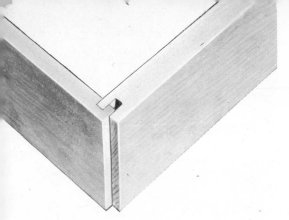

40–41d. Joint ready except for cutting off of tenon.

it should be located at least ½″ from the back edge of the drawer sides.

Cut the Pieces for the Drawer. If the drawer is to fit flush, the front should be cut ⅟₁₆″ narrower and ⅛″ shorter than the opening measurements. If a lip drawer is being constructed, add ¾″ to this width and length. The length of the sides is found by measuring the overall depth of the drawer opening and then allowing for the kind of joint used in the front. The back is cut ½″ narrower than the front so that it will rest on the drawer bottom. The back is also cut somewhat shorter.

40–42. The dovetail-dado joint used in a cabinet.

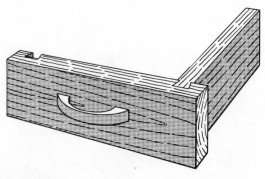

Join Sides to Front and Back. Follow the joinery construction that you have selected.

Cut the Groove for the Bottom. Cut a groove ⅛″ or ¼″ wide and ¼″ deep, at least ¼″ from the bottom of the drawer on the inside of the front and sides. Cut the bottom itself slightly smaller than the full width and length of the drawer to allow for expansion. If a center guide and runner (or slide) are to be used, the bottom may have to be located slightly higher than ¼″ from the lower edge of the drawer.

Assemble the Drawer. Assemble the drawer by fastening the sides to the front with glue and/or nails. Slip the bottom in place but never apply glue to the edges. Fasten the back to the sides.

Make the Drawer Guides. There are several kinds of drawer guides. The simplest is the guide and runner which is placed under the lower corners of the drawer. First, cut two pieces of stock long enough to go between the front and back rails. A rabbet which forms the guide and runner for the drawer is then cut out. These guides and runners are fastened in place by gluing and/or screws.

The side guide and runner is made by cutting a groove along both sides of the drawer. *Fig. 40–43.* This can be located anywhere on the side, usually toward or slightly above center. Two pieces of stock (cleats) are cut long enough to extend between the front and back of the chest or case. The cleat runners are fastened from

40–43. Here you see the use of a side guide and runner.

40–44. This drawer slides in dado slots cut into the side of the cabinet.

the front to the back on the inside sides of the case so the drawer can slide along them. The procedure can be reversed with a dado cut in the side of the chest or case. *Fig. 40–44.*

The best drawer guide is the center drawer guide and runner. The guide is fastened to the frame of the chest or desk, or between the front and back rails. *Fig. 40–45.* The runner or slide is then fastened to the center of the bottom of the drawer. The drawer guide is simply a rectangular piece of stock, usually rounded in the front. A second rectangular piece (slide) of stock has a groove cut along its length which slides over this guide. When installing the guides to a frame, such as in chest construction, a rabbet is cut out of the front of the guide; the guide is then glued and/or screwed in place. The slide or runner is glued to the bottom of

40–45. Center guide and runner.

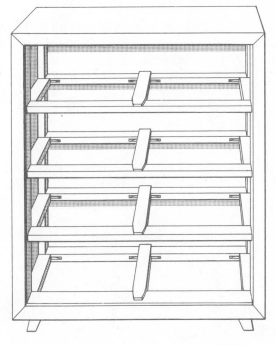

427

the drawer and oftentimes a few brads are installed to hold it firm. A notch must also be cut out of the bottom of the drawer back to provide clearance for the guide. Plastic-head tacks nailed to the frame under the sides of the drawer will make drawers open and close much easier. In commercial cabinet construction, the track and slide may be reversed. Drawers can also be made with tapered sides so that they will slide easier and stay in alignment. *Always apply a good coat of paste wax* to the guide and runner. *Never paint or finish* these parts of the cabinet. *Fig. 40–46.*

For heavy drawers such as those for letter files, special metal guides should be fastened to either side of the drawer or under the center. *Fig. 40–47.*

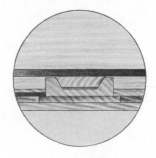

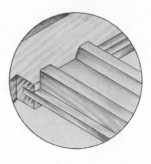

SOME COMMON OPERATIONS

Fastening Tops to Tables and Cabinets. The top on a table or cabinet can be fastened in place in several ways as shown in *Fig. 40–48.* The most common method is to install a metal bracket that will hold the top firmly in place.

40–46b. Typical commercial drawer guide construction with slide (guide) attached to the drawer bottom and the track (runner) below. The top picture is a sectional view showing the drawer bottom (heavy dark horizontal line) with the dovetail-shaped guide attached to it. The runner is also dovetail shaped so that the drawer will stay in perfect alignment even after the guide becomes worn. The lower picture shows how the runner is attached to the frame.

40–46a. Typical cabinet with four drawers removed showing track and frame support.

40–47a. Metal, commercial drawer-guide unit.

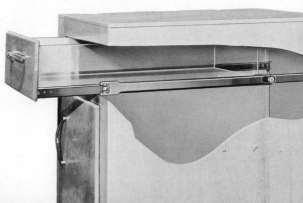

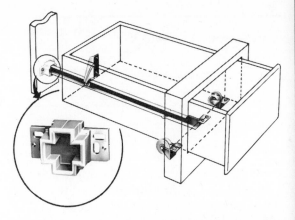

40–47b. Another commercial drawer-guide unit. The plastic end bracket (circled) can be nailed, stapled, or screwed.

40–48. Methods of fastening the tops to tables: (left to right) square cleat; square cleat with rabbet and groove; metal table top fastener.

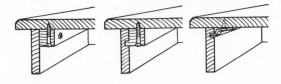

40–49a. Ways of installing shelves: *a.* Dowel pins. *b.* Metal shelf pins. *c.* Fixed shelf brackets. *d.* Adjustable shelf brackets.

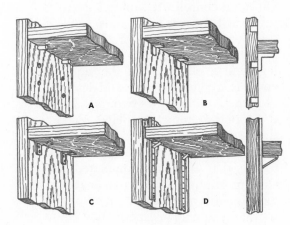

40–49b. Here you see the use of the metal shelf pins. Blind holes $\frac{5}{8}''$ deep are drilled in the side of the cabinet. Drill additional holes to permit moving the shelves when desired.

Installing Shelves. Modern furniture is often adaptable to several uses; therefore most shelves are made to be adjustable. There are several methods of doing this. *Fig. 40–49.* When installing the adjustable shelf brackets with snap clips, cut two vertical grooves for the hardware to fit into. Then the ends of the shelves can be cut square.

Commercial Legs. Many kinds of commercial legs are available for modern furniture. They are made of wood or metal in straight, round, tapered round, straight square, and

429

tapered square styles. Wood legs usually have a brass ferrule at the lower end. The metal legs are made of steel, aluminum, or brass. Steel and brass legs can be ordered with different finishes such as pewter, dull brass, chromium, or silver. *Fig. 40–50.*

Dropleaf Table Joint. A dropleaf table joint (sometimes called a rule joint) is used for many coffee and

40–51. Dropleaf table joint.

40–50. Types of commercial legs and brackets.

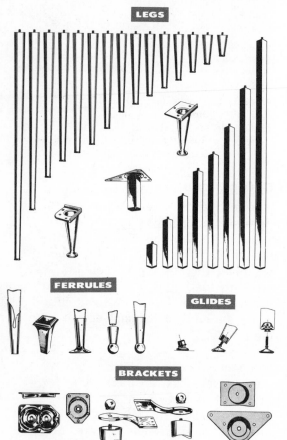

LEGS

FERRULES

GLIDES

BRACKETS

dining room tables. *Fig. 40–51.* The joint can be cut on a shaper or router. Two matching bits are required: a beading bit to use on the table itself and a cove bit on the table leaf. On scrap stock, use the beading bit first and adjust to the correct depth. Then make a cove cut on other scrap stock of the same thickness as the stock to be used. Check for fit. Use these pieces as templates in adjusting the machine for cutting the joint. Table-leaf hinges and supports are needed as hardware. See Unit 39.

ASSEMBLING FURNITURE

The steps in assembling a project are determined largely by how complicated it is. On simple projects, all parts can be assembled at one time. On more complicated ones, such as a table with four legs, rails, and a top, it may be a two- or three-stage job. It is often better to glue the two legs and a rail to form the sides or ends as a sub-assembly and later to glue these to the other two rails. Then the top is fastened in place. Follow these steps:

1. Get all parts together and check to see that they are completed, including sanding. Make sure that you have identification marks on all pieces so that you know exactly how they

430

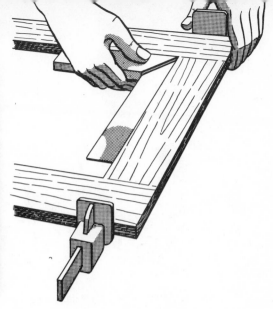

40–52. A project must be clamped properly before it is allowed to dry.

40–53. Checking the assembly with a square.

are to go together. Check this and see that all joints fit properly.

2. Decide on whether the project is to be assembled with glue, screws, or nails. Most furniture pieces have screws and glue as part of the assembly.

3. Cut a number of pieces of scrap stock that will be used to protect the wood from the clamps.

4. Get out the clamps and adjust them to the correct openings.

5. If sub-assemblies are to be glued up, decide on which parts are to be assembled first.

6. Make a temporary assembly of the parts to see that the piece will clamp up properly. *Fig. 40–52.* At this point check with a square and rule to see that the parts are parallel and level and at correct angles to each other. *Fig. 40–53.* This can usually be done by measuring at various points. *Figs. 40–54 and 40–55.* Sometimes it may be necessary to do a little hand trimming or to shift the clamps.

7. If screws are to be used, select the right ones by consulting the chart. In most cases, the size of the screw is shown on the drawing or print. For example, No. 9 R.H. $1\frac{1}{4}$, means that the screw is No. 9 gauge size, roundhead, and $1\frac{1}{4}''$ long.

8. When assembling with glue, mix only the amount needed at one

40–54.   Checking across the corners.

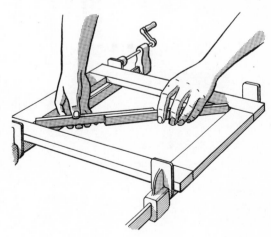

431

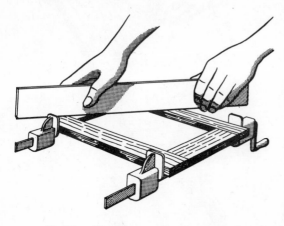

40–55. Checking with a straightedge for levelness.

time. Many kinds must stand for 10 to 15 minutes before they can be used. Cover the top of the workbench with paper. Lay the clamps out in proper position. Have the scrap blocks and a rubber mallet ready. Also have a square and rule nearby.

9. Carefully apply the glue to the joints. Be careful not to put on too much. Apply a little extra glue on the end grain, which soaks it up.

10. Quickly assemble the parts, place the scrap pieces over the project, and apply the clamps. Do not apply too much pressure. Then quick-

40–56. First step in completing the built-in is to install the dividers.

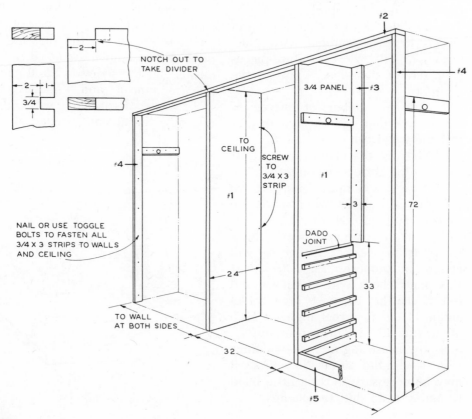

DRAWERS

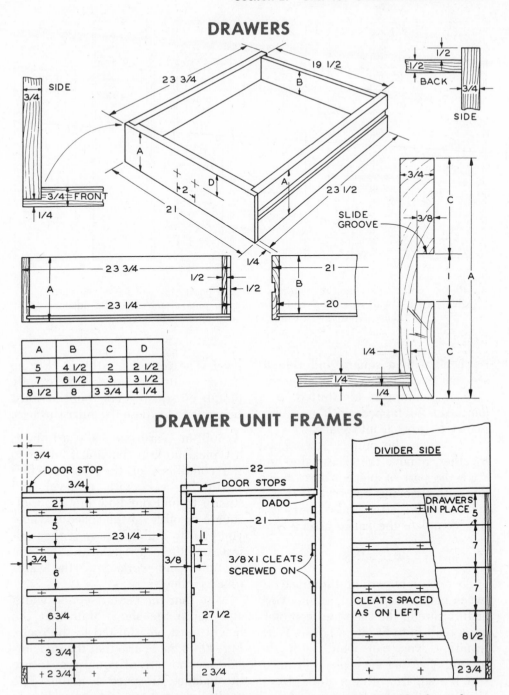

A	B	C	D
5	4 1/2	2	2 1/2
7	6 1/2	3	3 1/2
8 1/2	8	3 3/4	4 1/4

DRAWER UNIT FRAMES

40–57. Building one drawer unit for the closet. Cut and assemble the eight drawers according to the plans and dimensions in the top drawing.

433

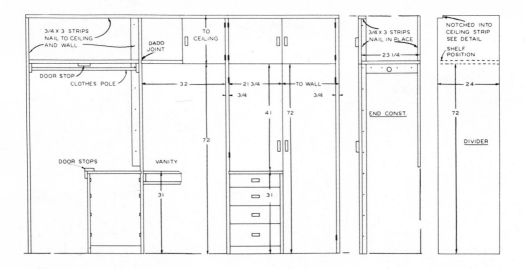

40–58. Schematic of entire wardrobe. At this point you will have two vertical dividers from wall to ceiling and two drawer units attached to the outside of these two dividers. From here on, progress will be rapid.

ly check with a square and rule to see that everything is true. If necessary, a clamp can be shifted or a joint can be tapped with a rubber mallet to bring it into place.

11. When the project is clamped together, remove the excess glue and store the part or piece where it can dry without being bumped. If it is a sub-assembly, after these parts are dry, complete the entire assembly.

BUILT-INS

There is an important difference between making a piece of cabinetwork or furniture in the shop and completing a built-in to fit into a house. With furniture, you can work with the square, checking each piece to make sure it is square with the other pieces. With a built-in, however, a good deal of preliminary work is done with the

level. The reason for this is that no house walls or floors are exactly plumb or square. The built-in must be made to fit these irregular surfaces.

A Built-in Wardrobe. A wardrobe is a typical built-in that must adjust to the conditions of the room. Before starting, check with a level and square to find out how much out-of-square or off-level the space is where you plan to build. You must then adjust for these irregularities as you continue your work. Start the wardrobe as follows:

Note that the center section width and depth are shown but that the height must be adjusted to the room. *Fig. 40–56.* Note also that the two outside sections are of equal size to use the balance of space available. The vanity section and the two drawer sections will be of definite size. The

434

outer doors must fit the opening. Locate and mark on the floor where the two dividers will be installed. From each of these marks measure from floor to ceiling to determine the height of the dividers. Cut the two vertical dividers (#1) out of $\frac{3}{4}''$ plywood. Cut the ceiling strip (#2) and notch it and the two dividers. Fasten the ceiling strip (#2) in place with

nails driven into the ceiling joists. You can use toggle bolts fastened to the lath and plaster. Use a level and a square to locate the position of the rear braces (#3). Fasten them with toggle bolts.

Cut dadoes on the inner faces of the dividers for the bottom of the storage section above the vanity, and on the outer faces for the two tops

40–59.   Building the second drawer unit.

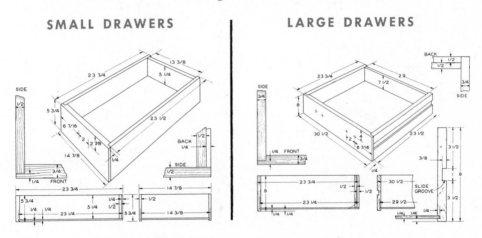

SMALL DRAWERS   LARGE DRAWERS

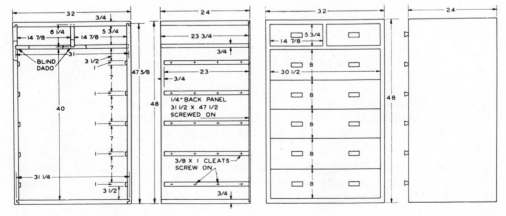

Make two of the small drawers shown first in the above illustration and five of the large drawers in the illustration.
Then construct the frame as shown in the plan below.

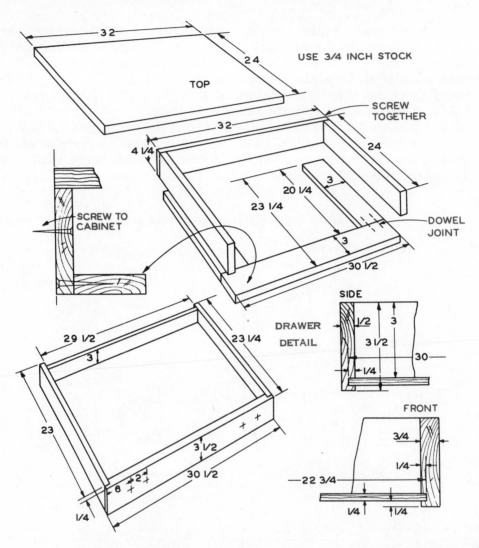

40-60. Building the vanity shelf drawer and support. Note that this complete unit is assembled and the frame screwed to the two vertical dividers. The vanity top is supported by the frame and the drawer fits flush below it.

of the drawer units. If there is slope in the floor, compensate for this when cutting these grooves. Notice in *Fig. 40-58* that the top of the drawer unit and vanity should be 31″ from the floor. To get these three surfaces level it may be necessary to vary this dim-

ension slightly on each vertical member. Cut the two grooves and nail the divider in place. Then stand the other divider in place and use a yardstick and level to mark the correct height of the corresponding dado in the left hand divider. Take this divider down and cut the grooves, and then install the left hand divider permanently.

Measure from the floor to the ceiling strip at each end. Cut two vertical end strips (#4). Lower braces (#5) will help hold vertical dividers solidly. Complete the drawer units as shown in *Figs. 40–57 through 40–59.*

In building the drawer sections, make adjustments for any slope in the floor. Before cutting the side support, hold the material in position at the proper distance from the main divider and, with the yardstick and level, determine the exact height needed. Front cross pieces below the lowest drawer (shown on the plan as

$2\frac{3}{4}''$ high) should be tapered to off-set for floor slope so that the top is level when the finished piece is in place. In other words, if there is a floor slant of about $\frac{1}{8}''$ between the two sides of the drawer units, this face should be marked $\frac{1}{8}''$ wider at the lower end. With this base as a guide, mark the positions of the drawer cleats and install them on both sides. Then fasten the frame in place as shown in *Fig. 40–58.* Cut and install the center shelf for the vanity table. *Fig. 40-60.* Cut the cleats and clothes poles as shown and install them. These cleats will support the two outside upper shelves which should be cut as shown in *Fig. 40–61.*

40–61.   Completing the base of the upper unit.

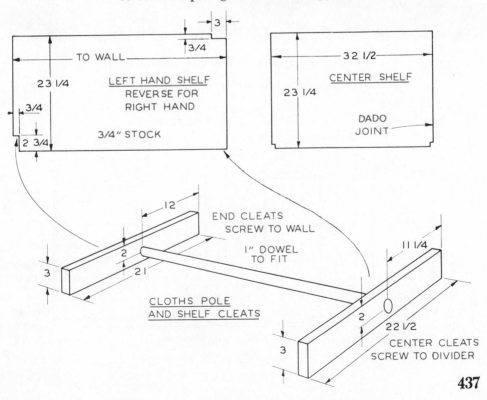

40–62a. Another example of built-in furniture.

40–62b. General suggestions for completing the back wall.

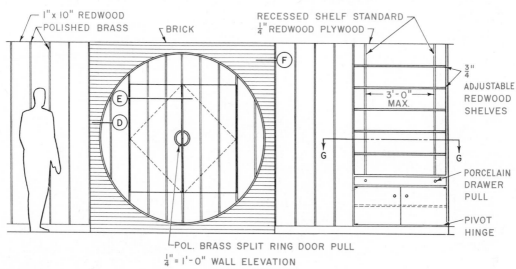

1" x 10" REDWOOD
POLISHED BRASS
BRICK
RECESSED SHELF STANDARD
¼" REDWOOD PLYWOOD

F

E
D

3'-0"
MAX.

G

¾"
ADJUSTABLE
REDWOOD
SHELVES

G

PORCELAIN
DRAWER
PULL

PIVOT
HINGE

POL. BRASS SPLIT RING DOOR PULL
¼" = 1'-0" WALL ELEVATION

438

Cut two lower doors to fit spaces above the drawer units with about $\frac{1}{8}''$ clearance below the upper shelf. Install these two drawers. Cut and fit the two upper center doors with the bottoms coming flush over the center shelf. Cut the two upper inside doors above the door and drawer units that have been completed. Measure and cut four outside doors to fit the actual dimensions of the spaces where they will go. In fitting, allow a little space between the doors and frames since all of the openings will decrease about $\frac{1}{16}''$ when the painting is completed. *Fig. 40–62.*

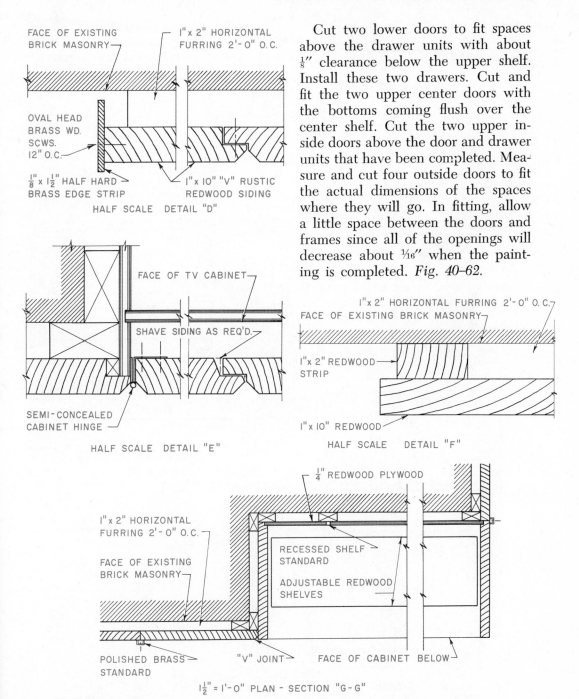

FACE OF EXISTING BRICK MASONRY

I" x 2" HORIZONTAL FURRING 2'-0" O.C.

OVAL HEAD BRASS WD. SCWS. 12" O.C.

$\frac{1}{8}$" x I$\frac{1}{2}$" HALF HARD BRASS EDGE STRIP

I" x I0" "V" RUSTIC REDWOOD SIDING

HALF SCALE DETAIL "D"

FACE OF TV CABINET

SHAVE SIDING AS REQ'D.

SEMI-CONCEALED CABINET HINGE

HALF SCALE DETAIL "E"

I" x 2" HORIZONTAL FURRING 2'-0" O.C.

FACE OF EXISTING BRICK MASONRY

I" x 2" REDWOOD STRIP

I" x I0" REDWOOD

HALF SCALE DETAIL "F"

$\frac{1}{4}$" REDWOOD PLYWOOD

I" x 2" HORIZONTAL FURRING 2'-0" O.C.

FACE OF EXISTING BRICK MASONRY

RECESSED SHELF STANDARD

ADJUSTABLE REDWOOD SHELVES

POLISHED BRASS STANDARD

"V" JOINT

FACE OF CABINET BELOW

I$\frac{1}{2}$" = I'-0" PLAN - SECTION "G-G"

40–62b. Cont'd. All four drawings on this page show details of the drawing on page 422.

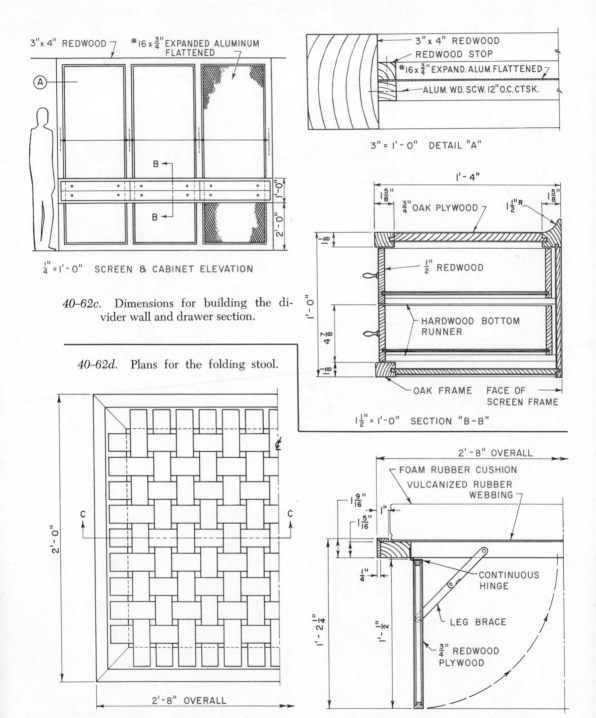

3"x 4" REDWOOD   #16 x $\frac{3}{4}$" EXPANDED ALUMINUM FLATTENED

(A)

$\frac{1}{4}$" = 1'-0" SCREEN & CABINET ELEVATION

3"x 4" REDWOOD
REDWOOD STOP
#16 x $\frac{3}{4}$" EXPAND. ALUM. FLATTENED
ALUM. WD. SCW. 12" O.C. CTSK.

3" = 1'-0" DETAIL "A"

40–62c. Dimensions for building the divider wall and drawer section.

40–62d. Plans for the folding stool.

1'-4"

$\frac{3}{4}$" OAK PLYWOOD   1$\frac{1}{2}$" R

$\frac{1}{2}$" REDWOOD

HARDWOOD BOTTOM RUNNER

OAK FRAME   FACE OF SCREEN FRAME

1$\frac{1}{2}$" = 1'-0" SECTION "B-B"

2'-8" OVERALL

FOAM RUBBER CUSHION
VULCANIZED RUBBER WEBBING

CONTINUOUS HINGE

LEG BRACE

$\frac{3}{4}$" REDWOOD PLYWOOD

2'-8" OVERALL

1$\frac{1}{2}$" = 1'-0" STOOL PLAN

1$\frac{1}{2}$" = 1'-0" STOOL SECTION "C-C"

440

Unit 41: MANUFACTURE OF FURNITURE AND OTHER WOOD PRODUCTS

The manufacture of wood products differs from other types of manufacturing, principally metal, plastics, and rubber, primarily because the raw material is a natural product and, therefore, has many variable features. *Fig. 41–1.* Each carload of lumber differs from every other in grain pattern, moisture content, density, and color. Veneer cut from two different logs of the same wood also varies in these respects. For this reason, wood manufacturing must adapt itself much more to the materials than most other industries.

PRODUCTION MACHINES

Many of the machines used in the manufacture of wood products are not found in the average school shop. These machines do the same operations as those performed on smaller woodworking equipment, but faster and more efficiently. A few of the more common pieces of machinery and equipment are:

Double Planer and Surfacer. This combines the operations of two machines: a power jointer and a planer. *Fig. 41–2.* When it is used to ma-

41–1. Two pieces of furniture are never exactly alike. Even these matching chairs vary slightly.

41–2. This machine does the work of both planer and jointer.

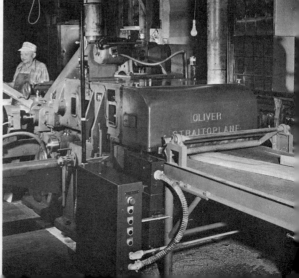

chine moderately warped or twisted stock, it takes boards up to 8′ long. In a standard planer it is necessary to plane one surface true before a board is run through the surfacer. However, on the double planer and surfacer both operations of straightening a board and planing it to thickness are done at the same time. The finished boards are perfectly straight and uniformly thick. *Fig. 41–3.*

Gang Rip Saw. The gang rip saw will cut off stock, rip it to width, and cut grooves. *Fig. 41–4.* For example, the eight identical drawer fronts

41–3. Before and after planing and surfacing. This is a pile of four-quarter stock as it usually appears after ripping and cut-off operations. These boards are warped, both lengthwise and crosswise. Formerly the only way to straighten these boards was to face joint one side and then plane to thickness. The double planer and surfacer does both operations in one pass. The finished boards are perfectly straight and of uniform thickness.

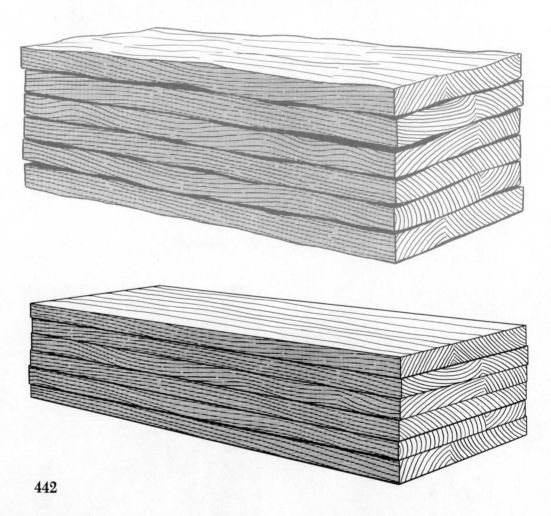

41-4.   A gang rip saw.

41-5.   These eight identical drawer fronts were ripped and grooved in one pass on a gang rip saw.

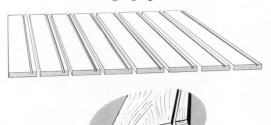

(*Fig. 41-5*) were ripped and grooved in one pass on this machine.

Tenoner. The tenoner is either a single- or double-end machine. The single tenoner works about as follows: two tenon heads on horizontal arbors are mounted on the front of the stand. The stand is placed on a frame to form the base of the machine. *Fig. 41-6.* The two arbors have independent horizontal adjustment and either independent or unison vertical adjustment. The machine is designed to do tenoning and joint cuts, and will cut off stock to length. The tenoner is used in furniture production for building cabinets, chairs, doors, and other millwork. A double tenoner can be set to the length of the piece and both ends cut and shaped at the same time. *Fig. 41-7.* Some other kinds of cuts that can be done on the

41-6a.   A single-end tenoner.

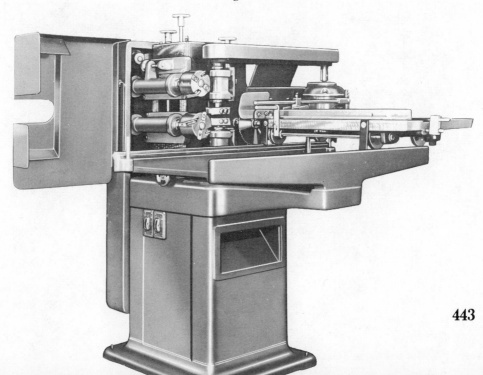

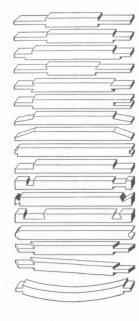

41-6b.   Samples of work done on a single-end tenoner.

41-7b.   Using cope heads on the tenoner to make end grain cuts.

double tenoner are shown in *Fig. 41–8.*

Double-End Cut-Off Saw. The double-end cut-off saw is similar to a double-end tenoner. It will not only cut stock to exact length or width, but also makes tongue-and-groove joints, special lock-miter box joints,

41-7a.   A double-end tenoner in use.

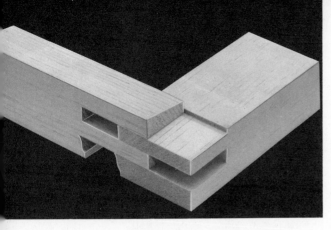

and open mortise-and-tenon joints. *Fig. 41–9.*

Automatic Lathe. The automatic lathe is used to turn parts such as legs, spindles, and arms. *Fig. 41–10.* It can also be used to shape the irregular fronts of drawers and other rectangular parts on one side only.

41–7c. The completed joint.

41–8. Examples of typical cuts and joints made on a double-end tenoner.

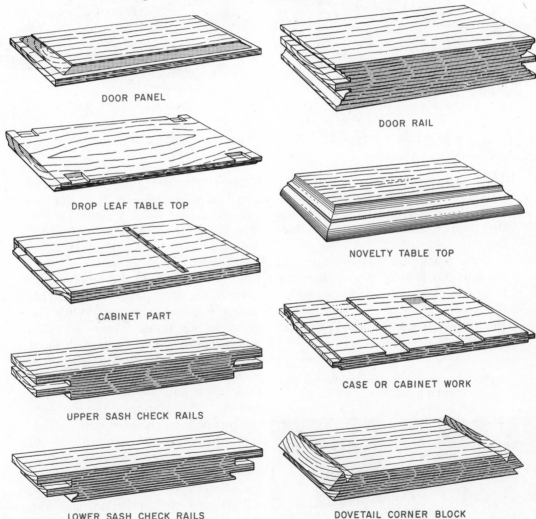

DOOR PANEL

DOOR RAIL

DROP LEAF TABLE TOP

NOVELTY TABLE TOP

CABINET PART

CASE OR CABINET WORK

UPPER SASH CHECK RAILS

LOWER SASH CHECK RAILS

DOVETAIL CORNER BLOCK

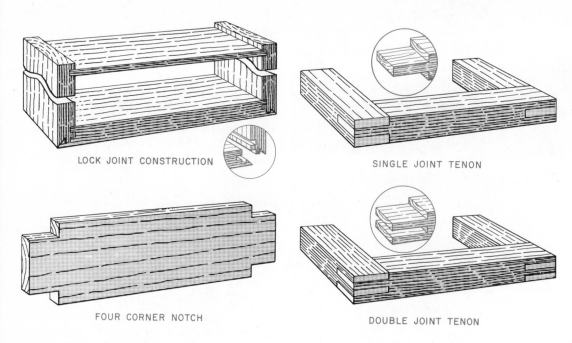

LOCK JOINT CONSTRUCTION

SINGLE JOINT TENON

FOUR CORNER NOTCH

DOUBLE JOINT TENON

41–8 Cont'd. Typical joints and cuts made on a double-end tenoner.

There are several kinds of automatic lathes. Many of them have automatic feed; the wood can be loaded into the hopper and the machine does the rest.

Basic parts of the lathe are: (a) A shaft on which the cutters are mounted. (b) Centers between which the pieces of stock fit; this unit is then moved against the revolving cutters.

41–9. Double-end cut-off saw being used to cut a panel door to width.

Shapers. Shapers are available in two common types. The *double-spindle shaper* is used with two cutters of the same shape which run in opposite directions. *Fig. 41–11.* With this machine the operator can shift from one spindle to the other as the grain in the workpiece changes. This makes it possible to work with the grain at all times. There are also *single-spindle shapers,* although these are not so common. The shaper is used to cut or shape the edges of table tops and to cut grooves and moldings. A variation of the shaper is the *molding machine* or *sticker*. This takes strips of wood and, with one to four cutters, shapes simple or complex forms. These machines are designed for straight work. As a result, the cutters are well guarded and the

446

41–10.   Automatic shaping lathe.

41–11a.   Double-spindle shaper.

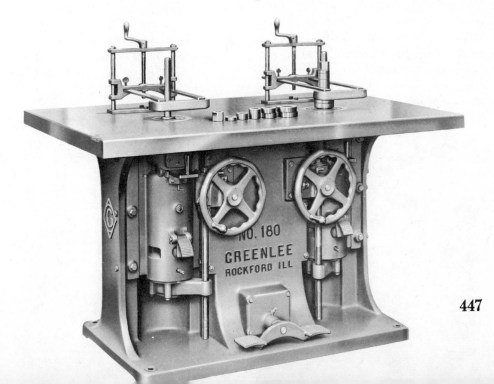

447

41–11b. Molding machine or "sticker."

work can be fed in at a predetermined rate.

Automatic shapers are very important in production work. On this machine the work is clamped to a table and the spindle guided in the desired path by a roller that forms the pattern. *Fig. 41–12.* The automatic shaper is capable of generating graceful curves and radii important in the shaping of wood parts, particularly legs and arms of chairs and tables. The operator loads the part into the machine one, two, three, or more parts at a time. The automatic shaper does the rest, forming each part identically.

Boring Machines. Boring machines are made to bore holes for dowel work. They can be horizontal or vertical, single or gang. (Gang means that several holes can be bored simultaneously.) *Fig. 41–13.*

41–12. Shaping furniture parts on an automatic shaper.

41–13. Hydraulic speed gang borer.

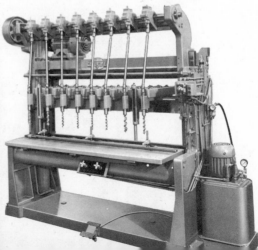

448

Gluing and Laminating Equipment. *Glue spreaders* cover wood surfaces with an even coat of adhesive. The pieces are held together by *presses* which may be mechanical, air operated, or hydraulic. Some presses operate cold. Others are called hot presses since heat and pressure both are used to dry the adhesive. See Units 35 and 37.

Sanders. *Drum sanders* are production machines used to sand doors, window frames, and other large, flat surfaces such as plywood or particle board. The machine looks somewhat like a large planer. *Fig. 41–14.* It has two to four big, revolving cylinders, above or below the bed, on which abrasive materials are fastened. As the stock is fed through the machine, both surfaces are sanded. Each drum is operated by a separate motor.

MAKING FURNITURE IN A FACTORY

Design. The designer creates ideas for new furniture. To do this he must use his own creativity, but he must also study the work of others. He must know the outstanding styles of the past as well as the modern

41–14. Drum sander.

41–15. Here management is reviewing wood products to be manufactured.

trends. The first step is to make several *sketches* of possible designs. From these, management chooses the ones to be developed. *Fig. 41–15.* Then the designer makes an *elevation,* that is, a front-view drawing of the new piece, to scale (usually 1½″ to 1′). *Fig. 41–16.* These drawings show more details than the first sketches did. At this point the drawings are usually discussed again, and changes may be suggested. When the drawings are approved, the designer makes a full-size *working drawing* of

41–16. The senior designer and the president of the company confer on the elevations, or front-view drawings, for the new designs.

the furniture piece. This gives very thorough details including kinds of materials, sizes, and method of construction. The working drawing is given to the engineering department where full engineering drawings are made and checked for accuracy. Next, a sample or experimental model is built. The cabinetmakers who work on samples are also responsible for building the jigs and fixtures used in the production of the furniture. *Fig. 41–17.* The sample piece helps the engineers and designers to check out errors in the drawings or design. This step is sometimes omitted if the furniture piece is very similar to one that has been previously produced.

The next step is done in the engineering department where the process route sheet is produced. These sheets are much like the plan-of-procedure sheets that you make out for a project you build, but they

41–17. Here you see the designer and the factory manager comparing the completed production model with the original model made in the sample or experimental room.

41–18. More than a year is required between the purchase of the lumber and the sale of furniture. Note the careful stacking that allows the air to circulate freely throughout, drying the lumber gradually.

have one sheet for each kind of part. This sheet includes a sketch of the part to be made, the number of pieces to be made, the kind of wood, the rough size, the sequence of operation, the finished size, the machines on which the operations are to be done, the number of men needed for production, and a great deal of additional information. Each furniture factory utilizes its own type of route sheet. The sheet stays with the piece from the time it is rough cut to size until it is ready to be assembled.

Conditioning of the Raw Materials. Lumber for furniture is usually purchased in the rough, in carload lots, and shipped to the factory where it

450

is stored in covered sheds. Here the lumber has a chance to air dry a little longer. *Fig. 41–18.* When ready for use, it is moved into drying kilns in the factory, where moisture is reduced to the desired percentage. *Fig. 41–19.* Most furniture factories keep raw lumber at a moisture content from 4 to 9 per cent just before processing it. The veneer for furniture is shipped to the factory in bundles or boxes containing one flitch. This makes it possible to match grain and pattern.

Making Lumber-Core Plywood. Most furniture manufacturers make their own lumber-core plywood for use in case goods, desk tops, and other large surfaces.

The first step in making lumber-core plywood is to make the core stock, usually of some fairly inexpensive material such as gum or poplar. The material is cut to narrow widths and the edges jointed. The stock is then made into wider boards by gluing the edges and curing the glue in a high-frequency electronic edge-gluing machine. Solid stock to match the veneer is glued to the edges of the core. At the same time the pieces of veneer are trimmed to width and matched. They are then glued together edge to edge to form the outer surface of the veneer core plywood. To complete the process, the crossbanding material is glued to the core and the veneer is glued to the crossband. This is all done in one operation in a batch press or hot press. The resulting pieces are just about the right size for use in the furniture. At the same time, solid lumber of the same kind as the plywood is roughed out to size. Solid stock is used for structural parts such as legs, rails, arms, drawer fronts, and other pieces that must be carved, machined, or shaped.

Rough Cutting and Planing. The first process in the factory is known as slashing or ripping. *Fig. 41–20.* This consists of running the boards through a ripsaw that cuts them to rough width. They are also cut to rough length, which is called slashing. The lumber is then put through a surfacer or planer that smoothes the top, bottom, and one edge. The pieces then proceed on a conveyor belt to the next step. *Fig. 41–21.*

Machining Straight Pieces. Many pieces that go into furniture such as legs, rails, drawer parts, sides, and the tops and bottoms of many case pieces, are rectangular. Many ma-

41–19. Kiln control room. Following the extensive drying period in the yard, lumber is kiln dried to very closely controlled limits of moisture content. This manufacturer keeps it between 4.5 and 5 per cent. Here you see the controls which carefully measure and control the temperature and humidity of the air circulating gently and evenly throughout the kilns.

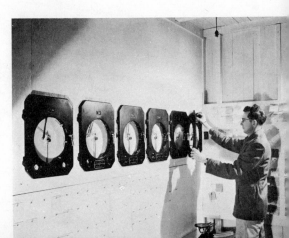

41-20a. Slashing or ripping denotes the first cutting down from full boards to rough dimensional length. Only about 35 per cent of the total lumber ends up in furniture. The rest is waste and, in the slashing operation, much defective or unusable lumber is discarded. This is a dual cut-off and planer unit which establishes the length and thickness of each stock piece. High-speed belt conveyors transfer stock from one station to the next.

chines can be used to process these parts. A gang ripsaw can be used, for example, to cut rectangular pieces. The double tenoner can make a wide variety of cuts on the ends or edges of pieces. It may also be used to join the parts or to shape the edges. The

shaper is used to cut moldings, to shape the edges of table tops, and to cut grooves for tongue-and-groove joints. Usually, the work is fed manually against the knives, although power is sometimes used in production. Double-spindle shapers, automatic shapers, and molding machines or "stickers" are sometimes used, as explained on page 446. Drum and belt sanders smooth the surfaces of machined parts. Boring machines and mortisers are used in joinery. Fig. 41-22. Boring machines are especially common because dowel joints are used extensively in the manufacture of chairs, tables, and cabinets. The mortiser is used less often. Sanding is done during every step of the production. Fig. 41-23.

Machining of Irregular Parts. The machining of curved and carved legs, arms, drawer fronts, and table-top edges requires many high-pro-

41-20b. Closer view of an automatic cut-off saw.

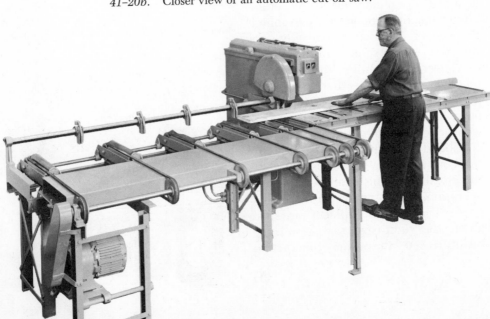

41-21. This production unit performs continuous ripping, jointing, and edge gluing of lumber for core stock.

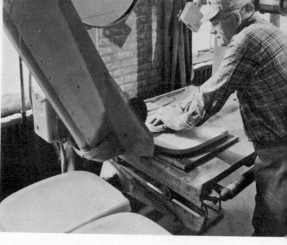

41-23. Sanding well done is an important part of all quality furniture. This worker is "rough" sanding a chair seat on a large belt sander.

duction machines. The automatic lathe turns out legs and irregular surfaces for the fronts of doors, drawers, and cabinets. A series of knives is mounted on a shaft. These rotate at high speed. The wood also rotates and moves against the knives. Routers are used to shape parts to a pattern. Multiple-spindle carvers are large machines that follow a pattern to make many identical parts at the same time. Fig. 41–24. Single-spindle carvers shape parts that are held freehand against a high-speed cutter.

Automatic shapers are also used to shape irregular parts. Fig. 41–25.

Even though machines do most of the work, skilled hand woodworkers are needed to do carving and fitting.

Bending and Laminating. A special department of a furniture factory is usually responsible for curved parts made by bending or laminating. For solid lumber a bending machine is used. Fig. 41–26. Laminated parts are clamped in a jig in a cold or hot press. Fig. 41–27. Molded plywood

41-22. This machine cuts off and then bores holes in the rails of chairs for a perfect hairline dowel.

41-24. A view of a multiple-spindle carver. This machine carves the legs in a mass-production operation.

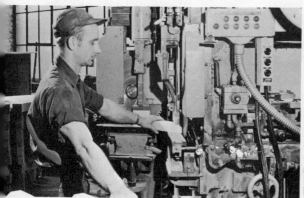

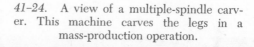

453

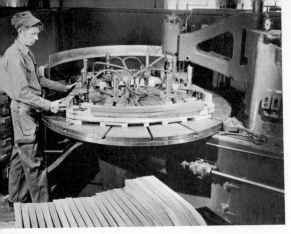

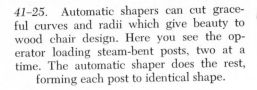

41–25. Automatic shapers can cut graceful curves and radii which give beauty to wood chair design. Here you see the operator loading steam-bent posts, two at a time. The automatic shaper does the rest, forming each post to identical shape.

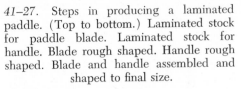

41–27. Steps in producing a laminated paddle. (Top to bottom.) Laminated stock for paddle blade. Laminated stock for handle. Blade rough shaped. Handle rough shaped. Blade and handle assembled and shaped to final size.

pieces such as chair seats and backs are made in a hot press. *Fig. 41–28.* See Unit 37.

Fitting and Assembly. When all of the parts have been machined on

41–26. Steam bending. This allows structural members, back posts, rails, and stretchers to retain the mechanical properties of the original flat stock without the shortcoming of "sawing away" the strength of the member. Here you see a modern forming bender undertaking a radial bend in what will become the back rim of a captain's chair. The unit at right is a steam retort used to plasticize (saturate) the flat lumber under conditions of controlled temperature and pressure before bending.

high-production equipment, they are brought on conveyer belts or by dollies to the assembly area. *Figs. 41–29 and 41–30.* Here the hand woodworker is all-important. He must do last-minute fitting of parts. *Fig. 41–31.* When all parts are ready, they are glued and clamped together to

41–28a. The parts of this laminated and molded plywood chair were made in a hot press. Beside the chair is a high-frequency operating center.

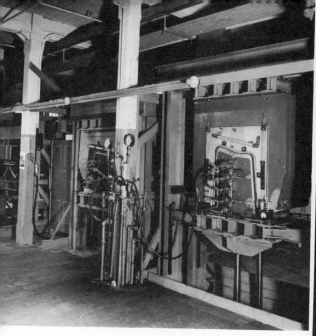

41–28b.   Hot presses for molded parts.

make the completed product. In large production, special fixtures replace clamps. *Fig. 41–32.* Many fixtures operate by means of air or hydraulics. The glues are applied by rollers or glue-spreading machines. After the case, chair, or cabinet is assembled, glue blocks, corner blocks, and metal fasteners (not hardware) are added. The drawers are fitted into the chests

41–30a.   Here you see the full machine parts for an occasional table. The turned parts were made on an automatic lathe. An automatic shaper made many of the flat parts. The holes were made on a boring machine and the joint cuts on a mortiser.

41–29.   Full machine parts for a chest. These parts are made in lots, anywhere from fifty to several thousand.

455

41–30b. The occasional table, completed.

41–32. Chair assembling. Here you see the essence of craftsmanship. In spite of exact operations and finest materials, it is here that materials would go to waste without the cabinetmaker's high skill and extreme care in assembly. Each item is completely assembled by one man who carefully controls the precise fit of each part.

and tables and the holes are drilled for hardware. Final hand sanding makes the item ready for finishing. The unfinished pieces are called white wood (regardless of the wood used). If finishing is not done immediately, white-wood products are stored in a room with humidity and heat control.

Finishing. Wood products may be finished with paint, enamel, varnish, lacquer, or combinations of materials. However, about 80 per cent of commercial furniture is given a sprayed-

41–31. Hand fitting a drawer for a fine chest.

41–33. Finishing actually starts with the many sanding operations. Then come the stain, filler, sealer, lacquer coats, and final hand rub.

41–34. Hand-rubbed finish is standard for high-quality furniture. This man is rubbing down the finish. He is using pumice and large bats of cotton waste.

41–35. Upholstery is another of the highly skilled crafts. It takes a person with aptitude about six years to become a completely accomplished journeyman upholsterer.

lacquer finish. *Fig. 41–33.* Finishing operations require a great deal of hand work including rubbing. *Fig. 41–34.* The finishing schedule in a factory is much like that for single pieces of furniture. See discussion of finishing in Unit 54. After finishing, the hardware, including handles, locks, hinges, catches, and so forth, is attached. Any upholstering is done at this point. *Fig. 41–35.* Last of all, products are inspected and packed for shipping.

Process Route Sheets. Some idea of the use of process route sheets can be obtained by studying the production materials for this lamp table. *Fig. 41–36.* This table has bright brass

41–36. This is the attractive decorator lamp table to be produced.

DRAWER RAILS

BANDING MITERED AT CORNERS

TREATMENT ON SIDE & BACK RIMS

TURNED LEG

$2\frac{1}{4}$

$10\frac{1}{4}$

$1\frac{15}{16}$ D.

BRASS RING - $1\frac{7}{8}$ I.D.

$\frac{3}{4}$ D.

41–37. An engineering working drawing of the table shown in *Fig. 41–36.*

457

trim and ferrules on its legs. It has one drawer. Its top measures 27" x 20½" and it is 24½" high. A full-sized engineering drawing is made first. *Fig. 41–37.* The next step is to make a stock list of the parts that will be required. *Fig. 41–38.* Notice that this list indicates the quantity of pieces needed for each table, the kind of material, the rough size (as to length, width, and thickness), the name of the piece, the finish or net size in

41–38.   Stock list of parts for the table.

Job No.   Stock No. 5567
Date   LAMP TABLE

NO. SQUARE FEET	QUANTITY	MATERIAL	ROUGH LENGTH	ROUGH WIDTH	ROUGH THICKNESS	NAME OF PIECES		NET LENGTH	NET WIDTH	NET THICKNESS	ITEM NO.
	1	African Mahogany Plywood	Net 22½	Net 16	3/4	Top		22½	16	3/4	1
	1	Oak Plywood	Net 15	Net 17½	3/16	Drawer Bottom		15	17½	3/16	2
	1	Mahogany	Net 16 7/16	Net 3 11/16	4/4	Drawer Front		15 7/16	3 7/16	13/16	3
	2	Mahogany	Net 28	Net 2 3/4	4/4	Top Side Bands		27	2½	13/16	4
	2	Mahogany	Net 21 ½	Net 2 3/4	4/4	Top End Bands		20 ½	2½	13/16	5
	2	Mahogany	Net 23	Net 3 3/4	4/4	Side Rims		22	3½	13/16	6
	1	Mahogany	Net 16½	Net 3 3/4	4/4	Back Rim		15 ½	3½	13/16	7
	2	Gum	Net 18 7/8	Net 2	4/4	Drawer Rails		17 7/8	1 3/4	5/8	8
	2	Gum	Net 18	Net 2	5/4	Drawer Guides		17	1 3/4	1	9
	1	Gum	Net 17	Net 7/8	4/4	Drawer Tilter		17	5/8	3/4	10
	2	Oak	Net 18 5/8	Net 2 7/16	5/8	Drawer Sides		17 5/8	2 3/16	3/8	11
	1	Oak	Net 16 3/8	Net 2 3/8	5/8	Drawer Back		15 3/8	2 1/8	3/8	12
	4	Mahogany	Net 24 1/4	Net 2 3/8	2 pcs. 5/4	Legs Turn		23 1/4	2 1/8	2 1/8	13
	1	Pull 3/4" Screws Brushed Brass									
	4	Brass Sockets Satin Brass Finish									
	4	Brass Rings Satin Brass Finish									
	6	Screws 1 1/4" #8 F.H.B.									
	2	Screws 1" #7 F.H.B.									
	4	1/2" Glides									

458

SPECIFICATION AND STANDARD COST SHEET

PAGE __4__ OF _____

SKETCH

Patt. Name	Lamp Table	Patt. No.	5567-9
Part Name	Top Side Bands	Part No.	4
No. Used Per Unit	2	Material	Mahogany

RIP MATCH		LENGTH	WIDTH	THICK	GRADE	FOOTAGE
21	ROUGH	28	2 3/4	4/4		GROSS
NO. OF PLY		MAKES	FINAL PIECES			
BET. SHO.		LENGTH	WIDTH	THICK	GRADE	NET
	FINISH	27 Miter	2 1/2 Moulder	13/16		

Oper. No.	Mach. No.	Rate	Set-up	OPERATION AND INSTRUCTIONS	Unit Equiv.	No. of Men	Total Oper. Time	Total Set-up Time
1	1	9.5	–	Cut off	2	2		
3	10	5.	2	Rough plane	2	2		
7	5	10.	–	Rip defects and gauge rip 75%	1	2		
5	5	5.	–	Rip match (7 in 1) 25%	1	2		
12	16	16.	–	Edge glue	1	2		
11	6	9.	–	Rip glued panels	1	2		
2	9	5.	Face plane	Face plane	2	2		
20	13	8.1	28	Moulder to pattern	2	2		
41A	25	18.	8	Miter 1 end	2	1		
41B	25	18.	8	Miter 1 end	2	1		
32	21	24.	23	Bore for dowels (1H2E)	2	1		
69	–	15.	–	Inspect and patch	2	1		

41–39a. Process route sheet (specifications and standard cost sheet) for one part of the table. Two of these pieces are needed for each table—one for each side of the top frame or band.

length, width, and thickness, and the item number (a factory code number). As you can see, the material includes mahogany veneer, mahogany, gum, and oak. The next step is to make a process route sheet or specifications and standard cost sheet for each of the thirteen major parts. This sheet includes a sketch of the piece, the rough and finish sizes, a list of the necessary operations, instructions, and information for figuring production costs. *Fig. 41–39.*

41–39b. This drawing would go in the space marked "sketch" at upper left on the process route sheet.

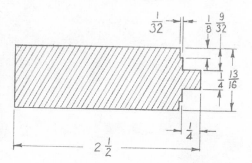

Unit 42: PATTERNMAKING

Wood patternmaking is the art of building a wood form or pattern to be used in the foundry for making a metal casting. It is the first important step in the manufacture of many metal parts. The patternmaker must be able to read a drawing or sketch and then imagine what the finished article will look like. *Fig. 42-1.* He must know foundry methods in order to make the pattern correctly. He must also know how to select woods, how to use hand and machine tools, and how to finish the pattern.

Look at the circular saw you have been using. How do you think the table of the saw was made? The table is a metal casting, like thou-

42-1. This man is working on a wood pattern for an automobile part.

42–3a.   The pattern with the draft side up is placed on the molding board.

42–2a.   This small gas engine has many castings.

sands of other items you see every-day. *Fig. 42–2.* Castings are also used to make such varied objects as decorative door knockers and the head of an automobile engine.

Before beginning the construction of a wood pattern, you should know how castings are made. The most

42–2b.   Many parts of this metal vise are castings.

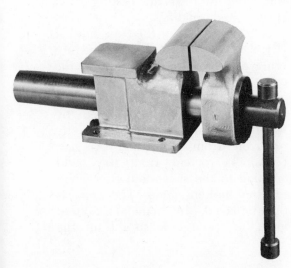

common way, called green-sand molding, is as follows:

The pattern is first made of wood, metal, plastics, or wax. It is slightly larger than the casting will be when finished. (The extra size is needed because metal shrinks as it cools.) The pattern must also be a little larger in places where the casting will require machining to a specified dimension.

The pattern is placed on a molding board and the *drag* (one half of an open box called a *flask*) is placed around it. *Fig. 42–3.* Molding sand is packed around the pattern. This process is called ramming-up. Another board (called the bottom board) is placed over the drag. The whole thing is then rolled over (turned over) with the molding board on top and the bottom board on the bottom. The molding board is removed and the *cope* (the other

42–3b.   Sand is packed around the pattern in the drag.

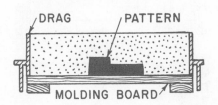

461

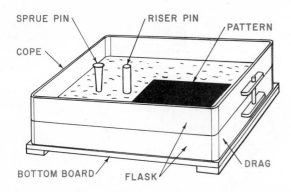

SPRUE PIN   RISER PIN
                      PATTERN
COPE

BOTTOM BOARD   FLASK   DRAG

42–3c. The cope section has been placed over the drag, and the riser and sprue pins are in place.

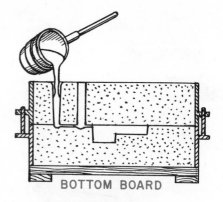

BOTTOM BOARD

42–3f. Molten metal is being poured into the sprue hole.

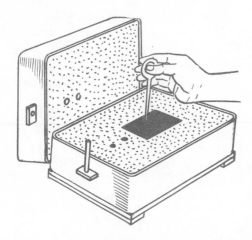

42–3d. The cope has been placed to one side. The pattern is being removed.

42–3e. The mold is closed.

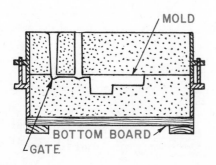

MOLD

BOTTOM BOARD
GATE

half of the flask) is placed over the drag. Fine *parting sand* is sprinkled over the surface to prevent the two parts of the mold from sticking. A *sprue* (tapered pin) is placed about two or three inches away from the pattern. This will provide the opening through which the molten metal is poured. Sometimes a *riser* (straight pin) is placed between the sprue pin and the pattern or on the opposite side of the pattern from the sprue. This will allow a column of metal in the mold to feed the casting as it shrinks and solidifies.

Sand is packed in the cope until it is full. The sprue and riser pins are removed, leaving holes through the cope half of the sand. The cope is carefully lifted off and placed on its side. The pattern is loosened by tapping it and then it is carefully removed from the sand. A *gate* (channel) is cut from the mold opening to the sprue and riser holes for the molten metal. The cope is then replaced. Molten metal is poured into the sprue hole to fill up the mold. The riser pin controls the reserve of molten metal, to fill in for metal shrinkage in the mold as it cools. When the metal is cool, the sand is broken up to remove the *casting*. The unusable parts such as the gate, sprue, and riser are cut off. The casting is then machined and finished.

COMMON TERMS AND MATERIALS FOR PATTERNMAKING AND FOUNDRY

• The *mold* is the cavity, or opening, made in the sand (or other materials) into which the molten metal is poured to make the casting.
• A *simple pattern* is a one-piece pattern used in making a casting. Several pieces of material may be

42–3g.   Here you see a student actually pouring a casting in the foundry.

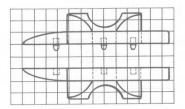

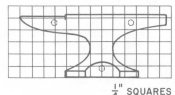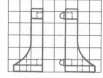

$\frac{1}{4}"$ SQUARES

42–4.   A split, or two-part, pattern for a paperweight anvil. Notice that the dowel pins should be twice as long as their diameter. The exposed half should be well rounded.

used in construction of the pattern, but all the parts are permanently fastened together.
• A *split pattern* is one that has two or more parts. These parts can be separated for greater ease in making a mold. A split pattern for a paperweight anvil, that can be cast of aluminum or brass, is shown in *Fig. 42–4.*
• A *dowel* is a pin of wood (or metal) placed between the parts of a split pattern. *Fig. 42–4.* Dowels are permanently fastened in one side of the pattern, with about half the length of the pin protruding. Matching holes are drilled in the other side of the pattern. The length of each dowel should be twice its widest diameter. The half that is exposed should be tapered, somewhat roundly, so that its end diameter is about half the diameter at the base. About

463

one-sixth of its protruding length at the base should have no taper. The part without the dowels is placed face down on the molding board in the drag section of the flask. When the drag is turned over, the half with the dowel pins is placed over the first half. When using a split pattern, part of the mold is in the cope section of the flask.

• *Shrinkage* is the decrease in size

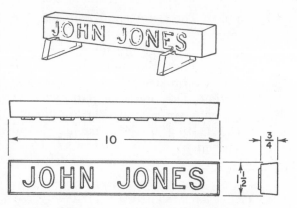

42–6. A one-piece pattern for a nameplate.

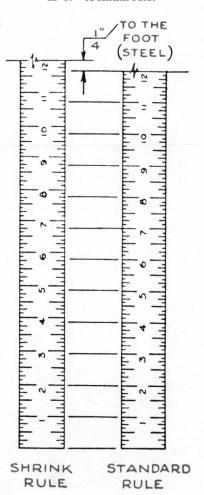

42–5. A shrink rule.

SHRINK RULE   STANDARD RULE

that takes place when the molten metal cools. Each kind of metal shrinks a different amount. For example, aluminum shrinks more than brass. To allow for this, the pattern must always be made a little oversize.

• A *shrink rule* is a scale on which each inch is slightly longer than a standard inch. There is a shrink rule for each kind of metal. For example, if the pattern is to be cast of aluminum, a shrink rule that is $\frac{1}{4}''$ longer per foot is used. *Fig. 42–5*. Brass shrinks $\frac{3}{16}''$ to the foot. Shrink rules are needed only in constructing production patterns. They are not necessary for making simple or decorative patterns in which shrinkage is unimportant.

• *Draft* is a slight taper on the vertical sides of the pattern to make it easier to draw the pattern out of the mold. Generally, a taper of $\frac{1}{8}''$ to the foot is considered "good draft." If the sides were a true vertical, the sand would crumble and ruin the mold as the pattern is drawn out.

42-7a.   Fillets.

42-7b.   Fillet tool.

To provide draft on a one-piece pattern for the nameplate in *Fig. 42-6*, the sides can be cut on a jig saw. Tilt the table two or three degrees and do all the cutting on one side of the blade.

• A *fillet* is a concave (curved in) piece of material (usually wax, wood, or leather) used to round off sharp inside corners of the pattern. The fillet lessens the danger of the mold's breaking at the sharp corners, and helps to avoid cracks or corner shrinkage. Fillets are made in sizes from numbers 1 to 16. *Fig. 42-7*. With wax fillets, a fillet tool is needed to push the material into the corners. The wax fillet can be forced into the corner cold, or the tool can first be heated slightly over a gas flame. Wood or leather fillets are fastened in place with waterproof cement.

• *Lumber and plywood for patterns.* Good, solid, white pine, mahogany, and cherry are the best materials for wood patterns. (White pine is preferred, since it is less affected by moisture in the sand.) Douglas fir plywood of the exterior type (with waterproof glue) is also good, especially for one-piece patterns.

• *Pattern letters and numbers* of cast white metal are available in many sizes and designs. These can be used for making a pattern for such things as house numbers and nameplates. *Fig. 42-8.*

• *Commercial patterns* are available that can be used in making such decorative items as wall designs and house signs. *Fig. 42-9.* The original of any decorative casting can be used as a pattern to make another casting.

• A *core* is a piece of hardened sand (usually baked) that is inserted in a mold to shape an interior opening. For example, the hole through the meat tenderizer (*Fig. 42-10*) can be made with a core. A core is made by packing sand into a mold called a *core box. Fig. 42-11.* Cores and core boxes are discussed further on the next several pages.

• The *finish for wood patterns* is usually two or three coats of shellac. Colors are discussed in the caption for *Fig. 42-19.*

42-8.   Pattern letters and numbers.

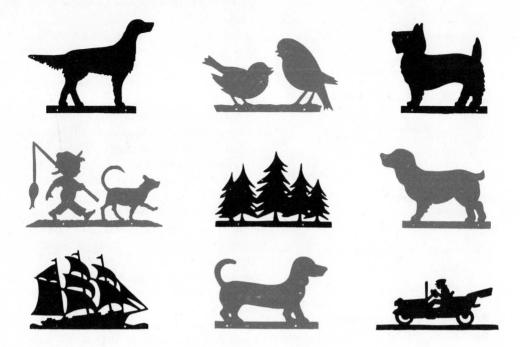

42–9.   A few examples of commercial patterns.

MAKING SIMPLE PATTERNS

A one-piece pattern such as a nameplate is a typical beginning project. *Fig. 42–6*.

1.   Obtain suitable material, such as a piece of soft white pine, $\frac{3}{4}''$ x $1\frac{1}{4}''$ x $10''$. Fir plywood, $\frac{3}{4}''$, could also be used.

2.   Square up the stock.

3.   Plane or cut a slight draft on the edges and ends.

4.   Cut out the letters of your name from $\frac{1}{4}''$ plywood. When cutting on the jig saw, remember to tilt the table to an angle of two or three degrees. Then do all the cutting with the work on one side of the blade in order to get the correct draft.

5.   Fasten the plywood letters to the background with waterproof glue and small brads. If metal letters are available, these can be fastened to the background with waterproof cement.

6.   Sand all surfaces thoroughly.

7.   Apply two or three coats of orange shellac to all wood surfaces.

To make a pattern for the "state" ash tray, *Fig. 42–12*:

1.   Using *Fig. 42–13* as a guide, make an outline of your state, about $8''$ to $10''$ long.

2.   Transfer the design to a piece of $1''$ mahogany.

3.   Cut out the design on the jig saw with the proper draft on the outside vertical surface.

4.   Shape the inside of the tray with a router to a depth of $\frac{3}{4}''$. Remember to provide draft on the inside vertical surface.

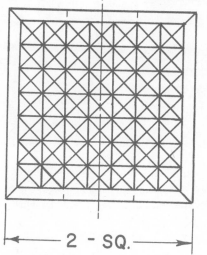

2 - SQ.

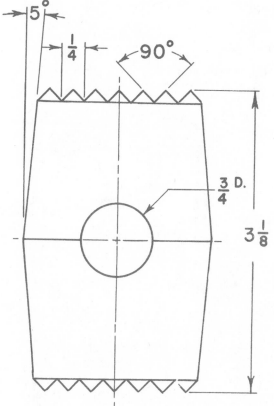

42-10a. Pattern for a meat tenderizer. A sand core is used to form the hole through it.

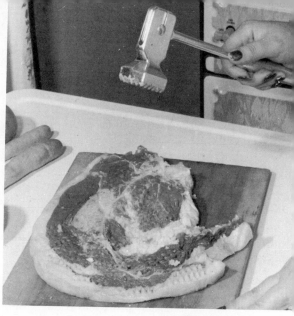

42-10b. Another cast aluminum meat tenderizer.

5. Fasten metal letters to the pattern.

6. Apply two or three coats of shellac to the wood.

CONSTRUCTING A SPLIT PATTERN

A simple split pattern (*Fig. 42–14*) is usually made of two parts, the drag and the cope, as explained on page 445. The parts are divided horizontally through the center. This dividing line is called the *parting line*. In a split pattern, the cope half has dowels, and the drag half has holes into which the dowels fit.

To make a pattern for a cylinder similar to the one shown in *Fig. 42–15*, proceed as follows:

1. Select two pieces of pine or mahogany that are about $\frac{1}{8}''$ thicker than half the diameter of the cylinder, about $\frac{1}{4}''$ wider than the diam-

eter, and about 2″ longer than the cylinder.

2. Surface the faces of the two pieces. Locate the position of the dowel holes on the matching faces. Remember that there must be at least two and preferably more dowels.

42-11a. A core is needed to form the hole in this washer casting. The pattern is made with a core print which supports the core as shown (top). The core box (bottom) is used for making the cores. They are made to take apart as shown. After the core is formed in the box it is hardened so that it can be handled easily without breaking.

42-11b. Making a sand core in a core box.

Be sure that dowels conform to the description on page 463.

3. Drill or bore the holes for the dowels. Glue the straight sections of the dowels in the cope half of the pattern.

4. Fasten the two pieces of stock together using small wood screws in the waste area. The two pieces can

42-12. A typical "your state" ash tray.

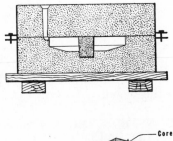

Core Print

Conventional Pattern

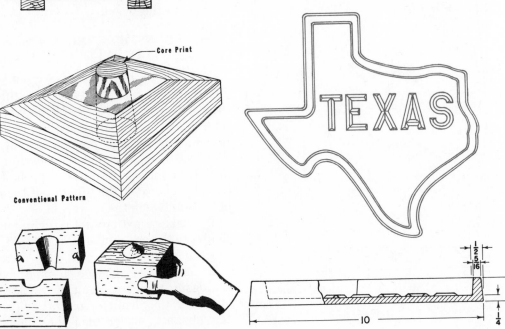

468

42–13. An outline map of the United States.

also be glued together with a piece of paper between for easy separation later.

5. Turn the pattern on the wood lathe. Be sure to use the correct shrink rule in adjusting the caliper.

42–14. A split pattern in a rammed-up mold.

42–15. A split pattern like this can be turned on a lathe.

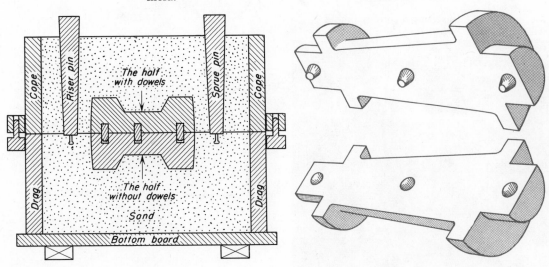

42-16a. Using a large split pattern to form the mold for an automobile housing.

6. After the pattern has been turned, cut off the excess stock at either end. Be sure to have the correct draft from the parting line to the largest diameter of the pattern.

7. Apply the necessary coats of shellac to protect the surface.

Constructing a Core Box for a Split Pattern. When a casting has an opening, the mold must have a core in it to form this opening. *Fig. 42–16.*

42-16b. Inserting a core in a mold.

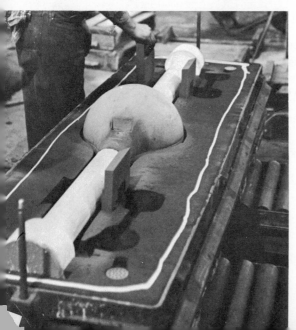

The core, which is a separate part of the mold, is usually made of sand. *Fig. 42–17.* When the sand core is used just as it comes from the core box, it is called a *green-sand core.* If the core is made from sand and a binder and hardened, it is called a *dry-sand core.* This core is made more durable by baking it in an oven or by using a gassing process with carbon dioxide. Gassing is excellent since it takes only 15 to 20 seconds. The core is used to make openings or different-shaped cavities in the casting. A *core print* must be added to the pattern to form a seat in the mold for the core.

42-17a. Note how a core is used in the mold to form the hole in the casting.

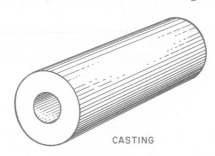

CASTING

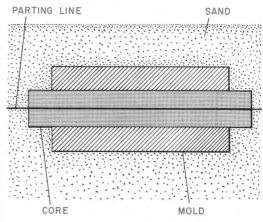

PARTING LINE   SAND

CORE   MOLD

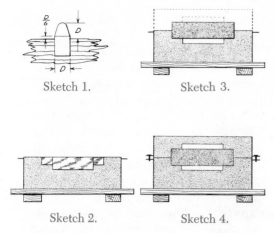

Sketch 1.   Sketch 3.

Sketch 2.   Sketch 4.

42–17b. Sketch 1 shows a well-designed wooden dowel pin. Unless the dowel pin fits snugly, it will cause trouble in ramming a mold. Sketch 2 shows the drag turned and swept clean, ready to receive the cope half of the pattern. The cope flask is placed over the drag flask and then rammed. The pattern is removed at this point. Sketch 3 shows the core in position in the drag half of the mold cavity. The cope half of the mold is then placed over it, completing the mold cavity as shown in sketch 4.

Before a core can be made, it is necessary to construct the core box. This is the mold in which the core is formed. Most core boxes are made in two parts, although some are made as half boxes only. *Fig. 42–18.* The half box is most often used when both sides are of the same size and shape, so that two half cores can be made and cemented together with a core paste. The core box can be made from a single, solid piece of stock, or by gluing up stock of several sizes. The size and shape of the core must be laid out on the core box and the excess material removed. On certain

types of rectangular boxes, the router can be used to remove this excess. On circular core boxes, the waste material can be removed by making several cuts with the circular saw. Then the additional stock can be removed with a gouge. A special-purpose *core box plane* can also be used.

After the core box is roughed out, it must be sanded smooth. The inner sides and/or the ends of the box must be tapered two or three degrees so that the core will come out easily. Often, a cylindrical core box can be made by clamping two pieces of stock together and boring a large hole of the correct size through the center of the two pieces. Then the length of the core print is laid out and the ends of the stock cut at an angle of two or three degrees. Next, pieces of wood must be glued and nailed to the ends of the core box to complete it.

Fig. 42–19 shows a complicated split pattern and the matching core box. This type of pattern is made of several pieces of wood glued together. In constructing a pattern like

42–18.   A half-core box.

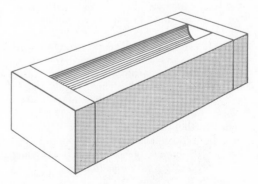

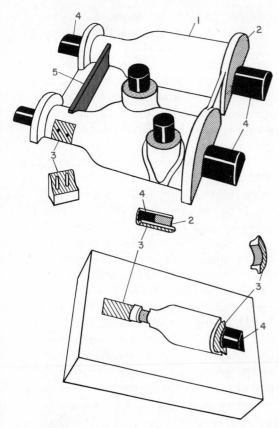

42-19. Standard wood pattern colors recommended by the American Foundrymen's Society. (Note: A new code has been devised, but not yet put into full effect. Some people now follow the new code, while others still use the old, which is actually considered to be the present code.) (1) Unfinished casting surfaces, the faces of core boxes, and pattern or core-box parting faces: new code—*clear coating;* present code—*black.* (2) Machined surfaces: new code and present code—*red.* (3) Seats of and for loose pieces: new code—*aluminum paint;* present code—*red stripes on yellow background.* (4) Core prints: new code—*black;* present code—*yellow.* (The new code further recommends that the core area be indicated in black.) (5) Stop-offs: new code—*green;* present code—*diagonal black stripes on yellow base.*

the one shown, the patternmaker must:

1. Determine the kind of metal that will be cast and then select the correct shrink rule. For example, if the casting is to be made of gray cast iron, an allowance of $\frac{1}{8}''$ per foot must be provided. *Fig. 42-20.*

2. Take into account the *finish allowance.* The purpose of this allowance is to supply a surplus of metal at such casting surfaces as may require machine finishing. These allowances are indicated on the drawing by a finish mark. The allowance is anywhere from $\frac{1}{8}''$ to $\frac{3}{8}''$ or more. Gray cast iron, for example, usually requires a finishing allowance of $\frac{1}{8}''$.

3. Determine if there is need for any *loose pieces* on the pattern. Many patterns could not be drawn from the mold without some parts or pieces being loose. These pieces are held in place with dowels to aid in making an easy draw from the mold. If the parts were made solid, as an integral part of the pattern, the mold would be torn up as the pattern was drawn from it.

4. Determine if a *stop-off* is needed. A *stop-off* is a piece of material or a cleat that is placed on a pattern to give it added support. In making a thin pattern for a casting that has a tendency to warp out of shape, one or more stop-offs are added. The sides and ends of the stop-off are shaped to an angle of 15 degrees for proper draft when drawing the pattern from the mold. After the pattern is removed from the mold, the impressions left by the stop-off are filled in and smoothed off.

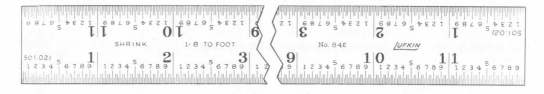

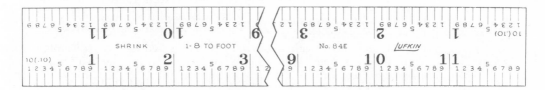

42-20.   A shrink rule for making a pattern to be cast from gray cast iron.

5. Cut and shape each part of the pattern with hand and machine tools. Then fasten the parts of the pattern together.

Constructing Circular Patterns of Segment Construction. Patterns of a circular shape are built of rows of wood pieces called *segments. Fig. 42-21.* This method is used to build curved shapes such as rings or ribs. A row of segments is called a *course.* A pattern of this type may be built of a single course or of three or five courses. Never attempt to construct it of two courses because it will not hold its shape. As the wood shrinks or expands, there is some distortion. If three courses are used, the stresses are equalized. Any number of spaces can be used to divide the circle, but six equal segments are best. An advantage of six segments laid lengthwise with the grain of the wood is that this number will turn clean and smooth on the lathe. If fewer segments are used, the wood

has a tendency to rough up as the tool turns against the grain.

Plain-sawed boards make the best segments because the annual growth rings of the wood have the toughest fibers and are vertical to the pattern

42-21. Checking the original wood pattern with the master metal pattern and the print. Note that the wood pattern is made up of segments.

473

surface. When a number of segments are needed, it is good practice to lay out and cut a template. Then stack the material, place the template over it, and mark an outline. The stacked pieces can then be cut in one operation.

42-22. Methods of segment construction: *a*. Courses with alternate joints overlapping. *b*. Single-course segments spliced with a spline. *c*. Multiple-spline system with splines as parts of the segments.

The three methods of joining segments are shown in *Fig. 42-22*. The single-course segment spliced at the joints with a spline is used for thin sections such as pipe flanges. After the segments are glued up, the pattern must be turned on the lathe.

Patterns on Match Plate. Sometimes a pattern is mounted on a plate, half on one side of center and half on the other. This is called *match plate* because, when used in making a mold, the two impressions that are formed will produce a perfectly matching mold. A match plate can be made of wood or metal. *Fig. 42-23*.

42-23. Six split patterns mounted on a match plate. One half of each pattern is mounted on one side and the mating half on the opposite side.

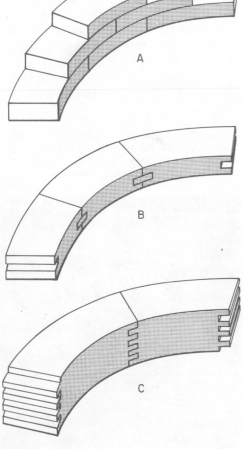

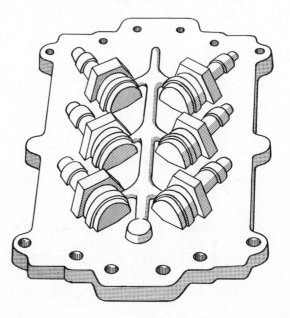

Unit 43: BOATBUILDING

More than thirty million people enjoy the pleasures of boating, water skiing, surfboarding, and other water activities. Marine projects can be built with relative ease, provided the correct materials are used and a few special procedures are followed. Many of the same basic techniques you have learned in hand and machine woodworking apply.

The methods of construction, however, are much different from those of cabinetmaking and carpentry. In these areas, most of the pieces must be level or plumb with square corners; therefore you can use the level and square for measuring, laying out, and checking. In boatbuilding, however, there are few if any square surfaces. Much of the layout, cutting, and fitting is done on curved surfaces. Because of this, the boatbuilder must have great skill in working with irregular pieces.

43–1a. This 16′ outboard runabout is a popular size. It is designed for smooth going at speeds up to 30 miles per hour. Boat builders will find this easy to make of fir plywood. Other boat plans are available from American Plywood Association.

43–1b. This 7′ 9″ pram dinghy is an ideal all-purpose small boat for the sportsman who needs a lightweight car-top boat. It is easy to row yet sturdy enough for a small outboard motor.

To do a good job, you must understand the terms used in boatbuilding and be able to read the prints. The project may be anything from a small dinghy to an outboard runabout. *Fig. 43–1.* You can order the necessary materials such as lumber, plywood, fittings, and finishing materials; or you can buy a kit that includes the drawings and pre-cut materials. Plans for boats and other marine projects may be secured from many sources.

BOATBUILDING TERMS

• *Batten.* A strip of wood used to strengthen and cover cracks.

43–2a. Study this sketch to learn the names of parts and how the boat is constructed.

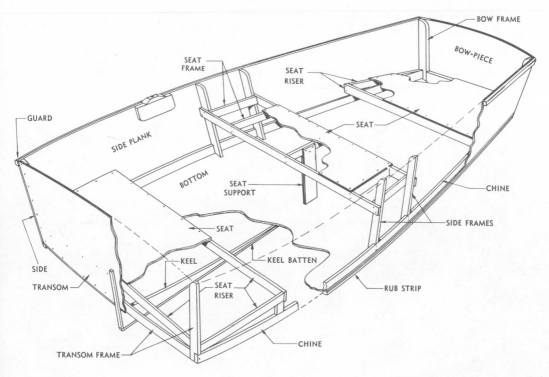

BILL OF MATERIALS

Item	No. Pcs.	Size	Kind
Planking	2	¼″ x 48″ x 96″	®EXT-DFPA•A-A grade G-1*
Transom	1	½″ x 16″ x 41″	®EXT-DFPA•A-A grade G-1*
Bow Piece	1	½″ x 16″ x 24″	®EXT-DFPA•A-A grade G-1*
Chines	2	⅝″ x 1¼″ x 8′	Oak
Framing, Trans., Bow- Piece & Midships	1	¾″ x 1½″ x 8′	Oak
Bottom Frame, Transom	1	¾″ x 2¾″ x 3′	Oak
Seat Risers & Supports	5	½″ x 1½″ x 4′	Oak or Mahogany
Rub Strips & Guard	5	½″ x ¾″ x 8′	Oak
Keel	1	¾″ x 3″ x 5′	Mahogany
Molds	1	½″ x 14″ x 8′	Fir Plywood; any grade suitable
Set-Up Stringers	2	1⅝″ x 3½″ x 8′	Fir or Pine
Rowlock Blocks	1	1″ x 3″ x 20″	Hardwood
Seats	Pieces Remaining from Plywood Planking		

*Special MARINE EXTERIOR panels can be used.

Use rust-proof hardware and fastenings.

Item	Quantity	Size	Kind
Frames to Bow-Piece & Transom	36	1″	No. 8 Flat Head Screws
Chines to Frames	4	1½″	No. 12 Flat Head Screws
Planking to Frames, Chines, etc.	200	¾″	No. 8 Flat Head Screws
Rub Strips	36	1¼″	No. 10 Flat Head Screws
Planking to Guard	36	⅝″	No. 6 Flat Head Screws
Planking to Rowlock Blocks	12	1″	No. 8 Flat Head Screws

43–2b.   Bill of materials and fastenings list for the pram dinghy.

• *Chine.* The piece at which the sides and bottom of the boat are joined. *Fig. 43–2a.*

• *Mold.* A shape or form around which the boat is built. Note that this same word is used in pattern-making and foundry to mean the opening into which molten metal is poured.

• *Stringers.* Long horizontal pieces of wood used in building the boat. The setup stringers, or jacks, are the frame on which the boat is built but which are not used in the finished boat.

• *Bow.* The part of the boat farthest forward.

• *Stern.* The part of the boat farthest to the rear.

• *Transom.* The back crosspiece of the boat.

• *Keel.* The ridge-like piece or combination of pieces that extends the entire length of the boat bottom.

• *Planking.* The outside shell of the boat that is exposed to the water.

• *Decking.* The floor or platform that extends from side to side in the boat.

BOAT DRAWINGS

When an architect designs a boat, he shows the shape or form of the hull with line drawings. These drawings show three main views of the hull, namely: the *profile view* or side elevation (sometimes called the *sheer plan*), the *plan view* or top view

477

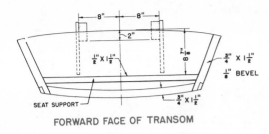

FORWARD FACE OF TRANSOM

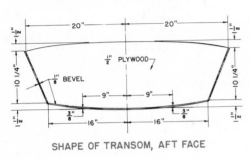

SHAPE OF TRANSOM, AFT FACE

43–3. Transom.

(sometimes called the *half-breadth plan*), and the *body plan* or end view.

Profile View. This is a side view showing the plank layout of the boat and indicating heights in true dimension. Heights are measured from a *base line* at the bottom (or top) of the view.

At each end of the profile the architect draws a line perpendicular to the base line. He measures the distance between these perpendiculars, then divides this distance into smaller divisions or sections by drawing other perpendiculars between the first two. *Fig. 43–9.* These *station lines* indicate the height of the boat at each point.

The profile also shows the contour of the bottom of the hull, its

keel, and how the chine sweeps from the bow to the stern. The transom appears as a line. This is also true of each station or frame.

Plan View. The *plan view* shows the boat from the top. All widths (or half widths if only half the boat is drawn) appear in true dimension. The center line of the boat is used as a common measuring point.

Body Plan. When looking at a boat from one end you can see only as far as the widest point. Therefore a plan is needed to show the rest of the boat's body. A body plan is actually two views in one. The half sections from the stern to the widest point are drawn on one side of a common center line, while the half sections from the bow to the widest point are shown on the other side. The body plan shows all half widths and heights in their true dimensions.

MATERIALS

The common materials are hardwood lumber such as mahogany, ash, oak, or spruce. Fir and mahogany plywood are also very popular. Oak is used for many parts that require great strength. Mahogany is excellent, since it can be easily shaped and resists moisture. Fir plywood for marine construction should be exterior type only. Standard, popular grades of exterior include: EXT-DFPA·A-A and A-B and EXT-DFPA·Marine (A-B). A-A and A-B, the highest standard grades, are used if both sides of the panel are to be smooth and tight, such as for transoms, bulkheads, or walls of

478

single-panel thickness; and for hull planking on small pleasure craft. *Fig. 43–2b.*

For decking and other places which expose only one side to view, specify EXT-DFPA·PlyShield (A-C).

For hull planking and transoms on boats subject to extreme wear or rigorous use such as racing craft, high-power outboards, cruisers, and commercial boats, specify MARINE EXTERIOR fir plywood identified by the grade trademark MARINE·EXT-DFPA. An exterior-type panel with special inner-ply construction, it is manufactured in A-A, A-B, and B-B grades.

Most Douglas fir plywood comes in 4′ x 8′ panels. However, there are extra long panels of 14′, 16′, 20′, and even longer. The most popular thicknesses are from $\frac{1}{4}''$ to $\frac{3}{4}''$.

If mahogany plywood is used, it should be Good grade of Type 1 (fully waterproof), made with a veneer core so that it can be bent and molded.

Nails, screws, and other fittings must resist rusting and corrosion. For fresh water, use only hot-dipped, galvanized steel fasteners. However, for exposure to water, especially salt water, the use of brass, bronze, or monel-metal fasteners is recommended.

BUILDING A DINGHY

Before you begin to work on this 7-foot, 9-inch dinghy, study this plan sheet a few minutes. Check through the steps in construction and note the various assembly details.

Layout. 1. With all materials on hand, start by drawing outlines of the bow and transom panels full size on $\frac{1}{2}''$ plywood. To draw the curved bottom lines, locate the dimension points along the curves shown in the plan and drive small brads at these points. *Figs. 43–3 and 43–4.*

2. Bend a $\frac{1}{4}''$ *batten* around the brads, drawing the curves along the batten.

3. Side and bottom edges of these panels are beveled. Either angle your saw to the bevels indicated as you cut them or saw them slightly oversize. Bevel to the outlines with a block plane.

4. Frame both panels with $\frac{3}{4}''$-thick hardwood. Note that notches for *chines* are cut in the hardwood frames only, not through the plywood.

5. Assemble the framing members on the panels with waterproof glue

43–4.   Bow.

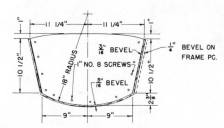

FORWARD FACE SHAPE OF BOW-PIECE

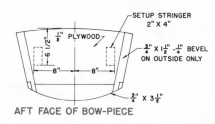

AFT FACE OF BOW-PIECE

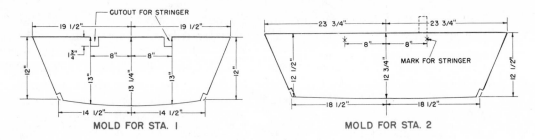

MOLD FOR STA. 1

CUTOUT FOR STRINGER

MOLD FOR STA. 2

MARK FOR STRINGER

43–5. Drawing of the molds for stations 1 and 2.

43–6. Assembly of setup stringers, transom, molds, and bow-piece.

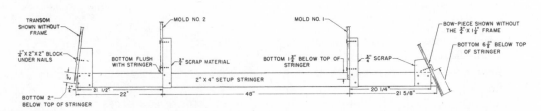

TRANSOM SHOWN WITHOUT FRAME

MOLD NO. 2

MOLD NO. 1

BOW-PIECE SHOWN WITHOUT THE ¾" X 1½" FRAME

BOTTOM 6½" BELOW TOP OF STRINGER

½" X 2" X 2" BLOCK UNDER NAILS

BOTTOM FLUSH WITH STRINGER

¾" SCRAP MATERIAL

BOTTOM 1¾" BELOW TOP OF STRINGER

¾" SCRAP

2" X 4" SETUP STRINGER

BOTTOM 2" BELOW TOP OF STRINGER

21 1/2"

22"

48"

20 1/4"

21 5/8"

480

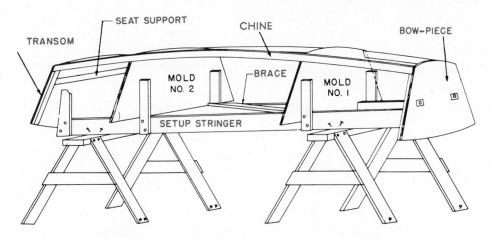

SEAT SUPPORT

TRANSOM

CHINE

BOW-PIECE

MOLD NO. 2

BRACE

MOLD NO. 1

SETUP STRINGER

43–7. Drawing showing the assembly of the bow and transom to the chine.

and 1″, No. 8 flathead brass wood screws.

6. Rough-bevel the frame edges with a plane.

7. Lay out and cut the two plywood *molds*. *Fig. 43–5*. It is not necessary to bevel the edges of these molds. Notch them for chines, however, and cut notches in the Station 1 mold for setup *stringers*.

Setup. 1. Assemble these *stringers*. They are the temporary backbone on which the dinghy is built. *Fig. 43–6*. Mount them on sawhorses or solid crosspieces. Check to see that they are parallel and level and that the ends are lined up exactly. Nail them down securely. Then measure off locations for the two molds. Nail cleats to the outer sides of the stringers at these marks and nail the molds to the cleats. *Fig. 43–7*.

2. To fasten the *bow* and *transom* panels in position on the stringers and cleats, nail through small scrapwood blocks. This will make it easy to pull the nails later.

3. Fit the oak chines. Mortise the ends of these strips carefully into the blind notches in the bow and transom panels.

4. After fitting, brush the ends of the chines liberally with glue and fasten them permanently with 1½″, No. 12 flathead wood screws. *Fig. 43–8*.

5. Countersink the heads of these screws deeply. The chines are not

43–8. Small boat with bow and chines in place. View taken from bow end.

481

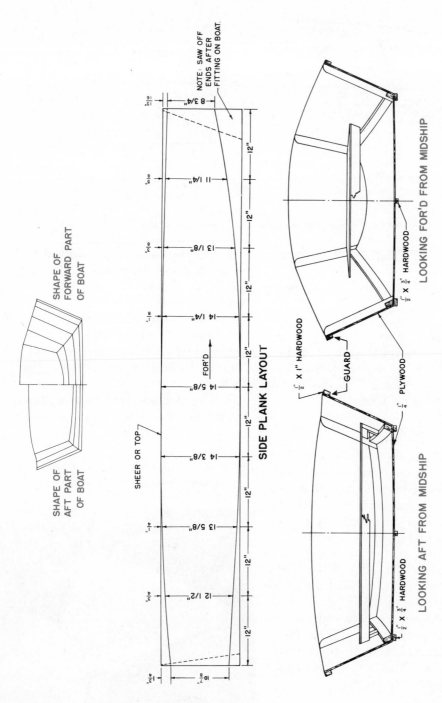

SHAPE OF FORWARD PART OF BOAT

SHAPE OF AFT PART OF BOAT

SHEER OR TOP

FOR'D

SIDE PLANK LAYOUT

NOTE: SAW OFF ENDS AFTER FITTING ON BOAT.

$\frac{1}{2}$" X 1" HARDWOOD

GUARD

PLYWOOD

$\frac{1}{2}$" X $\frac{3}{4}$" HARDWOOD

LOOKING FOR'D FROM MIDSHIP

$\frac{1}{2}$" X $\frac{3}{4}$" HARDWOOD

LOOKING AFT FROM MIDSHIP

43-9. These drawings show the side plank layout, a sectional view looking aft, another looking forward from amidships, and shape of both aft and forward parts.

43-10. Bottom planking partly shored in place, showing simple shoring method used to bend bottom planking to the form of the hull. View taken from forward end of hull.

fastened to the molds, but simply bent across them.

6. Plane each chine to blend smoothly with the bevels on the bow and transom panels. Also true up the bevels on the frames. Springing the strip of ¼" thick plywood across the framework will show the exact bevels required. Work carefully with the plane. Smooth off high spots and adjust the bevels until you are sure the side and bottom planks will fit tightly against the framework at all points.

Side and Bottom Planks. 1. Fit the side planks first. Rough-shape them somewhat oversize to allow enough material for trimming. Clamp them to the framework to check size and fit. *Fig. 43–9.*

2. Before fastening the planks, spread a full coat of waterproof glue along the bow, transom, and chines. Do not touch the mold edges with the glue. It is a good idea to lay several lengths of glue-soaked candlewicking or string along the edges of the frames as added insurance against any leaking.

3. Fasten the plywood in place with ¾", No. 8 flathead brass screws spaced about 2½" apart. Drive the screw heads flush with the surface. Use special bronze or monel nails instead of screws, if you prefer.

4. After trimming the side planks flush with the chines, mark the bottom plank for cutting. Bend the plank over the framework and draw around the side, bow, and transom. *Fig. 43–10.* Put glue-soaked candlewicking in the joints when you fasten the bottom.

5. When the glue dries, trim the bottom flush with the sides. Then fit rib strips, keel, keel batten, and guards. *Fig. 43–11.*

Finish Detail. 1. Turn the dinghy right side up. Drive small nails through the side planks into the molds to hold the molds in place temporarily, and remove the setup stringers.

2. Fasten seat framing with glue and screws driven through the side planks from the outside. *Figs. 43–12 and 43–13.* Then remove the molds by pulling the nails which hold them.

3. After installing seats, take a "dry run" in your dinghy on the shop

43-11.   Rough boat with hull completed. View from forward end.

483

43-12. Amidships and stern seat frame detail. View is from forward, facing down and aft.

floor to position rowlock blocks as you want them.

Applying a Finish. Commercial and amateur boat builders alike have found standard high-grade marine primers, undercoats, and finish coats very satisfactory for exterior plywood. The finishing materials you use should be made by a manufacturer of top-quality marine supplies. Generally speaking, it is wise to use products produced by the same manufacturer. In that way you can be sure that each coat of finish will go well with the others. Best results are obtained from finishes which retain a certain amount of flexibility when dry.

Be sure to prime the plywood well and seal all edges whether they are exposed or not. Use a good marine primer.

43-13a. Detail of drawing on page 485.

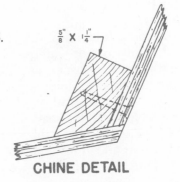

$\frac{5}{8}$" X $1\frac{1}{4}$"

CHINE DETAIL

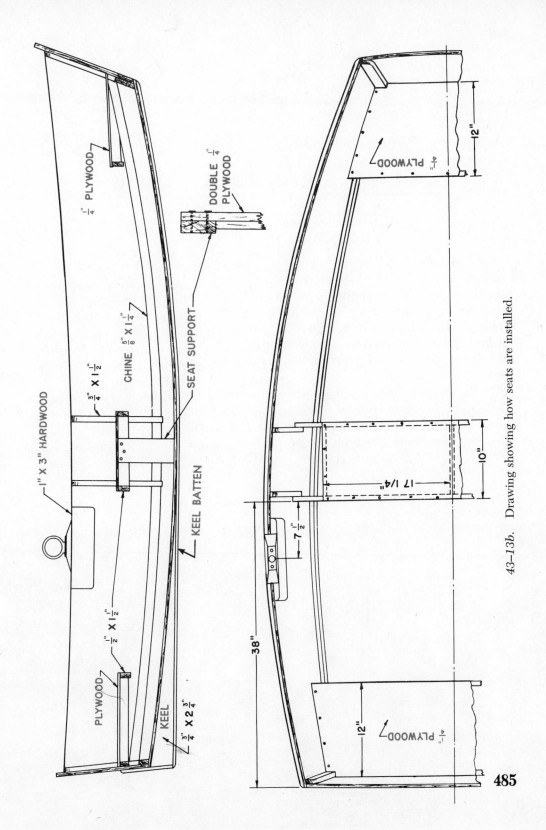

¼" PLYWOOD

DOUBLE
¼" PLYWOOD

CHINE ⅝" X 1¼"

SEAT SUPPORT

¾" X 1½"

1" X 3" HARDWOOD

½" X 1½"

KEEL BATTEN

PLYWOOD

KEEL

¾" X 2¾"

¼" PLYWOOD

12"

10"

17 1/4"

7 ½"

38"

12"

¼" PLYWOOD

43-13b. Drawing showing how seats are installed.

485

Unit 44: BUILDING A HOUSE

Most people hope some day to build or buy a home of their own. *Fig. 44–1.* In making these plans it helps to know the story of house building; this information is valuable to everyone, even to persons who may never do a bit of construction work in their lives.

While construction varies somewhat with house size and design, nearly every builder has to follow some of the same common procedures.

GETTING READY TO BUILD

There are several steps that must precede the actual building of the house itself. One of the first is to find a suitable lot on which to build. This is a very important decision. The following points should be considered in purchasing a lot:

• The neighborhood: Is it expanding or all built up? Will it be desirable for many years?

• Adjacent lots: If vacant, can they be purchased later by yourself

44–1.   A good place to live is important for everyone.

or someone you would like to have as a neighbor?

• Topsoil: Is it all right? What kind (rocky, sandy)?

• Neighbors: Are they desirable?

• Nearness of transportation.

• Nearness of schools, churches, and stores.

• Sewers, curbs, and gas lines: Are these already installed or will there be later assessments?

• Zoning: Will zoning restrictions protect you from future erection of undesirable commercial buildings?

• Deed restrictions: What are minimum lot and house size? Could a neighbor build a shack?

• Traffic: Is it through, dangerous, or fast?

• Lot shape: Is it wide and deep enough?

• Lot layout: Are the roads straight or curved? Are there adequate parks nearby?

• Lot cost: This should not exceed 14 per cent of the total building budget.

• Financing: Will the financing agent place an adequate mortgage in this neighborhood?

These are only a few of the important items that should be considered. The second step is to decide on the house plans. These should include the complete set of working drawings, materials list, and specifications. *Fig. 44–2.* If the house is to be individually designed, an architect must be employed. His fee usually ranges from 5 to 10 per cent of the total building cost. Many good stock plans are available from home-planning services, lumber yards, and lumber suppliers. *Fig. 44–3.*

After deciding on the lot and plans, the next step is to ask contractors to bid on the cost of construction. It is usually desirable to get two or three bids and to talk with each contractor about his bid. After a contractor is chosen, it is often necessary to obtain financing through a bank or loan company.

STAKING OUT THE SITE

The surveyor must set up a transit to mark the lot lines and the building lines. Stakes are placed at the corners to show the location of the home. The building contractor or his foreman has the job of supervising the actual construction.

EXCAVATING THE CELLAR

There are three common ways of providing a foundation for the house. Homes without basements are built on a concrete slab or with a crawl space under the house. *Fig. 44–4.* With both of these, a trench must be dug for the footings; these must go below the frost line.

For homes with a partial or full basement, after the layout is made, mechanical equipment is brought in to excavate the cellar. Then the foundation footings are dug, usually by hand. These are the poured-concrete base on which the basement walls are built. They should be deep enough to support the entire load of the house, and at least 6″ to 8″ wider than the walls. The footings must rest on solid earth. Sometimes wood forms are set up for the footings. In other cases, they are poured directly into the trench.

After the footings are cured, the

487

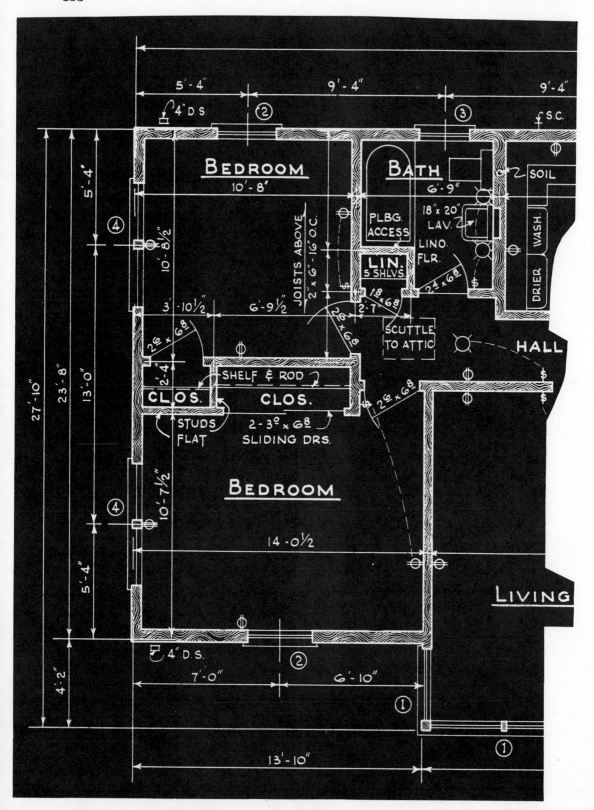

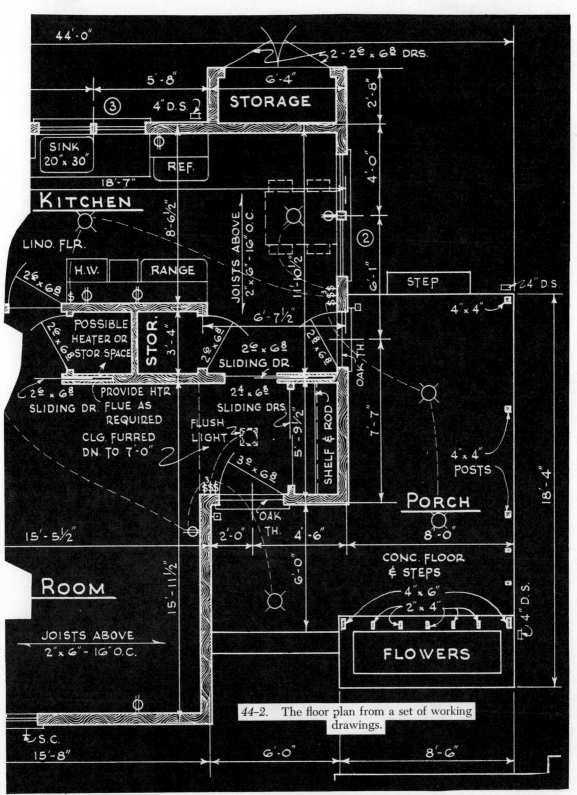

44-2. The floor plan from a set of working drawings.

44-3a. This attractive, well-planned home is typical of the excellent houses for which stock plans are available.

foundation wall itself is built. Either poured concrete or cement blocks can be used. Drain tiles should be laid around the outside of the foundation walls so that the basement will stay dry. The outside of the cement-block foundation wall should be treated to make it waterproof. The number of basement windows installed should be adequate to keep the basement fairly bright and airy.

If wood beam posts are used, it is necessary to pour concrete piers near the middle part of the house. These footings are like the wall footings except that the piers project up through the basement floor; also a metal dowel or rod sticks up from the center. Anchor bolts are imbed-

44-3b. Floor plan for the house in *Fig. 44-3a.*

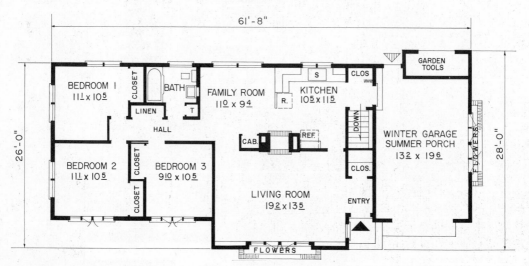

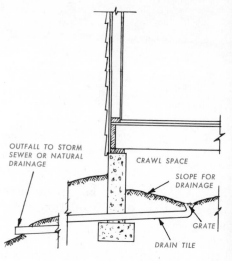

OUTFALL TO STORM
SEWER OR NATURAL
DRAINAGE

CRAWL SPACE

SLOPE FOR
DRAINAGE

GRATE

DRAIN TILE

44–4. This shows the construction of a
house over a crawl space.

44–5. Building the plywood subfloor.

ded in the cement every 6′ to 8′
around the top of the foundation
wall. The top of the basement wall
should be at least 6″ to 8″ above the
ground when the landscaping is
finished. At this stage of building,
trenches are dug for sewer pipe,
water, and gas. The pipes for these
are usually run just into the basement where a meter and a shut-off
valve are installed for the water and
gas.

FRAMING THE HOUSE

Lumber for framing the house is
delivered and stacked on the site. A
metal or wood girder or beam, which
is a horizontal load-supporting member, spans the distance between the
foundation walls and bearing posts.
This girder or beam is laid in pockets
in the basement wall, fastened to the
wood or metal bearing posts spaced

about 7′ apart across the basement.
Holes are drilled in a sill plate to go
over the anchor bolts.

After the plate is in place it is
tightened to the wall by fastening
nuts on the anchor bolts. In some
areas of the country it is important
to place a metal termite shield over
the foundation wall before putting
the sill plate in place. Then floor
joists are installed. Double joists are
used for all partitions. The double
header is used around the basement
stairwell and around an opening for
a fireplace. Bridging is placed between the floor joists.

The next major operation is to add
the subflooring. *Fig. 44–5.* If boards
are used, these should be placed
diagonally across the floor joists. This
will prevent the finished floor from
warping, opening, or squeaking.
Some homes have plywood subfloors. The wall framing includes the

491

44–6. The exterior framing has been completed.

44–8. Using plywood for the roof sheathing.

soleplate, studs, headers, top plates, and firestops. Usually the walls are assembled on the subfloor and then pushed up and nailed in place.

The areas for doors and windows must be adequately framed. To guard against plaster cracks, at least a double 2″ x 4″ should be placed over small window openings and a double 2″ x 6″, 2″ x 8″, or 2″ x 10″ on wider ones. Partitions are built for the rooms and closets according to the floor plans. Fig. 44–6. Ceiling joists are nailed to the top plates. Sheathing is added to the exterior.

This may be plain boards, tongue-and-groove boards, insulation board or plywood.

The roof is built by installing rafters nailed to the top plate and to a ridge board, or with a trussed rafter roof. Fig. 44–7. Rafters are usually braced to give added strength to the roof. Sheathing, nailed to the roof, closes in the house. Fig. 44–8.

After the sheathing has been added, a cover of building paper is tacked in place. Then the masons build chimneys, fireplace, and brick exterior, if any. The plumbers put in

44–9. The plumber installs pipes after the framing is completed.

44–7. Fastening a trussed roof in place.

44–10. Nailing siding to the exterior of the house.

the rough plumbing (Fig. 44–9), after which it is necessary to cut holes into the framing for the drain pipes. When this is done, as much wood as possible should be replaced so that the joists are not weakened. The carpenters may shingle the roof after the chimney is completed and metal flashing has been placed around it, in the corners, and at the edge of the roof.

COMPLETING THE EXTERIOR OF THE HOUSE

Windows are installed in the framed openings. They are always given a coat of paint before installation. Frames for the exterior doors are also put in place. Trim is added around doors, windows, and roof. The carpenters then add the exterior siding, shingles, or similar materials. Fig. 44–10. Flashing is always put across the tops of windows to prevent leaks. About this time, the sheetmetal men put up the gutters and

other drain pipes. Fig. 44–11. When this is completed, painters apply exterior paint. At the same time, the ground around the house is leveled out and sidewalks poured.

INSTALLING GAS, ELECTRICITY, AND OTHER UTILITIES

While the carpenters and sheetmetal men are working on the outside of the house, work is also progressing on the inside. If the cellar floor has not been poured, this is done at this point. Sheetmetal men install the furnace and the duct work for heating and air conditioning. Wires are strung and the rough wiring installed in the walls with locations marked for various outlets and switches. Fig. 44–12. After this is completed, insulation is fastened into the walls and ceiling. Large pieces of equipment, such as a hot-water heater, water softener, and bathtub, are put in place. Fig. 44–13.

COMPLETING THE INSIDE OF THE HOUSE

When all of the rough plumbing, heating, wiring, and similar installa-

44–11.   Fastening the downspouts to the walls.

44–12. Pulling wiring from a reel for overhead lighting circuits in a house.

tions are made and the insulation is in place, the inside walls are covered with gypsum board or panel (in drywall construction) or rock lath and plaster (for wet-wall construction). *Fig. 44–14.* After the plaster is dry, the finish flooring is installed and the trim around the doors and windows added. Cabinets and other built-ins are built by the carpenter or brought in ready-made and fastened in place. *Fig. 44–15.* A tile man completes the ceramic tile installation while the

flooring specialist installs flooring materials in the kitchen, bathroom, and utility room. *Fig. 44–16.* Counter tops of plastic laminates are also added. Interior doors must be hung including the door jambs, trim, and hardware. Electrical fixtures, plumbing fixtures, and similar accessories are added to complete the interior of the house. *Fig. 44–17.* Then all necessary interior painting and finishing is done.

SOME THINGS TO CHECK WHEN SELECTING A HOUSE

• Is the architecture pleasing?
• Do house and lot cost no more than 2 to $2\frac{1}{2}$ times your annual income?
• Is the lot in a good residential neighborhood?
• Is the contour of the lot to your satisfaction?
• Are there enough rooms now for any later expansion in the family?
• Are doors placed near corners where they will not waste wall space?
• Are there adequate closets?
• Are the bathrooms conveniently located and adequately equipped?

44–13. Getting the hot-water tank ready for installation.

44–14. Using plywood for the interior walls of a home.

44–15.　Fitting a door on a kitchen cabinet.

44–16.　Ceramic tile used in a bathroom must be installed by a tile setter.

• Is there enough work surface in the kitchen and enough cabinets?

• Is there a good dining space for the family and is it near the kitchen?

• Is the foundation solid?

• Will the basement walls and floors stay dry?

• Is the basement light enough?

• Are floor joists bridged?

• Is the basement ceiling height at least 7′ 6″?

• Will the furnace keep the house at 70 degrees when the temperature is 10 below zero outside?

• Is the hot-water heater insulated and of ample size? Two bathrooms require a forty-gallon tank.

• Is finish flooring laid on good subfloor?

• Are joists weakened by large notches for pipes?

• Are the stairs easy to climb? Not too steep or narrow?

• Do chimneys extend 2′ above the roof peak?

• Are chimneys and fireplaces kept free of the house framing?

• Are walls and ceilings insulated?

• Do bedrooms have cross-ventilation?

• Are there enough bedrooms and are they well planned?

• Do the windows open and close easily?

• Are windows big enough and placed well?

• Are windows and doors weather-stripped, and have storm doors and windows been provided?

• Is the attic or roof ventilated properly?

• If there is an attached garage, does it have fire-resistant walls and ceilings?

• Are there adequate electrical outlets?

• Is a termite shield provided?

• Are rust-proof nails used for siding?

44–17.　Painters and paper hangers are among the last craftsmen to work on a house.

495

Unit 45: CARPENTRY TOOLS, MATERIALS, AND METHODS

Nine out of ten homes in the United States are of wood-frame construction. Homes of this type often are enclosed with wood siding, wood shingles, brick veneer, or stucco.

Wood-frame houses have many advantages. They are relatively easy to construct, extremely sturdy, easy to maintain and repair, and relatively inexpensive.

KINDS OF CONSTRUCTION

Three kinds of wood-frame construction are in common use today.

Platform Frame Construction. This is an economical, strong, and simple framing method. *Fig. 45–1.* The subfloor extends to the outside edge of the building and provides a platform

45–1. The framing of this house is platform frame construction. Here you see conventional construction methods most common for one-story homes.

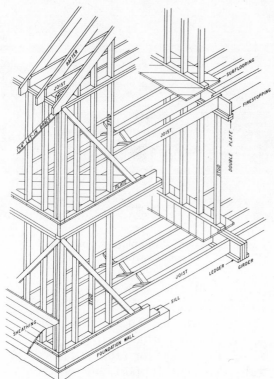

45–2. Platform frame construction as used in a two-story house.

Balloon Frame Construction. In this form of construction, the studs and the first-floor joists rest on the anchored sill. The second-story joists rest on a 1″ x 4″ ribbon strip which has been let into the inside edges of the studs. Balloon framing is excellent for two-story buildings with an exterior of brick or stucco. *Fig. 45–3.* The reason for this is that there is less likelihood that the wood framing and the masonry veneer will shift.

Plank-and-Beam Construction. The plank-and-beam method of construction of floors and roofs is particularly suited to modern designs for one-

45–3. Balloon-frame construction in a two-story home.

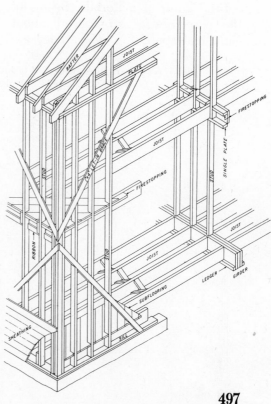

on which the exterior walls and interior partitions can be erected. Joists, headers, and subfloor of each story form an independent unit which rests on the sills or top plates of the story below. Platform construction is the framing technique most often followed in one-story houses. *Fig. 45–2.* It is simple because it provides a flat surface at each floor level on which to work. It is also best adapted to various methods of prefabrication. In platform framing, it is very common to assemble the wall framing on the floor and then raise the entire unit in place.

497

45–4. This attractive home has plank-and-beam construction.

45–6a. Another example of plank-and-beam construction.

story houses. *Fig. 45–4.* This is because this method features large glass areas, open-space planning, and natural finish of materials. Beams of the correct size are spaced about eight feet apart. *Fig. 45–5.* They are

covered with two-inch planks which serve as a base for the finished floor or roof covering. The ends of the beams are supported on posts. *Fig. 45–6.* Covering for the attached walls does not support any of the

45–5. A comparison of plank-and-beam construction with conventional framing. Notice the simplicity of plank-and-beam construction.

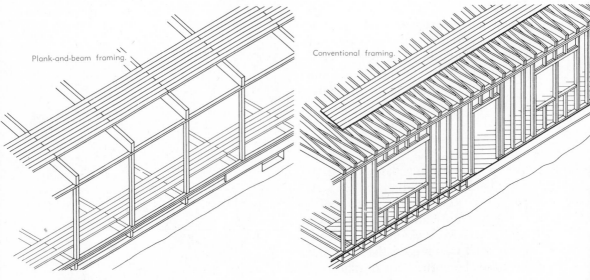

Plank-and-beam framing.

Conventional framing.

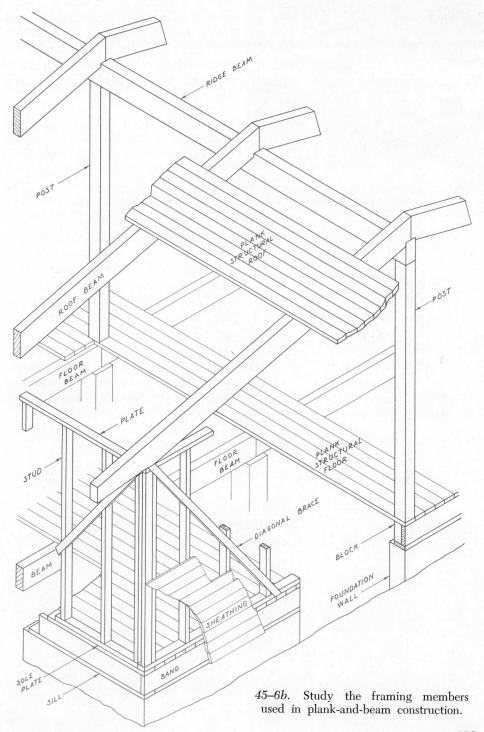

RIDGE BEAM

POST

PLANK STRUCTURAL ROOF

ROOF BEAM

POST

FLOOR BEAM

PLATE

PLANK STRUCTURAL FLOOR

STUD

FLOOR BEAM

DIAGONAL BRACE

BLOCK

BEAM

FOUNDATION WALL

SHEATHING

SOLE PLATE

BAND

SILL

45–6b. Study the framing members used in plank-and-beam construction.

499

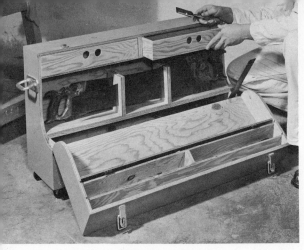

45-7a. A good tool chest is important if you do a great deal of carpentry.

roof. Ceiling height is measured to the underside of the plank.

CARPENTRY TOOLS AND MACHINES

The carpenter of today must have a good supply of hand tools and several pieces of power equipment. (See Units 14 through 33.) His hand tools should be kept in a sturdy chest. *Fig. 45-7.* By keeping tools in orderly arrangement and protecting the

cutting edges, time is saved and better craftsmanship is assured. In addition to the hand tools and machines described previously, there are two hand tools that are used constantly:

Carpenter's Square. The carpenter's square (framing or rafter) is his most common hand tool. *Fig. 45-8.* On every square are two kinds of information — scales and tables. The scales are the same as the ones on a try square. The inches are divided into halves, quarters, eighths, sixteenths, and thirty-seconds. On the reverse side of the carpenter's square, the inches are divided into hundredths. Also found on the square are the rafter table and the Essex board-measure table. The rafter table is used in layout and in cutting rafters. See Unit 47. The board-measure table gives the number of board feet in boards of different sizes. See Unit 10.

45-7b. Drawings for the tool chest. (Continued on next page.)

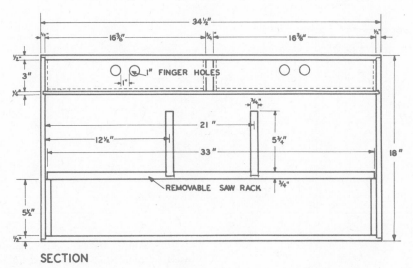

SECTION

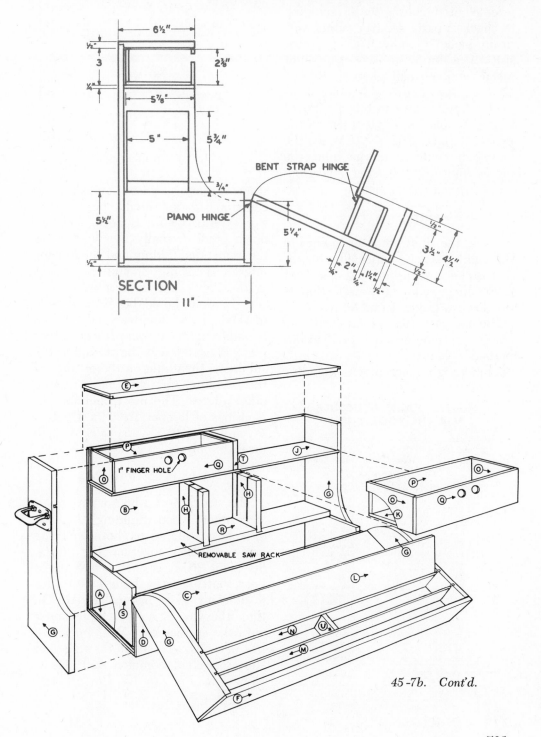

6½"

½"

3

2⅜"

¼"

5⅞"

5"

5¾"

¾"

BENT STRAP HINGE

PIANO HINGE

5½"

5¼"

½"

SECTION

11"

2"   1½"   ½"

½"   ⅛"   ½"

3½"   4½"

½"

E

P

1" FINGER HOLE

O

Q

T

J

O

B

H

H

G

P

R

REMOVABLE SAW RACK

O

Q

K

G

A

C

G

S

L

D

G

N   U

M

F

45-7b.   Cont'd.

501

Carpenter's Level. The carpenter's level is used constantly in building to check if parts are true either vertically or horizontally. The level consists of a frame of wood or light metal, and a small glass tube. *Fig. 45–9.* In the tube is a bubble, floating in liquid. You can tell if a board is level by placing the tool flat on the board's surface. *Fig. 45–10.* When the bubble is centered in the tube, the piece being tested is *level* if horizontal and *plumb* if vertical.

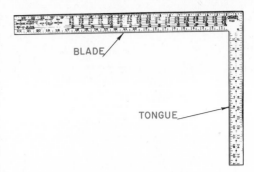

BLADE

TONGUE

45-8.   Carpenter's square.

LUMBER GRADES

Using the right grade of lumber in the right place is especially important for successful building. See Unit 9. Economy requires the selection of the lowest grade suitable for each particular part. *Fig. 45–11* shows the grades recommended for various parts of a house.

For rough carpentry, including studs, framing, joists, and rafters, common grade should be chosen. For exterior trim and finish flooring, finish grade (usually B or better) is recommended. Siding and lumber for interior finishing should be select grade. Plywood used in rough home construction should be exterior type marked "EXT" on every edge. *This is made with a special waterproof glue.* Plywoods can be used for the subfloors, sheathing on the outside of the building, for roofs, and in many other places. The most common dimensions of lumber are 2″ x 4″, 2″ x 6″, and 2″ x 10″. A dry 2″ x 4″ will measure only $1\frac{1}{2}″$ x $3\frac{1}{2}″$.

45–7c. PARTS SCHEDULE FOR THE TOOL CHEST

Code	No. Req'd	Size	Part Identification
A	1	11″ x 34½″	Bottom
B	1	17½″ x 34½″	Back
C	1	12½″ x 34½″	Front
D	1	5″ x 34½″	Front
E	1	6½″ x 34½″	Top
F	1	4½″ x 34½″	Top
G	2	10½″ x 17½″	Ends
H	2	5″ x 6⅛″	Saw Rack Support
J	1	6″ x 34″	Drawer Shelf
K	2	5⅝″ x 15⅞″	Drawer Bottom
L	1	4″ x 33½″	Level Box Lid
M	1	3½″ x 34″	Level Box Divider
N	1	3½″ x 34″	Level Box Back
O	4	2⅞″ x 5½″	Drawer Sides
P	2	2⅝″ x 15⅞″	Drawer Backs
Q	2	2⅞″ x 16⅜″	Drawer Fronts
R	1	5″ x 33″	Saw Rack Bottom
S	2	5½″ x 10″	Saw Rack
T	1	3″ x 6″	Drawer Divider
U	1	2″ x 3¾″	Level Box Divider
	1 Ea.	34½″	Piano Hinge
	2 Ea.	—	Strap Fasteners
	4 Ea.	—	Casters (Optional)
	2 Ea.	—	Metal Handles

Miscellaneous—4d and 6d Finish Nails
Waterproof Glue

NAILS AND NAILING

The strength of a house, garage, or any other wood building depends to a large degree on how well the parts are nailed together. *Fig. 45–12.* See Unit 36. It is not uncommon to hear that a hastily built house with insufficient nails has collapsed. On the other hand, a well built house with the correct kind, size, and number of nails will stand through bad storms. Actual common nail size is shown in *Fig. 45–13.* Correct nail

45–9.   Level.

sizes for parts of the house or garage are shown in *Fig. 45–14.* Common nails are used in all rough carpentry. *Figs. 45–15 and 45–16.*

Nailed joints are strongest when the load is acting at right angles to the nails. When the load is parallel to the nail in such a way as to cause withdrawal, the joint is extremely weak. Oftentimes the best way to fasten wood together is by *toenailing* in which nails are driven at approximately a 30-degree angle to the grain.

PROTECTING THE MATERIALS

Lumber and other items should be protected from the weather when they arrive at the building site. See Unit 8. Keep piles of lumber at least six inches above the ground and pro-

45–10.   Using a level.

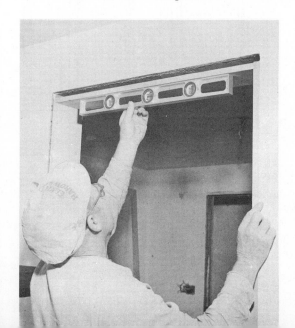

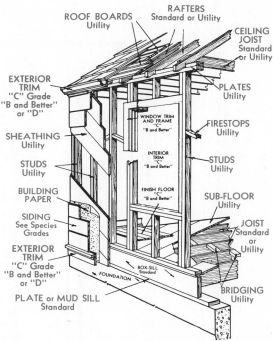

45–11.   Lumber grades for building as specified by the West Coast Pine Association.

45–12.   Ways in which pieces are nailed together. Arrows indicate direction of load. Nail in withdrawal is weakest, but is necessary in some jobs.

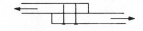

(a) Nail perpendicular to load.

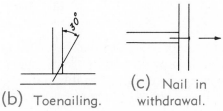

(b) Toenailing.

(c) Nail in withdrawal.

503

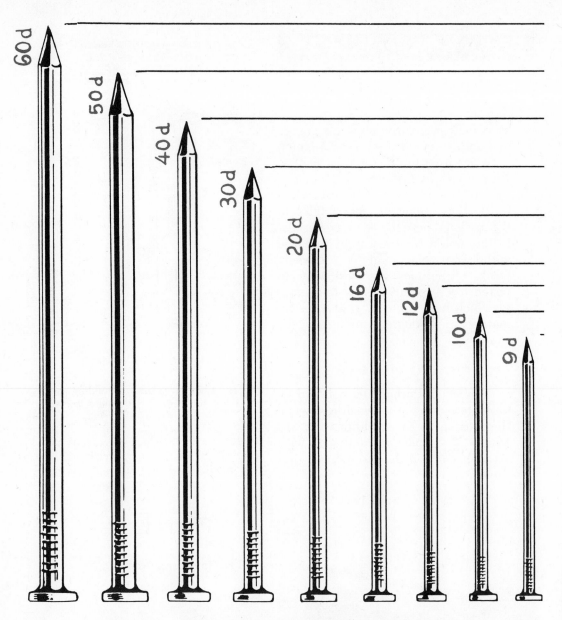

45–13. Actual common nail size.

tected with a waterproof cover. Finished lumber should be kept under cover at all times, preferably indoors, until it is needed. Doors, windows,

and exterior trim should be stored inside. When this is impossible, they should be off the ground and covered. Store interior doors, trim,

504

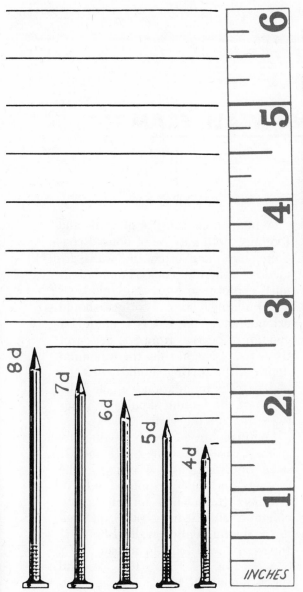

INCHES

45–14. RECOMMENDED NAILING SCHEDULE

Number and Size of Common Nails to Use on Various Members

Joist to sill or girder, toe nail................3-8d
Bridging to joist, toe nail each end............2-8d
Ledger strip...................................3-16d
                                          at each joist
1″ x 6″ subfloor or less to each joist,
    face nail..................................2-8d
Over 1″ x 6″ subfloor to each joist,
    face nail..................................3-8d
2″ subfloor to joist or girder, blind and
    face nail..................................2-16d
Sole plate to joist or blocking, face nail........16d @ 16″ oc
Top plate to stud, end nail.....................2-16d
Stud to sole plate, toe nail.....................4-8d
Doubled studs, face nail.......................16d @ 24″ oc
Doubled top plates, face nail...................16d @ 16″ oc
Top plates, laps and intersections, face nail.....2-16d
Continuous header, two pieces..................16d @ 16″ oc
                                       along each edge
Ceiling joists to plate, toe nail.................3-8d
Continuous header to stud, toe nail.............4-8d
Ceiling joists, laps over partitions, face nail.....3-16d
Ceiling joists to parallel rafters, face nail.......3-16d
Rafter to plate, toe nail........................3-8d
1-inch brace to each stud and plate,
    face nail..................................2-8d
1″ x 8″ sheathing or less to each bearing,
    face nail..................................2-8d
Over 1″ x 8″ sheathing to each bearing,
    face nail..................................3-8d
Built-up corner studs..........................16d @ 24″ oc
Built-up girders and beams.....................20d @ 32″ oc
                                       along each edge

45–15. NUMBER OF NAILS PER POUND

Size	Length and Gauge		Approximate No. to Lb.
2d	1″	No. 15	876
3d	1¼″	No. 14	568
4d	1½″	No. 12½	316
5d	1¾″	No. 12½	271
6d	2″	No. 11½	181
7d	2¼″	No. 11½	161
8d	2½″	No. 10¼	106
9d	2¾″	No. 10¼	96
10d	3″	No. 9	69
12d	3¼″	No. 9	63
16d	3½″	No. 8	49
20d	4″	No. 6	31
30d	4½″	No. 5	24
40d	5″	No. 4	18
50d	5½″	No. 3	14
60d	6″	No. 2	11

45–16. NUMBER OF NAILS REQUIRED IN CARPENTRY WORK

1 lb. of nails will case a door.
1 lb. of nails will case a window.
3 lbs. of nails per 1,000 ft. are required to put on rafters, joists, studding, etc.
15 lbs. of nails to the 1,000 feet are required to lay a 6″ pine floor.

flooring, and cabinetwork indoors. Interior finish, cabinets, flooring, or paneling should not be delivered to the building site until all wet plaster is completely dry.

505

Unit 46: FLOOR AND WALL FRAMING

A good foundation is essential to a wood frame house. While it is not the job of the carpenter to install the foundation, he must know how it is done so that he can always be sure the building is being started on a solid base.

46–1a. A foundation in which both footings and walls are of poured concrete.

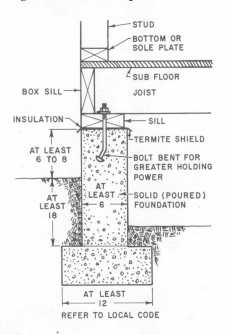

STUD

BOTTOM OR SOLE PLATE

SUB FLOOR

BOX SILL

JOIST

INSULATION

SILL

TERMITE SHIELD

AT LEAST 6 TO 8

BOLT BENT FOR GREATER HOLDING POWER

AT LEAST 6

SOLID (POURED) FOUNDATION

AT LEAST 18

AT LEAST 12

REFER TO LOCAL CODE

FOUNDATION

A foundation consists of walls and footings. Both may be of poured concrete, but more often the walls are made of concrete blocks. Foundations must conform to local soil conditions and building codes. Footings should extend below the exterior grade far enough to be free from the action of frost. As a general rule, the minimum depth of the footing should equal the width of the foundation wall, and the width of the footing should be about twice that of the wall.

Footings are of poured concrete. In most cases, after the basement has been dug, a trench is dug for the footings and cement poured into it. Footings are needed for pier posts, columns, and bearing posts, as well as for the foundation walls. *Fig. 46–2.* Blocks for walls should measure 8″ x 8″ x 16″ or 8″ x 12″ x 16″. Several types of concrete blocks used in foundations are shown in *Fig. 46–3.* After the footings are poured, the first course of blocks is laid out in order to check the layout. (A *course* is a series of building materials often stacked over one another such as shingles, siding, or concrete blocks.

Fig. 46-4.) Then a full mortar bed is spread with a trowel. *Fig. 46-5.*

The corner blocks should be laid first and carefully positioned. *Fig. 46-6.* All blocks should be laid with the thicker end of the face shell up as this provides a larger mortar bedding area. Several blocks are placed on end so that mortar can be applied to the vertical base shells of three or

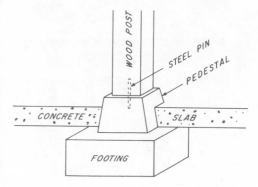

46–2.   The foundation and pedestal for a basement or cellar post. If the post is to be of wood, a steel pin should be fastened in the concrete to go into the post.

46–1b.   Foundations in which the footings are of poured concrete and the walls are of concrete blocks.

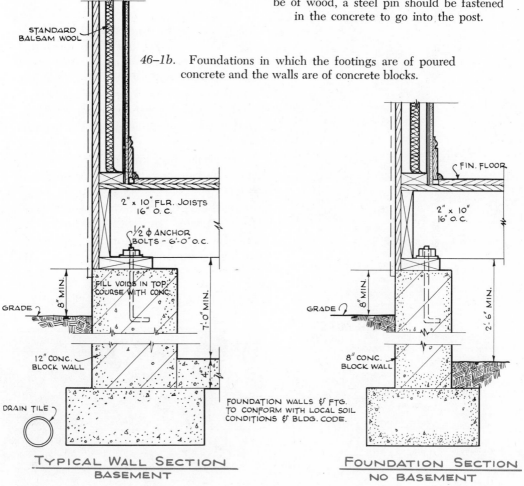

TYPICAL WALL SECTION
BASEMENT

FOUNDATION SECTION
NO BASEMENT

46–3a. Several common types of concrete blocks.

46–4. Checking the first course of blocks.

46–3b. Names of typical concrete blocks.

Stretcher (3 core)   Stretcher (2 core)   Solid Top

Header   Jamb   Corner

Partition

four blocks in one operation. *Fig. 46–7.* The blocks are then brought into final position and pushed into the mortar bed. *Fig. 46–8.* Blocks should next be carefully checked with a level, brought to proper grade, and made plumb. *Figs. 46–9 through 46–12.*

If the foundation wall is to be of poured concrete, the work should be done by experienced craftsmen who have the equipment to assemble the form. Anchor bolts ($\frac{1}{2}$″ x 8″ or 10″) should be placed 6′ or 8′ apart with at least two on each piece of sill. If

46–5. Using a trowel to spread the mortar.

46–3c. MORTAR MIXES
(PROPORTIONS BY VOLUME)

Type of Wall	Cement	Hydrated lime or lime putty	Damp, loose mortar, sand
Standard construction	1 masonry cement or	0	2 to 3
	1 portland cement	1 to 1¼	4 to 6
Construction to withstand heavy stress, severe frost	1 masonry cement plus 1 portland cement; or	0	4 to 6
	1 portland cement	0 to ¼	2 to 3

46–6.   Starting at a corner to lay the blocks.   46–9.   Making sure the blocks are aligned.

46–7.   Spreading mortar on the ends of the blocks.

46–8.   Pushing the blocks into place.

46–10.   Tapping a block with a trowel handle to level it.

46–11.   Making sure the block is plumb.

46–12.   The foundation going up.

concrete blocks are used, a ½″ layer of portland cement mortar should be applied to the exterior of the wall; then the wall should be covered with several coats of asphalt. Drain tile should also be installed around the exterior footings. *Fig. 46–13.*

When there is no basement, foundations may consist of free-standing piers, piers with curtain walls be-

46–13.   Correct foundation wall and footing with exterior covered with asphalt pitch, and drain tile installed.

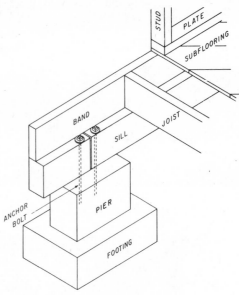

46–14.   Pier foundations for a house without a basement.

46–15.   Correct clearance between the bottom of a wood joist and the ground should be at least 18″ for a crawl space. Between the bottom of wood girders and the ground the clearance should be at least 12″. If the ground is damp it should be covered with a layer of asphalt-saturated felt.

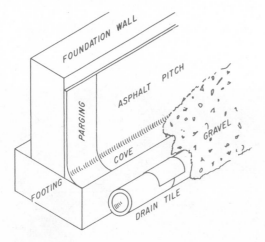

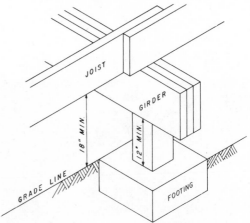

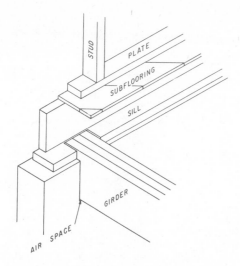

46–16. First-floor framing at the girder, and exterior wall platform frame construction. Review recommended nailing schedule before assembling any framing members. *Fig. 45–14.*

tween them, or piers supporting grade beams. In any of these methods, the piers and their footings must be large enough to carry the weight of the house and its contents. The spacing of the piers depends upon the arrangement of the floor framing and the location of the load-bearing walls and partitions. *Figs. 46–14 and 46–15.*

The working drawings of the house plans usually specify several alternate types of foundations.

FLOOR FRAMING

In a wood frame house, the floor framing consists of the following parts:

Posts. A post is a wood or steel member used in the basement to support

girders. If a wood post is used, it should be solid and not less than 6″ x 6″ in size. It should rest on the top of a masonry pedestal that is at least three inches above the floor.

Girders. Girders (beams) of wood or steel are large, principal beams used to support the floor joists. *Figs. 46–16 and 46–17.* When beams or girders are made of wood, they should be nailed together with two rows of 20d nails. The nails in each row should be spaced about 30″ apart with end joists over the supports. Glued laminated members are frequently used. The simplest method of floor framing is to place the joist on top of the girder; in this case, the top of the girder with wood sill should be even with the top of the sill plate on the foundation wall. *Figs. 46–18 and 46–19.*

Sill Plate. Sill or sill plate, the lowest member of the frame structure, rests on the foundation. *Fig. 46–20.* A metal termite shield should be placed under the sill. *Fig. 46–21.*

46–17. First-floor framing at girder, and exterior wall-balloon frame construction.

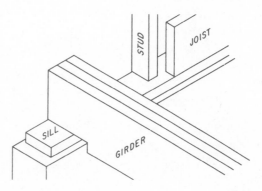

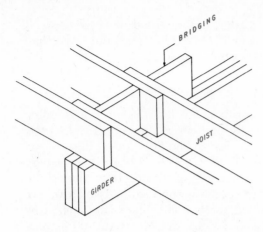

46–18a. Joists resting on wood girder.

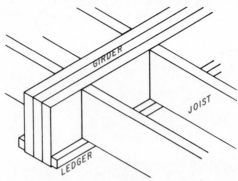

46–19. Two other methods of joist framing to the girder. (Neither of these methods reduces headroom in the basement as do the methods shown in *Fig. 46–18.*) *a.* Using a ledger strip nailed to the girder on which the joists rest.

Sometimes insulation material is also placed under it. The sill should consist of one thickness of 2″ lumber placed on the walls in such a way as to provide a full and even-bearing surface. Sills should be anchored to the foundation with $\frac{1}{2}$″ bolts spaced approximately 6′ to 8′ apart with at least two bolts in each piece of sill.

Two types of wood-sill construction are used over foundation walls, one for platform construction and one for balloon-frame construction. The "box" sill is usually used in platform construction. It consists of a sill or sill plate anchored to the founda-

46–18b. Joists resting on steel beam with wood sill.

46–19b. Using framing anchors.

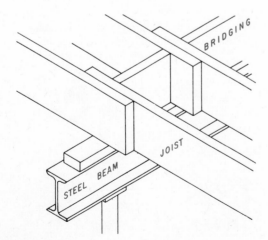

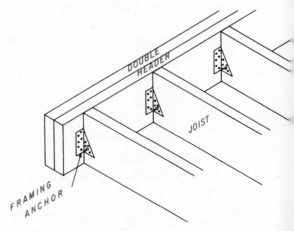

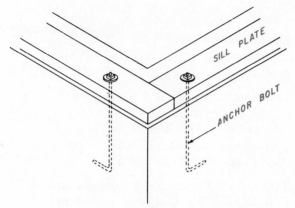

46–20. The sill plate is anchored to the foundation wall with anchor bolts.

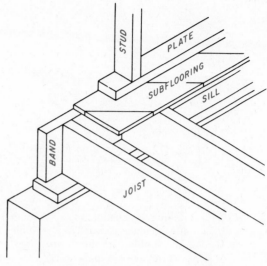

46–22. First-floor framing at the exterior wall in platform-frame construction.

tion wall for supporting and fastening the joists and a header (band) at the end of the joists. *Fig. 46–22.* Balloon-frame construction also has a sill plate upon which the joist rests.

46–21. Termite shields should be not less than 26-gauge galvanized iron, aluminum, or copper. They should be installed on top of all foundation walls, piers, and around pipes. The outer edges should be bent down slightly.

The studs also bear on this plate and are nailed both to the floor joist and to the plate. *Fig. 46–23.* The subfloor is laid diagonally or at right angles

46–23. First-floor framing at the exterior wall in balloon-frame construction.

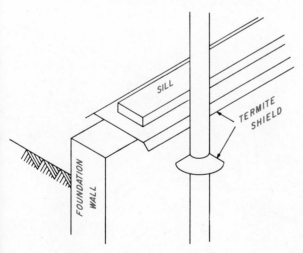

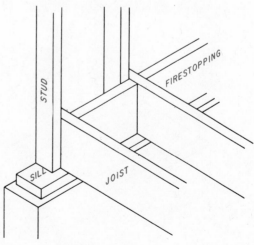

513

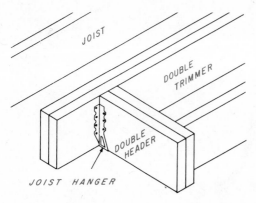

JOIST

DOUBLE TRIMMER

DOUBLE HEADER

JOIST HANGER

46–24. Framing a header to a trimmer with a joist hanger. Usually a double header and double trimmer are used around openings.

to the joist and a firestop is installed between the joists at the floor line.

Joists. Joists are a series of parallel beams which support floor or ceiling loads. Floor joists are usually a 2″ nominal thickness and either 6″, 8″,

10″, or 12″ deep. After the sills are level, the joists are fastened to the sill plate and girder, usually 16″ on center.

Headers. A header is a beam placed at right angles to joists. The joists are nailed to the header in framing a chimney, stairway, or other opening. *Figs. 46–24 and 46–25.*

Trimmers. A trimmer is a beam or joist to which a header is nailed in framing a chimney, stairway, or other opening. Trimmers and headers should be doubled when the span of the header exceeds 4′. Headers more than 6′ long should be supported at the ends by joist hangers or framing anchors unless they are supported on a partition, beam, or wall. Tail joists over 12′ long should be supported on a framing anchor or on a ledger strip not less than 2″ x 2″.

46–25a. Framing of tail joists to headers using a ledger strip.

46–25b. Framing of tail joists to header by framing anchors.

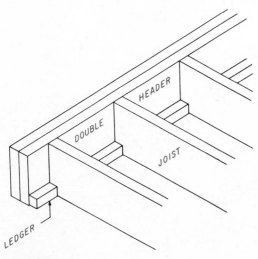

HEADER

DOUBLE

JOIST

LEDGER

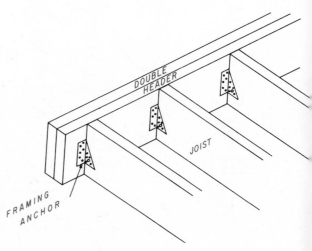

DOUBLE HEADER

JOIST

FRAMING ANCHOR

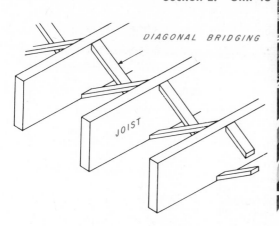

46–26. Diagonal bridging of floor joists. Nail at each end with two 8d nails. Nail the bottom ends after the subfloor has been installed. The photograph shows both diagonal and solid bridging.

Bridgings. Bridgings are small wood members (1″ x 3″, 1″ x 4″, or 2″ x 2″) inserted usually in a diagonal position between the floor joists for the purpose of stiffening the floor and helping to distribute the loads evenly on the joists. The bridging is cut at an angle to fit diagonally between the joists, and each piece is nailed at the top and bottom with two 8d nails. *Fig. 46–26.* Metal bridging of a rigid type can also be used. Sometimes solid bridging is installed.

Subflooring. This consists of the boards or sheet material laid over joists before a finish floor is laid. The material should consist of either $\frac{3}{4}$″ plywood, square edge, or tongue-and-groove boards no wider than 8″ and not less than $\frac{25}{32}$″ thick. *Fig. 46–27.*

46–27a. Subflooring installed diagonally.

46–27b. Using plywood sheets for the subfloor. Note the bridging between the joists.

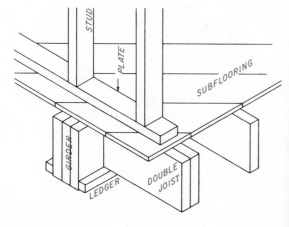

515

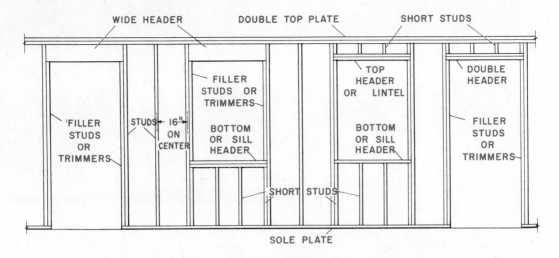

WIDE HEADER   DOUBLE TOP PLATE   SHORT STUDS

FILLER
STUDS OR
TRIMMERS

TOP
HEADER
OR LINTEL

DOUBLE
HEADER

FILLER
STUDS
OR
TRIMMERS

STUDS 16"
ON
CENTER

BOTTOM
OR SILL
HEADER

BOTTOM
OR SILL
HEADER

FILLER
STUDS
OR
TRIMMERS

SHORT STUDS

SOLE PLATE

46–28.   Parts of a typical wall. The fire block is not used in most one-story
homes. Nail soleplate to joist with 16d nails.

Subflooring can be laid either diagonally or at right angles to the joists. Diagonal subflooring is best because it makes the floor more rigid.

EXTERIOR WALLS

Exterior walls consist of the soleplate, studs, headers, top plates, and firestops. *Fig. 46–28.* The exterior wall framing should be strong and stiff enough to support the floors and roof. Generally 2″ x 4″ studs spaced 16″ or 24″ on center are used. The following is a description of the various parts of the exterior wall in platform construction:

Sole or Soleplate. This is a member, usually a 2″ x 4″, on which the partition studs rest.

Studs. Studs are a series of slender wood members placed in a vertical position as a supporting part of a wall or partition. Studs should be 2″ x 4″ for both one- and two-story buildings. Short studs that are sometimes added above and/or below the header (lintel) of doors and windows are called cripple studs or cripples.

Headers. As in floor framing, a header is a beam placed over an opening. In building exterior walls, headers (or lintels) are placed at right angles to the studs over a window or door opening. A double 2″ x 4″, 2″ x 6″, or 2″ x 8″ is used. The ends of the headers should be supported on studs or by framing anchors when the span does not exceed 3′. *Figs. 46–29 and 46–30.* When the opening exceeds 6′ in width it is good practice to install triple studs with each end of the header resting on two studs.

Plates. A plate is a horizontal member supported on studs and placed along the upper end of the wall. The

516

plate carries the trusses of a roof or carries the rafters directly. A double top plate is used in most construction.

Assembling Wall Sections. The most common method of assembling wall sections is to butt, nail, and fit the parts in a horizontal position on the subfloor. The plate or soleplate and the top plate are nailed to the pre-cut studs and the window and door headers are placed and nailed. Then the whole section is raised. The soleplate is nailed to the floor-framing member and temporary braces are added to hold the wall up. *Fig. 46–31.* Other wall sections are framed in a similar manner. For the exterior corners and at interior wall intersections, it is a good idea to install a multiple post in order to get a good tie-in between adjoining walls, and

46–29a. Framing around a window using a double header and double studs. Use 10d nails to fasten members together.

46–29b. Framing around a window, using a double header supported by framing anchors.

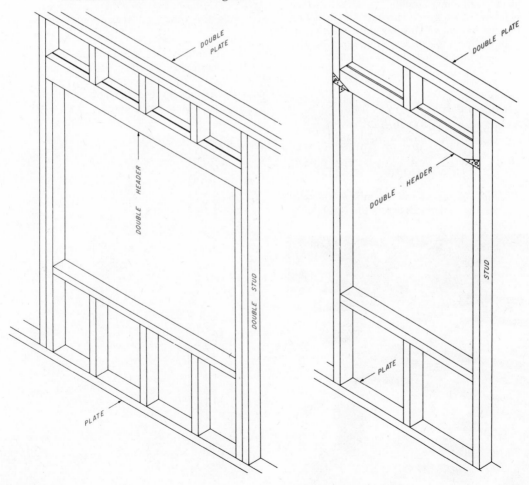

46–30. Framing around a large picture window. The exact method of installing the bottom or sill header varies with carpenters, as you can see by comparing this illustration with *Fig. 46–29.*

46–31b. Temporarily bracing a garage wall while the other walls are completed.

46–32. Three methods of assembling studs at outside corners. Use 16d nails staggered 24″ apart: *a.* Using three studs and space blocks. *b.* Using three studs and a shim. *c.* Using three studs.

to provide a nailing base for interior wallboard or plaster layout. *Figs. 46–32 and 46–33.* The exterior corner is usually made up of three 2″ x 4″ studs. Two 2″ x 4″ studs are nailed

46–31a. Checking the assembled wall section for squareness across the corners.

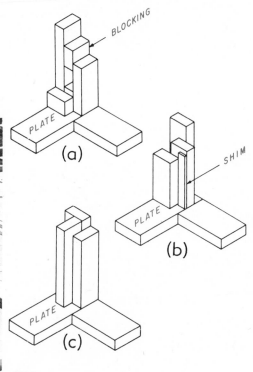

518

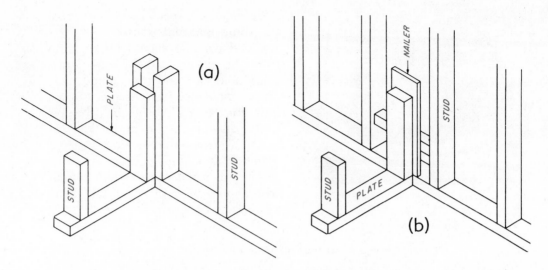

46–33. Assembly of studs where partition meets exterior wall. *a.* Using two studs spaced close together. *b.* Using a nailer strip fastened to blocks nailed between the studs.

together with short 2″ x 4″ spacer blocks. The third stud is nailed securely to the spaced studs with 10d nails. After the walls are up, they should be joined together at the corners. The top plate should overlap at the corners. *Fig. 46–34.*

All concealed spaces in wood framing are fire-stopped with wood blocking, accurately fitted to fill the openings and prevent drafts from one space to another. Stud spaces should be fire-stopped at each floor level with 2″ blocking. In one-story buildings, sills and plates will serve this purpose but, when they are not present, additional blocking is necessary. Additional strength for the walls can be provided by 1″ x 4″ members let into the outside face of the studs at an angle of 45 degrees. These are not found on most one-

46–34. Note how the corners of the double top plate overlap. Diagonal bracing is sometimes used to give added strength to the walls. Nail the plate to the studs with two 16d nails.

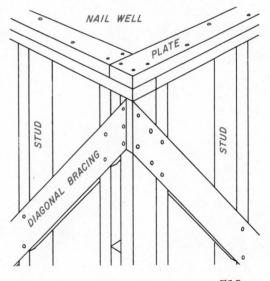

519

46–35. Here you see the framing for a fireplace opening.

story homes, especially when large sheathing material is used.

Wood framing should be separate from fireplaces and chimney masonry, and all wood trim should have proper clearance from fireplace openings. *Fig. 46–35.* All headers, beams, joists, and studs should be kept at least 2″ from the outside face of chimney and fireplace masonry. *Fig. 46–36.* All wood mantels and similar trim should be kept at least 6″ from a fireplace opening. *Fig. 46–37.*

46–36. Floor framing around a fireplace.

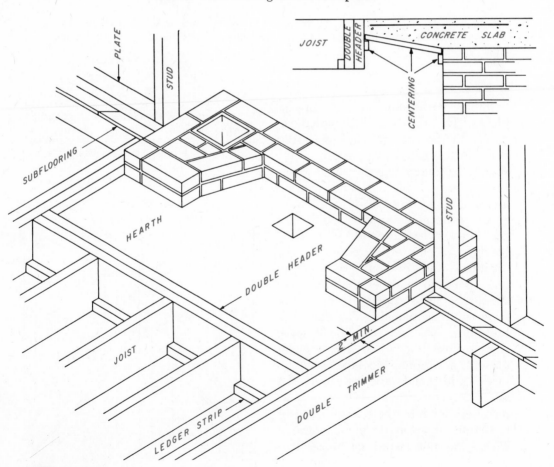

Section
through mantel.

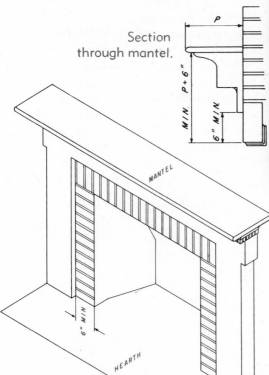

46–37. This is the correct clearance of trim around a fireplace opening.

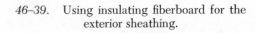

46–38. The carpenter is installing tongue-and-groove sheathing diagonally to the framing. This gives greater stability to the frame.

are provided by wood sheathing covered with asphalt-saturated felt weighing no less than 15 pounds for 100 square feet, or with other impregnated paper having equivalent water-repellent properties. Sheathing paper must not be of a type which will act as a vapor barrier. Starting

46–39. Using insulating fiberboard for the exterior sheathing.

The exterior wall is covered by sheathing which may be plain edge boards, tongue-and-groove boards, plywood, fiberboard, or gypsum. *Figs. 46–38 and 46–39.* Sheathing the end of the building before applying the siding is the usual practice, especially in mild climates. If wood sheathing is used, the exterior wall should be covered with asphalt-felt sheathing paper. The sheathing is nailed directly to the board studs. It forms a flat base on which the exterior finish is applied. Weather-tight walls

521

at the bottom of the wall, the felt should be lapped 4″ at horizontal joints and 6″ at vertical joints. Strips of sheathing paper about 6″ or 8″ wide are installed behind all exterior trim and around all openings.

PARTITION FRAMING

There are two types of interior partitions. *Fig. 46–40.* *Bearing partitions* support floors, ceilings, or roofs, and *non-bearing partitions* carry only the weight of the material in the partition.

Bearing Partitions. Studs for these should be at least 2″ x 4″, set with the wide dimensions perpendicular to the partition and capped with two pieces of 2″ lumber. Studs supporting the floor should be spaced 16″ on center while those supporting ceilings and roofs may be spaced 24″ on center. When openings occur, loads should be carried across the opening by headers similar to the exterior walls.

Non-Bearing Partitions. Studs may be 2″ x 3″ or 2″ x 4″ set with wide faces perpendicular or parallel to the partitions. Spacing of studs may be 16″ to 24″.

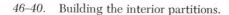

46–40. Building the interior partitions.

Unit 47: BUILDING THE ROOF

Roof framing may seem to be a complicated job because it involves a good many angle cuts. *Fig. 47–1.* However, since most small homes have fairly simple shed or gable roofs, the framing is not so difficult as it seems.

Roof construction and framing for the ceiling must be strong in order to withstand snow and wind. The parts are fastened together to provide continuity across the building; they are also anchored to exterior walls. There are two kinds of roof framing: the traditional method in which a ridge board and rafters are used, and the newer trussed rafters.

Ceiling joists are installed to support the finished ceiling. Sometimes they also act as joists for an attic floor and as a tie between exterior walls and interior partitions. The ceiling joists are nailed to exterior walls and to the ends of rafters. When joining over interior partitions, they are nailed to plates and to each other. Where ceiling joists are at right angles to rafters, short joists are nailed to the ends of the rafters and the top plate, and are fastened to the ceiling joists by means of metal straps or framing anchors.

KINDS OF ROOFS

The most popular roofs for homes and small buildings are flat, shed, gable, gable with dormer, gable valley, hip, and hip and valley. *Fig. 47–2.*

Flat and Shed Roofs. Roof joists for flat and shed roofs are laid level or at a slight slope with roof sheathing and roofing on the top. The underside of the rafters is utilized to support the ceiling. A shed roof has a slight slope to provide for adequate drainage. It may overhang beyond the wall. Insulation may be added just above the sheathing or in the spaces between the rafters. The

47–1. Building the roof is the most difficult part of house construction.

523

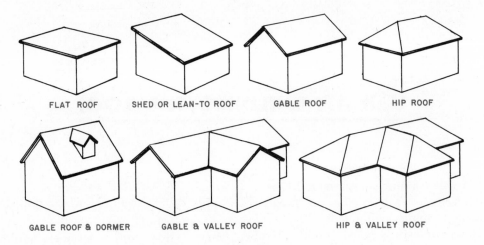

FLAT ROOF   SHED OR LEAN-TO ROOF   GABLE ROOF   HIP ROOF

GABLE ROOF & DORMER   GABLE & VALLEY ROOF   HIP & VALLEY ROOF

47–2. Common kinds of roofs.

insulation should be vented to remove hot air in the summer and to
provide protection from condensation
in the winter. This type of roof
generally requires larger-sized structural members than do pitched roofs.
In milder climates flat and shed
roofs may be built with 2″ matched
planks for roof sheathing supported
on large beams spaced about 6′
apart with the planking and beams
exposed on the underside.

Gable Roofs. To build a gable roof,
it is necessary to know how to lay
out and cut *common rafters.* This is
not difficult if you understand certain basic terms of roof construction.
Study *Fig. 47–3* and then review
these terms.

Span. The distance from one side
of the building to the other, or the
measurement between the outer
corners of the top plates.

Run. Equal to half the span (ex-

47–3. Terms used in roof construction.

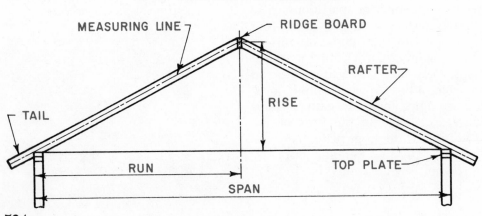

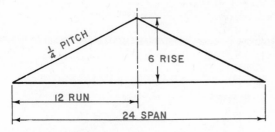

47–4. This roof has a ¼ pitch, or 6″ to the foot.

47–5. This roof has a ⅓ pitch.

cept when the pitch of the roof is irregular).

Rise. The vertical distance from the top of the plate to the upper end of the measuring line.

Measuring line. An imaginary line running lengthwise along the middle of the rafter.

Pitch. The pitch of a roof is the ratio of the rise of the rafter to the span (width) of the building. Pitch is really the slant or slope of the roof. It can be expressed in two different ways. Look at *Fig. 47–4.* Notice that the span is 24′ and that the rise is 6′. Therefore, the roof has ¼ pitch:

$$\frac{6' \text{ rise}}{24' \text{ span}} = \frac{1}{4} \text{ pitch}$$

The pitch may also be expressed on the basis of the number of *inches of rise* for each *foot of run* (½ the span). Look again at *Fig. 47–4.* The rise is 72″ (6 × 12″). The run is 12′ (½ of 24). The pitch is then expressed as a rise of 6″ to each foot of run:

$$\frac{72'' \text{ of rise}}{12' \text{ of run}} = 6'' \text{ to the foot}$$

The common roof pitches are ¼, ⅓, and ½. *Fig. 47–5.* A rise of a ½ pitch roof means that the roof rises one-half the distance of the span. For

example, if the span is 20, the rise would be 10. *Fig. 47–6.*

Ridge board. The horizontal piece that connects the upper ends of the rafters.

Tail. The overhanging part of the rafter. It must be added to the length of the rafter if the roof has an overhang or eave.

Laying Out and Cutting Common Rafters. The rafters are the skeleton of the roof. They must be carefully made and fitted if they are to support the roof weight. Cutting a rafter is not easy but it can be satisfactorily done by following instructions. Remember that the rise, the run, and

47–6. A roof with a ½ pitch.

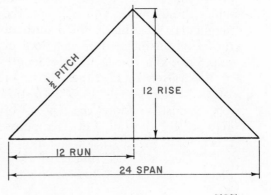

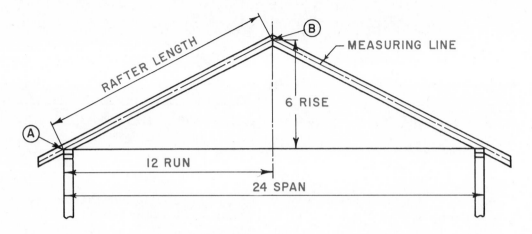

47-7. Note that the true rafter length is from point A to point B.

the rafter itself form a right triangle. The length of the common rafter is the shortest distance between the outer edge of the plate (A) and a point on the center line of the ridge board (B). *Fig. 47-7*. This length is found along the *measuring line*. Let's assume that you wish to cut a common rafter for this roof. This roof has ¼ pitch, or it rises 6″ for each foot of run. Proceed as follows:

1. Check the rafter table on the carpenter's square. *Fig. 47-8*. Look at the first line, marked "Length Common Rafters Per Foot Run." Since the rise is 6″ per foot, look under the 6″ mark. You will find the number 13.42. This is the length of the rafter in inches for each foot of run. Since the run is 12′, the length of the rafter is 12 times 13.42 or 161.04″. This equals 13′ 5″. To this length must be added the amount of material for the tail. Let us suppose this amount to be 12″, or one foot.

2. Select a 2″ x 4″ that is 16′ long. Place it over two sawhorses with the

top edge of the rafter away from you. Notice in *Fig. 47-9* that the top or plumb (sometimes called *ridge*) cut and the bottom or heel (sometimes called *plate*) cut are actually made at right angles to each other. Draw a line along the center of the rafter. This is to represent the *measuring line*.

3. Place the 6″ mark of the tongue and the 12″ mark of the blade over the rafter as shown in *Fig. 47-10* and mark the plumb cut.

4. Measure a length along the measuring line equal to 13′ 5″ and mark a point.

5. Hold the square as shown in *Fig. 47-11* and mark the heel cut. Square off the heel cut where the first layout line intersects the measuring line.

6. Measure the thickness of the ridge board. Measure back from the plumb line half this amount and mark a line that is parallel to the plumb line. *Fig. 47-12*.

7. Make the *top* cut and *heel*

526

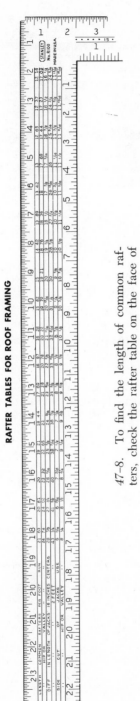

RAFTER TABLES FOR ROOF FRAMING

47-8. To find the length of common rafters, check the rafter table on the face of the steel square.

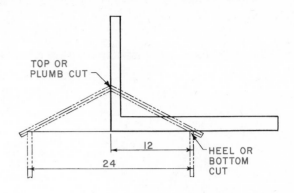

TOP OR PLUMB CUT

12

24

HEEL OR BOTTOM CUT

47-9. This enlarged square shows how the top and bottom cuts are made.

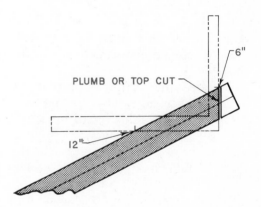

6"

PLUMB OR TOP CUT

12"

47-10. Layout of the plumb or top cut.

47-11. Layout of the heel cut. This is sometimes called a bird's-mouth cut.

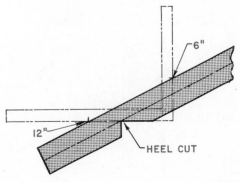

6"

12"

HEEL CUT

527

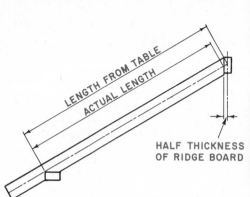

LENGTH FROM TABLE

ACTUAL LENGTH

HALF THICKNESS
OF RIDGE BOARD

47-12. Reducing the length of the rafter by half the thickness of the ridge board.

47-13b. Note how the studs have been notched out and securely nailed to the end rafters.

cuts. The notch formed by the heel cuts is sometimes called a *bird's mouth*.

8. Use this rafter as a pattern and cut a second rafter. Try the two rafters with the ridge board between

to see how the heel cut and the top cut fit. If they are all right, use one of these rafters as a pattern to cut all of the others needed. The tail can be cut off before or after the rafters are nailed in place.

47-13a. Exterior wall framing at gable end.

47-14. Roof framing around chimney masonry.

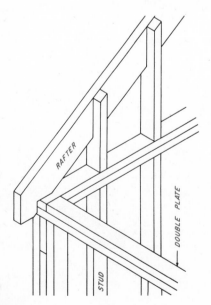

RAFTER

DOUBLE PLATE

STUD

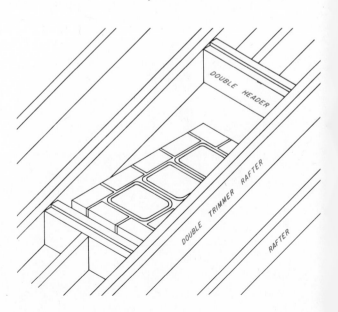

DOUBLE HEADER

DOUBLE TRIMMER RAFTER

RAFTER

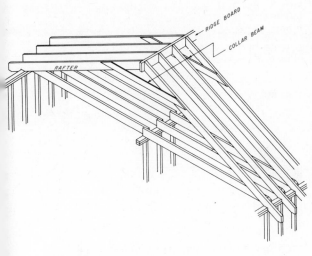

47-15. Roof framing with ceiling joist parallel to rafter and with a collar beam for added strength.

follows: Make a full-size pattern on the subfloor of the house. Draw a line across the subfloor at right angles to one side. Bisect this line and draw a perpendicular line. Measure along this line the total rise of the roof. Then draw a line from the end to the outside edge of the house. This will give you a full-sized roof triangle. You can then lay out the top or plumb cut and the heel or bottom cut by placing a rafter flat on the floor over the layout. Remember to allow for half the thickness of the ridge board. When you have cut one pair of rafters, check them to make sure they fit. Then use one of the rafters for a template, or pattern, for all the others.

9. The studs in gable ends should rest on the top plates with the tops of the studs notched to fit the end rafter to which they are nailed. *Fig. 47-13.*

10. When framing around a chimney use a double trimmer rafter on either side and a double header to block out the opening. *Fig. 47-14.*

11. For added strength, collar beams of 1″ x 6″ boards should be installed in the upper third of the attic space to every third pair of rafters. *Fig. 47-15.*

A dormer window is framed out from the gable roof so that the attic space can be used for rooms. *Fig. 47-16.*

A shed-type dormer is another way of enlarging the attic space for better use. *Fig. 47-17.*

A *second method* of laying out and cutting common rafters is as

47-16. This is the correct way of framing a gable dormer.

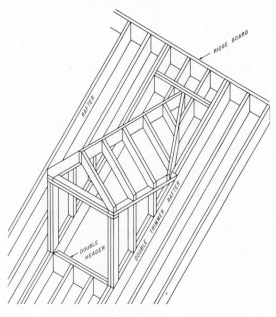

A *third method* for finding the length of common rafters is as follows: On the tongue of the square, find the number of inches the roof is to rise per foot; use the 12″ mark on the blade of the square, or the number of inches of rise for each foot of run. Then place the square on the rafter as shown in *Fig. 47–18*, as many times as the number of feet in half the width of the building. This will give the exact length of the

47–17. Framing in a shed-type dormer adds greatly to the usable space in an attic or half floor.

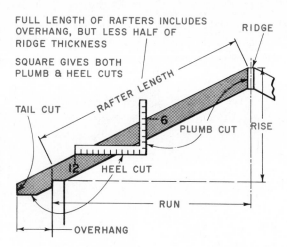

FULL LENGTH OF RAFTERS INCLUDES OVERHANG, BUT LESS HALF OF RIDGE THICKNESS

SQUARE GIVES BOTH PLUMB & HEEL CUTS

TAIL CUT

RAFTER LENGTH

PLUMB CUT

RIDGE

RISE

HEEL CUT

RUN

OVERHANG

STEP OFF RAFTER WITH THE SQUARE

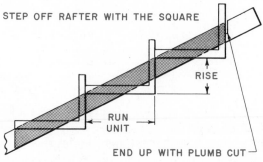

RISE

RUN UNIT

END UP WITH PLUMB CUT

47–18. Stepping off the length of a common rafter.

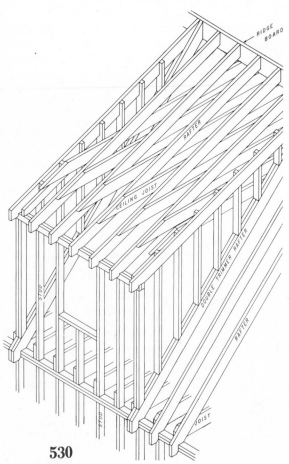

rafter. The line of the tongue gives the plumb or top cut and the line of the blade gives the seat or heel cut. Remember you must trim off half the thickness of the ridge board and provide material for the tail.

A fourth way of finding the lengths of common rafters for most common roof pitches is:

1. For ¼ pitch roof, multiply the width of the building by the decimal .56. For example, for a 12′ width house, 12W × .56 = 6.72 or 6′ 9″.

2. For a ⅓ pitch roof, multiply

47-19a.   Hip and jack rafters on a hip roof.

the width of the building by the decimal .71. For example, for a 12′
width house, 12W × .71 = 8.52 or 8′
6″.

HIP AND VALLEY RAFTERS°

The hip rafter is a roof member
that forms a raised area or "hip" in
the roof, usually extending from the
corner of the building diagonally to
the ridge. *Fig. 47–19.* The valley
rafter is similar, but it forms a de-
pression in the roof instead of a hip.

the width of the building by the
decimal .6. For example, for a 12′
width house, 12W × .6 = 7.20 or 7′
2½″.

3. For a ½ pitch roof, multiply

°The following material, up to but not including the discussion of lightweight rafters
on page 521, is reprinted by the courtesy of
Stanley Tools, from their booklet, *The Steel
Square,* by L. Perth. Illustrations are also
copied from this booklet which is a standard
reference in its field.

47–19b.   Roof framing at hip rafter.

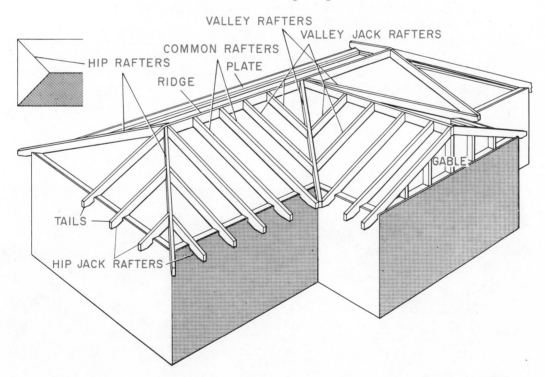

VALLEY RAFTERS
VALLEY JACK RAFTERS
COMMON RAFTERS
HIP RAFTERS
PLATE
RIDGE
GABLE
TAILS
HIP JACK RAFTERS

Fig. 47–20. It also extends diagonally from plate to ridge. Therefore the total rise of hip and valley rafters is the same as that of common rafters. *Fig. 47–21.*

The relation of hip and valley rafters to common rafters is the same as the relation of the sides of a right triangle. You may have learned in geometry that the square of the hypotenuse of a right triangle equals the sum of the squares of the other two sides. (The hypotenuse is the side opposite the right angle.) Therefore if the sides which form the right angle are each 12″ long, the hypotenuse will equal 16.97″, usually taken as 17″.

The position of the hip rafter and its relation to the common rafter are plainly illustrated in *Figs. 47–22 and 47–23* where the hip rafter is compared to the "diagonal" of a square prism. The prism has a base that is 5′ square and its height is 3′ 4″. D is the corner of the building. BC is

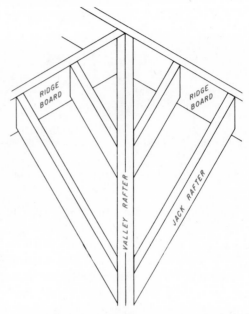

47–20b. Roof framing at valley rafter.

the total rise of the roof. AB is the run of the common rafter. AC is the common rafter. DB is the run of the hip rafter. DC is the hip rafter. It will be noted that the figure DAB

47–20a. Valley and jack rafters on a gable and valley roof.

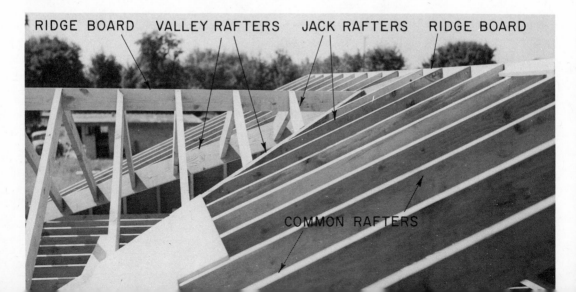

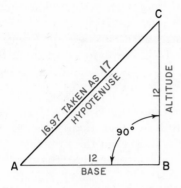

47-21. The hypotenuse of a right triangle with sides that equal 12″ will equal 16.97″. This is so close to 17″ that this number is used on the square.

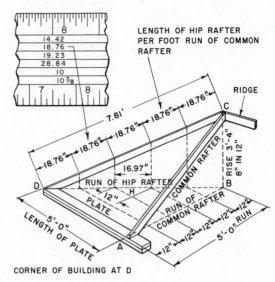

CORNER OF BUILDING AT D

is a right triangle whose sides are the portion of the plate DA, the run of common rafter AB, and the run of hip rafter DB. The run of the hip rafter, being opposite the right angle A, is the hypotenuse or the longest side of the right triangle. If we should take only one foot of run of common rafter and one foot of plate length we will have a right triangle

47-22. Here you see the relative position of hip rafter to common rafter.

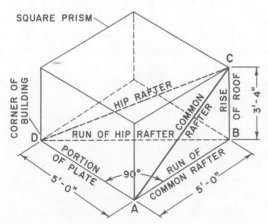

47-23. Here is an example of the way to find the length of a hip rafter.

"H" (*Fig. 47–23*) whose sides are each 12″ long and whose hypotenuse is approximately 17″. *Fig. 47–19.* The hypotenuse in this small triangle "H" is a portion of the run of the hip rafter DB which corresponds to one foot run of common rafter. Therefore the run of hip rafter is always 16.97″ for every 12″ of foot run of common rafter, and the "total run" of hip rafter will be 16.97″ multiplied by the number of feet run of common rafter.

Length of Hip and Valley Rafters. These lengths are found on the second line of the rafter table, which is entitled "Length of Hip or Valley Rafters per Foot Run."

Rule. To find the length of a hip or valley rafter, multiply the length given in the table by the number of feet of the run of common rafter.

533

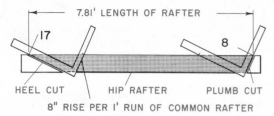

7.81' LENGTH OF RAFTER

17

8

HEEL CUT   HIP RAFTER   PLUMB CUT

8" RISE PER 1' RUN OF COMMON RAFTER

47–24. Marking the top or plumb cut and the seat or heel cut of a hip rafter.

Example. Find the length of a hip rafter where the rise of roof is 8″ per foot run, or ⅓ pitch, and the building is 10′ wide. Proceed the same as you did for common rafters, i.e., on the "inch line" of the body of the square, find the figure corresponding to the rise of roof which is 8. On the second line under this figure is found 18.76 which is the length of hip rafter in inches for each foot of run of common rafter for ⅓ pitch. The common rafter has a 5′ run; therefore there are also 5 equal lengths for the hip rafter as may be seen in the illustration. *Fig. 47–19.* We have found the length of the hip rafter to be 18.76″ per one foot run. Therefore the total length of hip rafter will be $18.76 \times 5 = 93.80'' = 7.81'$ or, for practical purposes, 7′ 9⅝″.

Top and Bottom Cuts. Use the following rule:

Rule. To obtain the top and bottom cuts of hip or valley rafters use 17″ on the body and the *rise per foot run* on the tongue. Number 17 on the body will give the seat cut, and the figure on the tongue the vertical or top cut. *Fig. 47–24.*

Measuring Hip and Valley Rafters. The length of all hip and valley rafters must be measured along the center of the top edge or back. Rafters with a tail or eave are treated similarly to common rafters, except the measurement or measuring line is the center of the top edge.

Deduction from Hip or Valley Rafter for Ridge. The deduction for the ridge is measured the same as for the common rafter except that half the diagonal (45 degrees) thickness of the ridge must be used.

Side Cuts. Hip and valley rafters, in addition to the top and bottom cuts, must also have side or cheek cuts at the point where they meet the ridge. The side cuts are found on the sixth or bottom line of the rafter tables, which is marked: "Side Cut Hip or Valley—Use." The figures given in this line refer to the graduation marks on the outside edge of the body. The figures on the square have been derived by determining the figure to be used with 12 on the tongue for the side cuts of the various pitches by the following method: From a plumb line, the thickness of the rafter is measured and marked at right angles as at A, *Fig. 47–25.* A line is then squared across the top of the rafter and the diagonal points connected as at B. The line B or side cut is obtained by marking along the tongue of the square.

Rule. To obtain the side cut for hip or valley rafters, on the body of the square take the figure given in the table, and take 12″ on the tongue. Mark the side cut along the tongue where the tongue coincides with the point on the measuring line.

Example. Find the side cut for a

534

hip rafter on a roof having 8″ rise per foot run or $\frac{1}{3}$ pitch. *Fig. 47–26* represents the position of the hip rafter on the roof. First locate the figure 8 on the outside edge of the body. Under this figure in the bottom line you find $10\frac{7}{8}$. Use this figure on the body and 12″ on the tongue. The square is applied to the edge of the back of the hip rafter. The side cut CD comes along the tongue. The deduction for half the thickness of the ridge must be determined and measured the same as for the common rafters except that half the diagonal (45 degrees) thickness of the ridge must be used. In making the seat cut for the hip rafter, an allowance must be made for the top edge of the rafter which would project above the line of the common and jack rafters if the corners of the hip rafter were not removed or "backed." The hip rafter must be slightly lowered by cutting parallel to the seat cut a distance which varies with the thickness and pitch of the roof.

It should be noted that the 12″ mark on the tongue is used in all angle cuts, top, bottom, and side. This leaves the workman only one number to remember when laying out side or angle cuts, namely the figure

47-25. Marking the side cut for a hip rafter.

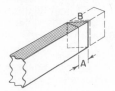

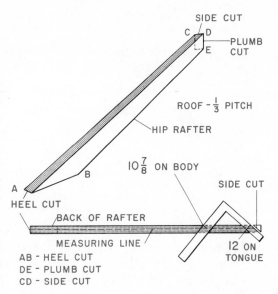

47-26. Marking the top or plumb cut, the heel cut, and the side cut for a hip rafter.

taken from the fifth or sixth line in the table.

The side cuts always come on the right hand or tongue side on rafters. When marking boards, these can be reserved for convenience at any time by taking the 12″ mark on the body and using the body references on the tongue. In other words, the square can be laid directly on the stock, and all necessary information and figures will be visible. There is no need to turn the square over.

JACK RAFTERS

Jack rafters are *discontinued* common rafters, that is, ones cut off by the intersection of a hip or valley before reaching the full length from plate to ridge. Jack rafters lie in the same plane with common rafters. They usually are spaced the same as

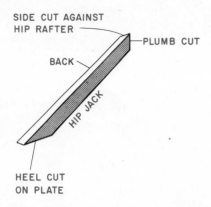

SIDE CUT AGAINST
HIP RAFTER

PLUMB CUT

BACK

HIP JACK

HEEL CUT
ON PLATE

47–27.   Layout for a hip jack.

common rafters and have the same pitch; therefore they also have the same length per foot run as common rafters have. Jack rafters are usually spaced 16″ or 24″ apart and, as they rest against the hip or valley equally spaced, the second jack must be twice as long as the first one, the third three times as long as the first, and so on. *Fig. 47–21.*

Lengths of Jack Rafters. The lengths of jacks are given in the third and fourth lines of the rafter tables and are indicated: 3rd line: "Difference in Length of Jacks—16″ centers." 4th line: "Difference in Length of Jacks —2′ centers." The figures in the table indicate the length of the first or shortest jack, which is also the difference in length between the first and second jacks, the second and third, and so on.

Rule. To find the length of a jack rafter, multiply the value given in the tables by the number indicating the position of the jack. From this, subtract half the diagonal (45 degrees) thickness of the hip or valley rafter.

Example. Find the length of the second jack rafter, if the roof has a rise of 8″ to 1′ of run of common rafter, when the spacing between jacks is 16″. On the outer edge of the body find figure 8 which corresponds to the rise of roof. On the third line under this figure find 19.23. This means that the first jack rafter will be 19.23″ long. Since the length of the second jack is required, multiply 19.23 by 2 which equals 38.46″ or, for practical purposes, 3′ 2½″. From this length deduct half the diagonal (45 degrees) thickness of the hip or valley rafter in the same manner as was done on the hip rafter for the ridge. Proceed in the same way when the lengths of jacks spaced with 24″ between centers are required.

Top and Bottom Cuts. Since jack rafters have the same rise per foot run as common rafters, the method of obtaining the top and bottom cuts is the same as for common rafters. Use the 12″ mark on the body and the *rise per foot run* on the tongue

47–28.   Layout for a valley jack.

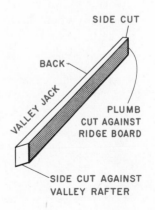

SIDE CUT

BACK

VALLEY JACK

PLUMB
CUT AGAINST
RIDGE BOARD

SIDE CUT AGAINST
VALLEY RAFTER

536

as in cutting a common rafter. The blade will give you the seat cut, and the tongue will give you the plumb cut.

Side Cut. At the end where the jack rafter meets the hip or valley rafter, a side cut is required. Side cuts for jacks are found on the fifth line of the rafter tables, marked "Side Cut of Jacks—Use."

Rule. To obtain the side cut for a jack rafter, take the figure shown in the table on the body of the square, and 12″ on the tongue. Mark along the tongue for side cut.

Example. Find the side cut for a jack rafter on a roof having 8″ rise per foot run, or $\frac{1}{3}$ pitch. *Figs. 47–27 and 47–28.* In the fifth line under the figure 8 find 10. This figure taken on the outside edge of the body, and 12″ on the tongue, will give the required side cut.

LIGHTWEIGHT TRUSSED RAFTERS

Framing for pitched roofs may be fabricated as light trusses and installed as complete units. This is a

47–29a. Trussed rafter assembled with gusset plates, glue, and nails.

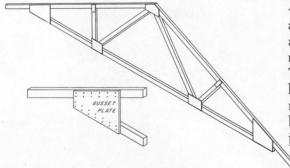

47–29b. Nailing plywood gussets in assembling trussed rafters. The operator is using a portable pneumatic (air operated) nailing machine.

common practice in pre-fabricated homes. These trussed rafters can be purchased as complete units for use in any conventional home building. The various members of the truss are joined by fasteners such as nails, nails and glue, bolts, connectors, and other framing devices. Trusses consist essentially of top and bottom cords connected by suitable diagonal and vertical members. Trusses must be designed in accordance with sound engineering practice. Complete information on how to design and use trussed roofs is available from the Timber Engineering Company, Washington 6, D. C.

There are two common ways of fastening trussed rafters—with gusset plates of plywood or metal (*Fig. 47–29*), and with timber connectors and nails. A simple lapped joint and a special metal ring combine to make an efficient fabricating system. The trussed rafter parts are cut and holes are drilled for bolts and the ring. *Fig. 47–30.* The parts can then be shipped flat and assembled on the job. *Fig. 47–31.* The use of trussed

537

538

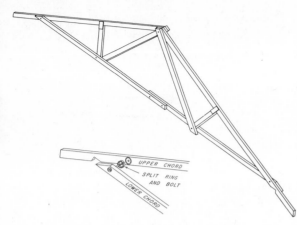

47–30a. Trussed rafter assembled with timber connectors and nails.

rafters eliminates the need for interior bearing partitions. This makes it possible to complete the inside of a home or building the same as one large room. For example, the insulation, ceiling, walls, and floor can be finished and then partitions can be built in any location desired. Spacing of trussed rafters is usually 16″ to 24″

47–30b. Cutting the holes for the split metal ring and bolt for assembling the trussed rafter.

depending on the kind of roof sheathing and ceiling covering used.

Overhangs at eaves can be provided by extending the upper cord of the trusses the required distance beyond the wall, or by nailing the overhang framing to the upper cord of the trusses.

ROOF SHEATHING

Roof sheathing is a covering over rafters. It usually consists of 1″ thick board or ¾″ plywood. *Fig. 47–32*. If boards are used, they are usually applied perpendicular to the rafters. Boards should be laid close together to provide a continuous support for roll roofing, asphalt shingles, and similar materials. When wood shingles are applied, open sheathing consisting of 1″ x 3″ or 1″ x 4″ strips may be used and spaced to coincide with the weather exposure of the shingles. When plywood sheathing is used, it should be laid with its face grain perpendicular to the rafters.

47–31. Assembling the trussed rafter on the job using the split ring and bolt.

47–32.   Using boards for roof sheathing.

47–33b.   Here you see a wide-box cornice with the lookouts nailed to a strip fastened to the studs on the outside of the sheathing.

CORNICE CONSTRUCTION

A cornice is a projection of the roof at the eaves that forms a connection between the roof and the side walls. There are four general types of cornice: (a) A *box cornice* uses the rafter projection for nailing surfaces for the fascia and soffit boards. The *fascia* is a flat board, usually in com-

47–33a.   A wide-box cornice with the lookouts nailed to the studs.

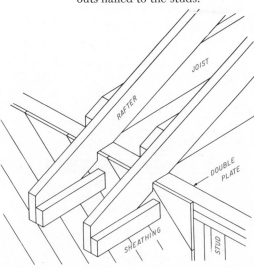

bination with molding, located at the outer face of the cornice. The *soffit* is the underside member of a building such as the board under a cornice. A *frieze* board is often used at the wall to receive the siding. (b) A *closed cornice* has no rafter projection. (c) The *wide-box cornice*, which is so popular in ranch home construction, requires framing members called lookouts which serve as a nailing surface and support for the soffit board. *Fig. 47–33.* The lookouts are nailed to the rafter ends and also toenailed to the wall sheathing or nailed directly to the studs. (d) The *open cornice* consists of a fascia board nailed to the rafter end. The rafters are exposed and can be seen projecting out through the wall. When used on a house, the roof boards that are seen from below are made of finished material *Fig. 47–34.* The *cornice return* is the end trim of the cornice on a gabled roof. This varies in design and is always shown on the blueprint.

47–34. Open cornice construction. Notice that you can see the roof sheathing.

47–36. Here you can see how the frieze board and molding are attached to the gable end just under the roof sheathing. Note the opening cut for ventilation. (The frieze board and molding have been cut for this instructional photo.)

RAKE OR GABLE-END FINISH

The rake section is the trim along the gable end of a house. In some house designs, the gable end has a projected roof. *Fig. 47–35.* The simplest gable-end finish is a frieze board installed along the edge just under the roof sheathing. Sometimes a molding is also added. *Fig. 47–36.* When a projected roof is used, a box-type finish is employed for the rake.

Fig. 47–37. In every case, all details are given in the house plans. Study one of the sets shown in Unit 4.

FLASHING

Flashing is thin metal sheets of galvanized iron, copper, or aluminum placed around chimneys, in roof valleys, over windows and doors, and in any other place where there is a change in the roof lines. Flashing

47–35. Roof framing for overhang at the gable end.

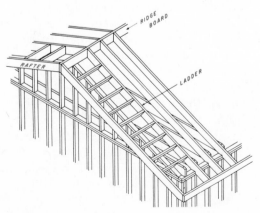

47–37. The rake detail for the house with a projected roof. Note that this information is available in the house plans.

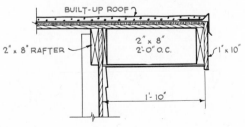

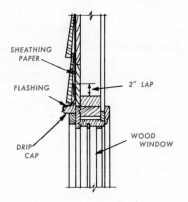

47–38a. Cutaway view showing flashing above a window. The location of flashing is shown in detail on a good set of house plans.

must be installed so that water will run off and over the shingles or siding and not under them. *Fig. 47–38.* Flashing must be installed before the final roof cover is put on.

ROOF COVERINGS

Roof coverings should be chosen for appearance, cost, and durability.

Common materials for covering pitched roofs are shingles of wood, asphalt, and asbestos. Tile, slate, aluminum sheets, galvanized iron, copper, and tin are sometimes used. For flat, shed, and low-pitched gable roofs, roof composition or built-up roofing with a topping of gravel, crushed stone, or marble-chip is often preferred. *Fig. 47–39.* Underlay or roof felt is normally required for asphalt, asbestos, or slate shingles. Asbestos shingles come in many colors, shapes, and surface textures. With these, a felt underlay is first attached to the roof sheathing. *Fig. 47–40.* Then the first course is started by laying a series of wood shingles along the edge covered by the asbestos shingles. *Fig. 47–41.* Shingles should project at least $1\frac{1}{2}''$ beyond the roof sheathing to provide a drip line. Gutters and downspouts are needed unless eave projection is $24''$ or greater. *Fig. 47–42.* The first course of asphalt shingles should extend downward beyond the wood shingles about $\frac{1}{2}''$. Each course up to that

47–38b. Flashing at a valley and dormer.

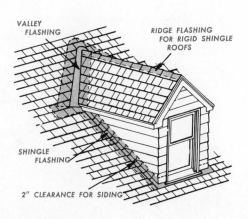

47–38c. Flashing around a chimney.

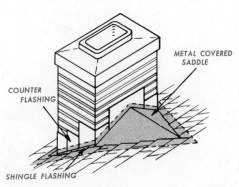

541

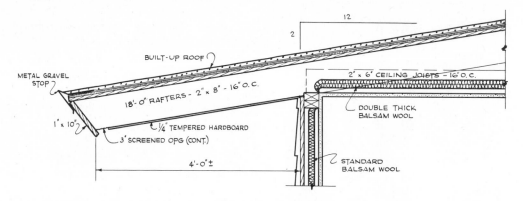

47–39.   Typical cornice section. Note the construction for a built-up roof with low pitch.

should allow about 5″ of exposure of the previous course. Wood shingles and shakes (hand-cut wood shingles) are usually made of western red cedar. When wood shingles are applied, open sheathing consisting of 1″ x 3″ or 1″ x 4″ strips may be installed and spaced to coincide with the weather exposure of the shingles. The first shingle course should be double, with the upper ones overlapping those beneath. It should extend about 2″ to 2½″ beyond the edge of the roof. Usually the second course is

47–41a.   Nailing the courses of shingles, using spiral-thread roofing nails.

47–40.   Flashing and roof felt have been installed before shingles are applied.

47–41b.   Applying asbestos roofing shingles.

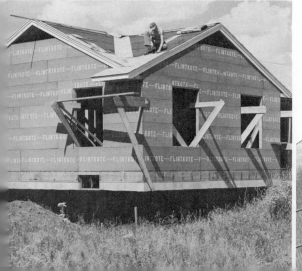

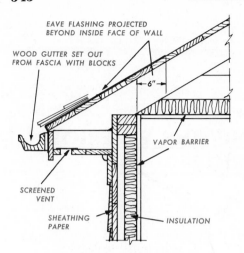

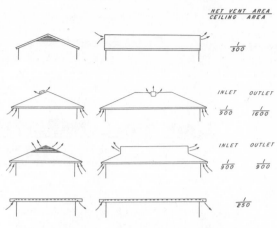

47–42.   Installing a wood gutter.

47–43b.   Methods of ventilating roof spaces and amount of ventilation required.

laid so that there is about 3″ to 5″ of exposure.

VENTILATION OF ATTIC SPACE

To eliminate the hazard of moisture condensation in cold weather and to permit the escape of heat in hot weather, ventilation of attic

47–43a.   A wood louver to be installed in the gable end just under the roof for ventilating the attic.

space is required. *Fig. 47–43.* For gable roofs, screened louvers generally are installed. The net area of the opening should be about $\frac{1}{300}$ of the area of the ceiling below. However, if there is to be an attic fan, the louver size should be increased. Ventilation can also be provided in the roof overhang or in the roof itself. *Fig. 47–44.*

47–44.   Method of installing ventilation in roof overhang.

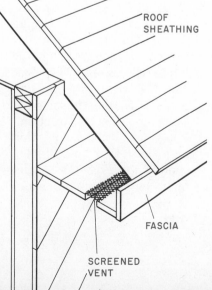

Unit 48: COMPLETING THE EXTERIOR AND INTERIOR

Much of the appearance of a house depends on the kinds and styles of materials used in completing its exterior and interior. A wide variety of building materials is available and the selection should be made in terms of house style and cost of materials. All of these materials are specified in the house plans. The exterior of the house, including doors, windows, and siding, is usually completed first. Then the interior of the house is finished. This includes insulation, walls, ceilings, trim, doors, floors, built-ins, and cabinets.

DOORS

Door styles include flush, panel, French, combination, and louver. *Fig. 48-1.* The first four are in common use for both exterior and interior doors. The louver door is usually chosen for closets or wherever ventilation is desired. The major difference between interior and exterior doors is in the thickness and sometimes in the construction. Interior doors are usually $1\frac{3}{8}''$ thick. Common door sizes and thicknesses are shown in *Fig. 48-2.* In general, main entrance doors should be 3'

48-1.   Common types of exterior and interior doors: *a.* Panel.

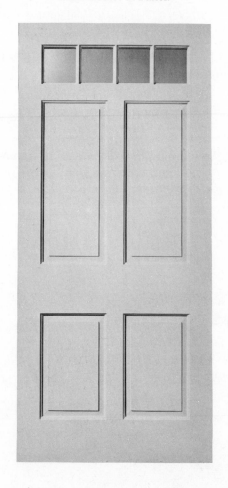

wide, 1¾″ thick, and not less than 6′8″ high. Other exterior doors may be 2′8″ wide. Exterior trim around the main entrance door can vary from a quite simple casing to an ornate, milled frame with decorative features including extra side windows. *Fig. 48–3.* Both interior and exterior doors must be hung in a door jamb. The jamb consists of two side jambs and a head jamb with separate moldings called doorstops. Jambs are made of nominal 1″ material 5¼″ wide for standard plastered walls. The jamb is purchased ready-made for installation in the rough opening which should be somewhat larger each way (3″ wider and 2″ higher) than the size of the door. The door jamb should be placed in the rough opening and lined up level and plumb. By inserting a temporary piece of wood (spreader) at the bottom, the sides can be held parallel until the jamb is securely in place. Usually shingles are used as wedges in lining up the door jamb before nailing it to the studs with 8d finish-

48–1b. Flush.

48–1c. French.

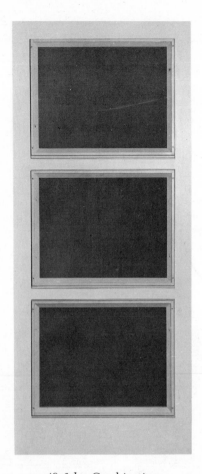

48–1d. Combination.

Hanging a Door. A door must be cut and planed to fit the jamb opening with enough clearance to allow it to operate freely. *Fig. 48–7.* The opening edge of the door is cut with a slight bevel toward the stop; this keeps the door from binding as it is opened and closed. Place the face of the door flush with the jamb and then temporarily nail the door stops in place. Wedge the door at the bottom and away from the hinge edge. Mark the location for the hinges. Cut the gains for the hinges by hand or with a router. Attach the hinges to the door. Block up the door in the opening and install one screw in each hinge on the jamb. Try the door. If it works well, install the other screws.

Many kinds of mortise lock sets are available. Each contains detailed instructions for installing. (See Unit 39.) Cut and fit the lock and the striker plate. After the hardware is

48–1e. Louver.

ing nails. *Fig. 48–4.* Today, many manufacturers feature pre-hung doors on jambs; this eliminates many of the details involved in hanging a door and fitting the hardware.

Casing (sometimes called trim) is nailed to the jamb around the door to provide a finish. *Figs. 48–5 and 48–6.* In installing the trim, a miter joint is cut at the upper corners. Interior doors are hung after the installation of the interior woodwork, but before decorating.

546

48–2. COMMON DOOR SIZES

WIDTH		HEIGHT	
2' 6"	4' 0"	6' 6"	7' 6"
2' 8"	5' 0"	6' 8"	8' 0"
3' 0"	6' 0"	7' 0"	
3' 6"	8' 0"		

installed, permanently nail the door stops in place. Nail the stop on the latch side first, then the top, and finally the stop on the hinge side. The one on the hinge side should have about ¹⁄₃₂" clearance so that the door will not scrape as it is opened and closed.

WINDOWS

Many types of windows are available for modern homes.

• *Double hung* consists of two sash which slide up and down in grooves of the window frame. The

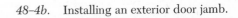

Wedges

Level and plumb jamb

Check carefully
before nailing

Wedges

48–4a.   A door jamb wedged in place.

48–3.   Entrance door with a complete frame.

48–4b.   Installing an exterior door jamb.

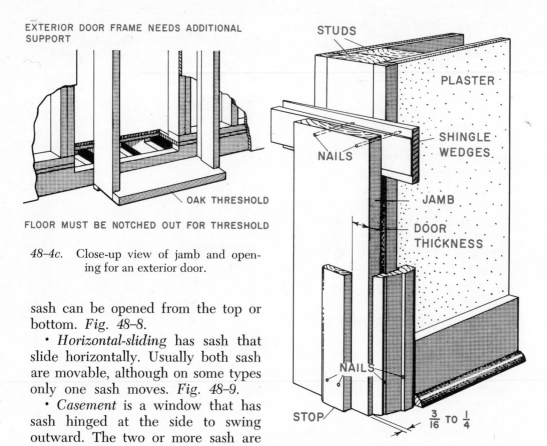

EXTERIOR DOOR FRAME NEEDS ADDITIONAL SUPPORT

OAK THRESHOLD

FLOOR MUST BE NOTCHED OUT FOR THRESHOLD

STUDS

PLASTER

SHINGLE WEDGES

NAILS

JAMB

DOOR THICKNESS

NAILS

STOP

$\frac{3}{16}$ TO $\frac{1}{4}$

48–4c. Close-up view of jamb and opening for an exterior door.

48–5b. Casing around a door.

sash can be opened from the top or bottom. *Fig. 48–8.*

• *Horizontal-sliding* has sash that slide horizontally. Usually both sash are movable, although on some types only one sash moves. *Fig. 48–9.*

• *Casement* is a window that has sash hinged at the side to swing outward. The two or more sash are separated by a mullion. *Fig. 48–10.*

• *A w n i n g-t y p e* windows are hinged at the top and open outward.

48–5a. Fitting a casing (trim) around an interior door opening.

When the sash are open they project out like an awning. *Fig. 48–11.*

• *Jalousie windows* consist of a series of small, horizontal glass pieces that are held by an end frame of metal. They open outward. *Fig. 48–12.*

• *Bottom-hinged or hopper windows* swing inward when open. *Top-hinged windows* are very similar. *Fig. 48–13.*

• *Fixed windows,* including picture windows, have glass that cannot be opened for ventilation. *Fig. 48–14.*

548

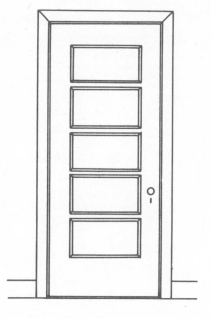

48–6.   Door frame and trim.

48–8.   Double-hung window.

48–7.   Door clearances.

48–9.   Horizontal sliding window.

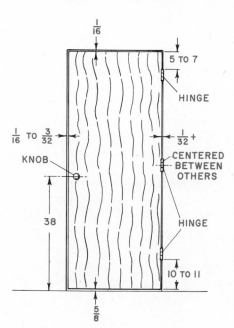

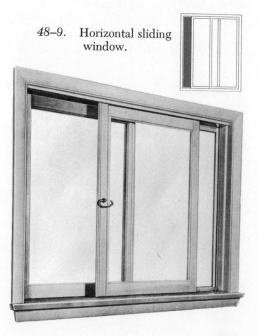

48–10. Casement window.

48–12. Jalousie window.

• *Combined windows* consist of a fixed window in combination with some other type to provide for ventilation. For example, a combined window might have a fixed window in the center with a double-hung or casement window on either side (*Fig. 48–15*), or there might be a fixed window above with jalousies below.

Window frames may be made of wood, aluminum, or steel. The wood double-hung window is still the most popular and is commonly used in much house construction. The parts of a double-hung window are shown in *Fig. 48–16*.

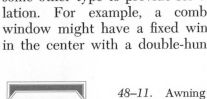

48–11. Awning window.

48–13. Bottom-hinged window.

YOU ARE AS BRIGHT AS THS LITTLE BOY IF YOUR A GUY IF YOUR A GIRL YOUR AS UGLY AN THIS LITTLR BOY.

TURN PAGE 603.

Installing a Window. The rough opening for a window must be determined by the glass size. On many house drawings, the exact rough-opening size is given for the windows. *Fig. 48–17.* The manufacturer of the window also provides the rough (stud) opening size. In the case of a double-hung window, the rough opening must be about 10″ larger each way than the glass size. For example, the double-hung windows to the right of the front door, *Fig. 4–6,* indicate the glass size as 24″ x 16″. To determine the rough opening, you must add 10″ to the 24″ for the width, making a total of 34″. Since there are two panes of glass, you must add 16″+16″+10″ for the height, or a total of 42″. This would be the rough (stud) opening size.

Before installing a window, apply a primer coat of paint all over to prevent undue warpage. If wood sheathing has been used, heavy building paper should be tacked around the window opening. Then place the frame in the opening, allowing the

48–15.   Combined window.

sub-sill to rest on the rough frame at the bottom. Level and plumb the window frame; then wedge with shingles to make it level. When everything is in order, nail the outside casing into the sheathing and/or studs. Before the siding or other exteriors are put on, a metal flashing should go over each window. All styles of windows are installed in a similar manner.

Window Trim. The casing for the window trim should match that used around the door. *Fig. 48–18.* The interior trim around the window includes:

• The *stool,* which is the horizontal piece that laps the sill of the window and projects beyond the casing. It is installed first and is nailed to the sill and the apron.

• The *apron,* which is the trim piece just below the stool. It is nailed to the stool.

48–14.   Fixed window.

551

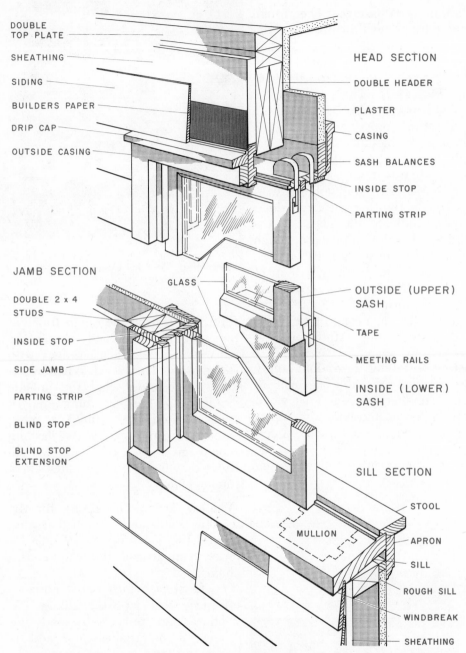

DOUBLE TOP PLATE

SHEATHING

SIDING

BUILDERS PAPER

DRIP CAP

OUTSIDE CASING

HEAD SECTION

DOUBLE HEADER

PLASTER

CASING

SASH BALANCES

INSIDE STOP

PARTING STRIP

JAMB SECTION

DOUBLE 2 x 4 STUDS

INSIDE STOP

SIDE JAMB

PARTING STRIP

BLIND STOP

BLIND STOP EXTENSION

GLASS

OUTSIDE (UPPER) SASH

TAPE

MEETING RAILS

INSIDE (LOWER) SASH

SILL SECTION

STOOL

MULLION

APRON

SILL

ROUGH SILL

WINDBREAK

SHEATHING

48–16. Parts of a double-hung window. There are two sash that slide up and down in the grooves of the frame and can be opened from either top or bottom. In some types the sash can be removed for cleaning. Balances at the sides support the sash and make them easier to raise.

552

WINDOW SCHEDULE

No.	GLASS SIZE	ROUGH OPG.	TYPE	MFGR. CAT. NO.
1.	39" x 49" OVER 39" x 18"	11'-0⅜" x 6'-7⅛"	FIXED OVER HOPPER.	
2.	22" x 44"	6'-10⁹⁄₁₆" x 4'-2¼"	TRIPLE - CSMNT.	
3.	39" x 22"	7'-4⁷⁄₁₆" x 2'-5⅜"	MULL - AWNING	
4.	22" x 44"	4'-7⁹⁄₁₆" x 4'-2¼"	MULL - CSMNT.	
5.	18" x 36"	3'-11⁹⁄₁₆" x 3'-6¼"	" "	
6.	39" x 22"	3'-8½" x 2'-5⅜"	SINGLE - AWNING	

48–17.   A window schedule from a set of house plans.

• The *casing* trim, which is nailed in place the same as around doors.

• The *stops*, that hold the window sash in place.

SIDING MATERIAL

There are many types of siding and other exterior covering materials that can be used over wood framing. These include wood siding, wood shingles, plywood, hardboard, brick, and other masonry materials. *Fig. 48–19.* There are many types and patterns of wood siding from which to choose. Among the most common are the bevel, drop, board and batten, and tongue-and-groove siding. *Figs. 48–20 through 48–22.* Wood siding, trim, and other exterior woodwork should be kept at least 6" to 8" above the ground. *Fig. 48–23.* These should be installed with corrosion-resistant nails, usually of galvanized steel or aluminum.

If wood sheathing has been used, the exterior must first be covered with building paper with a 4" lap,

48–18.   Parts of window trim.

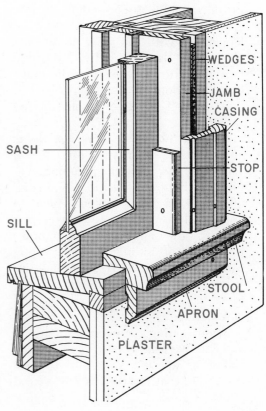

48–19. The exterior of this house has plywood siding with a flush door and horizontal sliding windows.

and siding may be nailed at 24″ intervals. With other types of sheathing, nails should be driven through the sheathing and into the studs. Bevelled and square-edge boards applied horizontally should be lapped 1″, with the nails driven just above the lap to permit possible movement due to changes in moisture conditions.

It is good practice to put on the siding with the bottom of the piece even with the top of trim over doors and window openings. *Fig. 48–24.* This requires careful planning before starting to apply the siding. *Fig. 48–25.* It is also a good idea to apply a heavy coat of water repellent to the end surfaces. Corner treatment of siding depends upon overall house design. This may involve corner boards, mitered corners, metal corners, or alternately lapped corners. *Fig. 48–26.*

Some siding, especially tongue-and-groove and board-and-batten siding, is applied vertically to produce an attractive architectural effect. *Fig. 48–27.* When tongue-and-

groove boards are used, the siding should be blind-nailed to the wood sheathing at 24″ intervals. If square-edge boards are used with battens, the boards should be spaced about ½″ apart and nailed only at the center. The batten is then attached by one nail driven through the center so that it passes between the boards. If shingles other than shakes are used, the exposed area of each shingle should be as follows: If the shingle length is 16″, then 7½″ is exposed in a single course, or 12″ in a double course.

When shingles are installed in double courses (one layer directly over the other before spacing for the next two layers), the butt of the shingle should extend about ½″ below the under course in order to

48–20. Four common types of siding.

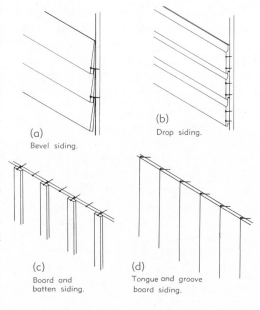

(a)
Bevel siding.

(b)
Drop siding.

(c)
Board and batten siding.

(d)
Tongue and groove board siding.

554

48–21. This home has a combination of bevel siding and tongue-and-groove board siding for an interesting effect. Note also the use of fixed and casement windows.

48–22. The exterior of this house has board-and-batten siding of Douglas fir.

48–23. The clearance between the exterior siding and the ground should be at least 6″. With wood sheathing, building paper must be applied before the siding is added.

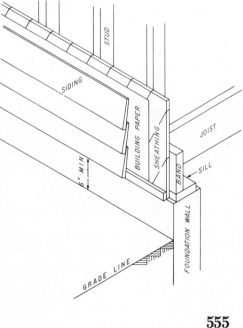

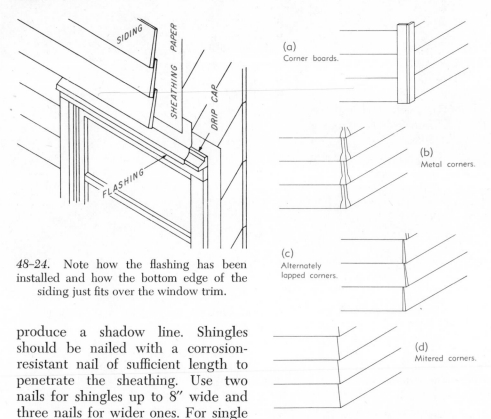

48–24. Note how the flashing has been installed and how the bottom edge of the siding just fits over the window trim.

produce a shadow line. Shingles should be nailed with a corrosion-resistant nail of sufficient length to penetrate the sheathing. Use two nails for shingles up to 8″ wide and three nails for wider ones. For single coursing, nails should be driven approximately 1″ above the butt line

48–25. Fitting bevel siding on the exterior over insulating board.

(a) Corner boards.

(b) Metal corners.

(c) Alternately lapped corners.

(d) Mitered corners.

48–26. Methods of finishing the outside corners of siding.

48–27. The exterior of this house has tongue-and-groove board siding.

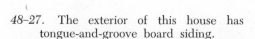

of the following course. *Fig. 48–28a.* For double coursing, the under course should be attached to the sheathing with 3d nails or staples, and the outer course attached with small-headed nails driven approximately 2″ above the butts and ¾″ from the edges.

When other than wood sheathing is used, it is necessary to apply 1″ x 3″ horizontal nailing strips over the sheathing, spaced to correspond with the weather exposure of the shingles. *Fig. 48–28b.* Masonry veneer should be supported on the foundation wall and attached to the wood framing with corrosion-resistant metal ties. *Fig. 48–29.* After the exterior has been completed, it should be given at least one prime coat of paint as soon as possible. This keeps it from absorbing too much moisture which causes difficulty later.

REDUCING THE CONDENSATION

Because of the construction of to-day's homes and the use of many appliances such as dishwashers and clothes dryers, there is a great deal of humidity in a house during cold

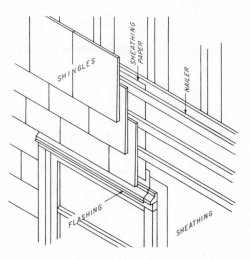

48–28b.   Putting nailing strips over sheathing before applying the shingles.

weather. This invisible moisture can cause much trouble, especially in exterior paint finish. The moisture vapor moves from the warm interior of the house toward the cold exterior. This vapor travels through plaster, insulation, and wood until it condenses into water at the colder exterior surfaces. *Fig. 48–30a.* The water increases the moisture content of the wood and causes such troubles as blistering, peeling, and staining. It is extremely important to prevent this by making sure that vapor barriers are used on the warm side of the walls between the insulation and the interior wall. When a vapor barrier is properly installed, the vapor leaves the house through the wall vents. Then it won't cause the trouble. This is also the reason why the attic of a home must be adequately ventilated. Some kinds of insulation are made with built-in vapor barriers.

48–28a.   Using annular-thread nails to hold wood shingles and shakes tight.

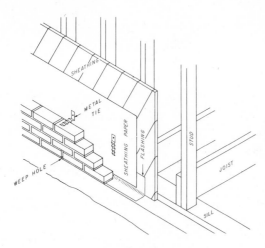

48-29. A masonry veneer over sheathing and wood framing.

INSULATION

There are many types of insulation for walls and ceilings. The most common are blanket, batt, fill reflective, and rigid. Any house that is heated or air-conditioned should be well insulated in the outside walls, ceiling, and floors. If the house has an unheated crawl space, insulation should be placed between the floor joists. Insulation should also be inserted around the openings of windows between the window frame and the rough frame. For new homes, blanket-type insulation is usually stapled in the walls and between the ceiling joists. *Fig. 48–30b.* This can be done after the exterior of the house is completed and before the interior walls are installed. All rough wiring, plumbing, and duct work must be completed first, however.

STAIRS

The stairway for most homes is a straight, continuous run, although a stairway with a landing platform is sometimes used to conserve space. *Figs. 48–31 and 48–32.* It is very important to make sure that the stairs

48–30a. This is what happens if the vapor is not checked.

48–30b. Note that blanket-type insulation has been installed in both the walls and the ceiling.

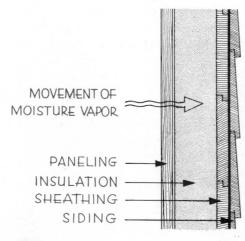

MOVEMENT OF
MOISTURE VAPOR

PANELING
INSULATION
SHEATHING
SIDING

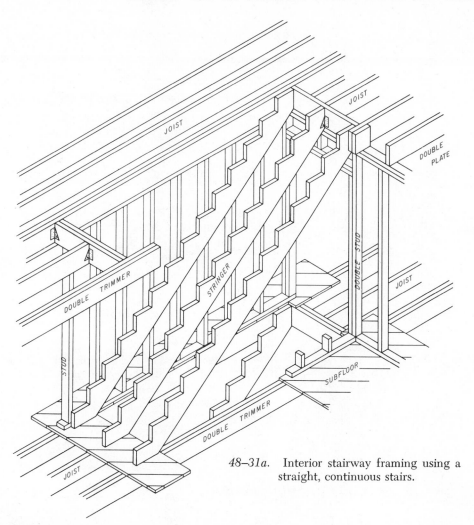

48–31a. Interior stairway framing using a straight, continuous stairs.

are designed for safety and convenience. A minimum of 6′ 6″ of headroom is essential for all stairs. Details for building the stairs are shown in the stairwell section of most house plans.

To design a stairway you will need the following information:

· *Total rise*—the total vertical distance from one floor to the next.

· *Total run*—the total horizontal length of the stairs.

48–31b. Exterior steps—structural portions should be at least 6″ above the finish grade.

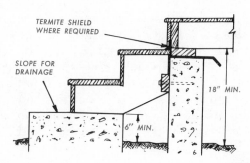

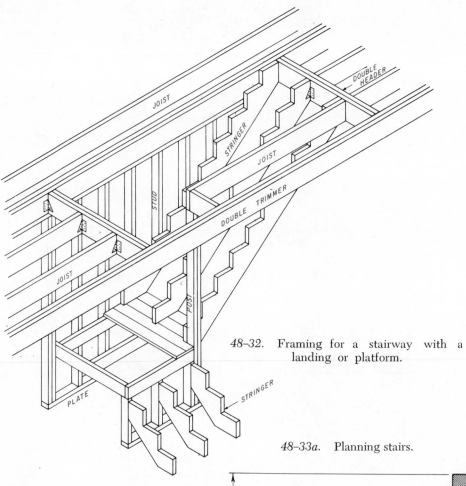

48–32. Framing for a stairway with a
landing or platform.

48–33a. Planning stairs.

· *Riser*—the vertical face of one
step.

· *Tread*—the horizontal face of
one step.

In general, the rise per step is
about 7″ to 8″. The width of the
tread should be about 9″ to 11″.
Fig. 48–33. In any case, the total
of one riser and one tread should not
be much less than 17″ or more than
18″, or the total of two risers and one
tread should be between 24″ and
25″.

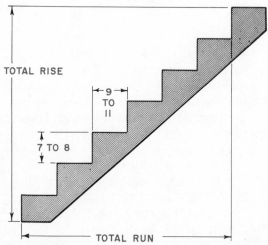

560

Let us see how the stairs shown in *Fig. 48–33b* were designed. The total rise is 7′ (84″) plus a 10″ floor joist for a total of 94″. Let us assume the rise is to be 8″. Divide 94″ by 8″ and you have 11¾. However, since the number of risers must be a whole number, let us use 12. Now, 94″ divided by 12 gives a rise of 7:83″ or, rounding this out to the nearest ⅛″, a rise of 7⅞″. The tread could be made either 9″ or 10″ to stay within the total of 17″ to 18″. A 9″ tread was chosen in *Fig. 48–33*. Remember that there is always one more riser than tread. The *total run* for these stairs would be 9″ times 11, or 99″, or 8′ 3″. This is the horizontal distance from bottom riser to top riser.

To lay out and cut the stairs, first get a 2″ x 10″ board that will be long enough for the stringer. Make sure that the top edge is straight and square with the sides. With the square set on the tread and riser measurements, mark the first notch near the lower end of the board. Now turn the square around and

48–33b. A stairwell section drawing for an actual set of house plans. Note that the architect has indicated the riser to be 7⅞″ and the tread to be 9″.

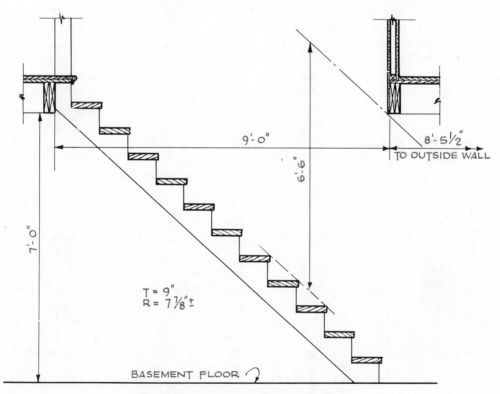

STAIRWELL SECTION

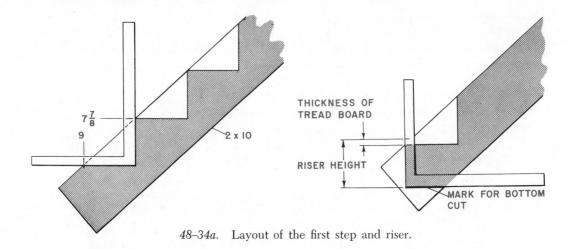

THICKNESS OF
TREAD BOARD

RISER HEIGHT

MARK FOR BOTTOM
CUT

7 7/8

9

2 x 10

48–34a. Layout of the first step and riser.

measure down a distance equal to the height of the riser less the thickness of the board used for the tread. *Fig. 48–34.* Then mark the bottom cut at right angles to the riser line. The first riser is shortened the thickness of the tread board so that all steps will have the same rise. Now mark the required number of notches (11 in all) with a square. Square off the top end of the stairs. Cut each notch carefully with a sharp saw. Check the first stringer. Then

48–34b. Completed stairs.

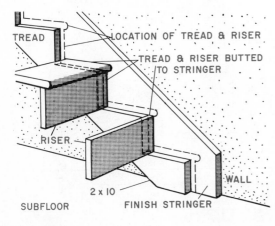

TREAD

LOCATION OF TREAD & RISER

TREAD & RISER BUTTED TO STRINGER

RISER

WALL

2 x 10

FINISH STRINGER

SUBFLOOR

use this as a pattern for cutting one or two more.

INTERIOR WALLS AND CEILING FINISH

Interior walls and ceilings are either plastered or dry-wall construction. For a plaster finish, gypsum board lath is usually nailed on as a base although other materials can be used. *Fig. 48–35.* The corners are reinforced with metal edges. The surface is given two coats of plaster —a rough and a finished coat.

Dry-wall construction is very popular because it can be done easily even by someone with limited skill. The most common materials are gypsum board, plywood, fiberboard, hardboard, and paneling. A gypsum board is sheet material composed of gypsum filler faced with paper. This usually comes in 4′ x 8′ sheets and is nailed directly to the studs. *Fig. 48–36.* The joints must be cemented and taped. Plywood can be used in large sheets and applied vertically or horizontally. *Fig. 48–37.*

562

48–35a. Installing gypsum board lath in preparation for plastering.

GYPSUM PANELS NAILED TO STUDS

FINISH WHITE

CORNER WIRE LATH

FIRST GROUT

METAL CORNER BEAD NAILED TO OUTSIDE CORNERS, OR USE WOOD PLASTER STOPS

PLASTER STOP BOARD

48–35b. Plastered walls.

48–36a. Fastening sheets of gypsum board to the walls. Annular-thread dry-wall nails are used.

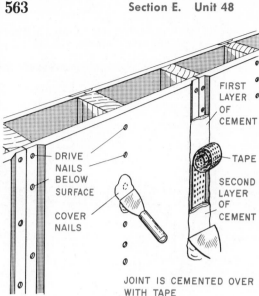

FIRST LAYER OF CEMENT

DRIVE NAILS BELOW SURFACE

TAPE

SECOND LAYER OF CEMENT

COVER NAILS

JOINT IS CEMENTED OVER WITH TAPE

48–36b. The joints must be cemented and taped with material especially designed for this type of wall covering.

Interior plywood comes in many textures. One kind has grooves cut into it to give the appearance of planking. Another kind has the wood grain in bold relief, an effect achieved by sand blasting. Hardboard sheets can also be used for interior surfaces. Wood and fiberboard can be installed by the so-

48–37. Using plywood for the interior of a home.

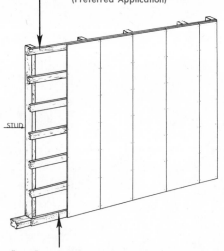

STUD

1″ x 2″ Furring Strips over studs spaced on 16″ centers.
1″ x 3″ Furring Strips over studs spaced greater than
16″ but less than 24″ centers.

48–38. Nailing 1″ x 2″ furring strips over
studs spaced 16″ on center. Arrows indicate that furring strips at top and bottom
of the wall support the planks.

called plank application. This is
usually put in vertically. Generally,
furring strips should be nailed to
the studs, and the planks nailed or
stapled to the furring strips. *Figs. 48–
38 and 48–39.* Many of these interior
wall materials have pre-finished surface so that it is not necessary to
apply paint or finish after installation. *Fig. 48–40.*

Ceiling tile of acoustical material
looks attractive and is easily installed.
The square-edged tiles can be applied with special adhesives, but
more frequently they are nailed or
stapled to 1″ x 3″ furring strips. For
this kind of installation, use tile with
edges that interlock, giving smooth
bevel joints so that all nails and
staples are concealed.

564

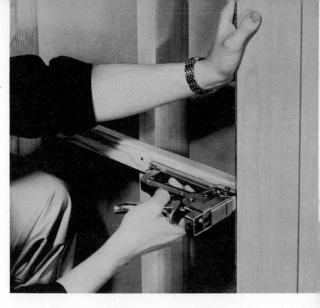

48–39. Stapling the planks to the furring
strips.

Before installing the ceiling, make
a scale drawing of it, indicating light
fixtures, outlets, and any other ob-
structions. Draw the tile pattern on
the diagram and then determine
the location of the furring strips.
Nail these to the ceiling joists on 12″
or 16″ centers, depending upon the

48–40. This interior has pre-finished plywood paneling with a matching flush door.
This is an easy-to-clean surface that resists
staining, scuffing, and fading.

48-41. Installing tile over furring strips that have been nailed to the joists.

tile size used. Install the tile, starting at one corner of the ceiling. Apply the border course of tile with the nailing flanges facing out from the wall so that both of them are accessible for nailing and stapling. Face nail the border course. Stapling with a trigger-type stapler is the best method of installing the tile. *Fig. 48-41.*

FLOORS

Although hardwood is very popular, many other materials can be used for the floors of a home. Tile made of rubber, linoleum, or plastic is common. If wall-to-wall carpeting is to be laid, the finish floor can be a good grade of plywood. *Fig. 48-42.*

Installing a Hardwood Floor. Cover the subfloor with building paper, preferably 15-pound, asphalt-saturated felt. Stretch a string the length of the room between two nails placed about 8" from a side wall. By lin-

565

ing up the first course of flooring at a uniform distance from the string, rather than from the wall itself, you assure a straighter course. This is because many walls are not perfectly true.

Place a long piece of flooring with groove edge about $\frac{1}{4}''$ from a side wall and groove end nearest an end wall. Space to be hidden by shoe mold is left for expansion. *Fig. 48-43.* Face nail the flooring piece near the end as shown. Measure as you nail progressively toward the other end, maintaining the same fixed distance from the guide string. Do likewise in lining up succeeding pieces in the course. Use one nail every 10" to 12".

Observe nailing recommendations of the manufacturer whose flooring is used. For example, with flooring $\frac{25}{32}''$ thick and $1\frac{1}{2}''$ or more wide, 7d or 8d screw nails or cut steel nails are best. If steel-wire flooring nails are used, they should be 8d, prefer-

48-42. Applying a plywood floor over subfloor and building paper in a living room where wall-to-wall carpeting will be laid.

48-43. Face nailing the first course from the string or chalk line.

at the point where the tongue of the flooring leaves the shoulder. This is an angle of about 50 degrees.

When a piece of flooring cannot be readily found to fit the remaining space in a course, cut one to size. Lay a piece down in reversed position from that in which it will be nailed. Draw a line at the point where it should be sawed. *Fig. 48–45*. Be sure the piece is reversed for this marking so the tongue end will be cut off. The groove end is needed for joining with the tongue end of the previous piece.

Stagger the joints of neighboring pieces so they will not be grouped closely. A joint should not be closer than 6″ to another in a previous course. To provide for this, arrange several pieces in their approximate positions in succeeding courses before they are nailed. After nailing each three or four courses, place a piece of scrap flooring at intervals against the tongue edges of pieces in the last course. *Fig. 48–46*. Strike the scrap piece a couple of good ham-

ably cement coated. After face nailing the first course, toenail the pieces through the tongue edge, employing the same spacing. For best installation, countersink the nails. *Fig. 48–44*.

Fit the groove edges of pieces in each succeeding course with the tongues of those in the preceding course. In toenailing, drive the nail

48-44. Toenailing the flooring.

48-45. Marking a piece to be cut.

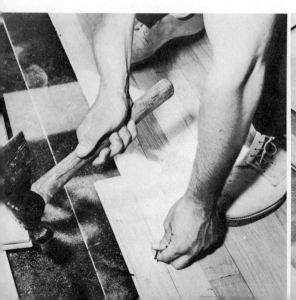

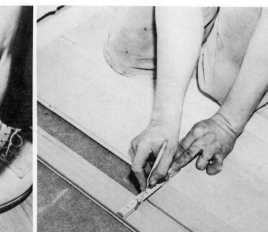

mer blows. This drives the nailed flooring pieces up tightly.

To fit flooring around a jutting door frame, place it flush against the frame, as shown. Measure the gap between the face of the previous piece and the groove edge of the piece to be nailed. Where the jutting begins, draw a straight line on the width of the flooring to the same distance as the gap. Do the same on other side of the door frame. Where the lines end, draw a straight line connecting them. Then cut the flooring along the lines. *Fig. 48–47.*

On reaching the opposite side of the room, you will find there is no space between the wall and the flooring to permit toenailing of the last two courses. Therefore just fit the pieces in. Face nail the last course, at the same time pulling the flooring up tightly by exerting pressure against it with a chisel or crowbar driven into the subflooring. *Fig. 48–48.* Protect molding with cardboard. After the last course, if the remaining space is too large to be covered by the shoe molding, cut pieces of

48–47. Layout of the flooring around a door opening.

flooring to the proper width and insert them in the spaces. Face nail these strips unless they are very narrow.

Installing a Tile Floor. Tile can be laid directly over a wood flooring or over a plywood floor. If a hardwood floor is to be used in one room and the adjacent room is to have a tile floor, a base is required for the tile so that it will be exactly the same height as the wood floor. In other

48–46.   Tightening the flooring.

48–48.   Tightening the flooring with a crowbar.

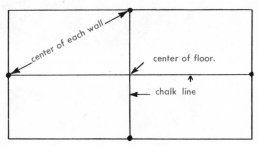

48–49.   Locating the center of the floor.

48–52.   Installing floor tile over a plywood base.

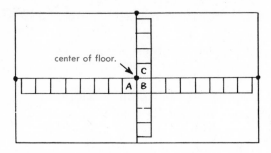

48–50.   Layout for even number of tiles.

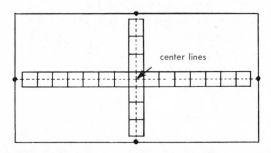

48–51.   Layout for odd number of tiles.

Locate the centers of opposite walls and draw a center line in either direction. The lines should cross at the center of the floor. *Fig. 48–49.* Place a row of uncemented tile along the line with the edge of the tile exactly on the line. Place another row of tile along the other line. Now shift the rows one at a time until the border space at the end of the rows is equal. Count the tiles in each row; if there is an even number of tiles,

48–53a.   The correct method of installing a base and shoemold or base shoe.

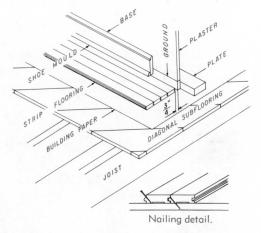

Nailing detail.

words, the thickness of the base floor plus the thickness of the tile should equal the thickness of the finished floor in the adjacent room. Some kinds of tiles require an underfelt that must be applied over the floor before the tiles are installed. Install tiles as follows:

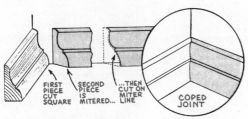

48–53b.   Fitting a coped joint.

the tiles on the center of each row should meet exactly on the center line. *Fig. 48–50.* If there is an odd number of tiles, the edges of the middle tile should fall at equal distance from the center line. *Fig. 48–51.*

Border tile should not be less than half a tile wide. Choose the correct adhesive for the tile you are using. Spread a thin coat over part of the floor, usually about two yards at a time. *Fig. 48–52.* Then install the tiles. The last row must be cut to fit snugly to the walls. Place a full tile over a tile in the last row. Push the top tile against the wall. Then make a line on the lower tile at the rear of the top tile. Cut the lower tile and slip it against the wall.

INTERIOR TRIM

Interior trim (casing) is installed around doors and windows and also used as a base molding at the floor and at wall intersections. In some cases, ceiling molding is also installed, but this is not a common practice today. The base molding is made in many styles to fit the architecture of the house. It consists of a base or baseboard and a base shoe (shoe-mold). *Fig. 48–53a.* The corners of the base are usually mitered, although a coped (fitted) joint is sometimes used. *Fig. 48–53b.*

KITCHEN CABINETS AND BUILT-INS

Kitchen cabinets and built-ins are really a form of cabinetmaking. You should review Unit 40 before doing any work of this type. The details for kitchen cabinets and built-ins are included in the working drawings of the house plans. *Fig. 48–54.* A kitchen cabinet may be purchased completely built so that the only thing required is mounting it to the wall. It may also be purchased in a

48–54.   Kitchen-cabinet elevations as they appear in a complete set of house plans.

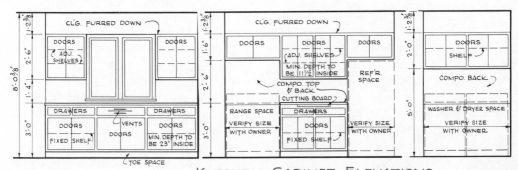

KITCHEN CABINET ELEVATIONS

48–55.   This is a commercial-type kitchen cabinet.

48–57.   Completing the carpenter-built kitchen cabinet.

knocked-down condition, or it may be built on the job by the carpenter. *Figs. 48–55 through 48–57.* General dimensions for both wall cabinets

48–56.   A carpenter-built sink base cabinet.

and base cabinets, as recommended by Douglas Fir Plywood Association, are shown in *Fig. 48–58.* The construction of cabinets depends to some degree on the architecture of the house. Some of the more common ways of building wall cabinets for kitchens are shown in *Fig. 48–59.* Another type of overhead cabinet for kitchen, utility room, basement, or garage is shown in *Fig. 48–60.* In general, the base cabinets in carpenter-built kitchens have the simplest type of cabinetry for doors and drawers. More elaborate construction techniques are evident in factory-built kitchen units.

In fitting (plumbing) factory-built kitchen cabinets to the walls, it is important to make sure that they will be plumb and level after mounting. Since no wall or ceiling is perfectly square, the back edge and

570

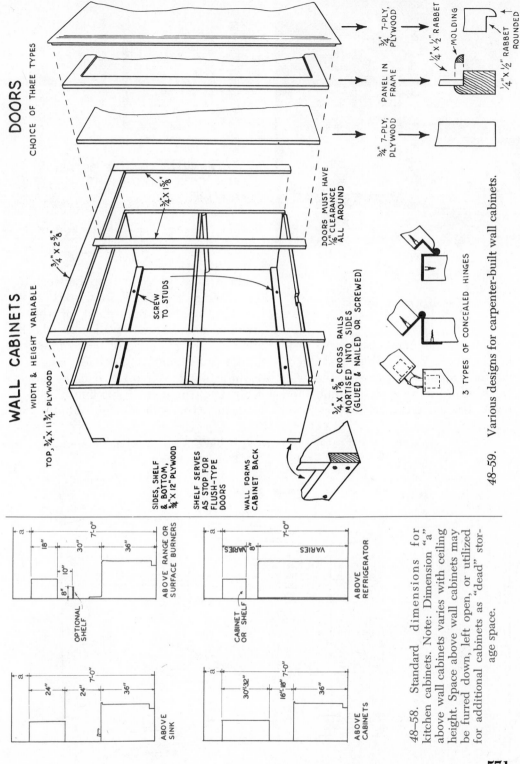

DOORS

CHOICE OF THREE TYPES

$\frac{3}{4}''$ 7-PLY, PLYWOOD

$\frac{1}{4}'' \times \frac{1}{2}''$ RABBET

MOLDING

$\frac{1}{4}'' \times \frac{1}{2}''$ RABBET ROUNDED

PANEL IN FRAME

$\frac{3}{4}''$ 7-PLY, PLYWOOD

WALL CABINETS

WIDTH & HEIGHT VARIABLE

TOP, $\frac{3}{4}'' \times 11\frac{3}{4}''$ PLYWOOD

$\frac{3}{4}'' \times 1\frac{5}{8}''$

$\frac{3}{4}'' \times 2\frac{5}{8}''$

SCREW TO STUDS

DOORS MUST HAVE $\frac{1}{16}''$ CLEARANCE ALL AROUND

$\frac{3}{4}'' \times 1\frac{5}{8}''$ CROSS RAILS MORTISED INTO SIDES (GLUED & NAILED OR SCREWED)

SIDES, SHELF & BOTTOM, $\frac{3}{4}'' \times 12''$ PLYWOOD

SHELF SERVES AS STOP FOR FLUSH-TYPE DOORS

WALL FORMS CABINET BACK

3 TYPES OF CONCEALED HINGES

48-59. Various designs for carpenter-built wall cabinets.

18"
30"
7'-0"
36"
10"
8"
OPTIONAL SHELF

ABOVE RANGE OR SURFACE BURNERS

a
VARIES
8"
7'-0"
VARIES
CABINET OR SHELF

ABOVE REFRIGERATOR

24"
24"
7'-0"
36"

ABOVE SINK

a
30"/32"
16"-18"
7'-0"
36"

ABOVE CABINETS

48-58. Standard dimensions for kitchen cabinets. Note: Dimension "a" above wall cabinets varies with ceiling height. Space above wall cabinets may be furred down, left open, or utilized for additional cabinets as "dead" storage space.

571

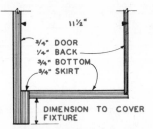

ALTERNATE BOTTOM DETAIL
FOR CONCEALED LIGHT
FIXTURE

48–60b. Alternate detail of cabinet drawing shown below.

48–60a. Another type of overhead cabinet that can be used in the kitchen, utility room, basement, or garage.

top of the cabinet must be made to fit the wall. To do this, first block up the cabinet as close to the wall as possible, so that it is plumb and level. Then open a dividers as wide as the widest space or gap between the cabinet and wall. Now start at the top, holding one point of the dividers against the wall and the other against the edge of the cabinet. Scribe a line along the back edges of the cabinet. When the back of the cabinet is trimmed to this line it will fit against the wall and be plumb.

48–60b. Drawing for the cabinet pictured at top left. Also see details shown at top right of the page and top of next page.

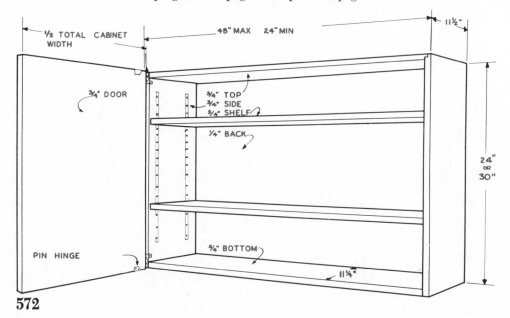

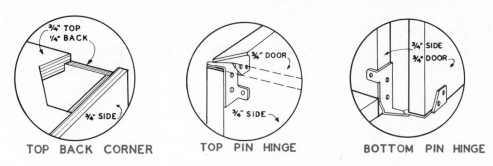

TOP BACK CORNER   TOP PIN HINGE   BOTTOM PIN HINGE

48–60b.   Additional details for drawing at bottom of page 556.

OTHER CABINETS AND BUILT-INS

Linen closets, wardrobe closets, storage cabinets, and other built-ins are an important part of the interior of a modern home. Many homes today are designed with no movable furniture in the bedrooms. *Fig. 48–61.* A well-designed home has storage facilities not only for the necessities, such as clothing, but also for extras such as recreational equipment.

48–61a.   Built-in clothes closet, chest, and storage cabinets in a bedroom.

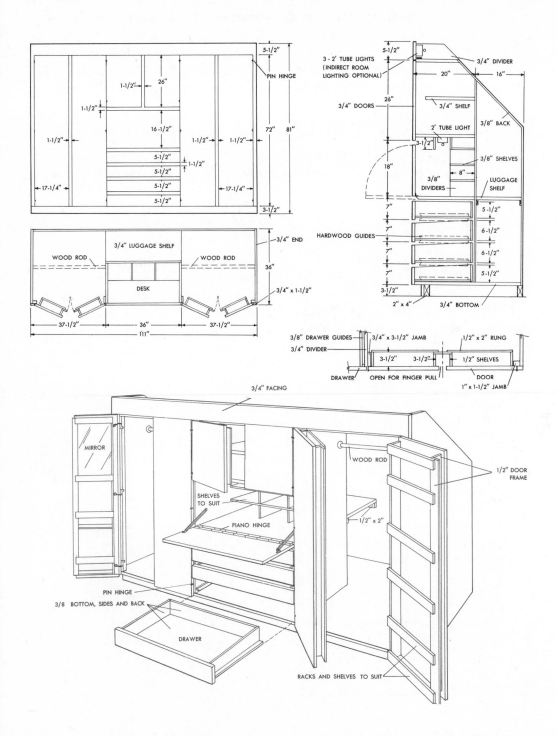

5-1/2"
PIN HINGE
1-1/2" 26"
1-1/2"
1-1/2" 16-1/2" 1-1/2" 1-1/2"
72" 81"
1-1/2"
5-1/2"
5-1/2"
17-1/4" 5-1/2" 17-1/4"
5-1/2"
3-1/2"

3/4" END
3/4" LUGGAGE SHELF
WOOD ROD WOOD ROD
36"
DESK
3/4" x 1-1/2"
37-1/2" 36" 37-1/2"
111"

5-1/2"
3 - 2' TUBE LIGHTS 3/4" DIVIDER
(INDIRECT ROOM
LIGHTING OPTIONAL) 20" 16"
26"
3/4" DOORS 3/4" SHELF
3/8" BACK
2' TUBE LIGHT
3-1/2" 3/8" SHELVES
18" 8"
3/8 LUGGAGE
DIVIDERS SHELF
7" 5-1/2"
HARDWOOD GUIDES 7" 6-1/2"
7" 6-1/2"
7" 5-1/2"
3-1/2"
2" x 4" 3/4" BOTTOM

3/8" DRAWER GUIDES 3/4" x 3-1/2" JAMB 1/2" x 2" RUNG
3/4" DIVIDER 1/2" SHELVES
3-1/2" 3-1/2"
DRAWER OPEN FOR FINGER PULL DOOR
1" x 1-1/2" JAMB

3/4" FACING
MIRROR
WOOD ROD
1/2" DOOR
FRAME
SHELVES
TO SUIT
PIANO HINGE
1/2" x 2"
PIN HINGE
3/8 BOTTOM, SIDES AND BACK
DRAWER
RACKS AND SHELVES TO SUIT

574

Unit 49: BUILDING A GARAGE

The **exact steps** in building a garage vary somewhat with the design and style of the building. Garage plans are available from many lumber yards and home-planning services. Many lumber companies have pre-cut materials available for a complete packaged garage. These "packages" consist of the lumber cut to size, doors, windows, hardware, and all the other materials needed. When not working with a package, it takes careful planning to get the correct kind and amount of materials. The design of the garage should be determined largely by the house design since the garage should be an asset to the overall appearance. Always consult a lumber dealer when working out your plans and material lists for a garage.

PREPARE THE SITE

Level the site of the garage and, if necessary, remove any top dirt, shrubbery, trees, and other things that might hamper your activities. Study the floor plan showing the overall size of the garage, and then decide exactly where the garage will be located. Usually, a garage is lo-

cated square with the lot line or the house. This can be done with a surveyor's transit by measuring from the house or lot line. If the garage is to be attached to the house or breezeway, you can measure the distance from the house itself. If the garage must stand by itself, measurements can be taken from the lot line. Stake out the location of the garage. Place batter boards (cross boards nailed to three stakes) about 4' outside each corner of the garage. *Fig. 49–1.* The top edges of the batter boards should be level; this can be checked with a carpenter's square. Make a saw cut or drive a nail into the upper edge of the batter boards to attach the cords. Tie a cord to the batter board at one outside dimension of the garage. Measure from it to locate the other cords. When the four cords or lines have been drawn tightly, they represent the outside of the building. Use a carpenter's level to level up the cord; this sometimes means that you need to drive the stakes of one batter board farther into the ground. After the cords are tight, check to make sure that the lines are square. First drop a plumb line at one corner and

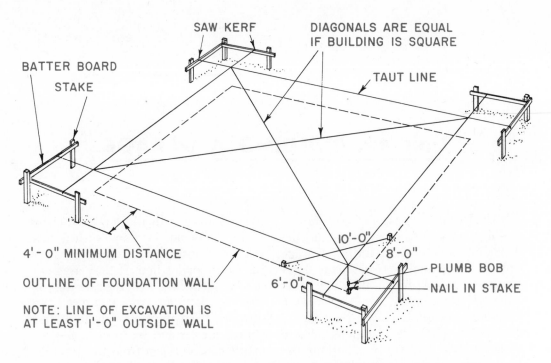

SAW KERF

DIAGONALS ARE EQUAL
IF BUILDING IS SQUARE

BATTER BOARD

STAKE

TAUT LINE

4'- 0" MINIMUM DISTANCE

OUTLINE OF FOUNDATION WALL

NOTE: LINE OF EXCAVATION IS
AT LEAST 1'- 0" OUTSIDE WALL

10'-0"

8'-0"

6'-0"

PLUMB BOB

NAIL IN STAKE

49–1.   The correct way to stake out the garage before digging the foundation.

drive in a wood stake. Two ways of checking for squareness are:

• Run diagonal cords between opposite corners, and measure them. If it is a square building, both cords should be the same length.

49–2.   The concrete slab has been poured and everything is ready for building.

• Let the two taut lines in one corner form two sides of a right triangle. On the ground directly under one taut line measure 6' from the corner of the garage. Under the other measure 8'. Connect these points. The third side must then measure exactly 10'. If not, move the cords until it does. *Fig. 49–1.*

CONSTRUCTION PROCEDURE

Provide for the Foundation. Dig a trench along the outline of the foundation wall. Make sure that it goes below the frost line. Pour 2″ or 3″ footing directly into the earth. Then lay a concrete-block foundation which is usually three blocks high around the perimeter of the garage.

576

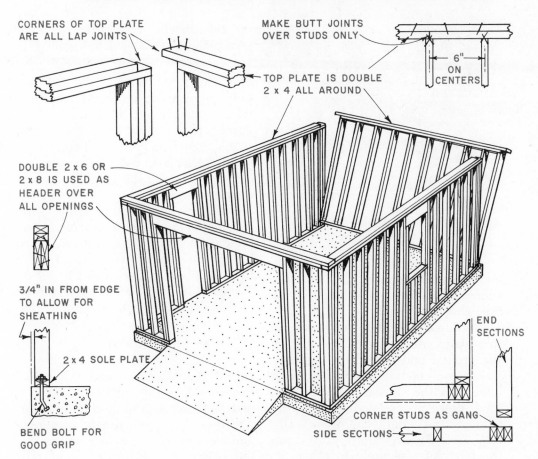

CORNERS OF TOP PLATE
ARE ALL LAP JOINTS

MAKE BUTT JOINTS
OVER STUDS ONLY

6"
ON
CENTERS

TOP PLATE IS DOUBLE
2 x 4 ALL AROUND

DOUBLE 2 x 6 OR
2 x 8 IS USED AS
HEADER OVER
ALL OPENINGS

3/4" IN FROM EDGE
TO ALLOW FOR
SHEATHING

2 x 4 SOLE PLATE

BEND BOLT FOR
GOOD GRIP

END
SECTIONS

CORNER STUDS AS GANG

SIDE SECTIONS

49–3.   The correct way of framing the garage walls.

Shovel 4" to 6" of crushed stone or gravel over the entire space inside the form. Level and tamp. Use ready-mix concrete; pour a 4" slab reinforced with No. 9 wire mesh. Have the mix dumped inside the form, or wheel the concrete in a wheelbarrow from the truck. The level of the breezeway can be slightly lower than the floor of the house. The garage slab can be poured at a level to meet the driveway. Sink ½" x 10" anchor bolts 24" apart around the edges to hold the floor or sole plates secure. Smooth and float the concrete surface. Then allow the concrete to cure for several days before beginning the carpentry. *Fig. 49–2.*

Frame and Walls. After the concrete sets, you are ready to build the exterior walls. *Fig. 49–3.* Bore holes through the sole plates (sill) to go over the anchor bolts in the concrete slab. Use 2" x 4"s on 16" cen-

577

49-4. Raising part of the wall after it has been nailed together on the ground.

ters for the exterior walls. Nail the framing together using one of the following methods:

• Arrange the material for the sole plates, studs, and top plates on the ground and nail them together. Raise a wall section into place, fitting holes over the bolts in the slab. *Fig. 49-4.* Brace up one wall temporarily with a 2" x 4". Raise the other walls. *Fig. 49-5.* Plumb carefully and nail the top plates securely together.

• Build the walls in a vertical position: sole plates, then studs, and finally the top plate. Remember to place the stud 16" on center. Make sure that you frame the window and door openings according to the garage plans, using double studs and double headers. For the garage-door opening, use double 2" x 6"s or a 2" x 8" as a header.

Sheathe the Exterior Walls. Sheathing material can be either fiberboard or plywood. Use large 4' x 8' boards for the side walls and 2' x 4' for the gable ends. Run the sheathing

up and around the rafter ends to give a tight, well-insulated wall.

Start the Roof. Review the unit on building a roof before cutting the rafters. Decide on the pitch of the garage roof. If possible, the pitch should match that of the house. Cut a pair of rafters. Put up one pair at a time, checking the ridgeboard frequently to make sure it is level. The rafters must fit smoothly against the ridgeboard and the top plate. Also, pre-cut the 2" x 4" ceiling joist and the 2" x 4" gable studs, and nail them in place as shown in *Fig. 49-6.* Toenail the rafters to the ridgeboard. A board running from the ridgeboard to the ceiling joist would help maintain the level.

Install the Windows and the Door Frames. Make sure that the windows match those in the house. Fit the windows into the rough openings and nail in place. The door frames for the overhead garage door and the smaller entrance door should be fastened in place. Make sure the jambs are level and plumb before nailing.

49-5. Bracing the wall temporarily with a 2" x 4". This gives you a chance to check whether the wall is plumb and level.

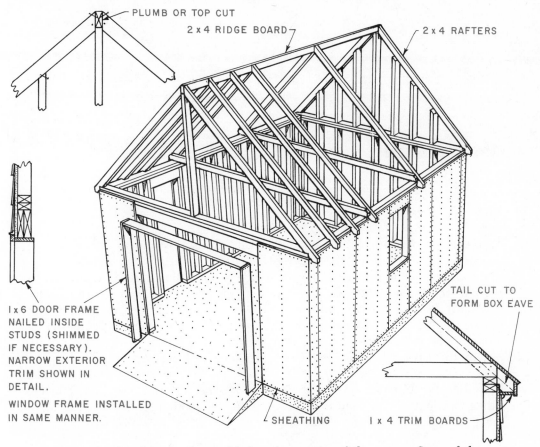

PLUMB OR TOP CUT

2 x 4 RIDGE BOARD

2 x 4 RAFTERS

1 x 6 DOOR FRAME
NAILED INSIDE
STUDS (SHIMMED
IF NECESSARY).
NARROW EXTERIOR
TRIM SHOWN IN
DETAIL.

WINDOW FRAME INSTALLED
IN SAME MANNER.

TAIL CUT TO
FORM BOX EAVE

SHEATHING

1 x 4 TRIM BOARDS

49–6. The sheathing has been added to the exterior of the garage. Some of the roof rafters are installed.

Apply Roofing Boards or Plywood Sheets to the Rafters. *Fig. 49–7.* Roofing boards should be 1″ x 6″. The material for the roof does not have to be cut to exact lengths until it is all nailed in place. It can then be trimmed with a cut-off or portable power saw. Attach the gable facing strips at either end.

Complete the Roof. If the shingles are to be asphalt, apply a layer of 15-pound felt on the roof and then a

49–7. Adding the wood sheathing to the roof.

579

49–8.   Applying the roof shingles.

double layer of shingles at the bottom row on each side. Extend the shingles $\frac{1}{2}''$ beyond the eave and $\frac{1}{4}''$ beyond the gable ends for a drip edge. *Fig. 49–8.* Use 1" galvanized roofing nails. Nail 1" x 4" trim boards to cover the ends of the rafters, and box in the eaves.

Complete the Exterior. Add exterior siding to match the house. Install metal corner caps. *Fig. 49–9.* Add

trim around windows and doors as necessary. Install the overhead garage door following the manufacturer's instructions. Hang any other doors and attach the hardware. Paint the garage to match the house. If necessary, electric wiring can be installed, built-ins can be added to the interior of the garage and, if you wish, the interior can be finished with plywood. *Fig. 49–10.*

49–9.   Here the siding has been added and the metal corners are being nailed in place.

49–10.   The completed garage.

Unit 50: "SHELL" AND PRODUCTION LINE HOUSES

The traditional method of building a home is to construct it of individual pieces of lumber and other building materials. *Fig. 50–1.* This is a slow and expensive way since each piece must be individually cut and fitted.

CUSTOM-BUILT HOUSES

The "industrial revolution" in house building is changing present-day building methods. Some builders are using components or manufactured parts to construct custom-built homes which are distinctly different from the prefabricated and manufactured homes discussed later in this unit. A *component* in building is a large, essential part of a house such as a wall section or roof trusses. Following are some of the processes and materials used in building a house with component parts.

Standard Sheet Materials. Most big sheet materials such as plywood, insulation board, and gypsum wallboard, come in 4′ x 8′ sheets and are made to be used on either 16″ or 24″ stud spacing. To use these materials, a house must be designed in multiples of 4′. This 4′ unit is a modular (or standard) dimension. Another modular dimension plan divides all spaces into 4, 16, 24 and 48 inches. *Fig. 50–2.*

Roof Trusses. Roof trusses are pre-constructed component units that can be put in place rapidly after wall sections are completed. They are used instead of joists and rafters. *Fig. 50–3.* The trusses are made in single units or, in some cases, are split in half for easy shipping. The two halves are then assembled on the job. Roof trusses have the following advantages:

• They make it possible to close in a house very rapidly.

50–1. This is the traditional method of constructing a home.

581

50-2. The use of large-sheet material, such as this plywood sheathing, speeds the building.

• They make it possible to finish much of the inside of the house as one large area before the partitions are installed.

• Partitions do not have to be load-bearing; therefore they can be put in any location. This allows much more flexibility in interior layouts.

Window, Door, and Wall Components. Manufacturers build walls with

several window sizes and styles. Walls with a variety of pre-fitted and hung doors are also available. These window and door parts are built in a shop and used as a component unit when fitted into the wall section.

Complete Modular Components. Many manufacturers produce standard wall units, roof components, and other large house parts. *Fig. 50–4.* These are of standard sizes such as the 4' x 8' wall component. These wall units include the frame, the insulation, and the interior and exterior wall.

Box Beams Made of Lumber and Plywood. These hollow beams are high in strength and stability and low in weight and cost. *Fig. 50–5.* They are used instead of solid timbers.

Stressed Skin Panels. These components are made as follows: 2" x 4" stringers, 8' long, are set in place 16" on center. Glue is applied and then

50-3. Roof trusses are fabricated on the ground and then placed on the wall frame.

50–4a. Using manufactured components for a conventional house.

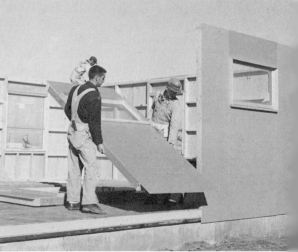

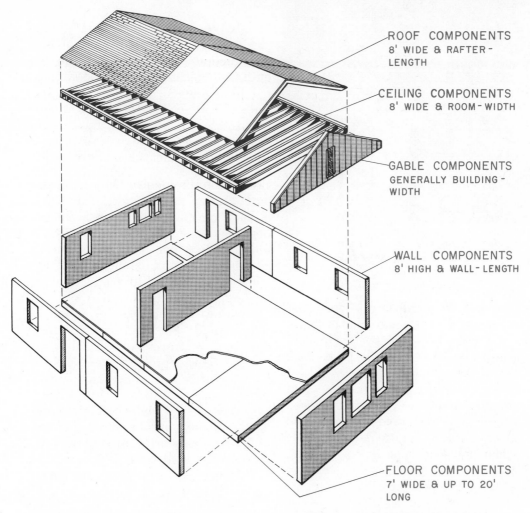

ROOF COMPONENTS
8' WIDE & RAFTER-
LENGTH

CEILING COMPONENTS
8' WIDE & ROOM-WIDTH

GABLE COMPONENTS
GENERALLY BUILDING-
WIDTH

WALL COMPONENTS
8' HIGH & WALL-LENGTH

FLOOR COMPONENTS
7' WIDE & UP TO 20'
LONG

50–4b. This house is being built with manufactured components. Note that the framing method shown in *50–4a* is quite different from that of a standard house.

a $\frac{3}{8}''$ plywood top skin is nailed in place. The panel is reversed and 3" of insulation is inserted. Glue is then applied to the tops of the 2" x 4"s and to the bottom skin of $\frac{5}{16}''$ plywood which is then tacked in place. The panels are placed in a press until the glue has cured. These panels are much stronger than any compo-nent unit that is merely nailed togeth-er. *Fig. 50–6.*

Other Standard Manufactured House Materials. Many kinds of manufac-tured materials save time and labor in completing a house. Some of them are:

• Pre-finished materials such as

583

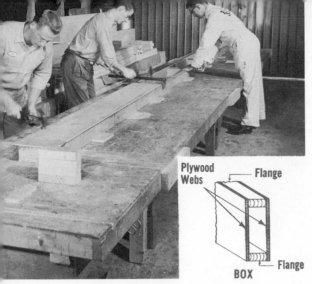

Plywood
Webs — Flange

— Flange
BOX

50–5a. These men are fabricating hollow beams. Insert shows a cross-section of a beam.

plywood or hardboard, doors and windows, flooring, and similar items.

• Pre-finished parts. There are many standard pre-built parts such as kitchen cabinets, chimneys, garage doors, and fireplace frames, that simplify building procedure, speed completion, and save material and labor. These are particularly valuable when only one home is to be built, or more than one if each is to have a distinct appearance.

THE PREFABRICATED HOME

The United States is known for its production methods. The symbol of mass production in this country is the automobile. In the automotive industry, all of the latest production techniques are employed, including precision measurement, jigs, fixtures, dies, interchangeable parts, a production line, and careful control. In contrast, most homes are built on a piece-by-piece procedure in which each piece must be fitted to the next

one. In other words, there is no interchangeability of parts in most house construction. The average home is built with techniques not too different from those of 100 years ago. In spite of the fact that well over a million and a half homes are built each year, building methods are, in many cases, rather ancient and out-of-date.

Production Problems. Only a small part of the prefabricated house is mass-produced. In building a three-bedroom home, the costs are about as follows: 25-35 per cent for the shell, 20 per cent for plumbing, including kitchen and bath, 10 per cent for heating, air conditioning, and electrical wiring; the balance for foundation, interior finishing, and for the cost and improvement of the lot. Today, most prefabricated home manufacturers are concerned largely with the construction of the shell. The shell is well under half the cost of the home, and because it is so bulky it is expensive to ship it any great distance from the factory.

Building codes vary from com-

50–5b. These hollow beams, made of lumber and plywood, could also be used as girders.

munity to community. Naturally
there are great differences in various
areas of the country. Building in-
spectors will not approve construction that does not follow these building codes (many of which are
out-of-date). Because of this, it is
quite difficult for the manufacturer
to meet the standards of all different
areas, particularly when he wishes to
use new construction techniques and
materials. Differences in weather also
cause problems for the manufacturer. In some areas of the country, roofs
must support heavy loads of snow,
while in others the problem of wind
damage is much more important. In
years past, construction has varied
greatly depending on the need for
heating; houses in colder climates require better insulation. Today, however, with air conditioning so common, insulation requirements are
much the same for most areas.

The cost of the manufactured utility core (bathroom, kitchen, and
heating) is important. A large part
of the cost of a home lies in the utilities, including heating and air
conditioning, plumbing, and basic

50-7. A typical prefabricated home of excellent design, workmanship, and materials.

wiring. Normally, these are installed
by tradesmen following traditional
methods.

Manufacturing a House Shell. The
techniques for manufacturing a shell
include the following: *Fig. 50–7.*

• The use of standard pre-cut
lumber, plywood, sheathing, and
other materials. In addition to the
standard large-sheet materials,
standard-dimension lumber is available from lumber mills, pre-cut for
use as studs, headers, and other
framing parts. *Fig. 50–8.*

• The use of jigs. House sections
are assembled on standard jigs that
hold parts in place during assembly.

• The use of power-operated
nailing and stapling equipment.
These air-operated machines fasten
the framing together and attach the
exterior and interior surfaces. *Fig.
50–9.*

• The use of a conveyor system
to carry the component parts along
in the factory, and special equipment

50-6. Using stressed skin panels for an
insulated roof.

585

50–8. Here pre-cut two-by-fours are placed in a jig.

50–9b. A nailing machine fastening wall board to the interior of a wall section.

to turn and handle the larger units. *Fig. 50–10.*

• The use of trucking facilities to move the completed parts to the building site. *Fig. 50–11.*

Assembling a Prefabricated Home. Before the shell of the house arrives at the building site the footings and

foundation have been completed. Completion of the shell on the site is a job for skilled workers, but with an adequate number of men the shell can be finished in less than one day. Common steps in the procedure are:

• The floor components are located in place. (This step is elimi-

50–9a. Placing large aluminum sheets of exterior material on a wall unit.

50–10a. Notice how the truss roof sections are fastened together with metal gussets as they roll through a rotary press.

586

50–10b. Whole wall sections can be turned over as they move along the conveyor.

50–12. The floor and walls have been fastened in place. Now the roof trusses are going up.

nated if the house is built on a cement slab.) The exterior wall units are fastened to the foundation or floor panels.

• The roof trusses are lifted into place and fastened to the side walls. *Fig. 50–12.*

• The roof is completed by installing the large sheets of roofing materials. *Fig. 50–13.*

50–11. Loading a complete home in sections on a truck.

• The exterior trim is added to complete the outside of the house.

• The insulation and dry wall for the ceiling are added.

• The finish flooring is installed.

• The interior partitions are put in place.

• The interior is completed. After this point much of the work is the same as in a conventional house.

50–13. Adding the metal roofing to the home.

finish. Besides the problem of varying local building codes, the manufacturer is also faced with high transportation costs and production problems in manufacturing the house and assembling it on the building site.

Despite these difficulties some manufacturers have succeeded in building complete houses in the factory. *Fig. 50–14* shows an all-factory-built house being assembled.

MOBILE HOMES OR TRAILERS

Mobile homes are built on a heavy steel chassis which can be moved. *Fig. 50-15.* Otherwise they are manufactured in much the same way as a factory-built house. The construction is especially similar if wood is used for the shell of the mobile home. *Fig. 50-16.* (Metal and fiberglass are also used for shells, and exteriors are mainly of metal or plastic.)

Interior cabinetwork is very similar to that in standard home construction, except that the units are scaled to the size of the mobile home. *Fig. 50-17.* (These homes are made in a wide range of sizes. Some are surprisingly large and well furnished.) *Fig. 50-18.* Mass production techniques are widely utilized in mobile home construction.

50–14. An all-factory-built home. This house is complete, including plumbing. heating, wiring, kitchen cabinets, interior trim, and floors: *a.* Back section.

However, the walls often contain the rough wiring and some rough plumbing. Kitchen cabinets and built-ins are pre-built at the factory, ready for installation.

THE ALL-FACTORY-BUILT HOUSE

If housing is to be produced with the techniques of automobile manufacturing, the all-factory-built house should include not only the shell, but completed heating, plumbing, siding, interior finish, and exterior

50–14b. Middle section.

50-14c. Front section.

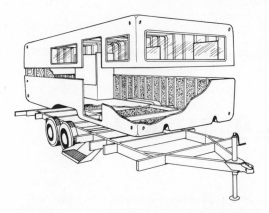

50-15. Exploded view of a mobile home showing the steel chassis.

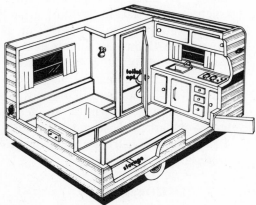

50-16. A trailer with structural members made of wood.

50-17. A cutaway of a small trailer showing the compact cabinetwork made of wood materials.

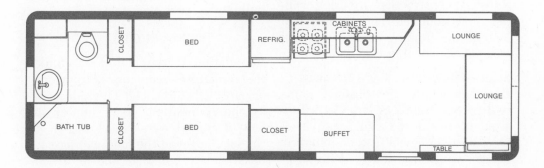

50-18. Typical floor plan of a medium-sized mobile home.

589

Unit 51: BUILDING A MINIATURE HOUSE

Nothing will replace the experience of actually cutting, fitting, and nailing full sized 2″ x 4″s and other structural materials in building a garage, an addition to a house, or a house itself. However, much can be learned about building construction by building a miniature or model house. This is an excellent way to study working drawings, to learn names of parts, and to get some idea of the way to construct a wood frame building. *Fig. 51–1.*

HOUSE PLAN

Use a modern set of standard house plans such as those included in Unit 4. Follow the plans just as though they were to be used for full-sized construction. By using well-designed, complete house plans that include the framing details, you will gain much valuable experience.

Scale. The best scale is 1½″ equals 1′. In other words, the finished home will be one-eighth as large as a full-sized house. If the real house itself measured 24′ by 40′, the miniature house would be 3′ x 5′. With this scale, a 2″ x 4″ measures ¼″ x ½″ and a 2″ x 6″ measures ¼″ x ¾″. You can use an architect's scale for most of the measuring and layout.

MATERIALS

Metal Fasteners. Nails and other metal fasteners should be in proportion to the size of the miniature. The nails for most of the house framing should be ¼″, 19- or 20-gauge wire nails. Best for nailing together joists, headers, and other larger members are ⅝″ or ¾″ nails. Use ¼″ nails or staples for attaching shingles.

Lumber. The lumber used for this home may be cut from poplar, pine, redwood, or other soft species that are also used for actual house construction. Much of this can be made from waste stock found around any building project.

CONSTRUCTION

Foundation. It is a good idea to build the miniature home on ¾″ plywood or particle board sheet. This can serve as the foundation. As a matter of fact, if the plywood sheet is cut to the lot size, even the landscaping can be added to complete the house. If a foundation wall is desired, it can be built from plaster of Paris.

Floor and Wall Framing. The floor and wall framing for a miniature house should be completed following the instructions given in Unit 46. Remember that the framing material will be slightly "oversize." As you know, a 2″ x 4″ actually measures $1\frac{5}{8}″$ x $3\frac{5}{8}″$, so a stud cut to exact scale would measure $\frac{13}{64}″$ x $\frac{29}{64}″$. However, it would be difficult to cut pieces to this exact size. Therefore material for the studs should be cut to $\frac{1}{4}″$ x $\frac{1}{2}″$. This slight difference in thickness and width will not affect the exterior dimensions of your house. Only the floors, walls, and roof will be slightly thicker than perfect scale for a standard house.

Roof. In order to make it possible to remove the roof to construct the interior partitions and also to study the construction after the model is completed, it is a good idea not to nail together the 2″ x 4″'s used for the top plates. If one top plate is nailed to the studs and the other top plate used to attach the ceiling joists and rafters, then the entire roof can be removed.

Exterior. Your main interest in constructing the miniature should be to gain experience in framing a house and building a roof; therefore it is not necessary to add many exterior materials. However, if you wish to do so, you can build and install simple windows and doors. You can make sheathing from thin veneer, and shingles from sandpaper. You can even install a low-voltage electrical wiring system.

51–1. Using a miniature house in an architectural drawing class to study house construction.

Unit 52: FINISHING TOOLS AND METHODS

The job of painting and/or finishing wood products is not strictly a woodworking occupation. It is, nevertheless, the last and most important step in the construction of most wood products. Painters and woodfinishers are skilled workers who prepare surfaces and then apply paint, varnish, enamel, lacquer, and similar materials, usually to furniture or buildings. Painters do both outside and inside work. *Fig. 52–1.*

In both painting and finishing much of the work is done in preparing the surface. This is especially true of repainting and refinishing, which are important parts of a painter's work. Irregularities must be sanded, holes filled, and imperfections removed. The wood must be primed and final coats applied with a brush, roller, or spray gun. A good painter must know how to use these and other painting and finishing tools. He must also be able to select and mix paint, and match colors. *Fig. 52–2.* He must know the common characteristics of paints and

52–1. Painters must know how to do both inside and outside painting.

52–2. Mixing and matching paint is an important part of the job.

other finishes as to their durability and suitability for different purposes. Especially important for safety is his knowledge of the way to erect and care for scaffolding.

A furniture finisher must be able do all of the jobs required to finish a good piece of furniture. *Fig. 52–3.* These include preparation of the surface and application of stains, sealers, fillers, and final coats of lacquer or varnish. He must know how to prepare materials in order to obtain desired colors and shadings. A good finisher must have experience in using a wide variety of finishing materials. In large furniture factories, finishing is broken down into a series of jobs including the preparation of surfaces, sanding, staining, filling, spraying, and rubbing.

In both furniture manufacture and the retail trade, the work of the finish patcher requires much skill. *Fig. 52–4.* He must be able to remove or camouflage all types of small defects. Because no wood object is really complete without some type of finish, fundamentals of finishing and painting ought to be part of the training of anyone who works with wood.

PREPARING WOOD FOR FINISHING

Before applying any finish or paint, be sure that the wood is ready.

Sanding the Surface. Sanding is needed to prepare surfaces for a finish. It must be done even when painting in order to correct such defects as small cracks and scratches. Scratches and saw marks should be removed by sanding before filler is applied.

52-3. Much of the beauty of this contemporary occasional table is in its fine finish.

Extra sanding is required for natural finishes. See Unit 38.

Applying Filler. There are several ways of filling nail holes, cracks, and spaces. *Fig. 52–5.* Some of them are:

Plastic Wood. This can be either natural or stain finish. Plastic wood closely resembles finished wood.

Stick Shellac. This is available in various colors. With a warmed putty knife this can be applied to the crack or hole.

Wood Dough. This is a synthetic wood that can be used to fill cracks or holes.

Sawdust and Glue. A thick half-and-half mixture of fine sawdust from the wood you are. finishing and powdered glue with a little water added makes a good paste for filling cracks and holes.

593

52–4. A finish patcher uses a chain and a coral rock, among other items, to produce a distressed effect. This finish, common on French Provincial furniture, imitates wear marks found on genuine antiques.

Plaster. Patching plaster or spackling material can be used to cover cracks if the surface is to be painted. *Shellac* can be used to cover knots; this prevents the sap from seeping through.

METHODS OF APPLYING PAINTS AND FINISHES

Paint Brushes. There are three common ways of applying paints or finishes. The first is with a paint brush. There is no standard style for paint brushes. However, it is very important to choose the correct size and type of brush to do the job. *Fig. 52–6.*

A *varnish* or *enamel brush* is sturdy. It is used for applying heavier paints, as well as varnish and enamel. It has a chisel edge. Nylon-bristle brushes, 3″ to 4″ wide, are best for most surfaces.

A *wall brush* is more flexible than a varnish brush, and it has longer bristles. It is usually 4″ to 5″ wide, with a straight-cut edge for use with sweeping strokes on large, flat surfaces.

A *utility brush* is a small brush for painting trim of window frames. It should be about 1″ to 1½″ wide.

Sash brushes are used for fine work in painting around windows and doors. These brushes have long handles and oval, round, or flat-bristle heads. They come in various bristle

52–5. Patching cracks and nail holes in a plywood wall before painting.

594

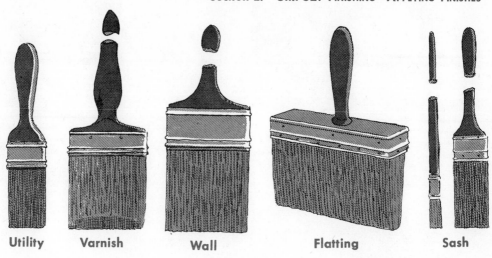

Utility   Varnish   Wall   Flatting   Sash

52-6.   Common kinds of brushes.

lengths, either straight-cut or chisel-cut.

To break in a brush, soak it in a solvent up to the metal cap for about one hour. *Fig. 52–7.* Then wrap the brush in a heavy piece of paper for some time before using it. After a brush has been used, keep it suspended in a solvent of the proper type, according to these rules:

• Varnish and enamel brushes in a solution of half turpentine and half varnish.

• Paint and stain brushes in one part turpentine and two parts linseed oil.

• Shellac brushes in alcohol.

To clean a brush, proceed as follows: Slosh the brush around in solvent to remove excess paint. Press out any excess solvent with a piece of smooth wood. Use a comb to remove paint imbedded in the bristles. Finish cleaning by pulling the brush against the palm of your hand, first

in the solvent and then inside the empty can. Wipe the bristles dry with a clean cloth. Use a commercial cleaning solvent mixed in water, or a

52-7. An old varnish can makes a good brush keeper. Solvent should cover the bristles.

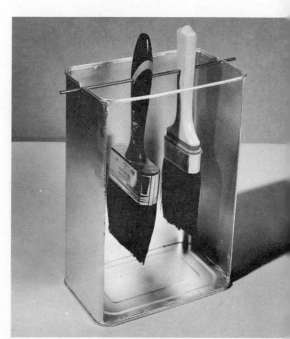

595

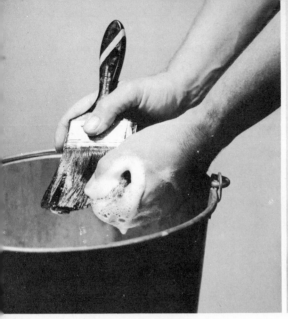

52–8. Before storing, wash brushes with detergent and lukewarm water.

52–10. This compressor is the stationary type commonly used in school and industrial shops.

good grade of detergent (*Fig. 52–8*) to wash the brush thoroughly. Wipe dry and comb straight. Wrap the bristles in brown paper. Store the brushes in a box or drawer, or hang them up.

Rollers. Roller coaters are ideal for painting large, flat surfaces. *Fig. 52–*

52–9. A roller provides a good method of applying paint on flat surfaces.

9. They cannot be used for finishes that dry rapidly such as shellac, lacquer, or fast-drying enamels. There are two kinds. One has to be dipped in the paint and the other is self-feeding because it carries a supply of paint inside the roller. Rollers come in lengths from 2″ to 9″ with the 7″ length the most popular. Various roller covers are available which make it possible to achieve different texture effects. Also, some covers are designed for painting screens, metal surfaces, and other special jobs. The dip-roller type is lowered into a special pan. Excess paint is pressed off before applying the roller to the wall.

Spray Painting and Finishing. Approximately 85 to 95 per cent of all industrial finishes are applied with a spray gun. Since finishing and painting can be done much faster this way, a spray gun should be used whenever possible. Spray equipment

596

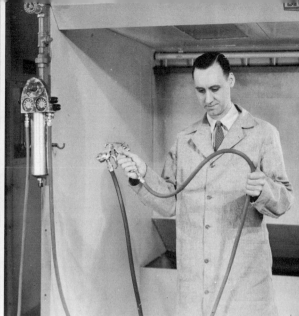

52–11. The transformer cleans the air and regulates its pressure.

52–12. A hose of the correct length and inside diameter is very important.

is essential to good lacquer finishes. Over 80 per cent of all furniture items, including almost all better-quality pieces have a sprayed-lacquer finish.

Basic equipment for spray finishing includes the following: The *compressor* is a machine that takes in air at atmospheric pressure, compresses it, and delivers it at higher pressure to operate the spray gun. Some compressors are stationary; others are portable, mounted on wheels. *Fig. 51–10.* The *transformer* controls the air pressure and also removes dirt, oil, rust, and moisture from the air. *Fig. 52–11.* Most small spray outfits do not have a transformer; therefore air pressure is controlled by the air-adjusting valve on the gun or by the air regulator on the tank. The *hose* carries air from the compressor and transformer to the spray gun. *Fig. 52–12.* In some types of machines, hoses also carry paint or finishing fluid from

the *paint* (or *fluid*) *container* to the gun. For most production work a *pressure-feed tank* holds the finishing fluid. Air pressure forces the fluid from the container to the gun. *Fig. 52–13.* For smaller jobs a *suction*

52–13. In some types of spray equipment, air pressure forces the fluid from the container to the gun.

597

52-14. With a suction cup only an air hose is needed.

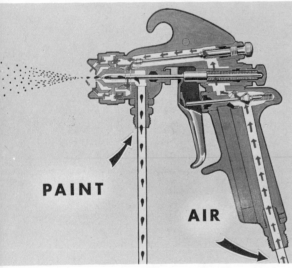

PAINT

AIR

52-15. Notice how paint and air come together.

52-16. The fluid is drawn up into a suction-feed gun without the extra pressure which is necessary in a pressure-feed gun.

cup, attached directly to the gun, does the feeding. *Fig. 52-14.* The *spray gun* itself is the key part. *Fig. 52-15.* As the trigger is pulled, the finishing fluid and air come together. The air breaks up (or atomizes) the fluid into a fine spray. In both pressure-feed and suction-feed guns, this mixing of air and fluid takes place outside the gun. This is called

52-17. On the pressure-feed gun, the fluid tip is nearly flush with the face of the air cap. However, on the suction-feed gun, the tip protrudes beyond the air cap, causing the air stream in front of the tip to create a vacuum. This vacuum pulls the paint out of the container and through the gun.

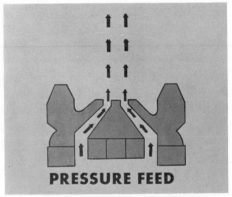

PRESSURE FEED

SUCTION FEED

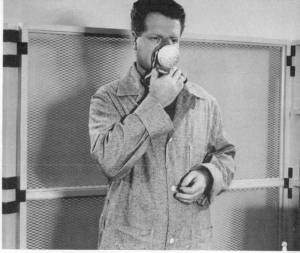

52–18. Spray booths are important. Some are dry and others are of the air-washed type. The booth must provide sufficient exhaust to keep the mist from coming back into the room.

52–19. If you are spraying and do not have a booth, always wear a respirator.

external mix. Fig. 52–16. There are other types of guns in which fluid and air are mixed inside. *Fig. 52–17.*

Whenever possible, spraying should be done in a spray booth with proper ventilation to carry exhaust away from the operator. *Fig. 52–18.* This eliminates the need for a *respirator.* When spraying outside a booth, the operator should always wear a face mask or respirator. *Fig. 52–19.*

Finishing fluids should always be carefully mixed before being placed in the container. Manufacturer's instructions should be carefully followed. Whenever necessary, fluids should be passed through a wire or metal strainer to remove impurities. Cheesecloth or fine window screening can also be used. *Fig. 52–20.* After the material is in the container, the spray gun or the cover should be locked in place. *Fig. 52–21.* There are two adjustments on the spray gun. The fluid-adjusting screw controls the amount of flow. *Fig. 52–22.* With a

52–20. Straining the fluid into a suction cup.

52–21. After filling and hooking up the fluid container properly, fluid pressure is adjusted with the regulator.

599

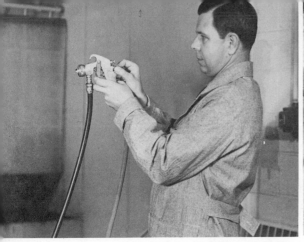

52-22a. When a transformer is used, the fluid-adjustment screw should be kept wide open and the fluid flow controlled at the tank.

52-24a. The fluid pressure gauge shows 15 pounds.

suction-feed spray gun, fluid flow can also be controlled by limiting the amount of trigger pull. The other adjustment is the *spreader-adjustment valve*. This changes the spray pattern. *Fig. 52-23*. Patterns may be round, flat, or fan-shaped. When a transformer and pressure-feed tank are used, start with the fluid pressure at 15 pounds and the air pressure at about 65 pounds. This should be changed as necessary until the best spray is obtained. *Fig. 52-24*.

Following are some helpful suggestions for spraying:

52-22b. When a suction-feed gun is used, the fluid-adjusting screws must be set to control the fluid flow. A limited or partial trigger pull also gives the operator some control of fluid flow.

52-24b. The air pressure gauge (left) is at about 65 pounds.

52-23. Patterns can be adjusted to various diameters or widths of round, flat, or fan patterns. This is done by changing the spreader-adjustment valve.

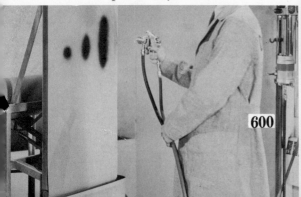

• Always keep the spray gun 6″ to 8″ from the surface. *Fig. 52–25.*

• Keep the gun at 90 degrees, or perpendicular to the surface. This will assure uniform deposit of finish material on the surface. It is very important that the gun be stroked at right angles. Pointing the gun to either side, arching, or up-and-down angling will result in an irregular deposit of finishing materials. *Fig. 52–26.*

52–25a. Right: Keep the gun moving back and forth with an even stroke at right angles to the surface. *Wrong:* Never use an arcing motion.

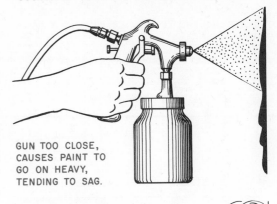

GUN TOO CLOSE, CAUSES PAINT TO GO ON HEAVY, TENDING TO SAG.

GUN TOO FAR AWAY, CAUSES EXCESSIVE DUSTING, AND A SANDY FINISH.

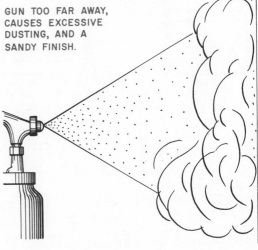

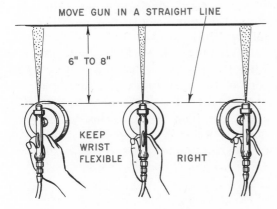

MOVE GUN IN A STRAIGHT LINE

6″ TO 8″

KEEP WRIST FLEXIBLE   RIGHT

52–25b. Keep the gun at the correct distance from the surface.

52–26. Do not tilt the gun in any direction as this man is doing because the spray will be uneven.

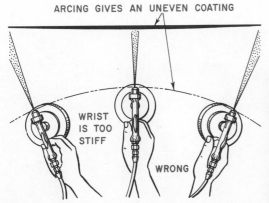

ARCING GIVES AN UNEVEN COATING

WRIST IS TOO STIFF

WRONG

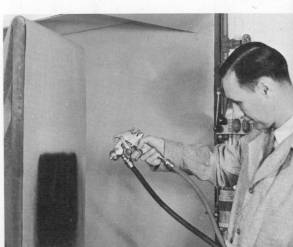

601

LONG PANEL CAN BE SPRAYED WITH UP & DOWN STROKES

LEFT:

52-27. *Banding*: Vertical bands sprayed at the ends of a panel prevent wasted spray from horizontal strokes. Long work is sprayed in sections of convenient length, each section overlapping the previous one by 4". When spraying a panel use alternate right and left strokes, releasing the trigger at the end of each stroke. The spray should overlap one half the previous stroke vertically.

• Overlap each space stroke 50 per cent as the gun is moved back and forth across the surface. This will eliminate the need for double or cross coats. *Fig. 52–27.*

• Release the trigger after each stroke so that the spray will stop while the gun is moving to position for the return stroke.

• When spraying corners, aim directly at the edge so that about 50 per cent of the spray goes to either side of the corner. The gun should be held about an inch or two closer than normal. After the edges are completed, spray the flat surface in the usual manner. *Figs. 52–28 and 52–29.*

52-28. Spraying the edges may be difficult at first, but with practice you will develop skill.

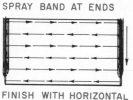

18" TO 36" STROKE   OVERLAP

FIRST   SECOND   THIRD

MOST WORK REQUIRES LAPS

SPRAY BAND AT ENDS

FINISH WITH HORIZONTAL STROKES

OVERLAP STROKES ONE-HALF

FIRST STROKE IS AIMED AT EDGE OF PANEL

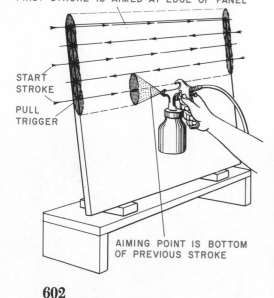

START STROKE

PULL TRIGGER

AIMING POINT IS BOTTOM OF PREVIOUS STROKE

52-29. When the edges are covered, spray the flat surface in the usual manner. Corners are always done first.

52-31. Cleaning out the gun.

• When spraying curved surfaces, keep the gun at the normal distance by using a curved stroke. *Fig. 52–30.*

Cleaning a Suction-Feed Gun. Loosen the air cap two or three turns and remove the fluid container. Hold a cloth over the air cap and pull the trigger. This will force fluid remaining in the gun back into the container. Then empty the container and clean it thoroughly. *Fig. 52–31.* Fill it about half full of thinner. *Fig. 52–32.* Reassemble the gun and spray

52-30. When spraying a curved surface, allow your stroke to follow the curve of the surface.

52-32. Filling the cup half full of thinner.

52-33. Spraying the thinner to clean out the passageways.

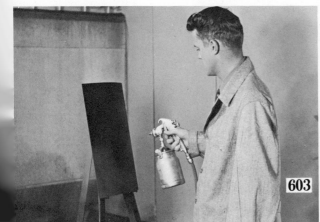

603

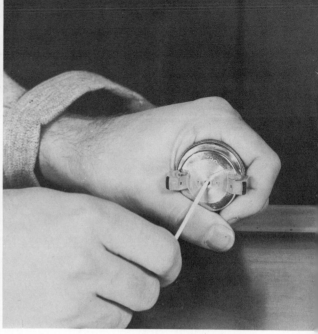

52-34. Brushing off the air cap with thinner.

52-35. A wood matchstick or toothpick is safe to use for cleaning the holes in the cap. A metal tool will damage the holes.

the thinner. *Fig. 52-33.* This will clean out the inside of the gun. Remove the air cap, if necessary, and let it soak in clean thinner to remove all traces of paint or finish. Later, brush and scrape it until it is perfectly clean. *Fig. 52-34.* If any holes in the cap are clogged, clean them out with a toothpick or matchstick. Never use a sharp wire or nail to clean out the air-cap holes. *Fig. 52-35.*

Unit 53: PAINTS AND PAINTING

Paints have been used for thousands of years to decorate and protect wood surfaces. A wide variety of surface appearances can be obtained through use of different kinds and colors of paints. For example, the surface can be made bright or dark, dull or glossy, smooth or textured. Exterior woods need some protection against weathering, roughing of the surfaces, and cupping or warping. The most important function of paint is to keep excessive moisture out of the wood. Interior wood surfaces are painted to keep them clean and smooth. Painting has other advant-

ages as well. In the summer, white and light-colored paints add to the insulating properties of wood by reflecting heat rays. *Fig. 53–1.*

Today the painter can choose from many kinds of paints. Some are designed for one kind of work or surface while others are better for another. *Fig. 53–2.*

CHANGES IN HOUSE PAINT

House paint of earlier years consisted primarily of white lead and linseed oil. While this is still available, it now represents only a small portion of the house paints that are

53–1. Painting the exterior of a home.

53–2. Applying a sealer to a fir-plywood cabinet before painting.

sold. Since 1920, industrial chemistry has revolutionized paint manufacture. The first new material introduced was titanium-dioxide which gave a marked increase in whiteness and provided for self-cleaning white paints. Changes have continued, providing paints with still greater whiteness, better wearing qualities, and more resistance to discoloration by fumes. As a result, most house paints today contain only small amounts of white lead, and some paints contain none at all. Also, house paints have been given superior qualities by the addition of chemicals made from petroleum. The first of these were the acrylic resins used in water-based wall paints. Then, alkyd resins were introduced to improve the wearing qualities of paints and finishes. More recently, still other chemicals such as isophthalic have further increased the wearing qualities of house paints and made them easier to apply. Many of these paints are guaranteed by the manufacturer to give a specified number of years of wear if properly applied. These "super" paints work equally well in bleaching sun or sleet and snow. Paints and finishes of all types will continue to improve as industrial chemistry develops still newer and more remarkable ingredients.

PAINTABILITY OF WOODS

While all woods can be painted, some take paint better than others. The painting characteristics of woods are judged by four standards: species, density and texture, grade, and kind of grain.

Species. Tests have shown that cedar and redwood hold paint best and that northern white pine, western white pine, and sugar pine are almost as good. Serious flaking of paint occurs sooner on southern yellow pine, Douglas fir, and western larch. Western yellow pine, white fir, and hemlock fall between these two groups.

Density and Texture. Summerwood is the dense, dark-colored portion of the wood. Because its wood cells have thick walls and small cavities, it does not hold paint as well as the more porous, light springwood. The relative weight or "heft" of softwood boards roughly indicates their ability to hold paint; boards are heavy or light depending on how much summerwood they contain. In boards which have many annual growth rings per inch, the summerwood may be confined to narrow bands, making the boards moderately heavy. This kind of board holds paint better than one of equal weight in which summerwood is present in wide bands.

Grade. Select grades hold paint better than lower grades which contain troublesome defects such as knots and pitch pockets. The knots of yellow and white pines cause more trouble than the sound knots of such woods as cedar, hemlock, white fir, and larch.

Kind of Grain. Edge-grained or quarter-sawed boards hold paint much better than flat-grained or plain-sawed boards because they are cut so that the bands of summerwood are very narrow. Flat-grained boards

606

hold paint better on the bark side than on the pith side.

EXTERIOR PAINTS

Some manufacturers print the composition or make-up of their paint on the label, but no quality standards apply throughout the industry. The well-known brand names are usually much higher in quality than the cheaper paints. Many manufacturers make several different-quality paints of the same kind, usually putting their own brand name on the best, and then selling the other kinds under a different label. Because the cost of paint is such a small portion of the total cost of painting a home, it is wise to insist on only top-grade, brand-name paints. Buying inexpensive or off-brand paint is likely to be more expensive over a period of years. Some of the more common types of paints available for exterior surfaces include:

White-Lead Paint (L). Pure white-lead paint consists of carbonated white lead, linseed oil, drier, and thinner. Tinting colors may also be used. This is a very durable paint that usually ages without checking or crumbling. It is one of the best kinds to choose if there is any question as to the paintability of wood, or if there is a moisture problem. It is available in ready-mix form and also as a soft paste to which the user adds an equal amount of boiled linseed oil. Pure white-lead paint is usually one of the more expensive varieties.

Titanium-Lead Zinc Paint (TLZ). A great majority of house paints on the market today are of this kind. Composition varies widely. The lower-quality kinds contain less white lead and linseed oil, and more mineral spirits and driers. TLZ paints are bright in color, usually stay cleaner, and are cheaper than the white-lead paints. Some paint stores stock several types of titanium-lead zinc paint, so you should inform the dealer as to where and how the paint is to be used. Some of these paints are designed for use in white only. They chalk freely to maintain whiteness and should *not* be tinted because the colors will soon fade badly. Others chalk less freely and may be tinted.

Titanium-Zinc Paints (TZ). This type of paint is sold in large quantities because it is less expensive than the other two. It is a satisfactory paint where conditions are ideal. It is particularly suited for surfaces exposed to industrial gases which discolor paints containing white lead.

Latex Paint. This is a family of paints made by mixing and emulsifying various chemicals in water, instead of dissolving them in such solvents as mineral spirits or turpentine. Many different kinds of resins are used in making latex paints, and these are being improved constantly. Latex paints were first developed for interior use but are now available for exterior painting. Their prime advantages are (a) ease of application, (b) rapid drying, (c) satisfactory application on damp surfaces, (d) ease of cleaning equipment (with water, if done before the paint dries), and (e)

607

transmission of water vapor, making blistering uncommon. Latex paints should not be applied if the temperature is below 40°F., nor should they be applied to a chalky paint surface.

Paints and Enamels for Metal. There are many kinds of metal primers, enamels, and paints designed to prevent corrosion of iron and steel. These should be used in painting metal downspouts, gutters, and other metal parts around the home. There is a special metal primer for use over new metal or rusted metal as a rust-inhibiting prime coat. Then, a high-quality gloss, rust-inhibitive enamel is used over the primer.

Metallic-Aluminum Paint. This consists of a powdered metallic pigment and a vehicle (the liquid portion). The aluminum paint possesses very good hiding powers to cover surface defects, and is commonly used as an undercoat for oil paints. It is an excellent paint for both metal and wood since it has high resistance to moisture.

Exterior Natural Finishes. There are two types of natural finishes—penetrating and surface—that are used on many homes which have exteriors of mahogany, redwood, or cedar. Penetrating finish soaks deep into the wood and does not lie on the surface like varnish. The wood, therefore, retains its natural appearance. There are many kinds of penetrating finishes designed expressly for exterior use. A popular surface finish is spar varnish which is made from gum, resin, and oils. It is an extremely hard, tough surface.

WOOD-PRESERVATIVE AND FIRE-RETARDANT TREATMENTS

The treatment of wood with chemicals to improve its properties is becoming very common. There are dependable preservatives that will protect against decay, insect, or marine-borer attack. Other chemicals will make wood more fire resistant. Before using wood in areas that are subject to termites or rotting, it is important to apply some kind of good preservative. However, dipping, brushing, and spraying are not very satisfactory because the penetration is too shallow to give good protection. The best method is to apply the chemicals with pressure so that they actually penetrate the cells of the wood. This must be done at a factory or large lumber yard that has the equipment for the job.

Creosote. Creosote is used to protect against decay and attack from termites and other wood-destroying organisms. It is a good material to use when painting is not required and when the slight odor of creosote is not objectionable. Creosote is sometimes mixed with coal tar when it is to be used in and around water. A creosote and petroleum mixture is used for land installations.

Oil-Borne Preservatives. These are used when the surface is to be painted. The treated wood is clean and odorless. Two common materials are Penta and copper naphthenate.

Water-Borne Preservatives. These are good for buildings which stand off the ground and particularly for interior surfaces. The wood can be kiln-

608

Colors suggesting the sea were used to paint this boy's room. Red is the accent color. Clever accessories complete the nautical theme. The built-ins illustrate fine cabinetmaking.

608 B

608 C

Warm tones in this bedroom are typical of the color qualities made possible through the development of chemical paint additives, such as those derived from petroleum. Available colors range from light pastels to deep, dramatic shades. Note also the beauty of furniture finish.

608 D

dried after this treatment. Many commercial materials are available for this purpose.

PAINTING

Supplies. In addition to brushes, thinners and solvents are needed. *Mineral spirits* are colorless liquids made from petroleum and used as solvents and thinners for paints. *Turpentine* is made from the resin drippings of pine trees. It is also used as a solvent and thinner for varnish, paint, and enamel. *Linseed oil* is a yellowish oil pressed from flax seed. It is available both raw and boiled. Boiling improves the drying quality. It is added to paints, fillers, and stains.

Methods of Painting. Paints are available for a one- two- or three-coat system of house painting. A one-coat white house paint should be used only for painting over a previously painted surface that is in very good condition. It is not intended for use on new wood. The paint should not be tinted or mixed with other paints unless so stated on the label.

For maximum appearance and durability, the two- or three-coat system is best. The first coat should be a good primer or undercoat. For some paints, such as pure white lead, the same paint can be used for the primer coat by mixing it with one-half boiled linseed oil and one-half paint thinner. Most paint manufacturers provide a special zinc-free house paint primer or undercoat for use with their house paints. As a rule, it is wise to choose a primer and finish paint of the same brand. Metallic-aluminum paint can also be used as a primer or undercoat.

As a rule, it is best to apply one prime coat and then two finish coats. As a matter of fact, approximately as much paint is used when a primer and a single finish coat are applied as when applying a primer and two finish coats, because more thinner is used in the three-coat process. Manufacturers also make a special paint for wood trim, screen frames, shutters, and similar areas. An undercoat of gray or other neutral color is used as a primer for trim or dark-colored house paints.

Common Paint Problems. • *Blistering and peeling* are caused by excessive moisture in the walls, either from the interior or entering through outside walls. Most cases of poor performance of exterior house paint can be traced to water in back of the paint film.

• *Excessive chalking.* Good-quality paints wear away normally in a period of four to six years. If a paint film becomes so thin that it needs repainting before that time, it is usually due to a previous coat that was applied too thin, to paint that was thinned excessively, or to poor-quality paint. The best way to correct this is to brush the surface thoroughly to remove the chalk, and then apply two or three coats of quality paint.

• *Wrinkling* occurs when paint has been applied too thick or when too much oil has been added in mixing.

• *Cross-grain cracking* is caused by the too-frequent application of paint. This builds up an excessively

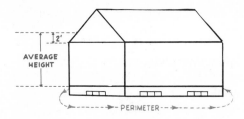

53-3. Measure this way to learn how many square feet of exterior surface are in a house.

thick, brittle coat which cracks and peels.

• *Mildew* is caused by continuous warm, damp conditions. Many paints are available that will minimize the mildew problem. Before repainting, the surface should be washed with strong soap and water or with a solution of two ounces of tri-sodium phosphate to a gallon of water. The surface should then be rinsed with cold water. Remember to use rubber gloves when handling tri-sodium phosphate.

• *Paint which weathers sooner in one location than another* is very common. With few exceptions, it is natural for paint to weather away earlier on the southern and western exposures. You should repaint when most of the old film has weathered away.

Most paint problems can be avoided by using a good-quality paint and applying it correctly.

Estimating Paint Needs. One method of estimating the amount of paint for the outside of a house is as follows:

1. Determine the coverage of the paint. Finish coats usually cover

about 500 to 600 square feet per gallon, primers about 450.

2. Measure the distance around the house and the average height. *Fig. 53-3.* For flat roofs, this distance should be from the foundation to the eaves. For a pitch roof, add two feet more than the height from the foundation to the eaves.

3. Multiply the average height times the perimeter and this will give you the area in square feet.

4. Divide the area in square feet by 450 to find the number of gallons of undercoat, or by 500 to 600 for gallons of finish paint.

Painting Outdoor Surfaces. 1. Make sure that all construction is completed.

2. See to it that all the lumber is dry. Green wood causes poor adhesion. Sap in the wood does not permit the primer to penetrate and form a good bond with the wood.

3. Seal all open joints with caulking compound.

4. Cover all knots with shellac or knot seal before applying the primer coat. *Fig. 53-4.*

5. Select a good-quality matching primer and finish house paint.

53-4. It is very important to seal knots with shellac or knot sealer before painting.

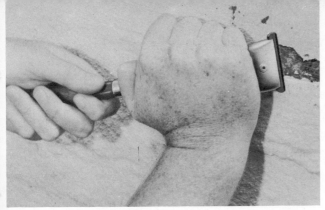

53-5. Scraping off loose paint before re-painting.

6. See to it that the nails have been set and covered with a glazing compound after the primer coat has been applied.

7. Mix the paint thoroughly. Pour off the top liquid into a clean container. Stir the pigments from the bottom with an upward motion. Gradually add the liquid poured from the can.

8. Cover with drop cloths anything which ought to be protected from splattered paint.

9. Carefully dust just before you apply paint. This will prevent a dust streak in the new paint.

10. Paint a side of the house just after the sun has passed over it. Morning dew or water from a brief shower should be wiped off and an hour of warm sunshine should follow before any painting is done. After many hours of hard rain, several days may be needed for drying. There are a few types of paints that can be used on a damp surface.

11. Start at the top of the house and work down. Always paint with the grain, in horizontal strips. Paint under the eaves as you go. After the peak of the house is painted, start at the corner and work across.

12. Paint windows with a narrow sash brush. Paint the pane divisions first, then the cross rails, and then the vertical stiles. Do casing, sash, and trim last. Move the sash up and down before it is dry to prevent sticking.

13. To paint a panel door, first paint the molding and then the panels. Next, do the crossrails and finally the stiles. For flush doors, paint across from top to bottom. Do the edges last with a sash brush.

REPAINTING

1. Wash or dust off the old painted surface.

2. Remove rust marks with sandpaper or steel wool and then reset the nails, apply primer paint to the spot, and putty.

3. Remove loose, flaking, or blistered paint with a wire brush or scraper. *Fig. 53-5.* If the blistering or cracking is extensive, it may be necessary to heat the paint with a blowtorch and then scrape the surface until the bare wood is exposed. *Fig. 53-6.*

53-6.   Using a blowtorch to heat the paint before scraping it off.

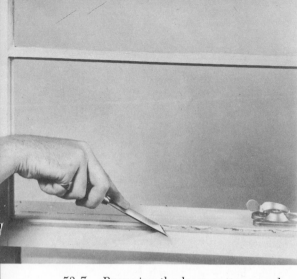

53-7. Removing the loose putty around a window.

to 1 part portland cement, mixed with water until creamy). Moisten the surface and then apply the grout with a trowel. Allow it to dry for 48 hours.

8. Remove scaling paint for gutters, downspouts, and other metal surfaces with a wire brush or scraper. *Fig. 53-8.* Brighten the rust spots with steel wool. Then apply a rust-inhibitor paint to the exposed surface.

4. Seal all open cracks or joints with caulking compound.

5. Repair all damaged surfaces. Clean out the dirt from boards close to the ground.

6. Re-putty window sash. Remove loose, cracked putty. *Fig. 53-7.* Spot prime the bare wood and then replace the glazier's points. When it is dry, reputty with glazing compound.

7. Fill masonry cracks with a grout mixture (3 parts sharp sand

INTERIOR PAINTS

Many different kinds of interior paints are available. The most popular are the latex paints because of their ease of application and quick-drying qualities. For a high-gloss or semi-gloss finish, a good-quality color enamel is better. Flat alkyd wall paints are also very popular because they are easy to apply, washable, odorless, and good for one-coat hiding. These paints are made from alkyds combined with special oils. They are an excellent material for covering almost any interior surface,

53-8. Scraping a metal post before repainting.

53-9. Using a putty knife and a filler to patch a plaster crack.

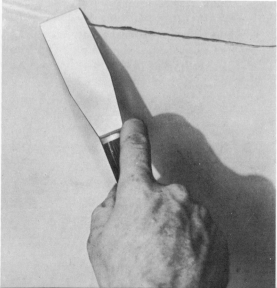

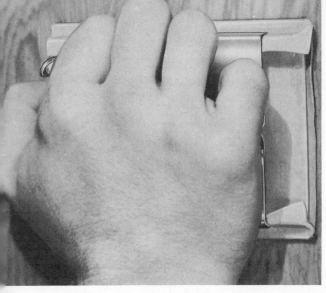

53–10. Sanding a glossy surface before repainting.

including plaster, wood, wallboard, metal, or wallpaper.

Interior Painting. 1. Remove all hardware and electrical switch plates. Apply masking tape to metal parts and switches that cannot be removed.

2. Fill all cracks so the surface is smooth and even. *Fig. 53–9.* Choose a good crack filler and apply it with a putty knife or old kitchen knife. After the filler is dry, sand it lightly. Fill holes in wood with putty. Remove mars and chipped paint with sandpaper.

3. Lightly sand all previously glossy surfaces before you start. *Fig. 53-10.* Wipe all sanding dust off with a damp cloth.

4. Choose the correct kind of paint and mix it thoroughly.

5. Cover the floor and all furniture with drop cloths. Before painting, wipe surfaces with a clean rag. *Fig. 53–11.*

6. Before using a roller, take a

brush and paint a narrow strip at all corners and around woodwork Always paint the ceiling first. For greater speed and to reduce the appearance of overlaps, work across the width of the room rather than the length. Start in the corner and roll a short distance, overlapping each stroke slightly. *Fig. 53–12.*

7. Never paint the woodwork until the walls are dry. Use a one-inch sash brush for windows and a two- or three-inch brush for other parts of the trim.

FLOOR FINISH

Many kinds of clear finishes can be used on wood floors. The selection should depend on the amount of time the room can be out of service, the durability desired, and whether or not a high-gloss finish is preferred. The more common types of finish are penetrating-seal and finish, fast-drying clear-gloss finish, or a slow-drying high-gloss finish.

The penetrating finish will give the

53–11.   Wiping the molding around a door before repainting.

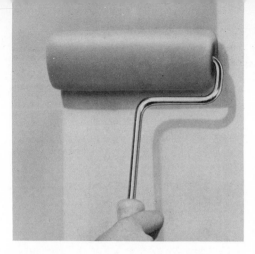

53–12. Overlap each stroke slightly as you apply the paint with a roller.

greatest durability because it becomes an integral part of the wood. This finish gives a soft, rubbed effect. It is light in color and not slippery. It is quite easy to maintain and only the sections showing wear need be refinished. A good coat of paste wax will keep the surface in excellent condition. Penetrating finish can be applied with a paint brush, a lamb's wool applicator, or with a cloth. Rub it thoroughly into the wood, first across, then with the grain. After it has dried about three hours it should be buffed lightly with an electric polishing machine. Then a second coat should be applied. This should be allowed to dry thoroughly and then buffed again. If a paste filler is needed it should be applied between the first and second coats.

Plastic varnish is usually used for a fast-drying high-gloss floor finish. If a stain and filler are desired for the floor, this should be applied first. Then at least two coats of the finish should be brushed on, allowing one hour or more between for drying.

A slower-drying floor finish that provides a high-gloss, non-slippery surface is also available. This is usually the most desirable of all and is often used on floors that will get extra hard wear. However, this type of finish usually must dry five or six hours between coats.

PAINTING PLYWOOD

Covering with three coats of good paint provides the best protection, in most instances. A dip or brush application of a top-quality water repellent (toxic or non-toxic) before panels are painted will provide additional protection.

The initial or prime coat is most important. A high-grade exterior primer, thinned according to directions on the container and thoroughly brushed on, is recommended. A top-quality, exterior, aluminum, house paint (long-oil spar-varnish-type vehicle preferred) makes an excellent outdoor primer for plywood. Greater than average opacity of finish coats may be required, however, to completely mask aluminum primer. Apply at least initial prime coat as soon as possible after construction.

Apply the second and third coats according to paint manufacturer's directions.

Marine Uses. On plywood boats very satisfactory finishes are obtained by using high-grade marine primers, undercoats, and finish coats. Seal edges with shellac or resin sealer, and prime plywood well; for proper adhesion, be sure all paint coats are completely compatible. Finishes which retain some flexibility give best results. Semi-gloss finishes usually perform better than high-gloss.

614

Unit 54: WOOD FINISHING

The wood finishing process varies with the kind of wood and the appearance desired. *Fig. 54–1.* Before applying a fine finish, make sure that the surface is really ready for it. A good finish will not cover up mistakes.

PREPARING WOOD FOR FINISHING

When the product is assembled and the glue is properly dry, plenty of time should be spent in preparing the piece for finishing.

1. Remove all excess glue. With a sharp chisel, remove carefully all traces of glue around the joints. If any glue has spilled on the surface, remove by scraping. Never attempt to sand off glue; this will force it into the wood and cause an imperfection.

2. Check the surface carefully for dents or irregularities. A small dent in the wood can be raised by applying boiling hot water to the area with a rag or sponge and allowing it to stand for some time. Then sand the surface. For deeper dents, cover the area with a heavy, wet cloth and then apply a hot soldering copper to the cloth. Fill cracks, dents, and nail or screw holes with stick shellac,

plastic wood, wood dough, or wood-sanding dust mixed with powdered glue.

Stick shellac (hard pieces of shellac) can be purchased in many shades resembling wood tones and also in transparent, white, old ivory, and similar varieties. To use, heat the end of the stick over a Bunsen burner until soft. Also heat the blade of a putty knife. Then press the shellac into the dent or crack with the

54–1. Much of the beauty and cost of fine furniture is in the excellent finish. More hand work is required in finishing than in any other step in furniture manufacture.

knife. Always add enough filler to make the area slightly higher than the surface.

Plastic wood can also be used. This comes in colors such as natural light oak, mahogany, walnut, and dark oak. Still another filler is wood dough, a synthetic wood. It comes in such common colors as cedar, walnut, pine, mahogany, fir, and oak.

3. Scrape and/or sand the surface thoroughly. On open-grained woods, scrape the surface with a hand or cabinet scraper. This should be done before any sanding.

FINISHING SUPPLIES

Mineral spirits is a pure distillation of petroleum that will do everything turpentine will do. It can be used as a thinner or solvent for paints, enamels, and varnishes.

Benzene, a material derived from coal tar, is widely used as a solvent.

Benzine, a colorless liquid made from petroleum, is used as a solvent in some cleaning fluids.

Alcohol, a colorless liquid made from wood drippings or chemicals, is used as a thinner and solvent for shellac.

Turpentine, made from the resin of pine trees, is used as a solvent for paint and enamel.

Linseed oil, made from flaxseed, is used in paints, fillers, and stains.

Pumice, a white powder that comes from lava, is used as a buffing and polishing compound. Use No. 1 for coarse rubbing and No. FF or No. FFF for fine rubbing.

Rottenstone, a reddish-brown or grayish-black limestone, is used for smoothing and rubbing. It is finer than pumice.

Rubbing oil, a good grade of petroleum or paraffin oil, is used with pumice or rottenstone for rubbing down a finish.

Wet-dry abrasive paper (waterproof aluminum-oxide paper), in grades 240 and 400, is used with water for sanding between finishing coats.

BLEACHING

Bleaching is a process of removing color from wood in order to obtain a full-blond effect. For simple bleaching operations, oxalic-acid crystals dissolved in hot water are satisfactory. However, for a more involved bleaching process, a commercial bleach will usually give better results.

Always follow the directions printed on the container. Apply the bleach to the surface with a sponge or rope brush, and work from the top down. Rinse the bleached surface with a 50-50 solution of water and white vinegar. Then allow it to dry for 12 hours. Sand the surface lightly with 6/0 garnet paper. Keep all bleaching rags in a closed metal container.

WIPE-ON FINISHES

There are many wipe-on finishes that can be applied with a cloth. Most of these penetrate into the wood. A finish of this type is particularly good when no spraying equipment is available or when a finish must be applied in places where dust is a problem.

A clear, semi-gloss interior finish,

such as "Deft," can be used on raw wood or over stains and filled surfaces. It seals and primes. The finishing procedure can be completed with three applications. The first coat seals the wood, after which the surface should be sanded with 6/0 sandpaper. The second coat can be rubbed with 4/0 steel wool or 400 wet-dry paper. The third and final coat can be sanded lightly with 600 wet-dry sandpaper or rubbed with pumice or rottenstone to a mirror-smooth finish.

"Sealacell" is another type of wipe-on finish. *Stain can be mixed with the first solution,* and this mixture applied as the first of three steps in the finishing process. Colored pigment ground in oil can also be added to get the desired shade. For open-grained wood a filler can be made by mixing natural filler with "Sealacell" until they reach the consistency of heavy cream; then add colored pigment ground in oil. This mixture is applied with a cloth and rubbed in. This first coat should be allowed to dry 12 hours and then buffed lightly with steel wool. Next, "Varno-wax," should be applied in a circular motion, using a pad or soft cloth. Only a small area should be waxed at a time. Twelve hours drying time should be allowed and the surface then buffed with very fine steel wool.

The last step is the application of a luster-producing finishing solution, "Royal Finish." Two or three applications can be made to get the degree of luster wanted.

Oil Finish. Some modern furniture, especially walnut, is given an oil finish to bring out the beauty of the grain and to preserve the wood. This is a long process which requires the application of oil every day for at least a week. Several different mixtures can be used, including:

• About two-thirds linseed oil and one-third hot turpentine.

• About one-third spar varnish, one-third boiled linseed oil, and one-third heated gum turpentine.

The finish is applied by saturating a cloth and rubbing the entire surface thoroughly until a uniform color is produced. After drying about 15 minutes, the surface should be rubbed with a clean cloth. About 24 hours should elapse between coats.

There are many other commercial wipe-on finishes that produce good results when spray equipment is not available.

ACHIEVING A FINE FINISH

Following are the basic steps necessary to obtain a fine wood finish. All are not required for every job. However, they should be carried out as necessary.

Sanding. (See also Unit 38.) A finish can be no smoother than the surface to which it is applied. Final sanding should be done with 3/0 garnet paper. Flat areas should be sanded with long, sweeping strokes. For grooves, molded curves, and crevices, bend the sandpaper so that it can be manipulated. After sanding, always clean the surface with a tack rag. This is a soft, lintless cloth such as an old handkerchief that has been dampened in water. Sprinkle the cloth liberally with turpentine, then pour two or three teaspoons of varnish on it and squeeze fairly dry. This cloth will pick up dust before a finish is applied.

Bleaching. Bleaching (see page 600) is done only when it is necessary to lighten the wood. Most furniture finishes do not include bleaching.

Staining. Staining provides an undertone color for a finish, or changes the tone or shade of the surface. Two types of fine-powder substances provide the colors in stains. They are *soluble colors or dyes*, which are dissolved in the stain, and *insoluble pigment colors*, which are dispersed in the stain but not dissolved. The soluble colors penetrate into the wood pores and actually make the color a part of the wood, while the insoluble colors remain on the surface, providing a uniform appearance.

The dyes are made from various chemicals, primarily coal tar. The insoluble colors are either natural pigments such as iron oxide, yellow oxide, raw sienna, burnt sienna, ochres, and umbers, or they are made from both dyes and pigment colors.

54-2.   Sponging the surface before applying water stains.

Some of the more common kinds of stains are:

• *Water stains.* These are made from dyes and sold as powders. They come in shades resembling many kinds of woods, such as walnut, English oak, golden oak, dark-red mahogany, antique oak, green maple, amber maple, brown mahogany, red mahogany, and fumed oak. The user purchases powdered dye and mixes it in water. One ounce of powder will usually make one quart of stain. Water stains are inexpensive, easy to use, give good, clear results, penetrate the wood very well, and accentuate the wood texture. They can be applied by brush. Their prime disadvantage is that they swell the wood and raise the grain, making another sanding necessary. Water stains are also slow to dry and should stand overnight before any additional finishing is done. Before applying water stains, sponge the surface lightly with water and then sand with 5/0 sandpaper. *Fig. 54-2.* Sponge end grain with water to keep it from absorbing too much stain and darkening too much. Apply the stain evenly, wiping off with a brush or sponge. Allow to dry and then sand lightly.

• *Non-grain-raising stains (NGR).* These are made with dyes mixed in a solvent of glycol and alcohol. These stains are available as ready-mixed colors and have most of the advantages of water stains, with none of the disadvantages. Widely used in industrial finishing, they are usually applied by spraying.

• *Spirit stains.* These are made by dissolving dyes in alcohol.

• *Oil stains.* Usually purchased

618

COMMON COLORS IN OIL
(TINTING COLORS)

Lt. Yellow	Raw Umber	Orange	Dark Green
Medium Yellow	Burnt Umber	Lt. Green	Blue
Raw Sienna	Ochre	Medium Green	Toluidine Red
Burnt Sienna			Deep Red

USING COLORS IN OIL FOR
FINISHING

White	Use zinc oxide ground in oil
Golden Oak	Use white zinc tinted with yellow ochre and raw sienna
Light Brown	Use Vandyke brown
Medium Oak	Use raw sienna and burnt sienna
Dark Brown	Use Vandyke brown and drop black
Walnut	Use half Vandyke brown and half burnt umber
Black	Use drop black

54–3.   Pigment colors used to make oil pigment stains and for adding color to fillers.

ready-mixed in cans, these are made from oil-soluble dyes dissolved in such materials as naphtha or turpentine. They are not commonly used for fine furniture finishes.

• *Pigment oil stains.* These contain pigment colors dispersed in oil. *Fig. 54–3.* They are used for an undertone color when filler is used. Pigment oil stains can be made by mixing ground pigments in a solvent of turpentine, linseed oil, or other light oil. Most oil stains used in finishing furniture in school shops are pigment oil stains. Before using, apply a thin coat of linseed oil to the end grain. Apply the stain with a brush or sponge. Wipe with a clean cloth.

• *Transparent lacquer toners.* Made from dyes and lacquer, these give a combined staining and sealing effect. However, their staining properties are not especially good. They are sometimes used over another stain or a filler to give added color.

Before staining, mix enough stain to cover the entire project. Test for color on a piece of scrap wood of the kind to be stained. It is better to apply two light coats of stain than one heavy one. It is much easier to darken the wood than it is to lighten it. *Fig. 54–4.*

Washcoating. Washcoating (sealing) is done to keep stain from bleeding, to provide a hard surface for applying filler, and to improve the toughness of the finish. Good sealer for many stains is a washcoat of shellac. This is a mixture of seven parts alcohol to one part of four-pound-cut shellac. In furniture production in which lacquer is used as the final finish, lacquer sealers are frequently

54–4.   Here you see the difference between a stained surface and the unstained (white wood) surface.

54-5. For finishing surfaces such as fir plywood, the first step after sanding is to brush on a clear resin sealer.

used. They are sprayed on with an air pressure of 40 to 50 pounds. After the sealer is dry it should be hand-rubbed with 5/0 to 7/0 sandpaper. Wipe off the fine sanding dust before applying additional finish.

Filling. Wood fillers are used to fill the pores of wood and to beautify the surface. When the pores are filled, the wood surface is smooth, hard, and ready for any finish. Walnut, mahogany, oak, hickory, and ash require a paste filler because the surface is covered with millions of small, open pores. Liquid filler only is needed for birch, maple, gum, and cherry. No filler is needed for such woods as poplar, fir, pine, and basswood, although a surface sealer should be applied. *Fig. 54-5.* Paste fillers are made from ground silicon, linseed oil, turpentine, dryers, and colors. Fillers can be purchased in cans in natural wood colors. Tints can be added to achieve any effect. Liquid fillers can be purchased, or they can be made by thinning paste fillers with turpentine. Before applying a paste filler, add turpentine, benzene, or naphtha and mix to about the consistency of heavy cream. Mix the oil color with a little turpentine and then add it to the filler until you get the color you want. Apply the

54-6a and b. Applying filler with a brush. Brush first with the grain and then across it. Fillers are also applied by spraying.

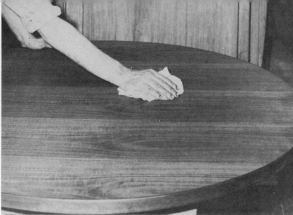

54-7. Rubbing in the filler, using pieces of burlap.

54-8. Wiping off excess filler with a clean cloth.

filler with a stiff brush, rubbing it into the pores. Brush both with and across the grain. *Fig. 54-6.* Rub in the filler with the palm of the hand or pieces of burlap. *Fig. 54-7.* Apply a little extra filler to end grain. Allow the filler to dry until the gloss disappears. Then rub across the grain with burlap or coarse cloth to remove excess filler. Wipe very lightly with the grain to make sure the filler is evenly applied. *Fig. 54-8.* Do not rub too hard as this will remove the filler from the pores. Allow it to dry for 24 hours.

Glazing. Glazing is a thin, transparent coat applied over filler or sealer to give a highlighted, shaded, or antiqued effect. It is used to even up the color and conceal areas which are too light. If used for this last purpose, the glaze coat is applied prior to the final top coat. Sometimes a thin glazing coat is applied over the entire piece of furniture. Antique glaze can be made by dissolving a tablespoon of burnt umber in one-half pint of pure turpentine, and then adding one teaspoon of drop black, a common tint. To give an antiqued effect, wipe the glaze com-

pletely off the flat surfaces and edges that are to appear worn. Leave the glaze in the recessed surfaces.

Sealing. After applying the filler, seal the surface with a shellac or lacquer sealer. Sand lightly with 5/0 finishing paper and clean off dust before applying the lacquer.

Applying the Finish. A varnish, synthetic finish, or lacquer finish can be applied as the top coat. Most furniture of quality has a good lacquer finish; this should be applied whenever spraying equipment is available. *Fig. 54-9.* It is important to choose a good, clear spraying lacquer when using spray equipment. Clear or transparent lacquer is a chemical

54-9. Applying a lacquer finish with a spray gun.

54-10. Rubbing with a rubbing machine. Back-and-forth movement of pads is supplied by air pressure.

compound of several ingredients. Clear lacquers are available from any large paint and varnish dealer. Spray on at least three to five coats of lacquer, allowing sufficient time for each to dry. If spraying equipment is not available, use brushing lacquer. When lacquer is brushed on, allow at least a day for each coat to dry.

Rubbing, Polishing, and Waxing. Rubbing can be done with 320 wet-dry paper dampened with rubbing oil. Another method is to use a felt pad. *Fig. 54–10.* When rubbing with a pad, mix pumice and water to paste consistency. *Fig. 54–11.* Sprinkle the surface with water; dip the pad in the water and then in the pumice paste. Rub along the grain of the wood. Use long strokes and uniformly moderate pressure. Do the ends of the grain first, using a full stroke. To get a satin finish, use 400 wet-or-dry abrasive paper and rubbing oil. Hand rub the entire surface. An even finer finish can be obtained with a felt pad by rubbing with rot-

tenstone mixed with rubbing oil. A final coat of paste wax should be applied over any finish to protect it. *Fig. 54–12.* The final appearance of the wood is determined largely by the color of the stain and the filler that is applied. Sample finishes for some of the common woods are shown in *Fig. 54–13.*

FINISHING FIR PLYWOOD

It is easy to get professional-looking results on clean, smoothly sanded fir plywood when you use top-quality materials, follow the manufacturer's directions carefully, and observe a few simple rules.

Prepare Surfaces Properly. Clean all surfaces thoroughly. Do not paint over dust or spots of oil or glue. Fill nail holes and blemishes in exposed edges with spackling compound or wood paste. Plywood already is sanded smooth, so it is not difficult to obtain proper surfaces. Always sand with the grain, using 3/0 grade sandpaper.

54-11. Using a felt pad to rub the surface of a table with pumice and water paste.

Interior Finishes. *Paint or Enamel.* Any standard woodwork finish is easy to use if manufacturer's directions are followed closely. For durability on frequently cleaned surfaces, use washable enamels.

• After sanding, brush on flat paint, enamel undercoat or resin sealer. Paint may be thinned slightly to improve brushability. Fill surface blemishes with spackling compound or putty when first coat is dry. Sand lightly and dust clean.

• Apply second coat. For a high-gloss enamel finish, mix equal parts of flat undercoat and high-gloss enamel. Tint undercoat to approximate shade of finish coat. Sand lightly when dry, and dust clean.

• Apply final coat as it comes from the can.

• A two-step finish, without the second undercoat, also may be applied.

Water-Thinned Paints. Seal plywood with clear resin sealer, shellac, or flat white oil paint to control grain rise.

Stippled Textures. Textured or roughened surfaces are obtained by "dabbing on" a heavy coat of stippling paint after priming. The paint coat is stippled with a stipple brush, roller, or sponge.

Clear or Colored Lacquer. You can spray, brush, or wipe on lacquer. Use the type made for your particular needs. Sand lightly or rub with steel wool between each coat.

Light Stain-Glaze. A natural finish which mellows the wood's contrasting grain pattern with effective warm colors is always popular. When

54-12. Always apply a coat or two of good paste wax to protect any finish.

using any finish which retains natural grain pattern, carefully select the plywood for pattern and appearance. A four-step procedure is recommended for fine work.

• Whiten panel. Use pigmented resin sealer or thin interior white undercoat one-to-one with turpentine or thinner. After 10 to 15 minutes (before it becomes tacky) dry-brush or wipe with dry cloth to permit grain to show. Sand lightly with fine paper when dry.

• Seal wood. Apply thinned white shellac or clear resin sealer. Sand lightly with fine sandpaper when dry. Omit seal coat for greater color penetration in the next step.

• Add color. There is almost no limit to the colors and shades you can get. Use tinted interior undercoat, thinned enamel, pigmented resin sealer, or color in oil. With care, light stains may also be used. Apply thinly and wipe or dry-brush to the proper depth of color. Sand lightly with fine paper when dry.

• Provide wearing surface. Apply one coat of flat varnish or brushing lacquer. For additional richness, rub with fine steel wool when dry.

Easy, Economical Finishes. An easy, inexpensive two-step procedure will give you a pleasant, blond finish. First, apply interior white undercoat thinned so wood pattern shows; tint undercoat if color is desired. Sand lightly when dry, then apply clear shellac, lacquer, or flat varnish for durability. The exact, natural appearance of plywood may be retained by applying a first coat of white shellac followed by flat varnish after sanding. Several coats of brushing lacquer may also be used. Attractive, economical one-coat stain waxes also are available in colors. If dark stain is wanted, first apply clear resin sealer to subdue grain.

Fig. 54–13. Sample Finishes. While specific finishes cannot be given for all woods, the following shows a number of selected finishes that have proved to be very popular. The first example describes in brief the step-by-step procedure. All of the others tell how to secure the correct color. The general procedure is the same in each case. The complete finish should follow the steps outlined in this unit.

WHEAT ON RED BIRCH

Brush and wipe on wheat oil stain. Allow to dry overnight.

Spray on lacquer sealer. Allow to dry 30 minutes to one hour.

Brush or spray on liquid filler.

Spray on lacquer sealer. Allow to dry 30 minutes to one hour.

Sand with 6/0 sandpaper.

Spray with first coat of gloss lacquer. Allow to dry one or two hours.

Spray with second coat of gloss lacquer. Allow to dry one or two hours.

Spray on the third coat of gloss lacquer. Allow to dry overnight.

Sand with wet-or-dry grade 240 sandpaper, using a mixture of half rubbing oil and half mineral spirits for lubricant.

Rub with rottenstone mixed with rubbing oil.

Apply paste wax.

CHAMPAGNE ON MAPLE

Brush and wipe on champagne oil stain.

Dry overnight.

NATURAL MAPLE

No stain used.

BLOND WALNUT ON WALNUT

Brush and wipe on blond toner, mixed as follows:

4 parts platinum oil stain
1 part gloss varnish

Dry overnight.

Brush and wipe on blond filler, mixed as follows:

3 parts natural transparent filler
1 part walnut oil stain

DRIFTWOOD ON MAPLE

Brush and wipe on driftwood oil stain, mixed as follows:

8 parts platinum oil stain
1 part raw umber first quality tinting color

Dry overnight.

BLOND FINISH ON RED BIRCH

Brush and wipe on platinum oil stain.

Dry overnight.

LIMED OAK ON OAK

Brush and wipe on limed oak filler, mixed as follows:

1 part natural transparent filler
1 part platinum oil stain

LIGHT WALNUT ON WALNUT

Brush on thin coat of shellac, reduced as follows:

1 part 4 lb. cut white shellac
5 parts denatured alcohol

Dry 1 hour.

Brush and wipe on brown filler, mixed as follows:

2 parts natural transparent filler
1 part walnut oil stain

Dry overnight.

ANTIQUE PINE ON PINE

Brush and wipe on dark oak oil stain, reduced 2 parts stain to 1 part solvent.

Dry overnight.

MAPLE ON RED BIRCH

Brush and wipe on maple oil stain.

Dry overnight.

COLONIAL PINE ON PINE

Brush and wipe on champagne oil stain, reduced by equal parts of solvent.

Dry overnight.

AMERICAN WALNUT ON WALNUT

Brush and wipe on walnut oil stain.

Dry overnight.

Brush on **wash** coat of white shellac, reduced as follows:

1 part 4 lb. cut white shellac
7 parts denatured alcohol

Dry 1 hour.

Brush and wipe on walnut filler, mixed as follows:

2 parts natural transparent filler
1 part walnut oil stain

Dry overnight.

WALNUT ON RED BIRCH

Brush and wipe on walnut oil stain.

Dry overnight.

BLOND MAHOGANY ON MAHOGANY

Brush on blond toner, mixed as follows:

4 parts platinum oil stain
1 part gloss varnish

Dry overnight.

Brush and wipe on blond filler, mixed as follows:

3 parts natural transparent filler
1 part walnut oil stain

Dry overnight.

MAHOGANY ON GUMWOOD

Brush and wipe on mahogany oil stain.

Dry overnight.

RED MAHOGANY ON MAHOGANY

Brush and wipe on mahogany oil stain.

Dry overnight.

Brush on **wash** coat of white shellac, reduced as follows:

1 part 4 lb. cut white shellac
7 parts denatured alcohol

Dry 1 hour.

Brush and wipe on mahogany filler, mixed as follows:

2 parts natural transparent filler
1 part mahogany oil stain

Dry overnight.

Unit 55: MATERIAL AND STRUCTURAL TESTING

Wood, metal and plastic are the three major materials used in manufacturing and construction. Wood has many advantages, including:

· It will not shatter when struck.

· It is the only common structural material which has a great capacity for absorbing impact and temporary overloads with a high safety factor.

· It is light in weight — pound for pound stiffer and stronger than structural steel.

· A high "fatigue limit" permits wood to withstand repeated loadings indefinitely.

· In heavy dimension, wood is fire-safe because of the slow rate at which it chars.

· Properly designed, fabricated, and finished wooden items are virtually permanent.

The knowledge necessary for proper use of wood has come from research. The Forest Products Laboratory at Madison, Wisconsin, one of many research centers, conducts hundreds of tests each year on wood materials and structures.

Research and experimentation have improved the design of roof trusses. Components made from plywood, particle board, laminated hardboard, and panels make it possible for builders to produce unusual designs in homes and commercial buildings. *Fig. 55-1.* Many fundamental tests that can be done in the lab will give you a better understanding of materials and products. Tests will help to answer such questions as:

· Which materials are best for a particular product?

· What are the best methods of assembling the parts? What kinds of joints and fasteners should be used? What are the best adhesives?

· How can the product be made to

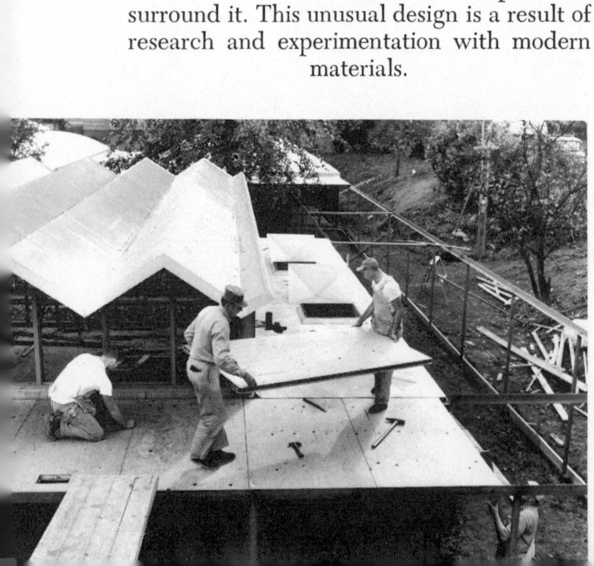

55-1. Glue-nailed plywood stressed skin panels are used both in the folded plate roof of this structure and the flat canopies that surround it. This unusual design is a result of research and experimentation with modern materials.

stand up under use? Which wood preservative should be used? What are the finest finishes?

PROPERTIES OF MATERIALS

All materials have a great number of properties including:

· *Physical:* dimensions, density, moisture content, and weight. Tests and studies of these were covered in Unit 13.

· *Mechanical:* bending strength, compressive strength, stiffness, hardness, and shock resistance.

· *Thermal:* conductivity, expansion.

· *Acoustical:* sound transmission and sound reflection.

Terms for Mechanical Properties. Stress usually refers to a force acting on a piece of wood (or other material) and tending to change the shape of the material. Stress may be *tensile, compressive, shear,* or *torsion. Fig. 55-2.* Tensile stress occurs when forces tend to elongate the piece. Compressive (or compression) stress is the result of squeezing or crushing. Shear stress is caused by opposing forces that meet almost head-on (like the blades of a pair of shears). Torsion stress is the result of twisting.

Stress is also related to the internal strength of a material by which it resists external force. For example, tensile strength refers to the ability of a material to withstand tensile stress—in other words, its resistance to being pulled or stretched apart. Wood is not used in many situations that require high tensile strength. It is also difficult to test the tensile strength of wood because the sample must be held with-

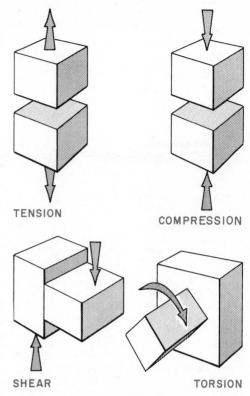

TENSION   COMPRESSION

SHEAR   TORSION

55-2.   Four common kinds of stress.

out crushing it. *Compressive strength* means resistance to loads which tend to push together or shorten a piece. The leg of a chair is compressed by the weight of the person sitting on it. The compressive strength of wood is good in the direction of the grain but poor across the grain. See Unit 13. For example, hickory has relatively high compressive strength with the grain. *Fig. 55-3.* This means it can stand up under a heavy load, thus resisting the compressive stress. *Shear strength* means resistance to forces tending to cause one part of a piece to slide over the other. *Torsion strength* refers to the ability to resist twisting.

627

COMPOSITE STRENGTH VALUES

Name	Weight* in pounds per cu. ft.	Bending strength	Compressive strength (endwise)	Stiffness	Hardness	Shock resistance
Hardwoods:						
Ash, white (avg. of 4 species)..........	41	110	106	161	108	139
Birch	46	117	105	207	104	159
Elm, American	36	85	74	130	66	123
Gum, red	34	86	77	134	60	99
Hickory and pecan (avg. of 8 species)	50	135	122	184	142	279
Maple, sugar	44	114	106	178	115	138
Oak, red and white	45	100	92	161	105	134
Softwoods:						
Cedar, western red	23	60	74	108	38	52
Cedar, southern white	23	53	61	93	35	51
Cypress	32	79	92	136	52	76
Douglas fir (coast type)	34	90	107	181	59	81
Douglas fir (mountain type)	30	75	83	142	52	67
Pine, southern yellow (long leaf)	41	106	123	189	76	103
Pine, ponderosa	28	65	69	112	41	58
Redwood	30	90	104	134	59	70

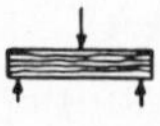

* **Weight at 12 percent moisture content.**

55-3. Comparative ratings in weight and strength properties of several important construction species of wood.

When a floor joist is under a bending load, it develops three kinds of stress. Compression develops along the upper edge of the joist, tension along the lower end, and shear through the middle. *Fig. 55-4.*

Strain is the deformation (physical change in form) which occurs in a material to which a load or force is applied. In other words, as a load or force is applied to a piece of wood, the size and shape of the material is *always* changed, at least slightly.

Deflection is the amount of bending that occurs in a piece when it is under a load. Deflection can be measured in inches or fractions of an inch at the center of the span. *Fig. 55-5.*

Load is an external force that is applied to a piece. It is usually given in pounds of weight or force. Loads can be classified as either *dead* or *live*. The dead load on any piece of material is its own weight plus its share of the total weight of the remainder of the structure. For example, a dead roof load includes the rafters, or trusses, and all the roofing material. A live load involves a weight or force besides that of the material itself and the structure of which it is a part. Live loads may be *static, repeated,* or *impact.*

628

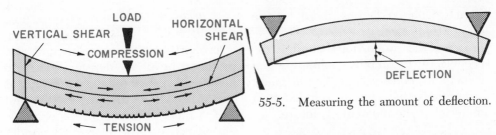

55-4.   Stress on a joist or beam.

55-5.   Measuring the amount of deflection.

Static loads are those which are applied slowly and remain constant or are repeated relatively few times. Furniture in a room is a static load. Loads applied a large number of times are called *repeated* or *fatigue* loads. People walking across a floor or cars driving over a bridge are illustrations of this. *Impact* load is a sudden or instantaneous force. A high wind or a tree falling against the roof of a home is an impact load. Dropping your full weight on a chair is an impact load; after that it becomes a static load.

Bending can be caused by a static, a repeated, or an impact load. Under a static live load, as the load is increased, the deflection increases proportionately up to a point called the proportional limit.

The *proportional limit* is the point beyond which the strain or deformation ceases to be proportional to the load applied. It is at this point that some of the wood fibers begin to be torn loose. *Fig. 55-6.*

Elasticity. Some people think that an elastic material is simply one which can be easily stretched, but this is not correct. A material with good elasticity is one which will *return to original size and shape* after being stretched or

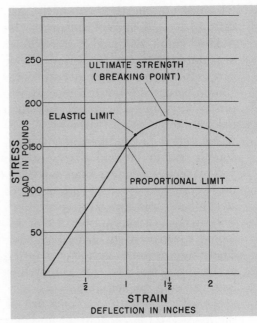

55-6.   Proportional limit is the point at which the strain (deflection) becomes no longer proportional to the stress (load). When shown on a graph, it is the point at which the line begins to curve.

otherwise deformed. The *elastic limit* is the greatest stress which can be developed in the material without permanent change in size or shape of the material after the load is removed. *Modulus of elasticity* is a measure of the stiffness of the material or a measure of resistance to deflection. For wood, this modulus is very low. For in-

629

stance, Douglas fir has about ¹⁄₁₅ the elasticity of steel.

When the proportional limit is exceeded, the wood fails completely and a *breaking point* occurs. The *ultimate strength* is the stress developed in a material at the moment of failure.

Strength Properties. Strength may refer to any one or to all the properties defined below that enable wood to resist different loads. When just one property is meant, that property should be named. For instance, southern yellow pine averages higher than oak in compression strength (endwise), but is lower in hardness. Therefore it cannot be said that southern yellow pine is stronger than oak without referring to a specific kind of strength. Simple comparative strength indexes for various properties of selected species are given in *Fig. 55-3*. These figures are merely comparative and cannot be used for calculating load-carrying capacity.

· *Bending strength* is a measure of the load-carrying capacity of horizontal structural parts between two supports. Examples of parts subjected to bending are joists, girders, stringers, and ladder steps.

· *Compressive strength* (endwise) is a measure of the ability to carry loads along the length of the member without deformation. Some examples of endwise compression members are columns and vertical posts. When columns exceed a certain length in comparison to cross section (usually 11 times the thickness or width, whichever is less), both stiffness and compressive strength affect the load capacity.

· *Stiffness* is a measure of resistance to deflection. The stiffness of a beam is proportional to its width and also to the cube of its depth. A joist 10 inches deep is about twice as stiff as one of equal width and quality but only 8 inches deep. Stiffness is an essential property of floor joists, ladder side rails, and girders. Floors in homes with 6″ joists will bounce up and down from normal traffic.

· *Hardness* is the property that makes the surface of timber resist denting or scratching. Hardness improves wearing qualities and resistance to crushing. On the other hand, hardness makes wood more difficult to cut and nail, and more likely to split. Hardness is a desirable quality for flooring and decking.

· *Shock resistance* is the capacity to withstand suddenly applied loads, blows, and repeated shocks without failure. It is an essential quality for tool handles, baseball bats, and wood used in operating parts of machinery.

Factors That Affect the Strength Properties of Wood. Most of the de-

55-7. Note that the strength properties of wood increase as the moisture content decreases.

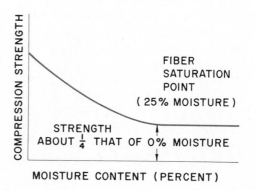

fects outlined in Unit 9—knots, pitch pockets, checks, and decay—exert harmful effects on the strength properties of wood. The actual degree of effect varies with the location and kind of defect and the strength properties being tested. For example, a knot on the compression side (upper side) of a floor joist affects its strength very little, while a knot on the tension (lower side) could have serious effects, particularly toward the middle of the joist. Knots on short compression pieces reduce the strength about in proportion to the knot size. The strength properties increase as the moisture content decreases until the fiber saturation point is reached. *Fig. 55-7.* Beyond this point, the strength

properties remain about the same. Strength properties of wood are related also to density—the denser the wood, the higher the strength—because the strength comes from the cell walls, not the space inside the cells.

BASICS OF TESTING

Equipment. Many kinds of testing machines and equipment are available from commercial sources. For truly scientific testing, it is important to have proper equipment. However, many of the elementary tests on wood and wood products can be made with laboratory-made equipment. The following are some common examples of testing equipment.

Universal testing machine with suitable accessories for making all kinds of mechanical tests of wood and wood products. These are available in many different models and sizes. *Fig. 55-8a.*

Bench-top testing machine. This smaller, commercial machine can be used to make many types of bending and compression-strength tests of woods and wood products. *Fig. 55-8b.*

55-8a.   This universal testing machine is rated at a capacity of 20,000 pounds in tension and compression.

55-8b.   This small bench-top testing machine can do a variety of the tests discussed in this unit.

55-9.   Lab-made testing machine. Note that a standard bathroom scale, a small hydraulic jack, and a 2′ rule are the only commercial items needed. The top of the scale must be reinforced with a piece of plywood.

A lab-made testing machine is fairly easy to build. Chiefly it consists of a standard bathroom scale and a small hydraulic jack. Bending, hardness, joint tests, and several other kinds of tests can be made. *Figs. 55-9 and 55-10.*

A *finish testing machine* can be made in the lab to test finishes on wood, plastic laminates, plywood, and many other surfaces.

55-10.   Drawings of lab-made testing machine. (A) shows its use for static bending. (B) shows use with a fixture for hardness testing. A ½″ steel ball is also needed. (C) shows use with a fixture for testing the strength of trusses. Note the shape of the jack cap. Bore a hole in the bottom of this cap so that it will fit snugly over the jack. For testing joints, make a metal spreader in the shape of a channel that is about 2½″ wide and 12″ long. See *Fig. 55-15.* Use the same jack cap.

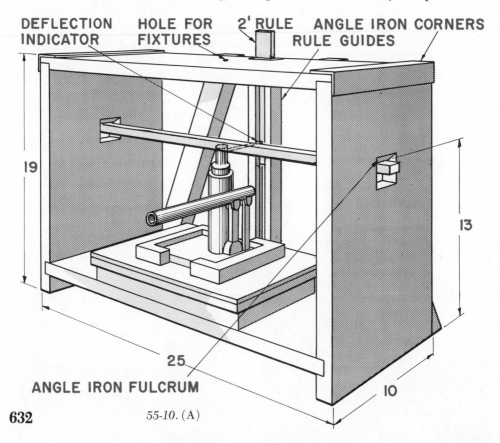

DEFLECTION INDICATOR   HOLE FOR FIXTURES   2′ RULE   ANGLE IRON CORNERS   RULE GUIDES

19

13

25

ANGLE IRON FULCRUM

10

55-10. (A)

FIXTURE 2 x 3 x 4 TO HOLD BLOCK $\frac{3}{8}$ x 2 x 2$\frac{1}{4}$

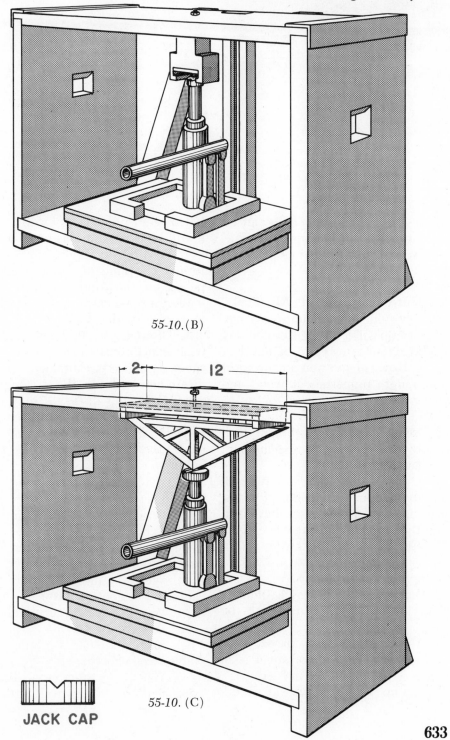

55-10.(B)

55-10. (C)

JACK CAP

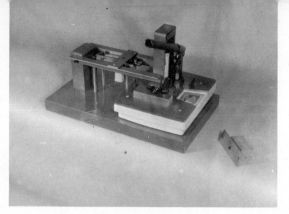

55-11a. Fastener testing machine. Note that the same scale and jack are used with this machine as with the one in *Fig. 55-9*.

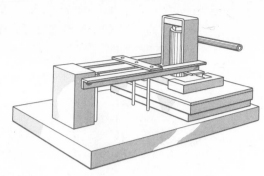

55-11b. Drawing of fastener testing machine.

A *fastener testing machine* can be made to test the holding power of nails, screws, and other metal fasteners. *Fig. 55-11.*

Procedure for Tests of All Types. While equipment limitations may make it impossible to secure precisely accurate results, tests can be made in the lab that will give you a concept of the strength properties of wood and wood structure. Guidelines for carrying out a test are:

1. Statement of the problem. Tell exactly what you are trying to find out, or what the purpose is.

2. Organize the problem. Study all available resources in technical books, magazines, and encyclopedias; and limit the problem to what you can do.

3. Get the necessary testing equipment and, if necessary, construct or modify the test apparatus.

4. Locate all the material. Indicate a specific list of all materials to be tested.

5. Check all safety precautions. This is particularly important if such things as chemicals are needed.

6. Set up the procedure. Make a de-

tailed set of precedures for the test so it will be as accurate as possible.

7. Record all results on suitable forms. The kind of form to use depends on the kinds of tests being made. In some cases, charts or graphs must also be developed.

8. Discuss the findings. Indicate what conclusions can be drawn from the tests and data obtained. Also indicate how and why the test might be repeated using different materials, procedures, or test equipment. In checking whether a good test has been made, the following questions might be answered:

   a. Was the problem well defined?

   b. Was it carried out as impartially as possible?

   c. Were the procedures for solving the problem fully explained?

   d. Were the materials used suitable and of good quality?

   e. Were the results accurately recorded?

   f. Were the charts, graphs, and tables well constructed?

   g. Were the summary, discussion, and conclusions well written?

Suggested Tests on Materials and Structures

Tests on Basic Wood
• Static bending tests using same species. Wood cut from different sections of log.
• Static bending tests of different species of wood.
• Static bending tests of dry and green wood.
• Hardness test.
• Fire-resistance test.
• Effects of moisture content on strength and bending.
• Impact bending tests.
• Stiffness.
• Shear parallel to the grain.
• Weight of different species.
• Comparison of bending strength of wood with holes bored at different locations similar to wood knots or the effect of holes in joists made by a plumber or an electrician.
• Comparison of solid and laminated woods.

Tests on Man-Made Material Such As Hardboard, Particle board, or Plastic Laminates
• Machining ability.
• Static bending.
• Stiffness.
• Abrasion resistance.
• Fire resistance.
• Effects of moisture.
• Water absorption.
• Hardness.
• Shock resistance.

Tests for Plywood
• Comparison of interior and exterior plywood.
• Weight of plywood.
• Bending strength.
• Stiffness.
• Surface hardness.
• Weight and strength of plywood in comparison with other materials such as steel or aluminum.
• Glue test.
• Bending radius test.

Tests of Structures or Assembly
• Strength of joints without reinforcements.
• strength of joints with dowels.
• Strength of joints with metal reinforcements —nails, screws, etc.
• Strength of wood trusses.
• Strength of box beam.
• Compare strength to weight ratio of solid wood beam to box beam.

Tests for Fasteners
• Nail withdrawal and holding power.
• Screw withdrawal and holding power.
• Nailing methods.
• Comparison of toenailing, straight nailing, and clinching.
• Comparison of holding power of different kinds of nail shanks.
• Tests for splitting, using nails of different sizes and woods of different species.

Tests for Adhesives and Glue
• Different kinds of adhesives on same wood species.
• Same adhesive on different kinds of joints.
• Different adhesives on same kind of joint.
• Effect of temperature on adhesives.
• Effect of moisture on adhesives.
• Strength test of joints such as compression, tension, shear, etc.

Tests for Abrasives
• Cutting ability of different abrasives of same grit.
• Cutting ability of different grits of same abrasive.
• Strength and durability of backings.

Tests for Finishes
• Resistance of different finishes to moisture.
• Resistance of different finishes to abrasives.
• Resistance of different finishes to light and/ or heat.
• Suitability of different paints for various purposes.

SAMPLE TESTS

Static Bending Test. Compare the bending strength of small, clear specimens of mahogany, walnut, and birch to determine deflection and breaking point with stock supported on edge and on face surface.

Materials: Cut several pieces ½″ x ½″ x 30″ of each species with the grain.

Equipment: Lab-made testing machine.

Procedure:

1. Select and cut stock to correct size.

55-12. Static bending test in a lab-made testing machine. Note that the pointer on the top of the jack shows the amount of deflection on the rule.

2. Mark edge and face surface of each piece, for easy identification.

3. Mark fulcrum points around each piece so that there is exactly 24 inches from point to point.

4. Position pieces over supports or edge and apply load slowly.

5. Keep careful track of load, deflection in eighths of an inch, and breaking point. *Fig. 55-12.*

6. Record correct information. *Fig. 55-13.*

7. Position pieces over supports on face surface and repeat.

Strength Comparison of Edge Joints. Select four joints used in cabinet construction such as the butt joint on edge *Fig. 34-20a;* the rabbet joint, *Fig. 34-37;* dado and rabbet joint, *Fig. 34-49;* and the edge miter with spline, *Fig. 34-63.* The strength of joints is determined by many factors including the kind of wood, kind of adhesive, method of reinforcing, fit and quality of joint, moisture content, and drying time, among others. In order to test only one factor—for example the kind of joint—cut all wood samples from the same piece, assemble without reinforcements, use the same kind of ad-

PROBLEM: Material Testing—Static Bending

Stick number_____

Species_____

Length_____

Span_____

Depth_____

Breadth_____

Weight_____

Moisture Content_____

Maximum load_____

Deflection at Max. load_____

Load at proportional limit_____

Kind of failure_____

Load—Scale reading in Pounds	Deflection to nearest 1/8"	
	Step	Total

55-13. Form for recording information on static bending. Note that the load is recorded in pounds and the deflection in eighths of an inch. Each step (under deflection) represents an additional five pounds of load. For kinds of failure, see *Fig. 37-9.*

hesive, apply the same pressure, and dry the same length of time.

Materials: Cut 16 pieces ¾″ x 2″ x 4″ of clear, straight-grained wood of any type.

Equipment: Make a clamping fixture. *Fig. 55-14.* Construct a metal spreader and a jack cap for the lab-made testing machine. *Fig. 55-10c.*

Procedure:

1. Make two each of the joints outlined above. Cut and fit all parts accurately.

2. Clamp in fixture and allow to dry the recommended length of time.

3. Set up the equipment and joints for making the test. *Fig. 55-15.*

4. Apply pressure slowly and evenly, keeping track of pounds of pressure and accurately recording when failure occurs. Make two tests on each of two different types of joints. Record all information.

5. Variations of this test can be made by using one of the following items as a variable and keeping all other items constant.

   a. Size of joint.

   b. Kind of joint.

   c. Type of joint.

   d. Kind of adhesive.

   e. Kind of reinforcement – dowel, spline, etc.

   f. Moisture content of wood.

   g. Drying time.

Effects of Knots and Holes on Joists. In house construction, it is important that the floor joists be high in stiffness and have good bending strength. Knots and holes weaken the joists, particularly on the lower (or tension) side. Frequently, plumbers and electricians drill and bore holes in floor joists with little regard for the location. Often the holes are drilled on the lower side of the joists. To check the effect of this practice, follow these steps:

1. Cut ten pieces of pine ¼″ x 1″ x 30″ (scaled size for 2″ x 8′ joists). See Unit 51.

2. Drill ⅛″ holes (equal to 1″ electrical conduit holes in full-size joist) so that you have five pairs as follows:

55-15.   Joint test being completed.

55-14.   Clamping fixture for gluing joints to be tested.

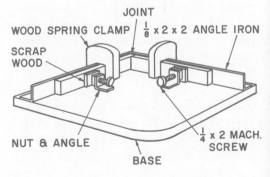

JOINT
WOOD SPRING CLAMP / ⅛ x 2 x 2 ANGLE IRON
SCRAP WOOD
NUT & ANGLE
¼ x 2 MACH. SCREW
BASE

a. One pair with holes toward upper edge (compression side).

b. One pair with holes toward lower edge (tension side). Actually pair "b" is drilled like pair "a" but is placed differently for testing. *Fig. 55-16.*

c. One pair with holes in center (edge to edge and side to side).

d. One pair with holes off-center (side to side).

e. One pair without holes.

3. Test comparative bending strength, stiffness, and breaking point of pairs.

Building Components. A number of experiments can be done by designing and testing different shapes of building components, such as roof trusses, stressed skin panels, box beams, and laminated beams. See Unit 50. The following is a suggested test of roof trusses: From clear pine, cut roof truss materials used for making a model house. See Unit 51. Cut small pieces of veneer or thin plywood for gussets.

55-16. Specimens for testing the effects of holes and knots.

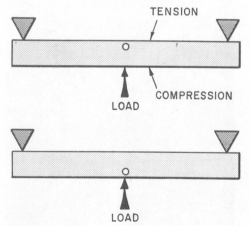

Make sample roof truss designs to scale. *Fig. 55-17.* Cut and fit the trusses, using glue and small nails or staples to fasten the parts together. *Fig. 55-17a.* To test, place truss on the lab-made testing machine and apply a load until the truss fails. *Fig. 55-18.* Record the destruct point. Note how the change in shape or design in the truss affects the strength of the unit. Architects and designers have worked out tables for the strength of these units. Tables have also been developed to enable designers to obtain the correct size and shape of other components, such as the box beam.

Surface Hardness. Surface hardness and resistance to indentation are important properties of wood. The standard commercial hardness test is to use a small steel ball slightly less than ½" (0.444") in diameter. The hardness value is the load in pounds required to impress this ball 0.222" into the wood.

A similar test can be made on the lab testing machine. First, make a fixture to hold the sample. Use a ½" steel ball on the jack. Cut different species of wood or different materials such as solid wood, hardboard, or particle board. Apply pressure up to 200 pounds on each material and measure the width of the indentation with calipers or a vernier scale. *Fig. 55-19.* This will give a fairly accurate idea of the hardness of the material.

Abrasion Resistance. Abrasion resistance is the ability of wood to keep from wearing under constant abrasive action. A relatively simple test is to

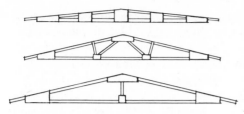

55-17.   Varieties of design in wood trusses.

hold the test specimens against an abrasive-coated wheel with the force of 10 pounds for 1,000 revolutions.

Fasteners. The best test of fasteners is to determine the load necessary to pull common fasteners out of materials. The following can be varied or kept constant in such tests:

1. Kind of material. Solid wood of high, medium, or low density; plywood, particle board, or hardboard.
2. Kind of fastener. Nail, screw, special fastener, other.
3. Size of fastener.
4. Kind of shank surface and shank treatment.
5. Fastener installed in face, edge, or end grain.
6. Moisture content of wood.

Nails should be installed not less than 10 times their diameter in woods of high density or 14 times in low-density woods. Screws should be turned—never driven—in place at least 7 times the shank diameter. Use a lab

55-19.   Making a hardness test.

testing machine to determine the load necessary to pull out the fastener. *Fig. 55-20.*

Plywood. Many experiments can be made to illustrate the value of plywood as a building material.

1. *Comparison of interior and exterior plywood exposed to moisture.* Cut four pieces of interior plywood and four of exterior, each ½″ x 1″ x 3″. Pair them, one piece of interior and one of exterior, so you have four pairs. Do not treat the first pair. The second

55-18.   Scale model of wood truss in lab-made testing machine.

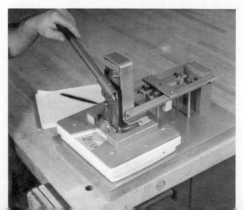

55-20.   Using a fastener testing machine.

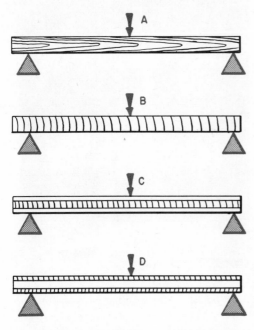

55-21. Comparative bending strength properties of lumber and plywood. Lumber is being bent with its grain parallel to the span at A and across the grain at B. At C, three-ply plywood has the two outer plies parallel to the span. At D, the two outer plies are perpendicular to the span, but the center ply is parallel to the span. In this experiment A is stronger than any of the others. C is nearly as strong as A, but D is considerably weaker. D is stronger than B.

pair should be covered with a penetrating finish, the third pair with a paint finish, and the fourth with an enamel finish. Make sure that each pair is carefully identified. Boil these pieces in hot water, then allow to cool. Repeat three or more times. Observe when the plies begin to separate, amount of warpage, which pieces lose the finish first, and similar tests.

2. *Weight of plywood.* Weight varies widely with the density and thickness of the various plies. Glue lines add to the weight. Cut plywood pieces of the same thickness but of different materials and compare the weights.

3. *Stiffness and strength.* Strength properties of solid wood can vary quite a bit, depending on whether the wood is tested across or with the grain. In plywood these properties tend to be about the same because the grain of one ply runs at right angles to the grain of the next. This crossing of plies also gives plywood much greater splitting resistance than hardwood. *Fig. 55-21.*

Plastic Laminate. Standard test data for plastic laminates have been established by the NEMA (National Electrical Manufacturers Association). *Fig. 55-22.* Many of the tests could be duplicated in a lab.

Wood Compression and Impact. Some types of testing require the use of commercial equipment. Compression and impact tests are generally of this type. Following are several examples of such tests.

• *Wood compression.* Cut several pieces of wood of different species. The pieces should have square cross sections and their length should be four times their thickness. A 1″ x 1″ x 4″ specimen is recommended. Make sure the ends are square. Center the piece in the machine and apply the load gradually. Record the maximum load and continue loading until the specimen fails completely. *Fig. 55-23.* Repeat for each kind of specimen. Longer pieces can be used to illustrate column loading, such as the load on a stud.

Property: NEMA Test	1/16" General Purpose	.050" Post-forming
Thickness	.062"± .005"	.051"± .004"

Wear Resistance
    Wear Value, cycles min.
    Rate of Wear, groove per 100 cycles
	400
	.08"
		400
		.08"

Boiling Water Resistance 20 minutes without surface disturbance	No effect	Slight dulling

High Temperature Resistance
    Bath Wax at 180° C in vessel
    in contact with surface
    20 minutes without surface disturbance
	Slight dulling	Slight dulling

Cigarette Burn Resistance
        Seconds:
    No blistering, charring, crazing
	110 sec.	75 sec.

Stain Resistance
    Alcohol (After 16 hrs. contact)
        Weak Acid 21-29
	No effect
	Superficial stains
		No effect
		Superficial stains

Color Fastness to Light
    (Exposure to carbon arc lamp or fading
    unit 48 hrs.)
	Slight change	Slight change

Moisture Resistance
    (2 hrs. in boiling water)
    Weight Increase
    Thickness Increase
	2-10%
	2-10%
		12% max.
		12% max.

Dimensional Stability
    24 hrs. in oven at 158° F high humidity—shrinkage with grain
    7 days at 100% relative humidity, 100° F—shrinkage cross grain
	.5%
	.9%
		1.1%
		1.4%

Flexural Strength
    Psi., face in tension
    Psi., face in compression
	12,000
	18,000
		12,000
		15,000

Formability		3/4" radius

55-22. These standards for plastic laminates have been set up by the National Electrical Manufacturers Association. The column at left shows the property and (in most instances) the test that is performed. Columns at right show the results which must be obtained if the laminate is to be considered up to standard.

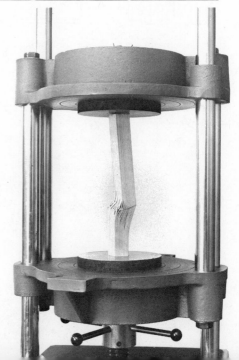

55-23. Making compression test in a universal testing machine.

• *Adhesive Joint*. Make several wood glue joint specimens. *Fig. 55-24a*. Different species of wood or different adhesives should be used. Place the specimens in the machine and gradually apply a load. Observe the behavior of the joint. Continue to load until it fails and record the maximum load reached. Also examine the broken specimen and determine whether the failure occurred at the glue line or in the wood. *Fig. 55-24b*.

• *Breaking strength*. Another test is to compare the breaking strength of a 2″ x 4″, placed first on edge and then flat, to determine the maximum load and the kind of failure. *Fig. 55-25*.

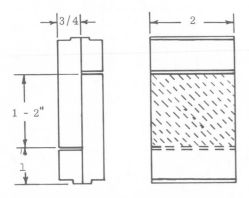

55-24a. Drawing of test specimens for making adhesive joints.

55-24b. Making an adhesive joint test.

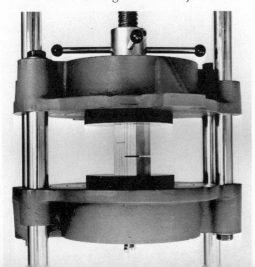

• *Impact Tests*. For many wood tests it is necessary to develop shock loads (rather than gradual loads) and to measure the amount required to break the piece. *Fig. 55-26* shows a testing machine for this purpose.

Structural Shapes. It sometimes happens that the parts of a wood product are strong enough and the joinery is sound, but the product itself is weak because its shape is wrong. Much can be learned about structural shapes through research and testing.

Most wood products such as houses and furniture are made up of basic geometric shapes such as the square, rectangle, triangle, hexagon, and octagon. To illustrate how the shape can affect the strength of the part, cut five pieces of smooth stock that are approximately 1″ x 3″ x 24″. Drill a series of equally spaced holes along each piece. *Fig. 55-27*. Fasten four of these pieces together with a loose pin (dowel) to form a square. Clamp one of the pieces to the table top so that it is held firm, resembling a piece of a framed wall nailed to the floor.

Now apply Force A. *Fig. 55-27*. Note what a small force is needed to collapse the sides. This illustrates how weak such a structure as the wall of a house or the base of a cabinet would be without additional support.

Now remove one piece and form a triangle. Note how much more rigid this shape is than the square. *Fig. 55-28*. The basic shape itself resists being distorted. The triangle is the basic shape for most roofs on homes and also is used for strengthening many furniture parts, as with corner blocks.

55-25. Testing a 2" x 4" for deflection and maximum load at point of failure.

55-26. Machine for making impact test.

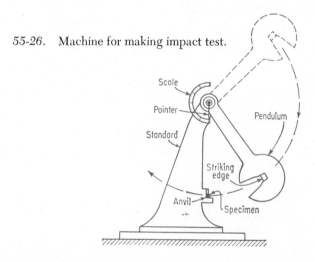

55-27. Testing the rigidity of a rectangular shape.

55-28. Testing the rigidity of a triangular shape.

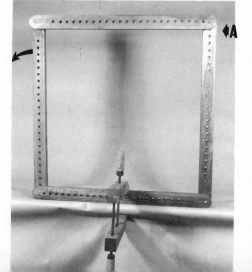

643

Note that in order to distort the triangle it would be necessary either to tear the unit away from the bench or to pull the sides away at the corners. The latter can occur when roof rafters are exposed to a high wind or an excessive snow load.

Now, replace the one leg and form a rectangle again. Use the fifth piece to form a support. *Fig. 55-29.* This kind of support is used in home and furniture construction. The triangular shape is added to provide additional strength and rigidity to the total unit. Many of the unusual shapes in homes and other buildings, such as "A" frames, are based on this fundamental idea of strength and rigidity of the triangle.

Section E
CHECK YOUR KNOWLEDGE

1. Give a description of cabinetmaking.
2. Describe five ways in which furniture and built-ins are assembled.
3. Name materials that are used to cover large areas or surfaces in cabinetmaking.
4. Describe several ways in which legs and rails can be joined together.

55-29. Improving the rigidity of a rectangular shape by adding a support to form a triangle.

5. Name several kinds of furniture that are included in case construction.
6. Describe several types of doors.
7. Describe a gain and tell how it is cut.
8. Name some of the joints used in drawer construction.
9. Describe some of the common drawer guides.
10. Tell where a dado joint is used in furniture construction.
11. Describe several ways of installing adjustable shelves.
12. Tell how furniture manufacture differs from the manufacture of metal products.
13. List several machines used in furniture manufacture that are not found in the average school shop.
14. Define a route sheet and tell its purpose.
15. Name two kinds of patterns.
16. Name the kinds of woods used to make patterns.
17. Describe how a pattern is used in foundry.
18. Explain the necessity for draft in a pattern.
19. Define a core and tell what purpose it serves.
20. Define shrinkage.
21. Tell how boatbuilding differs from other areas of woodworking.
22. List the kinds of metal fasteners that must be used in boatbuilding.
23. Name the kind of plywood that must be used in boatbuilding.
24. List the steps that must be taken before you are ready to build a house.
25. List the things that you should check before building or buying a house.
26. Describe the two types of foundations used in home construction.
27. Name the three basic methods of building a frame house. Describe the advantages of each.
28. Tell how materials should be stored on the job.
29. A girder is sometimes made of wood or steel. Give the advantages of each.
30. Tell why it is important to use bridging between floor joists.

31. Name the parts of an exterior wall.

32. Give another name for a header.

33. Name three kinds of roofs.

34. Define a common rafter and tell on what kind of roof it is used.

35. Tell the difference between a hip and a valley rafter.

36. Describe one method of figuring the length of a common rafter.

37. Define a trussed roof.

38. Tell why the attic space of a house should be ventilated.

39. Name four kinds of doors.

40. Name the most common type of window for frame homes.

41. Describe a casement window.

42. Name several kinds of wood siding.

43. Explain the importance of insulation in home construction.

44. Define dry-wall construction.

45. Name four common kinds of flooring material.

46. Give the first step in building a garage.

47. Describe some of the processes and materials used in constructing a custom-built house with component parts.

48. List some of the problems in building prefabricated homes.

49. List the ways in which a manufactured home differs from a prefabricated home.

50. Tell what is a good scale to use for building a miniature house.

51. Name three methods of applying paint or finish.

52. Describe the differences between a suction-feed gun and a pressure-feed gun.

53. Name three kinds of outside paint.

54. Define latex paint.

55. Name and describe the finish most commonly used for manufactured furniture.

56. Define the terms stress and strain.

57. Name the four common kinds of stress.

58. Explain the steps to follow in conducting a test.

59. Why is it necessary to have commercial equipment for compression testing?

THINGS TO DO

1. Design and construct a piece of furniture.

2. Visit a furniture manufacturing plant and find out how woodworking is done in industry.

3. Make a pattern for a part that you will use in the metal shop.

4. Visit a house under construction and report on the different craftsmen who are employed.

5. Visit a lumber yard that sells prefabricated garages. Report on the cost of materials.

6. Write for catalogs of prefabricated homes. Study the values of these homes.

7. Build a miniature home using a standard set of floor plans.

8. Make sample boards of different wood finishes.

9. Design and construct a device to do some kind of material or structural testing.

GLOSSARY*

A

Abrasives. Substances rubbed on wood to smooth it before or between applications of finish coats. Flint, garnet, aluminum oxide, and silicon carbide are common abrasives.

Adhesive. A material capable of holding other materials together by surface attachment. Glues, cements, pastes, and mucilage are some of the common adhesives.

Air-dried lumber. Lumber that has been dried by storage in yards or sheds for any length of time. For the United States as a whole, the minimum moisture content of thoroughly air-dried lumber is 12 to 15 per cent, and the average is higher.

Aluminum oxide. A common abrasive.

American lumber standards. Provisions or rules for softwood lumber, dealing with recognized classifications, nomenclature, sizes, descriptions, amounts, shipping provisions, basic grades, grade marking, and inspection. These are not commercial rules, so a purchaser must follow the rules of various lumber manufacturers' associations. Rather, these standards serve as a guide or basic example for the grading rules of the various associations.

Annual growth ring. The growth layer of a tree, put on in a single year, comprised of springwood and summerwood.

---

*Some of the terms in this Glossary have several meanings, but only the definitions which pertain to woodworking or closely related fields are included here. Many definitions are reprinted or adapted from *Wood Handbook* and *Wood-Frame House Construction,* by courtesy of The Forest Products Laboratory.

Annular. Ring-shaped. Often used to describe annual growth rings of a tree.

Apron. The flat part of the inside trim of a window, placed against the wall directly beneath the stool of the window.

Arbor. A shaft or spindle on which a tool is mounted.

Attic ventilators. Openings in the roof or in gables for the purpose of allowing air to circulate. Also, mechanical devices with power-driven fans to force the circulation of air.

B

Balanced construction. Man-made wood products so constructed that moisture content changes will be uniformly distributed, and therefore will not cause warping. An example would be symmetrical construction of plywood in which the grain direction of each ply is perpendicular to that of adjacent plies.

Balloon framing. The lightest and most economical form of construction. The studding and corner posts are set up in continuous lengths from first-floor line to the roof plate.

Bark. Outer layer of a tree, made up of a thin, inner, living part (phloem), and a corky, outer part which is dry, dead tissue.

Base or baseboard. A board placed along the bottom of a wall next to the floor.

Base molding. A strip of wood used to trim the upper edge of a baseboard.

Base shoe or shoemold. A strip of wood next to the floor on interior baseboard. Also called a carpet strip.

Batten. Narrow pieces of wood used to cover joints.

Batter boards. A pair of horizontal boards nailed to posts set at the corners of an excavation. They indicate the proper level and serve as a fastening for stretched cord to show the outlines of foundation walls.

Beam. A long, heavy piece of lumber. When used in construction it is usually supported at the ends, and it in turn supports a load which is laid across it.

Bending, steam. The process of forming curved wood members by steaming or boiling the wood and bending it to a desired shape.

Bending strength. A measure of the load-carrying capacity of a piece of lumber, such as a beam, which is loaded so that some bending is unavoidable. If a certain type of lumber tends to split easily when bent, it is said to have poor bending strength. (Not to be confused with *Stiffness.*)

Benzene (Benzol). A material derived from coal tar and widely used as a solvent. Also used for cleaning after finishing.

Benzine. A liquid obtained from petroleum. Used in dyeing, painting, and as a cleansing agent.

Bevel. An angular surface across an edge of a piece of stock.

Bevel siding (lap siding). A type of finish siding used on the exterior of a house. It is usually manufactured by resawing a dry, square, surfaced board diagonally to produce two wedge-shaped pieces.

Birdseye. Small, localized area in wood, where the fibers are indented and otherwise contorted to form few to many small circular or elliptical figures remotely resembling birds' eyes. Common in sugar maple and used for decorative purposes; rare in other hardwood species.

Bleaching. A method of lightening the color of wood by application of chemicals. seeping through the top coat, spoiling its

Bleeding. Color of a stain or lower coat appearance.

Blend. Mixture, as of two pigments to obtain a desired color.

Blind nailing. Nailing in such a way that the nailheads are not visible on the surface.

Blisters. Flat, cloudy, or milky-looking spots on finished surfaces.

Board. Lumber less than 2″ thick.

Board foot. A board 1′ square and 1″ thick, or the equivalent of this.

Boiled linseed oil. Linseed oil to which enough lead, manganese, or cobalt salts have been added to make the oil harden more rapidly when spread in thin coatings.

Bond. A joining or adhering, as of two surfaces; also a substance which causes such a joining to take place.

Bottom board. In foundry, the board upon which the mold rests.

Bow. (Rhymes with how.) The part of a boat farthest forward.

Bow. (Rhymes with low.) The distortion in a board that is no longer flat lengthwise, but has remained flat across its faces.

Brace. An inclined piece of framing lumber used to complete a triangle, thereby stiffening a structure. Also a hand tool.

Brick veneer. A facing of brick laid against the frame of a house.

Bridging. Small wood or metal members inserted in diagonal position between the floor joists. They brace the joists and spread the loads.

Building code. A collection of legal requirements designed to protect the safety, health, morals, and general welfare of those in and about buildings.

Building paper. An inexpensive, thick paper, used to insulate a building before the siding or roofing is put on. Sometimes it is placed between double floors.

Burl. (1) A hard, woody outgrowth on a tree, more or less rounded in form, usually resulting from the entwined growth of a cluster of buds. Burls are the source of highly figured veneers used for ornamental purposes. (2) A localized distortion of the grain, found both in lumber and in veneer. Generally rounded in outline, it is usually the result of an overgrowth of dead branch stubs. Burls may vary from $\frac{1}{2}$″ to several inches in

647

diameter. It frequently includes one or more clusters, each usually having a core or pith but no appreciable amount of end grain surrounding it.

Butt joint. The junction where the ends of two pieces meet in a square-cut joint.

C

Cambium. A thin layer of tissue, between the bark and the wood of a tree, that subdivides to form new wood and bark cells.

Casein glue. An adhesive substance composed of casein (the curd of milk), lime, and sodium salt. It comes as dry powder to which water is added.

Casement. A window sash which opens on hinges fastened to a vertical side of the frame. Windows with such sash are called casement windows.

Casing. Wide molding used to trim door and window openings.

Casting. In foundry, the shape or object formed by pouring molten metal into a mold and letting it harden.

Cell. A general term for the tiny, usually microscopic, units of which wood is formed. Wood fibers, vessel segments, and other structural elements all are cells.

Cellulose. The principal one of the substances which form the framework or walls of wood cells. Also, an organic substance obtained from the cotton plant and used as raw material in the manufacture of paints and other materials.

Chamfer. A beveled surface cut on the corner of a piece of wood.

Check. A lengthwise crack or separation of the wood, usually extending across the rings of annual growth. This defect commonly results from stresses set up in wood during seasoning.

Checking. Cracks or fissures that appear with age in many exterior paint coatings; superficial at first, they may in time penetrate the coating entirely.

Chine. The piece of a boat which lies along the junction of the sides and the bottom, and reinforces that junction.

Clamp. A device that holds things together, often used to hold pieces of wood together while glue on them dries.

Clapboards. One form of outside covering for a house; siding.

Cleat. A strip of material, such as wood, fastened to another piece to strengthen it or to furnish a grip.

Cold-setting resin glue. A resin-base glue that comes in powder form and is mixed with water.

Collar beam. A beam connecting pairs of opposite roof rafters.

Columns. A support (often square, rectangular, or cylindrical) as for roofs or ceilings.

Combination doors. Doors having a removable inside section. In warm weather a screen is inserted in the frame, and in cold weather a glass or glazed-and-wood-paneled section is inserted to make a storm door.

Compreg. Wood in which the cell walls have been impregnated with synthetic resin, and compressed, to reduce swelling and shrinking characteristics and give greater properties of density and strength.

Concrete. A combination of sand, broken stone, or gravel, and cement, used for foundations, building construction, walks, and many other purposes.

Conifer. Cone-bearing. (See *Softwood.*)

Cope. In foundry, the upper or topmost section of a flask.

Core. In foundry, a separate part of the mold, used to form openings or cavities in the casting. Usually made of baked sand.

Core (plywood). The center of the panel. May be either veneer or lumber.

Core box. In foundry, a mold in which a core is formed.

Corner block. A large triangular piece of wood or metal used for added strength at the corners of frames or where legs and rails join.

Cornice. A decorative member, usually molded, placed at or near the top of a wall.

Counterboring. Enlarging a hole so that the head of a screw or bolt inserted in it can be completely covered.

Countersinking. Removing stock around the end of a hole so heads of screws or bolts can be brought flush with the surface.

Courses. Alternate layers or thicknesses

of material, as in a masonry wall, or shingles on a roof.

Crawl space. A shallow space between the floor of a house and the ground, in no-basement construction.

Crook. The defect of a board the edges of which do not form a straight line from end to end.

Cross break. A crack or separation of wood cells across the grain of a board. Such defects may be caused by unequal shrinkage or by external forces.

Cross grain. (See *Grain.*)

Crossband. Layers of wood placed with grains at right angles to minimize shrinking and swelling. Also, in plywood of three or more plies, a layer of veneer whose grain direction is at right angles to that of the face plies.

Cup. Distortion or warping of a board which is no longer flat across its width.

D

d. (See *Penny.*)

Dado. A rectangular groove across grain in a board.

Deadening. Construction intended to prevent the passage of sound.

Decay. Disintegration of wood or other substance through the action of fungi.

Decking. The floor or platform that extends from side to side in a boat.

Defect. Any imperfection occurring in or on wood that may lower its quality.

Density. The mass or true quantity of wood (or any substance) in a unit of a given size. For instance, a board foot of white oak, a heavy hardwood, would have greater density than a board foot of a lighter wood such as ponderosa pine.

Dimension. (See *Lumber.*)

Dimension stock. A term largely superseded by the term hardwood dimension lumber. It is hardwood stock processed to a point where the maximum waste remains at the dimension mill, and the maximum utility is delivered to the user. It is stock of specified thickness, width, and length. According to specification it may be solid or glued up; rough or surfaced; semifabricated or completely fabricated.

Dimensional stabilization. Reduction in swelling and shrinking of wood through special treatment which causes the moisture content of the wood to change with changes in relative humidity.

Direct nailing. To install nails perpendicular to the surface or to the junction of the pieces joined. Also termed *face nailing.*

Dowel. A small, wooden pin used to strengthen a joint. Also, in foundry, a pin placed between the sections of parted patterns or core boxes to locate and hold them in position.

Drag. In foundry, the bottom part of a flask or mold.

Drawing. In foundry, removing the pattern from the sand.

Dressed and matched (tongue and groove). Boards matched in such a way that there is a groove on one edge and a corresponding tongue on the other.

Dressed lumber. (See *Lumber.*)

Drier. A solution added to drying oils to quicken the drying.

Drip cap. A molding placed above the exterior of a door or window, causing water to drip beyond the outside of the frame.

Drop siding. Exterior wall covering, usually $\frac{3}{4}$″ thick and 6″ wide, machined into patterns. Drop siding has tongue-and-groove or shiplap joints, and is heavier and stronger than bevel siding.

Dry kiln. (See *Kiln drying.*)

Dry rot. A term loosely applied to any crumbly decay of wood, but especially to that which, when in an advanced stage, allows the wood to be crushed easily to a dry powder. The term does not accurately describe decay, since fungi which cause the rot require considerable moisture for growth.

Dry-wall construction. A construction method in which the walls are installed dry, usually in the form of sheet materials.

Drying oil. An oil which, when a thin film of it is exposed to the air, takes on oxygen and becomes hard, tough, and elastic. Drying oils are used in the manufacture of paints and varnishes. Linseed oil is a common drying oil.

Ducts. Pipes which carry air from a furnace or an air conditioner to the rooms of a building. Usually they are round or rectangular and made of metal, although they may be made of asbestos and composition materials.

E

Early wood. (See *Springwood.*)

Edge-grained. (See *Grain.*)

Empty-cell process. A process for impregnating wood with preservatives or chemicals.

Enamel. A kind of paint in which the vehicle is a drying oil or combination of drying oil and resin. It dries to an even, hard finish. Usually it leaves a glossy surface, but the addition of a flatting agent can reduce the glossiness.

Equilibrium moisture content. The moisture content at which wood neither gains nor loses moisture when surrounded by air at a given relative humidity and temperature.

Evaporate. To pass off in vapor or to change a liquid into vapor or gas.

Extractives. Substances in wood, not part of the cellular structure, that can be removed by hot or cold water, ether, benzene, or other solvents that do not react chemically with wood components.

External-mix gun. A spray gun in which air and the fluid being sprayed are mixed outside the air cap of the gun.

F

Factory and shop lumber. (See *Lumber.*)

Fascia. A flat member, as on a cornice or an eave. Often, the board of the cornice to which the gutter for rain water is fastened.

Fiber saturation point. The point in the drying or wetting of wood at which the cell walls are saturated and the cell cavities are free from water. It is usually taken as approximately 23 to 30 percent moisture content, based on weight when oven-dry.

Fiber, wood. A comparatively long, narrow, tapering wood cell, closed at both ends.

Figure. The pattern produced in a wood surface by annual growth rings, rays, knots, irregular coloration, and deviations from regular grain such as interlocked and wavy grain.

Filler (wood). A heavily pigmented preparation used for filling and leveling off the pores in open-grained woods.

Fillet. A concave corner piece placed at the intersection of two surfaces to round out a sharp corner.

Finish. Wood products to be used in joinery, such as doors and stairs, and other fine work required to complete a building, especially the interior. Also, the process of adding stains, filler, and other materials to protect and beautify the surface of wood.

Fire stop. A solid, tight partition placed to prevent the spread of fire and smoke through a building.

Flakes. (See *Rays.*)

Flashing. Sheet metal or other material used in roof and wall construction to protect a building from seepage of water.

Flask. In foundry, a metal or wood frame, without top or bottom, in which the mold is formed.

Flat paint. An interior paint, containing a high proportion of pigment, which dries to a flat or lusterless finish.

Flat-grained. (See *Grain.*)

Flatting oil. A special liquid used with pigment-oil paste to produce a flat paint. It is a clear liquid, consisting primarily of thickened drying oils and turpentine.

Flitch. Portion of a log sawed on two or more sides and intended for remanufacture into lumber or veneer. The term is also applied to the sheets of veneer laid together in sequence of cutting.

Flue. The opening in a chimney through which smoke can pass.

Flush. Even, or in the same plane (with reference to adjacent surfaces of two structural pieces).

Footing courses. The bottom and heaviest courses of a masonry wall.

Foundation. The part of a building or wall which supports the superstructure.

Frame. The surrounding or enclosing woodwork, as around windows or doors; also, the skeleton of a building.

Frame construction. Construction in

650

which the structural parts are of wood or dependent on a wood frame for support. (See also *Balloon framing, Platform framing.*)

Framing. The rough structure of a building, including interior and exterior walls, floor, roof, and ceilings.

Frieze. A horizontal, often decorative, member of a cornice, set flat against a wall. More broadly, any sculptured or ornamental band in a house or on furniture.

Frostline. The depth of frost penetration in soil. This depth varies in different parts of the country. Footings should be placed below this line to prevent movement.

Full-cell process. A process for impregnating wood with preservatives or chemicals. In this process a vacuum is formed to remove air from the wood before adding the preservative.

Fungi, wood. Microscopic plants that live in damp wood and cause mold, stain, and decay.

Furring. Narrow strips of board nailed on the walls and ceilings to form a level surface upon which to fasten other materials.

G

Gable. A vertical, triangular part of a building, contained between the slopes of a double-sloped roof. Also, a similar part of a building, even though not triangular. Under a single-sloped roof, that vertical part of the building above the lowest elevation of the roof and below the ridge of the roof.

Gain. A notch or mortise, as in a beam or a wall, for a joist, girder, or similar member.

Gate. In foundry, a channel through which the molten metal enters the casting cavity.

Girder. A member used to support wall beams or joists.

Glazing. Application of a thin transparent color over a previously finished surface to produce a hard finish and provide luster, or to produce a blended effect.

Gloss. A shiny, lustrous finish which reflects light. The term also refers to paint or enamel that dries to a high sheen or luster, usually with a hard, smooth coat.

Glue. An adhesive, commonly used in joining wood parts. (See also *Casein, Cold-setting resin.*)

Glue block. A small piece of wood used to strengthen and support two pieces of wood joined at an angle.

Grade. The designation of quality, as of logs or plywood.

Grain. The direction, size, arrangement, appearance, or quality of the fibers in wood or lumber. The following terms describe specific types of grain.

CLOSE-GRAINED WOOD. Wood with narrow, inconspicuous annual rings. The term is sometimes used to designate wood having small and closely spaced pores.

COARSE-GRAINED WOOD. Wood with wide, conspicuous annual rings, indicating considerable difference between springwood and summerwood. The term is sometimes used to designate wood with large pores such as oak, ash, chestnut, and walnut.

CROSS-GRAINED WOOD. Wood in which the fibers deviate from a line parallel to the sides of the piece. Cross grain may be either diagonal or spiral grain, or a combination of the two.

CURLY-GRAINED WOOD. Wood in which the fibers are distorted so that they have a curled appearance, as in "birdseye" wood.

DIAGONAL-GRAINED WOOD. Wood in which the annual rings are at an angle with the axis of the piece. This effect is produced by sawing at an angle to the bark of the tree or log. A form of cross-grain.

EDGE-GRAINED LUMBER. Lumber that has been sawed so that the wide surfaces extend approximately at right angles to the annual growth rings. Lumber is considered edge grained when the rings form an angle of 45 to 90 degrees with the wide surface of the piece.

FLAT-GRAINED LUMBER. Lumber that has been sawed in a plane approximately perpendicular to a radius of

651

the log. Lumber is considered flat grained when the annual growth rings make an angle of less than 45 degrees with the surface of the piece.

OPEN-GRAINED WOOD. Common term for woods with large pores such as oak, ash, chestnut, and walnut. Also known as "coarse textured."

PLAINSAWED LUMBER. Another term for flat-grained lumber.

QUARTERSAWED LUMBER. Another term for edge-grained lumber.

SPIRAL-GRAINED WOOD. Wood in which the fibers take a spiral course about the trunk of a tree instead of the normal vertical course. The spiral may extend in a righthand or lefthand direction around the tree trunk. Spiral grain is a form of cross grain.

STRAIGHT-GRAINED WOOD. Wood in which the fibers run parallel to the axis of the piece.

VERTICAL-GRAINED LUMBER. Another term for edge-grained lumber.

WAVY-GRAINED WOOD. Wood in which the fibers collectively take the form of waves or undulations.

Green. Freshly sawed lumber, or lumber that has had no intentional drying; unseasoned.

Green sand. In foundry, molding sand tempered with water to proper consistency for use.

Green-sand core. A core made of molding sand, but not baked.

Groove. A long, hollow channel, cut by a tool, into which a piece fits or in which it works. Carpenters have given special names to certain forms of grooves, such as dadoes and housings. A *dado* is a rectangular groove cut across the grain the full width of the piece. A *housing* is a groove cut at any angle with the grain and partway across the piece. Housings are used for framing stair risers and treads.

Growth ring. (See *Annual growth ring.*)

Gum. A sticky substance obtained from the sap of certain trees and plants, and used in making varnishes and paints.

Gusset. A triangular or trapezoidal piece of wood or metal fastened to the exterior of a joint to strengthen it.

Hardboard. A man-made wood board produced by converting wood chips into wood fiber which is then formed into panels under heat and pressure.

Hardwood. In forestry, the wood of trees that have broad leaves, in contrast to the wood of cone-bearing trees which is called softwood. In this sense the term has no reference to the actual hardness of the wood.

Hardwood dimension lumber. (See *Dimension stock.*)

Header. In framing, a piece of timber, usually a short joist, which supports tail beams and is framed between trimmer joists; the piece of stud or finish over an opening; a lintel.

Hearth. The floor of a fireplace, usually made of brick, tile, or stone.

Heartwood. In a tree, the wood extending from the pith to the sapwood, the cells of which no longer help in the life processes of the tree. Heartwood may be infiltrated with gums, resins, and other materials that usually make it darker and more decay-resistant than sapwood.

Heel (of a rafter). The end or foot that rests on the wall plate.

Hip rafter. The rafter that extends from the wall plate to the ridge of the roof and forms the angle of a hip roof.

Hip roof. A roof which slopes up toward the center from all sides, necessitating a hip rafter at each corner.

Honeycombing. Checks, often not visible at the surface, that occur in the interior of a piece of wood, usually along the wood rays.

Humidifier. A device designed to discharge water vapor into a confined room for the purpose of increasing or maintaining the relative humidity.

Humidity. The moistness, dampness, or wetness of the air. "Absolute humidity" is the percentage of water vapor by weight, in a given volume of air. "Relative humidity" is the ratio of the amount of vapor in the air to the greatest amount possible at a given temperature or, in other words, the percentage of complete saturation.

I

I-beam. A steel beam which, when seen in cross section, resembles the letter "I".

Impreg. Wood in which the cell walls have been impregnated with synthetic resin so as to reduce greatly its swelling and shrinking. Impreg is not compressed.

Impregnate. To saturate, fill, or inter-penetrate one substance with another, as wood with chemicals.

Inflammable. Capable of being easily set on fire.

Inlay. A decoration in which the design is set into the surface.

Insulating board or fiberboard. A low-density board made of wood, sugar cane, cornstalks, or similar material. It is dried and usually pressed to a thickness of $\frac{1}{2}$" or $\frac{25}{32}$".

Insulation, building. Any material high in resistance to heat transmission that, when placed in the walls, ceilings, or floors of a home, will reduce rate of heat flow.

J

Jack rafter. A short rafter; often a rafter placed between the top plate and a hip rafter or from a valley rafter to a ridge board.

Jamb. The surrounding case for a door. It consists of two upright pieces, called jambs, and a head, fitted together and rabbeted.

Jig. A device that simplifies a hand or machine operation, usually by guiding a tool or serving as template.

Joint. The junction of two pieces, as of wood or veneer. (Specific types of joints are defined below.)

> BUTT JOINT. A square-cut joint where the ends of two pieces meet.
>
> DADO JOINT. A joint in which one piece is grooved to receive the piece which forms the other part of the joint.
>
> DOVETAIL JOINT. A joint in which one piece has dovetail-shaped pins or tenons which fit into correspond-ing holes on the other piece.
>
> GLUE JOINT. A joint held together with glue.

> LAP JOINT. A joint composed of two pieces, one overlapping the other.
>
> MORTISE-AND-TENON JOINT. A joint made by cutting a hole or mortise in one piece, and a tenon, or piece to fit the hole, in the other.
>
> SCARF JOINT. A joint made by fas-tening together two wedge-shaped pieces which have been cut to cor-respond to one another.

Jointing. (1) Smoothing and straighten-ing the edge of a board. A jointer is a machine which does this automatically. (2) Grinding or filing the teeth or knives of power tools to the correct height. Circular saws are jointed so that there are no high or low teeth. Knives of planers and jointers are jointed so that each knife makes the same depth of cut as all others.

Joist. One of a series of parallel beams which support floor and ceiling loads and which are supported in turn by larger beams, girders, or bearing walls.

K

Keel. The ridge-like piece or combina-tion of pieces extending the entire length of a boat bottom.

Kerf. The cut made by a saw.

Key. A small piece of wood inserted in one or both parts of a joint to hold it firmly together.

Kiln drying. Artificial drying of lumber in a specially designed furnace or heated chamber called a kiln.

Knot. A hard, irregular lump that occurs at the point where a branch grows out from the trunk or a large limb of a tree. As a knot appears on the sawed surface it is merely a section of the entire knot, its shape depending on the direction of the cut.

Knurled. Having a surface covered with small knobs or beads, as a nail which may have such a surface for greater holding power.

L

Lacquer. A varnish-type solution used for finishing wood, metal, porcelain, and similar materials. Lacquers dry quickly and leave a tough, durable, flexible, lightweight film. They should not be used over oil-base paints because they contain solvents that will cut such paints. There are several types of lacquers. Cellulose lacquers have a base of nitrocellulose or pyroxyline; others have a resin base.

Laminate. To form a product by bonding together two or more layers of materials. Also, the product so formed, such as a plastic laminate.

Laminate, paper base. A multi-layer panel made by compressing sheets of resin-impregnated paper together into a solid mass.

Laminated wood. A product made by bonding layers of veneer or lumber with an adhesive so that the grain of all layers is generally parallel.

Lap siding. (See *Bevel siding*.)

Layout. A full-sized drawing showing arrangement and structural features.

Level. A term describing the position of a line or plane which is parallel to the surface of still water; also, an instrument or tool used in testing for horizontal and vertical surfaces, and in determining differences of elevation.

Light. In builders' terminology, space in a window sash for a single pane of glass; also, a pane of glass.

Lignin. The second most abundant constituent of wood, located principally in the thin cementing layer between the wood cells. The chemical structure of lignin has not been definitely determined.

Linear measure. Measurement along a line.

Linseed oil. A yellowish drying oil obtained from flaxseed, widely used as a vehicle for lead-based paints. It is soluble in ether, benzene, and turpentine.

Lintel. A horizontal construction member, usually of stone, wood, or metal, which is placed over an opening and supports a superstructure; a header.

Log. A section of tree trunk suitable in length for sawing into commercial lumber.

Lookout. The end of a rafter, or a construction which projects beyond the sides of a house to support the eaves.

Louver. A kind of window, generally in the peaks of gables and the tops of roofs, provided with horizontal slots which exclude rain and snow but allow ventilation. Also a kind of door that provides ventilation.

Lumber. The product of the saw and planing mill not further manufactured than by sawing, resawing, passing lengthwise through a standard planing machine, crosscutting to length, and matching.

BOARD. Yard lumber less than 2″ thick and 1″ or more wide.

DIMENSION. Lumber at least 2″ but less than 5″ thick, and 2″ or more wide. Includes joists, rafters, studding, planks, and small timbers. (See also Dimension stock.)

DRESSED SIZE. The dimension of lumber after shrinking from its size when green, and being surfaced with a planing machine. Usually this size is $\frac{3}{8}$″ or $\frac{1}{2}$″ less than the nominal or rough size. For example, a 2″ by 4″ stud actually measures $1\frac{5}{8}$″ by $3\frac{5}{8}$″ under American lumber standards for softwood lumber.

FACTORY AND SHOP LUMBER. Lumber intended to be cut up for use in further manufacture.

MATCHED LUMBER. Lumber that is edge dressed and shaped to make a close, tongue-and-groove joint.

NOMINAL SIZE. As applied to lumber, the rough-sawed commercial size by which it is known and sold.

PATTERNED LUMBER. Lumber that is shaped to a pattern or to a molded form in addition to being dressed, matched, or shiplapped, or any combination of these.

ROUGH LUMBER. Lumber as it comes from the saw.

SHIPLAPPED LUMBER. Lumber that is edge dressed to make a lap joint.

STRUCTURAL LUMBER. Lumber that is 2″ or more thick and 4″ or more wide, intended for use where strength is required. The grading of structural lumber is based on the strength of the piece and the use of the entire piece.

TIMBERS. Lumber 5″ or more in its smallest dimension. Timbers may be classified as beams, stringers, posts, caps, sills, girders, purlins, etc.

654

Yard lumber. Lumber of all sizes and patterns, intended for general building purposes.

M

Mantel. The shelf above a fireplace. Originally referred to the beam or lintel which supports the arch above the fireplace opening. Used also in referring to the entire finish around a fireplace.

Masonry. Anything constructed of stone, brick, concrete, hollow tile, concrete blocks, gypsum blocks, or similar materials, or a combination of them.

Master pattern. In foundry, an original pattern made to produce castings which are then used as metal patterns.

Match plate. In foundry, a plate to which a pattern is attached at the parting line.

Matching, or tonguing and grooving. Cutting the edges of a board to make a tongue on one edge and a groove on the other.

Millwork. Generally, all wood materials manufactured in millwork plants and planing mills. Includes such items as inside and outside doors, window and door frames, blinds, mantels, panel work, stairways, moldings, and interior trim. Does not include flooring, ceiling, or siding.

Miter. The joint formed by two abutting pieces meeting at an angle.

Moisture content of wood. The amount of water contained in the wood, usually expressed as a percentage of the weight of oven-dry wood.

Mold. In boatbuilding, a shape or form around which the boat is built. In foundry, a body of sand or other heat-resisting material which contains a cavity and forms a casting when filled with molten metal.

Molding (moulding). In building construction, a strip of wood, often decorative, such as that on the top of a baseboard or around windows and doors.

Molding sand. In foundry, a sand which can be packed firmly, but which will still allow the passage of air or gases. Used in forming a mold.

Mortise. The hole which is to receive a tenon; or, any hole cut into or through a piece by a chisel or mortiser. Generally of rectangular shape.

Mullion. The construction between the windows on a frame which holds two or more windows.

N

Naphtha. Any of several volatile, inflammable liquids obtained by distilling certain materials containing carbon. Naphtha is used as a solvent or thinner in varnish making and as a fuel. Petroleum naphtha is also known as benzine.

Natural finish. A transparent finish, usually a drying oil, sealer, or varnish, applied to wood for the purpose of protection against soiling or weathering. Such a finish should not seriously change the original color of the wood or obscure its grain pattern.

Naval stores. A term applied to the oils, resins, tars, and pitches derived from oleoresin contained in, exuded by, or extracted from trees chiefly of the pine species or from the wood of such trees.

Newel. The principal post at the foot of a staircase; also the central support of a winding flight of stairs.

Nominal-size lumber. (See Lumber.)

Nosing. The part of a stair tread which projects over the riser, or any similar projection; a term applied to the rounded edge of a board.

O

O.C., on center. The measurement of spacing for studs, rafters, joists, and similar members in a building from the center of one member to the center of the next.

O.G., or ogee. In building construction, a molding with a profile in the form of a letter S having the outline of a reversed curve.

Oil paint. A paint in which the vehicle is oil.

Oil varnish. A varnish consisting of a hard resin combined with a drying oil and a drier thinned with a volatile solvent. After application, the solvent dries first by evaporation, then the oil dries by oxidation.

Oven-dry wood. Wood dried to constant weight in an oven at temperatures

655

above that of boiling water (usually 101 to 105 degrees C. or 214 to 221 degrees F.).

Oxidation. The process of combining with oxygen.

P

Panel. (1) A large, thin board or sheet of lumber, plywood, or other material. (2) A thin board with all its edges inserted in a groove of a surrounding frame of thick material. (3) A section of floor, wall, ceiling, or roof, usually prefabricated and of large size, handled as a single unit in the operations of assembly and erection.

Paper, building. A general term for papers, felts, and similar sheet materials used in buildings, without reference to their properties or uses.

Paper, sheathing. A building material, generally paper or felt, used in wall and roof construction as a protection against the passage of air and sometimes moisture.

Papreg. Any of various products made by impregnating sheets of specially manufactured high-strength paper with synthetic resin, and laminating them to form a dense, moisture-resistant product.

Particle board. A man-made board composed of wood chips held together with adhesive.

Parting. In foundry, the joint where the mold separates to permit removal of the pattern.

Parting sand. In foundry, a bondless sand dusted on the parting to prevent the parts of the mold from adhering to each other.

Parting stop or strip. A small wood piece used in the side and head jambs of double-hung windows to separate upper and lower sash.

Partition. That which subdivides space within a building; especially, an interior wall.

> BEARING PARTITION. A partition which supports any vertical load in addition to its own weight.
>
> NONBEARING PARTITION. A partition which extends from floor to ceiling but which supports no load other than its own weight.

Penny. As applied to nails it originally indicated the price per hundred. The term now serves as a measure of nail length and is abbreviated by the letter "d."

Piers. Masonry supports, independent of the main foundation.

Pigment. A substance which gives color, as in paint, enamel, dye, or lacquer. It is in the form of fine, powdery particles which are held in suspension, not dissolved, in the vehicle.

Piles. Long posts driven into the soil in swampy locations or wherever it is difficult to secure a firm foundation. Other timbers, or the footing courses of masonry, are then laid on these posts.

Pith. The small, soft core of a tree trunk, branch, twig, or log.

Pitch (roof). The incline or rise of a roof. Pitch is expressed in inches of rise per foot of run, or by the ratio of the rise to the span.

Pitch pocket. An opening on a piece of lumber, parallel to the annual growth rings, which contains or has contained solid or liquid pitch.

Pitch streak. A well-defined accumulation of pitch visible as a more or less regular streak in the wood of certain conifers.

Plainsawed. (See *Grain.*)

Plan (of a building). The representation of a horizontal section of a bulding, showing such parts as walls, doors, windows, stairs, chimneys, and columns.

Plank. A broad board, usually more than 1″ thick; especially, one laid with its wide dimension horizontal, and used as a bearing surface.

Planking. Planks, collectively. On a boat, the outside shell that is exposed to the water.

Plaster. A mixture of lime, cement, and sand, used to cover outside and inside wall surfaces.

Plasticizing wood. Softening wood by hot water, steam, or chemical treatment to make it easier to mold.

Plate. The top horizontal piece of the walls of a frame building, upon which the roof rests. (See also *Seat cut.*)

Platform framing. A system of framing a building in which the floor joists of each story rest on the top plates of the story below or on the foundation sill for the first story, and the bearing walls and partitions rest on the subfloor of each story.

Plough (plow). To cut a groove in the same direction as the grain of the wood.

Plumb. Exactly perpendicular; vertical.

Plumb cut. Any vertical cut; especially one at the top end of a rafter.

Ply. A term used to denote a layer or thickness, as of building or roofing paper, or a layer of wood in plywood.

Plywood. A wood product made by fastening together layers of veneer, or a combination of veneer layers with a lumber core. The layers are joined with an adhesive. Adjoining plies are usually laid with grains at right angles to each other, and almost always an odd number of plies are used.

MOLDED PLYWOOD. Plywood made to some desired shape other than perfectly flat. Often this shaping is done at the time when the layers are glued together. Two ways of molding plywood are (1) by applying fluid pressure, or (2) with curved forms.

Porch. A floor extending beyond the exterior walls of a building. It may be covered and enclosed or open.

Pores. Openings on the surface of a piece of wood. These openings result when vessels in the wood are severed during sawing. (See also *Vessels.*)

Porous woods. Another name for hardwoods, which frequently have vessels or pores large enough to be seen without magnification.

Post. A timber set on end to support a wall, girder, or other structural member.

Pouring. In foundry, filling the mold with molten metal.

Preservative. Any substance that, for a reasonable length of time, is effective in preventing the development and action of wood-rotting fungi, borers of various kinds, and insects that make wood deteriorate.

Pressure-feed gun. A spray gun in which the material to be sprayed is forced from a container into the gun by pressure.

Primer. The first coat of paint in a job that consists of two or more coats; also the paint used for such a coat.

Purlin. In a roof, a horizontal timber which supports rafters, or one that supports the roof sheeting directly.

Putty. A soft, pliable type of cement, having nearly the consistency of dough, used in sealing glass in sash, filling small holes and crevices in wood, and for similar purposes.

Pumice. An extremely light, spongy, or porous material used in powder form to smooth and polish surfaces.

Q

Quarter round. A molding which, in profile, appears as a quarter circle.

Quartersawed. (See *Grain.*)

Quill. The sleeve that carries the bearings and moves up and down in the drill-press head.

R

Rabbet. A rectangular groove cut in the corner of a board.

Radial. Coinciding with or pertaining to a radius, as of a tree or a log.

Rafter. One of a series of structural members of a roof, designed to support roof loads. The rafters of a flat roof are sometimes called roof joists. (See also *Hip, Jack,* and *Valley Rafters.*)

Rail. A horizontal bar or timber extending from one post or support to another, such as a guard or barrier in a fence or staircase. Also, the crosswise or horizontal members of the framework of a sash, door, blind, or any paneled assembly.

Raised grain. A roughened condition of the surface of dressed lumber in which the hard summerwood is raised above the softer springwood but not torn loose from it.

Rapping. In foundry, loosening the pattern from the mold by jarring or knocking.

Ramming-up. In foundry, the process of packing the sand in the mold or core box with a rod or rammer.

Rate of growth. The rate at which a tree has increased in its amount of wood. This is measured radially in the trunk or in lumber cut from the trunk. The unit of measure in use is number of annual growth rings per inch.

657

Raw linseed oil. The crude product expressed from flaxseed, usually without much subsequent treatment.

Rays, wood. Strips of cells extending radially within a tree and varying in height from a few cells in some species to 4″ or more in oak. The rays serve primarily to store food and transport it horizontally in the tree.

Reflective insulation. Sheet material of which one or both surfaces will reflect comparatively little heat; when used in building construction with the surfaces facing air spaces, such material reduces the radiation across the air space.

Relative humidity. (See *Humidity*.)

Resawing. Sawing lumber again after the first sawing; specifically, sawing into boards or dimension lumber.

Respirator. A covering for the nose and mouth, often necessary when using a spray gun.

Resin. A sticky material obtained from the sap of certain trees and plants (natural resins) or produced synthetically by chemical combinations of coal-tar derivatives and other organic substances (synthetic resins). Resins are widely used in making varnishes and paints.

R. P. M. (rpm). Revolutions per minute.

Ribbon. A narrow board let into the studding to add support to joists.

Ridge. The horizontal line at the junction of the top edges of two sloping roof surfaces. The rafters of both slopes are nailed to the ridge board.

Ridge board. The board placed on edge at the ridge of the roof to support the upper ends of the rafters.

Ripping. Sawing wood along the grain.

Rise. (1) The upward slope of a roof; also, a measurement of this upward slope, expressed as a comparison between the sloping part and a horizontal line beneath it. (See also *Run*.) (2) In stairs, the perpendicular height of a step or flight of stairs.

Riser. Each of the vertical boards closing the spaces between the treads of stairways.

Roll roofing. Roofing material, composed of fiber and saturated with asphalt, and supplied in rolls containing 108 square feet in 36″ widths. It is generally furnished in weights of 55 to 90 pounds per roll.

Roof. The covering or upper part of a building.

Roofing. Material put on a roof to protect it from wind and water.

Roof sheathing. Boards or sheet material, fastened to the roof rafters, on which the shingles or other roof covering is laid.

Rosin. A hard resin used in making certain varnishes.

Rotary cutting. A way of cutting veneer from a log. The log is fastened in a large lathe and a sharp knife cuts the veneer much as paper is unwrapped from a roll.

Rubber-emulsion paint. Paint, the vehicle of which consists of fine droplets of rubber or synthetic rubber dispersed in water.

Rubbing compound. An abrasive material used to produce a smoothly finished wood surface.

Run. (1) In reference to roofs, the horizontal distance that underlies the slope of the roof from a wall to the ridge. (2) Referring to stairways, the width of a step, measured from the face of one riser to the face of the next, and not including 'the nosing; also, the horizontal distance covered by a flight of steps.

S

Sag. An unevenness or irregularity in a coat of paint, varnish, or lacquer. It results if too much of the liquid is allowed to collect in one spot or area.

Sanding. Rubbing sandpaper or similar abrasive over a surface before applying a finish.

Sandwich construction. (See *Structural sandwich construction*.)

Sap. Most of the fluids in a tree. Certain secretions and excretions, such as oleoresin, are excepted.

Sapwood. The living wood, usually of pale color, near the outside of the tree. Under most conditions the sapwood is more susceptible to decay than heartwood.

Sash. The framework which holds the glass in a window.

Sawing. (See terms listed under *Grain* for explanation of certain sawing methods.)

Scaffold. A temporary structure or platform enabling craftsmen to reach high places.

Scale. A short measurement used as a proportionate part of a larger dimension. For example, the scale of a drawing may be expressed as ¼″=1′.

Scarfing. A joint between two pieces of wood which allows them to be spliced lengthwise.

Scotia. A hollow molding used as a part of a cornice, and often under the nosing of a stair tread.

Scribing. The marking of a piece of wood to provide for the fitting of one of its surfaces to the irregular surface of another. Also, the fitting of woodwork to an irregular surface.

Sealer. A finishing material, either clear or pigmented, that is usually applied directly over uncoated wood to prevent subsequent coats of paint or varnish from seeping into the wood.

Seasoning. Removing moisture from green wood in order to improve its serviceability.

Seat cut or plate cut. The cut at the bottom end of a rafter to allow it to fit upon the plate.

Second growth. New timber that has grown after the removal, whether by cutting, fire, wind, or other agency, of all or a large part of the previous stand.

Section. A drawing showing the kind, arrangement, and proportion of the various parts of a structure. It shows how the structure would appear if cut through by a plane.

Semigloss paint or enamel. A paint or enamel made so that its coating, when dry, has some luster but is not very glossy.

Shake. In lumber, a separation or crack along the grain, the greater part of which occurs between the rings of annual growth. Also refers to a hand split shingle, usually edge grained.

Sheathing. The material, usually wood boards, plywood, or wallboards, placed over exterior studding or rafters of a structure.

Shellac. A preparation made by dissolving lac in alcohol, and used commonly in the finishing of wood. Lac is a resinous substance secreted by a tropical insect.

Shingles. A covering applied in overlapping layers, as for the roof or sides of a building. Shingles are commonly made of wood, asphalt, asbestos, tile, and slate, among other materials, and are cut fairly small.

Shiplap. (See *Lumber.*)

Shrinkage. A decrease in volume, as of molten metal when it solidifies, or in wood when it dries.

Siding. The finish covering of the outside wall of a frame building. It may be made of weatherboards, vertical boards, battens, shingles, or other material. (See also *Bevel siding, Drop siding.*)

Sill. The lowest member of the frame of a structure, resting on the foundation and supporting the uprights of the frame. The member forming the lower side of an opening, as a door sill or a window sill.

Sizing. (1) Working material to the desired size. (2) A coating of glue, shellac, or other material applied to a surface to prepare it for painting or other method of finish.

Soffit. The underside of a staircase, cornice, beam, arch, or a similar member of a building; relatively minor in area as compared with ceilings.

Softwood. One of the botanical groups of trees that, in most cases, have needlelike or scalelike growths rather than broad leaves. (These trees are known as conifers.) The term *softwood* also applies to the wood produced by such trees. In this sense it has no reference to the actual softness of the wood.

Sole or soleplate. A member, usually 2″ x 4″, on which wall and partition studs rest.

Soluble. Capable of being dissolved.

Solvent. A liquid in which things can be dissolved. Also, more loosely, a liquid in which tiny particles of a substance can be dispersed in suspension, without actually dissolving. Solvents commonly used in wood finishing are turpentine, alcohol, and petroleum and coal-tar distillates. The solvent in a finishing material usually evaporates, leaving the pigment or other necessary ingredients dry on the finished surface.

Span. The distance between structural supports such as walls, columns, piers, beams, girders, and trusses.

Spar varnish. A varnish consisting mainly of drying oil and the harder types of resins. It is waterproof and strongly resists damage by moisture and sunlight.

Specific gravity. A measure of the relative density of a substance. For woods it is expressed as the ratio of the weight of a body to the weight of an equal volume of water at 4 degrees C. or other specified temperature.

Specifications. The written or printed directions regarding construction details, as for a building.

Spline. A thin strip of wood used to reinforce joints. Also known as a "feather" or "tongue."

Split pattern. In foundry, a pattern that is parted for convenience in molding.

Spray booth. A sheet-metal booth or small room used for spray finishing.

Springwood (early wood). The portion of a tree's wood that is formed during the early part of the season's growth, as indicated by the annual growth rings. It is usually less dense and weaker than summerwood.

Sprue. In foundry, the opening into which the metal is first poured.

Square (as a unit of measure). One hundred square feet. Usually applied to roofing material. Sidewall coverings are often packed to cover 100 square feet and are sold on that basis.

Stain. A discoloration in wood. It may have such diverse causes as micro-organisms, metal, or chemicals. The term also applies to materials that are used in coloring wood.

Stain, shingle. A form of oil paint, very thin in consistency, intended for coloring rough-surfaced wood, such as shingles, without forming a coating of significant thickness or gloss.

Stair rise. The vertical distance from the top of one stair tread to the top of the next one above.

Stickers. Wood strips or boards used to separate the layers of lumber in a pile

and thus permit air to circulate between layers.

Stiffness. A measure of how well a type of wood will resist bending under a load. (Not to be confused with *Bending strength*.)

Stool. The flat, narrow shelf which forms the top member of the interior trim at the bottom of a window.

Story. That part of a building between any floor and the floor or roof next above.

Strength. The term in its broader sense refers to all the properties that enable wood to resist forces or bear loads. In a more restricted sense, the term may apply to any one of these properties, in which event the property under consideration should be specified; for instance, strength in compression parallel to grain.

Stringers. In shipbuilding, long horizontal pieces of wood, laid fore and aft, and intended to give longitudinal strength. Also, the setup stringers, or jacks, which are the frame on which the boat is built. They are not used in the completed boat.

Structural sandwich construction. A construction in which layers of relatively high-strength facing materials are tightly bonded to, and act integrally with, a low-density core material.

Structural timbers. Pieces of wood of relatively large size, the strength of which is the controlling element in their selection and use. Framing for buildings, and cross-arms for posts are examples of structural timbers.

Stud. One of a series of slender wood or metal structural members placed as supporting elements in walls and partitions. (Plural: studs or studding.)

Subfloor. Boards or sheet material laid on joists, and over which a finish floor is to be laid.

Suction-feed gun. A spray gun which, by its own operation, develops a vacuum at the fluid tip, or nozzle. The vacuum draws the material to be sprayed, from a container attached to the gun. This type of gun is often used on smaller jobs.

Summerwood (late wood). The portion of wood that is formed after the springwood formation has ceased. It is usually denser and stronger than springwood.

660

T

Tack rag. A piece of cheesecloth or cotton rag moistened with thinned varnish. It is used to pick up small particles of dust.

Tacky. Not quite dry; sticky.

Tail beam. A relatively short beam or joist supported in a wall on one end and by a header on the other.

Taper. A gradual and uniform decrease in size, as of a round or rectangular piece or hole.

Template. A full-sized pattern from which structural layouts are made. They may be of paper, cardboard, plywood, or metal.

Termite shield. A shield, usually of non-corrodible metal, placed in or on a foundation wall or other mass of masonry, or around pipes, to prevent passage of termites.

Termites. Insects that superficially resemble ants in size, general appearance, and habit of living in colonies; hence, they are frequently called "white ants." Subterranean termites do not establish themselves in buildings by being carried in with lumber but by entering from ground nests after the building has been constructed. If unmolested, they eat out the woodwork, leaving a shell of sound wood to conceal their activities, and damage may proceed so far as to cause collapse of parts of a structure before discovery. About 56 species of termites are known in the United States. The two major species, classified from the manner in which they attack wood, are (1) ground-inhabiting or subterranean termites, the most common, and (2) dry-wood termites, found in this country almost only along the extreme southern border and the Gulf of Mexico.

Texture. A term often used interchangeably with grain. Sometimes used in referring to the density of a wood and the degree of contrast between springwood and summerwood. Texture often refers to the finer structure of wood (see *Grain*) rather than to the annual rings.

Thermoplastic glues and resins. Glues and resins which are cured by cooling, but which soften when subsequently subjected to high temperatures.

Thermosetting glues and resins. Glues and resins that are cured with heat and do not soften when subsequently subjected to high temperatures.

Thinner. A volatile liquid added to finishing material to make it flow more easily and smoothly.

Threshold. A strip of wood or metal beveled on each edge and used above the finished floor under outside doors.

Tie beam. A beam so situated that it holds the principal rafters of a roof together and prevents them from thrusting the plate out of line.

Timber. Wood suitable for construction; especially lumber with a cross section greater than 4″ x 6″, such as posts, sills, and girders.

Tint. A color produced by adding white pigment or paint to a colored pigment or paint, with the amount of white greater than the amount of colored.

Toenailing. To drive a nail so that it enters the first surface diagonally and usually penetrates the second member at a slant also.

Tongue. A projecting edge, as on a board, that fits into a groove of another piece.

Tracheids. Elongated cells that constitute the greater part of the structure of softwoods and are also present in some hardwoods. Tracheids are frequently referred to as fibers.

Transom. A transverse structural member, such as a lintel, or the horizontal crossbar in a window. In shipbuilding, the back crosspiece of a boat.

Tread. The horizontal board in a stairway; the part on which a person walks.

Trim. Finish materials in a building, such as moldings, applied around openings (window trim, door trim) or where walls join the floor and ceiling of a room (baseboard, cornice, picture molding).

Trimmer. A beam or joist to which a header is nailed in framing, as for a chimney or a stairway.

Truss. An assembly of members, such as beams, bars, and rods, combined to form a rigid framework that cannot be deformed by the application of exterior force without deforming one or more members.

661

Tung oil. A yellow drying oil obtained from the seed pods of tung trees, and widely used in water-resistant varnishes, lacquers, and high-gloss paints.

Turpentine. A volatile oil used as a thinner in paints and as a solvent in varnishes.

Twist. A wood defect characterized by a turning or winding of the edges of a board, so that the four corners of any face are no longer in the same plane.

U

Undercoat. A coating applied prior to the final or top coat of a paint job.

V

Valley of a roof. A low place in a roof, where two slopes meet.

Valley rafter. A rafter which runs from a wall plate to the ridge, along the valley of a valley roof.

Vapor barrier. Material used to prevent vapor or moisture from getting into walls and condensing. There are two common types of vapor barriers: (1) membrane-type, which comes in rolls and is applied as a unit in wall or ceiling construction; (2) paint-type, which is applied with a brush. The vapor barrier must be a part of the warm side of the wall.

Varnish. A thickened preparation of drying oil, or resin and drying oil. When applied to a surface it leaves a hard, glossy, transparent coating. It may also be mixed with pigments to make enamels. Clear varnish is a slightly yellow, semi-transparent liquid.

Vehicle. The liquid portion of a finishing material; it consists of the binder (nonvolatile) and thinners (volatile).

Veneer. A thin layer or sheet of wood; usually one that has beauty or value and is intended to be overlaid on an inferior surface.

    Rotary-cut veneer. Veneer cut in a lathe which rotates a log against a knife.

    Sawed veneer. Veneer produced by sawing.

    Sliced veneer. Veneer that is sliced off a log, bolt, or flitch with a knife.

Vent. An opening or a pipe to allow the flow of a gas or a liquid. In foundry, this term refers to the small opening in the mold to facilitate escape of air and gases.

Vessels. Wood cells of comparatively large diameter that have open ends and are set one above the other so that they resemble tubes. The cells themselves are sometimes called vessels, and so are the tube-like structures they form. The openings of the vessels on the surface of a piece of wood are usually referred to as pores.

Virgin growth. The original growth of trees on a piece of land. (To be distinguished from *Second growth*.)

Volatile. Easily vaporized.

W

Wallboard. Large, rigid sheets of wood-pulp, gypsum, or similar materials that may be fastened to the frame of a building, usually to form the interior walls.

Wane. The imperfect or missing portion of a defective board.

Warp. A variation from a true or plane surface, as in a piece of lumber. Warp includes bow, crook, cup, twist, and any combination thereof.

Water paint. A paint in which the vehicle is a water emulsion.

Water repellent. A liquid designed to penetrate into wood to make it resist water.

Water stain. A colored dye that is soluble in water.

Wax. A fatty material obtained from the honeycombs of bees or from similar plant, animal, or mineral substances, and used for providing an attractive, protective coating, as for wood. Waxes are used by themselves, and they are also combined with other ingredients to make certain paints, varnishes, and paint removers.

Weathering. The mechanical or chemical disintegration and discoloration of a wood surface, resulting from exposure to light, action of dust and sand carried by winds, alternate shrinking and swelling brought about by changes in the weather,

662

or a combination of these causes. Weathering does not include decay.

Weatherstrip. Narrow strips of material, such as metal, installed around doors and windows to retard passage of air, water, moisture, or dust.

Wind (rhymes with kind). The defect of a board which appears slightly twisted, or which rests on two diagonally opposite corners when it is laid on a flat surface.

Wood substance. The solid material of which wood is composed. Usually (but not always) this term refers to the extractive-free solid substance of which the cell walls are composed. There is no wide variation in chemical composition or specific gravity between the wood substance of various species; the characteristic differences of species are largely due to the differences in infiltrated materials and the variations in relative amounts of cell walls and cell cavities.

Workability. The ease with which wood can be smoothly cut and shaped with hand or machine tools.

INDEX